Managerial Economics
Text, Problems, and Short Cases

THE IRWIN SERIES IN ECONOMICS

Consulting Editor

Lloyd G. Reynolds Yale University

Managerial Economics

TEXT, PROBLEMS, AND SHORT CASES

MILTON H. SPENCER

Professor of Economics
Wayne State University, Detroit

K. K. SEO

Professor of Business Economics and
Quantitative Methods
University of Hawaii, Honolulu

MARK G. SIMKIN

Assistant Professor of Business
Economics and Quantitative Methods
University of Hawaii, Honolulu

1975 · Fourth Edition

RICHARD D. IRWIN, INC.   Homewood, Illinois   60430
Irwin-Dorsey International   London, England   WC2H 9NJ
Irwin-Dorsey Limited   Georgetown, Ontario   L7G 4B3

Fourth Edition

First Printing, July 1975

ISBN 0-256-01654-2
Library of Congress Catalog Card No. 74–31596
Printed in the United States of America

Preface

This book is aimed primarily at upper-division undergraduate and first-year M.B.A. students in economics and business administration. The present edition retains the major thrust of the previous one, although substantial changes have been made throughout to improve readibility as well as scope and depth of coverage.

The main purpose of the book is to develop and integrate principles and ideas from various fields of economics and business, with emphasis on management decision making and policy formulation within the firm. In view of the wide range of topics covered, each student will find some chapters more challenging than others, depending on his previous educational background. Our experience indicates, however, that the book as a whole is definitely within the grasp of the typical upper-division undergraduate or first-year M.B.A. student.

Particular attention is called to the following main features of the book:

- A level of discourse about equal to that found in standard intermediate texts in economics and business, presupposing nothing more than a typical introductory course in economics.
- Self-contained chapters, and self-contained major sections within chapters, thus permitting maximum teaching flexibility.
- Coverage of a wide variety of topics reflecting many modern developments in the field.
- Inclusion of many chapter-end problems and short cases, both qualitative and quantitative, thus providing ample material for class discussions, outside assignments and examinations.

In preparing this edition, we have benefited from the advice and criticisms of many people. William Long was particularly helpful at every stage of the book's development. In addition, we were fortunate to receive many helpful comments from Thomas Hailstones, Ibrahim

Ibrahim, Louise Lo, Barbara Newton, and Peter Vlachos, among others. Masayo Matsukawa and Gail Masaki typed and retyped many versions of the manuscript, and were helpful in other ways. To all of these people we offer our sincere thanks.

June 1975   M. H. S.
                                                                 K. K. S.
                                                                 M. G. S.

Contents

chapter I

Introduction: Risk, Uncertainty, and Theories of the Firm

Uncertainty and expectations are the joys of life.
William Congreve, *Love for Life*

Managerial economics, which is the subject matter of this book, may be defined as the integration of economic theory with business practice for the purpose of facilitating decision making and planning by management. But since decision making is so much a human activity, it is not surprising that it is largely subjective, depending upon the personality, temperament, and experience of the decision maker. Yet within the framework of subjective decision making, there are analytical tools that can be coupled with disciplined, logical thinking to provide at least a modicum of objectivity in the decision-making process. These tools and evaluative processes are usually discussed under the heading of decision theory, a complex and rapidly growing field which cannot be covered fully within the scope of this chapter. However, no book which purports to teach managerial decision making would be complete without at least partially drawing upon the wealth of models and prescriptive logic embodied in this disciplinary area. Hence, our first task is to examine some of the analytical tools of decision making, and to show how quantitative methods can be applied to the subjective, or so-called "nonquantifiable," factors in the list of available alternatives.

CLASSIFICATION OF DECISION MAKING

It is customary to classify decision making according to (1) the number of people who make the decisions and (2) the conditions under

1

which the decisions are made. Each of these may then be further partitioned, if desired, into subsets.

The first classification has to do with whether the decision maker is an individual or a group. This distinction is important for obvious reasons: a decision made by an individual whose motivation is based on unitary or integrated considerations may take one form; a decision made by a group with multiple motivations resolved by conflict or compromise may be expected to take quite a different form.

The bulk of decision theory literature has concentrated on the former type of situation, although much of the recent research has tended to focus on the latter. In "unitary" cases, a set of individuals comprising an organization such as a department or a business firm is considered as a single entity. On the other hand, in the study of group decisions, a chief task is to develop compromise preference patterns from the dissimilar and sometimes discrepant preference patterns of members. From the viewpoint of democratic theory, this involves the intriguing question of how to arrive at "fair" methods of amalgamating individual choices into optimum preference or social arrangements, a task which some writers have claimed is not possible. As regards group decision making, therefore, the chief conclusion is that the group process is usually more demanding of the time, energy, and patience of individual participants, more demanding of information, and consequently more costly. Hence, the desirability of the group process, as opposed to individual decision making, must ultimately be decided by weighing the additional expenses attendant with the aggregate approach against the perhaps better decisions and "democracy" to be gained.

The second classification refers to the particular state of knowledge under which a decision is made. In formulating plans for the future, a business manager may be operating under conditions of certainty, risk, or uncertainty. Business executives are prone to think of all conditions that may result in losses as risks, but there are some technical distinctions among the three concepts of certainty, risk, and uncertainty that are fundamental for purposes of analysis.

Each of the above classifications is important enought to warrant a brief but separate discussion of its overall scope and nature. As implied above, we shall deal primarily with decision making in the individual rather than group sense, although the distinction between the two is generally clear from the context.

THE CONCEPT OF CERTAINTY

Certainty has been defined as a state of knowledge in which the decision maker knows in advance the specific outcome of each alternative. In other words, the decision maker has complete information and perfect knowledge of the environment and of the result of his (or her) decision. The undergraduate level of economic theory or management theory is based mainly on an assumed condition of certainty. This underlying assumption is made in order to simplify the task of teaching and learning. To teach and learn concepts and tools we hold "all other things" equal.

How realistic is the assumption about our situation or environment? Are there really many examples of decision problems which can be logically placed in the category of certainty? The answer to this question is yes, even though we know that ultimately all decisions are made under conditions of either risk or uncertainty. No managerial decision maker will ever have perfect knowledge of future events which will influence the outcome of each of the possible alternatives faced. The outcome of a long-range investment, for example, is really impossible to predict when we consider the dynamic interaction of the huge number of unknown variables such as the general economic situation, the competition, consumer tastes, the political climate, and technological advances.

Despite the inevitability of long-range uncertainty, business administration, economics, and psychology abound with examples involving decision making under certainty. In fact, decision making under certainty includes most of the problems pertaining to theories of choice that arise in the economic and behavioral sciences. Thus, for example, short-run purchase decisions of the firm have virtually "certain" consequences, as do the immediate costs of very short-run resource allocation. Further examples of certainty may be found in classical applications of the calculus and algebra, and in many types of "optimization" models such as linear and nonlinear programming problems. For problems where the objective may be to maximize or minimize performance over time, an area of mathematics called the "calculus of variations" has been employed. In any event, these problems relate to traditional situations which have been typical of decision making under certainty—situations in which the alternatives are known and the problem is to find the resource allocation yielding the highest value of some index such as profits, or utility, or lowest value of some other index, such as costs.

Perhaps worthy of particular mention in a discussion of decision making under certainty are the contributions which linear programming has made in the field of business and economic analysis. Applications have been both far and wide, and clever definition of variables has enabled researchers to solve multiperiod resource commitment problems, "chance-constrained" models, and even certain nonlinear applications as well as more familiar problems of warehouse placement, manpower assignments, blending allocation, market distribution, and production scheduling. As more will be said of linear programming in Chapter 16, further discussion of this topic at this point is not necessary.

Selecting the Appropriate Objective

As noted above, decision making under certainty is typified by problems which can be expressed in the following form: given a set of possible alternatives, choose one or more that will maximize (or minimize) a particular index. But which index? This is often the most difficult part of the problem. In cases of an economic or business nature, quantities such as profit, sales, production, or cost are usually suitable indices. But in many problems of a behavioral nature, a desired index is not readily available. In such situation, how can a decision maker select an index function so that the decision maker's choice is then reduced to that of finding the alternative with the maximum index?

Psychologists and economists have long been interested in this question, and a considerable body of literature on the problem now exists. It is normally treated under the general heading of "utility"—a topic which is actually the basis of this and many other problems in modern decision theory. For our purpose, however, it can be simply stated that the individual might index his (or her) choices in an ordinal or ranking manner from most to least preferred. Then, if the individual were confronted with any pair of choices, the choice with the higher rank or index would always be selected. This assumes, however, that the individual's preferences satisfy the very important condition of *transitivity:* if the decision maker is confronted with all possible triples of alternatives A, B, and C, and prefers A to B in the paired comparison (A, B), and B to C in the paired comparison (B, C), then the decision maker always prefers A to C in the paired comparison (A, C).

The importance of this concept of transitivity as a cornerstone of modern decision theory cannot be overemphasized. The notion itself has some connection with many comparisons we make in our day-to-day activities: if A is larger than B and B is larger than C, then A is larger than C. Instead of larger, we can substitute other words such as "stronger" or "lighter." The point to be emphasized at this time is that this method of ranking permits an ordering of alternatives, or an *ordinal* preference pattern based on the amount by which one alternative is preferred to another. On this basis, economists after World War I developed the theory of demand in terms of indifference curves, thereby breaking away from the necessity of postulating an underlying cardinal utility function as done earlier by Alfred Marshall and the neoclassical school of economic thought.

THE CONCEPT OF RISK

Risk has been defined as a state of knowledge in which each alternative leads to one of a set of specific outcomes, each outcome occurring with a probability that is known to the decision maker. Risk may therefore be regarded as the quantitative measurement of an outcome, such as a loss or a gain, in a manner such that the probability of the outcome can be predicted. Thus among the central ideas in the concept of risk are measurement and prediction, their purpose being to estimate the likelihood of an eventuality or contingency. Let us note briefly, in an intuitive and conceptual manner, how this is accomplished.

Methods of Estimating Risk

There are two approaches that can be used in arriving at a probability measure or risk: one of these is *a priori*, by deduction; the other is *a posteriori*, by empirical measurement. Both methods attempt to provide the information needed to make decisions.

A priori is a Latin phrase which means, literally, "from the one before." It is used to describe a method of analysis by which we begin with a cause and deduce the effect. For example, we know that a coin has only two sides. Because of this, a tossed coin must come up either heads or tails. If we assume that the coin is evenly balanced, we can deduce that there is an equal probability of getting heads or tails on any one toss.

Thus, it is not necessary to toss a coin a large number of times in order to discover that the relative frequency of a head (or tail) approaches $\frac{1}{2}$, or one out of every two tosses. Likewise, it is not necessary to make a continuous drawing of cards from a deck containing 52 cards in order to conclude that the probability of drawing any particular card is $\frac{1}{52}$. And with continuous rolls of a perfect die, it can be predicted with confidence that over the long run, any given number will turn up one out of six times, so the probability can be written as $\frac{1}{6}$ or .17.

Are probability statements such as these intended to predict a particular outcome? The answer is no. They merely state that in a sufficiently large number of trials this is the outcome that will be realized. It follows, therefore, that the habitual gambler who is entertained with organized games of chance such as those encountered in "Lost Wages," Nevada, is faced with risks (not with uncertainty as we shall see below), and the only thing that is certain is that the gambler must lose over the long run.

The a priori method of estimating risk is appropriate whenever the decision maker can compute the probability of an outcome without having to rely upon past experience. When this is not possible, the decision maker must fall back on the a posteriori method. A posteriori is also a Latin phrase, meaning "from the one behind." In the a priori method, we proceed from cause to effect, but in the a posteriori method, we observe the effect and seek to establish the cause. The a posteriori method assumes that past performances were typical and will continue in the future. In order to establish a probability measure, the cases or observations included in the historical data must be numerous enough to exhibit stability, they must be repeated in the population or universe, and they must be independent.[1] Given these conditions, the statistical probability of an event can be computed and the likelihood of the outcome can be classified as a risk. Thus, insurance companies predict with a high degree of accuracy the probability of deaths, accidents, fire losses, and so forth, and thereby make decisions about premium levels and rates. Although they cannot establish the probability that a particular individual will die or that a particular house will burn, they can predict with small error how many people will die next year or how many houses out of a given type will burn.

Decision Making under Risk

For eventualities or outcomes that involve risks, a primary task of professional decision makers, managers, for example, is to develop techniques that will enable them to calculate and subsequently minimize the risks inherent in a particular problem. The method used to accomplish this is to calculate the probability distribution of possible outcomes from a set of sample observations, and then compute an *expected value.*

For example, suppose that it is now January and we have an automobile dealer who must order now the cars to be sold in June. From the historical data accumulated over several years and from estimates of the market, the dealer is able to construct a probability distribution table as illustrated in Exhibit 1.

EXHIBIT 1
Probability Distributions of New Car Sales in June

Number of Sales	Probability
Less than 5.	.00
5–15	.10
16–25	.20
26–35	.40
36–45	.25
46–55	.05
56 or more.	.00
Sum	1.00

Notice that in constructing a table such as this, the decision maker is not assigning an individual probability to each event. Rather, the decision maker is assigning a consistent and comprehensive set of

---

[1] Independency means that the observations are drawn at random and hence the magnitude of any particular random variable is not affected by the magnitude of another random variable drawn from the same population.

probabilities to some range of possible events. For the purpose of constructing the table, it is assumed that the actual event is certain to occur within this range; therefore, the total of all probabilities must be 1.0.

When a histogram is developed from these data, as in Exhibit 2A, the probability scale on the vertical axis must range from 0–1, since the proportion of outcomes can never be negative and since it can also never exceed 100 percent, or a relative frequency of 1.00. That is, a probability must always lie between 0 and 1. A probability of 0 means that the event is not expected to occur; a probability of 1 means that the event is expected to happen all of the time. (These two degenerate cases of risk were discussed in the previous section as decision making under certainty.) Values in between denote degrees of certainty (or degrees of uncertainty, if you prefer). On the horizontal axis, the outcomes being analyzed are scaled off. These might be wheat yields per acre, glass breakage in restaurants, or some other variable under consideration. A frequency or probability distribution of outcomes is then plotted.

EXHIBIT 2A
Probability Distribution Developed from Observed Frequency of New Car Sales in June

EXHIBIT 2B
Fitted Continuous Distribution of New Car Sales in June

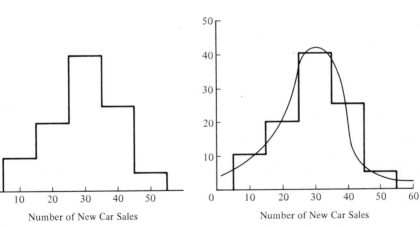

At this point perhaps a finer, more detailed probability distribution may be needed in order to determine the parameters necessary for the purposes of analysis. That is, a measure of central tendency is needed, such as the mean, median, or mode, to describe the typical size of the distribution; a measure of dispersion, such as the standard deviation, variance, or moments, to establish the scatter; a measure of skewness to denote the degree of symmetry; and a measure of kurtosis, or degree of peakedness. In particular, therefore, a smoothing of the probability distribution in the example would be of use, as suggested in Exhibit 2B. This smoothing process would reflect the facts that (1) distinct, and usually nonequal, probabilities are associated with each of possible numbers in the car sale intervals; and (2) the distribution empirically determined is merely an approximation of the "true" underlying probability function from which the graph was derived. Various smoothing devices are available for this purpose and need not concern us here. Note, however, that there is a distinction between frequency distribution and probability distribution. A frequency distribution is a tabulation of how many times certain events have occurred in the past. A probability distribution of the same events is a tabulation of the percentage of time that they are likely to occur in the future.

The simplest way to construct a probability distribution is to make a direct conversion of the frequency distribution. For example, if a certain event occurred during five of the past ten years, we might say that the frequency, and hence the probability, of occurrence next year is 50 percent.[2] However, the decision maker is not required to accept a direct conversion of the frequency distribution. The decision maker can modify the probability distribution to correct for the presence of new influential factors which might be expected to have important bearing upon later economic behavior, or to correct for past controls not continuing into the future.[3]

Risk Planning and the Cost of Risk

Two aspects of the theory of risk deserve some brief comments. One of these involves the notion of self-insurance or intrafirm risk; the other pertains to the idea of risk-shifting or interfirm risk. Both of these are intimately related to the general problem of *planning for risk.*

In its capacity as a decision maker and planner, management's activities are essentially forward-looking in nature. Plans are made in the present based on expectations of the future. Since it is a characteristic of risk that the parameters (mean, variance, skewness, etc.) of the frequency distribution of outcomes can be estimated statistically, the expected losses or gains can be incorporated in advance into the firm's

---

[2] Ideally, the decision maker will assign a probability to every possible event within the range that is to be examined. In actual practice, this course of action may not be practical. For example, our hypothetical car dealer may want to estimate the probability of all possible monthly sales between 20 and 60 in increments of one, but this would mean that the car dealer would have to calculate 41 separate probabilities.

[3] Of course, when the decision maker starts to inject his (or her) own opinions into the development of a probability distribution, subjectivity is introduced into what started out as an objective procedure. Whether this is good or bad depends upon how good the decision maker's opinion turns out to be.

cost structure. This is true whether the risk is of an intrafirm or interfirm nature, as explained below.

Intrafirm risk occurs when management can establish the probability of loss because the number of occurrences within the firm is large enough to be predicted with known error. For example, a factory may experience a loss of about 2 machine-hours out of every 100 machine-hours due to equipment breakdown. It might seem that management should protect itself against this type of loss through the purchase of insurance, but such is not the case. In reckoning profits, the cost of the production lost can be added to the cost of the production resulting from the remaining 98 machine-hours, and the profit rate will be altered accordingly by the revision in the cost structure. In other words, where the mean expected loss for the company can be predicted for the coming period, the loss can be "self-insured" by treating it as a cost of doing business, and hence no insurance from outside sources to cover the loss is necessary. In short, the probable future cost of the loss can, in such cases, be planned in advance of the company's fiscal period, thereby facilitating the decision processes of management. Thus, small-loan companies expect a certain percentage of defaults, banks charge off regularly a portion of their loans, and many companies have attempted to institute self-insurance programs for various kinds of risk to which they are subject, and against which they feel they can prepare themselves through the creation of loss or contingency reserves. These are only a few of many familiar examples that can be given to show how business executives adjust to, or plan for, intrafirm risks.

Interfirm risk occurs when the number of observations or cases is not large enough within any one firm for management to feel that it can predict the loss with reasonable confidence. However, when many firms are considered, the number of observations becomes numerous enough to exhibit the necessary stability for prediction. Examples of such risks are losses caused by floods, storms, fires, and so forth. Since managers are unable to predict such losses for themselves, they are able to shift the burden of the risk to insurance companies whose function it is to establish the probability of such losses based on a large number of cases. Under such circumstances, the probability of loss for a specific firm cannot be predicted, but the probability of loss covering many firms can definitely be established with a small amount of error. It follows, therefore, that since the insured pays a risk premium for insurance, this can also be recognized for purposes of planning future costs.

THE CONCEPT OF UNCERTAINTY

Uncertainty has been defined as a state of knowledge in which one or more alternatives result in a set of possible specific outcomes whose probabilities are either not known or are not meaningful. Unlike risk, therefore, uncertainty does not assume complete knowledge of alternatives. Furthermore, uncertainty is a subjective phenomenon: no two individuals will view an event and necessarily formulate the same quantitative opinion. This is due to a lack of knowledge or of sufficient historical data on which to base a probability estimate. This in turn is caused by rapid changes in the structural variables or "states of nature" that determine each economic or social environment.

Choices and decisions still must be made in such an environment, and one of the great challenges for the business executive lies in planning under conditions of uncertainty. Due to the complexity of our world, the analyst/decision maker's first step toward decisions must be to simplify the problem by identifying the structures and factors which are relevant to the executive's firm and its products. This may be done by forming mental images of future outcomes that cannot be verified in any quantitative manner. It follows from this that uncertainty is not insurable and cannot be integrated within the firm's cost structure as can risk. The parameters of the underlying probability distribution cannot be established empirically because all predictions are subjective and within the framework of each manager's own anticipations of the future. At best, it may be possible to assign subjective probabilities to these anticipated outcomes, but the distribution of expectations resulting therefrom cannot be established with any degree of precision.

For example, in marketing a new product, the decision may depend on whether management anticipates a period of prosperity, recession, transition, and so forth. These, then, represent the states of nature that may occur. The returns or payoffs that will result from a decision to market the product or not to market it will clearly depend on which state of nature is eventually realized. Of course, the decision maker may anticipate all three states of nature with varying degrees of uncertainty. Thus the decision maker may feel that there is a 70 percent chance of "no change," a 20 percent chance of prosperity, and a 10 percent chance of recession. In any event, to each state of nature, an act or strategy may be associated and an expected return or payoff established. The techniques of constructing or arraying the various payoffs—or, more generally, the methods of developing formal guides for making optimum decisions in problems such as these—are discussed in Chapter 2. At present our interest centers rather on the development of the broad concept of uncertainty as a background and framework for certain classes of decision-making problems.

Degree of Uncertainty

We begin by assuming that there is a true state of nature which is unknown to the decision maker at the time of choice. Three classes of uncertainty situations called "complete knowledge," "complete ignorance," and "partial ignorance" may then be distinguished.

Complete knowledge (or perfect knowledge) occurs when there is an a priori probability distribution over the states of nature—that is, *a distribution which the decision maker regards as meaningful.* This can occur when the decision maker assumes that he (or she) has complete knowledge even though this may not be the case. The decision maker has analyzed the relevant factors and decided more or less subjectively what are the chances that the state of nature will change. A decision has to be made based on something, so the situation is analyzed and the best decision made. When this has been done, the decision maker has changed the problem to one of decision making under risk, and can use specific analytical tools that have been developed for decision making within this environment.

Complete ignorance about the "true state" is the opposite situation of complete knowledge. In this case there is no assumption or knowledge on the part of the decision maker as to the probabilities of the various states of nature. Accordingly, the decision maker may use any one of a number of rational criteria for decision making. For instance, in the case of a business venture, the decision maker may adopt a pessimistic or conservative outlook. In that event the minimum outcomes or profit expectations of each combined strategy and state of nature might be examined and then the strategy chosen which yields the maximum of these minimum profits. Hence this is called the "*maximin* criterion." Alternatively, the decision maker may adopt an optimistic and speculative outlook. In that case the maximum profit expectations of each strategy and associated state of nature might be examined and then the strategy chosen which yields the maximum of these maximum profits. Hence this is called the "*maximax* criterion." Other criteria have also been established to meet the particular needs of decision problems under uncertainty where complete ignorance or complete lack of knowledge is the prevailing condition. These are discussed in Chapter 2.

Partial ignorance occupies the intermediate ground between complete knowledge and complete ignorance. Much of the pioneering research on decision theory in this area was done by the noted statistician L. J. Savage. In his monumental treatise, *The Foundations of Statistics* (1954), he develops a procedure for generating an a priori probability distribution over the appropriate states of nature in a decision problem. In this manner the decision problem is reduced from one of uncertainty to one of risk, with the a priori probability distribution called a *subjective* probability distribution. Since a great many decisions in business and the social sciences are made on the basis of partial ignorance or incomplete knowledge of the facts, a brief intuitive sketch of the notion of subjective probability distributions should be of interest.

Subjective Probability Distributions

Degrees of uncertainty may be illustrated by the set of probability or frequency distributions of expectations shown in Exhibit 3. Expected

EXHIBIT 3
Subjective Probability Distributions

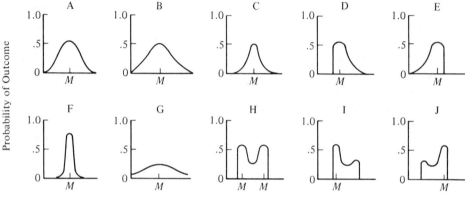

Expected Outcome

outcomes, such as profits, sales, GNP, and so forth, are plotted horizontally, while the subjective probability of the outcome is measured off vertically.

In the top panel of Exhibit 3 there are three normal distributions, but only A is of unit or standard normal form. In contrast with B and C (all of which are plotted in the same units), A represents greater uncertainty than C. This is due to the variance or spread of the distributions. If M is taken as the modal or most frequent outcome, the greatest variation in expectations (or greatest uncertainty) occurs in B because it has the widest spread; the least variation or uncertainty is in C because it has the least spread. Thus, as an indication of the degree of uncertainty, a measure of the *dispersion* of expectations such as the range, the standard deviation, or the variance could be used. The degree of uncertainty could be said to vary directly with the dispersion: a dispersion of zero would mean "perfect knowledge," or a single-valued expectation; a larger dispersion would indicate greater uncertainty or multivalued expectations.

In Exhibit 3, D and E illustrate the significance of *skewness*. Compare these curves with the normal curve of A, where the expected outcomes are arranged symmetrically about the modal outcome. In A, there is an even chance that a deviation from the most probable (modal) outcome will be greater or less than the mode. In D, a deviation from the mode M will most probably be in the direction of higher values, while in E the most probable deviation is toward lower values. Thus, a measure of skewness, since it describes the lopsidedness of the distribution, is a further indication of the degree of confidence or uncertainty.

A comparison of F with G reveals still further characteristics. The degree of peakedness of a distribution, called *kurtosis* in statistical terminology, is yet another indication of uncertainty. In F the probability of the particular modal outcome M is greater than for any other distribution shown. In G, however, where the distribution is relatively "flat topped," the subjective probability of the modal outcome is only slightly greater than outcomes higher or lower. In F, the decision maker is relatively certain of the modal outcome; in G, the decision maker's expectations cover a wide area of almost equal probabilities, and it would be difficult to formulate plans based on modal outcome or on outcome higher or lower than M.

Finally, H, I, and J represent a different pattern of distributions. The **U**-shaped distribution of H implies high, equal probabilities for outcomes whose values are either large or small, and a low probability for outcomes in between. The **J**-shaped curve of J shows a high probability of higher valued outcomes, while the reverse J curve of I implies a high probability for the lower valued outcomes. These latter two curves have statistical connotations similar to those of E and D, respectively.

It may be noted that, technically, there has sometimes been a disagreement among theorists as to whether the mode or the mean should be used as the most "representative" measure of central tendency. One group has contended that the mode is preferable because it is more realistic: it represents the most likely value to be chosen from the population since it is the observation with the highest associated probability. Further, for discrete probability functions, the mean usually calculates a fictitious value. In the June car sales example discussed earlier, the expected number of car sales (mean of the distribution) is 29.5 cars, a meaningless number in terms of the automobiles which can actually be sold.

Some have favored the mean over the mode as the most desirable statistic because (1) it is the theoretically correct one from which to compute the standard deviation and other, higher order moments of the distribution; and (2) the modal value is more likely to lie farther from specific sample observations if the true probability distribution is particularly skewed, such as in examples I and J of Exhibit 2. The ramifications of these arguments are unfortunately beyond the scope of this book. However, what concerns us most is not a detailed understanding of higher statistics but rather the development of a conceptual framework within which a more quantitative orientation towards uncertainty may be placed.

Economic Insurance and the Socioeconomics of Uncertainty

It is interesting to inquire why insurance against the uncertainty of losses has never been instituted in the business world. Enough has already been said to distinguish risk from uncertainty, and it should be clear that insurance can only be a response to the former rather than the latter. However, some further comments on the subject may be of interest here.

Fundamentally, there is no means known by which uncertainties can be isolated and generalized to the point where they can be classified as objective risks. Marketing researchers, for example, have yet to discover the economic laws (if any) that govern consumer behavior, and economists have yet to reduce to precise mathematical formulas the forces determining business cycles and the losses resulting therefrom. In short, there are simply too many imponderables to take into account in arriving at an exact method of prediction. Further, the creation of an adequate insurance program, if such were possible, would probably have to be based on long-run changes in both prosperity and depression.

During prosperity periods when most companies are profitable and losses are at a minimum, the total amount of insurance premiums paid should exceed the total amount of losses incurred. Conversely, in depression periods losses are more general and should exceed the premium payments. Over the long run, therefore, the insurance company's profit during prosperity would presumably be balanced by its deficits during depression. But this would assume that the amplitude and frequency of business fluctuations could be forecast with accuracy, which they cannot, and this is precisely the problem at hand. Moreover, if such accurate forecasts of depressions were possible, insurance would be unnecessary; action could be taken instead to avoid the setback, thereby eliminating the need for insurance.[4]

Uncertainty versus Security. The role of uncertainty also manifests itself with respect to income and employment. Broadly, as certainty increases in industries because of improved ability to predict, incomes there will tend to decline in the long run relative to the more uncertain fields of employment. At least this is true to the extent that individuals choose and train for occupations on the basis of their probability estimates of future earnings. The greater the uncertainties of the future in an occupational line, as indicated by the dispersion of earnings probabilities, the more attractive is the drive for security (in return for lower incomes)

---

[4] "It is fascinating to contemplate political or social institutions in a perfectly certain world. Policemen would be needed only at the moment of crime, firemen only at the time of fire; laws could be more pointed to cover precisely the specific objectionable future occurrence, and so forth. The mere knowledge of future developments would not always be sufficient to prevent antisocial outbreaks, for some of them may not always be amenable to advance control." (S. Weintraub, *Price Theory* [New York: Pitman Publishing Corp., 1949], p. 349.)

in the more certain fields of employment. Witness the fact that employees in civil service, banks, and public utilities generally earn less than their peers in the more uncertain though similar lines of activity in other industries. Admittedly these monetary differentials may be somewhat compensated by nonmonetary factors (longer vacations, shorter hours, retirement benefits, etc.). But the fact remains that coal miners earn more than ditchdiggers, window washers in skyscrapers command a higher wage than dishwashers in restaurants, and college professors earn less (but live longer) than corporation executives. The clash between uncertainty and security can manifest itself in many ways. The removal of uncertainty, if that were possible, would serve to modify the structure and pattern of resource allocation and income distribution, and would create a type of economy substantially different from that which currently prevails.

To what extent have the formal theories of risk and uncertainty influenced the development of management as a science? In the light of the foregoing discussion, the stage is now set for the development of a concept of management which reflects the trend in much of modern managerial theory and research. But first, a contrast between the old and the new should help sharpen this distinction.

MICROECONOMICS

Much of microeconomics is essentially a body of theory which describes the economic behavior of the individual firm under prescribed market conditions. Some of the fundamental properties of this aspect of microeconomics, discussed below, are summarized in Exhibit 4.

1. Economic Man. Underlying all of microeconomic theory is the assumption that the decision maker is omniscient and rational, or simply that the decision maker is an *economic man.* Thus, being omniscient means that the decision maker knows the alternatives that are available as well as the outcome of any action chosen. Being rational means that the decision maker can weakly order preferences[5] and can maximize the preference function or "utility" in a broad sense.

2. Transformation. The concept of the firm in microeconomic theory is that of an input-output process in which certain inputs or factors of production such as capital, land, and labor are *transformed* into finished outputs to be sold in the market. The inputs and outputs are valued at market prices; these serve to determine the explicit costs and

---

[5] The statement that an individual can order his (or her) preferences means (among other things) that given the two commodities A and B, the individual can decide whether (1) A is preferred to B, written $A > B$ or $B < A$; or (2) A is preferred or indifferent to B, written $A \gtrless B$ or $B \lesssim A$.

The first is an example of a strong ordering; the second illustrates a weak ordering. Concepts of preference arise in the economic theory of consumer behavior, especially in the study of indifference curves.

EXHIBIT 4

Some Basic Properties of Microeconomics:
The Equilibrium or Marginal Conditions

I. It is assumed that the firm's objective is to maximize profits, from which the following internal conditions of equilibrium may be deduced:
  A. Any output that is produced must be produced with factor combinations such that total cost is at a minimum. This results in two corollaries:
    1. The marginal productivity of the last dollar must be equal in every use.
    2. The price of each factor of production must be proportional to marginal physical productivity, the factor of proportionality being marginal cost.
  B. That output will be selected which maximizes net revenue, total cost being optimally determined by the previous conditions. This implies:
    1. The equality of marginal cost and marginal revenue, the slope of the latter being the smaller.
    2. In combination with the previous conditions under "A" we also have the marginal productivity of each factor equal to its price, the first term being defined as the product of marginal revenue and marginal physical productivity.
    3. If total cost exceeds total revenue, the firm will leave the industry.
II. If we impose by arbitrary assumption or hypothesis the external conditions that entry of firms into the market be free, that is, that total revenue be equal to total cost, then:
  A. Product will be exhausted by definition.
  B. The demand curve must be tangent to the unit cost curve. In the case of pure competition, this implies minimum average cost.

Source: Adapted with some changes from P. A. Samuelson, *Foundations of Economic Analysis* (Cambridge: Harvard University Press, 1947), p. 88.

revenues of the firm. In some cases the owner or entrepreneur may supply certain inputs and consume certain outputs, thereby incurring implicit costs and receiving implicit revenues. Nevertheless, whether explicit or implicit, it is assumed that costs and revenues can be valued, so that the difference between their totals is net revenue or profit (which may be positive, zero, or negative).

3. Constraints. Certain limitations are placed on the firm as a result of both its internal nature and external environment. A chief internal limitation or *constraint* is determined by the firm's production function, which embodies the technical and technological conditions of production that are available to it. Hence, the production function is even more fundamental than the cost function because the "shape" of the former determines the physical range of the firm's output and, given the market prices of the factors of production, the cost function can be derived from the production function. An important external type of constraint is given by the nature of the market in which the firm operates. Thus, the quantity of goods that the firm can sell is conditioned by price. This in turn is partly dependent on whether the market is one of perfect competition, monopoly, oligopoly, and so forth, since these market structures will determine the degree of competitive reaction to the particular price and output decisions of the individual firm.

The above assumptions and conditions permit us to define the *optimum* position of the firm as that position (out of the set of all possible positions) which maximizes net revenue. In this position, the marginal or equilibrium conditions in Exhibit 4 are satisfied. In essence, therefore, for optimality to exist, profit must be maximized, and this can occur only when marginal cost equals marginal revenue. Microeconomic theory is therefore concerned with the study of the optimization process and its consequences for the industry and the economy.

The "Firm" Is Not a Firm

To what extent can these ideas be utilized for the purpose of developing a managerial theory of the firm? That is, what are some of the difficulties in using microeconomic theory as an aid to the study of decision making at the level of the firm?

In the literature of economics and, more recently, in such areas as operations research, psychology, and sociology, the firm has come to be regarded in different lights and from different points of view, depending on the particular type of analysis that seems appropriate. Thus, within economics itself, for example, the firm may be viewed in one manner for purposes of accounting and in quite another manner for purposes of price determination and resource allocation. It is the latter sense to which microeconomics or the theory of the firm refers, and with which we are concerned at this moment.

For purposes of business decision making, microeconomics fails to provide sufficient analytical tools that are of use to managers. Some of the reasons may be noted briefly.

1. The model of "economic man" as an omniscient and high-speed computer who is confronted with a complete set of known or probabilistic outcomes is a distorted representation of reality. The typical business decision maker usually has limited information at his (or her) disposal, limited computing ability, and a limited number of feasible alternatives involving varying degrees of risk. Further, the net revenue function which the decision maker is expected to maximize, and the marginal cost and marginal revenue functions which the decision maker is expected to equate, assume a possession of information which is not known and, possibly, cannot be obtained even by the most careful analysis. Hence it is absurd to expect a manager to maximize and equalize certain critical functional relationships which the manager may not even know and cannot find out.

2. The property of "economic man" as a rational being who can weakly order the states or positions into which he can get, and then select the state which maximizes some known objective, is a gross oversimplification. With this property the theory of the firm and the theory

of consumer choice, that is, the theory of the household, are seen to be essentially the same, in that they both involve similar sets of objectives and relationships. Thus, as in the theory of consumer choice, the firm always maximizes "utility," but this may take the form of maximizing customer good will, security, liquidity, good labor relations, or possibly profits. The last variable, profits, is the one that is typically assumed, but the others are clearly possible objectives if "utility" is taken as the ultimate measure of effectiveness. Hence, something more specific than utility is needed if the objectives of the firm are to be given any concrete meaning.

3. The traditional theory of the firm neglects the internal problems and conflicts resulting from organizational structure because it is assumed that, in the long run, competition in the marketplace will permit the survival of only the most efficiently organized firms. This criticism alone is enough to undermine almost the entire system of microeconomics as a suitable basis for a theory of administrative or managerial behavior. Hence, we shall have more to say about the role of modern organization theory at a later point.

The Firm in Economic Theory

The above criticisms fall far short of exhausing the list of arguments against microeconomic theory, but they are indicative of the nature of these arguments. How relevant are these criticisms?

Educated business executives as well as professional economists who have studied the theory of the firm have been quick to recognize that the theory has very little to offer as a guide for business decision making. This should be no cause for alarm or even surprise, however, because *the theory of the firm was never intended to serve as a managerial or administrative theory.* It was constructed for one purpose only—to describe the determination of prices and resource allocation by business firms under specified market conditions. In this connection it should be clear that microeconomics must necessarily continue to maintain a central place in any theory of economic behavior because it serves as an *ideal type descriptive model* of the individual economic agent.

What microeconomics obviously fails to do, however, is to provide a normative discipline useful to the business executives in their daily decision-making role within the organization. Exhibit 4 is intended to portray the optimum position of the firm in terms of price and output adjustments exclusively. But these conditions cannot be viewed as "optimum" if the firm is considered in any context other than those imposed by the assumptions of the microeconomic model. In short, if we wish to deal with the firm in any other light than that of "price-and-output decision maker" operating under strictly prescribed market conditions, we are asking questions which the theory of the firm is not designed to answer.[6]

Hence, we see that managerial economics must begin where microeconomics leaves off: most of the problems which confront managers cannot adequately be handled by the convenient model of a firm faced with conventional cost and revenue curves in an environment of certainty. Before embarking on the development of a more prescriptive discipline, however, the recognition that managerial economics demands a more behaviorist approach first requires a little further examination into an already existing contribution towards this end—the field of behavioral science.

BEHAVIORAL SCIENCE

The approach to decision making and theories of the firm that has been discussed thus far is largely devoid of any "behavioristic" properties. By this is meant that the various theories identify the individual decision maker and the firm as one and the same entity—an organism bent on achieving specific goals under objectively defined conditions, without recognition of the complexities involved in predicting human behavior.

When the individual is recognized as an actor within the organization, the complexity and stability of the environment are introduced as elements which play a major role in affecting the individual's choices and plans. Drawing on psychology and sociology, concepts of role and status are introduced as vehicles for analyzing the interaction between the individual and the organization. Personality and environment are seen to play a part in the decision process, as do cognition, perception, and belief. The behavioral approach thus attempts to view the individual not as a mechanistically adaptive economic organism, but as a total human organism with multiple goals and with complex internal structures, all of which must be carefully analyzed if the processes and mechanisms through which adaptation takes place are to be understood and appreciated.

Following a fairly customary practice, we may classify most of the writings dealing with the behavioral theory of the firm under the heading of "organization theory." This grouping should be regarded in a broad sense as incorporating such related fields as administrative science,

---

[6] No wonder Boulding refers to the firm of economic theory as ". . . a strange bloodless creature without a balance sheet, without any visible capital structure, without debts, and engaged apparently in the simultaneous purchase of inputs and sales of outputs at constant rates." Kenneth E. Boulding, *A Reconstruction of Economics* (New York: John Wiley & Sons, Inc., 1950), p. 34. See also Edith Tilton Penrose, *The Theory of the Growth of the Firm* (New York: John Wiley & Sons, Inc., 1959), pp. 11, 14.

human relations, and the like, to the extent that these subjects contribute to our knowledge of the structure and operations of business firms.

Organization Theory

What is an organization? A "modern" theorist in this field might answer by saying that an organization is a network of interacting roles which are linked together by formal and informal lines of communication. But what does this mean? In order to appreciate the concept more fully, a brief sketch of the various approaches to organization theory is of use. For our purposes, three schools of thought may be identified: classical, neoclassical, and modern.

All three schools of thought, it may be noted, are largely concerned with achieving the optimum allocation of resources, particularly human resources, within the firm. This poses problems which traditional microeconomic theory has typically neglected because traditional microeconomics has been concerned only with *interfirm* relations and their overall economic effects in the resource allocation process, not with *intrafirm* relations and their internal effects on company profits and growth.

1. Classical Organization Theory. This theory is represented by a stream of literature which extends from the early 1900s to the present time. Historically, it is an integral part of the general scientific movement in industry which emerged around the turn of the century.[7] The main pillar of classical organization theory is the notion of division of labor and the benefits to be derived therefrom—concepts which were superbly expressed by Adam Smith more than a century earlier.

Thus, to the classical organizationist, the theory of organization involves the effective coordination of the work-division units of an enterprise. Maximum efficiency or productivity is attained when this division of work at *all* levels in the organization is achieved along natural lines and in natural areas of specialization, according to individual capacities and skills. Given this optimum division of labor, the structure and growth of an organization, its lines of authority or chains of command, and its span of control at various management levels can all be established logically and effectively.

It is clear, therefore, that classical organization theory tends to emphasize the formal anatomy and authoritarian aspects of organization. Like classical economics, it is strongly rationalistic and views workers

---

[7] Among the prominent early leaders of this movement were Frederick W. Taylor, Frank and Lillian Gilbreth, and Henry Gantt. Taylor was well known for his concern with functional foremanship and staff planning; the Gilbreths, for their contributions to time, motion, and fatigue study; and Gantt, for his integration of engineering concepts and techniques in cost accounting. Subsequent well-known writers include James Mooney, Lyndall Urwick, and Henri Fayol, as well as a number of others who are still active.

as commodities whose services are bought and sold in a competitive marketplace. By establishing as its chief measure of success the maximization of productive efficiency on the part of members of the system, it "dehumanizes" individuals and tends to regard them as a given rather than as a variable factor in the organization.

2. Neoclassical Organization Theory. This theory has been identified with the human relations movement which started in the 1930s.[8] This school of thought represents the reaction to the engineering-oriented, purely structural approach of the classicists and their hierarchical concept of organization. To a large extent, the reports of the famous Hawthorne studies done by the Harvard Business School under the leadership of Elton Mayo, with the cooperation of the managements of Western Electric and American Telephone and Telegraph, were responsible for spawning the human relations movement.

The Hawthorne studies indicated that people do not respond to variations in physical and environmental conditions in the predictable manner assumed by the classicists. Instead, from the viewpoint of the neoclassicists, an organization is considerably more than a well-designed machine. Indeed, it is a complex of interacting roles based on personal relationships, beliefs, perceptions, and cognition. These occur because division of labor creates specialization at all levels of the firm, and the result must be a greater interdependency among members of the system if the organization is to survive.

The neoclassical school regards the pattern of human relationships itself as the organization. Informal status systems emerge as part of the organization, with complex networks of communications among individuals and between groups. It is well known that the objectives of the organization do not necessarily coincide with the interests and motivations of its members. Internal frictions, or disequilibrium within the firm, can thus occur which if serious enough can lead to the demise of the system. In other words, the anticipated efficiencies that are gained from division of labor in the classical theory may, according to the neoclassicists, be more than offset by internal conflicts and frictions due to the interdependency which specialization breeds.

What sort of corrective actions can be taken? The neoclassical school makes several recommendations: encourage individual and group participation in decision making so as to give members of the organization a sense of "belonging"; develop a proper balance between the classical *top-down* or authoritarian type of managerial philosophy and the newer *bottom-up* concept in which it is recognized that the degree of effective authority of a leader is a direct function of the willingness of subordinates to accept it; and, last but not least, develop "human relations

---

[8] Among the early contributors to this field were Chester Barnard and Elton Mayo; subsequent well-known writers include Burleigh Gardner and William Foote Whyte, among many others.

training programs" so as to teach managers the art of leadership, coordination, and motivation.

The neoclassical school has been criticized for its overly descriptive and vague generalizations, frequently based on extremely narrow, often trivial, empirical research. Nevertheless, in the light of modern organization theory, it may have served as a significant counterbalance to the classical approach, and perhaps helped pave the way for the more recent lines of thought that have emerged in this field.

3. Modern Organization Theory. This theory is by no means a homogeneous body of thought. Yet, its main connecting thread or unifying theme is its emphasis on the study of total human systems. It seeks to achieve a more complete and thorough understanding of such systems by analyzing (1) the parts of an organization, namely, its members, its formal and informal groups, its status and role-expectancy patterns, and its physical work environment; (2) its linkages, including its communication and decision process; and (3) its goals, which involve stability, growth, and interaction. This, basically, is one way of representing the framework or background of modern organization theory. Against this background, some viewpoints propounded by Herbert Simon, one of the pioneering leaders of the modern school, are particularly worth noting.

In his discussions of the goals of firms,[9] Simon is particularly critical of the central assumption in the theory of the firm—the assumption that the entrepreneurs strive to maximize their residual share, or profit. Criticisms of this assumption, as was pointed out at the beginning of the discussion on microeconomics, are by no means new. The most important modifications of classical organizational objectives which emerge are as follows:

1. The theory is ambiguous as to whether it is short- or long-run profit that is to be maximized.
2. There is no allowance for the existence of "psychic income" which the entrepreneur might obtain from the firm, quite apart from the entrepreneur's monetary income.
3. The theory does not recognize that under modern conditions, owners and managers are separate and distinct groups of people, and the latter may not be motivated to maximize profits.
4. Under imperfect competition, maximization is an ambiguous goal, for actions that are optimal for one firm will depend on the actions of the other firms.
5. The entrepreneur may not care to receive maximum profits but may simply want to earn "satisfactory profits."

---

[9] See, for example, Herbert Simon, "Theories of Decision Making in Economics and Behavioral Science," *The American Economic Review,* June 1959, which presents a good survey of the current relationships between behavioral science and economic analysis.

The last point is particularly relevant from a behavioral science stand-point because it introduces a concept of *satiation* which is more meaning-fully related to the psychological notion of aspiration levels than to maximization. Thus, in Simon's words, a behavioral theory of organiza-tional goals may be described in the following manner:

> The notion of satiation plays no role in classical economic theory, while it enters rather prominently into the treatment of motivation in psychology. In most psychological theories, the motive to act stems from drives, and action terminates when the drive is satisfied. Moreover, the conditions for satisfying a drive are not necessarily fixed, but may be specified by an aspiration level that itself adjusts upward or downward on the basis of experience.
>
> If we seek to explain business behavior in the terms of this theory, we must expect the firm's goals to be not maximizing profit, but attaining a certain level or rate of profit, holding a certain share of the market or a certain level of sales. Firms would try to "satisfice" rather than maximize. . . . Models of satisficing behavior are richer than models of maximizing behavior, because they treat not only of equilibrium but of the method of reaching it as well. Psychological studies of the formation and change of aspiration levels support propositions of the following kinds. (*a*) When performance falls short of the level of aspira-tion, search behavior (particularly search for new alternatives of action) is induced. (*b*) At the same time, the level of aspiration begins to adjust itself downward until goals reach levels that are practically attain-able. (*c*) If the two mechanisms just listed operate too slowly to adapt aspirations to performance, emotional behavior—apathy or aggression, for example—will replace adaptive behavior.

The behavioral viewpoint thus appears to offer a more realistic ap-proach to the study of organizational objectives than do the classical or neoclassical schools of thought. But what are some of the business and economic implications of the satisficing model? Although empirical studies in these connections are still relatively limited, a few findings are worth mentioning.

1. Several studies of the pricing practices of business firms have indicated that managers tend to set prices by applying some sort of a standard markup on costs, rather than attempt to estimate marginal costs, marginal revenues, or demand elasticities, even if these could be accurately measured. For many firms, prices are more often set to attain a particular target return on investment—say 10 percent—than to maximize short- or long-run profits.

2. There is some evidence that firms experiencing declining market shares in their industry strive more vigorously to increase their sales than do competing firms which are experiencing steady or increasing market shares.

3. As for the economic implications, it has been argued by economists that the classical economic theory of the firm is necessary for
welfare economics—that is, that branch of economic theory concerned
with the behavior of the firm in achieving an efficient allocation of
resources. But, as Simon points out, not only does the satisficing model
vitiate all the conclusions that can be derived concerning resource allocation under perfect competition but it also focuses attention on the
fact that the *classical theory of the firm is empirically incorrect as a
description of the decision-making process!*

On this last basis alone, it appears that one of the main underpinnings
of classical economic theory has been seriously weakened. One cannot
help but wonder, therefore, whether the argument attributed to Hicks[10]
will be enough to retain the traditional system as an integral part of
general economic theory. Some comments along these lines are reserved
for the conclusions below.

A MODERN COORDINATIVE CONCEPT
OF MANAGEMENT

How can one reconcile the quest for normative models of managerial
decision making with the behaviorist conclusions that the firm is not
a firm but rather an organizational collective of individuals usually lack-
ing even a concensus on the objectives by which decisions may be made?
One approach would be to develop a modern coordinative concept of
management in which instead of trying to define management in terms
of routine functions such as organizing, planning, controlling, and so
forth, we can think of it as an integrated activity in which these functions
are *not* separated. This is a more abstract approach, but it permits a
classification of managerial activities in terms that are far more useful
for many conceptual and analytical purposes.

The functions of managers may be classified for purposes of analysis
into two distinct levels of activity: one is *coordination;* the other is
supervision. The coordinative function is that of decision making—the
process of selecting an action from alternative courses of action. The
need for this function is universal, since it arises in environments of
risk and uncertainty, that is, in situations where decisions must be made
and plans formulated on the basis of expectations. The other phase
of management, that of supervision, involves the fulfillment of plans

---

[10] The eminent British economist J. R. Hicks has pointed out that the various
attacks, irrespective of their sources, will never dislodge the theory of the firm from
its key position in economic theory, for to do so, even in the case of perfect competition, would involve the wreckage of "the greater part of general equilibrium theory,"
and this is not likely to occur until something better comes along to take its place.
J. R. Hicks, *Value and Capital* (2d ed.; Oxford: Clarendon Press, 1946), p. 84.

already established, and hence requires little if any coordination of a decision-making nature. It is management in the coordination sense which is now recognized by many modern scholars as a central concept of management theory. This classification of management functions may be somewhat different from, but is not in fundamental disagreement with, the analyses underlying the distinguished contributions to modern management theory by such writers as Andreas Papandreou, Herbert Simon, James March, Richard Cyert, and others.

The justification for viewing management in a coordinative or decision-making sense is easily established. All human behavior involves, by conscious or unconscious means, the selection of particular actions out of all those that are available to the individual and to those over whom the individual exercises influence and authority. The process of making selections has been called decision making. Behavioral scientists have shown that selections may themselves be the product of complex chains of activities which the traditional writers referred to above have called organizing, staffing, leading, and so forth. If these activities are true descriptions of the managerial process, then it follows that decision making is the core of that process. Thus, major advancements in management research in such areas as organization, leadership, planning, communication, control, and so forth, have been and are now being made by focusing on central concepts of decision making and decision theory. Many of these developments are emerging not only in the fields of operations research or management science where the impetus has perhaps been strongest, but in the fields of business, economics, and the behavioral sciences as well.

The fundamental role of the coordinating unit—management in its true sense—is that of choosing between alternatives. Problems of choice arise because the material and human resources available to an organization, such as capital, land, labor, and other inputs, are limited and can be employed in alternative uses. The executive function from the coordinative standpoint thus becomes one of making choices or decisions that will provide the optimum means of attaining a desired end, whether the end be the preservation of the existing situation between the organization and its competitors, or the long-run attainment of domination, or any other objective. But regardless of the goal, managers may classify outcomes as risks or as uncertainties. If knowledge of the future were perfect, decisions could be made and plans could be formulated without errors and hence without need for subsequent revision. In many cases, however, the time involved precludes perfect knowledge. Thus decisions and plans made at one point in time are based on current knowledge, in anticipation of results that will be forthcoming at future points in time. As more facts become known, new decisions may have to be made and old plans may have to be revised as new courses of action are adopted in order to achieve desired objectives. Managers are thus engaged in the continuous process of charting such new courses of action into hazy horizons.

CONCLUSION

The above ideas constitute the essence of the coordinative function, and hence the bare elements of the concept of management under risk and uncertainty. There is a fundamental point in all of this that is worth reiterating: *an organization* (as distinguished from a mere physical producing plant), *or management in the coordinative sense* (as distinguished from management in the supervisory sense), *exists largely as a device for adjusting to risk and uncertainty.* If the future were completely known, management in the coordinative sense would be needed for the most part only at the start or initial phase of an investment in order to formulate a plan for the future; thereafter, management in the supervisory sense would be all that is needed for the purpose of administering or carrying out the plan. Apparently, since risk and uncertainty constitute the environment in which business executives operate, planning, organizing, controlling, directing, and so forth, are actually inseparable activities of coordinative management. *Hence, the traditional classification and description of managerial functions along these lines is of doubtful value both on logical and operational grounds.*

The various approaches to organizational concepts of the firm that have been outlined above have far from exhausted the list that could have been compiled. They do, however, represent most of the main lines and patterns of thought. Some additional new and exotic areas in which research is underway for finding improved applications to managerial decision making can be classed under a general heading such as "information theory and intelligence." This would include the study of cybernetics, the use of computers for logical problem solving, and the analysis of business games and simulations. For the most part, these topics can be treated as special cases and applications of some of the previous approaches and concepts, and hence have not been given special attention in this discussion. Suffice it to say, however, that they share, with the other modern approaches and concepts, a strong emphasis on quantitative model building, experimentation, and empirical investigation.

PROBLEMS

1. How does decision making by individuals differ from decision making by a group?
2. List at least three types of business problems that involve decision making under certainty.
3. Why is the concept of *transitivity* important to decision making?

4. Suppose that you have before you an urn containing nine red balls, eight white balls, and seven green balls. If you shake the urn in such a way that the balls are thoroughly mixed and then draw out one ball, what is the probability that it will be green? Is this an a priori or an a posteriori probability? Why?

5. What is the distinction between a frequency distribution and a probability distribution?

6. Classify each of the following as an interfirm or intrafirm risk:
   a. Glassware and china breakage in a restaurant.
   b. Egg breakage on a chicken farm.
   c. Absenteeism in an industrial plant.
   d. "Acts of God" (cite examples).

7. Classify each of the following situations as decision making under certainty, risk, or uncertainty, and explain your answers.
   a. A farmer in Illinois must decide how many acres to plant in corn and how many in soy beans.
   b. In very hot weather at the baseball stadium, ice cream is the big seller with hot dogs a poor second; but if the weather is moderate or cool, the opposite occurs. Sanitary regulations do not permit the concessionaire to store either hot dogs or ice cream for more than two days. Because the concessionaire's orders are so large, suppliers require orders seven days in advance or else they can't guarantee delivery. Therefore the concessionaire must decide now what to order for next week's big game.
   c. Quality standards used by a maker of animal feeds set minimum percentages of protein, fat, and carbohydrates and a maximum percentage of inert ingredients in the final mixture. Three basic ingredients are available for mixing, each with different proportions of protein, fat, carbohydrates, and inert matter, and each with a different cost. The feed maker desires to meet or improve upon the quality standards at minimum cost and must decide what proportions of the basic ingredients to use in the final mixture.

8. In researching a new product, a marketing consultant has come up with four alternative brand names, five different package designs, and three alternative advertising campaigns.
   a. How many strategies must management consider?
   b. What states of nature might affect management's choice? Give examples.
   c. How can management take into account the reaction of competitors?

9. The *expected value* of an event is obtained by summing its "weighted" outcomes. A "weighted" outcome is simply the value of the outcome times its probability of occurrence.
   a. A salesperson makes 40 calls with an average sale of $30 per call and 60 calls with an average sale of $15 per call. What is the salesperson's expected sale per call?
   b. A certain stock has paid dividends of $2 per share in 30 out of the last 40 payment periods and nothing in the remaining 10 payment periods. What is the expected dividend?

10. An automobile dealer found that a new model was sold to 9 of the last 45 persons who took a demonstration ride. If the dealer's gross profit per car is $300 and the demonstration rides cost $5 each, what is the expected value of each demonstration ride?

REFERENCES

FERBER, ROBERT C.   "The Dark Side of Decision Making." *Management Review,* vol. 60, no. 3 (March 1971), pp. 4–13.

GREEN, PAUL E.; GROSS, IRWIN; and ROBINSON, PATRICK J.   "Behavioral Experiment in Two-Person Bargaining." *Journal of Marketing Research,* vol. 4 (November 1967), pp. 374–79.

KNIGHT, FRANK H.   *Risk, Uncertainty, and Profit,* p. 233. Boston: Houghton Mifflin Co., 1921.

LOASBY, BRIAN J.   "The Decision-Maker in the Organization." *The Journal of Management Studies,* vol. 5, no. 3 (October 1968), pp. 352–64.

McGUIRE, JOSEPH W., ED.   *Interdisciplinary Studies in Business Behavior,* chap. 6, "Uncertainty, Expectations, and Business Behavior," by Bryce B. Orton. Cincinnati: South-Western Publishing Co., 1962.

MILLER, DAVID W., and STARR, MARTIN K.   *Executive Decisions and Operations Research,* chap. 2. Englewood Cliffs, N.J.: Prentice-Hall, Inc., 1960.

PARSONS, JAMES A.   "Decision-Making under Uncertainty." *Journal of Systems Management,* vol. 23, no. 8 (August 1972), pp. 43–44.

PETERSON, RICHARD, and SEO, K. K.   "Public Administration Planning in Developing Countries: A Bayesian Decision Theory Approach." *Policy Sciences,* September 1972, pp. 371–78.

SIMON, HERBERT   *Administrative Behavior,* chap. 1. 2d ed. New York: Macmillan, Inc., 1961.

THOENIG, J. C.   "The Organization and Its Environment." *Management International Review,* vol. 11, no. 6 (1971), pp. 5–14.

chapter 2

Approaches to Management Decision Making

It is written, "In my Father's house are many mansions." Apparently, the house of administrative science also has many mansions, as evidenced by various developments that have occurred in the field since the late 1940s. We refer in particular to the many new concepts and analytical techniques, drawn from economics, the behavioral sciences, and mathematics, that appear to be revolutionizing the theories of management decision making at the level of the firm.

What are these new theories and procedures? How are they contributing to the advancement of managerial decision making? The purpose of the following sections is to survey these main lines of thought. As is typical of survey-type discussions, our primary objective is to organize and classify many separate and seemingly scattered strands of ideas in order to identify the main patterns of thought which have a bearing on the particular subject.

STATISTICAL DECISION MAKING

Statistical analysis has come to play an increasingly important role in the social sciences. This is due to a growing recognition on the part of social scientists that most branches of statistics deal, in one way or another, with the basic problem of decision making.

Modern statistics is based on the concept of probability which, despite some conflicting ideas among mathematicians and philosophers, has ordinarily been viewed for purposes of statistical analysis as the limit of the relative frequency of an event as the number of trials increases indefinitely. This, combined with the idea of a random variable, that is, a variable which can assume certain values with definite probabilities (as with the throw of dice), forms the basis of the science of statistical inference. Statistical inference is thus a probability process; it deals with the problem of making a probability judgment about the characteristic of a population on the basis of information derived from a sample.

Estimation and Hypothesis Testing

Statistical inference involves two classes of problems: one of these is the estimation of points and intervals; the other is the testing of hypotheses. Both topics are integral parts of classical statistical decision theory, and hence only some essential concepts need be reviewed here in order to pave the way for a few statments about some new developments that are revolutionizing this approach to decision making.

1.   The making of estimates consists of two parts, called point estimation and interval estimation. In *point estimation* the decision maker seeks to obtain a single figure as an estimate of the unknown parameter. In modern classical statistics, two methods have typically been used for this purpose: one is the method of least squares, which chooses as the estimate the particular value that minimizes the sum of the squares of the deviations from the chosen value; the other is the method of maximum likelihood, which chooses the particular value that maximizes the probability density. Both methods often lead to the same estimates, but the latter method is perhaps more frequently employed because it contains certain optimum properties which make it appealing to statisticians.

Point estimation is not a complete solution to the problem of estimation because the single estimate provides no measure of the degree of confidence which may be assigned to the estimate. Statisticians, therefore, prefer to compute interval estimates called *fiducial* or *confidence limits* which, though theoretically not the same, may be regarded as practically the same for elementary decision purposes. These interval estimates are computed such that the confidence coefficient is a preassigned number, usually 95 percent. If a great many such confidence or fiducial limits are computed, then on the average these confidence limits will include the true population value in 95 percent of the cases, and hence they will exclude the true population value in 5 percent of the cases. These procedures, of course, assume normality and independence of the observations which comprise the data—an assumption which may not always be justified where economic data are concerned.

2.   The second area of statistical inference deals with the *testing of hypotheses*. This is actually a special case of estimation in which

the decision maker seeks to determine which of two possible courses of action to adopt. The statistical principles of hypothesis testing were developed in the 1930s by Jerzy Neyman and Egon S. Pearson. This body of knowledge is often taken as the standard case exemplifying the modern classical approach to statistical decision theory. The following brief description is based on the theory of Neyman and Pearson, although the ideas have since been incorporated in modern textbooks on statistics and econometrics.

What is a statistical hypothesis? It is merely a supposition formulated by the decision maker as a basis for reasoning. The hypothesis is not derived from the data but is given independently of the statistical investigation on the basis of experience, observation, economic theory, or other considerations. Various kinds of hypotheses are possible, such as the hypothesis that one value is greater than another, or that one is smaller than another, or that the values are unequal. It is customary to call the hypothesis that is being tested the "null" hypothesis; the other hypothesis, which may include a range of values rather than a single point, is called the "alternative" hypothesis. The problem is to test the null hypothesis against the alternative hypothesis.

Two types of errors are distinguished in testing a hypothesis: Type I error occurs when we reject a hypothesis that should have been accepted, that is, a true hypothesis; Type II error occurs when we accept a hypothesis that should have been rejected, that is, a false hypothesis. The design of methods for testing hypotheses has been based on the criterion that for a given probability of Type I error (called level of significance) the test selected is the one which minimizes the probability of a Type II error.

These classical procedures, it may be noted, have been applied to a variety of practical problems such as tests or decisions involving means, proportions, standard deviations, the randomness of samples, time-series trends, relationships among variables, and so forth.

Recent Developments in Decision Theory

When probability considerations are introduced, the theory of choice may be extended to theories of decision making under risk and uncertainty. This leads to a discussion of choice of strategies, and to the role of "subjective" or "personal" probability theories developed mainly in the early 50s by L. H. Savage,[1] and extended subsequently to a more operational form by Robert Schlaifer and Howard Raiffa.[2] We

[1] L. J. Savage, *The Foundations of Statistics* New York: John Wiley & Sons, Inc., (1954).

[2] See Robert Schlaifer, *Probability and Statistics for Business Decisions* (New York: McGraw-Hill Book Co., 1959); Robert Schlaifer, *Introduction to Statistics for*

refer to these modern developments under the broad heading of "decision theory," a term resulting largely from the work of the eminent scientist Abraham Wald (1902–50), who is chiefly responsible for conceiving statistics in a decision-making context.

Bayesian Analysis

In the Bayesian probability approach, a procedure followed by the decision maker consists of listing the set of values of outcomes that the particular parameter may take and the corresponding subjective probability of each outcome or occurence. The expected value of an outcome, symbolized $E(X)$, is the weighted average of the values of the various outcomes, X_1, X_2, . . . , X_n, and may be expressed by the formula:

$$E(X) = P_1X_1 + P_2X_2 + \cdot \cdot \cdot + P_nX_n \tag{1}$$

where P represents the probability and X represents the reward or value of the outcome. Of course, $P_1 + P_2 + \cdot \cdot \cdot + P_n = 1$. The manner in which the decision maker's prior probability distribution is allocated over the range of possible values of the parameter will enable him (or her) to decide whether to act on the basis of subjective evaluation or whether to go ahead and gather further information (at further cost), with the possibility of revising prior probabilities in the light of the new information.

As an example of Bayesian analysis, let us say that an aerospace manufacturer has been invited to participate in design competition for the development of new weapons system for the Air Force. The company estimates that development of the design specifications will cost $2 million, which cannot be recovered if the design is not accepted. On the other hand, if its design wins the competition, the company can expect a profit of $50 million on its subsequent manufacture of the weapons system. The company has absolutely no information or knowledge of whether its design will win or lose, therefore the Bayesian probability is .5 for winning and .5 for losing.

The alternatives are (1) compete and (2) don't compete. If the company competes, the expected value is (in millions of dollars):

$$E(\text{profit}) = .5(-2) + .5(50) = \$24$$

If the company does not compete, there is neither cost nor profit, and the expected value is zero. Yet despite the fact that one alternative promises $24 million and the other nothing, the company may elect not to compete. Can you think of any reasons why not?

Business Decisions (New York: McGraw-Hill Book Co., 1961); and Howard Raiffa and Robert Schlaifer, *Applied Statistical Decision Theory* (Boston: Division of Research, Harvard Business School, 1961).

Transformation of Dollar Payoff Elements to Utility Measures

In the discussions which follow, a great deal more will be said about models which attempt to formulate "objective" procedures by which to reach business decisions under risk and uncertainty. However, the foregoing example may serve to illustrate the point that dollar payoffs only partially reflect the desirability of reward and that there is sometimes "more at stake," especially if losses are involved. Above, the $24 million expected value was simply a yardstick by which to measure the relative benefits to be derived from alternative courses of action. The actual benefit gained from competing is $50 million if the firm wins. If it loses, the loss will be $2 million. If such a loss would force the firm into bankruptcy, the firm would not risk its survival no matter how great the potential reward might be. On the other hand, if the company is in a position to absorb a $2 million loss, it might be more inclined to assume the risk.

The conclusion to be drawn from this little example is that a transformation of dollar payoffs into some other reward structure appears necessary before a proper analysis can be made. Conventionally, the firm's "utility function" is hypothesized, and potential profit or loss is therefore measured in terms of marginal utility rather than by absolute dollar values. In the above example, when the company cannot afford the loss, it will place a higher marginal utility on losses than on gains. In the discussions which follow, it is always assumed that *this utility transformation has been made before any other computations have been performed.*

The Payoff Matrix

The typical decision problem is sufficiently complex to permit a number of possible outcomes or payoffs for each strategy, depending on conditions beyond the control of the decision maker. How are problems of this type presented and analyzed?

Exhibit 1 presents a simple example of what is known as a "payoff

EXHIBIT 1
Payoff Matrix

Alternate Strategies	States of Nature				Expected Value $E(S_i)$
	N_1	N_2	N_3	N_4	
S_1	6	6	6	4	5.90
S_2	25	7	7	−15	9.50
S_3	20	20	7	−1	17.65*
S_4	19	16	9	−2	15.00
S_5	20	15	15	−3	15.10

matrix." The decision maker's alternative strategies, of which there are five in this particular problem, are listed at the left as S_1 through S_5. The decision maker envisions four possible environments or "states of nature" which are marked off along the top as N_1 through N_4. The numbers in the matrix represent the resulting (utility) payoffs or outcomes for each strategy and associated state of nature.

In this example, the separate strategies might represent different amounts of money to be spent on advertising; the different states of nature might represent the probabilities of economic states such as boom, stability, recession, and depression; and the various payoffs might denote some function of profits. These estimates, of course, are subjective with each decision maker.

THE DECISION ENVIRONMENT

Which strategy should the decision maker choose? This will depend first of all on whether the decision is being made under conditions of certainty, risk, or uncertainty. We will use the example in Exhibit 1 to illustrate a number of decision criteria that have been widely discussed in the literature of decision theory.

Decision Criterion under Certainty

Under conditions of certainty, the decision maker assumes complete knowledge of which state of nature will occur. This reduces the decision matrix to one column, and the decision maker chooses the strategy which yields the greatest payoff. Thus in our example (Exhibit 1) certainty of boom (N_1), would call for S_2, stability (N_2) for S_3, recession (N_3) for S_5, and depression (N_4) for S_1.

Decision Criterion under Risk

As noted in Chapter 1, the decision maker under conditions of risk is able to establish a probability distribution of the payoffs for each strategy, either by deduction or by empirical measurement. The decision criterion under conditions of risk is to maximize the expected value, or mean payoff.

To illustrate application of this criterion to the data in Exhibit 1, let us suppose that the decision maker assumes 20 percent chance of boom, 65 percent chance of stability, 10 percent chance of recession, and 5 percent chance of depression. (Note that the probabilities total 100 percent, which is a necessary condition; that is, one of the states of nature is certain to occur.) The expected value of each strategy, S_i, is calculated according to equation (1), and these calculations are summarized in the rightmost column of Exhibit 1. For example, the expected value of S_4 has been determined by:

$$E(S_4) = .20(19) + .65(16) + .10(9) - .05(2) = 15.00 \qquad (2)$$

As a result of our calculations, there is a clear decision for strategy S_3, which has the greatest expected value (17.65) and has thus been starred. But suppose we had a decision matrix as in Exhibit 2. If we

EXHIBIT 2
Example of Equal Expected Value

Alternative Strategies	States of Nature			Expected Value $E(S_i)$
	N_1	N_2	N_3	
S_1	20	10	20	15
S_2	40	10	0	15

further suppose that the probabilities of the states of nature are $\frac{1}{4}$, $\frac{1}{2}$, and $\frac{1}{4}$ respectively, the expected value for the strategies would be:

$$E(S_1) = .25(20) + .50(10) + .25(20) = 15.0$$
$$E(S_2) = .25(40) + .50(10) + .25(0) = 15.0$$

Since the expected value is the same for both strategies, the decision maker would have to look beyond expected value to reach a decision. A good place to look is at the variation, or spread, of the probability distribution, which, as we said in Chapter 1, is an indicator of the degree of risk.[3]

---

[3] To break the tie illustrated in Exhibit 2 the decision maker may calculate the standard deviation σ (read "sigma") as follows:

$$\sigma = \sqrt{\sum_i (x_i - \mu_x)^2 P_i} \qquad (3)$$

In the case of Exhibit 3, the calculations are:

	$(X_i - \mu_x)$	$(X_i - \mu_x)^2$	P_i	$(x_i - \mu_x)^2 P_i$	
S_1:	5	25	.25	6.25	
	-5	25	.50	12.50	
	5	25	.25	6.25	
			$\sigma_1^2 =$	25.00	$\sigma_1 = 5$
S_2:	25	625	.25	156.25	
	-5	25	.50	12.50	
	-15	225	.25	56.25	
			$\sigma_2^2 =$	225.00	$\sigma_2 = 15$

Dealing with Uncertainty

We have said that it is rarely possible to insure against uncertainty or to incorporate uncertainty into the firm's cost structure or forecasts. There are, however, a number of approaches that knowledgeable business executives commonly use to reduce the perils of uncertainty. Among these are reference to authority for guidance, attempts to control the environment, hedging, the introduction of flexibility into investments, diversification of the firm's interests, the acquisition of additional information, and the modification of goals.

Reference to Authority for Guidance

Perhaps the most pragmatic approach to the reduction of uncertainty, and in any event unquestionably a very common one, is to cast about for some authority to make the decision for us. In some cases, there is a literal authority, such as the Civil Aeronautics Board, the Securities and Exchange Commission, or the Labor Relations Board which dictates the choice of behavior whether the business executive wants it or not. But there are also "figurative authorities," such as tradition, rule of thumb, external suggestion, convention, peer group pressure, adherence to professional ethics, or simply imitation of what others are doing. For example, the corner grocer may adjust his financial structure in order to conform to the traditional "current ratio" of 2:1,[4] a figure of such universal acceptance as to assume the stature of dogma. He may establish his prices by a set percentage markup on cost (rule of thumb); by the manufacturer's suggested retail price (external suggestion); or by observing the prices of competitive grocers (imitation).

The trouble with this approach is that the decision maker is really just shifting the decision to others who may have even less knowledge of the firm's situation than himself. For example, a healthy current ratio depends upon the nature and liquidity of the firm's current assets rather

---

Another reason for examining variation is to compare the riskiness of two projects of different magnitudes. For example, suppose we have a choice between a project with expected return of $100,000 and a standard deviation of $30,000, and another project with expected return of $10,000 and a standard deviation of $4,000. The larger project requires more capital and a larger cash flow. Is it therefore more risky than the smaller one?

The comparisons can be made by means of the relative standard deviation, more commonly (but less accurately) called the coefficient of variation. The coefficient of variation is the ratio of the standard deviation to the mean. When calculated as a percentage, it provides an index of risk. The formula is:

$$C = \frac{\sigma}{\mu_x} (100) \tag{4}$$

To answer our question we see that $C_1 = 30$ and $C_2 = 50$. Therefore the smaller project is actually more risky than the larger.

[4] This is the ratio of current assets to current liabilities as taken from the firm's balance sheet.

than on some fixed yardstick. A set markup percentage ignores the rate of turnover, so that on some fast-moving items the price will be too high to meet the competition, while on some slow-moving items the price may be too low. The manufacturer's suggested retail price is a generality that may or may not apply to local markets. Finally, just following the lead of others may turn out to be a case of the blind leading the blind.

Reference to authority may yield satisfactory temporary solutions to short-run problems. In the long run, however, this approach cannot cope with the major changes that are bound to occur. Any number of new developments of a technological, institutional, legal, governmental, distributional, or consumer environmental nature can, and more importantly should, be anticipated which can not only quickly alter the firm's short-run situation but also render "remedial" decision making useless. Answers generated by rote are rarely satisfactory in time of transition, regardless of their source. In short, therefore, the firm is almost always better off to make its *own* decisions whenever possible.

Control of the Environment

A more sophisticated approach to the reduction of uncertainty is the attempt to gain some control over the business environment. This approach usually takes the form of attempts to gain a monopoly by means of patents, copyrights, exclusive dealerships, or just by being the first to "fill a hole" in the market. This approach also is of a short-run nature. Government casts a jaundiced eye on any reduction of competition, to say nothing of outright monopoly. In addition, if the market is profitable, competitors may be quick to enter despite patents or copyrights.

Hedging

Hedging is one of the most widespread methods by which business executives may replace the uncertainty of a future market with the security of a present contract. Hedging can of course take many forms, not all of which may be for the express purpose of reducing uncertainty; but most "futures" trading is specifically useful to the business executive interested in protection against loss due to price fluctuations in future markets.

The mechanics of hedging are perhaps best examined by specific reference to the commodities exchanges, by far the most common and largest volume example of "hedge" markets today. Trading in these markets is predicated upon a series of spot (current) prices, and a series of futures (forward) prices in various commodities such as corn, oats, soybeans, chicken fryers, and so forth. Suppose, for example, that it is now March and a flour mill has a large stock of wheat which it plans to sell in three months time, that is, in June. It can of course simply wait until June and take its chances on the price of wheat at that time. Alternatively, however, it has the option of "preselling" its wheat in a commodities exchange at the June futures price. Then, regardless of whether the June (spot) price of wheat is ultimately greater or less than the (June futures) selling price in March, the consequences to the flour mill are the same because the wheat has already been contracted at a fixed price. The mill's managers have clearly transformed a situation of uncertainty to one of certainty.[5]

Why is anyone willing to *buy* such a contract from the flour mill? Simply stated, the buyer is betting that the March futures price (for June wheat) will be lower than the June spot price. When the "day of reckoning" comes for the buyer, he (or she) will liquidate his position ("cover his contract") by selling an equal amount of wheat at the spot price, or, rarely, accepting delivery of the wheat itself. If he bets right, he will make money; if not, he will obviously lose money. Hence we see that hedging performs two vital roles in the theater of the commodities exchange; it not only provides an opportunity for suppliers to guarantee the future market price of their goods but also invites the speculative market participation, and therefore the financial liquidity, needed by the suppliers to complete these transactions.

There are yet other hedges against uncertainty beyond the utilization of the futures markets discussed above. Two other forms are (1) the inclusion of escape clauses in contracts and (2) the assessment of penalties for contract violation in the business agreement. The escape clause excuses the contractor from nonperformance caused by conditions beyond the contractor's control, such as strikes, natural disaster, or civil disorder.[6] These kinds of elements are particularly common in contracts depending upon volatile international relationships, for example, or situations in which disruptive labor disputes are probable. Where there is a high degree of uncertainty about costs, a cost-plus or cost-plus fixed fee may be preferable to a lump-sum contract, even though the latter may yield the higher profit if all goes well.

The alternate "nonperformance" clause is a kind of insurance. Penalty assessments are usually set high enough so that a firm may hire alternate contractors on an emergency basis to complete the job if it becomes

---

[5] If the flour mill wishes, it does not even have to deliver its wheat directly to the exchange buyer. An alternative is to sell its wheat locally and cover its "short" position in the market by *purchasing* a wheat contract at the spot price in June. The local selling price and the market spot price will always be very close (or else it would be profitable for someone to buy in one market and sell in the other), so these two transactions "cancel" out leaving the initial futures contract made in March the determinant of profitability.

[6] Insurance companies, for example, limit their coverages in these events. Ironically, the president of the United States is often hesitant to declare a given area a disaster area in the event of flood, say, because his word is often used as the measure by which insurance coverage is, or is not, applicable.

clear that the original contractor will fail. Treble damages are often sought in the courts if breach of contract occurs, so penalty clauses and the threat of lawsuits also clearly serve to limit the uncertainty surrounding the execution of a contractual agreement.

Flexible Investments

The wise manager remembers that change is inevitable and doesn't get locked into investments in specialized building or equipment unless it is clear that the specialized requirement will exist over the life of the investment. For example, a general-purpose machine may cost more than a specialized machine, but may also permit rapid changeover from one line of goods to another. Flexibility is particularly important for such long-term investments as land and buildings. While it may cost more to erect a general-purpose building than one tailored to the firm's current business, this flexibility will pay off if the nature of the business changes and the building must be sold or leased to another business.

Diversification of the Firm's Interests

Diversification is closely related to flexibility. This approach is summed up by the old adage, "Don't put all your eggs in one basket."

Diversification stresses stability and a long-run point of view. In the short run, maximum profit would result from concentration on the most profitable product. However, such a policy might well lead to the firm's demise if the market for that one product diminishes or disappears. Diversification of the product line may dampen fluctuations in the firm's profit function by stabilizing production and earnings. It may insure survival of the firm, and may even maximize profits in the long run. The manufacturer who produces a varied line of products, the investor who buys a diversified portfolio or stock in a mutual fund, and the conglomerate corporation all are examples of the diversification approach to reduction of uncertainty.

Acquisition of Additional Information

It seems obvious that the greater the information gathered about the future, the less uncertain it will be. This is true up to a point, after which the law of diminishing returns takes over. The collection of information is a costly business, and the benefits to be derived from additional information must be weighed against the additional cost.

It may be useful here to distinguish between information and data. Data are the facts, figures, and other raw materials that collectively serve as a basis for discussion, inference, and processing. Information may be defined as processed data ready for communication and use.

In some instances, the decision maker is faced with an enormous quantity of raw data. The collection of information then becomes a process of data reduction; that is, the consolidation of the raw data into a smaller quantity of more meaningful figures or work. In other instances, the decision maker is faced with a minimum of data from which useful information must be developed. In these instances, collection of information may depend upon statistical inference or operations research techniques. In either case, a computer can facilitate the process.

Where should one "draw the line" in the search for additional information by which to reach a decision? The answer has already been suggested above. The decision maker should continue to search for new alternatives, or process additional information about known alternatives, as long as the marginal expected gains of the work exceed their cost. For example a car buyer should continue to shop around for a new automobile up until the point where the cost of the trip to the next dealer, in terms of time, transportation, and so forth, is greater than the expected gain—in terms of, say, a better discount from the retail price. Beyond this point, further search is inadvisable: it costs more than it is worth.

Modification of Goals

In the face of complete uncertainty, an optimum decision may be impossible. However, if the decision maker is willing to settle for something less than a maximum, the problem may be reduced to manageable proportions. For example, break-even analysis can be used to establish a sales goal that will provide a satisfactory return on investment. Although some uncertainty remains as to whether or not the goal can be met, the higher degree of uncertainty (with reference to maximization) becomes less relevant to the decision. Thus it is that we find pricing objectives are commonly established to achieve a target return on investment, to stabilize prices and outputs, to realize a target market share, or to meet competition.

Decision Criteria under Uncertainty

There are a number of available criteria for decision making under uncertainty, and perhaps the most difficult task is to choose the one criterion most appropriate for the problem at hand. The choice of a criterion should not only be logical under the circumstances but should also be consistent with management's philosophy and temperament. Is the current management outlook optimistic or pessimistic? Conservative or adventurous? These characteristics may be, and should be, reflected in the criterion selected.

There are four basic approaches for decision making under uncertainty that have been widely discussed in the literature of decision theory. These criteria are (1) the *Wald* decision criterion, also called *maximin;* (2) the *Hurwicz alpha* decision criterion; (3) the *Savage* decision criterion, also called *minimax regret;* and (4) the *Laplace* decision criterion, also called the *Bayes* decision criterion. The first three are modern developments suggested by their originators during the period 1950–54. The Laplace criterion has been used for more than 2,500 years and was formally articulated by Laplace (a mathematician) early in the 19th century. We will discuss each of these criteria in more detail in the paragraphs that follow.

The Wald Decision Criterion

The Wald, or maximin, decision criterion has been described by various authors as the criterion of pessimism, the criterion of extreme conservatism, a manifestation of pure cowardice, and an attempt to maximize the security level. It envisions nature as perverse and malevolent with Murphy's law fully operational.[7] Therefore the criterion says: determine the worst possible outcome of each strategy and then pick the strategy that yields the best of the worst results.

The maximin criterion is essential to the theory of games, where it is assumed that each opponent is trying to gain what the other loses. Because the criterion is fiscally conservative, it is particularly well suited to small business firms whose survival depends upon avoiding losses. We may illustrate the maximin criterion by applying it to the example shown in Exhibit 1. Now, however, we assume nothing about the probability of events—these are unknown. As shown in Exhibit 3 below, the

EXHIBIT 3
Application of Maximin and Maximax Criteria

	States of Nature				Criterion	
Strategy	N_1	N_2	N_3	N_4	Maximin	Maximax
S_1	6	6	6	4	4*	6
S_2	25	7	7	−15	−15	25*
S_3	20	20	7	−1	−1	20
S_4	19	16	9	−2	−2	19
S_5	20	15	15	−3	−3	20

"most dismal" payoff from each row is chosen as the minimal security level associated with the row strategy. The largest of these, a value

---

[7] Murphy's law is the wry jest that if anything *can* go wrong, it *will.*

of 4, implies that strategy S_1 is the strategy of choice under this criterion.

Is this a good choice? It depends upon what you mean by "good". Note that if state of nature N_4 should occur, S_1 is the only strategy which avoids a loss. On the other hand, should any other state of nature occur, strategy S_1 repeatedly results in the poorest return. Is such a situation inconsistent with reality? Perhaps, but perhaps not. S_1 simply represents the "conservative banker's" strategy—it involves the smallest risks, but at the same time promises the smallest returns. It is up to the firm to decide just how much a minimal level of return is to be weighted in the decision-making process—how much it can afford to risk if things turn for the worse.

The Hurwicz Alpha Decision Criterion

The Hurwicz alpha decision criterion proposes to create a decision index (d) for each strategy, which is a weighted average of its extreme payoffs. The weighting factors are a "coefficient of optimism" (α), which is applied to the maximum payoff (M), and its reciprocal ($1 - \alpha$), which is applied to the minimum payoff (m). The "value" of each strategy is thus:

$$d_i = \alpha M_i + (1 - \alpha)m_i \tag{5}$$

The coefficient of optimism ranging from 0 to 1 enables the decision maker to reflect his (or her) attitude toward risk-taking and his subjective degree of optimism. If the decision maker is an incurable optimist who expects that the best will always happen, he may decide $\alpha = 1$. This is a special case of the Hurwicz criterion which often is treated as a separate criterion called maximax (maximum of the maximum).

The maximax is a criterion of optimism, focusing entirely upon the most welcomed outcome possible for each strategy. Under conditions of uncertainty, maximax is a nonsense criterion, as illustrated by Exhibit 3. Here the maximax criterion would call for S_2. This strategy yields the best possible results if, but only if, N_1 occurs. If N_2 or N_3 occurs, S_2 results are next to worst, and if N_4 occurs S_2 results are the worst possible.

You should also recognize that the maximin (Wald) criterion is a special case of the Hurwicz criterion where $\alpha = 0$. The Hurwicz criterion was advanced to enable the decision maker to consider both extremes and to assign a subjective probability to each. In our example, if the decision maker decided that $\alpha = .7$, the results would be as in Exhibit 4, with strategy S_3 being chosen as the alternative with the highest weighted average.

The decision indicated by the Hurwicz criterion depends upon the value of α, which in turn depends upon the decision maker's own attitude

EXHIBIT 4
Hurwicz Criterion Solution to Decision Problem

	M	α	αM	m	$1 - \alpha$	$(1 - \alpha)m$	d
S_1	6	.7	4.2	4	.3	1.2	5.4
S_2	25	.7	17.5	-15	.3	-4.5	13.0
S_3	20	.7	14.0	-1	.3	-.3	13.7*
S_4	19	.7	13.3	-2	.3	-.6	12.7
S_5	20	.7	14.0	-3	.3	-.9	13.1

toward risk.[8] It is suitable for use by business firms; but if the decision maker's degree of optimism proves to be unfounded, it can lead to substantial losses. Therefore, it must be used with caution.

The Savage Decision Criterion

The Savage criterion, sometimes called the "minimax regret criterion," seeks to minimize "regrets," that is, the opportunity cost of incorrect decisions. Regret is measured as the absolute difference between the payoff for a given strategy and the payoff for the most effective strategy within the same state of nature. After determining the maximum regret for each strategy, the strategy with the least maximum regret is chosen.

The regret matrix is constructed by modifying the payoff matrix. Within each column (state of nature) the largest payoff is subtracted from each payoff number in the column. The absolute difference between them is the measurement of regret. From our example in Exhibit 1, we construct the regret matrix of Exhibit 5.

EXHIBIT 5
Construction of a Regret Matrix

	Payoff Matrix				*Regret Matrix*				*Maximum Regret*
Strategy	N_1	N_2	N_3	N_4	N_1	N_2	N_3	N_4	
S_1	6	6	6	4	19	14	9	0	19
S_2	25	7	7	-15	0	13	8	19	19
S_3	20	20	7	-1	5	0	8	5	8
S_4	19	16	9	-2	·6	4	6	6	6*
S_5	20	15	15	-3	5	5	0	7	7

Exhibit 5 shows that if the state of nature turns out to be N_1 and the decision maker has chosen S_2, he (or she) will have no regret because he has chosen the right strategy to obtain the maximum payoff.

---

[8] The decision will tend toward maximax as alpha increases and toward maximin as alpha decreases. You should verify this by finding the value of alpha at which the decision is changed in our example. HINT: One shift point occurs when $d_2 = d_3$.

If he had chosen S_1, his regret is measured as $|6 - 25| = 19$; if he had chosen S_3, his regret would be $|20 - 25| = 5$; and so forth. After completing the regret matrix, the correct strategy is seen to be S_4 because it minimizes the maximum penalty for guessing wrong about the state of nature.

Note that the decision maker who uses the Savage criterion explicitly abandons attempts to maximize payoff in favor of attempting to achieve a satisfactory payoff with a lesser risk. The Savage criterion is therefore particularly useful for evaluating a series of projects over a long period of time.

The Laplace Decision Criterion

There is a Bayesian postulate which says that if the probabilities of occurrences are unknown, they should be assumed equal. The Laplace criterion uses this postulate to calculate the expected value of each strategy; hence the Laplace criterion is also called the Bayes criterion. The strategy selected is, of course, the one with the greatest expected value.

For strategies S_1, S_2, S_3, S_4, and S_5, from our example, the expected values then become $2\frac{2}{4}$, $2\frac{4}{4}$, $4\frac{6}{4}$, $4\frac{2}{4}$, and $4\frac{7}{4}$, respectively, and strategy S_5 would be selected. The effect of assuming equiprobability among the states of nature is to transform the decision problem under uncertainty into one under risk, and the previous discussion of the decision criterion under risk applies.

The Laplace criterion is a criterion of rationality, completely insensitive to the decision maker's attitude. It is, however, extremely sensitive to the decision maker's definition of the states of nature. For example, suppose the states of nature are hot, warm, and cool weather. In the absence of any weather forecast, the Bayesian probability of cool weather would be one third. But suppose the decision maker decided that it is sufficient to consider the major contingencies of hot and cool. Now the probability of cool weather has been raised to one half! In reality, of course, equiprobability of all states of nature is unlikely, particularly in the short run. Thus the Laplace criterion is more suitable to long-run forecasts by larger firms.

Conclusion

To conclude, we have seen that the process of decision making under uncertainty is essentially one of choosing a criterion, and then performing the calculations necessary to establish a choice within that criterion. We have also seen that the five decision criteria discussed above, when applied to the same decision matrix, can lead to five different strategy selections.

Which criterion is "best"? There is no universally correct answer. Each of the criteria is logically defensible under particular sets of circumstances and conditions, and each can be criticized upon one ground or another. The choice will often depend on personal considerations. In view of this, of what use is the notion of a payoff matrix? Perhaps the best answer is that it provides a useful tool for conceptualizing and formalizing the decision process into (1) a statement of objectives, (2) a selection of payoffs, (3) an evaluation of alternative payoffs, and (4) a selection of alternative strategies. Further, the payoff matrix plays a fundamental role in the theory of games, which represents another relatively new and exciting development in the science of decision making.

THEORY OF GAMES

Sometimes the state of nature or the conditions confronting the decision maker are influenced by the latter's choice of strategy. For instance, in a business situation, instead of trying to infer a competitor's actions on the basis of past behavior, we may seek to determine the competitor's most profitable counterstrategy in relation to our own "best" action, and thereby formulate appropriate defensive measures. This is the approach employed in game theory, about which much has been written since World War II.

What is the role of game theory as an approach to management decision making? How has game theory affected the concept of the firm from the standpoint of microeconomic theory? As in previous sections, it is useful to review some fundamental concepts before answering these questions.

Some Basic Concepts in Game Theory

In the theory of games, a *game* is conceived as a situation in which two or more parties (such as competitors in the marketplace, or unions and management, or even nations) are engaged in the activity of making choices, in anticipation of certain outcomes or payoffs which may take the form of rewards or penalties. The payoff matrix is thus a basic concept in game theory, as are the personal rules of choice or strategies adopted by each player. Thus, given a game involving, say, two players, each possible move on the part of either player may elicit a set of responses from the other. The specification or listing of these moves, based on all conceivable previous sets of moves in the particular game, is a strategy. Obviously strategies may run the range from simple to complex, depending on the nature of the game. Poker, business, and war provide many examples of activities in which both simple and highly elaborate formal games of strategy have been formulated and tested.

Games may be classified according to the number of players or opponents, and by the degree of conflict of interest among the opponents. Thus, by the first criterion, the simplest type of game is a two-person game, but more elaborate games involving any number of players are possible. By the second criterion, two different types of payoff arrangements may be distinguished. One type is called a *zero-sum game* because the amount that one player wins is equal to what the opponents have lost, so that the total payments for all players is zero. Thus the conflict of interest is complete. The other type may be called a *nonzero-sum game* because the total payments made as a result of the game is not zero. That is, the amount gained by one person is not necessarily equal to the amount lost by the others, and hence the conflict of interest is not complete. Considerable analytical complexities may arise in non-zero-sum games.

Often, it is of some use to depict graphically gaming problems for the purposes of analysis, and the two basic approaches are the "extensive" and the "normal" form of the game. The simpler, normal form, uses the payoff matrix concept developed in the last section; and an example is found in Exhibit 6. In this case, the diagram represents a

EXHIBIT 6
Strategies for a Zero-Sum, Two-Person Game
in Normal Form

	B_1	B_2	· · · · ·	B_j	· · · · ·	B_n
A_1	P_{11}	P_{12}				P_{1n}
A_2	P_{21}	P_{22}				P_{2n}
A_3	P_{31}	P_{32}				P_{3n}
A_i	P_{i1}	P_{i2}	· · · · ·	P_{ij}	· · · · ·	P_{in}
A_m	P_{mi}	P_{m2}				P_{mn}

Player B / *Player A*

Payoffs, P_{ij}, are to player A.

zero-sum, two-person game, with player A having to decide which of strategies A_1, A_2, . . . , A_m to adopt, and player B faced with a similar decision from among strategies B_1, B_2, . . . , B_n. The entries inside the matrix represent payoffs to player A, with a separate payoff, P_{ij}, either positive, negative, or zero, associated with each pair of strategies (A_i, B_j) chosen by the participants. (Of course the term "player" here is used in a symbolic sense: player A could just as easily represent a group, a company, a state or government, etc.) The payoff to player

B is easily computed, however, since the fact that this is a zero-sum game necessarily requires that B's payoff be the negative of A's. For nonzero sum games, this abbreviated system no longer works, and it is then required that two separate entries be made for each strategy set in the payoff matrix.

The normal form of the game obtains its compactness at the expense of detail. It does not indicate, for example, which player goes first, nor for that matter, how a sequence of choices might fit together to form a complete strategy alternative. For details of this type, the second, or "extensive," form of the game is required. Roughly speaking, the extensive form of the game looks very similar to the decision tree diagram discussed in the next chapter; choice alternatives for each player are represented by separate arcs from each decision point (node), and the tree terminates in payoffs representing the research outcome of the choice path through which the game was played.

The zero-sum, two-person game has been most successfully and extensively analyzed. In microeconomics, as we have seen, the decision maker's objective is to maximize a utility function (e.g., profits) or to minimize a disutility function (e.g., losses). In game theory a different decision rule is introduced which is already somewhat familiar from the discussion in the previous section. The decision maker can assign the worst or minimum possible payoff to each possible strategy that may be adopted. The strategy would then be selected that yields the maximum among these minimum payoffs, or simply the *maximin* strategy. On the other hand, the decision maker may think in terms of minimizing the maximum loss, or selecting the *minimax* strategy by assigning the greatest possible loss to each strategy and then selecting the strategy which minimizes the maximum loss.

Of course, it could happen that one player adopts a maximin strategy while the other player adopts a minimax strategy, and that a payoff exists in one of the cells of the payoff matrix such that the particular payoff is at the same time the largest value in its row and the smallest value in its column. When this occurs, the payoff matrix is said to possess an equilibrium point which, when expressed geometrically as the point P in Exhibit 7, is called a *saddle point* because, by analogy to a saddle,

EXHIBIT 7
Saddle Points

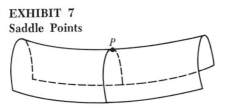

The point P is called a *saddle point*.
Note that it is a maximum in one direction and a minimum in the other.

it is a maximum in one direction and minimum in another. A payoff matrix does not always possess a saddle point. When it does, however, the minimax and maximin strategies have a number of interesting properties, and it can be proven that optimal strategies exist. On the other hand, where matrices exist without saddle points, mixed strategies may be employed in which players randomize their choice of strategies by assigning probabilities to their "pure" strategies. By incorporating utility theory, the concept of an optimum mixed strategy can be developed for a player, and further guides for decision making can then be formulated.

Summary

This brief account of the highly complex subject of game theory can provide at best only a small indication of its terminology, scope, and methodology. Nevertheless, it enables us to ask: What has this approach contributed to managerial decision making and the theory of the firm?

The pioneers in the theory of games, namely Von Neumann and Morgenstern, provided two theories for the behavior of individuals: one involves the two-person situation with complete conflict of interest; the other involves more general situations with two or more decision makers in which the conflict of interest is not necessarily complete (i.e., the goals of the players are not necessarily diametrically opposed). The purpose of the theory of games is to develop criteria for choosing strategies, and in this connection the Wald maximin criterion is of fundamental importance.

The two-person game has been applied successfully to some real problem areas, notably in the field of military warfare which appears to contain many situations that lend themselves to this type of formulation and analysis. Some applications have also been made to certain classes of problems in economics and business administration (e.g., certain relatives of duopoly theory). However, the major problems in the economic theory of the firm are not adequately handled in this manner. As for the more general theory mentioned above, this has been even less satisfactory as a universal theory because it does not appear to provide the kinds of models for most decision problems that are relevant to the firm. Instead, some of the two dozen or so theories of behavior in n-person games that now exist are more valuable for analyzing special types of situations such as bargaining, competition among a few firms in various oligopoly situations, voting and control, and the formation of power blocs.

Are we to conclude from this that the usefulness of game theory is strictly limited as an approach to business decision making and the theory of the firm? Perhaps not, for from a different point of view it may be shown that the theory of games can serve to supplement and reinforce the other approaches, particularly the approach of microeconomics. Thus, in economic theory, the firm's decisions reflect its reactions and adaptation to a given set of impersonal market forces. In the theory of games, the firm must be adoptive as well as adaptive, in the sense that it may continually seek new strategies and courses of action, as well as adjust to given market conditions. The conflicting and cooperating actions of others may thus play a more explicit role in game theory—a role which is not always brought into as sharp a focus in traditional microeconomic theory. That is, the relationships, goals, and states of information may differ substantially in game theoretic situations, laying bare a cross section of the firm's internal structure which is remarkably different from that which is ordinarily perceived in the neoclassical theory of the firm.

PROBLEMS

1. The Mark Shoe Company manufactures three types of shoes. Their sales records show that their sports line at $5 a pair accounts for 60 percent of their sales, dress shoes at $10 a pair account for 30 percent, and their premium line at $15 a pair accounts for the remaining 10 percent of sales. The company's profit margin is 20 percent on the sports line, 25 percent on dress shoes, and 30 percent on the premium line. The factory's capacity is 100,000 pairs of shoes per year. What is their profit at peak capacity if all production is sold?

2. Refer to Problem 1. The Mark Shoe Company estimates that it will cost $20,000 to double their capacity for manufacture of the premium line and would require an advertising campaign costing $25,000 to sell the increased production. Should they increase the production of the premium line?

3. A local department store finds that 9 percent of its charge customers default on 15 percent of their debt. What should be the store's allowance for uncollectible accounts?

4. A friend of yours is seeking financial backing for a speculative venture. You are asked to invest $5,000 which will either be totally lost or which will bring a return of $12,500. What is the largest probability of loss at which you would consider the investment to be profitable? (HINT: The investment is acceptable if the expected value of the return is zero and profitable if it is greater than zero.)

5. A Louisiana oil operator owns a $5 million off-shore drilling rig. It costs $75,000 to pull the drills to safety and batten down the rig in anticipation of a bad storm. An uninsured average loss of $400,000 results from a bad storm if such precautions are not taken. A weather-forecasting service provides an assessment of the probability of a bad storm. Four out of five times that a bad storm was predicted with a probability of 1.0, it did occur. Only 1 severe storm in 100 arrives unpredicted. Should the rig owner pull the drills when the forecasting service predicts a storm at probability 1.0?

6. Given the payoff matrix below, which alternative would be selected by applying the five criteria we have discussed: Laplace/Bayes, Hurwicz, Savage, Wald, and maximax? Assume that the coefficient of optimism is ⅗.

	States of Nature			
Strategy	N_1	N_2	N_3	N_4
A.........	11	15	9	6
B.........	13	4	14	7
C.........	10	10	10	10
D.........	9	11	15	13
E.........	8	3	7	5

7. A stock market advisory service offers three investment portfolios for its clients. Portfolio A contains speculative stocks which aim for capital gains through price appreciation; portfolio B's stocks emphasize stable dividend yields over the long run; portfolio C contains stocks with a moderate potential for growth as well as stable dividend yields.

You are considering investing in one of these portfolios for a period of one year, but you know that the return on your investment will depend on whether the economy (i.e., state of nature) during that period is in a stage of inflation, recession, or depression. Accordingly, you estimate your potential gains and losses after all taxes in the payoff table below, with your subjective probability estimate, P, for each state of nature as shown.

	States of Nature		
	Inflation $P = .7$	Recession $P = .2$	Depression $P = .1$
Portfolio A	100	50	−60
Portfolio B	50	45	40
Portfolio C	70	50	−10

  a. If your sole objective is to maximize the return on your investment, which portfolio should you choose?
  b. If you could not tolerate the chance of a loss, which portfolio should you select?
  c. Suppose that you had no knowledge of the various states of nature and hence were unable to assign any probabilities to them. What would be your maximin strategy? Explain.

REFERENCES

HALTER, A. N., and DEAN, G. W.   *Decisions under Uncertainty with Research Applications.* Cincinnati: South-Western Publishing Co., 1971.

LUCE, R. DUNCAN, and RAIFFA, HOWARD *Games and Decisions,* pp. 12–23, 275–78, 324–26. New York: John Wiley & Sons, Inc., 1957.

MURPHY, M. C. "Risk Evaluation in Farm Planning—A Statistical Approach." *Journal of Agricultural Economics,* vol. 22, no. 1 (January 1971), pp. 61–74.

PRATT, JOHN W.; RAIFFA, HOWARD; and SCHLAIFER, ROBERT "The Foundations of Decision under Uncertainty: An Elementary Exposition." *Journal of the American Statistical Association,* vol. 59, no. 306, pp. 353–75.

SPENCER, MILTON H. "Uncertainty, Expectations, and Foundations of the Theory of Planning." *Journal of the Academy of Management,* vol. 5, no. 3 (December 1962), pp. 197–206.

——— "Axiomatic Method and Accounting Science." *The Accounting Review,* vol. 38, no. 2 (April 1963), pp. 310–16.

TANNENBAUM, ROBERT "The Manager Concept: A Rational Synthesis." *Journal of Business,* vol. 22, no. 4 (October 1949), pp. 225–41.

WEISSELBERG, ROBERT C., and COWLEY, JOSEPH G. "Quicken the Queue." *Journal of Systems Management,* vol. 20, no. 10 (October 1969), pp. 30–35.

chapter 3

Some Decision-Making Models

Decision-making models are mathematical abstractions of real-life systems used to facilitate a choice among two or more alternatives. The application of such models in the field of business represents a trend in recent years to make management more a science and less an art; and while many professionals would debate this point, there is strong evidence to support the usefulness of many of these models in specific application areas. This chapter illustrates three decision-making models which have been successfully utilized by business executives: decision trees, Markov analysis, and Program Evaluation and Review Techniques (PERT).

DECISION TREES

A decision tree is a graphic device that shows a sequence of strategic decisions and the expected consequences under each possible set of circumstances. The construction and analysis of a decision tree is appropriate whenever a sequential series of conditional decisions must be made under conditions of risk. By conditional decision, we mean a decision that depends upon circumstances or options that will occur at a later point in the sequence of time.

Construction of the decision tree begins with the earliest decision and proceeds forward in time through a series of subsequent events and decisions. At each decision or event the tree branches out to depict each possible course of action at that point, until, finally, all logical consequences and the resulting payoffs are depicted. Exhibit 1 is an example of a decision tree.

EXHIBIT 1

**A Decision Tree Depicting the Consequences
of Marketing a New Product**

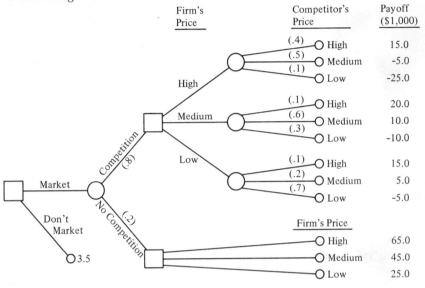

In Exhibit 1 a firm must decide whether to spend $35,000 to market a new product or to invest the money elsewhere for a 10 percent return. Taking the sequence of events from left to right, the first decision (a decision is symbolized by a square) is whether or not to market. If not, the payoff will be $3,500 from the alternative investment. If it markets, the next event (a noncontrollable situation, symbolized by a large circle) may be the entry of a competitor into the market. The probability of competition (.8) and the probability of no competition (.2) are entered beside the appropriate branches (in parentheses).

If there is no competition, the only remaining decision is whether to charge a high, medium, or low price. The three branches are drawn and labeled, and the payoff for each is noted. If there is competition, the same three branches are appropriate. However, each branch divides again into the competitor's options to price high, medium, or low. Each of these final branches is marked with a probability, and the payoff is noted at the end of each one.

The decision tree thus depicts in graphic form the expectation that the price a competitor charges will depend upon the price of the firm's product, and, in turn, the firm's sales and consequent profit will depend upon what price the competitor charges. The decision tree also depicts the range of events within which the actual event is certain to occur. Since it is certain that there will either be competition or there will

EXHIBIT 2
Analysis of a Decision Tree

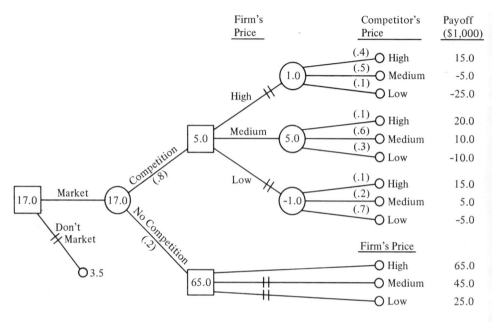

not, the sum of the probabilities for the competitor's pricing policy is
1.0 for each of the firm's three options.

Since each decision depends upon evaluation of events that take place
at a later time, analysis of the decision tree begins at the end of the
sequence and works backwards. Exhibit 2 depicts the analysis for our
example.

Beginning in the upper right of Exhibit 2, the analyst calculates the
expected value if the firm's price is high and there is competition. The
expected value is $(15 \times .4) + (-5 \times .5) + (-25 \times .1) = 1.0$. This expected value is noted in the event circle. The expected values of medium
and low prices are computed and noted in a similar manner. Since
the medium price gives the highest expected value, that value is noted
in the decision box, and the other two branches are slashed to indicate
they are nonoptimal. In the alternative state of no competition, the only
question is whether to charge a high, medium, or low price. The payoffs
indicate that a high price is optimal, and the other two branches are
marked out.

At the first event point (introduction of competitive product) the
expected value is $(5 \times .8) + (65 \times .2) = 17.0$. This value is also entered in the decision box at the first decision point. The firm is now
ready to make a decision. If it does not market, it gets $3,500. If it
does market, there is an expected return of $17,000. Clearly, then, the
firm should enter the market with a high price *if the decision criterion
is to maximize expected value.*

EXHIBIT 3
A Payoff Matrix Calculated from a Decision Tree

| | States of Nature | | | |
| | Competitor's Prices | | | No |
Strategies	High	Medium	Low	Competition
Don't market	3.5	3.5	3.5	3.5
Price—high	15.0	−5.0	−25.0	65.0
Price—medium	20.0	10.0	−10.0	45.0
Price—low.	15.0	5.0	−5.0	25.0

The diagram shows that this course has considerable risk. If competition develops—and there is 80 percent probability that it will—the high price will yield less than the medium price, and could result in substantial losses. In order to apply other decision criteria, the decision maker would have to use the information in the decision tree to develop a decision matrix, as in Exhibit 3. From this matrix, it is in turn possible to verify our conclusion by calculating the expected value of each alternative strategy, as illustrated in Exhibit 4.

EXHIBIT 4
Expected Values of Four Alternative Strategies

Strategies		Expected Value
Don't market		3.5
Price—high	$.8(.4)(15) + .8(.5)(-5) + .8(.1)(-25) + .2(65) =$	13.8
Price—medium	$.8(.1)(20) + .8(.6)(10) + .8(.3)(-10) + .2(45) =$	13.0
Price—low	$.8(.1)(15) + .8(.2)(5) + .8(.7)(-5) + .2(25) =$	4.2

The application of other criteria in the determination of a best-choice policy is also possible. From your understanding of the previous chapter's material, you should be able to confirm the best-choice strategy for Bayes, maximax, minimax, Hurwicz, and Savage assumptions as illustrated below:

Criterion	Best Strategy
Bayes	Price—medium
Maximax	Price—high
Maximin	Don't market
Hurwicz ($\alpha = .75$)	Price—high
Savage	Price—medium

You should also notice how the decision tree illuminates and gives logical meaning to the numbers in the decision matrix and to the wide range of decision options derived therefrom. The lesson to be learned here is that it behooves the decision maker to examine the problem from as many viewpoints as possible before making up his mind, but that the ultimate decision under uncertainty is personal and subjective.

STOCHASTIC DECISION MAKING
AND MARKOV ANALYSIS

Stochastic decision making concerns decision making over time. With the exception of the Bayesian expected value criterion, the foregoing models must be regarded as static; they are useful primarily for one-time investment or other types of commitments. If the decision is to be made over and over again, and the probabilities of outcomes do not change, then the expected value criterion will *always* yield the best results if a sufficient number of decision periods come to pass.

The problem is, of course, that when the decision maker first begins his (or her) task, nothing is known about the probabilities of events—the environment is, by definition, uncertain. Hence, it is at first impossible to perform the required calculations. The proper approach in such circumstances is to assign equal probabilities to each outcome (state of nature), then modify these to reflect what is learned about the system as time goes on.

For example, suppose that the problem associated with Exhibit 1, Chapter 2, requires a decision that must be made over and over again at the beginning of each period. Assume further that after 100 periods have passed, the states of nature N_1, N_2, N_3, and N_4 are observed 20, 65, 10, and 5 times respectively. It is obviously foolish to cling tenaciously to a belief in equiprobabilities in the face of such contrary evidence. Hence, when this additional information becomes evident, the proper approach would be to assign probabilities .20, .65, .10, and .05 to the four events and proceed with the foregoing analysis of expected value and risk.

Of course, systems are dynamic—they change over time. Therefore, the assumption of constant probabilities associated with events may frequently be thwarted. Two decision models commonly employed to handle problems involving dynamics are Markov decision models and PERT (Program Evaluation and Review Technique).

Perhaps the simplest and most straightforward of stochastic processes is the Markov model. Markov analysis is a technique which may be particularly useful in developing marketing strategy, as demonstrated in the example below, but notable success with Markov models has also been achieved in various fields of manpower, production, and financial management. In general, the Markov process may be used to describe any system in which the following assumptions apply:

1. The states of nature in which the system can reside are known and finite, and can be identified symbolically as the discrete entities $N_1, N_2, \ldots N_m$.
2. In each period there is a positive probability of transition from one state to another.[1] These transitional probabilities are either known, or can be approximated, by the decision maker.
3. At any given time, the probability of transition from one state to another is only dependent upon the current state of the system and not upon any states in which the system may have resided in the past.[2]

Illustration

To illustrate Markov analysis, let us visualize a market in which there are three competing brands of some product, and in which customers are free to switch from one brand to another for any reason that suits their fancy. Under these conditions how can we predict what the market shares of the respective brands will be at some time in the future?

If the buyers' behavior in switching brands follows a consistent pattern—and there is a considerable body of empirical data to indicate that it does—then Markov analysis can be used to analyze the pattern and make the desired prediction. The first step is to acquire empirical data regarding the customers' brand-switching behavior, and this is commonly obtained by interviewing a representative sample of buyers. Suppose that 600 buyers have been interviewed to determine which brands they had selected for their two most recent purchases, with the results shown in Exhibit 5.

The rows in Exhibit 5 indicate gains by the respective brands, while

EXHIBIT 5
Results of Market Survey

	Gains			Total Second Purchases
Losses	A	B	C	
A 200		20	10	230
B 15		225	0	240
C 10		5	115	130
Total first purchases	225	250	125	600

---
[1] Technically speaking, we ignore the special case of reducible models.
[2] This property is sometimes described by the statement "the system has no memory."

the columns indicate losses. For example, in the first column we see that brand A lost 200 customers to itself (i.e., retained 200), 15 to brand B, and 10 to brand C, thus accounting for its original market share of 225. In the first row, we see that brand A gained 200 customers from itself, 20 from brand B, and 10 from brand C, thus accounting for its second-purchase market share of 230, which is a net gain of five. The gains and losses by brand B and brand C may be interpreted in a similar manner.

When the numbers gained and lost by the respective brands are converted into fractions of the original market and the totals per brand are converted to fractions of the total sample, we have the following situation:

	Matrix of Transitional Probabilities			Vector of Market Shares, First Purchase	Vector of Market Shares, Second Purchase
	A	*B*	*C*		
A	.889	.080	.080	.375	.383
B	.067	.900	.000	× .417 =	.400
C	.044	.020	.920	.208	.217
	1.000	1.000	1.000	1.00	1.00

The transitional probabilities in the matrix may be interpreted as follows. The probability that the system (say, at present in state "purchased A") will remain in this state (i.e., the probability of exhibiting brand loyalty to A) is .889; the probability of brand loyalty to B is .900; and the probability of brand loyalty to C is .920. Also, we have transitional probabilities from one state to another: the probability of a customer's switching from brand A to brand B is calculated to be .067; of switching from brand B to brand C, .020; and so forth.

In order to calculate the market shares of the three respective competitors after a second "round" of purchases, we use matrix algebra to multiply the matrix of transitional probabilities by the vector of first purchase market shares, the result of which is another vector representing the new distribution. It is easily verified that this result agrees with the empirical data in Exhibit 5. The matrix multiplication may be calculated as follows: A's share of the second-purchase market equals:

A's ability to retain its own patrons times A's share of the first-purchase market . . . . $.889 \times .375 = .383$

Plus A's ability to attract B's patrons times B's share of the first-purchase market . . . . $.080 \times .417 = .033$

Plus A's ability to attract C's patrons times C's share of the first-purchase market . . . . $.080 \times .208 = .017$

Thus, A's share of second-purchase market is 383

Similar calculations for B and C may be computed using the second and third row of the matrix.

If we now want to determine the distribution of market shares in the third-purchase market, we multiply the transitional probabilities matrix by the second-purchase market share vector. Or we can get the same results if we raise the transitional probabilities matrix to a power of 2 and multiply by the first-purchase market share vector. In general, the forecast market shares for any purchase period n can be obtained by raising the transitional probabilities matrix to the $(n-1)$ power and multiplying the results by the original market share vector. Raising a matrix to a power is a tedious procedure when performed by hand, but it can easily be done on a computer.

Equilibrium Conditions

If none of the competitors does anything to alter the matrix of transitional probabilities, the market shares of each will eventually stabilize in a state of equilibrium, which may be defined as the condition in which, for each competitor, the net effect of gains and losses of customers "cancel out" and there is no change in market share. In the case of our example, if we let A, B, and C represent the market shares of brand A, brand B, and brand C respectively, then we may describe the market at equilibrium with the following set of equations:

$$A = .889A + .080B + .080C \qquad (1)$$
$$B = .067A + .900B + .000C \qquad (2)$$
$$C = .044A + .020B + .920C \qquad (3)$$
$$1 = \quad A + \quad B + \quad C \qquad (4)$$

These equations can be restated as:

$$0 = -.111A + .080B + .080C \qquad (5)$$
$$0 = \quad .067A - .100B + .000C \qquad (6)$$
$$0 = \quad .044A + .020B - .080C \qquad (7)$$
$$1 = \quad A + \quad B + \quad C \qquad (8)$$

Since the value of A in equation (5), (6), and (7) sums to zero, the equations are mathematically interrelated, and we may drop any one of them in order to have a set of three equations with three unknowns. Then, solving for A, B, and C, we find $A = .42$, $B = .38$, and $C = .30$.

Thus we conclude that the market shares will be at equilibrium where brand A has 42 percent, brand B has 28 percent, and brand C has 30 percent of the total market. To prove these results we once again resort to matrix multiplication:

	Transitional Probabilities			Equilibrium Market Shares	
	A	*B*	*C*		

$$
\begin{array}{c}
A \\ B \\ C
\end{array}
\begin{pmatrix}
.889 & .080 & .080 \\
.067 & .900 & .000 \\
.044 & .020 & .920
\end{pmatrix}
\times
\begin{pmatrix}
.42 \\ .28 \\ .30
\end{pmatrix}
=
\begin{pmatrix}
.42 \\ .28 \\ .30
\end{pmatrix}
$$

Using our computer, we learn that equilibrium occurs when the matrix of transitional probabilities is raised to the 11th power and multiplied by the first-purchase vector of market shares. This indicates that equilibrium of market shares will be reached in the 12th purchase period.

Marketing Strategy

In the preceding example we have seen that the manager of brand B, which started out with 50 percent of the market, can expect the market share of brand B to slide down to 28 percent when market equilibrium is reached—if he (or she) does nothing about it. If he wants to change this result, he can either try to retain more of his original customers or he can try to win more customers away from the other brands.

Let us say that the manager of brand B pursues the first strategy of increasing loyalty to brand B by, say, launching an advertising campaign stressing the quality of brand B. In so doing, the manager therefore affects the transition probabilities, as suggested in the new transitional matrix presented below. In particular, we see that the entries now reflect the desired increased brand loyalty to B because the "transitional" probability of B to itself has increased from .900 (see previous matrix) to .950; the probabilities of switching *from* brand B to alternate brands has also been reduced accordingly (second column of the matrix). If B is able to maintain this high level of customer loyalty, new equilibrium market shares will result, as indicated in the rightmost vector of the calculations below:

	Transitional Probabilities			Equilibrium Market Shares	
	A	*B*	*C*		

$$
\begin{array}{c}
A \\ B \\ C
\end{array}
\begin{pmatrix}
.889 & .040 & .080 \\
.067 & .950 & .000 \\
.044 & .010 & .920
\end{pmatrix}
\times
\begin{pmatrix}
.33 \\ .44 \\ .23
\end{pmatrix}
=
\begin{pmatrix}
.33 \\ .44 \\ .23
\end{pmatrix}
$$

Thus a marketing effort to increase brand loyalty by 5 percent will pay off for seller B by increasing its long-run equilibrium share of the market from 28 percent to 44 percent. On the other hand, suppose that seller B pursues the strategy of winning customers away from the other brands with this result:

	Transitional Probabilities			Market Shares		
	A	B	C			
A	.889	.080	.050	.39		.39
B	.092	.900	.030	× .41	=	.41
C	.019	.020	.920	.20		.20

Here we see that although the increase in customers is the same, the resulting market share is smaller. So, which strategy is better for the marketing manager of brand B? All other things being equal, the deciding factor would be the relative cost of the marketing effort. If it costs no more to increase brand loyalty than to win customers away from the competition, then the first strategy is better.

Conclusion

In conclusion, this brief foray into Markov analysis is intended primarily as an introduction to an increasingly popular approach to management decision making explicitly incorporating the dimension of time in the policy formulation process; it was not intended as an exhaustive review of discrete stochastic decision processes. Applications of Markov models in widely divergent fields such as operations research, demography, information sciences, and biology have already been made, and notable success has been achieved in the area of resource conservation, in which variations in game populations, water reservoir levels, or forest reserves have acted as the states of nature. Examples of applications in business have already been cited in the introductory remarks to this section. As in applications of other business models, however, the successful utilization of a Markov model is ultimately dependent not upon the power of the model but upon the judgment of the analyst in assessing its appropriateness for the environment under study.

PERT

Yet another type of stochastic decision making involves the use of PERT (Program Evaluation and Review Technique). Originally conceived by the Navy for use in its Polaris development program, the PERT approach applies to problems in which scheduling decisions are necessitated in the completion of a large project. Among other things, the manager presumably wishes to know which activities are the most crucial in the project's completion, which activities represent the most effective additional resource investment if the project lags behind, and of course, how much additional time savings for the entire project can be "bought" for each additional, say, thousand dollars of project money.

The basis of the PERT application is a schedule of activities as suggested in Exhibit 6 and an estimate of completion times for each of these activities.

EXHIBIT 6
PERT Activity Table

| Activity | Completed Prior Activities Required | Activity Duration Estimates (months) | | | Weighted Average | Updated Table— Expected Completion Times |
		Optimistic	Realistic	Pessimistic		
A	–	3	4	11	5	4*
B	–	5	8	11	8	7*
C	A	4.5	5.5	9.5	6	6*
D	B	2	5.5	6	5	8**
E	B	2	2.5	6	3	7**
F	E	.5	1	1.5	1	1
G	C, D, F	1	1.5	5	2	2
H	E	2	2.5	6	3	3

* Completed.
** New estimate.

As is evident from the table, all the activities need not be completed sequentially; many of them can be worked on in parallel, thereby saving time in the ultimate completion of the entire project. Among other things, PERT will be able to tell us just when each activity must start and end in order to achieve the most efficient schedule possible.

Usually, the exact completion time for each activity is not known in advance, and this is especially true for projects involving research or development. Customarily, it is the practice to use a weighted average of three estimates of activity duration: an "optimistic" estimate $\bar{a}$, a "pessimistic" estimate $\bar{b}$, and a "realistic" estimate $\bar{r}$, to calculate t_e, the expected duration of the activity according to the formula:

$$t_e = \frac{\bar{a} + 4\bar{r} + \bar{b}}{6}$$

It is this weighted estimation procedure which has been used to calculate the expected completion figures in the table.

Once the table has been constructed, a graphical display of the project's activities as a network usually proves helpful. This has been done for our example in Exhibit 7. Each activity is represented by a line;

EXHIBIT 7
A PERT Network

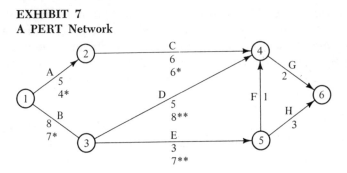

and the completions of activities, or "milestones," are designated by nodes or circles. The unstarred numbers under the lines represent the computed expected completion times of each activity, while starred numbers represent the updated expected completion times.

The Critical Path

The diagram makes clear that various sequences of activities must be accomplished *in order* before the entire project is completed. For example the network path corresponding to the sequence of activities B, E, F, and G must be completed before project termination (milestone 6) is attained. What is the sequence of activities most crucial to the successful conclusion of the project? This corresponds to the longest path through the project network, termed the "critical path." Several available computerized algorithms (computational procedures) permit the computation of this critical path, identifying these "crucial" activities. (In the simple example illustrated here, this may even be determined by inspection. However, we must bear in mind that PERT models of this type are typically applied to projects involving hundreds of nodes and thousands of activities.) The mechanics of these algorithms need not concern us here; of immediate importance is rather the fact that upon work commencement, the manager should obviously pay careful attention to activities lying on the critical path because delay in any of these will extend the completion of the entire project. In the present example, the critical path has been calculated to be the sequence of activities B, D, and G with a corresponding project duration of 15 time periods $(8 + 5 + 2 = 15)$, say 15 months.

Time and Cost Effectiveness of Additional Investments

Now assume that a period of time has passed. Some of the activities have been completed, and an update of the table is in order. This has been done in the rightmost portion of Exhibit 6. From the new information it appears that the project has had some successes and some failures. Most notable in the former has been the completion of activities A and B earlier than anticipated. Unfortunately, trouble has developed in activity D, extending its completion date to eight months; and to make matters worse, new information has been obtained indicating that activity E, formally thought to require only three months, is now likely to take in excess of seven. The starred numbers in Exhibit 7 represent the updated situation.

What of the critical path? Reevaluation of the situation reveals the fact that starting from node 3, there are now *three* "updated" critical paths: D–G, E–F–G, and E–H. Each of these paths takes ten months of expected project time, in addition to the seven months already expended, a total of 17 months. If the project must be completed in, say, 15 months (for the company to avoid heavy penalty), additional resources at additional cost must be obtained. But where can these additional resources best be allocated in order to achieve the most time savings for a given expenditure of money? The answer to this question lies in a cost-effectiveness analysis of the individual activities. Exhibit 8 illustrates the general approach.

EXHIBIT 8
Additional Resource
Requirements for a One- and
Two-Month Reduction in Project
Time for a PERT System

	Additional Resources (in dollars) Required for—	
Activity	One-Month Reduction	Two-Month Reduction
D.	$2,000	$4,000
E.	$1,500	$6,000
F.	Not possible	Not possible
G.	$3,500	Not possible
H.	$2,000	$3,000

The figures in the exhibit represent the project cost of one- and two-month time reductions in each of the critical activities and are obtained from sources closest to each activity. From this information, the project manager may now proceed to determine the most efficient expenditure plan required to "save" the project's completion time. If, for example, only activities D and G constituted the new critical path and a one-month savings were all that were needed, then clearly the cheapest corrective for the project would be a $2,000 investment (of resources) in activity D.

For the project illustrated here, however, a more difficult problem is at hand: a two-month savings is necessitated and three critical paths must be reduced simultaneously, timewise, in order to meet the project deadline. The schedule below outlines the various possibilities and their attendant costs:

Strategy	Description	Cost
1	Reduce D two months and reduce E two months	$10,000
2	Reduce D, E, G, and H each one month	9,000
3	Reduce D and G one month and reduce E two months	11,500

In order to achieve the time savings objectives, the project manager must now invest additional resources in such a way as to reduce the time requirement on three critical paths (D–G, E–F–G, E–H). From the above schedule, however, the manager's course of action is clear. Assuming the optimal decision is associated with the least-cost strategy, the most efficient way to obtain the desired two-month time reduction is to pursue strategy 2, which requires an investment of $2,000 of additional resources in activity D, $1,500 of additional resources in activity E, $3,500 of additional resources in activity G, and $2,000 of additional resources in activity H. The total cost of the two-month time reduction for the completion of the project is the sum of these investments, or $9,000.

For larger projects, a computerized approach is usually taken with regard to such questions, but the basis for the analysis remains the same. Project dollars are balanced against potential time savings along the critical path or paths, and a time/cost effectiveness schedule is constructed for the project as a whole as illustrated in Exhibit 9. Two points on a schedule such as this for the present problem, given the data above would be $3,500 for a one-month reduction (reduce D and E by one month) and $9,000 (as computed above) for the two-month reduction.

EXHIBIT 9
Time/Cost Tradeoffs in a PERT System

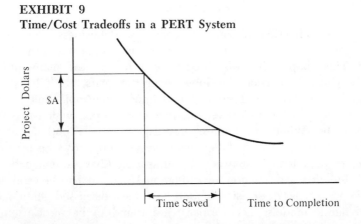

A Word of Caution

This brief review of PERT has provided some idea of the way in which large projects may be scheduled and phased, and how the network analysis along with other pertinent information may aid the manager in the necessary supervisory decision-making capacity as the project develops. PERT, along with CPM (critical path method) and other derivatives of the basic system, has been successfully applied by federal agencies such as NASA in the U.S. Space Program, by private industry such as developers planning large construction projects, and by other business firms preparing for large organizational changes in structure or location. But PERT is *not* a substitute for the discretion of the business manager and is limited in what it can do. It calculates critical paths for projects using only a single estimate of activity completion times, for example, and may therefore be calculating the "right" path for the wrong information. Further, the importance of activities is judged only by the magnitude of their completion times. Hence, the results of a PERT analysis may place the delivery of a nameplate as more critical to the delivery schedule than the assembly of a piece of electronic equipment necessary to the functioning of the completed product. Finally, there is a bit of circular reasoning in PERT in that there are many ways of doing things and usually the completion time of a project is dependent upon how much resource investment will be committed to each particular job. But this is sometimes decided after determining which activities are on the critical path so that we see that each estimation procedure must wait for the other before giving the desired information. For all these drawbacks, however, PERT is not without redeeming features and may prove useful to the business manager as one, if not the only, tool by which to plan and act. And, as in all key tools of management, discriminatory model application provides the key to better decision making.

CONCLUSION

Managerial decision making is a complicated business, and the risks and uncertainties of the decision environment do not make the job any easier. This chapter has discussed only a few of the many practical models which have been developed over the years. Underlying all of the analyses is a theme of fundamental importance: *objectivity.* A decision must always be subjective, but the criteria upon which it is based need not be. When criteria are established, usually both a rationale for choice and an implicit indicator of primary objectives become clear. Hence, communication between business executives is enhanced; and a basis for further discussion, investigation, or action, can be established.

Two basic types of decision models have been discussed: static models and dynamic models. The former were found to be most useful for the single, "one-time" problem, such as the investment decision; the latter explicitly included the dimension of time in the analysis for certain business problems in which decisions are time-dependent. Both types of models require discriminatory judgment if they are to be used successfully.

Decision trees enable the manager to trace through time the sequence of controllable and noncontrollable events which ultimately culminate in rewards or penalties to the firm. If the probabilities of outcomes are known, then an expected-value criterion may be applied to determine a specific course of action. If the probabilities of outcomes are not known, it is still possible to reduce the decision tree to a payoff matrix, then apply decision criteria under uncertainty in order to reach a business decision.

Stochastic decision making involves decision making over time. A Markov analysis permits the business manager to predict the consequences of certain decisions by enabling him to compute the ultimate "equilibrium" to which each contemplated decision might lead. PERT is most closely associated with project control, but is clearly a time-dependent decision-making tool. PERT enables the manager to keep track of those activities which are critical to completion of the entire project. If the project falls behind schedule, PERT enables the manager to decide how completion time may be accelerated at minimum additional cost.

PROBLEMS

1.* A logging company must decide the most advantageous duration for a paving project which must be completed during a period of expected foul weather. The beginning date of the project has been definitely set, and a critical-path analysis shows that three termination dates are feasible. If the paving is completed in four months, the basic project cost will be $80,000. A duration of five months will allow construction savings of $20,000, and it will cost an extra $40,000 over the basic cost to crash the project to three months. However, transportation expenses can be cut by $10,000 if the project is completed in three months, but will be increased by $15,000 if the project takes five months.

Extra expense for possible weather conditions must also be considered. Weather records indicate a .3 probability of mild rain, a .5 probability of heavy rain, and a .2 probability of wind and rain. Estimated costs under each of these conditions are given in the following table:

Weather Conditions	Three Months	Four Months	Five Months
Mild rain	$10,000	$15,000	$ 5,000
Heavy rain	10,000	40,000	60,000
Wind and rain	15,000	55,000	65,000

Which duration has the lowest expected total cost?

*Adapted from James L., Riggs, *Economic Decision Models for Engineers and Managers*. (New York: McGraw-Hill Book Co. 1968).

2.* A firm has produced a new product which has been unusually successful, and in order to meet the unexpectedly high demand it will be necessary to add additional production facilities. The troubling question is whether the high demand will continue, increase, or decrease. An eight-year marketing study has yielded the following results:

First Three Years	Last Five Years	Probability
High . . . . + ...	High	.4
High . . . . + ...	Low.	.2
Low. . . . . + ...	High	.3
Low. . . . . + ...	Low.	.1

Three plans are under consideration. Plan A provides a permanent increase in capacity at a cost of $100,000 and will yield a cash inflow of $40,000 per year if demand is high, $5,000 per year if demand is low.

Plan B is a stop-gap measure which can be converted to a permanent capacity by a supplementary investment, B', after three years when the demand pattern is better known. If demand is high, plan B will yield $30,000 per year for the first three years, and $20,000 per year thereafter without the supplement B'. With B' and high demand, the last five years will yield $40,000 per year. If demand is low, plan B will yield $30,000 per year for the first three years, and $30,000 per year thereafter without the supplement. With the supplement and low demand, Plan B will yield $10,000 per year during the last five years. Plan B will cost $70,000 initially, and the supplement, if added, will cost $45,000.

Use a decision tree to determine which plan or combination of plans appears most attractive. (Ignore time values of money, which will be considered in a later chapter on capital budgeting.)

3.* A small foundry is having trouble with its old arc furnace which has been completely depreciated for accounting purposes but which can be sold for $6,000. The immediate decision to be made is whether to modify the old machine or to buy a current model which has many desirable features which cannot be included in modification of the old machine. The decision is complicated by the general opinion in the industry that a breakthrough in furnace technology is coming within three years.

The best estimates the owners can get are that there is a 40 percent chance of a radically improved furnace in about three years. If the new furnace actually appears, the probability that it will make all current models noncompetitive is .9, and that it will amount to no more than a minor improvement is .1.

The cost of modifying the old furnace is $8,000, and the cost of a current model is $25,000. In either case, the furnace will be used

---

* Adapted from James L., Riggs, *Economic Decision Models for Engineers and Managers.* (New York: McGraw-Hill Book Co. 1968).

for eight years and then sold. The following table gives the expected annual savings and the salvage value under three conditions (states of nature):

N_1 = no technological breakthrough

N_2 = new furnace developed which makes all current furnaces obsolete

N_3 = new furnace developed which provides only minor savings

	Buy New Furnace		Modify Old Furnace	
States	Annual Savings	Salvage Value	Annual Savings	Salvage Value
N_1........	$6,000	$8,000	$2,000	$4,000
N_2........	2,000	2,000	1,000	2,000
N_3........	3,000	4,000	1,000	3,000

The table above is based on a study period and life of eight years for both furnaces. The sharp decrease in savings and salvage value in states N_2 and N_3 occur because the development of a radically different or even improved furnace would probably cut into the foundry's demand and its general competitive position.

Another alternative exists for the foundry. If the new type furnace is developed in three years, the modified old furnace could be sold at that time for $9,000 and the radical new furnace purchased for an estimated $45,000. There is a .9 probability of state N_2, in which case the new furnace would save $13,000 annually and be worth $20,000 at the end of five years; and a .1 probability of state N_3, in which case the new furnace would save only $8,000 a year and would be worth only $15,000 after five years. If a new machine is purchased now, it will be used for eight years, regardless of new developments.

Use a decision tree to determine whether the old furnace should be modified or a new, current model should be purchased. (Ignore the time value of money, which will be considered in a later chapter on capital budgeting.)

4. A market survey results in the following gains and losses for three brands of aspirin:

	Gains			Total Second Purchases
Losses	A	B	C	
A	150	80	70	300
B	20	80	40	140
C	50	50	60	160
Total first purchases	220	210	170	600

According to these data, what are the equilibrium market shares of the three brands of aspirin?

5. An electronics engineer is faced with the problem of deciding which series of parts should be used in the design of a new component system. There are three basic types of parts: A, B, and C. The engineer has two choices for part type A, three choices for part type B, and four choices for part type C. Using data from past experience, the engineer calculates the probability of successful operation between part types A and B and part types B and C. The diagram below illustrates the decision tree and calculated probabilities. Which combination of part types A, B, and C would be the most effective (have the highest probability of operation) for the data given?

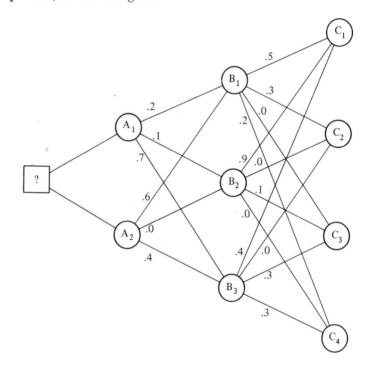

6. The diagram below represents a PERT network with activities A, B, C, D, E, and F.

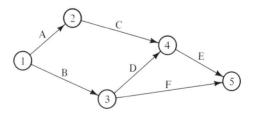

    a. Suppose the expected completion time for these activities were three, five, four, three, seven, and four months. respectively.
    Which activities lie on the critical path and what is the expected completion time of the project?

    b. Answer part (*a*) if the expected completion times for the activities were two, six, three, seven, eight, and one, respectively.

    c. Answer part (*a*) if the expected completion times for the activities were five, three, three, four, seven, and two, respectively.

    d. Using your answers for parts (*a*), (*b*), and (*c*), what is the probability that each activity will lie on the critical path?

7. The erection of a prefabricated house requires orderly construction through a number of major steps, including laying the foundation, raising the first floor walls, wiring, and so forth. For simplicity, identify these steps as A, B, C, and so forth.

    a. Below is a table identifying each activity and the steps required to precede each activity. Construct a PERT network from this information.

Activity	Immediately Preceding Activities	Expected Completion Time
A	—	4
B	—	6
C	—	3
D	A	2
E	A	8
F	B	5
G	B	7
H	C	4
I	D	3
J	E, F	5
K	E, F	5
L	G, H	5
M	I, J	7
N	K, L	6

    b. From the information provided in the table, determine the critical path and the expected completion time for a prefabricated house.

REFERENCES

BELLMAN, RICHARD E., and DREYFUS, STUART E. *Applied Dynamic Programming*. Princeton, N.J.: Princeton University Press, 1962.

BORCK, DAVID "Decision Theory: An Operations Research Tool." *Systems and Procedures Journal*, vol. 19, no. 3 (May–June 1968), pp. 24–26.

GRAY, CLIFFORD F., and REISMAN, ROBERT E. "PERT Simulation: A Dynamic Approach to the PERT Technique." *Journal of Systems Management*, vol. 20, no. 3 (March 1969), pp. 18–23.

GREEN, PAUL E. "Bayesian Statistics and Product Decisions." *Business Horizons*, vol. 5, no. 3 (Fall 1962), pp. 101–9.

HILLIER, FREDERICK S., and LIEBERMAN, GERALD J. *Introduction to Operations Research*. San Francisco: Holden-Day, Inc., 1975.

HIRSHLEIFER, JACK "The Bayesian Approach to Statistical Decision—An Exposition." *Journal of Business*, vol. 34, no. 4 (October 1961), pp. 471–89.

NIEDEREICHHOLZ, J.   "Business Simulation and Management Decisions." *Management International Review*, vol. 11, no. 1 (January 1971), pp. 47–52.

PAIK, C. M.   *Quantitative Methods for Managerial Decisions*. New York: McGraw-Hill Book Co., 1973.

PETERSON, R. E., and SEO, K. K.   "Benefit Cost Analysis: A Decision-Tree Approach." *Proceedings of Annual American Institute for Decision Science*, Western Conference, March 1974.

RIGGS, JAMES L.   *Economic Decision Models: For Engineers and Managers*. New York: McGraw-Hill Book Co., 1968.

WOLLASTON, JUSTIN G. F.   "Determining Optimum Policy Through Statistical Analysis." *Systems and Procedures Journal*, vol. 18, no. 6 (November–December 1967), pp. 20–23.

chapter 4

Forecasting

If we could first know where we are and whither we are tending, we could better judge what to do and how to do it.

Abraham Lincoln

These words, more than a century old, explain as well as any the necessity of forecasting. In a world where the future is not known with certainty, virtually every business and economic decision rests upon a forecast of future conditions. Successful forecasting aims at reducing the areas of uncertainty that surround management decision making with respect to costs, profits, sales, production, pricing, capital investment, and so forth. If the future were known with certainty, forecasting would be unnecessary. Decisions could be made and plans formulated on a once-and-for-all basis, without the need for subsequent revision. But uncertainty does exist; future outcomes are rarely assured, and therefore an *organized* system of forecasting is necessary.

Forecasting takes place at all levels of economic activity, with both long-range and short-range projections. In general, there are four different approaches that are commonly used to develop forecasts:

1. Mechanical extrapolations.
2. Barometric techniques.
3. Opinion polling.
4. Econometric models.

Although these methods are different, they should not necessarily be regarded as mutually exclusive. Indeed, some methods may be more suitable for preparing short-term forecasts such as monthly or quarterly predictions; others may be best for long-term projections of a year or

73

more. Some may be better for forecasting at the macro level, while others may be preferred for forecasting at the level of the firm. And in many organizations, two, three, or even all four approaches may be employed with various degrees of emphasis and sophistication.

MECHANICAL EXTRAPOLATIONS

Extrapolation procedures of one form or another are extensively used by business executives, economists, market researchers, and others engaged in forecasting activities. As a method of prediction, extrapolation may include procedures ranging from simple coin tossing to determine an upward or downward movement to the projection of trends, autocorrelations, and other seemingly more complex mathematical techniques. Typically, extrapolation techniques are distinguished from other forecasting methods discussed later in that they are essentially mechanical and are not closely integrated with relevant economic theory and statistical data. Nevertheless, they are widely used by professional forecasters, probably because they are convenient and, for reasons to be given later, often seem to "work." Hence, a few of the more common forms used in business should be worth noting.

Naive Models

Over the years, economists and statisticians have developed increasingly sophisticated theoretical and mathematical methods for predicting economic variables like production, income, and employment. Early in the game (mostly after World War II), the question arose as to how the errors of prediction made by these more elegant models and equations compared with the errors made by a "naive model," that is, by a very simple model or hypothesis set up as the straw man which the more sophisticated model could knock down.

The naive models that have been suggested may ordinarily be thought of as "continuity" models of one type or another, for they all state that the future value of the variable in question is in some way a function of its present or recent value. Thus, letting y denote the realized value of the variable under investigation, $\hat{y}$ (read: "y-hat") its forecast value, and letting the subscript t denote the time period, the following two naive models may be cited as typical examples:

1. *No change model:* The predicted value of the variable for the next period will be the same as its actual value in the present period:

$$\hat{y}_{t+1} = y_t$$

2. *Proportional change model:* The *change* in the value of the variable from the current period to the next period $(\hat{y}_{t+1} - y_t = \Delta\hat{y}_{t+1})$

will be proportional to the *change* in the value of the variable from the last period to the current period $(y_t - y_{t-1} = \Delta y_t)$, thus

$$\Delta \hat{y}_{t+1} = k\Delta y_t$$

where the parameter k may be estimated by sheer hunch if there is no adequate data, or by observation from historical data, or by more refined methods such as averaging or statistical regression. If $k = 1$, the equation may be said to represent an "equal change" model. On the other hand, with Δy positive, models of growth or decline would be represented by either $k > 1$ or $k < 1$.

It is an interesting fact that the great majority of all economic decisions (and probably political and social decisions as well) are made on the basis of naive models such as these. It is not difficult to see why this is so. Naive models are either straightforward or modified projections of the present or of the recent past. Hence for most short-term decisions they provide the only feasible guides for forecasting, since they are simple to apply and require a minimum amount of data or computation.

Naive models, as mentioned above, were originally developed for the purpose of providing a yardstick against which more elaborate forecasting models could be compared. Although they are still widely used for this purpose, they have also been extensively employed by various business firms as formal forecasting procedures, especially for short-term forecasting of one to several months.

On a number of occasions, it has been found that naive models proved to be better forecasting mechanisms than the more elaborate and sophisticated procedures with which they were compared. This situation is likely to arise when the system being forecast is relatively stable or if it is changing in a fairly uniform or gradual way so that a naive model serves as a reasonably good representation. However, for a complex, dynamic system in which fundamental changes occur frequently, it is likely that something more elaborate than a naive model is needed for making reliable predictions.

Time-Series Analysis

A *time series* is a sequence of values corresponding to particular points, or periods, of time. Data such as sales, production, and prices, when arranged chronologically, are thereby ordered in time and hence are referred to as time series. The simple line chart is the most common graphic device for depicting a time series, with the dependent variable such as sales or production or prices scaled on the vertical axis, and the independent variable, "time," expressed in years or months or any other temporal measure, scaled on the horizontal axis.

Why does a time series typically exhibit a pattern of fluctuations? The answer to this question has usually been that at least four sources of variation are at work in an economic time series:

1. Trend (T).
2. Seasonal variation (S).
3. Cyclical variation (C).
4. Irregular forces (I).

Trend represents the long-run growth or decline of the series. *Seasonal* variations due to weather and custom manifest themselves during the same approximate time periods each year (for example, Christmas, Easter, and other seasons of the year during which different types of purchases are made). *Cyclical* variations, covering several years at a time, reflect prosperities and recessions. And finally, *irregular forces,* such as strikes, wars, and boycotts, are erratic in their influence on the particular series, but nevertheless must be recognized.

Of the four forces affecting economic time series, the seasonal factor is fairly easy to measure and predict. The irregular factor is unpredictable but can be adjusted by a smoothing out process such as a moving average. Hence the trend, which represents persistent growth or decline, and the cyclical, which is presumably recurrent, are the forces which have occupied the chief attention of forecasters using time-series analysis. Comments as to the implications of trend projections and cylical analyses are therefore in order.

Trend Projections. As a forecasting procedure, the method of trend projection usually assumes that the recent rate of change of the variable will continue in the future. On this basis, expectations are established by projecting past trends into the future, using techniques such as regression analysis, for example. Thus, companies often project sales, GNP, and so forth, several years into the future by this procedure. In basing predictions on trends of past relationships, the trend may be a simple unweighted line, or it may be weighted by attaching greatest importance to the most recent period and successively lesser degrees of importance to periods in the more distant past.

A simple method of isolating the trend in a time series of data is to employ a moving average. A moving average is an "artificial" time series. It is constructed from a given time series by replacing each value in the given series by the mean of that value and some of the values immediately preceding it and directly following it. An illustration of a three-month, five-month, and seven-month moving average based on hypothetical sales data is presented in Exhibit 1.

Of course, moving averages of any desired length can be calculated, depending on the time unit in which the data are quoted and the number of observations. Ideally, the time length of the moving average should be equal to the average period of the cycle in the series, that is, the

EXHIBIT 1
Illustrative Moving Averages

| | | Moving Averages | | |
| | | Three | Five | Seven |
Month	Sales	Months	Months	Months
1	3	—	—	—
2	5	4.7	—	—
3	6	6.7	6.2	—
4	9	7.7	7.4	7.1
5	8	8.7	8.4	7.7
6	9	9.0	8.6	8.6
7	10	8.7	9.0	—
8	7	9.3	—	—
9	11	—	—	—

average distance from trough to trough or from peak to peak. The extent to which this can be done will determine how well the moving average has succeeded in smoothing out the fluctuations in the original series. The ultimate objective is to produce a series which changes gradually over time.

A moving average has both advantages and disadvantages. As a method of determining trend, it is simple and flexible to apply and tends to present a realistic portrayal of long-run movements. On the other hand, it misses turning points in the trend forecast, it assumes a definite and relatively stable periodicity for the series to which it is applied, and it necessarily misses as many observations as the length of the average, that is, half at the beginning and half at the end. (For example, in a three-month moving average, the first average represents the midpoint of the first three months and the last average represents the midpoint of the last three months. The moving average thus loses 1½ months at each end.)

Forecasting with a moving average thus becomes a problem of predicting the future course of the moving average based on its most recent level, which of necessity always trails behind the most recent observations of the original series from which the average is derived. The use of a moving average for forecasting can thus pose some difficulties unless the average is reasonably stable and easy to predict. Since this is not usually the case with economic data, moving averages have perhaps been more frequently employed as devices for studying the deviations from the trend of a series rather than the trend itself.

Trend models have been employed both successfully and unsuccessfully in the past. Forecasts based on 1929, 1933, 1937, and 1973 were disastrous for companies that employed this method. Yet the method continues in wide use, and for a simple reason. Many economic time series do, for the most part, show a persistent tendency to move in the same direction for a period of time because of their inherent cumulative characteristics. Therefore, a forecaster using the method of trend projection will be right as to direction of change more times than he (or she) will be wrong; and, in fact, the forecaster will be right in *every forecast except those at the turning points*. Thus, suppose a series rises for 28 months, waivers or runs about steady for 2 months, and then declines for 20 months—in all, a total of 50 months. A forecaster using the method of trend projection will forecast correctly the month-to-month direction of change at least 48 out of 50 times, which is a score of 96 percent. This is a remarkable record for a "mechanical" method! Yet, counting the percentage of correct forecasts appears to be a standard manner of evaluating a forecaster's performance.

Evidently it is in the prediction of the turning points rather than in the mere projection of trends that the challenge to forecasting really manifests itself. Only when the turning points can be detected in advance can management proceed to alter its plans with respect to sales effort, production scheduling, credit requirements, and the like. Otherwise, the mere projection of trends implies a forecast of continuance and no essential change in policy, and hence the coordinative (decision-making) function of management reduces to a mere supervisory one.

Cyclic Models. When the trend is removed from an annual series of economic data, the residual structure exhibits certain fluctuating characteristics that have been described by some economists as *business cycles*. Many years ago attempts were made to discover or to prove that a law of oscillation exists in such series, and in some instances the search for periodicity resulted in outstanding success with respect to prewar series. World War II, however, produced important changes in the structural variables of the economy and thereby altered the phase relationships between time series that had previously exhibited oscillatory characteristics. Nevertheless, the use of cyclic models as a prediction method continues in wide use among forecasters in many business firms.

At the present time, the use of time-series analysis in forecasting business cycles commonly employs what is known as the "residual method." The calculation techniques are described in all elementary textbooks on economic and business statistics and need not be illustrated here. What interests us is the nature and assumptions of the method, since the procedure in general plays such a dominant role in the forecasting activities of business firms.

The most common practice in constructing forecasting models is to assume a multiplicative structure for the elements so that the relationship is expressed by the formula $O = TSCI$. However, it is also possible to assume that they are additive, in which case $O = T + S + C + I$, or that there are both multiplicative and additive relationships such as $O = S + TCI$. Various theoretical possibilities may exist, but in most practical problems the above multiplicative structure is assumed. In any event, the problem for purposes of forecasting is to isolate and measure each of these four factors by separating out of the total behavior O, the gradual long-term change T, the regular oscillations S occurring within a year, and the regular oscillations C occurring over several years, each measured independently of the others. This problem of assumed relationships between the series, however, is relatively minor when compared to the following types of measurement problems that arise.

1. In explaining the cyclical mechanism, whether for the total economy or for a particular firm, there is a controversy over whether the methods of analysis are really valid. Analysts have shown that apparent cycles can result in a series not because a cycle actually exists but simply because of the way in which the data are processed. For example, the use of a moving average may induce an oscillation in a resulting series even if a real cycle is nonexistent, or in general, the summing or averaging of successive values of a random series can result in cyclical behavior by the very act itself (known as the "Slutsky-Yule effect"). For these reasons, the conventional method of residual analysis used by most business firms in separating cyclical and random components of time series is by no means a universally accepted procedure and, as a matter of fact, has been strongly questioned by analysts for many years.

2. The separation of trend and random forces in a time series has also been questioned. The assumption in the residual method is that the long-term and short-term movements are due to separate causal influences so that appropriate mathematical tools may accordingly be applied. But various studies of economic series reveal that perhaps the trend in a series is not separable from the short-term movements, and that both may perhaps be generated by a common set of forces. Where series of data are observed at fairly close intervals, the random changes from one term to the next may be large enough to outweigh substantially any systematic (causal) effect which may be present so that the data appear to behave almost like a "wandering series." In such instances it is difficult to distinguish by statistical methods between a genuine wandering series and one wherein the systematic element is weak. Hence, if the series really is wandering, any movements which appear to be systematic such as trends or cycles would be illusory, and their separation and measurement may be highly hazardous.

It is apparent that the traditional methods of processing time-series data—methods that are in extensive use by many business firms—are far from adequate, despite their wide acceptance by many professional business forecasters employed in industry. Nevertheless, this does not mean that such methods need be discarded. They definitely have certain specific uses and are often well employed as a part of the forecaster's total kit of analytical tools. Their limitations as discussed here are based on their shortcomings when used as the only forecasting technique in complex forecasting problems. When properly utilized, there are a number of advantages which can be derived from the traditional methods of time series analysis. These may be listed as follows:

1. The necessary data are usually minimal and often easily obtained either from within the company itself or from readily available outside sources.
2. The analytical calculations, such as the moving average, are usually simple and repetitive, and therefore suitable for computer processing. Hence, these techniques may be particularly well suited for problems in which a large number of variables must be forecast.
3. Only moderate analytical skills may be required of the forecasters themselves. The methods are fairly easy to understand and the data processing straightforward.
4. The method is largely objective, although judgment is involved in choosing additive or multiplicative decomposition, fixed or changing seasonal factors, type of trend to use, and extrapolation of the cyclical component.
5. The resultant forecasts are usually reasonably accurate for the short run, say, a 12-month period.
6. Time-series analysis usually permits the calculation of the degree of error in the forecast. Hence an interval of confidence attendant with the predicted value strengthens the quality of the forecast itself. Forecast errors can be further reduced where identification of dependable trend and seasonal patterns can be made.
7. Once decomposition of the time series has been accomplished, the way is open for a causal analysis of the separate components.

Despite these advantages, time-series analysis, like every other tool, must be used with full cognizance of its limitations:

1. Time-series analysis cannot be used in situations where time-series data have not been accumulated; for example, projections for a new product or a new environment for which no historical records have been kept.
2. Forecasts based on extrapolation of trend, cyclical, and seasonal components of a series assume a strong persistence of time patterns from the past into the future. This may not always be a valid assumption.
3. Strict adherence to the time-series analysis techniques will fail to take advantage of the forecaster's knowledge of prospective developments. For example, the forecaster might know that advertising effort will be greater than anything in the past, and such knowledge should be used to modify the extrapolation.

4. Time-series analysis gives no information as to the causal factors influencing the time-series components. It merely provides a basis for causal analysis.

BAROMETRIC TECHNIQUES

Whereas mechanical methods of forecasting, particularly time-series analyses, imply that the future is some sort of extension of the past, the use of barometric techniques is based on the idea that the future can be predicted from certain happenings in the present. Specifically, barometric methods usually involve the use of *statistical indicators*— selected time series which, when used in conjunction with one another or when combined in certain ways, provide an indication of the direction in which the economy or particular industries are heading. The series chosen thus serve as barometers of economic change. Two particular applications of the barometric approach are commonly employed: leading series and pressure indexes. To some extent they may be overlapping, but we will discuss them separately for convenience.

Types of Indicators

The basic concept underlying the statistical indicator approach to business cycle analysis and forecasting is that various economic activities exist which tend to move through the course of the business cycle in consistent but different time sequences. *Coincident indicators* are those that move approximately in phase with the aggregate economy, and hence are measures of current economic activity. *Leading indicators* are measures that tend to reflect future changes in the trend of the aggregate economy. *Lagging indicators* are those that trail behind aggregate economic activities. The relative position of these indicators in the business cycle is illustrated in Exhibit 2.

The relationships between leading, coincident, and lagging indicators are not purely geometrical but usually have an economic basis. In many

EXHIBIT 2
Economic Indicators

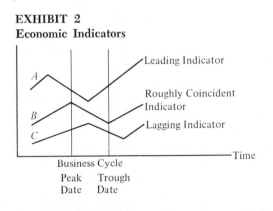

Leading Indicator

Roughly Coincident Indicator

Lagging Indicator

Time

Business Cycle

Peak   Trough
Date   Date

instances of leading indicators, for example, there are planning, contracting, or purchasing commitments which systematically lead to the realization of further economic activities or which are symptomatic of such further activities. Coincident indicators reflect concurrent economic activities and are therefore the most direct of the three relationships. Current sales and production levels, for example, contribute toward establishing a more general level of economic activity. Finally, lagging indicators may sometimes be viewed as the residual in economic activities, as in the case of post-Christmas business inventories, or as a reflection of business or governmental commitments already underway. But though experience is gained through historical evaluation, business executives are not nearly as interested in hindsight as they are in foresight. Consequently, of the three series discussed so far, lagging indicators are the least useful as an aid in formulating future business policy.

There are also two refinements of statistical indicators that are often used in forecasting. One is the diffusion index, which shows the direction and intensity of a majority of selected economic time series in a particular category, such as production or consumption. The other is the composite index, which highlights the timing and pattern of business cycle expansion and contraction. These indexes will be discussed in more detail below, after we first take a closer look at the nature of leading indicators. Exhibit 3, which displays a number of leading indicators, will facilitate the discussion. Each of the time series displayed in Exhibit 3 portrays some facet of business activity during the years 1948–74. The vertical scale differs for each series as indicated in the title of the series. For example, the title of the first series indicates that the average workweek is measured in hours.

Leading Indicators

In the history of forecasting, no method has been given more attention than the leading indicator approach. If a series or index could be discovered that showed leads of, say, six months with substantial regularity, it would end the quest for a universal "predictor" (and, of course, the need for several thousand professional forecasters currently employed in industry).

Forecasters have long sought leading indicators for predicting the future course of business. Andrew Carnegie used to count the number of factory chimneys belching smoke to tell whether business would rise or decline. The Brookmire Economic Service as early as 1911 utilized successive leads in stock, commodity, and money market series to forecast economic change. Today, many business executives employ their own leading indicators based on personal experiences and observations.

The most extensive periodic reports on business cycle indicators have appeared, since October 1961, in a monthly magazine entitled *Business*

EXHIBIT 3
Early Warning Signals by Leading Indicators

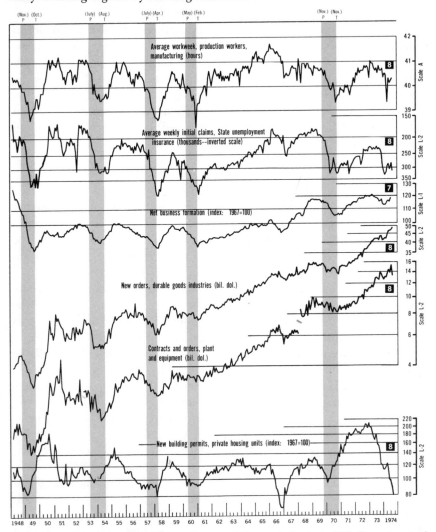

Source: *Business Conditions Digest*, Bureau of Economic Analysis, U.S. Department of Commerce (September 1973), p. 39.

Conditions Digest, published by the Census Bureau of the U.S. Department of Commerce. This widely quoted source consists for the most part of many pages of tables and charts showing the movements of several hundred economic indicators over the business cycle. Accordingly, it is closely related to the work of the National Bureau of Economic Research, a private organization in New York which, for decades, has been the world's leader in business cycle research and analysis.

Each issue of *Business Conditions Digest* contains, in addition to the numerous tables and charts, descriptions and sometimes technical discussions of various series and their usefulness in the story of business cycles.

For forecasting purposes, chief interest centers on the several dozen economic series that in the opinion of the Census Bureau may be classified as "leading" indicators—economic measures that quite consistently precede the upturns and downturns of business activity as a whole. The movements of the series usually are shown against the background of the expansions and contractions of the general business cycle so that "leads" and "lags" can be readily detected and unusual cyclical developments spotted.

Diffusion Indexes

The diffusion index was developed to answer the question of whether a change in any particular indicator series is really forecasting a reversal in the general trend or whether it is just an isolated development. The large aggregate statistics developed by government agencies are extremely useful in macroeconomics as measures of the prevailing level of economic activity. For example, the Commerce Department's measure of gross national product (GNP) aggregates all production of final goods and services into a single dollar-value figure; the physical output of all manufacturing industries lumped together is measured by the Federal Reserve's industrial production index; and the Bureau of Labor Statistics publishes figures on the volume of employment in nonfarm industries.

As useful as these figures may be, they mask the important changes that may be taking place in individual industries or markets, even though these changes may in time have a major impact upon the aggregate statistics. The overall economy may be expanding or contracting, but there will be some business activities that are bucking the trend, moving in the opposite direction. The diffusion techniques look at these variations of economic activity rather than at the trend as a whole, and attempt to measure the degree of dispersion.

To construct a diffusion index, the analyst first chooses a number of indicator series (all of which are either leading, coincident, or lagging) and smooths each of the selected series, say, by means of moving averages. Then for each time period, the analyst counts the number of series that exhibit an increase in economic activity, converts that number to a percentage of the series examined, and plots it on the chart. Therefore, whenever the plot point is above the 50 percent line on the chart, it means that the majority of indicators is predicting expansion of the economy. Below the 50 percent line means, of course, that the majority of indicators is predicting contraction. The intensity of the trend in either direction is reflected in the distance of the plot point from the 50 percent line.

Diffusion indexes thus measure rates of change of the aggregates to which the indexes apply; hence diffusion indexes tend to change direction before the aggregates do. This is a useful characteristic for forecasting purposes. Unfortunately, however, the lead of a diffusion index is erratic. Many indexes tend to peak in the early stages of a business expansion, then settle down at a moderate level until the onset of recession. At that point they may fall spectacularly, but much too late to be of any value in forecasting.

The prime difficulty with diffusion indexes is that efforts to increase their lead make them harder to interpret, while efforts to simplify their interpretation reduce their lead. Efforts to improve their lead usually require the inclusion of more and more leading series, but this results in increasing instability of the index. Despite the fact that diffusion indexes appear to derive reliability from the aggregation of more than one series, they must be used with caution. Leading indicators often give false signals, such as an indication of a downturn in the business cycle that turns out to be merely a slowdown in the rate of expansion. Also, there is the danger of combining some indicators which may be potentially unreliable for a given situation with those of greater accuracy. In such cases, the probability of successful prediction is not increased with the weight of additional series. Diffusion indexes become more reliable if three are constructed: one for leading indicators, one for coincident indicators, and one for lagging indicators. However, the student is well advised to regard the diffusion indexes as *aids* to careful study and analysis of underlying economic phenomena rather than substitutes therefore.

In spite of their shortcomings as reliable indicators of a coming trend, diffusion indexes provide a useful way of examining the breadth and vigor of movement in the business cycle. They cannot substitute completely for the judgment and experience of the forecaster, but they do provide a means of cross-checking his judgment against the raw data of business statistics.

Composite Indexes

Composite indexes are weighted amalgamations of various leading, coincident, and lagging series. When used with comprehensive diffusion indexes, they highlight the timing and pattern of business cycle expansions and contractions. Additional "timing distributions" of current highs or lows may be used to show the number of individual series reaching highs during an expansion or lows during a contraction. Comparisons of the current timing distributions with those of earlier troughs and peaks are helpful in appraising the evidence of a prospective business cycle turning point.

How Useful Are the Indicators?

How does the Census Bureau's approach—with its close resemblance to the indicator techniques long used by the National Bureau of Economic Research—avoid the difficulties that have plagued indicator methods in the past? Does the indicator approach give false signals of a recession or recovery when a real recession or recovery is under way?

A number of leading series are available monthly. Hence, it seems that they should provide a useful guide for predicting the future course of the economy. Unfortunately, however, they are not as useful for this purpose as might at first seem because of the following limitations:

1. They are not always consistent in their tendency to lead. Frequently, some of the series will signal what turns out later on to be a true change, while the remaining series either fail to signal at all or else signal too late to be of much value for prediction purposes.

2. It is not always possible to tell whether the series is signaling an actual future turning point of the economy or whether it is merely exhibiting a wiggle which is of no real significance. In order to be sure whether the variation is actually a true signal of impending change or merely a false start, it may be necessary to wait a few months for confirmation. But this of course destroys any forecasting advantage which the series may have in the first place, since the leading series, whether taken individually or as a composite, can at best be used only for short-term forecasts up to about six months or so.

3. Even if the leading indicators could consistently signal the true turning points of the economy, they would still indicate only the direction of future change, while disclosing little or nothing about the magnitude of the change.

4. Indicator forecasting is not applicable to new product situations. The development of indicators requires historical records that do not exist for new products.

5. Indicator forecasting cannot make use of the forecaster's knowledge of prospective market developments. It gives no information on the response of sales to company marketing strategy or to external forces. These are probably the most cogent reasons why indicator forecasting should be used only in conjunction with other forecasting tools more specific to an industry or geographic area of interest.

6. There are certain technical difficulties inherent in indicator forecasting. Sometimes, indicators which lead company sales are very hard to find. At other times, it requires a historical record extending over several cycles, a longer span than that required for short-run extrapolation procedures. This consideration also may necessitate the accumulation of considerable data for a number of possible indicators until a

good one is found. Other technical shortcomings include the fact that there is no way to obtain an estimate of error in the forecasts.

7. Much skill and experience is necessary for the use of indicators as a forecasting tool. Forecasts of turning points require very fine judgment not only in the interpretation of historical records but also in the interpretation and evaluation of current evidence.

In the light of these criticisms, the use of leading series as a forecasting device would seem to be a very limited approach at best. However, despite their shortcomings, indicators can be valuable forecasting tools when used in conjunction with other forecasting analyses for several reasons:

1. Indicators can be readily understood by those who make business decisions. Understandability is a very important consideration for any tool.
2. The indicator technique can be a great help in detecting turning points so that extrapolations of sales can be modified. Even an indication that the probability of a turning point in the near future may be at hand is useful information which can suggest that provision for flexibility in plans is advisable.
3. The quantity of data required for indicator forecasting is usually moderate once the right indicator has been found; periodic updatings of an already available statistic may be all that is needed. Usually if the data used need adjustment, they can be computerized.

Pressure Indexes

Based largely on the idea that amplitude differences play a decisive role in the analysis of business cycles, economists have developed various ratio and difference measures called "pressure indexes" as guides to forecasting. Some examples of such indexes used in economic and business forecasting are the following:

1. Durable goods production fluctuates much more widely than nondurable goods production over the course of a business cycle. Hence the ratio of durable to nondurable goods production is sometimes used as an indicator of cyclical change, the ratio tending to increase in prosperity periods and to decline before a business cycle downturn, although there is no clear-cut evidence of the latter.
2. Purchasing agents, in predicting raw materials prices, frequently use a ratio of raw materials inventories to new orders for finished goods. Also, a somewhat rougher indication is given if production of finished goods rather than new orders is used in the denominator.
3. The difference between the rate of family formation and the rate of housing inventory growth is a pressure indicator of the long-term

demand for new housing. In the short run, on the other hand, factors such as disposable income and mortgage conditions are usually more influential in determining the actual rate of construction.

4.　Railroads approximate from six months to a year in advance the demand for new orders for railroad cars from the ratio of carloadings (seasonally adjusted) to cars in serviceable condition.

5.　The spread between common stock yields and corporate bond yields has sometimes been used as a predictor of stock prices. Classical market theory states that as the spread narrows, the advantage of owning stocks rather than bonds declines, and money flows out of the stock market into the bond market.

These ratio and difference measures, as well as numerous others that can be devised, may not always be helpful in forecasting the magnitude of change. However, they do serve the useful purpose of providing warning signals of impending developments, and frequently an indication as to the future direction of change. When used in conjunction with other forecasting methods, pressure indexes can accomplish much in the way of establishing guideposts for better prediction.

OPINION POLLING

The opinion polling or sample survey technique of forecasting is a subjective method of prediction, amounting largely to a weighted or unweighted averaging of attitudes and expectations. The underlying assumption is that certain attitudes affecting economic decisions can be defined and measured well enough in advance so that predictions can be made of changing business trends. The results are arrived at by asking people who are directly involved about their expectations as to future economic happenings. Various forms or types of surveys are employed both in economic and in sales forecasting and are discussed below.

Surveys of Economic Activity

Among the best known opinion-polling studies made for forecasting economic activity or some particular phase of it are the following:

1.　Surveys of business executive's intentions on what to spend on plant and equipment, made independently by the McGraw-Hill Publishing Company, the Department of Commerce, the Securities and Exchange Commission, and the National Industrial Conference Board.
2.　Surveys of consumers' finances and buying plans, made primarily by the Survey Research Center of the University of Michigan under the sponsorship of both industry and government.

3. Surveys of business executive's plans regarding inventory changes, made by the National Association of Purchasing Agents.

All of these surveys are made periodically. On the whole, the more successful ones, perhaps, have been the McGraw-Hill survey of expenditure plans for plant and equipment (capital-consuming plans) and the Survey Research Center's surveys of consumers' intentions. These account for most of the investment undertaken by the important capital-consuming industries. The "record" of these surveys has agreed rather well with actual expenditures, except for a few scattered years where the errors could be accounted for by unexpected international political events such as war or the threat of war. Capital expenditure plans, since they are so dependent on changes in the structural environment of the economy, could not be expected to remain the same under such unusual circumstances. Other than these, however, the McGraw-Hill surveys have provided a basically sound analysis of capital expenditure plans. The surveys cover much the same ground as the government survey mentioned above but are available earlier (published in *Business Week* magazine) and are widely used for forecasting purposes.

The Survey Research Center of the University of Michigan prepares surveys of consumer finances and buying plans. The surveys, based on samples of several thousand respondents, are designed to (1) evaluate recent developments among consumers; (2) provide data for testing hypotheses about economic behavior, that is, functional relationships between variables; and (3) determine expectancies for consumer purchases of automobiles, houses, and major appliances. A single survey provides a cross section of data, while consecutive surveys yield time series of such data.

The results of these surveys have been both good and bad. On the one hand, the surveys seem to do well in foretelling some of the more important turning points of business. On the other hand, the surveys are not as useful for predicting the magnitude of change. They have been best suited to predictions covering only a few months at a time because the average consumer is not a very rational planner and his (or her) decisions are affected by a wide array of economic and emotional complexities which he cannot unravel and use as a basis for future buying plans beyond several months.

Sales Forecasting

Opinion-polling methods are not used just to forecast changes in economic conditions; many business firms employ variations of the method in forecasting sales.

1. *Executive polling*, whereby the views of top management are combined and (subjectively) averaged, is frequently employed. The

assumption in the use of this approach is that there is safety in numbers, in that the combined judgment of the group is better than the forecast of any single member. Hence the executives sit as a jury and pass judgment on the sales outlook for the coming year. Generally represented on the jury are those with a divergency of opinions—the firm's sales, production, finance, purchasing, and administrative divisions. In those companies where forecasts of probable events are derived after a sifting and analysis of market reports, sales data, and formal economic forecasts, the executive-polling approach may be quite successful. Without such careful evaluations, however, the method can easily degenerate to the level of a guessing game yielding nothing more than sloppy and unfounded predictions. Companies employing the executive-polling approach may also combine it with statistical measures of trends and cycles, or other analytical tools, by raising or lowering the statistical forecast according to their subjective judgments.

2. *Sales force polling* is another variation whereby a composite outlook is constructed on the basis of information derived from those closest to the market. The sales forecast may be built up from the estimates of salespeople made in cooperation with branch or regional managers, or by going directly to jobbers, distributors, and major customers in order to discover their needs. The advantage claimed for the method is that it utilizes the firsthand, specialized knowledge of those nearest to the market, and thereby gives salespeople greater confidence in their quotas developed from forecasts. Obviously, however, salespeople may be quite unaware of structural changes taking place in their markets, and hence incapable of shaping their forecasts to account for those future changes. Also, sound forecasting requires more time and effort than most salespeople can ordinarily devote, and the result is more likely to be an off-the-cuff guess than a prediction. Accordingly, firms using this method may set up a system of "checks and balances" whereby the estimates of salespeople are compiled, checked, adjusted, and revised periodically in the light of past experience and future expectations.

3. *Consumer intentions surveys* are still another version of the opinion-polling method applied to sales forecasting. Some of the automobile companies, for instance, make sample surveys of automobile buying intentions which they then project to a national level of weighting the estimate with the average purchase rate and an index of predicted incomes. Similar techniques are used by other firms in forecasting the sale of appliances, furniture, and other durable goods.

ECONOMETRIC MODELS

Based on the idea that changes in economic activity can be explained by a set of relationships between economic variables, there has grown a branch of applied science known as *econometrics*. Breaking the word into its two parts, "econo" and "metrics," it is evident that its subject matter must deal with the science of *economic measurement*. And this is precisely what econometrics does: it explains past economic activity and predicts future economic activity by deriving mathematical equations that will express the most probable interrelationship between a set of economic variables. The economic variables may include disposable income, money flows, inventories, government revenues and expenditures, foreign trade, and so on. By combining the relevant variables, each a separate series covering a past period of time, into what seems to be the best mathematical arrangement, econometricians proceed to predict the future course of one or more of these variables on the basis of the established relationships. The "best mathematical arrangement" is thus a model which takes the form of an equation or system of equations that seems best to describe the past set of relationships according to economic theory. The model, in other words, is a simplified abstraction of a real situation, expressed in equation form, and employed as a prediction system that will yield numerical results. To the extent that economic theorems and relationships can be verified by subjecting historical data to statistical analysis, then, at least in principle, econometrics as a system of measurement stands as a compromise between pure "ivory tower" economic theory on the one hand and sheer description of facts and occurrences on the other.

Single–Equation Models

Economic theory deals with the science of choices among alternatives, and its method is to construct simplified models of economic reality on the basis of which certain laws describing regularities in economic behavior are derived. When these models are quantitatively formulated, they may take the form of econometric models. Such models may be constructed for the total economy for the purpose of predicting future levels of income, employment, and other aggregate economic variables, or they may be constructed for a particular firm or industry in order to predict sales, production, costs, and related economic variables. Both types of models can be useful, of course, in facilitating decision making and planning by government agencies, business executives, labor unions, political organizations, and similar groups with a direct interest in economic and business conditions. Hence, both types of models are often discussed and illustrated in the literature of econometrics.

One of the first steps in the construction of an econometric model is to specify the hypotheses which purport to explain the economic phenomena under investigation. Then, these hypotheses are translated into a form suitable for testing, usually into one or more mathematical equations.

For example, consider an elementary demand problem in which it is hypothesized that the industry sales (S) of a certain product during any given time period (t) is a function of the number of households (H) during the period and of consumers' disposable personal income (Y) during the previous period. This model is expressed by the unspecified equation:

$$S_t = f(H_t, Y_{t-1})$$

If it is further hypothesized that the relationship among the variables is linear and that the relationship is not exact, the model becomes the specified equation

$$S_t = a + bH_t + cY_{t-1} + u_t$$

where a, b, c are parameters to be estimated from the available data by certain statistical techniques, and the variable u is a "disturbance" term. Thus, if u had been excluded from the equation, the relationship would be interpreted to mean that sales are completely determined by the household and income variables. However, by including u, recognition is given to the fact that sales will be affected by additional factors besides households and incomes, and hence the forecasted estimates of sales that are derived from the equation will deviate from the actual or realized sales. Hopefully, these "other" factors represented by u will be random in nature and, in a statistical sense, normally distributed so that u will average out to zero. Then, once the parameters are estimated, certain statistical tests may be applied to evaluate the adequacy of the equation as a forecasting device. These are discussed with specific reference to demand forecasting in a later chapter.

Simultaneous–Equation Models

There are many relatively uncomplicated problems in business and economics which can be solved by expressing the underlying structure in the form of a single mathematical equation. However, when a theoretical structure is found to be complex, as is usually the case, there are simultaneous interrelations among the variables in the system. In that event it is no longer correct to employ a single-equation model of the system; instead, a system of equations must be developed which expresses the complex interactions among the variables, and which undoubtedly requires a computer solution. The construction of such a model can be illustrated by the following simplified version of an actual model. Let:

C = consumption
G = government expenditures on goods and services
I = investment (net)

K = net capital stock at end of period
P = nonwage income
W = wage income
Y = national income (or net product)
t = a given time period; $t - 1$ denotes the previous time period
a, b, c = parameters
u_1, u_2, u_3 = disturbance terms or random influences affecting the dependent variable but which are assumed to average out to zero

In order to construct an econometric model, we must now specify various hypotheses which purport to explain the phenomena under investigation. These hypotheses are based on previous studies, empirical findings, or a priori reasoning. Then the hypotheses are translated into a form that is suitable for empirical verification and testing, usually into mathematical equations.

1. Consumption in the current period depends on the current period's income and on consumption in the previous period:

$$C_t = a_0 + a_1 Y_t + a_2 C_{t-1} + u_{1t}$$

2. Investment in the current period is determined by nonwage income earned in the current period and by the net capital stock available at the end of the previous period:

$$I_t = b_0 + b_1 P_t + b_2 K_{t-1} + u_{2t}$$

3. Wages in the current period depend on income in the current period and on time. ("Time" is used as a substitute variable for all other variables which are unspecified, but which nevertheless exert an influence on wages.)

$$W_t = c_0 + c_1 Y_t + c_2 t + u_{3t}$$

4. National income or net product in the current period is the sum of consumption in the current period, investment in the current period, and government expenditures in the current period. (In the real world there are some accounting differences between national income and net product, but these differences are assumed to be sufficiently unimportant to be neglected for purposes of this model.)

$$Y_t = C_t + I_t + G_t$$

5. Nonwage income in the current period is the difference between national income in the current period and wage income in the current period:

$$P_t = Y_t - W_t$$

6. Net capital stock at the end of the current period is equal to the last period's net capital stock plus current net investment:

$$K_t = K_{t-1} + I_t$$

This completes the set of hypotheses which we have expressed both in words and in equations for the purpose of explaining the phenomena being investigated. Note that the last three statements are actually nothing more than definitions or mathematical identities which are needed to complete the model. For convenience, the six equations which comprise the model may now be grouped together as a system of equations.

$$C_t = a_0 + a_1 Y_t + a_2 C_{t-1} + u_{1t} \tag{1}$$

$$I_t = b_0 + b_1 P_t + b_2 K_{t-1} + u_{2t} \tag{2}$$

$$W_t = c_0 + c_1 Y_t + c_2 t + u_{3t} \tag{3}$$

$$Y_t = C_t + I_t + G_t \tag{4}$$

$$P_t = Y_t - W_t \tag{5}$$

$$K_t = K_{t-1} + I_t \tag{6}$$

It may be worth noting again that there is a reason for the use of the variables, u_{1t}, u_{2t}, and u_{3t} on the right side of the first three equations. These variables, called "disturbance" terms, represent the fact that the other explicit independent variables in the equations do not account completely for the variations in the dependent variables.

For example, in equation (1), consumption in the current period is, in reality, determined by other factors in addition to income in the current period and consumption in the previous period. Some of these other factors may be both economic and psychological. Further, there may be errors in the data employed to represent the relevant variables. All of these "disturbances" are represented in (1) by the variable u_{1t}. If we assume that no important independent variables have been omitted, then the disturbance terms may be thought of as reflecting all of the unknown and unpredictable factors. Ideally, the variations in these "all other" factors will be small and random in nature, and will tend to cancel each other out so that their overall net effect on the dependent variable is zero. To the extent that this assumption is realized in practice, the remaining explicit variables in the equation will account for the systematic or "causal" movements in the dependent variable.

The reader should be aware that there is considerably more involved in the subject of econometric model building than the brief sketch presented herein. Many deep problems of a theoretical and statistical nature exist which must be handled in actual model construction. However, these paragraphs have conveyed a bit of the flavor of the subject for those who are unfamiliar with it.

EVALUATION OF FORECASTING

If forecasting is to be effective, there has to be some way of measuring its performance. Having one's forecast checked against actual results and against the forecasts and opinions of others can be a disenchanting experience. For their own protection, as well as to encourage intelligent use of their products, economic forecasters should insist upon objective and systematic procedures for review and rigorous evaluation of their work.

These procedures must recognize that forecasting with complete accuracy is impossible, and, fortunately, unnecessary, provided the forecasts are evaluated and used in the proper manner. Even if the forecaster's estimate of some economic indicator is pretty far from the mark, the correct operating decision can be reached if the forecaster is generally correct in the appraisal made of the other forces at work in the economy.

Actually, forecasts seem to be getting better, at least on the national indicators. For example, the United California Bank (UCB) boasts that its 1973 forecast dealt with more than 550 economic and business indicators, of which more than 90 percent accurately predicted the directions which actually prevailed in 1973. The UCB's Forecasting Score Board, as published in their 1974 forecast, is reproduced as Exhibit 4.

Procedures for evaluating forecasts are required at three different stages. In reverse time sequence these are:

1. After the forecast event has happened or not happened, the accuracy of the forecast should be evaluated and the value of the forecast to those who may have acted upon it should be appraised.
2. Between the time the forecast is released and the time of the forecasted events, an interim review should be made to determine whether or not to revise the forecast.
3. While the forecast is being prepared or just prior to its release, an evaluation of its quality should be made in full recognition that important and perhaps costly decisions might be based upon it.

Auditing Past Performance

Checking a short-range forecast against the record, when all the data are in, is a fairly simple process. Evaluating long-range forecasts may be somewhat more complicated. Sometimes the statistical series has been altered; sometimes the forecast was hedged by unrealized assumptions or other restrictions. In either case, comparison with actual results may be difficult.

Forecast versus Actual. The simplest way to evaluate an unequivocal forecast is to compare numbers with actual results and state the difference either in dollars or as a percentage of error. In Exhibit 4, for

EXHIBIT 4

Self-Evaluation of United California Bank's 1973 Forecast

UCB'S FORECASTING SCOREBOARD
GROSS NATIONAL PRODUCT

Constant (1958) Dollar GNP

Year	UCB Forecast	Actual	% Variance Forecast vs. Actual
	. . . .(billions).		
1971.	$ 750.0	$ 745.4	+0.6%
1972.	790.0	790.7	−0.1%
1973.	836.0	838.0	−0.2%

Current Dollar GNP

1971.	$1,050.0	$1,055.5	−0.5%
1972.	1,150.0	1,155.2	−0.5%
1973.	1,260.0	1,285.0	−1.9%

UCB FORECAST OF 10 MAJOR INDICATORS COMPARED WITH ACTUAL DATA — 1973

MAJOR INDICATORS	UCB Forecast 1973	Actual Data 1973 [1]	Percent Variance Forecast from Actual
Plant and Equipment Expenditures (billions of dollars)	$100.0	$100.0	0.0%
Corporate Profits After Tax (billions of dollars).	$ 62.3*	$ 69.0	−9.7
Corporate Dividends (billions of dollars)	$ 26.9*	$ 28.0	−3.9
Money Supply (M1) (billions of dollars)	$268.3*	$267.0	+0.5
Housing Starts (thousands of units)	2,100	2,100	0.0
Mobile Homes (thousands of units)	620	600	+3.3
Unemployment Rate (percent)	5.1%	4.9%	+0.2pp
Savings Rate (percent of disposable income) . .	5.9%*	6.0%	−0.1pp
Inflation Rate (CPI percent increase)	3.5%	6.3%	−2.8pp
California Personal Income (billions of dollars).	$111.0	$112.0	−0.9%

(1) Actual data represents an estimate of the year's results based on the first three quarters of actual data. This establishes the basis for UCB's 1974 FORECAST.

*Data base adjusted to reflect revisions by official reporting agencies.

pp = percentage point change

example, the UCB Forecasting Scoreboard presents the comparison both ways. In a statistical series subject to erratic movement, this method of appraisal may be adequate. However, if the series had only limited room to move, this yardstick may make the forecast look better than it really is. We hasten to add that no criticism of the UCB Forecasting Scoreboard is intended, as we are not in a position to evaluate the statistical series which it depicts.

With respect to some indicators, it may be enough to forecast success-fully the direction of change, and the magnitude of the change is unim-portant. Similarly, the critical element may be the timing of a change rather than either its direction or magnitude. Examples where the critical factor is either direction or timing of change are common in connection with forecasting inventories, balance of payments, and commodity prices.

Subjective Tests. Objective tests are not always fair or relevant, and some subjective considerations seem to be appropriate. Among these are the questions:

1. Did the forecast do what it was supposed to do?
2. Were the important changes forecast with respect to magnitude? Timing? Direction?
3. Should the errors have been anticipated by the forecaster?
4. Did the forecast enable better decisions to be made than would have been possible without it?

Whatever tests are made, they should be realistic and practical, keep-ing in mind that even in the most elaborate statistical techniques leave wide margins for error. Bald comparisons with perfection prove nothing.

Interim Review

The appropriate timing for interim review of forecasts depends upon so many factors that it is difficult to generalize about it. The best guide is to keep in mind what the interim review is for, which is to enable management to change an operating policy based on an erroneous fore-cast before it is too late. The interim review also enables the forecaster to update the forecast to reflect new developments, and enables him to perform a running check on his sources and methodology.

Sometimes the requirement for interim review is inherent to the fore-casting schedule. This is common in short-range forecasting where quar-terly forecasts running four or five quarters ahead are made. For longer term forecasts, reviews might be instituted—

1. when the basic data from which the forecast was developed is changed, as when a published statistical series is revised;
2. when a key assumption undergoes an important change, such as a technological breakthrough; or
3. when anticipated bounds on the forecast variable have been breached.

When there is a substantial deviation in the behavior of the forecast data, it is important to determine whether or not the validity of the forecast has actually been impeached. If the forecast represents an antici-pated trend, then seasonal, cyclical, or random aberrations do not neces-sarily invalidate the trend. In the case of long-range forecasts, such as for ten years, there is no reason to panic if the trend is off the forecast in the first two or three years even by a wide margin. However, the interim review provides the opportunity to look again.

Any revisions brought about by the interim review should be announced promptly to all concerned. Reasons for the revisions should be explained concisely and frankly, but without apology. Perfect forecasting does not exist and is not to be expected; therefore no apology is in order when perfection has not been achieved.

Appraising New Forecasts

This is the most difficult of all evaluations, simply because there are no yardsticks; yet it is the most crucial appraisal since the action it inspires may be important and costly.

The observations that went into the forecast should be double-checked for accuracy; and statistical tests might be helpful, depending upon the process used to develop the forecast. For the most part, the forecast must be evaluated mostly on the question of whether it is reasonable and relevant. Critical appraisal should cover every step of the forecasting process: the raw data, construction of the model or hypothesis, the assumption about the variables, and the forecast itself.

Trial Runs. If it can be demonstrated that a forecasting model applies to situations or periods different from those which entered its construction, such a "trial run" might provide a measurement of the validity of the model. For example, suppose a regression analysis has been made utilizing data for the years 1960 through 1970. If the resulting equation successfully replicates the data for those years within some acceptable range, then confidence in its ability to forecast 1980 will be considerably enhanced. Such a trial might also be useful to uncover abnormalities in behavior of the basic data which should therefore be eliminated from the model in order to give it "normal" characteristics.

Statistical Tests. Many textbooks in statistics and econometrics caution that uncritical statistical tests of time-series data may lead to unwarranted conclusions.[1] Fortunately some practical alternatives to the standard error are available. Although not elegant, they have the virtue of simplicity, and may be better suited to economic data.

1. The absolute and percentage ranges of the source data may provide a rough indication of the probable range of future values.

---

[1] Time-series data are typically heteroscedastic, meaning that the variances of the data are not uniform from time period to time period, and serially correlated, meaning that the variables lack independence (being influenced by the preceding value). Methods for detecting and dealing with heteroscedasticity and serially corrected data are discussed in standard textbooks in econometrics.

2. The standard error of estimate of the trend or regression line may be used as a range encompassing approximately two thirds of probable values.
3. Two or more projections based on different assumptions will produce "high" and "low" estimates to be used as a probable range of values.
4. Several different methods of forecasting may produce differing results whose extremes can be used as limits of the probable range of future projections.

Despite the difficulty of making statistical tests, there is a growing tendency to submit a confidence estimate along with the forecast. Although couched in statistical terms, the confidence estimate is more likely to represent subjective judgment. There is nothing wrong with this, for in the end the economic forecaster is in the same position as the professional handicapper setting the morning line for pari-mutuel odds at the race track—both must rely upon experience, intuition, and professional judgment to find the meaning of masses of intractable data.

SUMMARY AND CONCLUSIONS

In this chapter, we have reviewed some of the tools and techniques available to the art and science of economic forecasting, and have looked at some of the ways in which they are used. We have seen that mechanical extrapolations, barometric techniques, opinion polling, and econometric models all have uses in both long-term and short-term forecasting at all levels of economic activity.

The econometric method, rather than rivaling the other methods, is probably the only approach which is logically suitable for incorporating or utilizing the best features of them all. Thus to an increasing extent, econometric models that are now being constructed are making greater use of other forecasting methods such as leading indicators and the results of up-to-date survey data. These statistics are incorporated as variables in the model, and the latter is continually revised as new information becomes available and new "weights" become necessary.

It has sometimes happened that econometric models have failed, under certain conditions, to provide better predictions for the following year than less costly models such as simple trend projections. Does this mean that econometric methods should be abandoned? Not at all; where our theoretical understanding and statistical data are good, econometrics can illuminate the darker areas and enhance our ability to predict. For econometrics, to a greater degree than other forecasting methods, is analytical in nature and process-oriented in approach. Its chief concern is to identify and measure changing cause-and-effect relationships through time.

In any forecast, certain strong forces always come into play and serve to modify existing relationships. The econometrician is aware of this and constantly watches for the emergence of new forces or for changes in existing ones so that allowances can be made for these in the operating model. In this manner, a good econometric model automatically incorporates the necessary degree of built-in flexibility, thereby facilitating the model's use for forecasting purposes. Perhaps the most important use of naïve models, therefore, is that they provide a benchmark—a null hypothesis—against which the more sophisticated forecasting methods can be compared.

Whatever method is used, it seems likely that the forecaster's role in the decision-making activities of the firm is apt to grow rather than to diminish. The forecaster's contribution to the welfare of the firm is to make management aware, on a timely and continuing basis, of the economic forces at work; and this requires that the forecaster must subject his (or her) own work to constant critical review. However, despite the improved techniques offered by use of a computer, forecasting remains in large part an effort to predict human behavior. Forecasting, therefore, is at least as much art as science, and seems likely to remain so throughout the foreseeable future.

PROBLEMS

1. Trend models or projections will usually yield correct forecasts, at least as to direction of change, more often than not. If the distinction between a forecasting artist and a forecasting scientist is that the later is correct more than half the time, the use of trend models would seem warranted. Yet we have been critical of their use. Why? Discuss.

2. "After all, in the final analysis, the best forecasting method is obviously the one that yields the highest percentage of correct predictions." Comment, in the light of this chapter.

3. Briefly discuss the nature and pros and cons of the following methods for forecasting business cycles:
    a. Trend projections.
    b. Leading indicators.
    c. Survey methods.
    d. Econometric model building.
    e. Any other method or technique.

4. Identify which indicator is considered leading or lagging and explain why.
    a. Durable goods orders.
    b. Book value of manufacturing and trade inventories.
    c. Changes in inventories.

5. An economist at the Reading Company conjectured the naive model that sales in any given month are directly proportional to the square of buyers' incomes in the preceding month, plus a random disturbance.

    a.   Write an equation for this month's sales, and another equation for next month's sales, using the symbols y = sales, x = income, t = time, and u = disturbance term.

    b.   Assume that the disturbance term averages out to zero. If sales this month are 36 and income last month was 3, what should sales be next month if income this month is 5?

6.   If the growth (y) of an organization is proportional to the number of its line personnel (x) and to the square of the number of its staff personnel (w) and if y = 36 when x = 2 and w = 3, find y when x = 3 and w = 4. (Assume that any disturbance term, if it exists, averages zero.)

7.   A naive model for a demand problem has been suggested which states that the quantity demanded of a certain product during any given week is inversely related to the price of the product in the previous week. Two weeks ago the price, P, was 6. Last week the quantity demanded, D, was 3 and the price was 12. What should the quantity demanded be this week? Assume that the relationship is exact.

8.   A naive model of the demand for television sets asserts that annual sale of television sets varies *jointly* with the number of families during the year, income per family in the previous year, *plus* "all other factors."

    a.   Letting X = sales, Y = income per family, Z = number of families, t = time in years, and u = "all other factors," write the equation of the model.

    b.   Assume that you are presented with the data in the following table:

Television Sales Data

Year	Sales	Total Family Incomes	Number of Families
1.....	5	18.0	3
2.....	8	20.0	4
3.....	10	21.6	6
4.....	6	21.0	5

Assuming that the "all other factors" have always averaged out to zero, does the model seem to forecast accurately? If the number of families for year 5 is predicted to be 7, what will your sales forecast be?

9.   According to a naive model employed by an economist at the Deward Corporation, sales (x) vary jointly with income (y) and population (z), and inversely with the square of the price (w). It has been found that x = 4 when y = 2, z = 4, and w = 2. What is x when y = 3, z = 5, and w = 3, assuming that the relationship is exact?

10. Consider the forecasting model

$$Y_t = AK^t$$

where A and K are known constants. It is interesting to gain an apprecia-tion of the time path of the dependent variable Y_t for different values of A and K, and integer values of t representing *discrete time periods*.

a. Let $K = 1$ and A = any positive constant. Graph the time path of Y_t from $t = 0$ to $t = 5$, that is, $0 \leq t \leq 5$.

b. Let $K = 2$ and $A = \frac{1}{4}$. Graph the time path of Y_t for $0 \leq t \leq 5$. If your graph is correct, you will see why the time path of Y_t is said to *explode*. The direction of the explosion (i.e., positive or negative) de-pends on the algebraic sign of A. What happens if $A > 0$? $A < 0$? What does the magnitude of K determine?

11. What are the four major sources of variation in a time series? Explain.

12. The Universal Appliance Store has accumulated the following sales data and has asked you to isolate the trend:

| | Monthly Sales (in thousands of dollars) | | |
Month	1971	1972	1973
January	10	11	12
February	11	12	14
March.	12	12	15
April	15	14	18
May.	14	17	20
June	18	18	22
July.	16	17	21
August	17	15	22
September	15	16	23
October	14	16	25
November	14	16	25
December	20	19	30

a. First you plot the sales data on a graph and note that there seems to be a 12-month cycle with peaks in December and troughs in January. Therefore you decide to use a 12-month centered moving average to isolate the trend. You proceed as follows:

(1) Calculate 12-month moving totals for each successive 12-month period beginning with January–December 1971, then February 1971–January 1972, and so forth. These totals are centered be-tween June–July 1971, July–August 1971, and so forth, as illustrated below.

(2) Calculate 2-month moving totals by adding together each ad-jacent pair of 12-month moving totals, as illustrated below. These two-month totals are centered on the months beginning with July 1971.

(3) Divide the 2-month total by 24 to obtain the centered 12-month moving average for each month July 1971–June 1973.

The following table illustrates the necessary calculations which you should complete:

Year and Month	Monthly Sales	Twelve-Month Moving Total	Two-Month Moving Total	Centered Twelve-Month Moving Average
1971:				
January.	10			
February	11			
March.	12			
April	15			
May.	14			
June	18	176		
July.	16	177	353	14.7
August	17			
September	15			
October	14			
November	14			
December	20			
January	11			

b. Next you plot the 12-month centered moving averages on a graph and attempt to fit a trend curve. What kind of curve does it appear to be?

13. ## CASE PROBLEM: GENERAL STEEL CORPORATION
CONSTRUCTING AN ECONOMETRIC MODEL

General Steel Corporation is a major manufacturer of iron and steel. For the past ten years the company has been actively working with several foreign governments in the planning of heavy industrialization programs. As a result, General Steel now has subsidiary iron and steel manufacturing corporations in three foreign countries.

Two years ago, the management of the company began exploring the possibility of opening a subsidiary corporation in Arcadia, a major industrial nation. Since the economic future of Arcadia is of obvious interest to the parent firm, General Steel's economists have been actively engaged in collecting data for the purpose of constructing an econometric model of that country.

Thus, according to General Steel's recent studies by its economic research department, last year's rate of corporate profits in Arcadia was about $42 billion. Although there is no way of being certain of what Arcadia's federal, state, and local governments will spend next year, General Steel's economists estimate from present budget information that the amount should be around $75 billion. Also, an analysis of the most recent business cycle in Arcadia covering a number of years indicates that annual consumption expenditures have averaged $40 billion plus 70 percent of national income; investment expenditures have averaged about $20 billion plus 90 percent of preceding year's profits; and tax receipts have averaged about 20 percent of gross national product. GNP, of course, is composed of consumption, investment, and government expenditures, while national income represents the difference between gross national product and tax receipts.

Questions:

Let C = next year's consumption, Y = next year's national income, I = next year's investment, P_{-1} = preceding year's profits, T = next year's tax receipts by government, G = next year's gross national product, E = next year's government expenditures. Assume that all disturbance terms average out to zero.

a. Construct an econometric model of Arcadia. [SUGGESTION: You should construct a five-equation model on the basis of the facts in the problem. Thus, your first equation should be an equation for consumption, the second for investment, the third for tax receipts, the fourth for gross national product, and the fifth for national income. You may find it helpful to construct the model first by using small letters such as a, b, c, d, e to represent the constants, and then substituting the correct numbers for the constants.]

b. Solve the system. [HINTS: You want values of C, I, T, G, Y. The equations are not to be solved in chronological order. First solve equation (2). Then, in solving (1) and the remaining equations, look for substitutions that can be made.] Here are the correct answers. See if yours check. For next year: C = \$259.9 billion, I = \$57.8 billion, T = \$78.5 billion, G = \$392.7 billion, Y = \$314.2 billion.

REFERENCES

BURCH, S. W., and STEKLER, H. O. "The Forecasting Accuracy of Consumer Attitude Data." *Journal of the American Statistical Association,* vol. 64, no. 328 (December 1969), pp. 1225–33.

BUTLER, W. F., and KAUESH R. A., EDS. *How Business Economists Forecast,* part 3–4 and parts 5–1, 2, and 3. Englewood, N.J.: Prentice-Hall, Inc., 1966.

CUMMINGS, J. M. "How Good Is Your Sales Forecasting?" *The Business Quarterly,* vol. 26, no. 1 (Spring 1971), pp. 54–63.

KIERULFF, HERBERT E. "Best Estimate Forecasting—A Better Alternative." *California Management Review,* vol. 15, no. 1 (Fall 1972), pp. 79–85.

LIPPITT, VERNON G. *Statistical Forecasting,* chaps. 11, 12, and 13. New York: Random House, Inc., 1970.

McKINLEY, DAVID H., ET AL. *Forecasting Business Conditions.* New York: Banking Education Committee, American Bankers Association, 1969.

OKUN, ARTHUR M. On the Appraisal of Cyclical Turning-Point Predicators." *Journal of Business,* vol. 33, no. 1 (April 1960), pp. 101–20.

———. "The Predictive Value of Surveys of Business Intentions." *American Economic Review,* Papers and Proceedings, May 1962, pp. 218–25. See also the discussion by Daniel Brill, pp. 226–28.

SILK, LEONARD S., and CURLEY, M. L. *Business Forecasting,* chaps. 3 and 4. New York: Random House, Inc., 1970.

SUITS, DANIEL B. "Forecasting and Analysis with an Econometric Model." *American Economic Review,* vol. 52, no. 1 (March 1962), pp. 104–32.

chapter 5

Demand

If we define profit as the difference between revenues and costs within some unit of time, then we may fairly say that profits are a function of demand. Thus the study of demand becomes of central importance to the profit-seeking firm as well as to the economist. However, unlike the traditional economics textbook approach to demand analysis, the profit-seeking firm cannot afford to content itself with a descriptive investigation of demand—rather, it must come to grips with the forces that affect demand. The profit-seeking firm must determine whether and how those forces can be manipulated, and it must make and execute plans based upon forecasts of future demand for its products in the predicted environment.

In some markets, such as monopoly or oligopoly, the firm may have some measure of control over the market forces which determine demand. In other markets closer to pure competition, the firm may have to pursue policies of a more adaptive nature. But, regardless of the specific type of market in which the firm operates, the necessity to generate the information required for decision making leads inevitably to some sort of study of demand relating to the firm and to the industry of which it is a part.

From a managerial viewpoint, then, the purpose of demand analysis is to identify and measure the forces that affect the purchase of a product, to define more precisely the relationship between those forces and resultant sales, and, most importantly, to *use* such information in diverse planning activities such as capital budgeting, preparing advertising campaigns, or initiating adjustments to inventories and production.

The intent of this chapter is to provide an analytical framework within which demand determinants may be examined, and to explore some analytical approaches to demand measurement. We therefore begin with a discussion of the market forces which may favorably or adversely affect consumer behavior, after which the stage will have been set for a more quantitative analysis of such forces and some illustrative examples of representative empirical studies.

DETERMINANTS OF DEMAND AND THE DEMAND FUNCTION

To a professional economist, the term "demand" has specific meaning: it refers to the number of units of a particular commodity or service which consumers would be willing to purchase (per unit time) under explicitly stated conditions of time, place, price, and so forth. In elementary economics, you were introduced to the concept of a demand schedule and the demand curve, in which *price* "calls the tune." Demand as a functional concept was expressed algebraically in the equation form:

$$Q_d = f(P)$$

which states that the quantity demanded of a commodity is a function of price and that a particular (but in the form of the equation above, unspecified) *law of behavior* exists between the two variables.

Realistically, business executives and economists know that the demand for most products is affected by many factors other than, or in addition to, price. These other factors may include such diverse elements as income level, the availability of substitute products, advertising and sales promotion, population, geographic location, and so on. Accordingly a demand function expressed in the simple form above may be inadequate to explain the variations in the quantity demanded, and a multiple relation may therefore be necessary. The latter would be expressed as the function:

$$Q_d = f(X_1, X_2, \ldots, X_n)$$

where Q_d represents the quantity demanded, or dependent variable, and each of the X_i variables denotes a specified independent demand determinant with X_n representing the last of these. Thus, for example, if we allow price, income, advertising expenditure, and the price of tea to stand for the independent variables, and the quantity of coffee purchased (Q_d) as the dependent variable, the above equation would read, "the demand for coffee (Q_d) is a function of, or dependent upon, the price of coffee (X_1), income level (X_2), advertising expenditure (X_3), and the price of tea (X_4).

In the foregoing model, four independent variables have been specified. In general, the number of demand determinants for a product may be quite large, and no single set of determinants for any one product is necessarily applicable to another product either in the same combination or to the same extent. Yet, if for any given commodity a few of the most important demand determinants could be isolated and their joint effects on the total demand for the product could be established, a more comprehensive demand or sales function would be available. A demand function of this type would provide a more general statement as to the nature of the multiple relationship between the dependent variable, sales, and two or more independent variables, such as those stated above. This is precisely what analysts try to do by the use of statistical demand analysis. By encompassing more than one demand determinant, they develop more comprehensive predicting equations that serve to improve their ability to forecast.

In our analysis of demand, therefore, a first step must be to identify those variables that might reasonably be expected to affect consumer purchases of the product under study, after which the functional form of the equation relating the dependent variable to the hypothesized independent factors may be fruitfully explored.

Price

In demand analysis, one of the first questions that concerns us is the *shape* of the demand curve. Very often, elementary expositions of demand present the demand "curve" as a downward-sloping straight line. This presentation can be quite misleading. There is no strong evidence to suggest that, a priori, the price-quantity demand relationship is a linear function. Indeed, just the reverse (a curvilinear relationship) can be just as likely. It is, of course, true that linear demand curves are easy to draw, impart much of the flavor of the negative or inverse relationship between price and quantity, and are highly practical from the standpoint of statistical estimation as we shall see. But you should bear in mind that the linear models which may have been presented in past expositions of demand analysis, as well as those presented below, are but a small subset of possible formulations from a much larger class of functional forms.

A second point is that from a managerial perspective, price is important for its prescriptive merits rather than for its descriptive quality. In particular, therefore, the business manager is interested in price-quantity relationships because a firmer understanding of such relationships provides a better basis for pricing, demand manipulation, and therefore, ultimately, profitability.

Despite the advantages of such knowledge to all profit-oriented firms, empirical demand-price studies have been less common in manufacturing than in agriculture. In the latter sector of the economy, there are wide variations in prices, and the effects on consumption are often discernible in the short run. In manufacturing, on the other hand, prices remain stable for long periods of time and the effects of price changes are usually combined with general business conditions, thereby complicating still further the problems of separation and measurement. Hence, to a large extent, controlled experiments offer a promising approach to the study of short-run sales-price relationships, particularly where manufactured goods are concerned.

Income

Empirically, the negative relationship between price and quantity demanded, derived in elementary economics, is rarely directly observed because the ceteris paribus assumption of "all other things being equal" is almost invariably violated. Take, for example, the purchase of automobiles. In 1950 the average price of a passenger car at the factory was $1,270, and 6,666,000 such vehicles were sold. By 1955 the price had risen to $1,572, yet there was a record production and sale of 7,920,000 passenger cars. The annual sales and average wholesale prices for passenger vehicles from 1958–68 were as shown in Exhibit 1. Although both

EXHIBIT 1
Factory Sales of Passenger Cars, 1958–68

Year	Number Sold (thousands)	Average Price
1958	4,258	$1,881
1959	5,591	1,884
1960	6,675	1,822
1961	5,543	1,856
1962	6,933	1,886
1963	7,638	1,889
1964	7,752	1,917
1965	9,306	1,975
1966	8,598	2,042
1967	7,437	2,105
1968	8,822	2,194

Source: U.S. Department of Commerce, *Statistical Abstract of the United States.*

sales and price exhibit a cylical variation with record production in various years, the trend clearly is toward rising sales despite rising prices, and this is true even when prices are adjusted for inflation.

How can one reconcile the fact that more cars were sold at a higher price than a lower price? One explanation is that the incomes of automobile purchasers have risen in greater proportion than has the price. Of course, similar conclusions can be drawn for many other types of commodities.

Finding the relative strength of income versus price as a demand determinant is, of course, an empirical task which requires direct investigation for each specific commodity under study. Further, there are implications to the business manager. For example, charging a higher price becomes a more viable alternative if it is known that buyers' incomes, rather than price, are the more influential variable in the purchase decision. Although the problem must be attacked on a case by case basis, certain generalizations with regard to the relative strength of price and income as demand determinants are possible:

1. Nondurable goods are usually more dependent upon price while durables tend to depend more heavily upon incomes.
2. Items which may be purchased on credit tend to depend more heavily upon income levels than items normally purchased with cash.
3. More expensive items, such as those representing large, one-time purchases, may be expected to depend more heavily upon income than on price.

Closeness and Price of Substitutes and Complements

Different commodities may be related to one another with respect to demand in one of three ways. They may be nearly interchangeable, in which case they are substitutes for one another; they may be independent; or they may enhance each other's use, in which case they are complements. Commodities are substitutes when the purchase of one usually precludes a purchase of the other, as for example, when a family buys a Ford instead of a Chevrolet. Commodities are independent when the purchase of one has no direct influence upon the demand for the other. Examples of such products are numerous, although it can be argued that out of any given income, all products stand in competitive relation with one another and with saving, as far as the buyer is concerned. For purposes of demand measurement, however, the relevant criterion is whether the product purchased has a direct (and usually immediate) effect on the decision to purchase any other products such that the relationship can be "justified" economically.

Finally, commodities are in complementary demand when an increase in the purchase of one causes a rise in the consumption of the other. Examples here are strawberries and cream, pizza and beer, automobiles and service stations, good girdles and sleek dresses. There are, of course, degrees of substitutability and complementarity. Some products may have a one-to-one relationship, for example, houses and furnaces; others may vary in widely differing ratios, for example, shirts and ties. The broader the variation in the ratios, the more difficult it may be to determine the competing or complementing effects for prediction purposes.

From the standpoint of sales, management should be most favorably disposed to circumstances in which the price of substitutes goes up and the price of complements goes down, as both of these situations encourage purchases of the original product or service, thereby increasing demand and, hopefully, individual company sales. In most instances, the fewer the available substitutes, the better, in that fewer substitutes may give the firm a greater control over the price of its own product, enhance its ability to differentiate its product, and thus permit management to assume a more active role in setting price for profit maximization. In some instances, however, the existence of substitutes may actually increase the sale of the original product. This may occur through identification with a luxury item such as a copy versus an original Paris "creation," through recognition of a useful item at a cheaper price, such as generic drugs versus brand-name drugs, or through exploitation of consumer acceptance of a particular product, such as cola soft drinks.

Direct Demand versus Derived Demand

Some products and most services are purchased for final consumption, while others are required mainly as inputs for the production of still further goods. The term "derived demand" is used to describe this latter circumstance because, in effect, the demand for the primary good is dependent upon the demand for the final good. Examples of this type of relationship are wheat and bread, steel and cars, cotton and cloth. Of course, it is also possible to have several intervening stages between primary and end products, as for example the demand for baked cakes determining, in part, the demand for chicken eggs. Some products may also have uses both as final consumption items and intermediate productive factors; for example, leather. Hence the distinction between what is clearly a "directly demanded" good and what is an "indirectly demanded" good soon becomes a question of degree.

Of specific relevance in distinguishing between derived versus directly demanded goods is the question of demand volatility. In the particular case of durable or "producer's goods"—that is, goods whose demand is to a high degree indirectly determined in a separate market—demand usually experiences much sharper fluctuations than "consumer's goods." Why? Because small fluctuations in demand for a given end product may be expected to result in substantially greater fluctuations in the intermediate producer's markets, if demand variations are expressed in percentages. (The analogy is to the floorboard accelerator of a car, in which slight incremental pressure on the pedal moves the accelerator only a little but results in much greater traveling distance of the car per unit time.)

It may also be pointed out that derived demand or input factor markets may sometimes be distinguishable from consumer's markets in other ways which have an important bearing upon the successful sale of the individual firm's product. In general, input factor markets tend to involve more homogeneous goods and there is consequently less opportunity to product-differentiate among primary inputs as opposed to final products. Thus, factor markets tend to be more competitive and therefore more sensitive to price disparities between products than may be characteristic of final (output) markets. Further, the purchasers of producer's goods may be expected to be more knowledgeable of prices and physical characteristics than might purchasers in consumer markets, be less sensitive to promotional activity, be more "demanding" of product quality and supplier integrity, and may often seek long-range supply commitments at fixed prices. Over the long run, the substitutability of labor for capital will also play a part in these purchasers' decisions, with an understandable slackening in demand for certain production equipment if, for example, economic forces result in a decrease in the relative price of labor.

Finally, the demand for producer's goods may be distinguishable from consumer's goods in that demand for producer's goods is often dependent upon long-term contractual agreements between producer and purchaser. Among the other implications of this characteristic are the possibilities of greater intransigence in the market itself, a great reliance on purchaser credit (especially credit extended by suppliers), and perhaps the opportunity for the supplier to maintain lower levels of inventory in the event that "back orders," rather than "off-the-shelf" sales, is the chief demand characteristic of the firm.

Durable versus Nondurable Goods

Another important factor influencing the sale of a commodity is its durability. As was true in the previous discussion of consumer's versus producer's goods, the distinction between durable and nondurable goods is not always clear-cut. There are some products which might best be classified as a "semidurable." However, this categorization is not always very meaningful. As an operational definition, the Bureau of Labor Statistics requires that a good be classed as a durable if its expected life of service extends beyond 12 months, and as a nondurable if the service life expectation is 12 months or less.

The distinction between durable and nondurable goods is important from the standpoint of demand because durables may be stored and because their replacement may be postponed. In times of inflation, consumers are motivated to purchase increased amounts of durables, and perhaps even stockpile some goods, in anticipation of higher prices in the future. During such periods, price, more than income, may play the prominent role as a demand determinant. During economic down-turns, however, income considerations appear to play the dominant role in the consumer's purchase, or replacement, decision.

Other Determinants of Demand

There are other demand determinants worthy of mention. For example:

1. Sociological Influences. In a local market, homogeneous ethnic backgrounds or other sociological similarities sometimes create a highly discriminating market element. A naive example would be the demand for christmas tree lights in a non-Christian neighborhood. Marketing managers are wise to be both knowledgeable of, and adaptive to, the sensibilities of such market groups.

2. Quality. From a theoretical perspective, it does not make sense to talk about the change in demand resulting from quality improvements in a particular product, for essentially, the "old" and "new" models are different entities and the comparison becomes one of the "apples and oranges" variety. From a more pragmatic standpoint, however, substantial evidence points to the desirability of product improvement as a means of stimulating consumer demand. Among other things, product improvement is a key method of product differentiation to the noncolluding oligopolist. If the firm can establish its own product or service as unique—and hopefully uniquely *better*—in the minds of purchasers, it is clearly in a much better position to control price. Hence, to the extent that product improvement is motivated by product differentiation for increased profitability, there is a pervasive likelihood of continued product change in the general direction of quality improvements.

3. Demographic Variables. Perhaps the most obvious demographic variable would be age distribution. This factor would be expected to have substantial influence on the demand for a wide range of products which are age dependent (for example, toys or baby food). In the United States, the age distribution of the population is significantly non-uniform, a fact which obviously has important bearing upon the demand for any number of purchasable items.

4. Demand Saturation. The consumption of some products is bounded by an upper limit of some form. Especially in the case of certain consumer durables, for example, there is some point beyond which gains in consumption should be considered negligible. For example, the stock of refrigerators is presumably limited by the number of households; the number of tickets sold for a play or an airline flight is limited to the number of seats available; and so forth. Naturally, there are ways of getting around each of these apparent constraints. The point is simply that projections of demand must necessarily take demand saturation into account.

MEASURES OF DEMAND RESPONSIVENESS:
ELASTICITY

The relevant determinants of demand have now been qualitatively examined, and it remains to explore some quantitative measures in order to pave the way for empirical studies.

One such measure of demand—the concept of elasticity—is already familiar from elementary economics. We recall that *price elasticity* is a measure of the responsiveness of buyers' purchases to price changes. Since elasticity is a relative and not an absolute measure, it is quoted in percent rather than units of something, and hence permits comparisons of demand sensitivity to be made for different products, irrespective of the units in which the prices are quoted. (A 10 percent change has the same meaning whether it is measured in ounces, bushels, or pounds.)

Many specific types of elasticity are encountered in the literature of economics, especially in the study of demand, production, costs, and prices. Some general statements about the interpretation and measurement of elasticity should therefore be of use.

Consider the function $Y = f(X)$, which may represent a demand function, a production function, a cost function, or any functional relationship in economics. For purposes of interpretation, we might say: *elasticity is the percentage change in the dependent variable, Y, resulting from a 1 percent change in the independent variable, X.*

When it comes to measuring elasticity, however, a distinction should be made between two types of measures: one is *point* elasticity; the other is *arc* elasticity. Geometrically, if we want to think in terms of the graph of the function, such as a demand curve, for example, we could say that point elasticity measures the elasticity at a particular point on the curve, whereas arc elasticity measures the elasticity over a range or segment of the curve. The following definition of elasticity refers to point elasticity, e, from which a general formula for arc elasticity, E, may be derived.

> DEFINITION. The elasticity e, of the function $Y = f(X)$ at the point X is the percentage change in the dependent variable, Y, relative to a slight percentage change in the independent variable, X, thus:

$$e = \frac{\dfrac{\Delta Y}{Y}}{\dfrac{\Delta X}{X}} = \frac{X\Delta Y}{Y\Delta X}$$

The elasticity of a function is simply the rate of change, $\Delta Y/\Delta X$, combined with a multiplicative factor X/Y, which makes it independent of units. Note, therefore, that a function may have a different elasticity at each point, depending on the values of these factors.

The above formula for point elasticity refers to very small incremental movements from point to point along a curve. For practical purposes, therefore, it makes little difference in the result whether the percentage changes are based on X and Y either before or after their changes. There are many instances, however, when all we have are a few observations for X and Y rather than a complete curve or function. Or, we may know the curve and its equation but be interested in only a segment of it. In such cases, a general formula for arc elasticity, E, for measuring the average elasticity over the range in question is:

$$E = \frac{Y_2 - Y_1}{\dfrac{Y_2 + Y_1}{2}} \div \frac{X_2 - X_1}{\dfrac{X_2 + X_1}{2}} = \frac{\dfrac{Y_2 - Y_1}{Y_2 + Y_1}}{\dfrac{X_2 - X_1}{X_2 + X_1}}$$

where the pairs (X_1, Y_1) and (X_2, Y_2) represent, respectively, the coordinates of X and Y before and after their change. Note that in dividing by 2, it is the average change in X and Y that is being used as a base from which to measure percentage changes. The 2's, of course, cancel out in the calculation.

These general concepts of elasticity will now be given concrete meaning as we discuss the following specific measures of elasticity that are related to demand:

1. Price elasticity of demand.
2. Income elasticity of demand.
3. Cross elasticity of demand.
4. Cross elasticity of prices.
5. Elasticity of substitution.
6. Market share elasticity.

Measuring Price Elasticity

When the subject of demand is discussed in elementary economics, emphasis is placed on distinguishing between (1) a change in the quantity demanded and (2) a change in demand. As you probably recall, the first refers to a movement along a demand curve due to a change in price; the second refers to a shift in a demand curve to a different level due to a change in one or more of the underlying factors which are assumed constant when a demand curve is drawn (e.g., tastes, incomes, etc.). The latter concept is obviously the more complex one, for it requires the estimation of two demand curves from the available data. For the present discussion, we shall concentrate on changes in the quantity demanded.

Exhibit 2 illustrates the results of two demand studies, one for beef and one for pork, based on the period 1942–69. When one variable is plotted against another, as in each of these charts, the resulting pattern

EXHIBIT 2. Demand for Beef and for Pork

A. Demand for Beef (price of beef divided by per capita income, plotted against per capita beef consumption, annually, 1942–69)

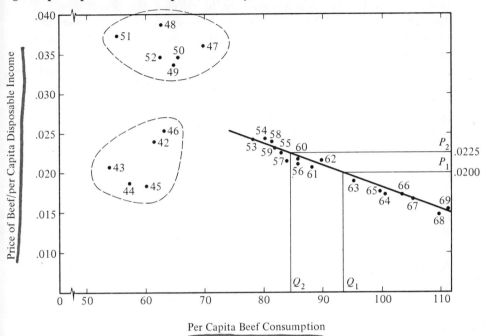

Per Capita Beef Consumption

B. Demand for Pork (price of pork divided by per capita income, plotted against per capita pork consumption, annually, 1942–69)

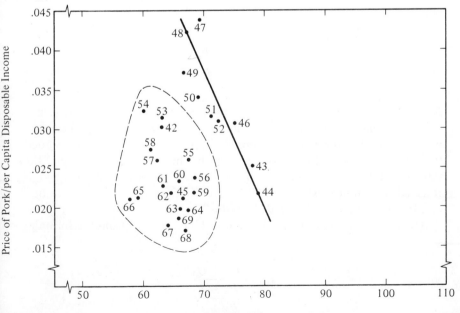

Per Capita Pork Consumption

of dots is called a *scatter diagram*. The numbers next to the dots represent years and hence are a means of identifying the observations. A line which is drawn through a set of dots is called a *regression line*. Each regression line represents a "best fit" to its set of dots. The fitting of regression lines can be done either mathematically or freehand. An example of the mathematical method is the method of least squares as described in elementary statistics textbooks. Freehand fitting, however, is obviously simpler, faster, and, with practice, can yield extremely close approximations to the least-squares result.

It is important to note the "per capita" form in which the price and consumption variables are expressed. Per capita data are used in order to adjust both for the growth of population during the study period and for income disparities. More will be said about such adjustments in the next chapter. Also note that several observation years, appearing in dotted circles, have not been included in this regression analysis. For the most part, these observations covering the war years 1942–45 are considered exceptional because price ceilings and rationing depressed beef consumption during this period. Hence, prices do not represent the interplay of free market forces.

Applying the Formula for Price Elasticity of Demand.   One of the chief purposes of constructing simple demand models of this nature is to obtain estimates of elasticity. The general elasticity formulas given previously may be adapted to this problem by letting P and Q denote price and quantity, respectively. The point elasticity formula for measuring the price elasticity of demand, e_D that is, the ratio of the percentage change in quantity demanded to a slight percentage change in price, would then be:

$$e_D = \frac{\dfrac{\Delta Q}{Q}}{\dfrac{\Delta P}{P}} = \frac{P\Delta Q}{Q\Delta P}$$

Note that although demand curves are usually negatively sloped (since price and quantity demanded are normally inversely related), the negative sign is often omitted in economic discussions because it is assumed to be understood. Thus, disregarding the implicit negative sign, the ratio can range from zero to infinite values. When $e_D = 1$, demand is referred to as unit elastic. Elasticities greater than 1 are termed "elastic," and those less than 1 are called "inelastic."

The arc elasticity of demand, E_D, may be calculated from the formula:

$$E_D = \frac{\dfrac{Q_2 - Q_1}{Q_2 + Q_1}}{\dfrac{P_2 - P_1}{P_2 + P_1}}$$

where Q_1 and Q_2 represent the quantity demanded before and after the price change, respectively, and P_1 and P_2 are the prices that correspond with these quantity figures. Thus, in measuring the demand elasticity on D_2D_2, we may determine the elasticity for the curve as a whole. If the elasticity over a smaller price range is desired, the P_1P_2 band (and hence the Q_1Q_2 band) can be narrowed accordingly. From the above formula, the elasticity of the demand for beef (upper panel, Exhibit 2) is about .7, which means that demand is inelastic.

$$E_D = \frac{\dfrac{85 - 92.5}{85 + 92.5}}{\dfrac{.0225 - .0200}{.0225 + .0200}} = \frac{-.042}{.059} = -.71$$

The minus sign, as explained above, is understood in economic discussions, since price and quantity demanded are inversely related. Hence the sign, though included here, may often be omitted from the final answer. Also, it should be noted that the choice as to which end of the curve to designate as P_1Q_1 and P_2Q_2 is immaterial, since the same answer will be obtained either way. Interpreting the result, the elasticity coefficient means that a 1 percent increase (or decrease) in price may be expected to bring about a .7 percent decrease (or increase) in quantity demanded. Similarly, a 10 percent change in price will be associated with approximately a 7 percent opposite change in quantity demanded.

Price Elasticity and Marginal Revenue

One major reason for the estimation of the individual firm's price elasticity is its usefulness in the determination of marginal revenue. When profit is defined as the difference between revenues and costs, it is easily shown that in order to maximize profits, the firm must equate marginal cost with marginal revenue. But since revenues will depend upon market price—a variable which may not always be within the control of the individual firm—marginal revenue is not usually an easy figure to calculate. For example, consider the demand curve illustrated in Exhibit 3. Total revenue is defined as price times quantity, which is the total area of the rectangles $OP_1M_1Q_1$, $OP_2M_2Q_2$, and $OP_3M_3Q_3$. Which is the largest of these, and what is the direction of change in the magnitude of total revenue for small price and quantity movements?

Elasticity measures at each of the three points tell us the answer. In particular, marginal revenue at price P and elasticity e is given by the formula:

$$MR = P\left(1 + \frac{1}{e}\right)$$

EXHIBIT 3
Typical Demand Curve

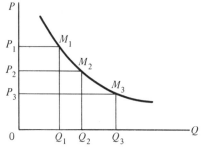

It should be pointed out that since this formula is applicable for a point estimate of elasticity, it is independent of the shape of the demand curve (linear or curvilinear). Also note that in order to apply the formula, the *sign* of the elasticity component must be explicitly taken into account.

Observe further that the formula obtained is consistent with theory. For the pure competition model, elasticity is infinite and hence, $MR = P$ (that is, the firm can sell the next unit of output at the same price as the previous one—the firm's own demand curve is horizontal). For other types of firms, notice that an elasticity of 1 (i.e., −1 including the sign) results in marginal revenue equal to zero, that an elasticity greater than 1 (i.e., less than −1) results in a positive marginal revenue and therefore increasing total revenue, and that an elasticity less than 1 (i.e., greater than −1) results in a negative marginal revenue and therefore decreasing total revenue.

Product Consumption Functions: Income Elasticity

Despite the technical difficulties in estimating aggregate consumption functions, the fact remains that total consumption usually exhibits a more stable relation to income than do broad product groups such as consumers' durables and nondurables. The reason for this is not hard to find: given the decision to spend, the choice of how to spend depends on relative prices, consumer stocks, and other factors as well as income. Nevertheless, despite the somewhat greater difficulties of prediction where product groups are concerned, some useful product consumption functions can be derived for estimating sales-income relations.

Exhibit 4 illustrates the sales-income relation, or product consumption function, for six product groups. The regressions were derived by correlating dollar expenditures for each item with disposable income over the periods 1952–70.

Exhibit 4
Product Consumption Functions

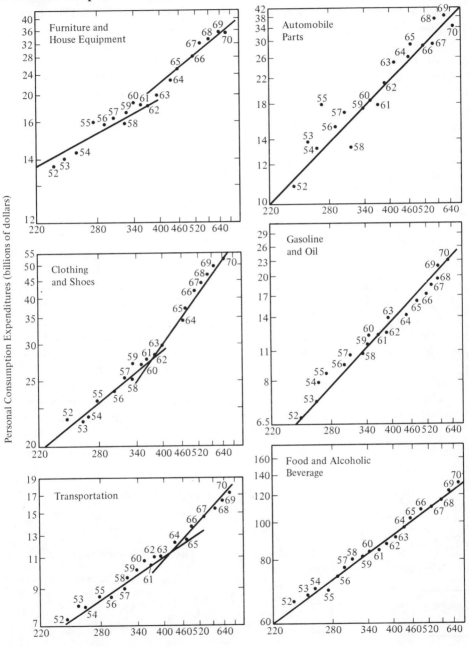

Disposable Personal Income (billions of dollars)

Source: USDC, Office of Business Economics. See also "Personal Consumption Expenditures by Type of Product," reported annually in the *Statistical Abstract of the United States*.

Note that the data in each of the charts have been plotted on *double logarithmic* paper, that is, paper on which both axes are scaled in logarithms. This is because a series whose underlying trend is curved when plotted on an arithmetic scale may sometimes come closer to approximating a straight line when plotted on a logarithmic scale. In this case, all of the series exhibited a curved pattern when they were plotted over time on regular arithmetic scales. When they were plotted against each other on the logarithmic scales in Exhibit 4, they yielded the one or two simple linear regression lines as shown.

It is quite possible that if these series were updated to the most recent year for which data are available, the underlying trend of one or more of the series when plotted over time on arithmetic scales would appear to be linear. In that case, the series would be plotted on an arithmetic scale when constructing the scatter diagram. In other words, since we don't always know the real underlying economic forces that are at work in affecting the trend of a particular series, we often end up choosing the type of relationship that produces the best statistical fit. The fact that the trend of a series of economic data appears to be curved over, say, a ten-year period does not necessarily mean that it will continue on its curved path for the next five years. And when judged in final perspective over the entire 15-year period, it may even turn out to be best represented by a linear rather than curvilinear trend. However, unless we know enough about the underlying economics of the series, it usually turns out that we can only estimate on the basis of the data at hand, with little or no guidance from economic theory.

Applying the Formula for Income Elasticity of Demand. The general elasticity formulas given earlier can be adapted to measuring the income elasticity of demand, e_Y that is, the ratio of the percentage change in quantity Q, demanded to a slight percentage change in income or purchasing power, Y.

$$e_Y = \frac{\dfrac{\Delta Q}{Q}}{\dfrac{\Delta Y}{Y}} = \frac{Y \Delta Q}{Q \Delta Y}$$

This, of course, is a formula for point elasticity. As a measure of arc elasticity, E_Y, the formulas is:

$$E_Y = \frac{\dfrac{Q_2 - Q_1}{Q_2 + Q_1}}{\dfrac{Y_2 - Y_1}{Y_2 + Y_1}}$$

Note that in measuring the income elasticity of demand, quantities purchased are used. In the present problem our dependent variable is personal consumption expenditures rather than quantities purchased. Hence the derived measure is, technically speaking, the "income elasticity of personal consumption expenditures" and thus reflects the influence of income on consumption. (NOTE: Purchasing power is sometimes a better measure than income for certain kinds of problems. The two are not always the same. Can you see why?)

Mathematical Considerations. The above formulas are applicable to a straight line on arithmetic scales. In the present problem, we have a straight line on double logarithmic scales. How can we estimate the elasticity in such cases? What is the relation between elasticity and slope? These are mathematical considerations which arise in the use of logarithmic scales and which warrant our attention at this time.

Let us recall that on an arithmetic scale, equal distances are represented by equal *amounts* of change. Therefore, when a series plots as a straight line on regular arithmetic scales, the slope of the line measures the *amount* of change in the vertical distance divided by the *amount* of change in the horizontal distance, or simply the change in Y per unit change in X. Elasticity, on the other hand, measures the *percentage* change in the vertical distance divided by the *percentage* change in the horizontal distance, or simply the percentage change in Y relative to a 1 percent change in X.

When a series plots as a straight line on double log paper, an interesting and sometimes convenient mathematical property of the line is that its slope is also the elasticity. In other words, if the equation is logarithmic, that is, linear in the logarithms as is the equation:

$$Y = aX^b$$

or

$$\log Y = \log a + b \log X$$

the elasticity is revealed directly by the exponent, b, in the former equation or by the slope, b, in the latter equation. Intuitively, the reason for this is that on a log scale, equal distances are represented by equal *ratios* or *proportions*, or in other words by equal *relative* changes. Since elasticity is, after all, a measure of relative change, the slope of a straight line on double logarithmic paper will be the same as its elasticity. Therefore, elasticity in this case can be estimated by using the ratio of the logarithmic expressions in the slope portion of the two-point formula. Thus, for a straight line on double logarithmic scales, the arc elasticity is given by the ratio:

$$\frac{\log Y_2 - \log Y_1}{\log X_2 - \log X_1}$$

NOTE: We now see that the arc elasticity formula for a straight line on semilogarithmic scales represents a combination of two parts:

one is a portion of the elasticity ratio for a straight line on logarithmic scales as shown above; the other is a portion of the elasticity ratio for a straight line on arithmetic scales which we have been using all along. There are thus two arc elasticity formulas for a straight line on semilogarithmic scales. One formula applies to the case where the vertical axis is logarithmic and the horizontal axis is arithmetic. The other formula applies to a situation in which the vertical axis is arithmetic and the horizontal axis is logarithmic. You should be able to write the correct formula for this case.

Three Measures of Elasticity for Substitute or Complementary Products

Several different measures of elasticity may be developed for interpreting the economic effects and interactions of substitute and complementary products. Letting P_X denote the price of X, and P_Y the price of Y, three of the more common measures are the following.

1. Cross Elasticity of Demand. This measures the rate of percentage change in the quantity demanded of Y relative to a slight percentage change in P_X, with P_Y constant. The point formula is:

$$e_C = \frac{\dfrac{\Delta Y}{Y}}{\dfrac{\Delta P_X}{P_X}}$$

and the arc formula is:

$$E_C = \frac{\dfrac{Y_2 - Y_1}{Y_2 + Y_1}}{\dfrac{P_{X_2} - P_{X_1}}{P_{X_2} + P_{X_1}}}$$

The cross elasticity can be positive, negative, or zero. It will be positive if the products are substitutes. Thus, other things remaining the same, if the price of butter increases, the consumption of margarine should also increase (to replace the decrease in butter consumption).[1] On the other hand, when commodities are complementary their cross elasticities are negative. Increases in the prices of cameras, for example, should bring decreases in the purchases of film, again assuming a constancy of other factors. Finally, a small or zero cross elasticity would indicate that the products (or the markets in which they are sold) are effectively

---

[1] Substitutes defined in this way (in terms of cross-demand elasticity) are called gross substitutes. If we separate the income effect of ΔP_X from the total effect, we have a *substitution* effect. Substitutes defined in terms of a substitution effect only are called *pure substitutes.*

independent, since variations in the price of one produces no appreciable changes in the purchase of the other.

2. Cross Elasticity of Prices. If products (or markets) are interrelated, a change in the price of one product may produce a change in the price of the other. The point formula is thus:

$$e_{pp} = \frac{\dfrac{\Delta P_Y}{P_Y}}{\dfrac{\Delta P_X}{P_X}}$$

and the arc measure is:

$$E_{pp} = \frac{\dfrac{P_{Y_2} - P_{Y_1}}{P_{Y_2} + P_{Y_1}}}{\dfrac{P_{X_2} - P_{X_1}}{P_{X_2} + P_{X_1}}}$$

Theoretically, the value of the cross elasticity of prices should range from $+1$ for products which are perfect substitutes to -1 for those which are perfect complements. (Why?) In reality, the measure may sometimes fall a bit beyond these limits, due to errors in the data and to various extraneous factors that may be at work and which are not usually taken into account in simple studies of the type discussed here.

3. Elasticity of Substitution. This coefficient relates relative changes in the consumption of products to relative changes in their *marginal rate of substitution*. The latter expression, abbreviated *MRS*, is defined in demand theory as the change in the consumption of Y which will just offset a unit change in X, leaving the consumer as well off as before. In other words, the *MRS* is the decrease in Y per unit increase in X along an indifference curve, or simply $MRS = -\Delta Y/\Delta X$. Accordingly, the elasticity of substitution may be defined as the rate of percentage change in the consumption ratio of X to Y relative to a slight percentage change in the marginal rate of substitution. However, in literature dealing with the economic theory of demand, it is shown that when the consumer's expenditure-preference pattern is in equilibrium, $MRS = -\Delta Y/\Delta X = P_X/P_Y$. Hence we may use these equalities and the above statements to develop the following point formula for the elasticity of substitution:

$$e_{ss} = \frac{\dfrac{\Delta(X/Y)}{X/Y}}{\dfrac{\Delta MRS}{MRS}} = \frac{\dfrac{\Delta(X/Y)}{X/Y}}{\dfrac{\Delta(P_X/P_Y)}{P_X/P_Y}}$$

The expression on the right, since it employs objective prices rather than a subjective marginal rate of substitution, is more easily applied in empirical work. The arc measure using price would thus be:

$$E_{ss} = \frac{\dfrac{(X/Y)_2 - (X/Y)_1}{(X/Y)_2 + (X/Y)_1}}{\dfrac{(P_X/P_Y)_2 - (P_X/P_Y)_1}{(P_X/P_Y)_2 + (P_X/P_Y)_1}}$$

What does the elasticity of substitution tell us? Basically, it is a measure of the *degree* or ease of substitutability between X and Y along an indifference curve or at a given level of well-being. (In production economics, where the concept is also employed, it measures the degree or ease of factor substitutability along an isoquant or at a given level of output.) It assumes, therefore, that total utility or well-being remains constant as product prices change. This assumption, obviously, may not always be realistic, and hence some special care may have to be taken in interpreting the measure. In any event, an elasticity of zero would mean that the products are being used in the same proportions irrespective of the changes in their relative prices. What would a positive elasticity indicate? A negative elasticity?

Market Share Elasticity

The percentage of a firm's sales relative to that of its industry's is termed *market share*. Clearly, formulas for a company's market share could be established in which the percentage change in market share is dependent upon relative prices between the firm and the industry, or between, say, relative advertising expenditures for the firm and the industry. Of course, any other appropriate independent variable may also be employed.

The third proposition above tends to explain why it happens that for an industry composed, say, of two firms selling an undifferentiated product (i.e., a perfect duopoly), any price difference between the producers will result in a 100 percent market share for the seller who charges the lower price. This principle could be extended, of course, to three or more sellers of an undifferentiated product (i.e., perfect oligopoly). Further, it could be generalized to include several producers selling similar but not identical products (i.e., imperfect oligopoly) except that the lowest priced seller is not likely to receive as much as a 100 percent market share.

It is possible to develop some interesting relationships between market share elasticity and one or more of the other types of elasticity mentioned above. However, to do so would raise certain complexities, a discussion of which is beyond our scope.

ELASTICITY INTERRELATIONS

For most types of demand analyses, the price of the product, the income or purchasing power of buyers, and the prices of competing products or substitutes are generally taken as major demand determinants. Accordingly, it is meaningful to talk of such things as price elasticity, income elasticity, and substitution elasticity, and to measure their effects in particular demand situations.

Are each of these factors independent of the others? Clearly not. If income rises while the price of the product remains constant, the consequent increase in purchases will depend on both the price and income elasticities of the product. On the other hand, if income remains the same while the relative prices of the product and its substitutes change, the change in purchases will depend on both the price and substitution elasticities. Apparently, therefore, the three types of elasticities are related to each other. But how?

A Price-Income-Substitution Relation

Assuming two products, X and Y, can we state a relation between the price elasticity of demand for X, the income elasticity of demand for X, and the elasticity of substitution between X and Y? If K represents the proportion of income spent on X, we can write the relation:

Price elasticity $= (-K)$ (Income elasticity)
$$+ (1 - K) \text{ (Substitution elasticity)}$$

If three or more products are involved, the formula is more complex. However, it is always possible to lump all other commodities together as one good by employing index numbers or some other amalgamation device which permits an "averaging" of diverse items.

The formula exhibits a number of interesting properties, a few of which may be stated as follows:

1. If the substitution elasticity is zero, the price elasticity will depend on the income elasticity and the proportion of income spent on the product.
2. If the income elasticity is zero, the price elasticity will depend on the substitution elasticity and the proportion of income *not* spent on the product.
3. If approximately equal proportions of income are spent on both products, the price elasticity will depend on the relative magnitudes of the income elasticity and substitution elasticity. The latter will be large—theoretically infinite—in the case of products that are perfect substitutes, in which case the price elasticity would be very high even if the income elasticity, or K, were zero.

SUMMARY

The analysis of demand is important to a firm because demand determines revenues and therefore influences profits. Hence, analysis of demand provides a useful operational tool for business management—particularly in the areas of forecasting, budgeting, and planning. The most well-known determinants of demand are price and income. However, a complete analysis of demand requires an understanding of all the important factors that influence a company's sales. Among these factors are product quality, product durability, and industrial market structure, as well as sociological, demographic, and saturation level characteristics.

One of the most common measures of demand responsiveness is demand elasticity. Six different types of elasticity were presented: price elasticity, income elasticity, cross-demand elasticity, cross-price elasticity, elasticity of substitution, and market share elasticity. All of these may be estimated either with a point formula or an arc formula, the difference depending upon whether a specific or average measure is desired. The especial usefulness of price elasticity to compute marginal revenue for the individual firm was discussed, and an empirical example using beef and pork consumption has been presented.

PROBLEMS

1. The J. P. Jackson Company, a department store, conducted a study of the demand for men's ties. It found that the average daily demand, D, in terms of price, P, is given by the equation $D = f(P) = 60 - 5P$.
   a. How many ties per day can the store expect to sell at a price of $3 per tie?
   b. If the store wants to sell 20 ties per day, what price should it charge?
   c. What would be the demand if the store offered to give the ties away free?
   d. What is the highest price that anyone would be willing to pay for these ties?
   e. Plot the demand curve.

2. The demand for sugar in the United States was once estimated to be $D = 135 - 8P$. If this equation were valid today:
   a. How much would be demanded at a price of 10?
   b. What price would correspond to a demand of 95?
   c. How much would be demanded if sugar were free?
   d. What is the highest price anyone would pay?

3. The demand for widgets is given by the equation $3D = 3a - 3bP$, where a and b are positive constants.
   a. Find the price if the quantity demand is $a/2$.
   b. Find the quantity demanded at a price of $a/3b$.
   c. How much will be demanded if widgets are free?
   d. What is the highest price anyone will pay for widgets?

4. PRINCIPLES OR PROVERBS? Many statements in economics and business parade as principles when in reality they are hardly more than proverbs. The differences between the two are by no means trivial. For one thing, principles are never contradictory whereas proverbs often are. (EXAMPLE: *"Look before you leap"*; however, *"He who hesitates is lost."*) Statements like the following are often heard. Are they principles or proverbs? Explain. Rephrase if necessary to improve the statement. Use examples.

   a. "Inexpensive products tend to have inelastic demands."
   b. "The demands of rich consumers are less elastic than the demands of poor consumers."
   c. "Products whose purchases are closely correlated with income are elastic in demand."

5. "Demand elasticity measures percentage changes in quantity demanded relative to percentage changes in price. It follows that with ten equal demanders for a product, the elasticity will be ten times as great as it is for one." True or false? Explain.

6. "The elasticity of demand for a product usually increases with the length of time over which a price change persists. Thus, a 1 percent decrease in price may result at first in a less than 1 percent increase in quantity demanded, but eventually the quantity may increase by 2 percent, 5 percent, or even more." True or false? Explain why.

7. In economics textbooks we usually see *price* scaled on the vertical axis of a chart and *quantity* on the horizontal axis. This implies that price is to be viewed as a dependent variable and quantity as an independent variable. In the case of demand curves, for example, it would mean that price is a function of quantity demanded. In most business demand studies, however, where price and quantity are the only variables being considered, we tend to think of quantity demanded as a function of price; that is, we regard demand as the dependent variable and price as independent. Can you explain the reason for this seeming inconsistency between economic theory and the business world? Discuss.

8. Each of the following demand functions expresses price, P, as a function of demand, D. Rewrite each equation so that D is expressed as a function of P. In all cases the variables D and P take on only positive values and a, b, and c are positive constants.

   a. $P = a - bD$

   b. $P = \dfrac{a}{D + b} - c$

   c. $P = \sqrt{a - bD}$

   d. $P = (a - bD)^2$

   e. $P = a - bD^2$

   f. $P = \left(\dfrac{b}{D - c}\right)^{1/a}$

   g. $P = \left(\dfrac{1}{b}\right) \log \dfrac{a}{D}$

9. Generally speaking, would you expect the cross elasticity of demand to be positive, negative, or zero for each of the following pairs of products? What general rule, if any, can you infer from your answers?
   a. Convertibles and sedans.
   b. Coca-Cola and Pepsi-Cola.
   c. Textbook sales and school enrollments.
   d. Desks and chairs.
   e. Chinese egg rolls and children's socks.

10. Central City Meat Packers has noted that the demand (Q) for its smoked breakfast sausages is affected by changes in per capita personal income (I) such that $Q = 1,000 + .2I$.
    a. Calculate quantity demanded at each $1,000 of per capita income from $2,000 to $6,000.
    b. Calculate the income elasticity of demand if income changes from $3,000 to $5,000.
    c. How are changes in income elasticity of demand related to changes in income?

REFERENCES

ALLEN, C. L.   *The Framework of Price Theory*, pp. 45–82. Belmont, Calif.: Wadsworth Publishing Co., Inc., 1967.

FERGUSON, C. E., and GOULD, J. P.   *Microeconomic Theory*. 4th ed. Homewood, Ill.: Richard D. Irwin, Inc., 1975.

HENDERSON, JAMES M., and QUANDT, RICHARD E.   *Microeconomic Theory*. 2d ed. New York: McGraw-Hill Book Co., Inc., 1971.

KATONA, GEORGE   "Consumer Behavior: Theory and Findings on Expectations and Aspirations." *The American Economic Review*, vol. 58, no. 2 (May 1968), pp. 19–30.

WANG, Y., TOLLEY, G. S., and FLETCHER, R. G.   "Reexamination of the Time Series Evidence on Food Demand." *Econometrica*, vol. 37, no. 4 (October 1969), pp. 695–705.

chapter 6

Analytical Framework for
Demand Measurement

The theory and measurement of demand, which is the essence of demand analysis, is subject to a number of difficulties both in methodology and interpretation. In any empirical investigation, the nature of these difficulties should be understood if proper use is to be made of the analysis. For the most part the problem consists of bridging the gap between the concept of demand as it exists in economic theory and the measurement of demand by statistical methods. The former provides a guide for judgment, while the latter, we shall see, attempts to yield quantitative estimates within the limits of actual experience.

SOME STATISTICAL CONSIDERATIONS

The measurement of demand can be divided into two problems. The first attempts to estimate the nature of the price-quantity relation, that is, the demand schedule or curve, on the assumption that other demand-determining factors remain constant. This type of measurement can be used, for example, as a means for determining elasticity. The second aspect of the problem is to measure changes in the intensity of demand. This type of measurement can be used in determining shifts in the demand curve. Thus, where management is contemplating a change in price and its subsequent effect on the quantity demanded, it is the first concept of demand in the schedule or curve sense that must be measured. Alternatively, if price remains the same and there are changes in other demand-determining factors such as income, advertising expenditures, and so forth, it is the shifts in the demand curve as a whole that are of immediate concern. Realistically, however, in the actual work of demand measurement, these two problem areas are not regarded as mutually exclusive. In most practical situations we must usually be concerned both with the nature of the demand curve and with its shifts, for rarely is it possible to measure one without measuring the other in the same process.

Economists have developed two different methods for making quantitative estimates of demand: one involves the use of time-series data; the other employs cross-sectional statistics.

1. Time-Series Data. Data are sometimes used in which the historical changes in prices, incomes, population, and other variables affecting demand are observed and their interrelationships with demand are measured. Since a demand relation with only certain independent variables is wanted, it may be necessary to eliminate the influence of other independent variables that have a significant effect on demand. Thus, in a demand-price study where the influence of price is the only independent factor under consideration, it is often necessary to make two types of adjustments in the data.

a. Population Adjustment. In order to eliminate the effect of population variation on the sale of the product, incomes and demand quantities are reduced to a per capita basis. This adjustment is usually made, however, when the data cover a number of years, since population figures do not usually show sharp fluctuations from year to year. The result of the adjustment is to enable the changes in demand to be attributed to factors other than population. Where the product being analyzed is a family-type good, such as an automobile, washing machine, and so forth, a better demand estimate is often obtained by reducing the relevant data to a per household or per family rather than per capita basis. In any event, it should be realized that such reductions do not, of course, adjust for changes in the age distribution, racial composition, or other elements in the population that may affect demand over the long run. These are additional factors which, if they are deemed to be important in a particular demand study, will require separate consideration and adjustment.

b. Deflation Adjustment. A similar reduction, usually called "deflation," is to adjust for changes in the purchasing power of money by dividing the series which is expressed in current dollars by an average price index. An example of the latter and one that is commonly used in consumer demand studies is the Consumer Price Index, since it reflects the weighted average of prices paid by consumers for most goods and services, relative to a previous base period. The result of this division is to convert the first series from current dollars to "constant dollars" of the base period. Although this procedure yields fairly satisfactory results, it should be kept in mind that deflation methods of this sort do not give precise measures of price changes, mainly because no perfect index has yet been constructed and because the time period covered may be too long.

In addition to the population and deflation adjustments in time-series analysis, other adjustments are also sometimes made, such as removal of trend, seasonal, and cyclical influences. These as well as deflation adjustments are discussed and illustrated in elementary statistics textbooks.

2. Cross-Sectional Analysis. This attempts to discover how consumption by individuals or families varies with prices, incomes, geographic differences, and the like, at the present time rather than over a period of time. Variations in the data may thus be current rather than historical. For example, in establishing a sales-income relationship for the purpose of measuring the income elasticity of demand, the time-series approach would employ past variations in the data as a basis for measurement. The cross-sectional approach, on the other hand, would compare the different levels of sales at a given time among different income groups, and the elasticity measure would be based on these differences. But as in the time-series method, adjustments in the data may also be needed in order to eliminate the effects of other factors (in this case all factors other than income) that may affect the demand for the product. In any event, the choice of either approach may often depend upon time and expense considerations, and the data already available. For these reasons, the time-series method is perhaps more commonly employed in demand studies—the data being already available from published sources—with some use made of cross-sectional information when it seems appropriate.

CONSTRUCTING ELEMENTARY DEMAND MODELS

You will find it instructive to go through the procedure of constructing an elementary demand model. The following two studies, one for beef and one for millinery, illustrate some of the typical situations that are encountered in demand analyses, and hence provide a basic guide for conducting an independent research project.

1. Demand for Beef

World War II brought many structural changes in consumption patterns, as evidenced by the new demand relationships for various products that developed after the war. One such change occurred in the case of beef, where the demand for this product took on a new form beginning with 1947. Let us, therefore, develop a simple *freehand* or *graphic* demand model for beef based on the period 1953–69.

Step 1. Construct the Variables. Our objective is to see whether a simple relationship can be established between beef consumption and beef prices, based on a time period covering a number of years. During this period, various factors affecting beef consumption, such as population and purchasing power, as well as beef prices, underwent important changes. Hence, if we are to express beef consumption as a function of beef prices, we can adjust for the influence of population and purchasing power (or income) by expressing the dependent variable as "beef consumption per capita" and the independent variable as the ratio "price of beef/disposable income per capita."

The procedure for constructing the necessary variables is illustrated in columns 1 through 6 of Exhibit 1. One of the first problems in performing studies of this sort is finding good sources of data, and we are indeed fortunate in the United States that more and more governmental agencies and private institutions have begun to keep records yielding the kinds of information required for this type of demand analysis. Usually, these publications are available in college and public libraries. The *Statistical Abstract of the United States* is always a good first source to consult, since it abstracts from all other sources and gives specific references to other publications which may also be of assistance. Other periodicals containing fairly extensive economic statistics are the *Annual Economic Report to the President*, published yearly by the Council of Economic Advisors; the *Survey of Current Business*, published monthly by the U.S. Department of Commerce; *Business Statistics*, published biennially by the U.S. Department of Commerce; and a summary of business indicators published weekly by *Business Week* magazine. *Agricultural Statistics*, published yearly by the U.S. Department of Commerce, is an extremely useful general source for data relating to agriculture.

A word as to the price of beef in column 5 may be of interest, especially for updating this study. *Agricultural Statistics* reports annually the average wholesale prices per 100 pounds of steer beef, dressed, at Chicago and New York, for grades of prime, choice, good, and commercial. The price at New York for each grade is never more than one or two dollars above the Chicago price, the difference being primarily a reflection of transportation costs. Although an average price for the two cities could have been used, an examination of the data in *Agricultural Statistics* reveals that the price movements tend to parallel each other. Hence the price of choice grade at Chicago was taken as representative for the country as a whole.

Step 2. Plot the Variables over Time. It is helpful, especially in graphic or freehand regression analysis, to plot the variables over time, as in Exhibit 2, so that a visual comparison can be made of their fluctuations. This step may permit the discovery of leads and lags between the variables, as well as serve as a guide for deciding on the ways

EXHIBIT 1
Beef Demand Study

Year	(1) Civilian Population (millions)	(2) Disposable Personal Income (billion $)	(3) Disposable Income Per Capita (dollars) (2) ÷ (1)	(4) Beef Consumption Per Capita (pounds) Y Exhibit 2	(5) Price of Beef, Dressed, Wholesale, Choice, Chicago ($ per 100 lbs.)	(6) Price of Beef/Disposable Income Per Capita (ratio) X Exhibit 2 (5) ÷ (3)	(7) Regression Estimates $Y_c = 142.5 - 2500 X$ Exhibit 3 (4) vs. (6)	(8) Deviations $d = Y - Y_c$ (4) − (7)	(9) Deviations Squared $d^2 = (Y - Y_c)^2$ (8)²	(10) Beef Consumption Per Capita, Squared Y^2 (4)²
1953	156.6	252.5	1,612.4	77.6	39.98	.0248	80.5	−2.9	8.41	6,021.76
1954	159.7	256.9	1,608.6	80.1	40.10	.0249	80.2	−.1	.01	6,416.01
1955	163.0	274.4	1,683.4	82.0	39.24	.0233	84.2	−2.2	4.84	6,724.00
1956	166.1	292.9	1,763.4	85.4	37.89	.0215	88.7	−3.3	10.89	7,293.16
1957	169.1	307.9	1,820.8	84.6	39.38	.0216	88.5	−3.9	13.27	7,157.16
1958	172.2	316.5	1,838.0	80.5	45.05	.0245	81.2	−.7	.49	6,480.25
1959	175.3	337.3	1,924.1	81.4	45.24	.0235	83.7	−2.3	5.29	6,625.96
1960	178.1	350.0	1,965.2	85.2	43.98	.0224	86.5	−1.3	1.69	7,259.04
1961	181.1	364.4	2,012.1	88.0	41.14	.0204	91.5	−3.5	12.25	7,744.00
1962	183.7	385.3	2,097.4	89.1	44.84	.0214	89.0	.1	.01	7,938.81
1963	186.5	404.6	2,169.4	94.5	40.83	.0188	95.5	−1.0	1.00	8,930.25
1964	189.1	438.1	2,316.8	99.9	39.48	.0170	100.0	−.1	.01	9,980.01
1965	191.6	472.2	2,464.5	99.5	42.61	.0173	99.2	.3	.09	9,900.25
1966	193.4	511.9	2,646.8	104.2	43.04	.0163	101.7	2.5	6.25	10,857.64
1967	195.3	546.3	2,797.2	106.5	43.37	.0155	103.7	2.8	7.84	11,342.25
1968	197.1	591.0	2,998.5	109.7	43.84	.0146	106.0	3.7	13.69	12,034.09
1969	199.1	634.2	3,185.3	110.8	47.75	.0150	105.0	5.8	33.64	12,276.64
				ΣY = 1,559.0					Σ(d²) = 119.67	ΣY² = 144,981.28

Source: Columns 1 and 2: *Statistical Abstract of the United States* (annual). Columns 4 and 5: USDA, *Agricultural Statistics* (annual). Other general sources such as USDC, *Business Statistics*, published biennially, carry most of these data.

EXHIBIT 2
Beef Demand Study

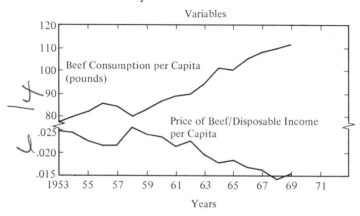

in which the variables are to be combined. In this case, visual inspection of Exhibit 2 seems to indicate the following:

1. There is no apparent lead-lag relationship between the variables, nor is there reason to expect such a relationship according to economic theory.

2. The underlying trend of each series appears to be linear, and there are no reasons to expect any curvilinear trends on the basis of economic judgment.

3. There is an inverse relationship between consumption and price, which is in accordance with what we would expect on the basis of economic theory.

This information gives us a background for plotting the scatter diagram.

    Step 3. Plot the Scatter Diagram. The scatter diagram of beef consumption against beef prices is shown in Exhibit 3. Since it was decided in the previous step that there was no lead or lag relation between the variables, we can plot each year's consumption variable against the same year's price variable, without having to "shift" one of the series forward or backward. Also, since it was decided that the underlying trend of each series was linear, the scatter diagram can be plotted on ordinary arithmetic scales. On the other hand, if the trends of the variables were approximately geometric, they could be plotted on logarithmic scales in order to express them more simply as linear relationships. Examples of such cases will be given later.

    Step 4. Fit the Freehand Regression Line. How is a regression line fitted to a set of dots? A widely used mathematical procedure which is learned in elementary statistics is the method of *least squares*—so called because the regression line is such that it minimizes the sum

EXHIBIT 3

Beef Demand Study (beef consumption per capita versus price of beef/ disposable income per capita, 1953–69)

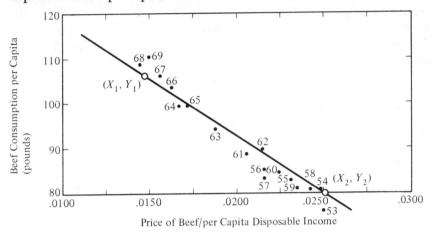

Price of Beef/per Capita Disposable Income

of the squared deviations of the dots from the line. The mathematical method of least squares produces the regression equation, and this equation is then used to draw in the regression line on the scatter diagram.

In the graphic method, the mathematically correct regression line is approximated by sketching it *freehand*. After this is done, the equation for the line can be estimated directly from the chart. In sketching the freehand regression line, the following suggestions may be useful to keep in mind:

1. The direction of the line, that is, whether it slopes upward or downward, should accord with economic theory and judgment. Thus, in the case of Exhibit 3, the line slopes downward, since it has already been decided in step 2 above that the price-quantity relation is an inverse one.

2. Roughly, about half the dots should be above the line and half below.

3. The *vertical* deviations of the dots from the regression line, when squared, should total to less than the sum of the squared vertical deviations of the dots from any other regression line that might be drawn.

It should be emphasized that the second suggestion is only a rough guide and not a rigid rule. The third suggestion is a technical one which provides a logical basis for the mathematical method of least squares. In the graphic or freehand method, this third rule is admittedly a difficult one to apply. However, there is some consolation in the fact that with practice, you can learn to fit freehand regression lines with considerable accuracy.

Step 5. Estimate the Regression Equation. The equation for a regression line can be estimated directly from the chart by utilizing the *two-point* formula from analytic geometry. This formula, as its name suggests, requires only that we know the coordinates of any two points on the regression line. Hence, it is the most suitable of several straight-line formulas that might be employed, since other formulas require a knowledge of other properties of the line (e.g., slope, intercept) which are not always as readily available from freehand analysis.

In the two-point formula, we choose any two points on the line and read off their coordinates, X_1, Y_1, and X_2, Y_2, directly from the chart. These coordinates are then used in the formula to estimate the equation for the line. Thus, let us estimate the equation for the line in Exhibit 2, using the following two-point formula which expresses the *computed* values of the dependent variable, Y_c, as a function of the independent variable, X.

$$Y_c = Y_1 + \frac{Y_2 - Y_1}{X_2 - X_1}(X - X_1)$$

From the line in Exhibit 3, choose any two points on the line and read off their coordinates directly from the graph. Thus, we choose two points whose coordinates appear to be:

$$X_1 = .0150$$
$$Y_1 = 105$$
$$X_2 = .0250$$
$$Y_2 = 80$$

Substituting these visual estimates in the above formula,

$$Y_c = 105 + \frac{80 - 105}{.0250 - .0150}(X - .0150)$$
$$= 105 - 2{,}500(X - .0150)$$
$$= 105 - 2{,}500X + 37.5$$
$$= 142.5 - 2{,}500X$$

This is our estimated equation for the freehand regression line in Exhibit 3.

Step 6. Compare Calculated and Actual Values. How close are the calculated values of the dependent variable to the actual values? In other words, how well does our regression equation succeed in predicting the beef consumption variable on the basis of the price variable? A visual answer to this question is obtained by plotting the actual and calculated values over time. These data are obtained from columns 4 and 7 of Exhibit 1 and are graphed in Exhibit 4.

EXHIBIT 4
Beef Demand Study

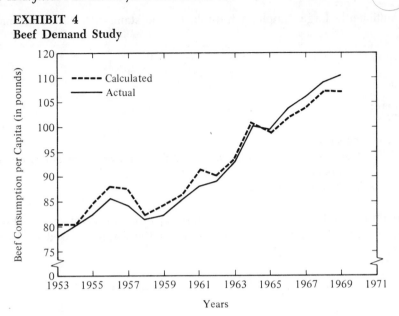

The deviations of the dashed or calculated line from the solid or actual line is a reflection of the fact that all of the dots in Exhibit 3 did not fall along the regression line. For, if they did, the variations in Y would be completely explained or accounted for by X, and hence Y would equal Y_c. The fact that the dots depart from the regression line may indicate that forces other than price affect beef consumption. In a multiple regression analysis, one or more of these other forces would be incorporated in the regression equation.

Step 7. Calculate Supplementary Measures. How meaningful or accurate is this analysis? A number of statistical measures exist which, when applied to this study, will serve as a guide for interpreting the results. For our purposes, a few of the more simple and widely used ones may be reviewed at this time. A fuller treatment of these and various other measures can be found in elementary statistics textbooks.

1. Standard Error of Estimate. Our simple demand model has obviously left out a number of variables, such as the price of beef substitutes, which might be expected at least marginally to affect the per capita consumption of beef in future periods. In demand models such as this, the effects of such omitted variables are assumed to be minor; and it is further assumed that their influences, being both positive and negative, will tend on average to cancel each other out. Yet for any given year this may not be true; and hence it is useful to provide a range of values for the predicted variable, rather than only a single value, within which the forecast-year figure may be expected to fall with given probability. The standard error of estimate permits us to calculate this range. For a sufficiently large sample, a formula for the standard error of estimate s_y, is

$$s_y = \sqrt{\frac{\Sigma(d^2)}{N}}$$

where:

Σ = the sum of

d = deviations of the actual values of the dependent variable from its calculated values

N = number of observations

Columns 8 and 9 of Exhibit 1 show the steps that are involved in obtaining the data for this calculation. Applying the formula based on these columns:

$$s_y = \sqrt{\frac{119.67}{17}} = \sqrt{7.04} = 2.65$$

The standard error of estimate, 2.65, represents the average error of estimate that may be expected in predicting the dependent variable on the basis of the independent variable in the regression equation. If we assume that the errors are normally distributed, then we may say that about 68 percent of the estimates based on the regression equation will come within a range equal to Y_c plus or minus 1 standard error (or 2.65). Similarly, about 95 percent of the estimates for Y will include a zone of $Y_c \pm$ two standard errors (or $2 \times 2.65 = 5.30$), and practically all estimates will incorporate a range of three standard errors (or $3 \times 2.65 = 7.95$). These concepts should be familiar to you if you have studied elementary statistics.

2. *Coefficient of Determination.* This measure, symbolized r^2 in simple regression problems (and R^2 in multiple regression problems), gives the proportion of variations in the dependent variable which is explained by the independent variable in the analysis. The following formula, employing some of the above symbols, is useful for models based on freehand methods:

$$r^2 = 1 - \frac{\Sigma(d^2)}{\Sigma(Y^2) - (\Sigma Y)^2/N}$$

Column 10 of Exhibit 1 gives the Y^2 figure needed for this formula. Applying the appropriate data from Exhibit 1:

$$r^2 = 1 - \frac{119.67}{144,981.28 - (1,559)^2/17} = .9405 \text{ or } 94.05 \text{ percent}$$

Thus, more than 94 percent of the variations in the beef consumption variable are explained or accounted for by the price variable. The coefficient of determination, r^2, is thus a very practical and useful concept.

Values of r^2 may range from 0 to 1 (or in percentage terms, from 0 to 100 percent). The square root of the coefficient of determination gives the *coefficient of correlation, r,* which is a measure of the degree of association between the variables. Since r^2 may range from 0 to 1, r will range from -1 to $+1$. In the present problem, $r = \sqrt{.9405} = -.97$. The minus sign indicates that the correlation is negative or inverse, a fact which we know from the slope of the regression line.

> NOTE: A short-cut graphic device that may be used to approximate the standard error and the coefficient of determination is as follows:
>
> 1. Estimate the standard error, s_y, by drawing two lines *parallel* to the regression line so as to include approximately ⅔ of the dots (and hence exclude ⅙ on each side). The vertical width of the resulting band, measured on the Y axis, is roughly $2s_y$, so one half of this is approximately s_y.
>
> 2. Estimate the standard deviation, σ_y, by drawing two *horizontal* lines to include approximately ⅔ of the dots (and hence exclude ⅙ above and below). The width of this band is roughly $2\sigma_y$, so one half of this is approximately σ_y.
>
> 3. The coefficient of determination, r^2 is then computed from the formula
>
> $$r^2 = 1 - \left(\frac{s_y}{\sigma_y}\right)^2$$

It is perhaps worth repeating that various other tests and calculations may be performed in evaluating the results of a statistical model. Those given above are a few of the more common ones.

II. Demand for Millinery

In contrast to the previous study in which the data were derived from a times series covering a number of years, Exhibit 5 and Exhibit 6 show some sales and price data derived from controlled experiments. The data are expressed as index numbers, that is, percentages of a previous period. The indexes refer to sales and prices for a group of millinery products in a multiple-branch department store. The data were obtained from controlled experiments among the store's branches covering a period of 15 midweek shopping days (Tuesdays to Thursdays) over five weeks. The short time period allowed for wide price manipulations while other influential factors, such as income, seasonal changes, fashion variations, and competitors' price reactions could be assumed to remain constant. This made it possible to confine the analysis to one of simple correlation between demand and price.

EXHIBIT 5
Millinery Demand Study

Week	Sales Index (previous year's same 15-week period = 100%)	Price Index
1	560	105
2	571	102
3	408	110
4	466	114
5	232	122
6	310	113
7	319	124
8	200	122
9	180	122
10	182	126
11	178	133
12	175	142
13	129	139
14	101	149
15	120	150

Note in Exhibit 6, just as in the previous study, that the variables are first plotted over time so that they may be compared. If a freehand imaginary trend, shown by a dashed line, is passed through each of these series, it is apparent that the sales series is best represented by a curved trend, while the price series is best represented by a linear trend. Since we want to derive a relation between sales and price and already know how to determine statistical estimates of such relationships when the association is linear, the problem would be simplified somewhat if we could get the sales series into linear form.

One manner by which this might be done would be to hypothesize an exponential model of the form:

$$Y = aX^b$$

and then transform the data *logarithmically* into:

$$\log Y = \log a + b \log X$$

If we let $Y' = \log Y$; $a' = \log a$, and $X' = \log X$, we see that

$$Y' = a' + bX'$$

or that the transformed data can be used to estimate the newly determined linear relationship in exactly the same manner as was conducted for the previous problem. In practice, we rarely encounter curved lines which are precise geometric progressions. Nevertheless, it is often the

EXHIBIT 6
Millinery Demand Study

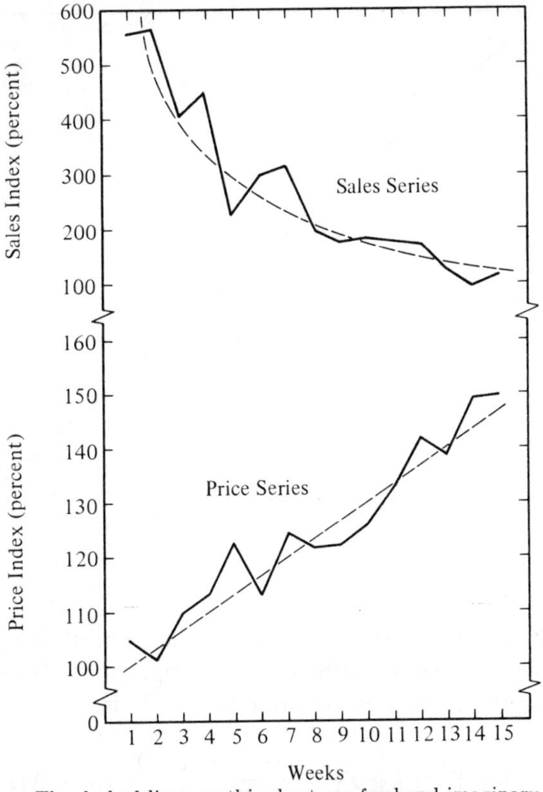

The dashed lines on this chart are freehand imaginary trend lines. They have been included to show the underlying pattern of the series. The sales series is represented by a curved trend, whereas the price series is represented by a linear trend.

case that the curve will roughly approximate a geometric progression, and hence will tend to "straighten out" somewhat and come closer to approximating a straight line if it is plotted on a logarithmic scale.

Since one of the variables (price) exhibits a linear trend, as opposed to the curvilinear tendency of the other variable (sales), a slight variation of this model seems appropriate. In particular, the "semilogarithmic" model

$$\log Y = a + bX$$

is suggested, in which sales (the dependent variable) has been "transformed" logarithmically but price (the independent variable) has not. Applying this model to the data at hand yields the approximating relationship presented in Exhibit 7.

EXHIBIT 7
Millinery Demand Study (sales index versus price index)

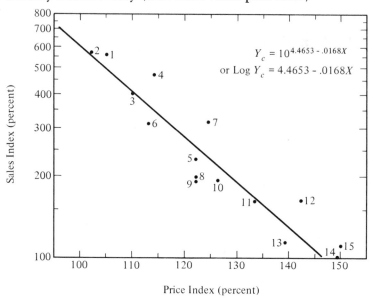

Price Index (percent)

For quick, freehand estimation, when the vertical axis is logarithmic and the horizontal axis is arithmetic, the appropriate two-point formula for computing the regression equation for $\log Y_c$ is:

$$\log Y_c = \log Y_1 + \frac{\log Y_2 - \log Y_1}{X_2 - X_1}(X - X_1)$$

Thus, from Exhibit 7, select any two points on the line and estimate their coordinates as follows. (The logarithms are obtained from a table of common logarithms as in the Appendix or from a slide rule or calculator.)

$$X_1 = 100$$
$$Y_1 = 610 \qquad \log Y_1 = 2.7853$$
$$X_2 = 140$$
$$Y_2 = 130 \qquad \log Y_2 = 2.1139$$

Inserting these values in the above formula:

$$\log Y_c = 2.7853 + \frac{2.1139 - 2.7853}{140 - 100}(X - 100)$$

$$\log Y_c = 4.4653 - .0168X$$

or

$$Y_c = 10^{4.4653 - .0168X}$$

or

$$Y_c = 10^{\log 29200 - .0168X}$$

The last three equations are in equivalent final form. However, the one for log Y_c is more convenient for calculation purposes. Accordingly, we may use this equation to verify our calculations in the above procedure. Thus, suppose we let $X = 120$. According to Exhibit 7, Y_c should equal about 280. Substituting in the above equation for log Y_c:

$$\log Y_c = 4.4653 - .0168(120)$$
$$= 2.4493$$
$$Y_c = \text{antilog } 2.4493 = 281$$

This accords with our visual inspection, so we are inclined to judge that our calculations in estimating the above regression equation are correct. One or two more verifications of this type for other values of X should serve to confirm our judgment.

Estimating Elasticity. In Exhibit 7, how do we estimate the arc elasticity of sales or demand, E_D, directly from the chart? For convenience, let us use the same coordinates as employed above; we will then obtain an average estimate of elasticity for the range of the curve between the two chosen points. First, however, let us recall that on an arithmetic scale, equal distances are represented by equal *amounts* of change, whereas on a logarithmic scale equal distances are represented by equal *ratios* or *percentage* changes. Therefore, since the vertical axis is logarithmic and the horizontal axis is arithmetic, we may employ the following elasticity formula. (What formula would you use if both axes were logarithmic?)

$$E_D = \frac{\dfrac{\log Y_2 - \log Y_1}{X_2 - X_1}}{\frac{1}{2}(X_2 + X_1)}$$

$$= \frac{\dfrac{2.1139 - 2.7853}{140 - 100}}{\frac{1}{2}(140 + 100)} = \frac{-.671}{.333} = -2.02$$

This means that for the range in question, a 1 percent change in the price variable produces about a 2 percent opposite change in the demand or sales variable. The minus sign, as mentioned earlier, is often omitted because it is understood.

INCOME AS A DEMAND DETERMINANT

The previous chapter stressed the theoretical importance of income as a demand determinant. How well does empirical evidence support this theory? Reference is made to Exhibit 8, in which the relationships between aggregate personal consumption expenditures and personal disposable income have been plotted. The fact that these two variables have fluctuated closely during the period of study lends ample evidence to support both the importance of income as a demand determinant

EXHIBIT 8

Consumption Expenditures Related to Income

Consumer Expenditures Fluctuate Closely with Income Changes

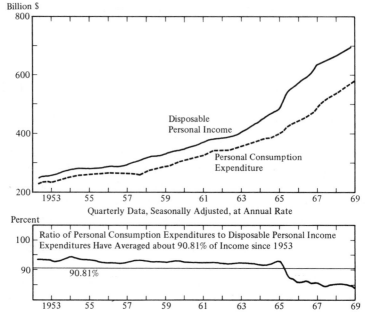

Personal Consumption Expenditures for Goods Related to Disposable Personal Income

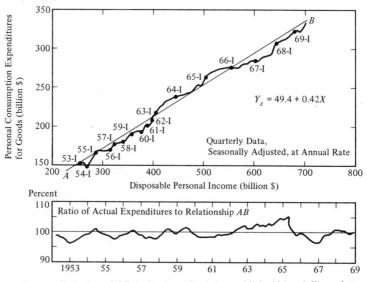

Source: Data from USDC, *Business Statistics*, published biennially, or from *Survey of Current Business*.

and the stability of this relationship over a long span of time (see second panel of the figure).

The relationship between income and selected durable goods, consumption goods, and services has already been presented in the discussion of income elasticity. Further studies of this nature for many other classes of products and services represents an area of considerable research effort today. The ramifications of the various analyses are numerous, but a few of the many interesting and important conclusions for the time-series studies of aggregate consumption and budget data can be stated briefly as follows:

1. Some studies, notably those based on annual time-series data extending back over many decades, have shown a highly stable relationship between consumption expenditures and income, or between saving and income (since consumption and saving are complementary). In particular, these as well as some quarterly studies have indicated, as in the second panel of Exhibit 8, that consumption expenditures are usually in the vicinity of 90 to 95 percent of disposable personal income. On the other hand, some budget studies have appeared to contradict these findings by showing that the ratio of saving to income, rather than remaining virtually constant, has risen substantially with income.

2. Short-run, such as quarter-by-quarter, analyses usually tend to show greater instability between consumption and income as compared to studies based on annual data. (Why?) An illustration of a type of quarterly analysis is shown in the third panel of Exhibit 8, along with the corresponding regression equation.

3. Some studies have found pronounced tendencies for consumption expenditures to increase in absolute amounts, but decrease as a percentage of income, during the upswing of a business cycle, and to decrease in absolute amounts, but increase as a percentage of income, during the downswing. In other words, total consumption expenditures are a larger percentage of income in depression periods and a smaller percentage of income in times of prosperity. Savings, of course, since they are the difference between consumption and income, are a larger percentage of income in prosperity and a smaller percentage in depression.

4. In the long run, an individual's spending habits are based on the distribution of income within his community, his place within that distribution pattern, and his desire to emulate the consumption of others (i.e., keep up with the Joneses). Therefore, as long as the pattern of income distribution remains about the same, the proportion of consumption expenditures to total income, called the "average propensity to consume," will remain fairly stable.

5. It appears to be easier for consumers to raise their standard of living than it is for them to lower it. Therefore, the rate of consumption increase is greater in periods of prosperity than is the rate of consump-

tion decrease in periods of recession. When the economy is in a down-swing, consumers try to maintain their standard of living in the face of falling incomes, and thus consumption expenditures become a larger proportion of income. Cultural lags, of course, are also a dominant factor in the analysis of consumption-income dynamics. When a family experiences a change in income, the family may take a substantial period of time before adapting to the new income level. Until the full adjustment is made, the family's consumption habits and patterns may be substantially different from the average for its income group.

6. Some of the recent investigations of consumer behavior have been concerned with the adequacy of current income as the most significant determinant of consumption behavior. Thus, extensive studies of non-wage-earner families have shown that although the income receipts of such families may vary substantially from period to period, their consumption outlays exhibit a relatively high degree of stability. This has led to a new theory of consumption-income relations—one which hypothesizes that people do not relate their consumption expenditures to income received in the current period but rather to their average and anticipated income over a number of periods. Accordingly, economists who have attempted to test this hypothesis have had to distinguish, among other things, between such concepts as wealth versus income, stocks versus flows, present versus future values, and transitory versus permanent income, to mention only a few of the technical difficulties. For clearly, when income streams are taken as variables in an analysis, dynamic problems arise in the separation and treatment of certain elements which might not otherwise be important in a less subtle type of static analysis.

Conclusion. The above characteristics of aggregate consumption functions reflect some of the main lines of investigation that have been pursued by economic researchers during the past several decades. This research is still under way, more actively today than ever before. We may summarize the seemingly separate lines of thought discussed above by noting that the various approaches and assumptions can be conveniently grouped into three classes of theories:

1. The *absolute income hypothesis,* which expresses the level of saving, or of consumption expenditures, as a function of income and perhaps of other variables.

2. The *relative income hypothesis,* which attempts to reconcile inconsistencies in the former by stating that the saving or consumption rate depends not on the level of income but on the *relative position* of the spending unit (such as the individual or family) on the income scale.

3. The *permanent income hypothesis,* which postulates that consumer expenditures in a given period are a function of average and anticipated income over a number of periods.

State and Regional Income

Business executives are often interested in regional as well as national markets and hence are frequently concerned with the purchasing power of specific states or groups of states which comprise a particular section of the country. Various sources of data may be used for such purposes. Three in particular that are readily available in most libraries, and widely used by marketing researchers as well as others interested in demand analysis, include:

1. Index of buying power for states, counties, and major metropolitan areas in the United States, published annually in *Sales Management* magazine.
2. Personal income, by states, published monthly in the last issue of each month's *Business Week* magazine.
3. Personal income, by states, total and per capita, compiled by the U.S. Department of Commerce and published each year in its August issue of the *Survey of Current Business*. The *Statistical Abstract of the United States*, as well as several other annual publications, also report these data.

Exhibit 9 shows some relationships between state personal income payments and the nation's total for the years 1947–69, which can be readily revised and updated by obtaining data from the sources mentioned above. Problems of this type are practical and useful for anyone interested in economics, marketing, and related areas involving demand analysis.

Exhibit 9 shows the remarkably close relationship that exists between state income payments and the nation's total, particularly with respect to the direction of movement, for example, chart A for Ohio and the United States as a whole. The relationships may be estimated by plotting the data on scatter diagrams as done in charts B, C, and D for states chosen at random. Note that these scatter diagrams have been plotted on ratio or double logarithmic scales in order to make the percentage changes in income for the state and for the nation comparable. Thus, a straight regression line on these charts indicates a constant percentage change in the vertical distance per unit of percentage change in the horizontal distance, or, in other words, a slope and elasticity which are the same, since the regression line is linear in the logarithms. As another illustrative exercise, let us estimate the regression equation for New Hampshire, using the appropriate two-point formula given earlier. The slope of the equation will also be the elasticity, as we have already seen.

Taking any two points on the line, preferably two points that are far apart, we estimate the following coordinates from the Chart D. (In

EXHIBIT 9

Relationship between Income Payments for Specified States and the United States

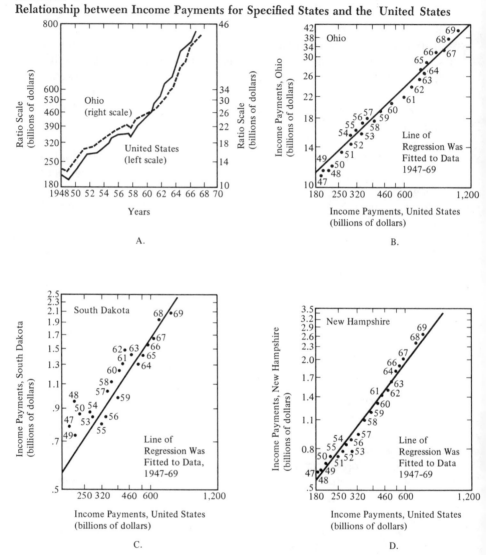

A.

B.

C.

D.

Source: USDC, *Survey of Current Business*; USDC, *Statistical Abstract of the United States*.

applying the formula, note as was done earlier that the negative form of a logarithm may be used for computational convenience, but it must be converted back to a positive mantissa to obtain the antilog, since published tables of mantissas are always positive. The conversion may be made by simply adding the negative number to 10 and subtracting 10 at the end.)

$$X_1 = 218.5 \qquad \log X_1 = 11.3395$$
$$Y_1 = .65 \qquad \log Y_1 = 8.8129$$
$$X_2 = 530.0 \qquad \log X_2 = 11.7243$$
$$Y_2 = 1.70 \qquad \log Y_2 = 9.2304$$

$$\log Y_c = \log Y_1 + \frac{\log Y_2 - \log Y_1}{\log X_2 - \log X_1}(\log X - \log X_1) \qquad (1)$$

$$\log Y_c = 8.8129 + \frac{9.2304 - 8.8129}{11.7243 - 11.3395}(\log X - 11.3395) \qquad (2)$$

$$\log Y_c = -3.4905 + 1.0850 \log X \qquad (3)$$

$$\log Y_c = 6.5095 - 10 + 1.0850 \log X \qquad (4)$$

$$\log Y_c = \log .0003 + 1.0850 \log X \qquad (5)$$

or

$$Y_c = .0003X^{1.0850} \qquad (6)$$

The last four equations are in equivalent final form, but (3) is probably the most convenient for calculation purposes. Since the exponent or slope is the elasticity, this may be interpreted to mean that for the analysis period, a 1 percent change in the nation's income was associated with about a 1.085 percent change in New Hampshire's income. It is an instructive exercise to see how these results compare with a study covering the period since 1970, not only for New Hampshire but for other states. Such comparisons can be readily made by obtaining the data from the sources described above.

> NOTE: There may be a number of cases in which a simple regression between two variables may not be sufficient to explain all the variations, in which case a time trend of the residuals may be used as a second independent variable. A procedure that may be employed is indicated by the following worksheet column headings with application to the formula derived above for New Hampshire.

(1) State Income	(2) Nation's Income	(3) Regression Equation— Eq. (6)	(4) Residuals	(5) Trend of Residuals	(6) Final Calculated Values
Y	X	$Y_{1c} = .0003X^{1.0850}$	$Y \div Y_{1c}$ $(1) \div (3)$	$Y_{2c} = T$	$Y_c = .0003X^{1.0850}T$ $(3) \times (5)$

Thus, in column 3 we compute the first approximation of Y, called Y_{1c}. [For computational convenience, use the logarithmic form of the regression equation, namely equation (3) derived above, and enter the antilogs in column 3.] After filling in column 3, we obtain the residuals or deviations in column 4 by dividing the actual values of column 1 by the computed values of column 3. These residuals, entered in column 4, represent the variations in state income payments (Y) which have not been accounted for by the nation's income payments (X). We can then plot these residuals over time, fit a freehand time trend to the graph, and enter the values of this trend, T, in column 5. This represents our second approximation to Y, and hence may be symbolized Y_{2c}. The product of the two approximations then becomes the final computed regression equation shown in column 6.

This procedure is the beginning of freehand multiple regression analysis since two independent variables, X and T, are being employed. Of course, additional variables may also be introduced if they are believed to affect significantly the dependent variable.[1]

Studies of this type illustrate the sort of use that can be made of readily available income data as a basis for sales planning and forecasting on a local or regional level. The techniques are relatively simple and the results can be derived either by freehand or mathematical methods. For many products a functional sales-purchasing power relation is relatively easy to determine. More difficult is the choice as to the type of purchasing power variable to use. For instance, if a product is usually purchased for both cash and credit, a weighted total of both of these may turn out to be a better measure of purchasing power than cash income alone. Thus, in a study of the demand for major appliances, an examination of the data indicated that on the average, major appliances are purchased for about 25 percent in cash and 75 percent in credit. Hence, the purchasing power variable selected was .25 (disposable income) + .75 (net credit extension, excluding automobiles). The former series (disposable income) is readily available in many published sources; the latter is reported monthly in the *Federal Reserve Bulletin*. The new weighted series may then be adjusted for price changes, or it may not, depending on the circumstances of the problem.

More complicated weighting problems may arise in analyzing demands for consumer or capital goods. In each case, economic judgment plays the key role in deciding on the weights to be employed.

---

[1] In column 4, the *ratio* deviations of the actual values to the calculated values were taken because the vertical axis of the chart is logarithmic. If the vertical axis were arithmetic, the difference deviations, or the actual values minus the calculated values, could be taken. In practice, it usually makes little or no difference in the final results of a freehand model whether ratio or difference deviations are used. However, the use of ratio deviations has certain advantages in freehand multiple regression analysis. Hence, as a rule of thumb, it can be said that ratio deviations may (almost) always be used (with relatively few possible exceptions), irrespective of whether the vertical scale is arithmetic or logarithmic. By following this rule fairly consistently, the analyses will usually gain more in clarity than they may lose in precision or technical accuracy.

EMPIRICAL STUDIES OF CROSS-DEMAND ELASTICITY

How might the formulas for cross-demand elasticity be determined in practice? One example can be given for two classic substitute products: butter and margarine. Prices and consumption data are contained in Exhibit 10 for the period 1947–69 and are depicted graphically in Exhibit 11. The source of these data, *Agricultural Statistics*, published annually by the USDA, contains similar information for hundreds of other

EXHIBIT 10
Butter and Margarine Data

Year	(1) Margarine Consumption Per Capita (pounds) Y	(2) Margarine Prices (average wholesale price per pound, white, domestic, vegetable, Chicago) (cents) P_y	(3) Butter Consumption Per Capita (pounds) X	(4) Butter Prices (average wholesale price per pound at New York) Grade A 92 Score (cents) P_x	(5) Consumption Ratio X/Y (3) ÷ (1)	(6) Price Ratio P_x/P_y (4) ÷ (2)
1947 . . .	4.0	36.9	11.2	71.3		
1948 . . .	4.9	27.1	10.0	75.8		
1949 . . .	5.7	26.7	10.4	61.5		
1950 . . .	6.1	27.9	10.7	62.2		
1951 . . .	6.6	31.8	9.7	69.9		
1952 . . .	7.9	26.9	8.6	73.0		
1953 . . .	8.1	27.4	8.5	66.6		
1954 . . .	8.5	26.6	8.9	60.5		
1955 . . .	8.2	26.0	9.0	58.2		
1956 . . .	8.2	26.9	8.7	59.9		
1957 . . .	8.6	27.4	8.4	60.7		
1958 . . .	9.0	26.5	8.3	59.7		
1959 . . .	9.2	24.2	7.9	60.6		
1960 . . .	9.4	22.2	7.5	59.9		
1961 . . .	9.4	25.5	7.4	61.2		
1962 . . .	9.3	24.3	7.3	59.4		
1963 . . .	9.6	23.2	6.9	59.0		
1964 . . .	9.7	23.4	6.8	59.9		
1965 . . .	9.9	24.2	6.4	61.0		
1966 . . .	10.5	23.2	5.7	67.2		
1967 . . .	10.5	22.8	5.5	67.5		
1968 . . .	10.8	21.2	5.7	67.8		
1969 . . .	10.8	15.6	5.4	68.5		

Source: USDA, *Agricultural Statistics*.

EXHIBIT 11
Butter and Margarine Data

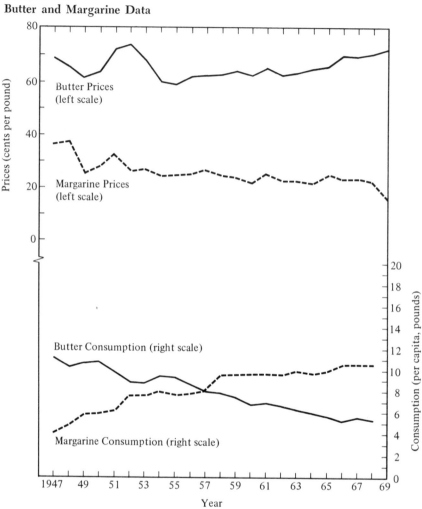

Source: Exhibit 10.

goods, including specific kinds of meats, dairy products, fruits, vegetables, and so forth, so that many interesting demand and elasticity studies can be done by utilizing this handy source of information.

In Exhibit 11, the inverse relationship between the consumption of both products is clearly indicated, with the trend being to substitute margarine for butter to such an extent that in 1957 margarine consumption exceeded butter consumption for the first time. Prices for both products show an unusual peak during the Korean War years, but after that the trend seems to be upward for butter and downward for margarine. The trends of all of the series appear to be approximately linear on the arithmetic scales of Exhibit 11; hence, their regression lines will also be sketched on arithmetic scales.[2]

Exhibit 12 shows a freehand regression line of margarine consumption on butter prices, based on the data obtained from Exhibit 10. A "full-

EXHIBIT 12
Margarine Consumption versus Butter Prices

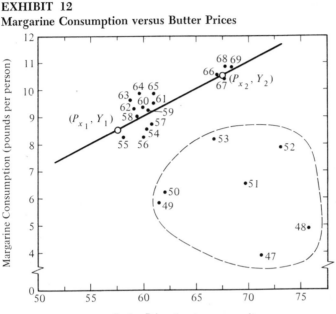

Butter Prices (cents per pound)

scale" least-squares regression analysis of the data, as illustrated above, is of course also possible. Selecting any two points on the line, preferably two points that are far apart (e.g., those shown by the hollow circles), the cross elasticity of demand is computed. A similar calculation may be employed to calculate the arc measure of cross-price elasticity.

Cross elasticity of demand:

$$E_c = \frac{\dfrac{Y_2 - Y_1}{Y_2 + Y_1}}{\dfrac{P_{x_2} - P_{x_1}}{P_{x_2} + P_{x_1}}} = \frac{\dfrac{10.5 - 8.5}{10.5 + 8.5}}{\dfrac{67.5 - 57.5}{67.5 + 57.5}} = \frac{25}{19} = 1.32$$

---

[2] Admittedly, it could be argued that butter prices and butter consumption appear to be better represented by a curved trend, in which case a better fit might be obtained if semilog paper were used and these variables were plotted on the log scale. Experimentation with both arithmetic and semilog scales would therefore be warranted in this case. However, we shall content ourselves with using only arithmetic scales at this time, and leave the alternative semilog case as an exercise for you to try.

Strictly speaking, this is not the "true" measure of cross-price, or cross-demand elasticity, for it is necessary to hold P_y constant when making the estimates. Therefore, to the extent that other important determinants of demand have not been held constant, we must consider our measures of cross-demand or price responsiveness as a "gross" rather than a "net" estimate.

What do we obtain from our analysis? First, the fact that the cross elasticity of demand is positive gives us the ability to conclude that the goods under study are substitutes—that a *positive* additional amount of margarine will be demanded for a *positive* price increase in the price of butter. Secondly, we are given at least a rough measure of *how much* additional margarine will be purchased by examining our elasticity estimates and remembering that cross-demand elasticity measures the percent increase (decrease) in the purchase of one good or service for each unit percent increase (decrease) in the price of the other. In this case, we may therefore conclude that the demand for margarine may be expected to increase an average 1.3 percent for a unit percent increase in the price of butter. Finally, and perhaps most importantly, we can profit from our analysis by now being in a position to make some quantitative forecast of margarine sales based on estimates of future butter prices. In particular, we know from our calculations that rising butter prices implies an increase of margarine demand which we can project either directly using our regression results or indirectly using our elasticity analysis.

A second empirical study of cross-demand elasticity involving the substitutibility of three competing brands of canned peaches is graphically illustrated in Exhibit 13. The data were derived from controlled experiments as part of a supermarket study. Note that double logarithmic scales have been used because, as mentioned earlier, the regression lines "straightened out" on these scales, whereas they were distinctly curved when the data were plotted on arithmetic scales. These regression lines are therefore linear in the logarithms; and hence their slopes, as we have already learned, are equal to their elasticities.

The calculations of the elasticities are shown beneath the chart, using methods which have already been described. The hollow circles on the regression lines represent the coordinates of the points which were chosen for the calculations. The elasticity of substitution, E_{ss}, between brands A and C (upper line) is about −.63, while that between B and C (lower line) is about −.15. This means that consumers found it easier to substitute A for C than B for C. (Can you see why? What would an elasticity of zero mean?)

It would be a simple matter to estimate the equations for these regression lines by employing the appropriate two-point formula given earlier. These equations could then be used for making predictions of the expected quantity ratio based on given price ratios. However, the elasticities rather than the regression equations are probably of greater practical

EXHIBIT 13

Elasticities of Substitution between Three Competing Brands of Canned Peaches

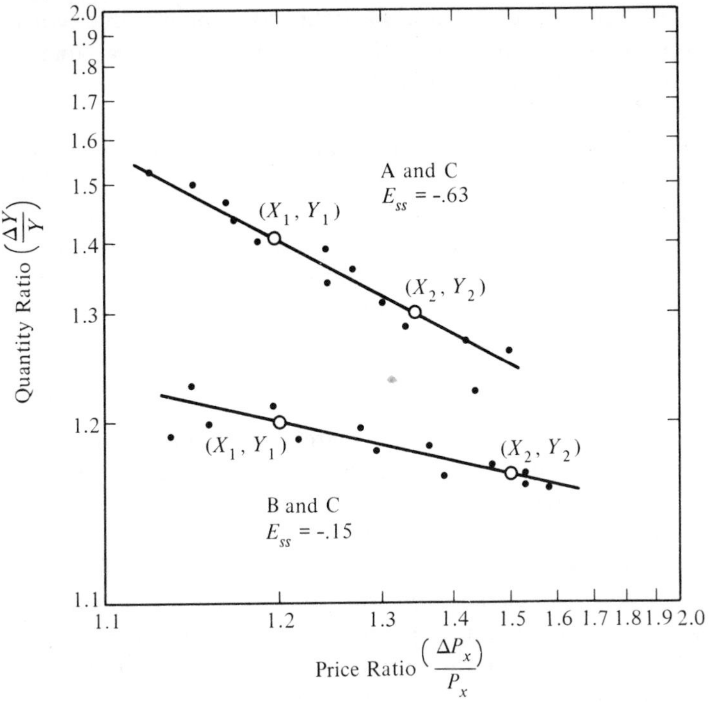

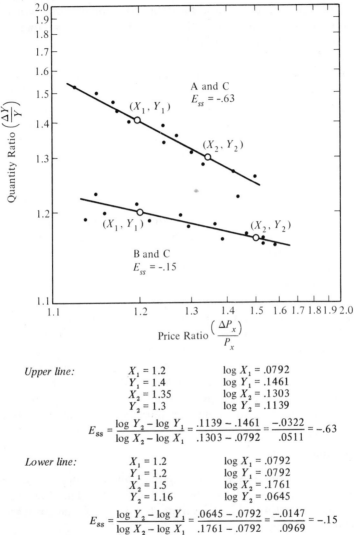

Upper line:

$X_1 = 1.2$ $\log X_1 = .0792$
$Y_1 = 1.4$ $\log Y_1 = .1461$
$X_2 = 1.35$ $\log X_2 = .1303$
$Y_2 = 1.3$ $\log Y_2 = .1139$

$$E_{ss} = \frac{\log Y_2 - \log Y_1}{\log X_2 - \log X_1} = \frac{.1139 - .1461}{.1303 - .0792} = \frac{-.0322}{.0511} = -.63$$

Lower line:

$X_1 = 1.2$ $\log X_1 = .0792$
$Y_1 = 1.2$ $\log Y_1 = .0792$
$X_2 = 1.5$ $\log X_2 = .1761$
$Y_2 = 1.16$ $\log Y_2 = .0645$

$$E_{ss} = \frac{\log Y_2 - \log Y_1}{\log X_2 - \log X_1} = \frac{.0645 - .0792}{.1761 - .0792} = \frac{-.0147}{.0969} = -.15$$

value in this type of problem. (Why? What use could management make of this elasticity information as a guide for pricing decisions? Can you think of its value for other purposes?)

THE MULTIVARIATE REGRESSION EQUATION

The foregoing studies have discussed demand responsiveness to particular demand determinants on a variable-by-variable basis. In effect, therefore, the analysis required us to assume either that other influential factors (such as population change, inflation, etc.) were constant or unimportant for the application at hand, or that we explicitly "control" the other factors through data adjustment. But what if we wish to examine demand responsiveness when several variables fluctuate simultaneously? Are we limited to an analysis of demand on a "piecemeal" basis?

The answer is no. Recall that in the previous chapter we formulated a demand equation of the form: $Q_d = f(X_1, X_2, \ldots, X_n)$ with Q_d representing the dependent, or demand, variable and the various X's representing independent, or demand determinants. One extremely popular method of analysis permitting a multivariate study of demand determinants is the econometric approach discussed in an earlier chapter. The linear model for the present problem would be:

$$Q_d = \beta_0 + \beta_1 X_1 + \beta_2 X_2 + \cdots + \beta_n X_n + \mu \tag{1}$$

in which $\beta_0, \beta_1, \ldots, \beta_n$ are the regression parameters to be estimated and μ is a disturbance, or error, term representing the presumably minor effects of nonincluded variables and other random fluctuations which are not explicitly related to the independent variables.

Once data are obtained for a proposed model, usually some variant of the "ordinary least squares" method already discussed with single variable models is used to perform the computations necessary to estimate the coefficients of the equation model. Although straightforward, the calculations are distinctly long and arduous, and most researchers usually take recourse to packaged computer regression programs to accomplish the task. Several such programs are available for this purpose, and most large university and commercial computer centers maintain program libraries in which one or more of these may be found.

Interpreting Results

Once the calculations are completed, however they are done, it remains for the researcher to interpret the results. The "success" of the model may sometimes be judged on the basis of the answers to the following questions.

Do the Independent Variables "Explain" the Fluctuations in the Dependent Variable? The answer to this question is usually determined by an examination of the coefficient of determination which has already been discussed above. A high (percent) R^2 statistic means that a large proportion of the variance in the dependent variable is "explained," or attributed to, the fluctuations of the independent variables. A low statistic means the opposite. Exactly what is an "acceptable" figure is by and large a matter of individual judgment. Because a large number of variables will usually provide a higher resultant R^2 than will fewer variables, there is often the temptation to include as many as possible in the regression model to achieve the R^2 "goal." It should be kept in mind, however, that little can be said for a model which includes variables that have little or no theoretical justification.

Are the Regression Parameters of Correct Sign? Each independent-variable coefficient in the linear model represents the marginal response of demand quantity to a unit change in the value of the independent variable, holding all other independent variables fixed. For example, let us examine the coffee model hypothesized in the preceding chapter, in which the quantity of coffee demanded, Q_d, depended upon price (X_1), income levels (X_2), advertising expenditure (X_3), and the price of tea (X_4). Our econometric formulation of the demand equation is therefore:

$$Q_d = \beta_0 + \beta_1 X_1 + \beta_2 X_2 + \beta_3 X_3 + \beta_4 X_4 + u$$

and our task is to determine values for the regression parameters β_0, β_1, β_2, β_3, and β_4. Upon completion of the estimation task, we find values for these parameters which are, of course, either positive or negative in sign. The value of β_1 may be interpreted as the *change* in quantity demanded attributable to a unit change in the price of coffee. Clearly we expect the quantity of coffee demanded to be negatively related to the price of coffee; hence, we look for a negative sign for β_1. Similarly, we anticipate a positive sign for β_2 and β_3, which relate the quantity of coffee demanded to income and advertising expenditures; and assuming tea may be considered a substitute for coffee, a positive sign for β_4 as well.

What can one say when the regression estimates do not yield results as dictated by theory? In actuality, sometimes very little. Often times, "wrong" signs result from econometric models which have been (in some way) mis-specified, as for example, when an important variable has been left out of the equation. In such cases, the corrective is comparatively easy—reformulate the model to include the appropriate variable, or in some other manner reflect the proper demand relationship. A more difficult situation occurs when specific statistical problems of estimation are present in the model or in the data which preclude "accurate" measurement of the regression parameters using conventional techniques. But a detailed discussion of each of these problems is beyond the scope of this book. Suffice it to say, therefore, that the linear econometric model, for all its simplicity, does not guarantee estimation results which are necessarily consistent with theory, and that further, there should clearly be a wide avenue of question and discussion when the model does not yield the "good" results that theory and common sense would dictate.

Are the Estimated Regression Parameters Reasonable in Magnitude? The test of reasonableness is clearly a test of judgment since degrees of tolerance and acceptability will vary from one researcher to another. Even in the absence of conventional limits, however, most economists have implicitly defined intervals associated with certain coefficients beyond which, the associated regression model becomes untenable. Take for example, a consumption model in which aggregate consumption demand, C_d, is "explained" by three elements: a constant, β_0, the price level, X_1 (say, quantified by a price index); and disposable income, X_2. Our model is:

$$C_d = \beta_0 + \beta_1 X_1 + \beta_2 X_2 + u$$

and our task is to determine values for β_0, β_1, and β_2. Suppose β_0, β_1, and β_2 all come out with the "right" sign (β_1 negative, β_2 positive), but with β_2 assuming a value of 1.3. Does this make sense? Clearly not; β_2 represents the aggregate marginal propensity to consume or, in more familiar language, the additional consumption which could be anticipated from a unit increase in income. Hence, the estimated value of 1.3 is clearly unreasonable because it states that the average consumer will spend $1.30 of the next $1 of incremental income he receives! Similar regions of legitimacy are easily determined for regression parameters in other types of models, as, for example, the test of elasticity measures through the log models discussed previously. In summary, therefore, we see that econometric estimates of the regression parameters should stand a test of reasonableness as well as a test of sign, and that further, the correctness of one is not a guarantee of the propriety of the other.

Are the Estimated Values of the Regression Coefficients Significant? This is usually a difficult question to answer, not so much because of computational barriers but because of a semantic issue over the interpretation of the word "significant." The importance of this point cannot be overemphasized, for perhaps no other word in economic literature has been used to convey so many meanings. And if this were not bad enough, proper interpretation of a particular researcher's conclusions often hinges precisely on the specific meaning which the author has implicitly assumed in his use of this word. A few of the most common interpretations may be noted.

Some economists have used the word significant to convey the idea of importance due to size, as for example when it is said that the value of one coefficient is "significantly larger" than the others. In this sense of the word, "significance" is associated with the value of magnitude, as might be attributed to a regression parameter whose units were hundreds as compared with other parameters estimated in the same equation expessed in units or tenths of units. The danger of such a particular interpretation is twofold: not only does this interpretation preclude other possible meanings of the word but also it has the potential to ignore the fact that the data may be scaled in such a way as to result in "artificially" larger estimates for some coefficients than for others.

A second interpretation of the word significant is to connote "appropriateness"—as for example when it is said that "the independent variables proved significant in the model, attaining an R^2 of .96." But, as we have already seen, the values of the coefficient of determination, R^2, is of limited use as a test of a demand model's acceptability as a mathematical abstraction of the market system. In fact, some well-known writers have gone so far as to say that high R^2's are much more reliable as a measure of a particular researcher's stamina and search persistence for new variables than they are meaningful in and of themselves. Hence, the use of the word "significant" 'in this sense is far from the flattering adjective some would have us believe, and may even have negative connotations in the minds of some.

A third definition of "significant" is a statistical one which conveys the results of a particular statistical test, namely the test to assess the likelihood of any particular regression coefficient differing ("significantly") from zero. This type of usage is also quite common in the literature and no doubt owes at least some of its popularity to the fact that the "different from zero" statistical calculations required to reach a conclusion are usually performed as an integral part of the estimation procedure of most regression programs. In part, this is understandable because a regression coefficient which cannot be statistically distinguished from a value of zero (that is to say, a regression coefficient for which the likelihood of assuming a value of zero is large) has obvious implications in the assessment of the associated variable as a demand determinant—namely, that quantity demanded does not appear to be appreciably affected by the fluctuations of this variable.

A final usage of the word significant is somewhat related to the third—the use of an adjective attempting to state that values of estimates of the parameters are narrowly defined and that the values thus determined are unlikely to be attributed to chance. The use of the word significant in this sense is therefore also observed to hinge on the relative magnitude of the parameter variances as compared with their absolute levels. Hence, a parameter with a comparatively small variance would be termed significant, whereas one with a relatively large variance would not.

Which of these meanings is the "correct" one? Actually, this should not be the question, for what is important is not so much the many definitions of the word "significant" as the clear communication between writer and reader which is hindered by potential ambiguity. In the absence of explicit definition, therefore, the researcher using multivariate statistics is well advised not to use the word at all!

Constructing and Testing a Multivariate Demand Equation

Having explained the demand theory of Chapter 5 and the demand analysis of Chapter 6, we are now in a position to construct multivariate demand models of our own. Let us suppose, for example, that we are interested in forecasting the demand for a durable good, such as automobiles or washing machines, for the forthcoming year, given that we have available to us sales data for several previous years.[3] Our first task is to specify the demand variables which are most likely to affect appreciably the demand for the good in question. A review of the material in Chapter 5 would indicate that several factors could be expected to play an important role in the determination of durable purchases, of which prices, incomes, population, consumer credit, new housing starts, and even perhaps the number of recent marriages might play some role.

For concreteness, suppose that we intend to estimate the demand for washing machines and we select wired dwelling units, disposable income, net credit extended, and price as the major demand determinants. Our next step is to specify the form of the demand equation, and several types of relationships may suggest themselves. Linear models are simplest as they require no data transformation. Log models require data transformations but may yield better "fits" between actual and computed values of the dependent variable. In addition, log models are convenient for estimating elasticities. Higher order polynomial models are probably the most general but are also most difficult to estimate due to technical statistical barriers, and hence usually give the poorest results.

For simplicity, let us assume a linear model. Our demand equation is therefore:

$$Q_d = \beta_0 + \beta_1 X_1 + \beta_2 X_2 + \beta_3 X_3 + \beta_4 X_4$$

where:

Q_d = total demand for washing machines per year, in thousands
X_1 = wired dwelling units, in millions
X_2 = disposable income, in billions of dollars
X_3 = net credit extended (excluding automobiles), in billions of dollars
X_4 = price index of house furnishings
β_0, β_1, β_2, β_3, and β_4 are parameters to be estimated by the regression analysis.

Once the model has been specified, data must be obtained for the regression estimate. Sources for such data are, of course, highly dependent upon the model's requirements, but the *Survey of Current Business,* the *Statistical Abstract of the United States,* or the *Annual Economic Report to the President* are usually good starting points. The question of how many observations to obtain in order to get "good" results is not easily answered. If the model has been mis-specified, then no amount of data

---

[3] Sometimes, the demand for consumer durables is divided into two parts: replacement demand and new owner demand, and separate equations are estimated for each type. This point is ignored in the present analysis.

will yield good results; however, even a properly specified model will require at least as many observation years as there are parameters to be estimated, and a good rule of thumb is to obtain at least three to four times this number of observations to permit the least squares estimation technique to work well.

A further question usually raised concerning the data is whether to use monthly data, quarterly data, or yearly data. Often, this question is answered simply on the basis of availability, as many data sources do not publish economic series as often as the researcher would desire, and he is forced to accept annual data by default. As more data observations usually permit greater estimation efficiency, however, quarterly data are often also highly desirable. (If it is available, though, it is also important to account for any seasonality by making sure that seasonal fluctuations do not affect the specification of the model. Since many economic phenomena respond to changing conditions only after a lag, econometric models using quarterly data may be constructed with lagged, rather than current, variables on the right-hand side of the equation.)

Again for simplicity, let us stick to yearly data. One more pitfall remains, and that is to recognize that certain years are indicative of unusual conditions which are unrepresentative of "normal" relationships. For example, economic data for the war years are sometimes omitted from time-series regressions because such years do not represent "normal" times. Similarly, the more recent national price freeze during the years 1971–73 also represents an era in which supply and demand were not able to respond to free-market pressures.

With these data considerations taken care of, the regression analysis may now proceed by running the model on the computer. The results might be presented in the following conventional form, in which the numbers in parentheses on the lower line are standard deviations of the respective parameters:

$$Q_d = -751.39 + 34.17X_1 + 2.84X_2 + 450.81X_3 + 17.56X_4$$

(1,534.89)   (75.58)   (12.68)   (245.75)   (17.63)

$$R^2 = .91$$

To assess the validity of the model, we might first start with the coefficient of determination, or R^2. The value of .91 reported in the results would have to be considered relatively high since the scale of this statistic is from zero to one. The value of .91 means that 91 percent of the fluctuations in the dependent variable (demand) has been "explained" by the variability of the independent demand determinants, and hence that there is good reason to believe that at least some of the "causal" elements of demand have been identified.

The constants in the equation represent the estimates of the regression coefficients β_0, β_1, β_2, β_3, and β_4 in the original model, and the numbers underneath them represent the standard deviation of each estimate, based on the assumption that the disturbance term u in the original model (see equation (1) above) is normally distributed with a mean of zero. As an alternate to this form, the numbers found in parentheses are sometimes not the standard deviations but rather the t-statistics which are used to test whether the regression coefficients are statistically different from zero. Large t-statistics mean that it is unlikely that the regression coefficient is close to zero (and hence the associated regression variable is not an important demand determinant); small t-statistics mean the opposite. Exactly how large these t-statistics must be before confidence may be placed in the regression coefficients is dependent upon the number of parameters in total to be estimated, and the number of observations with which the model was run.

It is not necessary, however, to resort to t-statistics to assess the precision of the regression in estimating the values of the coefficient. Like small t-statistics, large standard errors relative to the values themselves foretell the existence of a poorly defined parameter which may in fact be close to zero or even possibly of opposite sign. This situation is noticeably the case here: most of the standard errors equal, or even exceed, the values of the coefficients themselves, giving us little confidence in their values.

Had the standard errors been smaller, we may have wanted to apply the further tests of reasonableness and sign. In the foregoing model, we might note that the test of sign is particularly appropriate since theory would dictate a positive relationship between demand and income, credit, and dwelling units, and a negative relationship between demand and price. Turning to the results, we see that the model's findings are inconsistent: three out of the four coefficients are of "right" sign but the fourth, price, enters the equation with a positive, rather than negative, sign. As it is unreasonable to expect more washing machines to be purchased at higher prices, we must question the validity of the model. One explanation for the sign discrepency would be that some "confounding" has taken place between price and the other variables. This happens when two independent variables are highly correlated with each other and the resultant *multicollinearity* makes it difficult to distinguish the separate effects of each of the independent variables upon the forecast variable. High correlation between any two independent variables are symptomatic of this problem and thereby serves as a guide to detection: this has been the problem here, because several of the variables are actually highly correlated with one another. The presence of multicollinearity also manifests itself in the unusually high standard errors associated with the regressor estimates, as noted above.

In summary we must conclude that the formulated model has met with mixed success. The high R^2 appears to validate the use of several of the independent variables as demand determinants, but the multicol-linearity discovered in the model has rendered their separate effects impossible to assess. Several remedies are possible, but unfortunately their mechanics will take us too far afield. Our purpose here has merely been to introduce you to the basics of building linear regression models and a few of the better-known tools used to evaluate them.

SUMMARY AND CONCLUSIONS

In demand analysis we seek to measure relationships between the purchases or consumption of products and the factors which are primarily responsible for those purchases. Accordingly, the demand for a product may be expressed as a simple relation or as a multiple relation: the former treats the dependent demand variable as a function of a single independent variable; the latter views it as the result of two or more independent variables.

The data employed in statistical analysis may be of a time series or cross-sectional nature. Time-series data are available from company records, trade associations, government agencies, and various public and private sources, whereas cross-sectional data are usually less readily available and must often be compiled from specific research studies. In any case, the use of times-series data, in particular, will often require that statistical adjustments in the data be made to eliminate effects of general price changes, population changes, and other factors that may have an unwanted influence on the variables involved. Cross-sectional data may also sometimes require statistical adjustments, depending on the particular circumstances.

One objective of demand analysis is to derive estimates of elasticity. Since price, income, and substitutes or complements are among the most important factors entering into a typical demand study, measures of elasticity may be established for each of these variables. Thus the more common measures include price elasticity of demand, cross-elasticity of demand, cross-elasticity of prices, elasticity of substitution, income elasticity of demand, and market share elasticity, all of which were discussed in the preceding chapter.

Statistical regression methods exist which are employed for deriving demand curves, and from which elasticity estimates are made. Both mathematical and freehand methods of regression analysis exist. The latter is a convenient intuitive device which, with practice, yields good approximations to the more elegant mathematical methods that are learned in elementary and advanced statistics. Simple formulas exist which can be used to estimate equations for regression lines and their elasticities directly from graphs. The particular formulas employed depend on whether the graphs are on arithmetic, semilogarithmic, or logarithmic scales.

PROBLEMS

1. (Library research.) Obtain price and consumption data covering the most recent ten or more years for any two competing or complementary products. (SUGGESTION: USDA, *Agricultural Statistics,* published annually, provides data for numerous agricultural products. Check the index of the most recent volume for price and consumption statistics for various products.) Examples of products that may be selected include *meat:* beef, veal, lamb, pork, ham; *dairy:* cheese, milk, ice cream; *citrus:* oranges, lemons, and so forth. A pair of products may be selected from different product groups, such as ham and eggs, or meat and cheese, and so forth, if it makes *economic* sense to do so. Of course, you may choose nonagricultural products if you wish, from any source you can find.

   Analyze the data for the two products you have selected by estimating the arc measures for the *cross elasticity of demand, cross elasticity of prices,* and the *elasticity of substitution.* Interpret your results. Choose a third substitute or complementary product and estimate the "ease" of substitutability or complementarity. (HINT: All of these procedures have been illustrated in this chapter. Use these illustrations as guides for doing your own study. In particular, review the discussion of substitutes and complements in the chapter where the above three measures of elasticity are explained and demonstrated for butter and margarine, and for three competing brands of canned peaches.)

2. A manufacturing firm is currently making and selling 100,000 units of a product priced at $20 per unit. However, they have the capacity to make 150,000 units per year without increasing the fixed costs of $1,000,000. Current profit margin is 10 percent of sales. The sales manager tells the president that profit can be increased by 50 percent if the price is cut by 10 percent. If the sales manager is right,

   a. How many units must be sold at the new price?

   b. What would be the necessary price elasticity of demand?

3. Refer back to Exhibit 2, Chapter 5, dealing with the demand for beef and for pork. Would there be anything wrong with simply plotting prices against total consumption in each case, instead of first putting the data on a per capita basis? Explain.

4. Refer back to Exhibit 8 and the corresponding discussion dealing with the relationship between consumption expenditures and income. Using appropriate charts and tables, develop a report on the absolute income hypothesis by doing the following:

   a. Test the regression equation in Exhibit 8, up to the most recent quarter for which data are available. (See sources to Exhibit 8.) How well has the equation held up? Explain.

   b. Develop a new study following the procedures indicated by Exhibit 8, based on the most recent ten quarters for which data are available. (You may fit a freehand regression line if you wish.) Compute the coefficient of determination and the standard error of estimate. Discuss in a few paragraphs the major similarities and/or differences between your findings and those in the text.

5. Refer to Exhibit 9 in which regressions are developed for state income payments as a function of the nation's income.

    a. Each student in the class should choose one of the 50 states in the U.S. and develop a regression equation for the years since 1947. If there are more than 50 students in the class, two or more states may be combined, thereby permitting some students to construct regional regression estimates. (NOTE: Remember that the data should first be plotted as time series in order to decide on the type of scales to employ in constructing the regression chart. If you are still in doubt after plotting the time series of the data, try both arithmetic and logarithmic scales for your regression line, and choose the one that gives the best fit.) Calculate r^2 and S_y as part of your analysis.

    b. Interpret your results and discuss briefly the practical value of this type of analysis for a firm interested in marketing its products at the state or regional level.

6. Refer back to Exhibit 10. Fill in the necessary information up to the most recent year for which data are available. Then estimate the arc measures for the elasticity of substitution and the coefficient of price interdependence, and interpret your results briefly.

7.   **CASE PROBLEM: GALAXY DEPARTMENT STORE**
                      INSURANCE PLAN FOR MAJOR APPLIANCES

The Galaxy Department Store chain is one of the largest in the United States. Twelve years ago, after only moderate success in the sale of major appliances, the management of the store introduced a unique service insurance plan which had a significant effect on improving the store's sales of these products. Basically the plan provided that a customer who purchased any major appliance (e.g., washer, dryer, television, etc.) could

EXHIBIT 14
Item: Automatic Washing Machines under $250

Year	Premium for Two-Year Contract	Number of Two-Year Contracts Purchased	Average Family Income	Premium for One-Year Contract
1.	$50	1,000	$5,000	$35
2.	55	950	5,000	35
3.	55	1,000	5,500	40
4.	55	1,050	5,500	45
5.	50	1,000	5,500	35
6.	50	1,050	5,500	40
7.	50	1,000	5,000	40
8.	60	1,050	5,500	40
9.	60	950	5,500	35
10.	65	900	5,500	35
11.	65	1,000	6,500	40
12.	65	1,050	7,000	40

also purchase either a one-year or two-year complete service contract covering both labor and parts for a specified future period. The contract, which was really an insurance policy, had no limit as to the number of service calls, and covered any defects or breakdowns resulting from normal operation of the appliance. The only conditions were that the customer must: (1) buy the contract before the end of the normal factory warranty period; (2) renew the contract upon its expiration, that is, the contract could not be reinstated once it had lapsed; (3) pay a $1 flat fee for each service call; and (4) pay the required premiums when due.

Several months ago the president of Galaxy instructed the sales manager of the store to review the history of this insurance plan and to present an evaluation of it. The sales manager recently completed the report and submitted it to the president. Exhibit 14 is one of the tables reproduced from his report, based on a study of one of the company's branch stores.

Questions:

In the section of the sales manager's report dealing with this table of figures, the sales manager made the following statements:

a. "The trend in premiums for two-year contracts has been upward while the number of contracts sold has exhibited long-run stability. It appears, therefore, that the premium charge for two-year contracts could undergo a substantial increase without seriously affecting sales."

b. "In the future, as the income of buyers continues to rise, we may expect substantial increases in sales of two-year contracts."

c. "The premium for one-year contracts seems to have a strong correlation with the sale of two-year contracts. I suggest that there is a close relationship here which warrants further examination. Perhaps we should think twice before altering the premium for one-year contracts, because of the adverse effect it may have on our sales of two-year contracts."

These statements imply certain things about elasticity. What type of elasticity is involved in each statement? Compute all of the *meaningful* elasticities. (HINTS AND SUGGESTIONS: Remember that an elasticity computation is meaningful only when "all other things" remain constant. Why? When tastes change, it would not make sense to compare years before and after the change of tastes. Hence, you should always compare years as close together as possible, on the assumption that tastes do not change during the short run. As a further hint, note that there are three types of elasticity to be identified. Once this is done, there are 198 possible computations! However, there are only seven that are meaningful. Can you explain why the remaining 191 are useless?)

REFERENCES

ADDISON, WILLIAM, and NERLOVE, MARC   "Statistical Estimation of Long-run Elasticities of Supply and Demand." *Journal of Farm Economies,* vol. 40, no. 4 (November 1958), pp. 861–80.

ALCALY, ROGER E., and KLEVORICK, ALVIN K.   "Food Prices in Relation to Income Levels in New York City." *The Journal of Business*, vol. 44, no. 4 (October 1971), pp. 380–97.

HOUTHAKKER, H. S., and MAGEE, STEPHEN P.   "Income and Price Elasticities in World Trade." *The Review of Economics and Statistics*, vol. 51, no. 2 (May 1969), pp. 111–25.

HUGHES, JOHN J.   "Note on the U.S. Demand for Coffee." *American Journal of Agricultural Economics*, vol. 51, no. 4 (November 1969), pp. 912–14.

METCALF, DAVID, and COWLING, KEITH   "Demand Functions for Fertilizers in the United Kingdom, 1948–1965." *Journal of Agricultural Economics*, vol. 18, no. 3 (September 1967), pp. 375–86.

SAMUELS, STUART A.   "New Product Demand Estimation in the Pharmaceutical Industry." *American Statistical Association 1969 Proceedings of the Business and Economic Statistics Section*, pp. 334–40.

SLATER, JOHN M.   "Regional Consumer Expenditure Studies Using National Food Survey Data." *Journal of Agricultural Economics*, vol. 20, no. 2 (May 1969), pp. 197–212.

chapter 7

Production

What are the economic problems that confront managers in organizing and planning the firm's production? What should management know in order to make the most profitable decisions concerning the employment of resources and the scheduling of output?

The answers to questions of this nature involve a study of what economists call "production functions." These describe the input-output relationships within the firm, or the physical (technical and technological) conditions under which production takes place. Hence the study of production functions is even more basic than the study of cost functions, for once the physical relationships between a firm's productive input services and its output are known (i.e., its production function), the firm's cost function can be derived from the production function when the market prices of the input services are given.

This chapter is devoted to a discussion of some of the elementary economics of production theory and measurement, and to some related problems of an economic nature that may be included under the broad heading of production management.

THEORETICAL PRODUCTION FUNCTIONS

Taking as synonymous the terms "resources" and "factors of production" to represent the inputs (men, machines, materials, etc.) required in production, the procedure followed below is to set forth the basic relationships between resources and products in a production process. By "production process" is meant the *transformation* of inputs into output. Such transformations of factors into product may occur within a single time period such as a year, or they may occur over several time periods, or they may never occur completely. The transformation (production) period thus varies between resources and thereby complicates the problems confronting the decision maker. In a static economy where the future is known with certainty, production would take place in a timeless vein without errors in estimation. But in the real world where uncertainty prevails, the recognition of time (uncertainty) excludes the possibility of perfect knowledge, and resources (representing investments over the years) must be analyzed for their effect upon output in terms of both fixed and variable costs. Time, and hence uncertainty, are the real causes of complexities in decision making with respect to a company's resource use.

Input-Output or Factor-Product Relations

The economics of production management takes as its starting point the study of the entire group of possible factor combinations that could be used to produce a certain output, within a given state of technology. The heading under which this type of analysis goes is that of the "production function." A *production function* is an expression of the dependent or functional relationship that exists between the inputs (factors) of a production process and the output (product) that results. Hence it is also sometimes called the "input-output" relation. Like a demand function, a production function can also be expressed in the form of a schedule or a graph as shown subsequently, or algebraically by an equation such as $Y = f(X)$. This is a simple relations type of function.

Realistically, the output of a product can never be ascribed to a single factor of production but is rather the result of combining several factors. A more accurate expression of the production function, therefore, would be $Y = f(X_1, X_2, X_3, \ldots, X_n)$, where Y refers to the specific output as a function of the various input factors specified and unspecified. The only real requirement is that each of the letters represents a well-defined homogeneous class of factors. This is a multiple relations type of function.

The most elementary form of production analysis and the one which provides the basis for more complex considerations in production management is the single factor-product relationship. It is concerned with the transformation of a single input into a single output and hence for estimational purposes may be expressed conceptually by writing it in the form $Y = f(X)$. However, since the product Y will be the result of combining the input factor X (e.g., labor) with other factors (such as capital, land, management, etc.), the functional relationship may more appropriately be written $Y = f(X_1 | X_2, X_3, \ldots, X_n)$. The vertical bar indicates that the input factors to the right are regarded as fixed in the production process under analysis, the factor to the left being varied.

The fundamental problem in the study of the production function is to discover the probable nature of the input-output relationship. This is discussed in the literature of economic theory under several synonymous headings such as the "Law of Variable Proportions," the "Law of Diminishing Returns," or simply the "Laws of Return." Regardless of the name, it represents an explanation of one of the most widely held and best developed set of principles in economic science. The nature and ramifications of these laws are presented in elementary economics, and are reviewed briefly in the paragraphs below.

Properties of the Production Function: Simple Relations

Exhibit 1 presents a production function as it is typically shown in standard economic texts. The total product curve, *TP*, average product,

EXHIBIT 1
Theoretical Production Function

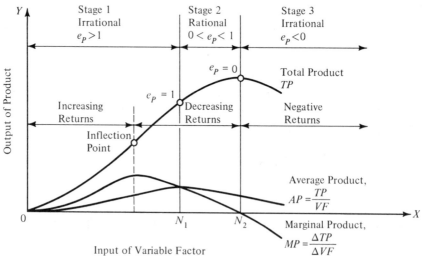

Input of Variable Factor

AP, and marginal product, *MP*, comprise the production function as a whole; these curves refer, of course, to the output of the product scaled along the vertical axis of the chart, expressed as a function of the variable input factor, *VF*, measured along the horizontal axis. All other input factors that may have an influence on production are assumed to be held constant.

What does the chart reveal? In other words, what are some of the fundamental properties of the production function?

Law of Variable Proportions. First, the chart as a whole reveals the operation of the *law of variable proportions* or the *law of diminishing returns*. It shows that in a given state of technology, the addition of a variable factor of production, keeping other productive services constant, will yield increasing returns per unit of variable factor added, until a point is reached beyond which further additions of the variable factor yield diminishing returns per unit of variable factor added. This is the nature of the law as it is usually expressed in economics textbooks. It encompasses virtually all types of production functions ranging from agriculture and automobile production through retailing and textile operations to the manufacture of zinc and zippers. It is thus a law of enormous significance as well as generality, as the discussion below will indicate.

Total-Marginal Relationship. Second, the chart reveals what may be called the *total-marginal relationship.* The marginal productivity curve expresses the change in total product resulting from a unit change in input. Since total product is plotted on the Y axis, marginal productivity can be expressed as $MP = \Delta Y/\Delta X$. As long as this ratio $\Delta Y/\Delta X$ is increasing, that is, the MP curve is rising, the total product curve is increasing at an increasing rate and is *convex* to the X axis. The point at which the TP curve changes its curvature is the point of inflection and corresponds vertically with the peak of the MP curve as shown by the broken line in the diagram. In the law of diminishing returns stated above, it is the peak of the marginal product curve that is referred to as the point of diminishing (marginal) returns—the point prior to which there are increasing returns to the variable factor and beyond which there are decreasing returns. (The peak of the average product curve represents the point of diminishing average returns.)

When the total product curve reaches its maximum, at that point it is neither rising nor falling and hence its slope is zero. Since the ratio $\Delta Y/\Delta X$ also defines the slope of the total product curve at a given point, it follows that when TP is a maximum, MP is zero. Beyond its maximum point the total product is declining and hence must have a negative slope; the marginal product, therefore, is also negative, that is, goes below the X axis. Increasing returns to the variable factor exist, therefore, when MP is positive and rising; decreasing returns occur when MP is positive and falling; and negative returns are realized when MP is negative and falling.

Average-Marginal Relationship. Third, the chart reveals what may be called the *average-marginal relationship.* This is such that as long as the marginal product exceeds the average product, the average productivity of the variable factor increases; when the marginal product is less than the average product, the latter decreases; and when the average product is constant at its maximum, the marginal product is equal to it. A simple example illustrates this point. If to a class of students there is added a student whose age is above the average age of the class, the average age is increased; if the student's age is below the average age, the average decreases; if the student's age is equal to the average, the average remains the same. It should be noted from the diagram that even when the marginal productivity of the input turns down from its maximum point, the average productivity of the factor is still rising as long as its marginal productivity is greater than the average.

Three Stages of Production. Fourth, economists customarily divide a production function of the type shown into what are known as the *three stages of production,* as illustrated in the chart. Stage 1 extends from zero input of the variable factor to where the average productivity of that factor is a maximum; stage 2 extends from the end of stage 1 to where the marginal product of the variable factor is zero (or to where total product is a maximum); stage 3 occurs where marginal product is negative (or total product is falling). Stages 1 and 3 are defined as *irrational* in that management, if it is to maximize profits, will never knowingly apply the variable to the fixed factors in any combination that will yield a total product falling in either of these two stages. The explanation follows.

In stage 1 the fixed factors are excessive relative to the variable factor and output can always be increased by increasing the variable relative to the fixed (or by reducing the "fixed" relative to the "variable"). In a large department store understaffed with clerks, for example, sales can be increased by employing more clerks (the variable factor) relative to counters, floor space, and so forth (the fixed factors), or by closing off sections of the store relative to the number of clerks. In stage 3 the variable factor is excessive relative to the fixed, and total output can be increased by reducing the variable relative to the fixed (or increasing the fixed relative to the variable). In the case of the department store again, if it were so overstaffed with clerks that they hampered each other or perhaps even kept customers from getting into the store and hence sales were declining, sales could be increased by reducing the number of clerks (or by increasing the size of the store). Stage 2 is the only *rational* stage of production, that is, the only area within which profits can be maximized. Accordingly, management will seek to operate in the second stage because neither input is then being used in such excessive quantity as to reduce total output. Hence, the decision maker will employ a quantity of variable factor somewhere between ON_1 and ON_2 to maximize the economic returns of the firm.[1]

---

[1] The precise amount of factor hire will depend upon the price of the factor and the price of the product. The ratio of the two is the economic choice indicator

The fundamental concepts underlying the three production stages can be further developed from Exhibit 2, in which the vertical axis measures physical products and the horizontal axis measures the *ratio* of variable product to fixed product, v/f. The plotted curves are total

EXHIBIT 2
Total Product, Average Product, and
Marginal Product Curves

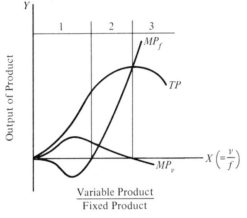

product *TP*, the marginal product of the variable factor MP_v, and the deduced marginal product of the fixed factor MP_f. The diagram illustrates the symmetry of the relations. In stage 1 the marginal product of the variable factor is positive while that of the fixed factor is negative; in stage 3 the reverse is true. Only in stage 2 are both marginal productivity curves positive. If the variable factor is available free, the manager will go to the end of the second stage; if the fixed service is free, the manager will stop at the beginning of the second stage. (Why?) The former principle is indicative of agricultural practices where labor is abundant relative to land, as in parts of the Far East; the latter helps to explain the lavish use of land by the colonists in early American history.

Elasticity of Productivity. Fifth and finally, Exhibit 1 reveals certain values of the *elasticity of productivity* or the *elasticity of production*, symbolized e_P. This may be defined as the rate of percentage change in total product relative to a slight percentage change in variable input. Thus, the elasticity varies at every point on the total product curve. It is demonstrated below that e_P is algebraically equivalent to the *ratio of the marginal product to the average product*, that is, $e_P = MP/AP$. The range

---

which, when equated to the marginal product ratio, determines the maximum profit position. More will be said of this later.

of e_P will thus depend on the values of MP and AP, or whether MP lies above, intersects, or lies below AP in Exhibit 1. This relationship accounts for the various values of e_P shown in the diagram.[2]

Referring back to Exhibit 1, the elasticity of production thus helps to explain the three stages of production outlined earlier. In stage 1 the e_P coefficient is greater than unity (written $e_P > 1$), since $MP > AP$; hence a 1 percent change in variable input brings a more than 1 percent change in output. In stage 2 the percentage change in output is less than proportional to the percentage change in input but greater than zero (written $0 < e_P < 1$), since $MP < AP$, but both are positive. In stage 3 where total product is falling, the percentage change in output is negative with respect to any percentage increase in variable input.

Production Function: Multiple Relations

In a factor-product or simple relations type of production function, changes in total output are expressed as a function of one variable input. A more general and realistic kind of production function is a multiple relations type in which changes in total output are expressed as a function of two or more variable inputs. The problem, as will be seen, then reduces to either of two considerations:

1. Determining the minimum amount of variable factors needed for producing a given output.
2. Determining the maximum output that can be produced from a given amount of variable factors.

As a beginning, let us assume a production function in which total output, Y, is expressed as a function of only two variable inputs, X and Z. Thus: $Y = f(X, Z)$. As examples, X might represent labor and Z might represent capital, both combined with other fixed factors in the production of a manufactured product; or X might represent nitrogen and Z might represent phosphate, both applied to an acre of land to produce an agricultural product. In any case, with output expressed as a function of two variable inputs, the resulting relationships can be illustrated by the three-dimensional "pie wedges" shown in Exhibit 3.

The diagram in Exhibit 3A is a *production surface*. Note that the inputs are scaled along the two horizontal axes of the plane, while output is measured vertically and hence is indicated by the height of the surface.

What determines the shape of a production surface? Actually, many kinds of surfaces are possible, depending on the nature of the underlying

---

[2] When two or more variable inputs are involved, the above definition of elasticity refers to the amount of fixed proportionate change in *all variable* factors. However, if *all* inputs are allowed to vary, there arise considerations of "returns to scale," a concept to be discussed at a later point.

EXHIBIT 3
Production Surfaces with Increasing and Decreasing Returns to Both Factors

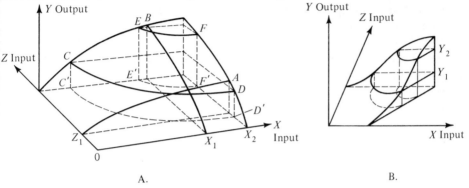

A.　　　　　　　　　　　　　　B.

production function. A brief review of some of the properties of the diagram in Exhibit 3A should therefore be of interest.

Input-Output Curves and Relationships

The production surface may be viewed as a mountain or hill, with greater outputs represented, as mentioned above, by greater height of the surface. It is apparent, therefore, that output is increased by moving "up" the hill. This can be accomplished by increasing either one of the inputs, X or Z, while the other is held constant, or by increasing them both.

Thus, if the quantity of Z input is held constant at OZ_1, a vertical slice parallel to the X axis produces the surface line Z_1A. This line or curve expresses the partial relationship between total output and the variable input X, at the constant OZ_1 level. Similarly, if the quantity of X input is held constant at OX_1, a vertical slice parallel to the Z axis results in the surface line X_1B, which reveals the partial Y-Z total output relationship at the constant OX_1 level. These surface lines, therefore, are simply input-output curves, and each expresses a partial relationship between output and one variable input while the other input is held constant at a specified level. Obviously, since infinitely many vertical slices can be made, there are infinitely many input-output curves that can be drawn.

What do these curves show? As in the simple relations or factor-product type of production function, the slopes of the individual input-output curves indicate the marginal products of the variable input. In this particular illustration we know that diminishing marginal productivity holds for both factors. (How do we know?) Also, the elasticity of production is first greater and then less than 1.0 for both inputs. Thus, under increasing returns to both factors, the surface is first convex to the X-Z base plane; it then becomes concave as decreasing returns to the input sets in. On the other hand, if constant productivity and perfect divisibility of both factors prevailed, the production surface would be linear in all directions.

Exhibit 3B presents a different view of a production surface in which the alternating cases of increasing and decreasing elasticities of productivity, along with the change in the surface from convexity to concavity, is more clearly in evidence. (Can the input curves in this diagram be developed and interpreted in the same way as those of Exhibit 3A?)

Factor-Factor Relationships: Isoquants

A second type of relationship is revealed when the production surfaces in Exhibit 3 are sliced horizontally instead of vertically. Thus, the height of each horizontal slice represents a specific output level, as indicated by Y_1 and Y_2 in Exhibit 3B. Associated with each horizontal slice is a contour line around the surface representing a constant level of output. Such contour lines are called *isoquants*. In Exhibit 3A, line CD is one such isoquant, while line EF is another isoquant representing a greater level of total output than CD. Obviously, the "higher" we go up the hill, the greater the level of total output represented by a particular isoquant. Also, since each isoquant is the result of various combinations of inputs, analyses of this type may be said to involve the study of factor-factor relations.

Since it is somewhat awkward to work with three-dimensional diagrams, we can project the isoquants down to the base as shown by the dashed lines C'D' and E'F' in Exhibit 3A. Clearly, any number of such isoquants can be developed, depending on how thin we want to make the horizontal slices or layers in the production surface. In any event, it is customary in economic theory to work with the two-dimensional version of the isoquants rather than their more cumbersome three-dimensional counterparts. Accordingly, it is in the two-dimensional framework that analyses of isoquants and other concepts of production are developed in the field of production economics. These concepts provide a powerful set of tools for management choice and decision making in business and economics.

ANALYTICAL FRAMEWORK FOR PRODUCTION MEASUREMENT

In this section we are concerned with outlining some of the elementary conceptual problems that arise in the statistical measurement of production functions—a subject which has had a long and fascinating history. Several types of mathematical functions are commonly employed in the measurement of production functions, but four in particular, namely *linear functions, power functions, quadratic functions,* and *cubic functions* have had the widest use in applied research. Hence this section will be devoted mainly to a discussion of the economic and mathematical properties of these functions, since an understanding of them provides a basis for deciding which type of function to employ in a particular empirical study.

Some Basic Formulations

The relationships and properties usually derived from the production function—namely average product, marginal product, and elasticity of production—can be expressed in simple algebraic terms as well as geometrically. This is illustrated in the following paragraphs, which serve as a basis for the discussion of specific types of production functions.

Average Product. This is the ratio of output to input. Thus, given a production function $Y = f(X)$ in which output, Y, is expressed as a function of input, X, the average product function is obtained by dividing through by X:

$$\text{Average product:} \quad \frac{Y}{X} = \frac{f(X)}{X}$$

To illustrate, suppose an empirical study results in a linear production curve. Its equation would then be of the form

$$\text{Total product:} \quad Y = a + bX$$

and hence the corresponding average product equation would be

$$\text{Average product:} \quad \frac{Y}{X} = \frac{a}{X} + b$$

In this form it is easy to judge the shape of the average product graph and come to some conclusions about the meaningfulness of the production curve itself.

Marginal Product. This is the rate of change of output with respect to a one-unit change of *any one* input. Like the measures of demand elasticity discussed in the previous chapter, we distinguish between an instantaneous rate of change at a point on the curve and an average rate of change over a segment of the curve. Thus, given a production function of two variables, $Y = f(A, B)$, the "point" measure of marginal product of A, for ΔA sufficiently small, would be $\Delta Y / \Delta A$; the marginal product of B, for ΔB sufficiently small, would be $\Delta Y / \Delta B$. For larger changes the "average" marginal product of A would be

$$\frac{\dfrac{Y_2 - Y_1}{2}}{\dfrac{A_2 - A_1}{2}} = \frac{Y_2 - Y_1}{A_2 - A_1}$$

which is the ratio of the average change in Y to the average change in A. Similarly, the marginal product of B would be $(Y_2 - Y_1)/(B_2 - B_1)$. In examining output response to a change in either input, it is understood that the other is held constant at some predetermined level.

The instantaneous measure of marginal product is more analytically precise as well as more easily calculated for production functions whose equations are known. The instantaneous rate of change of output with respect to a one-unit change of one input factor, holding all others constant, is given by the first partial derivative, $\partial f/\partial A$ or $\partial f/\partial B$. For the linear production function in the previous example, therefore, the marginal product is:

$$\text{Marginal product} = MP_X = b$$

Since the function is linear and therefore has constant slope, this equation expresses both the average as well as the instantaneous measure of the marginal product. (For other forms of production functions, however, the measures will almost always differ slightly.)

The derived result for the linear case is unusual in that marginal product is constant at the same level, b. This means that regardless of the level of output, an additional unit of input X would be expected to yield b units of output. In practice. however, the curvature of the MP curve at low or high levels of output is likely to be pronounced rather than flat. Therefore, linear production functions are not usually encountered in empirical studies.

Elasticity of Production. As discussed above, the elasticity e_P of the production function $Y = f(X)$ at the point X is the rate of percentage change in the dependent variable, Y, relative to an infinitesimal percentage change in the independent variable, X, thus:

$$e_P = \frac{\dfrac{\Delta Y}{Y}}{\dfrac{\Delta X}{X}} = \frac{\Delta Y}{\Delta X} \cdot \frac{X}{Y}$$

The elasticity of the function is therefore seen to be the rate of change, $\Delta Y/\Delta X$, combined with a multiplicative factor, X/Y, making it independent of the units in which the variables are quoted. Now, keeping in mind that marginal product is $\Delta Y/\Delta X$ and average product is Y/X, we can manipulate the terms in the above formula and rewrite elasticity as

$$e_P = \frac{\dfrac{\Delta Y}{\Delta X}}{\dfrac{Y}{X}} = \frac{\text{Marginal product}}{\text{Average product}}$$

thus showing that elasticity may be expressed in either of the above two ways. Using our linear production function as an example,

$$\text{Elasticity:} \quad e_P = \frac{b}{\dfrac{a}{X} + b}$$

In this form it is clear that since a and b are constants, the elasticity of production will vary at each point according to the value of X. Since elasticity is a fundamental concept in economic theory, the above formulation suggests, as we shall soon see, a useful way of employing this important notion in empirical research.

The above formulations yield the elasticity near any point along the total product curve. In many cases it is also desirable to have a means of estimating the elasticity over an arc or segment of the curve. The following arc elasticity formula for E_P which measures the average elasticity between two points with coordinates (X_1, Y_1) and (X_2, Y_2) along a total product curve, can be used to give a satisfactory estimate of the elasticity of the segment as a whole. In applying this formula, it is assumed that the curve segment in question can be adequately approximated by a straight line—an assumption which turns out to be reasonably realistic in many practical problems, especially if the curve segment chosen is not too long.

$$E_P = \frac{\dfrac{Y_2 - Y_1}{Y_2 + Y_1}}{\dfrac{X_2 - X_1}{X_2 + X_1}}$$

It is to be emphasized that the above definitions of average product, marginal product, and elasticity of production are based an fundamental concepts drawn from economic theory. Hence the investigator who wishes to fit production curves to empirical data would be wise to familiarize himself with the ways in which these concepts can serve as useful guides for judging the type of curve to be fitted. This is illustrated by the properties of production functions developed in the following paragraphs.

Power Production Functions

A power function which expresses output, Y, as a function of input, X, in the form

$$Y = aX^b$$

has frequently been employed in research investigations. Some of the properties of this type of function are as follows.

1. If we assume that the constant $a = 1$, a look at Exhibit 4 shows that the curvature of the function depends on the exponent b, which in all practical problems is always assumed to be positive. (A negative exponent would not make economic sense.) Thus if $b = 1$, the curve

EXHIBIT 4
Examples of the Power Function
$(Y = aX^b$ for $a = 1$ and $b > 0)$

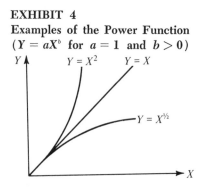

is a straight line. For $b > 1$ the curve is convex to the base, and for $b < 1$ it is concave to the base. The constant b may be thought of as defining the *transformation ratio* for different magnitudes of X.

2. The equation is linear in the logarithms; that is, it can be written

$$\log Y = \log a + b \log X$$

Graphically, this means that the equation plots as a straight line when expressed in its logarithmic form, or when plotted in its original form on double logarithmic scales. Hence, for simplicity and convenience the equation is estimated statistically in logarithmic form.

3. An interesting and sometimes convenient mathematical property of this function is that the exponent, b, in the original equation or the coefficient, b, in the logarithmic equation is the *elasticity of production*. The elasticity is thus the same for all values of X, that is, for whatever amount of dollars we may assign to X. Intuitively you can visualize this by the fact that on a log scale equal distances are represented by equal *relative* or *percentage* changes (as compared to an ordinary arithmetic scale on which equal distances are denoted by equal *amounts* of change). Since elasticity is nothing more than a measure of relative change, the slope of a straight line on double logarithmic scales will be the same as its elasticity.

4. One of the important properties of this function is that it allows for either increasing, constant, or decreasing marginal productivity, but not all three. This can be "seen" by visualizing the slopes at various points along the curves in Exhibit 4, or by analyzing the following marginal product equation:

$$MP_x = baX^{b-1} = \frac{baX^b}{X}$$

Thus if $b = 1$, both marginal and average product will be constant at the level a. This is the case for the linear production function $Y = X$ in Exhibit 4. If $b > 1$ the magnitude of marginal products will increase with increasing X, depending on the magnitude of b. For example, if $b = 2$, then $Y = X^2$, and the graph in Exhibit 4 rises by increasing amounts. In this case, for X values of 1, 2, 3, and 4, the corresponding marginal products are ba, $2ba$, $3ba$, and $4ba$.

These mathematical properties impose certain severe limitations on the use of power functions as appropriate curves in production studies. *The limitations, however, come primarily from economics rather than mathematics.* For example, a power function would not be satisfactory where the data exhibit ranges of both increasing and decreasing marginal productivity or both positive and negative marginal productivity. Yet these are precisely the kinds of marginal product curves that form the basis of the economic theory of production, and which have been verified by various empirical studies during the past several decades.

Among the three (total) product curves illustrated in Exhibit 4, the upper curve assumes an increasing marginal product, the middle or linear one assumes a constant marginal product, and the lower curve assumes a diminishing marginal product. Economists would generally agree that for logical consistency in the theory of production, the upper curve would have to be rejected as manifestly unrealistic; the other two may be acceptable, but only under special conditions and within specified limits if the data.

It might also be noted that none of the three curves in Exhibit 4 obtains an economic "optimum." Even the lower curve, for example, will only tend to "flatten out" as the variable input increases, without ever reaching a maximum. In the economic theory of production, the optimal amount of variable input would be determined by equating the marginal revenue product with the marginal cost of the input. If we employ this economic criterion of optimality, therefore, it is necessary to define an economic optimum for small magnitudes of X, or else the power function will have a tendency to overestimate the value of X which equates the two marginal functions.

The Two-Variable Cobb-Douglas Production Function

One of the pioneering econometric studies of production functions was done in the late 1920s by Paul H. Douglas, at that time professor of economics at the University of Chicago and subsequently (until 1966) United States Senator from Illinois. Together with C. W. Cobb, he laid the groundwork in a 1928 journal article by deriving a production function for American manufacturing as a whole. This and subsequent studies later resulted in what has come to be known as the "Cobb-Douglas function." It is the best known of numerous empirical studies that have since been done, and has served as an analytical basis for a great deal of later production research by other econometricians. In view of their importance, some of the highlights of the Cobb-Douglas studies, and the criticism they experienced, are worth reviewing.

Cobb and Douglas were the first to fit a formal empirical production function to time-series data. Moreover, they used two independent variables instead of one. Thus, the function they fitted was of the form

$$P' = bL^kC^{1-k}$$

where

   P' = calculated or expected index of manufacturing output over the period
   L = index of employment in manufacturing industries
   C = index of fixed capital in manufacturing industries

Thus, using annual data for the United States based on the period 1899 to 1922, the function which Cobb and Douglas derived for American manufacturing as a whole was

$$P' = 1.01L^{.75}C^{.25}$$

$R^2 = .9409$

with all three indices on the base period 1899 = 100. R^2 is the coefficient of multiple determination and represents the proportion of variations in the dependent variable which were explained by the independent variables in the analysis. Thus, about 94 percent of the variations in P' were accounted for by L and C in this equation.

Let us examine some of the interesting implications of their analysis:

1. Note that this equation, a power function, is linear in the logarithms but not in the original functional form. Thus the equation expressed in its equivalent logarithmic form is

$$\log P' = \log 1.01 + .75 \log L + .25 \log C$$

2. Since the equation is linear in the logarithms, the exponents of the original equation give the elasticities directly: an increase of labor by 1 percent results in a three fourths of 1 percent increase in product; an increase of capital by 1 percent results in a one fourth of 1 percent increase in product. Production is thus seen to be relatively inelastic with respect to *each* of these two independent variables.

3. One of the main problems which Cobb and Douglas sought to

solve concerned the economic theory of *imputation:* how is the value of the final product divided among the factors of production (that is, capital, land, labor) which collaborated to produce it? To answer this question, they computed (by partial differential calculus) the marginal productivities of labor and capital, obtaining $.75PL^{-1}$ and $.25PC^{-1}$, respectively. On the basis of these quantities, they imputed the proportion of total product going to labor as $.75P$, and the proportion of total product going to capital as $.25P$, where P represents the actual index of production in any one year (as compared to P' which is the calculated index obtained from the derived production function).

4. An important *assumption* concerning the production function fitted by Cobb and Douglas was that the sum of the elasticities is 1. They made this assumption because, as stated above, they wanted to impute the total product back to the two categories of productive factors, labor and capital. Hence, if the sum of the elasticities were greater than 1, the total product would have been less than the total amount imputed to the resources; on the other hand, if the sum of the elasticities were less than 1, the total product would have been greater than the total amount imputed to the resources. (Why?)

Cobb and Douglas, it should be noted, also considered other possible exponents such as $k = .67$ and $1 - k = .33$. However, they finally decided on values of $k = .75$ and $1 - k = .25$ as reasonably accurate approximations to the true state of affairs for the period of the analysis.

5. An important assumption is involved in utilizing a production function in which the sum of the elasticities is unity, namely that the production function is linearly homogeneous, or homogeneous of degree one. This concept is discussed in greater detail below, but basically it means that if inputs are doubled, output is doubled, if inputs are trebled, output is trebled, and so forth, or that the production function is assumed to exhibit constant returns to scale.

Does this mean that decreasing returns to scale will never actually set in, that small and large firms are about equally profitable, and therefore that the law of returns to scale as discussed in economic theory is not actually valid? Not necessarily. Intuition alone correctly leads us to believe that decreasing returns to scale must eventually be realized, although possibly over a wide range of inputs, or else firms could continue go grow without limit. The economic explanation for the existence of constant returns as exhibited by the studies of Douglas and his associates can probably be given by the fact that not all productive services were included in the analysis. At least one factor of production—management—was necessarily excluded from the empirical relationship, and it is likely that the omission of this scarce factor resulted in the appearance of constant rather than decreasing returns to scale as would otherwise have been expected.

This work on production functions became the object of a considerable amount of controversy and criticism in the professional economic journals. Accordingly, Douglas and his associates, by the late 1930s, began to relax the assumption that the sum of the elasticities in a production function should total unity. Accordingly, they began to employ a power function of the form

$$P = bL^kC^j$$

where the exponents k and j were free to assume any values.

The above power function has come to be known as the *Cobb-Douglas function*. It has been employed in many production function studies utilizing time-series as well as cross-sectional data, and it has been applied at various times to countries, industries, and firms. However, it has not gone without criticism.

Criticisms of the Cobb-Douglas Function

1. The production function that is ordinarily discussed in economics is a rigorously developed microeconomic concept which occupies a strategic role in the general theory of the firm. Douglas and his colleagues, by estimating production functions for entire nations, for manufacturing sectors, and even for industries, "transferred" a strictly microeconomic concept to a macroeconomic setting without sufficiently justifying their act on logical economic grounds. Therefore, the results of their studies, in the form of the equations they derived, may be incorrect; and hence the interpretations based on their equations are suspect.

2. The production function of economic theory assumes that the quantities of inputs employed are those that are actually used in production so that no variable input is ever redundant. In the Douglas studies, however, only labor was measured by the quantity actually used in production, whereas capital was measured by capital investment, that is, the quantity available for production. Therefore, with the possible exception of the years in which full employment and prosperity prevailed and industry made reasonably full use of available inputs, the measure of capital employed was not the theoretically correct one. Only if annual capital input always remained a constant proportion of total capital investment would the elasticities be the same.

3. In cross-section studies where several firms are analyzed at the same point in time, the resulting production functions that are derived, whether short or long run, are probably "mongrel" or "hybrid" rather than pure functions of the type discussed in economic theory. This is due to the varying degrees of adaptation which firms make to changing prices and other conditions within specified periods of time. For example, changes in input and output prices result in some firms adjusting their

plant structure and utilization more quickly than others. This is reflected in their actual production functions at any given time, thereby making it questionable whether the derived production functions are actually of a short- or long-run nature.

4. Ideally, the data or observations that are employed to estimate production functions should be derived from scientifically controlled experiments in which different input mixes are systematically manipulated and the corresponding effects on output are measured. In reality, the data that are actually employed, whether historical or cross-sectional, are not derived by controlled experimentation, and instead are reflections of management decisions. Consequently, the observations usually cover a very small segment of the production surface; and errors may arise due to incomplete or delayed adjustments to price changes, to errors on the part of management, or to changes in the underlying function itself.

These are some of the main economic criticisms of the production function studies done by Douglas and his associates. For the most part these criticisms revolve around the idea that the derived functions were of an *interfirm* rather than *intrafirm* nature, thereby leaving some doubt as to whether they could be said to represent the traditional production function of microeconomic theory.

In addition to these economic shortcomings, there are criticisms of a statistical nature. These can be largely grouped under the headings of "identification," "estimation," and "specification"—three broad problem areas that form a major part of the literature of modern econometric science. We shall content ourselves, however, with the brief sketch of economic criticisms that has been outlined above, and not undertake a discussion of the various statistical and econometric problems at this time.

Some Advantages of the Cobb-Douglas Function

If the Cobb-Douglas type of function has so many shortcomings, why has it been widely used by economists who are interested in estimating statistical production functions? At least two reasons may be cited, both of which serve to emphasize the advantages of this particular form of algebraic equation.

1. It is convenient for interpreting economic results, since the elasticities of production are given directly by the exponents when the data are in original form, or by the regression coefficients when the data are in logarithmic form.
2. The estimation of parameters involves fewer statistical degrees of freedom than other algebraic forms which allow increasing or decreasing returns to scale.

It should be emphasized, of course, that where the Cobb-Douglas type of production function has been used, especially at the intrafirm level, it has typically been in the later, "unrestricted" form rather than in its original (restricted) form. Also, with the exception of the work done by Douglas and his associates, most of the others who have applied this type of equation have not ordinarily done so for the purpose of estimating the functional distribution of income factors of production, as was the intent of Cobb and Douglas, but rather for the more immediate purpose of estimating the parameters of empirical production functions. Exhibit 5 illustrates an agricultural application, in which feed

EXHIBIT 5

Power Production Functions (relationship between feed input and pork output—Iowa experimental data)

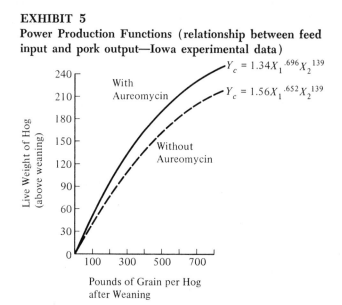

Pounds of Grain per Hog
after Weaning

Production functions have been applied extensively to agricultural and feeding experiments. These power functions illustrate the results of two feeding studies involving hogs. The inputs are aureomycin, X_1, and protein, X_2. The latter was held constant to obtain the corn-pork, input-output relationships of $Y_c = 2.41X_1^{.696}$ with aureomycin. Protein was "fixed" at 70 pounds for both curves by "feeding" it in constant amounts spread over feeding "periods" of different lengths and including various amounts of grain.

Some important special properties of such power functions are:

1. The exponents are the elasticities of production and remain constant over the curve, since the equations are linear in the logarithms.
2. The total product tends to "flatten out" as input increases since a maximum product is not defined.
3. If one input is increased while all others are held constant, marginal product will decline.

These are some of the factors to consider in selecting this type of production function.

input was varied in order to derive a production function for pork output.

Other Forms of the Production Function

Although many other forms of production functions besides the exponential Cobb-Douglas function are possible, only a few are reviewed here. One example is a simple quadratic of the form where the depen-

$$Y = a + bX - cX^2$$

dent variable Y represents total output and the independent variable X denotes (a single) input. The small letters again represent parameters; estimates of their values are determined, of course, by a statistical analysis of the data. Four examples of this type of production function are shown in Exhibit 6 based on fertilizer-vegetable input-output studies

EXHIBIT 6
Quadratic Production Functions (fertilizer-vegetable input-output data, four successive years in Alabama)

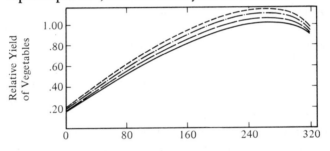

Input of Phosphate Fertilizer (pounds)

Eutaw soil:
  1st year—$Y = .13 + .492X - .07X^2$
  2d year—$Y = .1128 + .5304X - .0786X^2$
  3d year—$Y = .137 + .5854X - .0936X^2$
  4th year—$Y = .1498 + .6324X - .1071X^2$

Some important special properties of quadratic production functions of the above type are:

1. The minus sign in the last term denotes diminishing marginal returns.
2. The equation allows for both decreasing and negative marginal products, but not for both increasing and decreasing marginal products.
3. A maximum total product can be defined for some level of input.
4. The elasticity of production is not constant at all points along the curve as in a power function but declines with input magnitude.

These are some of the factors to consider in selecting this type of production function.

over a four-year period in Alabama. Also included in the example is a brief list of the more important properties of the quadratic form of the production function, of which the possibility of a decreasing marginal productivity would usually be considered the most notable.

Also worthy of specific mention is the derivation of the elasticity of production. In the case of the quadratic production function, the elasticity is not constant at every point along the total product curve. Instead, it declines as input is increased. The following formula, representing the ratio of marginal product to average product, may be used to measure the elasticity of production at any point along the total product curve, provided that we know the values of the parameters a, b, and c.

$$\text{Production elasticity:} \quad e_P = \frac{b - 2cX}{\dfrac{a}{X} + b - cX} = \frac{\text{Marginal product}}{\text{Average product}}$$

NOTE: You should recall that the elasticity of production has already been shown to be equivalent to the *ratio of marginal productivity to average productivity*. If you are familiar with elementary calculus, therefore, you should know how the numerator of the above formula was obtained. As for the denominator, its derivation involves only elementary algebra, since average product equals total product divided by input, that is, the total product equation divided by X.

An empirical investigation of a production process usually begins not with the functional form—that is, a "ready-made" production function—but rather with a series of production observations generated by either historical or cross-sectional analysis. When these data are plotted on an input-output chart (we assume that there is only one variable input; all others are held constant at some fixed level), a dot pattern similar to the one illustrated in Exhibit 7 may be determined. The reason for the apparent concentration of dots is explained on the chart.

Because of the dispersion pattern of the sample data, the analyst might try to fit a cubic equation to the sample observations, as suggested by the solid curve TP in the exhibit. This curve is the classic production function of economics textbooks, similar to the type discussed earlier with reference to Exhibit 1. As such, this curve has a range of increasing marginal productivity and a range of decreasing marginal productivity, that is, a range over which the elasticity of production is greater than one and a range over which it is smaller than one. Note also that in contrast to the quadratic curve, this curve has two bends instead of one.

The most general form of the cubic equation is:

$$Y = a + bX + cX^2 - dX^3$$

and it is this curve which has been graphed as the curve TP in Exhibit 7. In accordance with the fact that for this particular example, output

EXHIBIT 7
Cubic Production Function
(total product curve fitted to observed data)

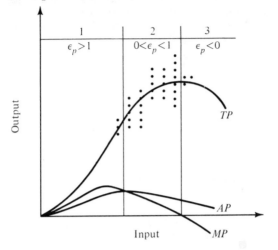

The "vertical" pattern of dots indicates that the inputs were available only in discrete units. Note that almost all of the dots fall within the rational area, stage 2. This indicates that management was usually able to maintain the input level within the optimum range on the basis of its intuition and experience.

Some important special properties of a cubic production function such as this are:

1. It allows for both increasing and decreasing marginal productivity. However, this property is rarely needed for a single variable resource. (Why?)
2. The elasticity of production varies at each point along the curve as illustrated in the diagram.
3. Marginal productivity decreases at an increasing rate in the later stage.

These are some of the factors to keep in mind in selecting this type of production function.

(Y) equals zero when input (X) equals zero, we assign a value of zero to the parameter "a" in the above formula. The total product equation therefore becomes:

$$\text{Total product:} \quad Y = bX + cX^2 - dX^3$$

If the curve and equation for Exhibit 7 are all that we know, how might we derive the corresponding average and marginal product curves? Can a formula be developed for measuring the elasticity of production? What can we say about the minimum input quantity that management should hire? These questions can be answered arithmetically by constructing a production schedule similar to Exhibit 8 and plotting the graphs. Alternatively, the questions can be answered algebraically in the following manner.

EXHIBIT 8
Production Function Data

Input X	Output Y	Average Product $Y \div X$	Marginal Product $\Delta Y \div \Delta X$
0	?	?	?
20	?	?	?
40	?	?	?
—	—	—	—
—	—	—	—
—	—	—	—
320	?	?	?

Average product is equal to total product divided by input, or the above equation divided by X.

$$\text{Average product: } \frac{Y}{X} = \frac{bX + cX^2 - dX^3}{X} = b + cX - dX^2$$

Marginal product, utilizing some elementary calculus, is obtained by differentiating the total product equation. Thus, for ΔX sufficiently small:

$$\text{Marginal product: } \frac{\Delta Y}{\Delta X} = b + 2cX - 3dX^2$$

(You should now be able to state a formula for measuring the elasticity of production, as was done in the previous section for the quadratic production function.)

We know that the minimum amount of input to hire is found at the beginning of stage 2 of a cubic production function (see Exhibit 1) where average product and marginal product are equal. Therefore, equating the above marginal product and average product equations, we get

$$b + 2cX - 3dX^2 = b + cX - dX^2$$

Collecting terms and solving for X, we obtain the equation

$$X = .5cd^{-1}$$

This indicates the least amount of factor X that should be used per unit of fixed resources if input is to be greater than zero.

An example of a cubic production function expressing a relation between feed consumption and hog production is

$$Y_c = 65.2X + 7.0X^2 - .8X^3$$

where

Y_c = calculated output in dressed weight of hogs

X = feed input, measured in terms of the amount fed to hogs of different weights (values of X tend to range from about 150 pounds to 300 pounds)

The average and marginal product data for this equation can be derived by constructing a table as described earlier. The curves can then be plotted on a chart. Alternatively, the equation for average product can be obtained by dividing the above equation by total input, X. The equation for marginal product is for ΔX small: $\Delta Y/\Delta X = 65.2 + 14.0X - 2.4X^2$.

Conclusion: Which Function Should We Select?

As noted, numerous forms of algebraic equations can be fitted to input-output data in order to derive production functions. It is, of course, obvious that different processes will be expected to determine different functions: magnitudes of coefficients will vary with such factors as floor area, arrangement of machines, work flows, quality of equipment, degree of mechanization, magnitude of "fixed" inputs, and so forth. In view of the wide spectrum of different productive processes, guidelines are needed for choosing a function that fits correctly.

In addressing this problem, perhaps the most important thing which can be said about the choice of algebraic production functions is that they are mathematical models which can, at best, only approximate the "true" input-output relationship. Probably very few production managers have ever even heard of the production function, let alone are familiar with the mathematics used by Cobb and Douglas to manipulate them. But this does not matter. What is important is the fact that the hypothetical production function serves a vital analytic purpose as an abstraction of the real production process under the manager's supervision. However, to the extent that intangible factors, catalytic agents, and the uncertainties attributable to breakage, spoilage, mistakes, miscommunication, errors in judgment, and so forth are not accounted for in the algebraic formulation, the model must necessarily be accepted only as an incomplete approximation of the system rather than a precise formula.[3]

With this point made, it is perhaps equally important to stress that the researcher's inability to describe completely the production process

---

[3] It is perhaps ironic to note that the field of cost accounting, a relatively descriptive discipline, has long recognized the "variances" associated with the production process, while managerial economics, a comparatively prescriptive discipline, until very recently has not.

should not preclude any attempt at all. To begin an empirical analysis, the most formidable guide to choosing an approximating function is the underlying theory. By this is meant that, to the extent possible, the selected function should reflect the physical properties of the underlying biological, psychological, economic, or other environmental factors or processes from which the derivation is to be made. As a simplistic example, a linear production function would have to be rejected if the likelihood of a constant marginal product was quite small.

By the same token, the ease with which the researcher is able to match theory with algebraic form is admittedly less than one would like. For example, various biological investigations have viewed the production phenomenon as a study similar to the process of organic growth; some psychological studies have approached the problem within a framework of learning theory, and so on. Accordingly, it may be quite possible, depending on the problem, to give equally valid reasons for selecting one type of function over another, and there is probably no single mathematical function that could be used for all economic situations.

Does this mean that we cannot develop criteria which can serve as guides for selecting the appropriate type of production function in a given problem? The answer is no. A considerable number of criteria, both economic and statistical can be derived, based on the special properties of the various types of production functions discussed thus far. A few of these have already been indicated in previous charts and in the text. They involve such factors as the shape of the different curves, their marginal productivity properties, their elasticity properties, their relative ease or difficulty with respect to computation, and so forth. These are the kinds of guides that must be considered in selecting the most logical function for a given situation.

TECHNIQUES OF OPTIMUM INPUT ANALYSIS

The production function provides a useful model for decisions involving minimum cost or maximum profit input rates. If inputs are measured in terms of dollars, and if it is assumed that the costs of all input combinations are known, the optimum input combination is the one which yields either:

1. Minimum total costs for a given level of output, or
2. Maximum output for a given level of total costs.

There are many different combinations of inputs that will yield a given level of output, but obviously the cheapest combination will maximize the producer's profit. Clearly, the cheapest combination depends on the relative prices of the inputs. This leads to the following principle or decision rule which is learned in elementary economics:

PRINCIPLE: The least-cost combination of inputs is achieved when a dollars worth of any input adds as much to total output as a dollar's worth of any other input.

Thus, letting MP_A denote the marginal product of A, and P_A the price of A, and similarly for other inputs $B, C, \ldots, N$, the equation of minimum cost is:

$$\frac{MP_A}{P_A} = \frac{MP_B}{P_B} = \frac{MP_C}{P_C} = \cdots = \frac{MP_N}{P_N}$$

This rule of minimum cost states that if the price of an input rises, the producer should use less of it thereby increasing its marginal product, and more of other inputs thereby decreasing their marginal products. As an example, suppose a producer employs two inputs, A and B, and at some given volume of output, a dollar's worth of each factor yields:

$$MP_A = 10 \text{ units}$$
$$MP_B = 8 \text{ units}$$

Assuming that the producer wants to minimize his costs at the prescribed output level, he should proceed as follows:

1. Buy \$1 less of B, thereby reducing production by 8 units.
2. Buy \$0.80 more of A, thereby increasing production by 8 units ($= \frac{4}{5}$ of the marginal product of a dollar's worth of A).
3. Save \$0.20.

This example shows how a producer would go about minimizing his costs for a given level of output. By a similar process it could be demonstrated how the same producer would proceed to maximize his output for a given level of costs. Either process is aimed at achieving the minimum cost or maximum profit input rate combination.

Minimum Cost/Maximum Profit Input Rates

Consider a production function with two variable inputs, L and C, representing units of labor and units of capital, respectively. The marginal product of an input is then the change in output quantity ΔQ resulting from a unit change in that input. Thus, $MP_L = \Delta Q/\Delta L$ and $MP_C = \Delta Q/\Delta C$. If P_L denotes the price of labor and P_C the price of capital, the condition for minimum cost can be written as

$$\frac{MP_L}{P_L} = \frac{MP_C}{P_C}$$

or

$$\frac{\Delta Q/\Delta L}{P_L} = \frac{\Delta Q/\Delta C}{P_C}$$

or

$$\frac{MP_L}{MP_C} = \frac{\Delta Q/\Delta L}{\Delta Q/\Delta C} = \frac{P_L}{P_C} \qquad (1)$$

The last equation, namely equation (1), can be conveniently used to solve some practical problems. This equation says that production costs are minimized when the input factors are combined so that the *ratio of their marginal products equals the ratio of their corresponding prices* (*or marginal costs*). This is one of the basic principles of production theory that is learned in elementary economics. (NOTE: Are the prices of the inputs always the same as their marginal costs?)

An Illustrative Example

A certain production process is given by the equation

$$Q = C^{\frac{1}{2}}L^{\frac{1}{2}} \qquad (2)$$

Let us analyze this production function in several steps by posing some interesting problems and answers.

Step 1. Assuming that $C = L$, what is the graphic "shape" of the equation? The answer is obtained by substituting values for C and L in (2). Note, for example, that when $C = L = 1$, $Q = 1$; when $C = L = 2$, $Q = 2$; and so on. The resulting graph is shown in Exhibit 9.

EXHIBIT 9
Production Surface for $Q = C^{\frac{1}{2}}L^{\frac{1}{2}}$

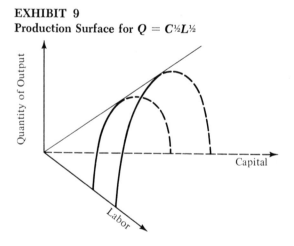

Step 2. Suppose that the cost of labor is $10 per unit and the minimum acceptable return on capital is also $10 per unit. What is the minimum cost combination of labor and capital?

Since equation (1) states the condition for minimum cost, the answer to this question can be obtained by applying partial differential calculus to equation (2):

$$\frac{\partial Q/\partial L}{\partial Q/\partial C} = \frac{C^{\frac{1}{2}} \frac{1}{2} L^{-\frac{1}{2}}}{L^{\frac{1}{2}} \frac{1}{2} C^{-\frac{1}{2}}} = \frac{\$10}{\$10}$$

Dividing through as indicated:

$$C^{\frac{1}{2}-(-\frac{1}{2})} L^{-\frac{1}{2}-\frac{1}{2}} = 1$$
$$CL^{-1} = 1$$
$$C = L$$

Thus the minimum cost input combination requires that $C = L$.

Step 3. Assume that the production budget is $1,000 and that the prices of labor and capital are the same as in the previous step, that is, $P_C = P_L = \$10$ per unit. What is the optimum input combination of C and L? What will be the corresponding output?

Obviously, since the prices of C and L are each $10 per unit, an expenditure of $1,000 will purchase a total of 100 units. And since the optimum (minimum cost) input occurs when $C = L$, mangement should purchase 50 units of each, resulting in an output of

$$Q = 50^{\frac{1}{2}} 50^{\frac{1}{2}} = 50 \text{ units}$$

Step 4. Let the price which the seller receives for each unit of output be denoted by the symbol P_Q. Suppose that this price is a function of the seller's total output as given by the equation

$$P_Q = \$30 - \frac{Q}{1,000} \tag{3}$$

Keeping in mind that $P_C = P_L = \$10$ per unit, can you write an equation for profit or net revenue in terms of C and L?

Since profit, π, is equal to total revenue, TR, minus total cost, TC, we have

$$\pi = \overbrace{(P_Q)Q}^{TR} - \overbrace{[P_C(C) + P_L(L)]}^{TC} \tag{4}$$

Substituting equation (3) in (4):

$$\pi = \left(\$30 - \frac{Q}{1,000}\right)Q - [\$10(C) + \$10(L)]$$

$$= \$30Q - \frac{Q^2}{1,000} - [\$10(C) + \$10(L)] \tag{5}$$

But since we know that

$$Q = C^{\frac{1}{2}} L^{\frac{1}{2}}$$

we can substitute this in (5) to obtain

$$\pi = \underbrace{\left[\$30(C^{\frac{1}{2}}L^{\frac{1}{2}}) - \frac{CL}{1,000} \right]}_{TR} - \underbrace{[\$10C + \$10L]}_{TC} \tag{6}$$

Step 5. This equation for net revenue can be employed to find the profit (or loss) resulting from the employment of various combinations of capital and labor. For example, let $C = L = 100$. Then $C^{\frac{1}{2}} = L^{\frac{1}{2}} = 10$, and substituting in (6):

$$\pi = \left[30(10 \cdot 10) - \frac{10,000}{1,000} \right] - [10(100) + 10(100)]$$
$$= [3,000 - 10] - [1,000 + 1,000]$$
$$= \$990$$

It should be evident that different combinations of C and L will yield different levels of profit. But assuming that $C = L$, which combination will yield maximum profit? One way of answering this question is by a "trial-and-error" method of substituting different quantities of input levels in (6) above until the maximum profit figure is attained. An alternative and far more efficient method is to deduce the profit-maximizing equations directly. This again requires some familiarity with partial differential calculus as illustrated by the following procedure.

Step 6. (*Optional*) In order to find the combination of C and L which maximizes profit, we take the partial derivative of net revenue with respect to C, and then with respect to L, and set the resulting equations equal to zero. Then, after performing some substitutions and solving for the unknowns, we arrive at the maximum profit input combination. Thus, from equation (6) we derive:

$$\frac{\partial \pi}{\partial C} = L^{\frac{1}{2}}15C^{-\frac{1}{2}} - \frac{L}{1,000} - 10 = 0 \tag{7}$$

$$\frac{\partial \pi}{\partial L} = C^{\frac{1}{2}}15L^{-\frac{1}{2}} - \frac{C}{1,000} - 10 = 0 \tag{8}$$

From equation (7) we solve for $C^{\frac{1}{2}}$, obtaining

$$C^{\frac{1}{2}} = \frac{15,000L^{\frac{1}{2}}}{L + 10,000} \tag{9}$$

Squaring both sides,

$$C = \left(\frac{15,000L^{\frac{1}{2}}}{L + 10,000} \right)^2 \tag{10}$$

Alternatively, we could solve equation (8) for $L^{1/2}$ and get

$$L^{1/2} = \frac{15{,}000C^{1/2}}{C + 10{,}000} \tag{11}$$

and by squaring both sides,

$$L = \left(\frac{15{,}000C^{1/2}}{C + 10{,}000}\right)^2 \tag{12}$$

We can now either substitute (9) and (10) into (8) and solve for L, or (11) and (12) into (7) and solve for C. Suppose we arbitrarily select the former alternative, thus:

$$\left(\frac{15{,}000L^{1/2}}{L + 10{,}000}\right) 15L^{-1/2} - \frac{1}{1{,}000}\left(\frac{15{,}000L^{1/2}}{L + 10{,}000}\right)^2 - 10 = 0$$

from which we find that

$$L = 5{,}000$$

Substituting $L = 5{,}000$ in either (9) or (10), we get

$$C = 5{,}000$$

Therefore, $L = C = 5{,}000$ is the maximum profit input combination.

Once we know the best actual imput combination, the resulting maximum profit can be found by substituting in equation (6):

$$\pi = 30(5{,}000)^{1/2}(5{,}000)^{1/2} - \frac{(5{,}000)(5{,}000)}{1{,}000} - 10(5{,}000) - 10(5{,}000)$$

$$= 150{,}000 - 25{,}000 - 100{,}000$$
$$= \$25{,}000$$

The output which corresponds to this maximum profit is

$$Q = (5{,}000)^{1/2}(5{,}000)^{1/2} = 5{,}000 \text{ units}$$

Of course, if the price of one input should increase relative to another, the producer will tend to shift the pattern of resource use by substituting cheaper inputs for the more expensive one. The producer's ability to do this will depend on the elasticity of substitution between inputs, that is, the ease with which one input can be substituted for another. It should be apparent that for any given production function, this elasticity will be determined by various technological and institutional constraints.

THEORY OF RETURNS TO SCALE OF PLANT

The law of returns to scale is a topic of extraordinary importance in production economics. It is also a far more complicated problem than the familiar law of variable proportions (or as it is more popularly called, the law of diminishing returns). Fundamentally, the differences hinge on the following considerations:

1. In the theory of variable proportions, all inputs but one are held fixed so that the effects of *proportionality* relationships can be analyzed.
2. In the theory of returns to scale, all inputs are varied simultaneously so that the effects of *scale* relationships can be analyzed.

The theory of variable proportions thus deals with "short-run" production functions whereas the theory of returns to scale is concerned with "long-run" production functions. It is the latter theory, of course, that is of interest to us in the following paragraphs.

Constant Returns to Scale

The simplest and most common type of situation is the case of constant returns to scale. This occurs when equal proportional changes in all inputs lead to equal proportional changes in output, or in other words when the input of each factor of production is multiplied by a constant amount and the corresponding output is multiplied by a like amount. (In mathematical terminology, a production function which exhibits constant returns to scale would be called homogeneous of the first degree, or linearly homogeneous). In this case the marginal and average productivity of all factors depends only on the ratio between the factors and not on the amounts of the factors.

Thus, consider a production function which is defined as

$$P = f(A, B)$$

and assume that the inputs A and B are each multiplied by a constant k. The right side of the equation would then become $f(kA, kB)$ or $kf(A, B)$. If the output is increased by the same proportion so that it too is multiplied by k to become kP, the resulting production function is

$$kP = kf(A, B) = f(kA, kB)$$

thus denoting that the product is increased by the same constant ratio as all factors.

Implications of Constant Returns to Scale

Does the case of constant returns to scale contradict the law of variable proportions? Clearly not. The law of variable proportions states, for example, that if two inputs A and B yield an output of P, then $2A$ and B will yield an output of less than $2P$. On the other hand, the concept of constant returns to scale implies that if A and B yield

P, then $2A$ and $2B$ will yield $2P$. The two notions are thus quite different in both principle and application.

One of the interesting features of a production function characterized by constant returns to scale is the fact that all sizes of plant with this production function will be equally efficient. This means that if Company X produces only half as much as its competitor Company Y, then Company X will require only half as many resources as Company Y. If both firms pay the same prices for their resources, then Company X's total cost of production will be half that of Company Y's, whereas their average costs will be equal. From a managerial viewpoint, therefore, it is a matter of complete indifference as to which size of plant should be built.

In statistical studies of production functions done both by economists and engineers, the type of equation often employed has been the power (or early Cobb-Douglas) function of the form

$$P = bC^j L^k \qquad (j + k = 1)$$

where P is product, C is capital, and L is labor. As previously noted, such a function is logarithmically linear and therefore easy to estimate; the exponents are the elasticities; the total product tends to "flatten out" as output increases, but a maximum output is not defined. Most important, however, is that since $j + k = 1$, the function *yields constant returns to scale* (as well as diminishing returns to each factor separately). Thus, if each input is varied by a given proportion, that is, multiplied by the same constant, m, the product increases in the same proportion. In terms of the above function:

$$b(mC)^j (mL)^k = bm^{j+k} C^j L^k = bmC^j L^k = mP$$

This property of constant returns to scale is more than just a convenient assumption. In the early production function studies done by Cobb and Douglas, it was assumed that the sum of the exponents (or elasticities) was unity so that the entire product could be imputed to the input factors which produced it.

Conclusion: Variable Returns to Scale

It seems appropriate to summarize briefly what we now know about the theory of constant returns to scale, and in the process say a few words about the causes of a related class of phenomena, namely *variable* returns to scale.

An important principle which differs from the law of variable proportions as discussed in the factor-product analysis or simple relations type of production function is the *law of returns to scale*. That is, instead of varying only one input and noting the effect on output, we can consider the possibility of varying *all* inputs and measuring the change in output.

For example, suppose that all of the factors in a production process could be varied in the same proportion, say doubled or trebled. It seems that the consequent change in total output would also be altered in the same proportion, being doubled if all inputs were doubled and trebled if all inputs were trebled. A relation of this type, where the percentage change in output is exactly proportional to the percentage change in all inputs as a whole (so that $e_P = 1$) is known as constant returns to scale, and a production function that exhibits this characteristic is said to be *linear and homogeneous*. In reality, conditions are rarely if ever encountered in which a production function is characterized by constant returns to scale over the full range of inputs, despite the fact that it might seem very plausible for constant returns to scale to be the rule rather than the exception. Actually, a production function would almost always exhibit alternating stages of both increasing ($e_P > 1$) and decreasing ($e_P < 1$) returns to scale due to the following two categories of phenomena.

1. Indivisibility of Productive Services. The first condition which tends to prevent the occurrence of constant returns to scale over the full range of inputs is the indivisibility of productive services. Rarely is it possible to increase all of the productive factors in the same proportion; as a consequence, some of the factors are always being underworked or overworked relative to others at most levels of output, and this results in alternations of increasing and decreasing returns.

For example, doubling the rate of output of an assembly line may still require only one final inspector instead of two; one locomotive may have sufficient horsepower to pull 40 freight cars as adequately as 20; a salesperson may be able to take on a full line of goods instead of a single item at no significant increase in costs; and to a bank, the expense of investigating and managing a loan does not increase in proportion to the size of the loan. These examples from the fields of production, marketing, finance, and so forth, serve to illustrate that the advantage of size may result in economies that yield increasing returns to scale.

What about decreasing returns to scale? This is beautifully illustrated in the following passage from a classic work:

> There is a story of a man who thought of getting the economy of large scale production in plowing, and built a plow three times as long, three times as wide, and three times as deep as the ordinary plow and harnessed six horses to pull it, instead of two. To his surprise, the plow refused to budge, and to his greater surprise it finally took fifty horses to move the refractory machine. In this case, the resistance, which is the thing he did not want, increased faster than the surface

area of the earth plowed, which was the thing he did want. Furthermore, when he increased his power to overcome this resistance, he multiplied the number of his power units instead of their size, which eliminated all chance of saving there, and since his units were horses, the fifty could not pull together as well as two.[4]

2. *Decision-Making Role of Management.* The second factor tending to upset the plausibility of constant returns to scale lies in the decision-making role of management. In its function as a coordinator, management may be able to delegate authority, but ultimately decisions must emanate from a final center if there is to be uniformity in performance and policy. As the firm grows, increasingly heavy burdens are placed on management so that eventually this class as a factor of production is overworked relative to others and "diminishing returns to management" set in. Thus it is the growing difficulty of coordination that eventually stops the growth of any firm. To some extent, the development of new scientific methods and techniques of decision making may have the effect of (*a*) reducing the time necessary to make a given number of correct decisions, or (*b*) increasing the number of correct decisions that can be made in a given time period. However, this would only tend to prolong the realization of decreasing returns to scale rather than eliminate it. Further, even if advances in decision science could eventually overcome the limitational factor due to management, there is still the indivisibility consideration discussed previously that serves as a major factor preventing constant returns to scale over all ranges of inputs.

Homogeneous Functions

Suppose we have a relationship in which the dependent variable is expressed as a function of two independent variables, such as $z = f(x, y)$. We can think of the independent variables as "inputs" and the dependent variable as the "output." In general, if the input variables are increased or decreased in a fixed proportion, the corresponding change in output may be proportionately greater than, equal to, or less than the change in x and y. This fact prompts us to consider an interesting concept in mathematics which goes by the technical name of "homogeneous functions."

A *homogeneous function* is a function such that if each of the input variables is multiplied by a power of k, then k can be completely factored out of the function. The power of k which can be factored out of the function is called the *degree of homogeneity* of the function. Thus the function $f(x, y)$ is homogeneous of degree n, if and only if, for any

---

[4] J. M. Clark, *Studies in the Economics of Overhead Costs* (Chicago: The University of Chicago Press, 1923), p. 116.

point (x, y) and for any value of k,

$$f(kx, ky) = k^n f(x, y)$$

The degree n in this definition may be any real number, and the function may be extended to include any number of variables. These ideas can be illustrated with the following examples.

EXAMPLE 1: Suppose we have the input-output function

$$z_1 = f(x, y) = 5x + 3y$$

Then

$$\begin{aligned} f(kx, ky) &= 5kx + 3ky \\ &= k(5x + 3y) \\ &= kf(x, y) \end{aligned}$$

Thus in multiplying the inputs x and y by k, the output z_1 has also been multiplied by k. And since the power of k is 1, that is, $n = 1$, the original function $z_1 = 5x + 3y$ is said to be homogeneous of degree 1, or linear and homogeneous.

EXAMPLE 2: Let

$$z_2 = f(x, y) = \frac{3x - 5y}{4x + 2y}$$

Then

$$\begin{aligned} f(kx, ky) &= \frac{3kx - 5ky}{4kx + 2ky} \\ &= \frac{k(3x - 5y)}{k(4x + 2y)} \\ &= \frac{3x - 5y}{4x + 2y} \\ &= f(x, y) \end{aligned}$$

Thus $n = 0$; that is $k^0 = 1$. Therefore the original equation is homogeneous of degree zero.

EXAMPLE 3: The function

$$z_3 = f(x, y) = (x + y)^{3/2}$$

is homogeneous of degree $3/2$ because with $k > 0$,

$$\begin{aligned} f(kx, ky) &= (kx + ky)^{3/2} \\ &= k^{3/2}(x + y)^{3/2} \\ &= k^{3/2}f(x, y) \end{aligned}$$

It should be clear from these examples that a function is homogeneous of degree n if when each of the independent variables is multiplied by a positive constant k, the new function is k^n times the original function.

Using Homogeneous Production Functions as a Test for Returns to Scale

An immediate application of the homogeneity property of a production function is to test whether the production function exhibits increasing, decreasing, or constant returns to scale. Not all hypothetical production functions are homogeneous, of course; but if they are, then a homogeneous production function of degree less than 1 ($n < 1$) will exhibit decreasing returns to scale, a homogeneous production function of degree n equal to 1 ($n = 1$) will exhibit constant returns to scale, and a homogeneous production function of degree greater than one ($n > 1$) will exhibit increasing returns to scale.

To illustrate, first recall that a simpler test of returns to scale is to examine how output responds to a doubling of all input factors simultaneously. If output more than doubles when inputs are doubled, increasing returns are in evidence. If output less than doubles when all inputs are doubled, the production process is characterized by decreasing returns to scale. Finally, if output just doubles when all inputs are doubled, constant returns to scale are said to exist.

Letting $k = 2$ for the foregoing Examples 1, 2, and 3, and setting $x = 4$ and $y = 2$, we are now in a position to examine what happens to outputs when inputs are doubled.

$$z_1 = f(x, y) = 5x + 3y = 26$$

and

$$z_1' = f(kx, ky) = k^n f(x, y) = 2^1 z_1 = 52$$

$$z_2 = f(x, y) = \frac{3x - 5y}{4x + 2y} = \frac{1}{10}$$

and

$$z_2' = f(kx, ky) = k^n f(x, y) = 2^0 z_2 = z_2 = \frac{1}{10}$$

$$z_3 = f(x, y) = (x + y)^{3/2} = 6\sqrt{6} = 14.7$$

and

$$z_3' = f(kx, ky) = k^n f(x, y) = 2^{3/2} z_3 = 24\sqrt{3} = 41.6$$

The first example illustrates a production function which is homogeneous of degree 1. Hence, 2 to the first power is just two, or in other words, doubling inputs just doubles output: the production function exhibits constant returns to scale. In the second example, the production function is homogeneous of degree zero. The factor 2 raised to the zero power is just one; and therefore a doubling of inputs does not affect output at all, indicating decreasing returns to scale. Finally, the production function in Example 3 is found to be homogeneous of degree $3/2$. The factor 2 raised to the $3/2$ power implies that doubling inputs more than doubles output, and hence the production function exhibits increasing returns to scale.

It is interesting to note that the Cobb-Douglas production function is always homogeneous of degree n equal to the sum of the exponents. This is true regardless of the number of productive input factors (independent variables) in the equation. In the earlier Cobb-Douglas model, input factors were restricted to capital and labor, and their exponents were chosen to sum to one, which restricted the model to production functions yielding constant returns to scale. Later models have relaxed these restrictions so that more than two input factors may be considered, and the sum of the exponents may be more or less than one. Returns to scale may be quickly determined by simply adding up the exponents of the independent variables.

We note again that the homogeneous functions comprise a special class of functions. Many functions are *not* homogeneous, such as $f(x, y) = 3x^2 + y$, $f(x, y) = x + y^2$, or $f(x, y) = x^3 + y^3 + 7xy$. Non-homogeneous functions can still be tested for returns to scale, of course; but the simple test afforded by the homogeneity property is not available.

Euler's Theorem on Homogeneous Functions (Optional)

Euler's theorem, named after the 18th-century mathematician Leonard Euler (pronouced "oiler"), entered economic theory in the latter part of the 19th century, although the theorem itself was formulated on a purely mathematical basis. It states that given a homogeneous function of degree n, then n times the function is equal to the sum of the independent variables when each is first multiplied by the partial derivative of the function with respect to that variable. In symbols, Euler's theorem says

$$nf(x_1, x_2, \ldots , x_m) = x_1 \frac{\partial(f)}{\partial x_1} + x_2 \frac{\partial(f)}{\partial x_2} + \cdots + x_m \frac{\partial(f)}{\partial x_m} \qquad (13)$$

To illustrate the operation of Euler's theorem, let us take the same three examples as in the preceding section,

$$z_1 = 5x + 3y \qquad (14)$$

which is homogeneous of degree 1,

$$z_2 = \frac{3x - 5y}{4x + 2y} \qquad (15)$$

which is homogeneous of degree 0, and

$$z_3 = (x + y)^{3/2} \qquad (16)$$

which is homogeneous of degree $3/2$.

From equation (14) above,

$$\frac{\partial z_1}{\partial x} = 5 \quad \text{and} \quad \frac{\partial z_1}{\partial y} = 3$$

Therefore, by Euler's theorem,

$$x \frac{\partial z_1}{\partial x} + y \frac{\partial z_1}{\partial y} = 5x + 3y = nz_1$$

since $n = 1$. In the case of equation (15) above, let $u = 3x - 5y$, and let $v = 4x + 2y$. Since

$$\frac{dz_2}{dx} = \frac{d\left(\frac{u}{v}\right)}{dx} = \frac{v \frac{du}{dx} - u \frac{dv}{dx}}{v^2}$$

then

$$\frac{\partial z_2}{\partial x} = \frac{(4x + 2y)3 - (3x - 5y)4}{(4x + 2y)^2} = \frac{12x + 6y - 12x + 20y}{(4x + 2y)^2} = \frac{26y}{(4x + 2y)^2}$$

and

$$\frac{\partial z_2}{\partial y} = \frac{(4x + 2y)(-5) - (3x - 5y)2}{(4x + 2y)^2} = \frac{-20x - 10y - 6x + 10y}{(4x + 2y)^2}$$

$$= \frac{-26x}{(4x + 2y)^2}$$

Then from Euler's theorem,

$$x \frac{\partial z_2}{\partial x} + y \frac{\partial z_2}{\partial y} = \frac{26xy}{(4x + 2y)^2} - \frac{26xy}{(4x + 2y)^2} = 0 = nz_2$$

since $n = 0$.

In the case of equation (16)

$$\frac{\partial z_3}{\partial x} = \frac{3}{2}(x + y)^{\frac{1}{2}} \quad \text{and} \quad \frac{\partial z_3}{\partial y} = \frac{3}{2}(x + y)^{\frac{1}{2}}$$

Then from Euler's theorem,

$$\frac{3}{2}x(x + y)^{\frac{1}{2}} + \frac{3}{2}y(x + y)^{\frac{1}{2}} = \frac{3}{2}(x + y)(x + y)^{\frac{1}{2}} = \frac{3}{2}(x + y)^{\frac{3}{2}} = \frac{3}{2}z_3 = nz_3$$

since $n = \frac{3}{2}$.

In economic theory, the marginal product of an input factor may be expressed as the partial derivative of the production function with respect to that factor. If the production function is homogeneous of degree 1, and if each input factor is paid according to its marginal productivity, then, by Euler's theorem, the total output will be fully and fairly distributed among the various factors.

The Cobb-Douglas studies centered on this application of Euler's theorem. Following their original macro studies of American industry as a whole, Douglas and his associates subsequently used time-series data to estimate some industry production functions of the form

$$P' = bL^kC^{1-k}$$

where the sum of the exponents would be forced to unity. In all cases their interest centered on equations of the type

$$P = \frac{\partial P}{\partial L} \cdot L + \frac{\partial P}{\partial C} \cdot C$$

where the marginal product of labor, $\partial P/\partial L$, times the quantity of labor, L, plus the marginal product of capital, $\partial P/\partial C$, times the quantity of capital, C, always yielded a sum equal to the total product, P. During the 1930s they estimated production functions of this type for various states and countries, including Massachusetts, Victoria, New South Wales, and New Zealand, each of their studies covering different time periods.

MULTIPLE PRODUCTS AND PRODUCT-LINE POLICY

What are the typical kinds of policy decisions relating to product diversification and specialization that must be made by management in achieving an economic balance of its end products? In economic theory, problems of this type come under the heading of *multiple products;* business executives, on the other hand, are more apt to use the term *product line*. In this discussion we use both terms interchangeably.

Problems of multiple products fall into three broad categories for purposes of analysis:

1. Product-line coverage or combination, which, as stated above, involves the establishment of policies for obtaining an economically balanced company output.
2. Product-line pricing, which concerns the separate interrelationships between multiple product costs and multiple product demands.
3. Product-line improvement, which involves problems of a valuation nature over time.

The first is discussed in this section, while the second and third are treated in the literature of pricing and capital budgeting, respectively.

Economic Bases of Multiple Products

In the final analysis, the reasons why management would be interested in expanding its product line are to increase profits and/or strengthen its market position with respect to competitors. The drive to expand profits by manipulating the product line is usually the result of excess capacity and thus places management on the offensive; keeping up with competitors, economies of scale, and certain other factors are sufficiently important, however, to warrant a separate discussion for each.

Excess Capacity. The presence of excess production capacity is perhaps the most important single factor prompting product-line diversification. If all productive services are not being fully utilized in an optimum manner, fixed costs are spread over fewer units and average total costs (i.e., unit costs) are thereby increased. The typical reaction, therefore, is to expand the product line, thereby reducing unit costs by obtaining a better utilization of capacity.

Integration. The causes of integration—the reasons why a firm may embrace a variety of products, markets, and functions—are attributable to a complex of historical, economic, and technical circumstances. The most obvious motive, however, is to get a strategic market advantage, thereby reducing competitive uncertainties and enhancing profits. There is an economic motive to integrate whenever lower production costs will result. These reductions in costs may come about through a fuller utilization of plant capacity and other productive factors, or by creating new market opportunities. To the purchasing firm, the intermediate factors that it must buy from other companies in order to carry on its operations constitute a part of its costs. When the purchasing firm can supply its own resource needs more economically through integration than it can by securing these resources in the markets, profits will be increased by integrating. Similarly, in integrating forward, the additional (and average) costs at the new output level must not exceed the difference between the market price at the new and the old output level.

Economies of Scale. Frequently, a firm can produce two goods more cheaply together than separately: meat-packers produce soap and other products from formerly wasted animal parts; grocery delivery trucks carry many products rather than a few; and salespersons can handle a full line instead of a few items at little extra cost (and, as a matter of fact, the products often complement one another thereby increasing sales). In chemicals, oils and electronics, long-term fundamental research has been particularly exploited by integration in an attempt to discover new and better product uses. These considerations, along with the importance of assuring sources of supply in order to maintain continuity of operations, have been major incentives accounting for the drive toward integration. The results, however, have often been dislocations in economies of scale along with technological and cyclical changes that serve to create an unbalanced product line from the company's profit-making standpoint.

Competition. Keeping up with or ahead of competitors is another broad motive for product diversification. In industries where exact duplication is difficult or illegal due to secret processes, patent rights, and so forth, or where entry into the industry is relatively obstructed by economic or institutional obstacles, the need to produce similar (if imperfectly substitutable) products prevails.

Industries characterized by monopolistic competition (many sellers, heterogeneous products) provide the most notable examples, though certain types of oligopoly structures are also illustrative. Profitable decisions in such circumstances require that the firm adhere to what has been called by some economists (e.g., Boulding) the "Principle of Minimum Differentiation": *make the product as similar to competing products as possible without destroying the differences,* thereby capturing part of the competitors' markets while at the same time instilling sufficient consumers' loyalty to minimize the shifts in buying due to minor price differences.

Modern business abounds with illustrations of this principle. Breakfast cereals, automobiles, and women's clothing are only a few of the many industries whose products could be cited as indicative, the last two particularly as examples of product variation or differentiation in the short run due to style and fashion changes, and in the long run of product diversification as well.

Stability. From a long-run standpoint, management may diversify its output in order to achieve an optimum product line that will maximize the profits from its resources. In the short run, on the other hand, it may decide to adopt as a "safeguard" against uncertainty a more immediate objective of income stability rather than profit maximization. In this case an optimum product line would be one which does not "place all of the eggs in one basket," in the hope that profits from the sale of certain products will offset losses incurred on others. In the long run, however, the goal of income stability merges with that of profit maximization and hence the concept of an optimum product line as one which fulfills this requirement remains essentially unaltered.

Joint Products. A final explanatory factor for multiple products may be the existence of production processes which naturally yield more than one output. Classical examples of such processes are sheep raising, which results in the production of both wool and mutton, and steer raising, which results in the production of both beef and leather. Non-agricultural situations also abound, however, as in oil refining. The case of joint products is distinguished primarily on technical rather than categorical grounds, and is said to be found whenever the production of one product automatically implies the production of a second. By-products may or may not fit this definition, therefore, depending upon whether or not additional processing is necessary to "obtain" the second or third commodity.

Optimum Product Line

The previous discussion outlined the nature of the underlying pressures that prompt management to examine the production of multiple products. Granted that these pressures are sufficiently strong to cause diversification in production, what are the goals that may be adopted by the firm if it is to expand its output offerings?

In the short run, the optimal production level is found for the case of independent products by equating marginal cost with marginal revenue for each product. Those products for which marginal cost is always greater than marginal revenue are unprofitable items and should not be produced. In such computations, it is important to remember that marginal costs do not include any pro rata portion of fixed or overhead costs: only direct costs are used in the analysis.

In the case of joint products, the necessary theoretical requirement for profit maximization is that the marginal revenue product of an input with respect to every output must be equated to its price. However, empirical considerations often forestall any direct application of this result, and only rough approximations may be possible.

Viewed as a long-term problem, the decision as to what constitutes an optimum product line boils down to one of maximizing the *return on investment*. Thus, the production of goods represents an investment in resources (time, money, materials, etc.) which over the life of the product line gives rise to a series of expenses. Over the same period of the product-line's life, the firm will also enjoy receipts as the goods are sold. Thus production gives rise to a stream of costs over time and sales give rise to a stream of revenues over time. The difference between these two streams, the economic revenues less the economic costs, represents the stream of economic net profits or the return on investment, the *present value* of which is to be maximized over the life of the product line. The optimum product line is thus the combination of products that accomplishes this end. When the problem is framed in this manner, product-line policy takes the form of making decisions in the present based on expectations of the future, and is thus a recognition of the uncertainty inherent in forward planning by management.

In view of the foregoing, the practical aspects of establishing the optimum product line resolves itself into two problems:

1.   Forecasting demand and costs for each new product to be added.
2.   Arriving at a relevant concept of profit.

On the revenue side, forecasting demand involves estimates of the product's price, advertising effectiveness, and other demand determinants; on the cost side, the problems are largely those of predicting the labor, materials, and other expenses that will be incurred at given levels of output. For new products such forecasts are rarely more than pure speculation to begin with and are nothing but visions if they extend beyond a short-range (three- to five-year) period, at least in the product's early stages of development.

Establishing an appropriate profit concept means that, in principle, the *incremental profit* attributable to the addition of the new product should exceed the incremental returns that would be incurred by investing the resources in the next best alternative use; in practice, this means that the income expected over the life of the product less the outlay and investment (i.e., economic cost) must be greater than the income received from any other investment alternative, including considerations of discounting and compounding.

Problems of this and a related nature, which involve investment decisions over time, form part of the subject known as capital budgeting. Our purpose at this point has been to emphasize that the relevant profit concept is one that is expressed in a form which permits comparisons to be made with alternative uses of the same resources (labor, plant, materials, etc.) over time. The cost to the firm is thus measured by the sacrifice it incurs or the return it foregoes by not using these resources in their most profitable alternative.

> NOTE: Products are thus portrayed as competing for the firm's limited resources; hence, the market cost of new capital to the firm should be the true profit standard, as pointed out in the literature of capital budgeting. When resources are not limited, a profit rate based on historical average earnings for a past period may be quite practical.

Product-Line Expansion

If greater net profits are realized from additions to the product line, it may frequently be the result of at least two separate but related underlying factors: one of these is *product interdependence;* the other is *excess capacity.* Each of these represents a class of causes in many and varied forms that may be sufficient to prompt a product-line expansion.

Product Interdependence. The relationships that may exist between the products of a multiple-product firm may be of a competing, complementary, or independent nature.

> Competing (substitute) products, from a demand standpoint, often serve as a precaution against uncertainty by reducing the probability of sales variations due to changing demands, tastes, and so forth, while recognizing that satisfactions rather than products are what buyers are purchasing. In other words, a company must always face the real possibility of product obsolescence either by itself or by competitors, and firms that offer a wide array of substitutes in their respective product lines (e.g., Lever Brothers, Procter and Gamble, etc.) are frequently hedging against this type of uncertainty.
>
> Complementary products, on the other hand, provide the firm with a profitable opportunity to fill the related needs of the buyer (e.g., shoe stores selling polish, hose, etc.). The hope on the part of management in expanding the product line is either that the existing products are well enough known to sell the new product, or that the

new product will perhaps excite enough sales to increase the demand for the existing products.

Finally, when products are independent, they are supplementary to one another and have no direct effect on the sale of other products by the firm. From a production standpoint, however, all products in the line, regardless of the relationships between them, compete for the firm's resources (including management) and may thereby raise important opportunity cost considerations in deciding on the optimum product line.

Excess Capacity. Product-line expansion to utilize available capacity may be motivated by a variety of considerations. Thus it may be the result of an effort to fill in seasonal dips in sales, as when a firm sells air conditioners and heaters; it may be the result of utilizing common advertising media and distribution channels, for example, supermarkets; it may be the result of management's desire to provide a "full line" to customers by utilizing the excess capacity that exists in the company's brand name or reputation. (Can you cite examples?) Numerous other possibilities exist and you can undoubtedly think of several. In any event, the considerations in expanding the product line involve, from the standpoint of excess capacity, questions of both productive and distributive efficiency.

Production aspects include:

1. The integration of existing facilities for the new product in the form of plant space, machinery, and so forth, with seasonal and/or cyclical variations in production.
2. The proportion of the firm's present resources to be allocated to the product and the proportion to be acquired from outside (e.g., should the company manufacture the product and farm it out for assembly?).
3. The availability of materials in sufficient quantity to assure required output levels.

To a large extent these factors are conditioned by the existence of common production facilities for the new product and the existing product line, thereby making possible a fuller utilization of excess capacity and thus the sharing of overhead costs.

Distribution aspects involve:

1. The place of the product in the company's regular distribution pattern (e.g., whether the product can be sold through the same or regular channels, which will be partly determined by the opinions of the product held by jobbers and wholesalers).

2. Whether the present sales force can handle the new product without prohibitive increases in salespeople's costs and time, and without neglecting other products.
3. The amount of advertising and promotion needed in the product's introductory and early growth stages.

Integrated with both the production and distribution aspects, of course, are various financial considerations such as manufacturing costs, sales and advertising costs, capital requirements, inventory levels to be maintained, pricing methods, and profit planning.

Product-Line Contraction

For the most part, the converse of the rules stated above with respect to product-line diversification also apply to product-line contraction. In principle, the optimum product line is the one which yields the greatest long-run rate of return for a given investment of resources, or yields a given long-run rate of return for a minimum investment of resources. Hence a product can be dropped if the same resources used to produce it could be used more profitably in a better alternative, provided that net returns on the company's total resource investment would be thereby increased. Usually, if a product is not evidencing profitable performance, management can consider the three alternatives of make, buy, or drop.

  Make. If the firm continues to make the product, it may require an improvement in production and/or distribution efficiency as outlined above to yield adequate returns. If the commodity is a by-product, it may be sufficient to retain it as long as its *contribution profit* (revenue minus variable cost) is positive. Advertising, promotion, and other selling expenses may even have to be minimized for the product in order to raise the contribution margin. A further cut in distributive costs might be realized if the product were manufactured by the firm and farmed out to others for final sale. The practices of Sears-Roebuck, Montgomery Ward, and other mail-order houses are notable examples of companies that assume the marketing functions which manufacturers may not otherwise be equipped to handle.

  Buy. A decision to buy the product rather than make it is justifiable if the supplying firm can provide the product in adequate volume and at low enough costs to make it sufficiently profitable for resale by the buying company. For the buying firm this alternative has the following consequences: (*a*) it makes the firm more dependent on others, which may not be a disadvantage if the supply of the product can be assured; and (*b*) if the supplying firm is part of an oligopolistic industry, its pricing practices may be sufficiently erratic to complicate profit, cost, and sales planning by the buying company.

Drop. The decision to drop the product entirely is warranted if its long-run net profit is below what would be attained from an alternate product using the same resources. It is important to emphasize long-run and not short-run profits (or even losses). In the short run, only contribution profit is the relevant consideration, since earnings above variable expenses go to sharing the overhead and the earning of profit. In the short run, resources are a sunk cost and any spreading of fixed expenses over more products is justifiable. Long-run considerations, however, allow for greater resource mobility, and hence all fixed costs become variable. Net profits resulting from various alternatives thus become the only relevant criterion as a basis for decision making.

LIMITED RESOURCES

The foregoing analysis has been based upon the assumption that the production process(es) of the firm were a function of unlimited resource inputs, an assumption which permits direct computation of marginal product and hence optimum resource distribution in accord with the least-cost input principles developed in the previous section on Techniques of Optimum Input Analysis. Whereas this assumption may not always have been overly unrealistic for actual manufacturing in the United States, more recent economic experience has witnessed a substantial amount of supply failures, the most notable of which, of course, was petroleum and petroleum products. The discontinuities and irregularities which result in the production function in the presence of restricted resources require that we reexamine the firm's production decision in light of these new limitations.

In terms of the production surface, the presence of resource constraints implies a reduction in the total surface area of the production function. For example, referring back to Exhibit 3, the restriction of input Z to Z_1 units and input X to X_2 units would imply that only the production surface OZ_1AX_2 would be relevant for the firm. In terms of production measurement, any hypothetical production function must now be redefined in terms of a limited domain for the argument variables since inputs are no longer in unlimited supply. Hence, traditional production curves (total product, average product, and marginal product) do not extend indefinitely along the X (Input or Variable Factor) axis, as might be suggested by Exhibit 1; nor, for that matter, do they necessarily have to extend beyond the second stage of production. A priori, it is conceivable for the firm to find itself limited to a quantity of input X (Exhibit 1) which falls short of N_2 or even N_1 units, and hence severely limits the productive efficiency of the firm.

In terms of normative policy for the production of a single economic good, the firm's chief question is whether to maintain its present production processes, or switch to alternates which utilize less intensively the restricted input or inputs. To answer this question, the firm must distinguish between short-run input restrictions versus long-run input limitations. If the firm considers its factor constraint to be a temporary supplier failure, then the concern must weigh the advantages of utilizing the alternative production strategy against the transition costs of the changeover. If the costs of the conversion are small, however, this does not necessarily mean that a "switch" is optimal, for the abandonment of the "old" process presumably also implies a switch from a (former) least-cost production system to a system of higher costs. The decision cirteria therefore must also include this factor if the firm is to profit-maximize, as opposed to output-maximize.

As a practical matter, the easiest analysis for the firm would be to first compute approximately how many units can be produced under (1) the present productive process and (2) any alternative production process. The firm may then proceed to calculate total costs and revenues for the alternate schemes and determine the appropriate policy by choosing the productive process for which total profit is greatest.[5]

Input restrictions which are viewed as long-run affairs by the firm can be handled in a similar fashion, except that in the long run, conversion costs cease to assume as important a role. This is because the firm can more flexibly adjust its technology if given enough time to exhaust existing fixed resource commitments. In fact, technological adjustment is expected to be the norm, rather than the exception, in long-run considerations; and hence the adjustment process would probably be viewed as an expected concomitant of industry recognition of factor input limitations.

For the multiproduct firm, the presence of restricted resources normally constrains the firm on several production "fronts," and the firm must now face the problem of allocating its limited resource, or resources in such a way as to maximize the total profit contribution from the various products it still has the capacity to make. Where the production processes assume linear relationships, this problem is ideally suited for solution by a linear programming model, and in fact represents the classical production problem often used to illustrate the technique. Because of its importance, a separate chapter of this book has been devoted to linear programming and production management and hence these subjects are not discussed in detail here.

PROBLEMS

√1. Fill in the following table representing a classical production function. Sketch the corresponding graph and label your chart showing the titles

---

[5] This assumes that the resource constraints are sufficiently strong to deter the firm from expanding output to its unconstrained optimum. If this assumption is violated, then the firm does not really face the problem of a limited resource.

of the curves, the stages of production, phases of returns, and so forth, as done in the chapter.

Production Function

(1) *Variable* *Input* *X*	(2) *Total* *Product* *Y*	(3) *Average* *Product* *(AP)*	(4) *Marginal* *Product* *(MP)*
0	0		
10	22		
20	48		
30	76		
40	98		
50	116		
60	122		
70	118		
80	110		

NOTE: In plotting the curves, you may find it desirable to use a scale break on the vertical axis to distinguish average and marginal product from total product.

2. The law of diminishing returns was originally intended to serve as an explanation of an historical process. In England, for example, as the population grew during the 18th and early 19th centuries, it was predicted (e.g., by David Ricardo) that the marginal productivity of labor on land would decline. If this were true: (*a*) What would happen to aggregate values of agricultural land? (*b*) What could happen to total land rent as a percentage share of national income? (*c*) What would happen to the price of food relative to nonfood goods?

3. How would you answer the questions in Problem 2 with respect to India and the United States?

4. Explain the underlying differences between the following two statements:
   a. "If it were not for the law of diminishing returns, it would be possible to grow all of the world's food in a flowerpot."
   b. "If proportional changes in agricultural inputs, say labor and land, resulted in proportional changes in the output of food, and if labor yielded increasing marginal products, then the world's food could be grown in a flowerpot if the pot were small enough."

5. Evaluate the effect of a technological improvement on a company's production function.

6. What characteristics or environments of today's industry make it difficult to apply marginal theory?

7. Explain underlying differences between the law of diminishing returns and return to scale.

8. What is an "optimum" product line? Outline and discuss the types of factors that often motivate managements to expand or contract their product lines.

9. A certain production function is given by the equation $Q = 8X - X^2$, where X denotes input and Q is output.

    a. Sketch the total output, average output, and marginal output curves for the range $X = 0$ to $X = 6$.

    b. Write the equations for average output and marginal output. (Suggestion: If you calculated your marginal products directly from your table of values, then each MP figure should be plotted midway between successive integer values of X on your chart. On the other hand, if you calculated each MP value directly from your derived equation for MP, you should plot the points in the conventional manner, that is, to the corresponding X values.)

    c. Assume that X is hundreds of units of input and Q is tens of units of output. If the output sells at $100 per unit and the input costs $3 per unit, what is the largest profit the seller can incur? At what level of input and output is the largest profit realized?

10. Does the production function $Y = 10C^{.25}L^{.75}$ show constant returns to scale? Demonstrate algebraically.

11. Matlin Commercial Farms derived the following production function, where Y = value of farm production, R = real estate (including land and buildings), L = labor, M = machine services, and Z = miscellaneous resource services:

$$Y = .27R^{.25}L^{.05}M^{.10}F^{.30}Z^{.40}$$

    a. What is the economic meaning of the exponents? Explain.

    b. What kind of returns to scale are indicated by this production function? Explain your answer.

12. Blake Machine Engineering, Inc., estimated by means of simultaneous equations the following production function, where L = labor, C = capital, and R = real estate (including land and buildings):

$$Y = 1.62L^{.05}C^{.50}R^{.40}$$

If all of the inputs are doubled, will the output be doubled? Explain your answer. What kind of returns to scale are indicated here?

13. This problem continues the illustration of a maximum profit input rate which was given in the third section of the chapter. Thus, the production function was assumed to be

$$Q = C^{1/2}L^{1/2}$$

and the price of output

$$P_Q = \$30 - \frac{Q}{1,000}$$

The optimum input rate was then found to be $C = L = 5,000$ units; the total profit, assuming that capital and labor inputs each cost $10 per unit, was $25,000.

Suppose now that the price of capital changes from $10 per unit to $12 per unit while the price of labor remains constant at $10 per unit. Determine the following: (a) optimum input mix of capital and labor; (b) total profit equation; (c) maximum profit combination of capital and labor; and (d) maximum profit and corresponding output. (e) Interpret your results.

14.   a.   A clothing manufacturer doubled the size of the factory manufacturing garments, the number of machines in it, the number of employees, and the quantity of materials employed. As a result the manufacturer's output increased from 200 to 420 garments per day. Is this an example of increasing returns to scale, or, as it is often called, the economies of large-scale production?

b.   The manufacturer then doubled the quantity of managers and found the output fell to 370 garments per day. What do you suppose might have happened?

15.   MC & D is the largest manufacturer of concrete products in Honolulu. The firm has three processes available to produce H-shaped concrete tile. By process A the firm can produce an output of 1,000 units per time period with 10 units of labor and 30 units of capital; by process B the firm can produce 1,000 units of output with 15 units of labor and 20 units of capital; by process C the firm can produce 1,000 units of output with 30 units of labor and 5 units of capital. Assume that each process represents a linear and homogeneous production function. (a) If the price of labor is $4 per unit and price of capital is $11 per unit, which is the lowest cost process to produce 3,000 units? (b) If the price of labor is $7 per unit and the price of capital is $9 per unit, which is the lowest cost process to produce 1,500 units?

16.   **Biological Growth Analogies of Returns to Scale**

a.   There is a relationship between the volume, V, and the surface area, A, of physical bodies. This relationship may be approximated by the formula

$$V = A^{3/2} = \sqrt{A^3}$$

For example, if the surface area of an object increases 4 times, its volume should increase about $\sqrt{4^3} = 8$ times. Can you use this notion to explain why there are no small warm-blooded animals in the Antarctic or in the ocean, and why the largest insect is about as large as the smallest warm-blooded animal?

b.   There is often a tendency to think that constant returns to scale should be common in economic life, yet variable returns (i.e., both increasing and decreasing) are frequently encountered. For example, we should expect that by doubling all inputs to a production process, including the quantity of management, the output ought to double. Yet there are examples from nature to illustrate why this is not so. Thus, if a house were scaled down so that it stood in the same proportion to a flea as it now stands to a person, the flea would be able to jump over it. However, if a flea were scaled up to the size of a person, the flea would not be able to jump over the house. In fact, it couldn't jump at all because its legs would break. Can you explain why?

c. What conclusions relevant to the size and growth of organizations can you draw from these notions? (HINT: It has been said that prehistoric monsters became extinct because they could not adjust to their changing environment. Why not?)

17.   **CASE PROBLEM: NATIONAL TOBACCO COMPANY**
       FUTURE EXPANSION FROM DIVERSIFICATION

National Tobacco Company is a large producer of cigarettes. It manufactures eight different brands, three of which have been major sellers for many years while the remaining five have usually ranked between 7th and 12th place.

As a result of adverse publicity relating cigarette smoking to lung cancer, the company, along with American Tobacco, Reynolds Tobacco, and others in the industry, has embarked on a planned diversification program. Although the manufacture and sale of cigarettes is still the company's main source of income, it has acquired six additional manufacturing businesses completely unrelated to tobacco. These include the following: canned fruit, frozen foods, soft drinks, clothing, textbook publishing, and school furniture. Each of these subsidiaries reflects the company's desire to avoid acquiring businesses which are strongly cyclical in nature.

The management of National Tobacco now feels that it has a well-rounded, diversified corporation. Profits from cigarette sales and from all of the six subsidiaries are satisfactory. However, management is always interested in using its limited resources, financial and otherwise, to encourage the expansion of those subsidiaries which show the greatest relative promise over the long run.

Some time ago a team of economists working for the parent company started conducting extensive research investigations of the six subsidiaries. Their analyses will eventually include the development of various detailed studies ranging through many areas of marketing, finance, and production, for the purpose of advising management on policy pertaining to future expansion of the subsidiaries. The first phase of this research project is concerned with the derivation of production functions for each of the subsidiaries. As of now the following tentative production functions have been hypothesized.

a. Canned fruit: $Y = cX_1^{1/5}X_2^{1/10}X_3^{1/20}X_4^{1/20}X_5^{3/5}$
b. Frozen foods: $Y = \frac{1}{4}X + 500$
c. Soft drinks: $Y = cX_1X_2X_3X_4$
d. Clothing: $Y = 3X_1 + 5X_2 + 4X_3$
e. Textbook publishing: $Y = cX_1^{1/3}X_2^{1/3}X_3^{1/4}$
f. School furniture: $Y = \sqrt{-aX_1^2 - bX_2^2 + cX_1X_2}$

Questions:

a. On the basis of this information, can you suggest the subsidiaries to which management should devote the relatively greatest increase in total resources in order to encourage future expansion? (HINT: This question involves a problem of returns to scale.)

b. What conditions, qualifications, and so forth, do you suggest adding to your answer in question (a)?

Problems on Homogeneous Functions and Euler's Theorem

Find the degree of the following homogeneous functions by multiplying each of the input variables by k.

18. $z = \dfrac{ax - by}{cx + dy}$

19. $z = \sqrt{ax^2 + 2hxy + by^2}$

20. $z = ax^2 + 2gxy + by^2$

21. $z = ax^b y^c$

22. $z = x^2 + 4xy + 3y^2$ (Verify Euler's theorem for this function.)

23. $v = 3x - 2y + 4z - u$ (Verify Euler's theorem for this function.)

24. A production function for a small farm was found to be given by the equation

$$z = f(a, b) = 3a^2 + 4ab + b^2$$

where z is total output, a is the amount of land employed, and b is the amount of labor used.

a. Determine whether this function is homogeneous.
b. Verify Euler's theorem for this function.
c. If the manager of the farm employs three units of land and five units of labor, what will be the total product?
[Assume $a = 3$, $b = 5$ in answering (d), (e), and (f) below.]
d. If labor is paid its marginal productivity, what is the wage rate?
e. What is the total payment to labor?
f. Assuming that land is the "residual claimant," what rent will the owner of the land receive?

25. In his labor theory of value, Karl Marx (1818–83) advanced the proposition that in a capitalist society, workers do not stop producing when the value of what they produce is equal to the value (i.e., wages) they receive. Instead, they continue to produce goods and services the value of which exceeds the value they receive. This excess becomes the capitalist's *surplus*. Workers, according to Marx, are thus exploited by capitalists, the latter thriving off the "sweat" of the former.

How might your knowledge of homogeneous functions and Euler's theorem be used to evaluate Marx's theory?

REFERENCES

BAUMOL, WILLIAM J. *Economic Theory and Operations Analysis*, chap. 11, "Production and Cost," pp. 250–69. Rev. ed. Englewood Cliffs, N.J.: Prentice-Hall, Inc., 1965.

FERGUSON, C. E., and **GOULD, J. P.**   *Microeconomics Theory,* chaps. 5 and 6. 4th ed., Homewood, Ill.: Richard D. Irwin, Inc., 1975.

——— *The Neoclassical Theory of Production and Distribution,* chap. 5. London and New York: Cambridge University Press, 1969.

HEADY, EARL O.   *Economics of Agricultural Production and Resource Use.* Englewood Cliffs, N.J.: Prentice-Hall, Inc., 1952.

LLOYD, PETER J.   "Elementary Geometric/Arithmetic Series and Early Production Theory." *Journal of Political Economy,* vol. 77, no. 1 (January–February 1969), pp. 21–34.

McELROY, F. W.   "Returns to Scale, Euler's Theorem, and the Form of Production Functions." *Econometrica,* vol. 37, no. 2 (April 1969), pp. 275–79.

MINASIAN, JORA R.   "Research and Development, Production Functions, and Rates of Return." *The American Economic Review,* vol. 59, no. 2 (May 1969), pp. 80–84.

TINTER, GERHARD   *Econometrics,* pp. 47–77. New York: John Wiley & Sons, Inc., 1952. Presents a brief sketch of some statistical cost studies and a brief sketch of statistical production functions, especially Douglas' work.

WALTERS, A. A.   "Production and Cost Functions: An Econometric Survey." *Econometrica,* vol. 31, no. 1–2 (January–April 1963), pp. 1–66.

WHITE, LAWRENCE J.   "A Note on the Influence of Monopoly on Product Innovation." *The Quarterly Journal of Economics,* vol. 86, no. 2 (May 1972), pp. 342–45.

chapter 8

Cost

"A graduate class in economic theory would be a success if the students gained from it an understanding of the meaning of cost in all its many aspects."

These words were written as long ago as 1923 by the noted economist J. M. Clark in his classic work, *Studies in the Economics of Overhead Costs*—a book which is undoubtedly one of the most important contributions to economic and business literature in the 20th century.

What prompted Professor Clark to make this statement is the fact that the study of cost is extraordinarily complex, embracing all kinds of accounting, financial, economic, engineering, and even legal implications. Accordingly, it is probably impossible to treat the subject with much justice within the limits of one or even a few chapters. Our approach, therefore, will be to cover certain topics in the study of costs— topics dealing with some important aspects of cost theory and measurement that are of interest for business decision making.

NATURE AND TYPES OF COST

The general idea of cost covers a wide variety of meanings, but there is one meaning that is common to all types of costs and is summed up in the single word "sacrifice." The nature of the sacrifice may be tangible or intangible, objective or subjective, and for this reason a chief difficulty for decision purposes is to represent costs by appropriate numbers that can be readily manipulated. It is common, therefore, but not always correct, to avoid such concepts as psychic costs or sacrifices in the form of mental dissatisfactions, social costs such as the smoke nuisance of a factory, and sometimes "real" costs, for example, sacrifices in purchasing power.

Actually, most of the controversy over the existence of various kinds of costs evaporates once it is realized that there are different kinds of problems for which cost information is needed, and that the particular information required varies from one problem to another. The fact that accountants, economists, and engineers are each concerned with the study of costs for different purposes explains why there is a large variety of ideas about costs, many of which are adapted to different purposes. The following classification of some common cost concepts will help fix certain basic ideas and relations.

Cost Concepts for Decision Making

A classification of important cost concepts for decision making should dispel immediately the notion that conventional accounting practice provides the firm with all its necessary cost information, and should drive home the fact that cost concepts differ depending on managerial uses and viewpoints. In practical work, the historical costs provided by accounting are often sufficient to fulfill certain legal and financial requirements, but for economic decision making where the problem is to predict costs under alternative courses of action, conventional accounting usually leaves much to be desired. As will be seen below, the most useful estimates are frequently those that are derived by combinations and adjustments in the data, evidencing the fact that in the well-managed firm the accounts are a source of basic information rather than an end in themselves.

1. Absolute Costs and Alternative Costs. One of the most fundamental distinctions between two general classes of ideas of costs is that between absolute or outlay costs and alternative or opportunity costs. *Absolute costs* involve an outlay of funds or, in fact, all reductions in assets such as wages paid, materials expense, rents, interest charges, and so on. *Alternative cost,* on the other hand, concerns the cost of foregone opportunities, or in other words a comparison between the policy that was chosen and the policy that was rejected.

For example, the cost of lending or using capital is the interest that it can earn in the next best use of equal risk. The alternative uses of capital measure the marginal cost of capital to a given borrowing or lending firm. If capital funds can earn 15 percent in their most productive employment, then that is their cost to the firm employing the funds. Similarly, assuming full capacity operations, the cost of a product in the product line is not merely the outlay on resources but also the profit that would have resulted from the best alternative product produced with the same facilities. Evidently, the basis of choice or decision where alternative costs are involved hinges on a comparison between what the firm is doing and what it could be doing, and it is the *difference* between those alternatives that constitutes the critical cost consideration.

A subdivision of opportunity or alternative cost is *imputed costs*. These never show up in the accounting records but are nevertheless important for certain types of decisions. Interest (never paid or received) on idle land, depreciation on fully depreciated property still in use, interest on equity capital, and rent on company-owned facilities are examples of imputed costs.

To illustrate, in evaluating the relative profitability of two warehouses owned by a company in order to decide whether to continue, discontinue, or lease them requires supplementary calculations of rent and interest on investment. In deciding how much to impute to each, the answer rests on the uses to which the space released could be put and the relative profitability of each use. Although precise calculations are rarely possible, the concept nevertheless provides for a correct way of thinking about such problems and a basis for establishing at least rough estimates for better decisions.

2. Direct and Indirect Costs. *Direct costs* are costs that are readily identified and visibly traceable to a particular product, class of products, operation, process, or plant. The concept may also be extended beyond the sphere of manufacturing costs; thus, overhead may be direct as to departments, and manufacturing costs are frequently direct as to product lines, sales territories, customer classes, and the like.

Indirect costs are costs that are not readily identified nor visibly traceable to specific goods, services, operations, and so forth, but are nevertheless charged to the product in standard accounting practice. The importance of the distinction between direct and indirect cost from an economic standpoint is that some indirect costs, even though not traceable to product, may nevertheless bear a functional relation to production and vary with output in some definite way. Examples of such costs are electric power, heat, light, and depreciation based on output.

Practically synonymous with indirect costs are common costs. *Common costs* are costs that are incurred for the general operations of the business and yield benefits to all products, for example, the president's salary. When the outputs involved are related to each other, common costs are also known as *joint costs*. Thus, the cost of crude petroleum is common to gasoline, kerosene, and so forth; the cost of raising cattle is common to the yield of beef and hides.

The significance of cost traceability becomes considerable when management must make decisions in such areas as product-line policy and pricing policy. Most industrial firms produce multiple products for which there are at least some common costs, but for which there may be substantial differences in production and marketing processes. Cost tracing all the way back to the individual product is not necessary and is not the basis for intelligent pricing policies in such firms. Instead it is sufficient for management to know the separate cost of classes of output and to price on the basis of typical conditions rather than accidental variations resulting from irregularities and imperfections in various resources and markets.

3. *Fixed Cost and Variable Cost.* Economists generally distinguish between two major categories of cost as fixed cost and variable cost. *Fixed costs,* or "constant" costs as they are sometimes called, are those costs that do not vary with (are not a function of) output. They are costs that require a fixed outlay of funds each period such as rent, property taxes and similar "franchise" payments, interest on bonds, and depreciation when measured as a function of time (without any relation to output).

It should be emphasized that the term "fixed" refers to those costs that are fixed *in total* with respect to volume, for they may still be a function of capacity and hence vary with plant size. In other words, fixed costs are not fixed in the sense that they do not vary; they may vary and frequently do, but from causes that are independent of volume.[1]

A term synonymous with fixed cost, at least to the economist, is *overhead cost.* To the cost accountant, however, the meaning of this term is virtually the same as indirect cost. Overhead, in accounting literature, usually is composed of some fixed costs and some costs that are variable in nature. The distinction is unfortunate and can lead to misinterpretations in technical discussions if care is not taken in defining terms.

Variable costs are those costs that are a function of output in the production period. Unlike fixed costs the resource services of which are given off in a constant flow irrespective of the output quantity, variable costs emanate from the stock services that are transformed or "used up" as output is produced. Variable costs vary directly, sometimes proportionately, with output. Over certain ranges of production they may vary less or more than proportionately with output depending on the utilization of fixed facilities and resources. The sum of these two categories of cost, total fixed cost and total variable cost, at any given output level, yields the total cost at that output level, that is, $TFC + TVC = TC$. When derived for successive levels of output, the resulting TC series thus represents a functional relationship between total cost and output. Examples of variable cost include materials utilized, power, direct labor, factory supplies, salesmen's commissions, and depreciation on a production (rather than time) basis.

---

[1] It follows of course that since fixed costs are constant in total, they will vary *per unit* with the rate of output, continuously decreasing as output increases within the production period.

Since total variable costs comprise the only changing portion of total cost in the above equation, any change in the aggregate will be equal to the change in total variable cost. These changes, due to changes in output, are called *marginal costs*. That is, marginal cost is the change in total cost (equals the change in total variable cost) resulting from a unit change in output. In economic theory, marginal cost is important for decisions involving the company's allocation of resources and in product pricing, and it has other practical implications as well. At the present time it is sufficient to note that the concept of marginal cost should not be confused with the notion of differential or incremental cost discussed below.

In economic and accounting theory it is often assumed that variable costs are continuous functions of output when, in reality, some costs that remain fixed over considerable ranges of production increase by jumps, discontinuously, at various levels of output. Costs that exhibit this tendency have been classified as *semivariable* (*semifixed*) *costs*. They consist of a fixed and a variable portion, such as telephone expense, foremen's wages, and certain other expense elements which may remain constant for a wide range of production but then increase by definite jumps as output expands beyond certain levels.

4. Short-Run and Long-Run Costs. The above distinction between fixed and variable costs bears a close tie-in with another kind of cost dimension used by economists, short-run costs and long-run costs.

Short-run costs are costs that can vary with the degree of utilization of plant and other fixed factors, that is, vary with output, but not with plant capacity. The short run is thus a period in which fixed costs remain unchanged but variable costs can fluctuate with output; accordingly, it is a period in which a flow of output emerges from a fixed stock of resources.

Long-run costs, in contrast, are costs that can vary with the size of plant and with other facilities normally regarded as fixed in the short run. The latter is an interval of time in which plant, equipment, labor force, and so forth, can be expanded or contracted to meet demand requirements. It is thus a period in which the firm's output emanates from a variable stock of resources and, therefore, a period in which there are no fixed costs, that is, all costs are variable. These concepts are discussed further in later sections, where it is shown how distinctions between fixed and variable costs and between short- and long-run costs are useful for predicting the effect of temporary and permanent output decisions on costs, prices, and profits.

5. Incremental Costs and Sunk Costs. When a decision has to be made involving a change in the volume of business, the difference in cost between the two policies may be considered to be the cost really incurred due to the change in business activity. This change in cost is the *incremental cost* (or *differential cost*) of a given amount of business. It represents the change in costs resulting from a change in business activity, where the latter may include any type of change such as the introduction of new machinery, development of a new product, or expansion into different markets. In estimating costs for this purpose, it is necessary to include any interest charge that is actually incurred in the one case and could be avoided in the other case. Thus, cost in this sense depends as much on one of the proposed alternative policies as it does on the other. The cost of remaining in business and producing a product is one thing if the alternative is to go out of business entirely, or it may be another if the alternative is to keep a skeleton force on hand even if the plant is not running at all.

The concept of incremental cost forces recognition of the fact that expenses vary according to different dimensions of the business. For example, a trucking company, in considering the taking on of new business, may be confronted with the two alternatives of utilizing (1) more trucks per day, or (2) more payload per truck. The choice of either alternative will result in separate incremental costs, and the most economical policy would be to maintain a balance between the two, using each to the point beyond which the other would be cheaper, that is, where the incremental costs are equal. And in many agricultural processing operations, for example, meat-packing, sugar refining, and so forth, the incremental cost of processing the main products is not the same as the separate incremental costs of the various by-products nor of their sum.

Evidently, certain costs will not be altered as a result of a decision that will change business activity. Such costs that are not assignable by the differential method are called *sunk costs*, and hence are irrelevant as far as the future effects of the decision are concerned. Since incremental cost includes interest on investment, that is, the interest on additional capital that may be required because of the added business, sunk cost would include interest on the entire investment to the extent that it is not traceable differentially to some part of the product. It should be noted, however, that incremental costs need not be variable with output, nor traceable to a product, nor absolute (cash outlay) costs. They may in some situations be placed in the same family with opportunity or alternative costs so that the incremental cost becomes the foregone opportunity of using limited resources in their present activity as compared to their most profitable alternative activity.

6. Shutdown and Abandonment Costs. *Shutdown costs* may be defined as those costs that would be incurred in the event of a temporary cessation of activities and which could be saved if operations were allowed to continue. The concept is important because of a widely recognized economic principle that so long as a firm is at least covering its variable costs, it will not cease operations in the short run because any excess will be applied to the recovery of its fixed costs.

This principle, though broadly correct, contains certain ramifications. In reality, to suspend operations temporarily involves certain costs that must be considered, such as the compounding and storing of machines, the boarding of windows, and the construction of shelters for exposed property. These are classes of expenses which must also be reckoned as shutdown costs. Further, additional expenses are incurred when operations are resumed, including the cost of recruiting and training new workers, of reopening plant facilities, of restarting processing equipment, and so forth. In essence, therefore, the point to be emphasized is that in the long run there may be less of a loss if management keeps a few products before consumers, even if revenues fail to cover variable cost, than to close temporarily if shutdown costs (including the costs of reestablishing marketing contacts when business is resumed) are expected to be unduly high.

Unlike shutdown costs which are incurred because of a temporary suspension of activities, *abandonment costs* are the costs of retiring a fixed asset from service. The situation may arise, for example, in the abandonment of an obsolete plant or part thereof not useful in modern production, of an exhausted mine or oil well, or of bus facilities upon the institution of mass transit. Abandonment thus involves a permanent cessation of activities and creates a problem as to the disposal of assets. Briefly, the correct accounting procedure in such instances is to consider implicit interest on the current market value of the facilities and to depreciate on the basis of sales value. Depreciation based on original cost is manifestly irrelevant for this type of management decision. (Why?)

7. Urgent and Postponable Costs. Those costs that must be incurred in order to produce a finished product are classified as *urgent costs*. Examples include the outlays on materials and the expenses of labor in working them up. Costs that may be put off, at least within limits, on the other hand, are called *postponable costs* and include such expenses as maintenance of buildings and machinery.

This distinction is important because, in a certain sense, postponable costs cannot really be postponed. Physical deterioration and obsolescence will reduce the value of a plant whether maintenance is provided for or not. Hence, it is not the cost that is actually postponable but rather the rate at which it is provided for. Railroads have made fairly common use of the urgent-postponable cost distinction, incurring expenditures for maintenance in periods of low activity in order to repair and maintain equipment that was worn down in periods when activity was high. In the modern firm, however, the postponing of such costs is decided automatically by recording a regular accrual of depreciation irrespective of whether expenses in a particular period have been large or small. This serves to minimize, though not necessarily eliminate, the postponable outlays, thereby stabilizing costs and, from a social standpoint, reducing cyclical unemployment and fluctuations in purchasing power. The problem has become less serious over the years, as accountants have increasingly accepted the practice of recording an expense before the cost is actually incurred. Management, however, still tends to look upon the postponability of expenses as a lifesaver by allowing for retrenchment when times are hard.

8. Escapable and Inescapable Costs. A cost that may not only be postponed but may be avoided entirely as a result of a contraction of business activity is called an *escapable cost*. It is important to note that such cost is conceived as a *net* figure: the decrease in cost by curtailing or terminating an activity, less any added cost incurred by other operating units as a result thereof. For example, the escapable costs by eliminating a middleman may turn out to be less than originally anticipated if the same functions must be assumed by the selling firm which is less equipped to handle it. Similarly, railroads, for instance, sometimes find it cheaper to retain or perhaps reduce operations on a seemingly unprofitable line than to incure the costs of eliminating it entirely.

An *inescapable cost* (or "unavoidable" cost) is a cost that must be continued in the face of a business retraction. Airlines, for example, must incur certain periodic maintenance expenses irrespective of the volume of business. Manufacturing plants must incur prescribed minimum power costs regardless of the level of sales. Some costs, however, though unavoidable, are nevertheless postponable, as is the case with many types of fixed assets, and frequently costs that appear to be avoided are really only postponed. (Can you give examples?)

Occasionally the escapable-inescapable grouping is employed in place of the more usual fixed-variable classification by some accountants and business executives. From an economic standpoint, before the enterprise is started and resources are committed, all costs may be viewed as escapable and all expected costs as variable. (Why?)

9. Controllable and Uncontrollable Costs. This classification of costs is useful mainly as a means for fixing responsibility and measuring efficiency. The distinction may not be too meaningful over the long run, for over the life of the enterprise as a whole all costs are controllable, at least in the sense that they are someone's responsibility. The ability to control costs, however, should not be confused with the ability to reduce costs. Over the long run, not all costs are either equally controllable (e.g., property taxes as compared to materials prices) nor equally reducible (e.g., skilled union labor as compared to institutional advertising).

10. Replacement Cost and Original Cost. In establishing costs so as to determine income, an asset is conventionally valued on the books at its original or historical cost, or at the cost of replacing it in the current market. Many accountants and economists have advocated the latter procedure so that with regard to inventories, the profit figure in the event of substantial price-level changes will represent a more realistic situation, as well as improve the results of cost projections as a basis for management decisions.

When substantial changes occur in the general price level, the firm still has the alternatives of (1) using its materials to produce and sell a finished product, or (2) disposing of the materials at current prices. The sacrifice is thus measured by the market price of the materials and not by their original cost. The difference between the two, assuming that the price has fallen, is a loss due to holding goods during the period, and this loss should not be charged as a cost of making the materials into finished goods.

Thus, more than one firm has been known to lose contract bids because it figured price on the basis of original cost of materials after the market price had dropped significantly. Management refused to make bids low enough to secure orders because the lower price would not cover certain costs incurred in the past. Actually, the determining criterion should be based on *what the costs will be at the time the order is filled, compared to what they will be at that time if the order is not taken.* It may be easier to charge materials at their original cost, but it is more accurate to charge them at the market price prevailing at the time they are used, thereby separating gains and losses arising from production from gains and losses due to changes in the value of materials in stock. Original costs are bygones and should be reexamined in the light of present market values if it appears likely that such reexamination would give rise to a different decision with respect to pricing. (Note that this discussion is using replacement cost in the last-in, first-out sense.)

Conclusion

The foregoing classification of cost concepts reveals various distinctions from both the economic and accounting standpoints.

> This being the case, the thing to do is to cease trying to make one concept do the work of several. After all, the obligations a corporation must meet before dividends are paid are one thing, and the whole financial outgo or sacrifice attributable to the act of producing certain goods is another thing, and a conservative stand for valuing unsold goods is still a different thing. Undoubtedly the ultimate solution lies in the development of systems of cost analysis which shall be separate from the formal books of account, though based on the same data.[2]

There thus cannot be found any single meaning for "cost of production" that would be universally applicable in all situations. At best,

[2] J. M. Clark, *Studies in the Economics of Overhead Costs* (Chicago: University of Chicago Press, 1923).

the analyst can only attempt to translate the many current usages into consistent language in order to be certain that the given concept is being used for its proper purpose.

INCREMENTAL COST IN DECISION MAKING

For many practical decision problems, the terms *marginal cost, incremental cost,* and *differential cost* may be used synonymously. That is, the underlying concept common to all three terms is the notion of a *change in the level of total costs resulting from the implementation of a decision.* The decision may frequently involve a change in production, but just as frequently it may not. Thus it may be a decision involving the flotation of a new security issue, the closing down of a department, the installation of a data processing system, the launching of a new advertising campaign, or any other type of activity which is not directly reflected by a change in production but for which there is nevertheless a change in the level of total cost. The increase (or decrease) in cost which results from the change in activity, and which would have been avoided if the decision had not been made, is the incremental cost of the activity.

How are incremental costs employed in decision making? According to the above explanation, it is evident that the prospective *differences* between alternatives are the relevant factors to be considered in making a choice. In any going business all past receipts and expenses as well as many future ones will be unaffected by a particular choice. Likewise, average or unit costs are frequently irrelevant and should not enter into many types of decisions. Business executives who fail to understand these notions and apply them correctly will always make incorrect decisions.

Illustrative Examples

Perhaps the best way of learning to use incremental cost analysis in decision making is to study some concrete examples. In the following illustrative cases, keep in mind that it is the *difference between alternatives* that provides the basis for making the correct choice.

Example 1. Cost of an Automobile Trip

PROBLEM: Fred, a college student, wants to drive home for Christmas recess in his own car. The driving distance from the college to his hometown is 250 miles. He figures that he can't afford to make the trip unless he takes other students along to share the driving cost. In order to decide how much to charge the other riders, he compiles the following total cost data from which he estimates his cost per mile as shown in Exhibit 1.

On the basis of these calculations, Fred concludes that the cost of the

EXHIBIT 1
Estimated Annual Cost of Automobile
(assuming 10,000 miles of driving per year)

1.	Depreciation this year	$ 800
2.	Interest on investment in car (at 10%)	400
3.	License fees and taxes	50
4.	Parking fees (at $10 per month)	120
5.	Insurance	400
6.	Gasoline (10,000 miles at 3¢ per mile)	300
7.	Oil and grease	30
8.	Tires (replaced every 20,000 miles for $160)	80
9.	Repairs and maintenance	120
	Total annual cost:	$2,300

$$\text{Cost per mile:} \quad \frac{\text{Total annual cost}}{\text{Annual mileage}} = \frac{\$2,300}{10,000} = 23¢ \text{ per mile}$$

Therefore, total cost of 500-mile round trip is $500 \times 23¢ = \$115$.

---

trip, namely $115, can be shared equally among himself and his riders. He therefore offers to take four riders at a charge of $23 each for the round trip.

Assuming that the figures in the tables are reasonably accurate, is Fred's reasoning about the cost of the trip correct?

SOLUTION: Ask yourself, What is Fred's objective? According to the problem, it appears that he merely wants to cover the cost of the trip on an equal-share basis. Therefore, he has two alternatives:

ALTERNATIVE A: Make the trip, and charge each rider (including himself) enough to cover the cost.

ALTERNATIVE B: Don't make the trip if the cost can't be covered.

In comparing these alternatives, the only relevant costs are those that will be incurred if the trip is taken, and avoided if it is not. These increased costs are the *incremental costs* which must be identified. They are estimated as follows, based on the data in Exhibit 1.

Incremental costs of 500-mile trip:

Gasoline (3¢ per mile)	$15.00
Oil and grease $\left(\dfrac{\$30}{10,000 \text{ mi.}} = .3¢ \text{ per mile} \right)$	1.50
Tires $\left(\dfrac{\$80}{10,000 \text{ mi.}} = .8¢ \text{ per mile} \right)$	4.00
Repairs and maintenance $\left(\dfrac{\$120}{10,000 \text{ mi.}} = 1.2¢ \text{ per mile} \right)$	6.00
Total incremental cost	$26.50

An increase of 500 miles in driving will thus increase Fred's total cost by $26.50, not $115 as he originally assumed. The unit incremental cost is 26.50/500 mi. = 5.3 cents per mile, as compared to his original estimated cost of 23 cents per mile. The difference, of course, reflects the fact that his original estimate is based on all (fully allocated) costs, whereas the incremental estimate is based only on the added costs of the trip. In any case, by charging a price per rider high enough to cover his original estimate of $115, he might not get any customers and thus end up not making the trip, all because of his failure to realize that in any decision-making problem *it is better to have a rough estimate of the right concept than an accurate estimate of the wrong one.* (NOTE: It might be argued that for this particular trip, the only realistic incremental cost would be the cost of the gasoline. However, this is at best a very short-run view. If he were to make a number of special trips like this one, he would obviously have to include the other incremental cost items since they would have a significant long-run effect on the cost of these trips.)

Example 2. Cost of Household Electricity

PROBLEM: Assume that you received the monthly bill shown in Exhibit 2 from your electric company, based on 1200 kilowatt-hours of electricity consumed in your home last month.

EXHIBIT 2
Your Friendly Electric Company
Monthly billing for *1200* kwh. of electricity

Basic service charge.	$ 1.00
First 40 kwh. at 10¢ per kwh..	4.00
Next 60 kwh. at 8¢ per kwh.	4.80
All over 100 kwh. at 3¢ per kwh..	33.00
Subtotal	$42.80
Fuel adjustment.	10.00
Total due	$52.80

Suppose that this is fairly typical of your recent monthly electric bills, and you feel that these bills are too high. Someone therefore suggests that you economize by cutting down if not eliminating the use of certain lights or electrical appliances.

Can you evaluate this suggestion?

SOLUTION: The bill of $52.80 amounts to an average or "total unit cost" of $52.80/1200 kwh. = 4.4 cents per kilowatt-hour. However, unless the monthly consumption of electricity is reduced by more than 1100 kilowatt-hours, the unit saving will be only 3.8 cents per unit (which includes a proportionate reduction of the fuel adjustment surcharge of $10.00/1200 kwh. = $.008 per kilowatt-hour). As a concrete example, a reduction in electricity consumption of 400 kilowatt-hours (33⅓ percent) would reduce the monthly bill by $15.20 (only 28.8 percent). The average or "total unit cost" is thus irrelevant for any decision involving the reduction in use of an electrical appliance or lights; likewise, it is also irrelevant for any decision involving a proposed increase in load.

Example 3. Incremental Cost versus Sunk Cost

Problem: A few years ago, several young doctors, while still serving their internships, pooled their limited funds to make a down payment on a desirable lot in an expanding suburb of a large midwestern city. It was their ultimate intention to construct a medical professional building on the lot, and to locate their offices in the building so that they could function in group practice.

The purchase price of the lot was $9,000. The doctors made a down payment of $1,000 and monthly payments including taxes and interest of $100. Under the terms of the contract, they would not secure legal title to the lot until it was completely paid up; however, they could choose to pay off the unpaid balance at any time in a lump-sum amount if they wished, and thereby secure legal title immediately. The contract further stipulated that in the event of default on any monthly payment, they would lose their entire equity.

Several years later, after the doctors were reasonably well established, they decided that they were ready to contract with a builder for the construction of a building. At that time the unpaid balance on the lot was $5,000. The doctors had the cash available and were prepared to pay it in order to take title to the lot. However, land prices in the area had become depressed, and the owner of an adjacent lot who was in financial difficulties offered to sell his lot for $4,000 cash. As far as the doctors were concerned, this second lot was as satisfactory as the first in all respects. Nevertheless, they decided to go ahead as originally planned; that is, they paid the $5,000 due on the first lot and acquired title to it in accordance with the contract. When asked why they chose this lot rather than the other, they answered, "Because we didn't want to lose the $3,000 that we had already put into it."

Evaluate their decision.

Solution: The doctors failed to recognize that it is the *difference* between alternatives that is relevant to their decision. Whatever has happened before the moment of decision is history and cannot affect their choice among alternatives for the future.

Thus, the doctors were confronted with two clear-cut possibilities:

a.   Pay the $5,000 balance and acquire legal title to the lot.
b.   Pay $4,000 and acquire legal title to a lot which they agreed was equally satisfactory in all respects.

They chose the first alternative, whereas they should have chosen the second and saved themselves $1,000 immediately. In other words, they should have defaulted on the original agreement, but they didn't do so because they had paid out $3,000 (including interest and taxes) over the past several years, and this amount would appear to be "lost" by breaking the contract. They thus deluded themselves into thinking that to default on the contract would be to acknowledge a past error of judgment which would not be acknowledged by selecting the first alternative.

To summarize, the fundamental principle involved in this problem is that the $3,000 has already been spent regardless of which alternative is selected for the future. Hence the $3,000 is a *sunk cost* or past outlay, and is irrelevant as a basis for choosing between these two alternatives.

THEORY OF COST: COST–OUTPUT FUNCTIONS

If any practical use is to be made of cost-output relationships, it is necessary to know the nature of these relationships. The following treatment, though far short of being exhaustive, provides a brief sketch of the essential nature of cost-output functions under both short- and long-run conditions. In both cases the relevant cost concepts involved are the ones commonly employed by economists, namely the fixed-variable classification and the subdivision of marginal costs. These costs apply even in the most simple production processes and are the ones that are derived by econometricians and engineers when they construct cost curves from actual company data.

Some Assumptions and Definitions

In production economics, the short run is defined as a period of time long enough for the firm to vary output by altering some, but not all, of the firm's input factors. Inherent in the notion of short run, therefore, is the idea of temporarily fixed resource commitments whose expense the firm incurs regardless of level of output. What constitutes the short run for a given firm is usually dependent upon a wide spectrum of factors including, but not limited to, the intensity of capital versus labor necessitated for the product or industry involved, flexibility of the financial structure of the company, and, of course, the duration of contractual agreements between the firm and its suppliers. As such, two seemingly identical firms may in reality have very different time frames constituting their short-run situations, making it virtually impossible to say, a priori, what is *the* short-run period for a given firm in a given industry.

The *long run* refers to the cost structure of a firm over a period of time long enough so that no factors need be considered as fixed, or in other words a period of time long enough so that all of the firm's costs are variable. In the following paragraphs *short-run* costs are discussed first, including their more important ramifications; the nature of long-run costs is then outlined so as to unify the logic into a consistent body of doctrine.

The level of the various cost curves—fixed, variable, total, and marginal—will be affected by factor prices. If these are constant, the exact nature (curvature) of the curves will depend on the nature of the underlying production function. The fundamental starting point in the development of cost theory is that a unique functional relationship exists between cost and the rate of output for a firm. Admittedly, there may be independent variables other than output that will affect cost (e.g., lot size, plant utilization, etc.), but these are assumed to remain constant in constructing the cost curves. The curves thus derived are static in nature, meaning that they show only the various costs that will prevail under alternative output levels, all other things being equal.

Short-Run Costs

Exhibit 3 illustrates three kinds of short-run total cost curves under conditions of constant, decreasing, and increasing productivity. Thus,

EXHIBIT 3
Three Kinds of Short-Run Total Cost Functions

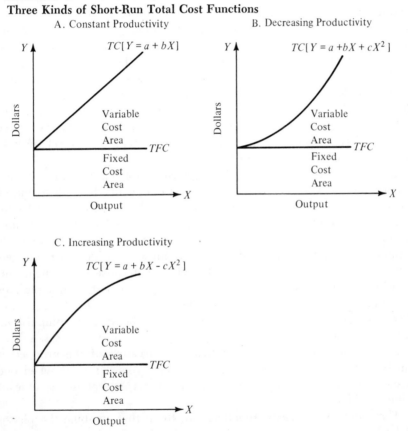

A. Constant Productivity

$TC[Y = a + bX]$

B. Decreasing Productivity

$TC[Y = a + bX + cX^2]$

C. Increasing Productivity

$TC[Y = a + bX - cX^2]$

even if the prices of the inputs remain constant as the firm purchases more of them in order to expand its production, the cost curves can still take the shapes shown in Exhibit 3 due to the nature of the under-lying production function.

Thus, in chart A of Exhibit 3, the *TC* curve is linear. Assuming a constant price per unit of variable input purchased, each unit of input adds the same amount to total output and hence to total cost. This type of linear cost function exists over a range of output when, assuming constant input prices and technology, the fixed factors are readily divisible so that the fixed and variable resources can be mixed at minimum-cost proportions for each output level. At zero output, fixed cost (cash rent, property taxes, insurance, and depreciation as a function of time and obsolescence) equals total cost, while at higher output levels the difference is represented by variable costs. The total cost curve, it may be noted, would turn sharply upward for output levels beyond the physical capacity of the equipment.

Chart B shows a parabolic total cost function where the underlying production function or factor-product relationship is one of diminishing marginal productivity throughout the entire range of output. The reason for this is that even if each unit of the variable factor costs as much as any previous unit, each additional unit of the input adds less to total output than the previous unit. (The elasticity of the production function is less than 1 throughout.) This illustration of diminishing returns throughout the entire output range occurs when the fixed factor is limited and not divisible. The shape or curvature of the *TC* curve is due solely to the technical nature of the input-output relationship and not to market conditions or factor prices.

Chart C shows a parabolic total cost curve for a production process under conditions of increasing returns throughout the entire output range. This means that each unit of output adds less to total cost than the previous unit, and this in turn is due to the fact that each unit of input in the underlying production function (whose elasticity is greater than 1 throughout) adds more to output than does the previous unit of input. Actually, the possibility of an enterprise experiencing increasing returns for all output levels is unlikely; at best, it may perhaps be found at the lower levels of production where the fixed factors are excessive relative to the variable, and before the stage of diminishing productivity sets in.

Incidentially, it may be noted that the curvature of the production function and the total cost curve is always reversed in that when one is concave, the other is convex, and vice versa, except in the case of a linear relationship.

The most common cost functions are those that combine the phases of both increasing and decreasing returns. Most cost functions that appear to be of a constant or increasing returns nature are more likely to be only segments of curves; and if they could be extrapolated, they would eventually exhibit a phase of decreasing returns. Exhibit 4 illustrates this generalized type of cost function with increasing returns resulting at all levels of output to the left of the vertical dashed line (because total cost rises at a decreasing rate) and decreasing returns to the right of the dashed line (because total cost is rising at an increas-

EXHIBIT 4
Generalized Short-Run Total Cost Function

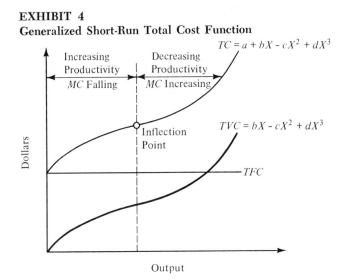

ing rate). The curve as shown is a cubic function of the type commonly encountered in economics textbooks and is based on the classic production function of increasing-decreasing returns. It is thus the most widespread kind of total cost function in economic theory, although quadratic and linear types have more often been used in empirical studies.

To improve comprehension of a firm's cost structure as well as serve as a better basis for various kinds of decision problems confronting management, the average and marginal cost curves are necessary. For most purposes these include average total cost, ATC, average variable cost, AVC, and marginal cost, MC. All of these can be derived from the total cost data. Thus, if Q represents output, then $ATC = TC/Q$; $AVC = TVC/Q$; $MC = \Delta TC/\Delta Q$. Numerous other methods can be employed in deriving these curves from given output and total cost data, since $TC = TFC + TVC$ is the basic relationship and the quantities can be algebraically transposed as desired.

In Exhibit 5, the ATC, AVC, and MC curves corresponding to the generalized total cost curve of Exhibit 4 are presented. Note that the MC curve passes through the minimum ATC (at Q_3) and AVC (at Q_2) in accordance with the rule of the "average-marginal relationship." (Can you explain?) Other than this, the various curve relationships should already be familiar to you from your elementary economics and hence require no further discussion at this time. The only point that need be mentioned is to stress again that the shape (curvature) of the average and marginal curves is conditioned by the technical nature of the underlying production function and not by factor prices. A change in the latter will shift the curves up or down but will not affect the slopes as such, or the spatial relationships among the three curves.

EXHIBIT 5
Generalized Short-Run Average and Marginal Cost Functions

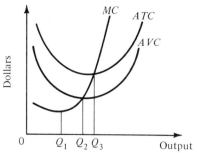

In summary, we have for output level Q the information shown in Exhibit 6.

EXHIBIT 6
Relationships of Short-Run Cost Curves

Cost Curve	Abbrevi-ation	Formula	Curve Reaches Minimum Value at*—	Comments
Total fixed costs	TFC	None	Not applicable	Costs not traceable to variations in output level
Total variable costs	TVC	Many algebraic forms possible (see text)	0	Costs which directly vary with output level
Total costs	TC	$= TVC + TFC$	0	Total of fixed plus variable costs
Average total costs	ATC	$= TC/Q$	Q_3	At Q_3; $MC = ATC$
Average variable costs	AVC	$= TVC/Q$	Q_2	May coincide with ATC if TFC = 0; at Q_2, $MC = AVC$
Marginal cost	MC	$= \Delta TC/\Delta Q$ or $\Delta TVC/\Delta Q$	Q_1	If cost function known, $MC = d(TC)/dQ$

* See Exhibit 5.

Long-Run Costs

The analysis of short-run costs reveals how a firm's costs will vary in response to output changes within the limits of a time period short enough so that the size of the plant may be regarded as fixed. By extending the logic one step further, it is possible to develop a *long-run cost curve* or function which, correspondingly, is one that shows the variation of cost with output for a period long enough so that all productive factors, including plant and equipment, are freely variable in amount.

The knowledge of such a long-run cost curve, or "planning curve" as it is also called, can be of use to management in determining output rates over periods long enough so that assets acquired for use during the period can be fully amortized, and in establishing rational policies as to optimum plant size, location, and general operational standards.

Because of the flexibility afforded management in the long run, the cost structure associated with it is determined in an entirely different way than for the short run. In particular, in the long run, management is now free to think in terms of what output level it would like to produce, rather than the output level it finds itself constrained to produce. For each possible output level in the long run, it is assumed that there is "least-cost" combination of input factors which can produce it. This least-cost combination of input factors will usually include such things as raw materials and labor which may be short-term purchases, but also investment in plant, equipment, and so forth, that is, long-term acquisitions. Also, because of this mixture of short- and long-term productive factors, there is, in addition, a short-term "flexibility schedule" or short-run average (total) cost curve, indicating a range of costs for producing neighboring output levels once the firm has made its commitment to certain kinds of plants, technology, and so forth. These ideas are graphically represented in Exhibit 7, in which the short-run cost curves asociated with five arbitrary output levels, Q_1, Q_2, Q_3, Q_4, and Q_5 for the given firm have been depicted. The construction of the long-run average cost curve (LAC), and some of the more salient relationships between the LAC and SAC curves, may be summarized as follows:

1. There will exist a different short-run average cost curve, SAC, for each possible plant size or for each technique of production (production function). There is thus an entire family of short-run cost curves, each corresponding to a particular point on the long-run average cost curve. That is, although only five SAC curves are shown, infinitely more

EXHIBIT 7
Short- and Long-Run Average Cost Functions

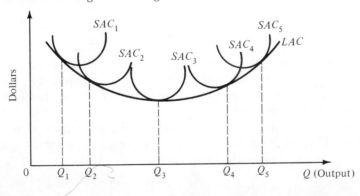

could be drawn, depending on the divisibility of productive units and their technical nature.

2. The *LAC* curve generalizes the entire family of *SAC* curves by enveloping them together. The U shape of the long-run curve implies at first lower and lower average costs until the "optimum" scale of plant shown by SAC_3 is reached, and thereafter successively higher average costs with larger plants.

3. The *LAC* curve is tangent to only one point on each *SAC* curve. The tangency point occurs: (*a*) to the left of the minimum-cost point on all short-run curves that are to the left of the optimum curve SAC_3, and (*b*) to the right of the minimum-cost point on all short-run curves that are to the right of the optimum curve. For the optimum curve, however, the tangency occurs at the minimum point on that curve, that is, at the lowest point on SAC_3. Therefore, for outputs less than Q_3 for which the optimum scale is SAC_3, it is more economical to "underuse" a slightly larger plant operating at less than its minimum-cost output than to "overuse" a smaller plant. For example, it would be cheaper to produce output Q_2 with a plant designated by SAC_2 than with one represented by SAC_1 Conversely, at outputs beyond the optimum level Q_3, it is more economical to "overuse" a slightly smaller plant than to "underuse" a slightly larger one. Thus, it is cheaper to produce Q_4 units with plant SAC_4 than with SAC_5.

4. Finally, the tendency for long-run average costs to fall as the firm expands its scale of operations is a reflection of cost economies that are frequently encountered with increasing size, while the ultimate rise in the long-run curve is due largely to the eventual generation of diseconomies of large-scale management. The latter is illustrated by the principle (or perhaps "proverb") that as the firm becomes larger and decision making more complex, the burden of administration becomes disproportionately greater and "diminishing returns" to management set in. (NOTE: Would this be true of well-managed firms like General Motors or Procter and Gamble? That is, do all firms seeking expansion face eventual "diminishing returns" to management? Of what significance is technology, organizational structure, managerial ability, and so forth?)

Elasticity of Total Cost

Since the economic theory of cost deals with relationships between cost and output, can we measure responsiveness or sensitivity between these variables? The answer to this question, of course, involves the familiar concept of elasticity.

The elasticity of total cost, e_c, measures the percentage change in total cost, *TC*, resulting from a slight percentage change in output, *X*. Thus, at any point along the total cost curve:

$$e_c = \frac{\dfrac{\Delta TC}{TC}}{\dfrac{\Delta X}{X}} = \frac{X \Delta TC}{TC \Delta X}$$

Keeping in mind that marginal cost, MC, is $MC = \Delta TC/\Delta X$, and average total cost, ATC, is $ATC = TC/X$, we can manipulate the terms in the above formula and rewrite it as

$$e_c = \frac{\dfrac{\Delta TC}{\Delta X}}{\dfrac{TC}{X}} = \frac{MC}{ATC}$$

In this form it is apparent that the elasticity of total cost is the *ratio of marginal cost to average total cost*. The range of e_c will thus depend on the values of MC and ATC, or whether MC lies below, intersects, or lies above ATC as shown in Exhibit 8.

EXHIBIT 8
Cost Curves and the Elasticity of Total Cost

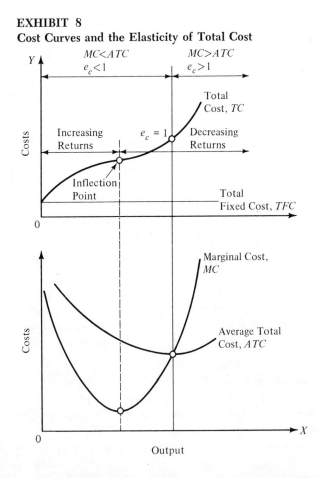

NOTE: In Exhibit 8, if $e_c = 1$ at all levels of output, the *MC* curve would be a horizontal line and would coincide with the *ATC* curve; the *TC* curve would be a straight line emanating from the origin and running upward to the right. (Can you explain why?)

If the total cost curve is linear, or if it is nearly linear within the range desired, the arc elasticity of total cost, E_c, can be estimated with the formula

$$E_c = \frac{\dfrac{TC_2 - TC_1}{TC_2 + TC_1}}{\dfrac{X_2 - X_1}{X_2 + X_1}}$$

where (X_1, TC_1) and (X_2, TC_2) are the coordinates of the two points on the total cost curve which determines the segment being measured. This formula gives a measure of the average elasticity for that segment.

Conclusion

The above discussion of cost theory could only touch upon some of the barest essentials. Nevertheless, these theoretical principles are the framework for conducting statistical cost analyses. It should be borne in mind that cost-output relations are *anticipated* relations drawn, frequently, from past experience. As such, they are subject to uncertainty and it can only be hoped that their measurement will be of some aid in reducing the degree of uncertainty inherent in a decision problem. Where the uncertainty is great, management's knowledge of strategic costs may at best be sketchy, but some measure of important relationships is better than none at all. It is on this basis that statistical cost functions are estimated.

ANALYTICAL FRAMEWORK FOR COST MEASUREMENT

In this section we are concerned with the conceptual problems of constructing empirical cost functions or, in other words, the methodological problems of measuring the actual cost-output relation for a particular firm or group of firms. Several methods exist by which an analysis of costs can be undertaken, but three of these, embracing accounting, engineering, and econometric approaches, are the most common.

Accounting Method. Essentially, the method used by cost accountants is to classify the data into various cost categories (e.g., fixed, variable, semivariable) and then to take observations at the extreme and various intermediate output levels. In this manner linear or curvilinear cost functions are estimated and built up from the basic data, with little or no attention normally paid to formulating hypotheses or accounting for changes in factor prices or other conditions that may have affected costs.

Engineering Method. In the engineering approach, emphasis is placed primarily on the nature of physical relationships such as pounds of supplies and materials used, rated capacity, and so forth, and these relationships are then converted into dollars to arrive at an estimate of costs. The method may be particularly useful when good historical data are difficult to obtain and the analysis may therefore require a relatively greater utilization of engineering rather than economic theory.

Econometric Method. The econometric or statistical approach uses statistical analysis, combined with economic theory, to measure the net effect of output variations on cost. Frequently, the goal is to construct a cost function from historical or cross-sectional data that will reflect as closely as possible the static cost curve of economic theory. However, since the empirical curve is at best only an average of past relationships, it is not an exact replica of the theoretical cost curves discussed in economics textbooks.

These three approaches to cost measurement should not be regarded as mutually exclusive or even competitive, but rather as supplementary and complementary to one another. As always, the emphasis placed on any method depends on the purpose of the investigation, that is, what it is that management really needs and wants, and the time and expense considerations as well as the availability of data.

Objectives and Problems of Cost Measurement

Certain measurement problems concerning various adjustments in the data and other considerations must be taken into account when attempting to derive empirical functions from economic data. As in the measurement of demand and production, so too in the measurement of cost, there are problem areas of a methodological nature to be considered. Some of the more essential ones may be sketched briefly at this time.

Basically, the problem is to derive a cost function, expressed mathematically as an equation or geometrically as a curve, that will show the net relationship between the firm's costs and its rate of output. If the shape of the cost curve depended solely on the rate of output, solving the problem would be fairly simple. Unfortunately, costs depend on a number of factors in addition to output, so the problem resolves itself into eliminating these other cost determinants in order to arrive at a cost function that reasonably expresses the cost-output relation. Generally speaking, the following problem areas are among the important preliminary ones that must be handled in preparing the empirical analysis.

1. Time Period

The choice of an appropriate time period on which to base the analysis involves three important considerations: normality, variety, and length of observation.

Normality. The time period should be a "normal" or typical one for the firm, so far as this is possible. This means that the period covered should be one which was reasonably static in that changes in technology, plant size, efficiency, and other dynamic occurrences that may have a significant bearing on costs were either nonexistent or at least at a minimum. Admittedly, a completely static period would probably be impossible to find. However, a period in which changes were relatively minor would be acceptable if the data could be adjusted to compensate for the differences; if not, the cost function will not reflect the typical type of cost behavior desired. Recent inflationary experience in particular makes it extremely difficult to assess accurately cost functions for current processes.

Variety. The period should be one in which there were sufficiently wide variations in output so a good curve "fit" can be obtained. Further, if the results are to be used as a guide for future planning, the period should be recent enough to include data that will be basically relevant for the future. In many instances a minimum of three to five years has been used as a source for the data within a period of a business cycle, say seven to ten years or thereabouts. On the other hand, if the normality conditions stated above are satisfied, a full business cycle may be preferable as an analysis period.

Length of Observation. The period chosen should be one in which the observational unit (week, month, quarter, or year) will be a minimum to the extent that completeness of the data will permit. A small observation unit such as a week or perhaps a month will allow measurement of slight output variations more readily, say, than will a year. Further, the cause-effect relationship between output and cost is more readily discernible with small rather than large observational units. Frequently, the month is a typical unit chosen in cost studies, although analyses have also been conducted on quarterly and annual bases because of technicalities involving inventory changes, cost reporting dates, and so forth.

2. Technical Homogeneity

In order to minimize the effect on costs of differences in product, equipment, frequency of production lags, and so forth, the plant chosen for a statistical cost study should be characterized by an input and output structure that is as technically homogeneous as possible. This means that on the input side, the use of identical or very similar units within factor classes is necessary, for example, equipment, so as to prevent variations in cost due to different machines being brought into production at different output levels. On the output side it means that the number of different products produced should, ideally, be small enough to facilitate measurement, and these products should not undergo significant cost changes (due, for example, to changes in composition or style) during the analysis period. If these conditions of output homogeneity are not met, the analysis may require that a weighted index of output be constructed for products or for classes of products, according to some logical criterion. Various approaches and techniques are possible.

Thus, in a study of production costs for steel, tons shipped rather than tons produced was found to be more useful because inventory fluctuations (the difference between production and shipments) were relatively small. In a cost study made for a clock manufacturer, the weights used for the output index were based on direct labor costs; in a cost analysis of a men's clothing factory, on the other hand, square feet of wool of a specific grade was chosen as the measure of output, from which conversion coefficients were derived so as to apply to other types of materials used by the company. In short, a number of preliminary measures must frequently be developed based on theoretical considerations, and then the particular one chosen is the one that accords best with economic analysis and statistical criteria.

3. Cost Adjustment

The third problem area in cost analysis involves decisions as to the proper choice of data and the types of adjustments needed to correct the figures if they are to be recast into a meaningful cost function. The problem as a whole breaks down into three subclassifications: cost inclusion, deflation, and cost-output timing.

Cost Inclusion. Since the object is to arrive at a cost-output relation, the problem is to select only those elements of cost that vary with (are functionally related to) output. Thus, various kinds of overhead and allocated expenses that do not bear any relation to production rates should be excluded. Sometimes a series of preliminary correlations must be made to determine which costs should and should not be included in the final analysis. Also, it should be mentioned that total rather than unit (average) costs should be used in conducting most statistical cost analyses, for two main reasons: (1) the results are likely to be more reliable statistically because average cost is a ratio of two variables and therefore more susceptible to error, which in turn may cause magnified errors in the derived marginal cost function; and (2) the marginal and average cost functions can be readily derived mathematically from the total cost function if desired, or the marginal and average cost figures can be derived by simple arithmetic if a cost table or schedule is constructed from the total cost equation.

Deflation. In the construction of empirical cost functions, the data must often be "reduced" or deflated to a particular base period if the results are to be meaningful. Wages and equipment price indexes are readily available and are frequently used for such purposes, or the analyst may construct his own indexes if it seems desirable. In any event, the purpose of deflating the data is to adjust for significant inflationary changes in input prices during the analysis period.

Cost-Output Timing. The third area of an adjustment nature involves the problem of obtaining the correct correspondence of cost and output. Costs are not normally recorded in the books of account in such a manner that they are readily traceable to the output variations that created them. Usually, technical engineering estimates will be necessary if the correct timing associations are to be established between the two variables, cost and output. Of particular importance in this respect are certain costs that are usually charged as a function of time, such as depreciation (normally on a "straight-line" basis). These costs, or portions thereof, must first be adjusted or recalculated as a function of output rate before they can be incorporated in the overall cost function.

STATISTICAL COST FUNCTIONS

If a researcher wishes to make an empirical analysis of short-run costs, his first task would be to generate the kind of information presented in Exhibit 9. In light of the many entries of the table, it might

EXHIBIT 9
Derivation of Cost Schedules

(1)	(2)	(3)	(4)	(5)	(6)	(7)
Output (units) X (given)	Total Cost TC (given)	Total Fixed Cost TFC (given)	Total Variable Cost TVC (= TC − TFC)	Average Total Cost ATC $\left(=\frac{TC}{X}\right)$	Average Variable Cost AVC $\left(=\frac{TVC}{X}\right)$	Marginal Cost MC $\left(=\frac{\Delta TC}{\Delta X}\right)$
0	$100	$100	$ 0	(meaningless)	(indeterminate)	
50	230	100	130	$4.60	$2.60	$2.60
100	285	100	185	2.85	1.85	1.10
150	360	100	260	2.40	1.73	1.50
.	.	.	.	.	.	.
.	.	.	.	.	.	.
.	.	.	.	.	.	.
500	890	100	790	1.78	1.58	.

Cost schedules can be constructed from given data without having to know the cost equations. After filling in the required information from the data given in the first three columns, the entries of the remaining columns may be calculated using the known relationships among variables.

at first appear that a great deal of information, and therefore effort, is necessitated. In reality, however, due to the interrelationships of the cost functions as summarized in Exhibit 6, only the first two columns of Exhibit 9, plus an estimate of fixed costs (column 3) is required. All other information may be derived from this basic data. Again, it is emphasized that care must be taken in the mechanics of the data-gathering task because the problems of appropriate time period, technical homogeneity, and cost adjustment are not only very real in this type of analysis but also very common.

One further word of caution concerns the choice of output-unit increments. This choice should not be arbitrary but rather should reflect whatever "natural" cost breaks are inherent in the underlying production process itself. Moreover, this methodology should be followed even if it results in uneven increments in the production units (column 1) of the table. Thus, for example, if in a study of the costs of a rock-crushing process it is found that additional (but available) machines are needed at unit intervals of 2, 5, and 10 thousand-pound units of rock, then these output units should be chosen when performing the calculations.

The reason for this care is found in the calculation of marginal costs. When "natural" cost breaks are reflected in the choice of incremental units of output, the marginal cost statistics generated will accurately reflect the additional costs of additional units of output. Notice, however, that if in our rock crushing example, arbitrary units of 2, 4, 6, 8, and 10 had been chosen, the marginal cost associated with the two-thousand-pound unit increment between 4 and 6 would be calculated incorrectly because it would actually reflect the "average" marginal cost of two different machines.

Exhibit 10 illustrates a few of the simplest types of cost functions, along with derived cost curves and elasticity measures. Naturally, empirical investigations are not limited to these types of examples, and the researcher must look to the individual data and underlying cost structure before any definitive choice of function can be made. Of course, each type of cost function will possess unique mathematical properties; those associated with the equation forms of Exhibit 10 are explored in the problems at the end of the chapter.

Long-Run Costs

The measurement framework discussed above is applicable primarily to the derivation of short-run cost functions, but some of the same considerations and others, too, apply to the measurement of long-run costs as well. Basically, these other difficulties break down into three classes of problems: choice of method, measurement of size, and measurement of cost.

EXHIBIT 10
Parametric Cost Curve Calculations for Selected Types of Total Cost Equations

Type of Equation	General Form	Total Fixed Costs	Total Variable Costs	Marginal Costs	Average Total Cost ATC	Average Variable Cost AVC	Cost Elasticity
Linear	$Y = a + bx$	a	bx	b	$\dfrac{a}{x} + b$	b	$\dfrac{b}{\dfrac{a}{x} + b}$
Quadratic I	$Y = a + bx + cx^2$	a	$bx + cx^2$	$b + 2cx$	$\dfrac{a}{x} + b + cx$	$b + cx$	$\dfrac{b + 2cx}{\dfrac{a}{x} + b + cx}$
Quadratic II	$Y = a + bx - cx^2$	a	$bx - cx^2$	$b - 2cx$	$\dfrac{a}{x} + b - cx$	$b - cx$	$\dfrac{b - 2cx}{\dfrac{a}{x} + b - cx}$
Cubic	$Y = a + bx - cx^2 + dx^3$	a	$bx - cx^2 + dx^3$	$b - 2cx + 3dx^2$	$\dfrac{a}{x} + b - cx + dx^2$	$b - cx + dx^2$	$\dfrac{b - 2cx + 3dx^2}{\dfrac{a}{x} + b - cx + dx^2}$

Choice of Method. There are two choices open to the analyst who wants to derive a long-run economic cost function:

1. He can analyze changes in the same plant's costs at different points in time.
2. He can analyze changes in costs of different size plants at the same point in time.

The first approach requires, among other things, a virtual constancy of such dynamic factors as technology and product line to say the least, or else the data will probably be impossible to adjust. From a practical standpoint, therefore, the method could be considered as a possible approach only for a plant that has remained relatively static for long periods of time.

The second approach is usually the preferred one for these reasons, but it also raises several difficulties. In particular, where the industry is not sufficiently homogeneous, differences in accounting methods, management, technology, and so forth, tend to cloud the relationships of cost to plant size. If the various plants are owned by a single firm, some of these obstacles are avoided, but this becomes a special rather than a general case. Accordingly, despite the difficulties, empirical cost studies involving a number of plants under separate ownerships have been made.

Measurement of Size. Some measure of size of plant that accords with theoretical considerations is necessary if an empirical long-run cost curve is to be meaningful. Several typical *physical* measures of size include rated capacity, number of workers, man-hours, and machine-hours; *economic* measures include various balance sheet items such as total assets or net worth, and "normal" or "average" output expressed, perhaps, as a percent of capacity.

Unfortunately, there is no simple solution to the problem of choosing an appropriate measure of size. This is because (1) most of the various physical measures require certain conditions of homogeneity within and between plants if the firms are to be ranked in size; and (2) the economic measures do not meet the theoretical requirement that the long-run curve be an envelope of the various short-run curves, that is, the latter will not produce the correct long-run curve unless a correct measure of economic capacity is established. However, to the extent that an engineering measure of capacity is roughly equal to minimum average cost, which is also an approximate concept of economic capacity, it may be possible to average statistically the various cost-output observations in industries with a wide array of plant sizes in order to arrive at a meaningful function whose curvature approximates theoretical requirements.

Measurement of Cost. Finally, as with short-run cost functions, there is the problem of removing those factors that are irrelevant to the analysis so that a cost–plant-size function can be obtained. Some of these "other" variables to be removed or accounted for are differences in accounting procedures, changes in factor prices, locational differences, product differences, and differences in output rates. If the effects of these variables are not removed, they will affect average costs and thus conceal the true relationship between cost and size of plant.

To some extent the various adjustments discussed thus far will serve to eliminate some if not most of these differences in many instances. Other than this, no general set of rules or procedures can be laid down that will be universally applicable in all cases. Each cost–plant-size study involves a different set of circumstances to be handled separately, and at best only illustrative models can be analyzed (many of which have been published elsewhere in various books and articles). In the end, the investigator must formulate his own critical evaluations.

Managerial Decision Making with Long-Run Cost Curves

Although many managerial decision-making problems are short run in nature, the relevance of a long-run cost analysis to a firm should not go unnoticed. One question which the long-run curve can answer is whether or not management has achieved an optimal scale of plant, given the technological level of manufacturing applicable to its industry. Consider, for example, the firm whose short-run situation develops the SAC_1 curve in Exhibit 7. If all firms were similarly poised, and assuming there were no barriers to entry or expansion, there would be a tendency for firms with larger scaled plants (closer to SAC_3 situations) to enter the industry. There would also be a tendency for existing firms to expand their own facilities either through investment or mergers. In both cases, these movements would be made to obtain a more efficient base of operations, that is, lower per-unit costs. Further, as a result of such activity, the individual competitor might soon find a decline in output price brought about by the efficiencies of these larger firms. Hence, forward planning by management would benefit from a long-run cost curve study by enabling it to make provision for appropriate expansion, thus enabling it to "keep up" with the industry.

A second advantage of the long-run cost curve, somewhat related to the first, is that it helps management decide the advisability of a merger. As already noted, a concern which expects economies of scale as a result of expanding its base of operations has a positive incentive to do so as long as the costs of such an expansion do not exceed the benefits obtained. The long-run cost curve can at least serve as a guide in arriving at an answer.

A final reason for studying the individual firm's long-run cost curve is that economies of scale are sometimes considered a public issue, especially in the case of antitrust. For example, where a potential merger has been shown to result in an "unfair" competitive advantage due to anticipated cost savings among industry giants, the antitrust division of the Justice Department has sometimes stepped in to bar the arrangement. Alternatively, the federal government has also encouraged the merger or expansion of large companies when the public interest was thought to be involved and/or the firms were controlled through further federal regulation. The economies of scale wrought by an integrated telephone system, the formation of the quasi-public Amtrak passenger rail system, and the "rescue" from bankruptcy of several aerospace and air carrier concerns through mergers provide examples. Similarly, the breaking up of General Motors into smaller units has successfully been thwarted to date, perhaps in part because it has been successfully argued that the American consumer would ultimately suffer by paying higher prices for the passenger cars and other transport products produced by less efficient, independent firms.

Empirical Studies of Long-Run Cost Curves: Findings and Limitations

Due to a number of statistical and technical difficulties, empirical studies have met with limited success in assessing the long-run cost curve for the individual firm or industry. By and large, the research that has been conducted has tended to support an "L-shaped" pattern of long-run average cost instead of the more familiar "U-shaped" curve. This implies that in most cases, particularly manufacturing, the likelihood of constant, or slightly increasing, returns to scale is the norm, with perhaps slight increases in long-run costs for a minority of select firms.

The concept of a constant long-run average cost is suggested in Exhibit 11, that is, long-run average cost curve *LAC*. It may be noted that

EXHIBIT 11
An "L-Shaped" Long-Run Average
Cost Curve

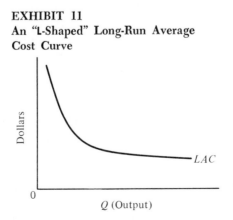

the empirical results appear to conflict with the traditional **U**-shaped model of long-run average cost, but this conflict may be more apparent than real. In particular, theory does not preclude a wide range of relatively stable, or even slightly decreasing costs. Theory and empirical findings may be reconciled if the theoretically increasing portion of the long-run cost curve falls outside the range of the studies in question.

CONCLUSION

In conclusion, it may be stated that the purpose of derived statistical cost functions is to isolate, from among the many factors that influence costs, the *net* effect of changes in output rates. In most of the studies that have been made, problems have been encountered that may be classified into two broad categories: statistical and economic. The statistical problems relate to difficulties in methodology and measurement; the economic problems concern the nature and validity of the results. Each may be treated separately for discussion purposes, even though there may be some overlapping in certain respects.

Statistical Problems. In this category there are at least four broad classes of problems that may be distinguished.

1. The first difficulty relates to the measurement of a diversified output for a firm producing multiple products. Attempts to solve the problem have usually taken the form of weighting the quantity ratios of the various commodities by the relative direct, or variable, costs which they respectively cause. In effect, this amounts to determining output by costs, introducing a spurious dependence where it is actually the measurement of an independent relationship that is wanted. Despite this objection, however, it is difficult to see what other solution might be better, for the problem cannot easily be solved regardless of the sort of statistical procedures that may be employed.

Paralleling this problem is the difficulty of measuring the size of the firm in long-run studies. The more common practice has been to use assets or number of workers, the primary justification being that this provides a convenient way of measuring output by one input. A more accurate measure, however, would appear to be sales, because in sales the various outputs are combined in proportion to their relative importance (prices).

2. Next, there are the problems of technological change, and here the difficulties appear insurmountable. Whenever such change occurs, a new cost function comes into being, if not a new production function, and no amount of curve fitting will really compensate. At best, the results can only roughly be adjusted rather than accurately accounted for.

Closely related to this is the problem of variations in the size of the firm. Assuming that technique remains constant, full "harmony" exists in the structure of the enterprise when, given marginal costs, minimum average costs cannot be further lowered. This would occur when an increase in fixed costs causes no more than a proportional increase in output rate without increasing average costs. Thus, there is a risk of overstating marginal costs to the extent that variations in the size of a firm are not taken into account for the observation period.

What most analysts have done to solve this problem has been to avoid it, although carefully, by choosing firms and periods in which technological change and variations in size are absent. Thus, Joel Dean, exclusive of the excellent nature of his statistical work, stated many years ago in his classic cost study of a leather belt shop: "The period . . . was chosen because it fulfilled the following conditions most satisfactorily: (1) The rate of output and other measurable determinants varied sufficiently to yield observations over a wide range . . . (3) The plant and equipment remained unchanged during the analysis period, permitting the observation of short-run adjustments uninfluenced by long-run changes. . . ." Despite the fact that this study is now quite old, the same criticism could be leveled against more recent authors, but there is no need to belabor the point. The conclusion to be drawn is that when a problem is solved by avoiding its inherent difficulties, the solution is usually not a very satisfying one.

3. Statistical difficulties exist in the measurement of costs. Thus, with respect to asset valuation, there is a problem of valuing raw materials (inventory) at cost or market. One argument is that they should not be valued in a cost study because they are not part of production. The other argument is that they should be valued because an index of sucessful management is its ability to buy raw materials at low prices. A further problem is the valuing of land. Accountants would value it at its definite and objective historical cost, but economists would hold that historical costs are irrelevant for decisions affecting the future. Nor would economists hold to current market value, because this is approximately equal to discounted future earnings and the firm would always be earning the going rate of return on investment. (Problems of this type are discussed in the literature of capital budgeting.)

4. Finally, there are statistical considerations to be made in choosing a measure of efficiency. For example, if rate of return on investment, a common measure, is used, companies paying high executive salaries instead of high dividends in smaller owner-officer corporations will appear inefficient. One approach that has been suggested is to accept the corporation's decision as final; another is to adjust the salaries of officer-owned corporations to equality with nonofficer-owned corporations of equal size. Both methods are questionable, however, and the results of the two methods are quite different.

Still other problem areas could be mentioned, but enough has already been said to indicate the sorts of difficulties frequently encountered in the empirical study of costs. It should be evident, therefore, that although studies of this kind can provide a useful guide for management planning, ambiguities can be attached to almost all such studies and hence their practical value will depend upon how carefully they are interpreted.

Economic Problems. Many of the analysts who have investigated statistical cost functions have found a tendency for short-run total costs to be linear and hence marginal costs to be constant. Since this seems to contradict certain assumptions of economic theory, could it be that the theory is incorrect, unrealistic as to the facts, and hence in need of basic revisions? Various closely related explanations can be offered, all of which appear to contribute to the correct answer.

1. It is possible that the assumptions of economic theory are approximately correct, but total costs tend to be linear or nearly so within the practical operating range. If in empirical studies, wider ranges could be covered closer to the output extremes of the total cost curve, the curve would bend in the end areas and thus yield decreasing and increasing marginal costs at these extremes.

2. It is possible that the assumptions of economic theory are approximately correct, but constant marginal costs prevail in industry, at least over wide ranges of total cost. If this is true, it means that within the relevant range of the data there is a constancy of input or factor proportions and therefore no signficant economies or diseconomies of large-scale production. This leads to the inference that in the final analysis, the only comprehensive test of efficiency is *survival*. If small firms tend to disappear and large ones survive, as in the automobile industry, we must conclude that small firms are relatively inefficient. If small firms survive and large ones tend to disappear, as in the textile industry, then large firms are relatively inefficient. In reality, however, we find that in most industries, firms of very different sizes tend to survive; and hence we conclude that usually there is no significant advantage or disadvantage to size over a very wide range of outputs. In other words, it seems plausible to conclude that in many different industries, constant returns to scale are a good approximation to reality.

3. It is possible that since the cost curves of economic theory are static, they can at best provide only an approximate explanation of the organization of enterprise in a fluctuating dynamic economy. When firms have to contend with business cycles, they must of necessity be flexible so that they can adapt to changing business conditions. This means that they must be able to produce efficiently over a wide (normal) output range, and this in turn requires flat or nearly flat average and marginal costs at least within that range.

It should be pointed out again that these three sets of explanations are not mutually exclusive. They each give a valid partial account of why statistical total cost functions in industry have often been found to be linear, and marginal cost, therefore, to be constant.

PROBLEMS

1. a. Write an expression for incremental cost in terms of a change in cost, ΔC, and a change in activity, ΔA.
   b. Give some examples of a change in "activity."
   c. Is incremental cost the same as marginal cost? Explain.

2. Differentiate between—
   a. The accountant's and the economist's version of cost.
   b. The terms "short-run" and "long-run" as they affect a firm's expense classification.
   c. Incremental and sunk costs.

3. "There is no such thing as costs of production." Discuss.

4. "For outputs less than the long-run optimum level, it is more economical to 'underuse' a slightly larger plant operating at less than its minimum-cost output." Illustrate this proposition graphically, and also its converse.

5. If $TC = Y = aX^2$ where a is a constant, what are AVC, TVC, AFC, TFC, ATC, and MC? For what value of X will $ATC = TC$ and $MC = TC$?

6. a. Are opportunity costs entered in the accounting records of a firm? If yes, what are they used for? If not, what good are they?
   b. In estimating the annual cost of owning a fully paid up $4,000 automobile, you might show the following cost entry: "Interest on investment at 10 percent: $400." What would this mean? Explain.

7. Road-Ready Tire Company manufactures and sells about 1,000 tires a day at a unit cost of $14 and a wholesale price of $21. The company has an unexpected opportunity to sell additional tires under private labels to three different retail outlets. Thus, Able's Auto Accessories offers to buy 100 tires for $19 each; Baker's Auto Accessories offers to buy 100 tires at $17 each; and Charlie's Auto Accessories offers to buy 100 tires for $16 each. Road-Ready figures its unit costs on these additional tires to be $15 for the first 100 tires, $16 for the second 100 tires, and $17 for the third 100 tires.
   a. Which of these orders should Road-Ready agree to fill?
   b. What fundamental principles are involved here?

8. The total daily fuel cost, Y, for operating a manufacturing plant was found to be $Y = 20 + .15X - .005X^2$, where X = output (as a percentage of capacity).
   a. What is the equation for average total cost?
   b. What is the equation for average variable cost?
   c. What is the equation for marginal cost?
   d. What is the total cost of fuel when the plant is:

1. Shut down?
2. Operating at half-capacity?
3. Operating at full capacity?
   e.   Construct a cost schedule from shutdown to full capacity in increments of 10 percent showing total cost, average total cost, average variable cost, and marginal cost; then plot *ATC*, *AVC*, and *MC*.

9. The total cost function of a shirt manufacturer is $Y = 10 + 15X - 6X^2 + X^3$, where Y represents total cost (in hundreds of dollars per month) and X is output (in hundreds of shirts produced per month).
   a.   What is the equation for average total cost?
   b.   What is the equation for average variable cost?
   c.   What is the equation for marginal cost?
   d.   Plot the total and fixed-cost curves for $X = 0, 0.5, 1, \ldots, 5$. Plot the *ATC*, *AVC*, and *MC* curves for these values of X. Show your work by constructing a complete cost schedule.
   e.   Compare these curves with those obtained in Problem 8 and comment on the important similarities and differences.

10. Dream Furniture Company has been experiencing operating losses in its plant for a number of months.
   a.   What cost factors should management consider in deciding whether to shut down its factory?
   b.   Is there a difference between abandonment and shutdown?
   c.   Is it possible for the company to recover part of its plant cost while operating at a loss? (HINT: What is the role of depreciation and its influence on cash flow?)

11. The Devlin Manufacturing Company classifies the costs of operating a machine as follows:

        C_f = fixed costs per year (including depreciation, space charges, maintenance, interest, indirect labor and supervision, insurance, taxes, etc.)

        C_v = variable costs per hour of operation (including power, supplies, and similar items but excluding direct labor)

        N = number of hours of operation per year

        A = annual total cost of operation

        C_h = hourly cost of operation

        t = time in hours required to process one unit of product

        M_p = machine cost of processing a unit of product

        n = number of units of product processed per year

   a.   Using these symbols, write formulas for A, C_h, and M_p.
   b.   If $C_f = \$400$, $t = .2$, and $C_v = \$0.50$, write the equation for M_p and then use it to complete the table below. Sketch the graph of M_p as a function of N.

N	0	1,000	2,000	3,000	4,000	5,000	6,000	7,000	8,000	9,000	10,000
M_p											

c. Let C_w represent the hourly wage cost of direct labor necessary for operating the machine. Write the equation for C^*, which represents the total of direct labor and machine cost per unit of product.

12. Accuro Division of Metropolitan Instruments Company manufactures miniature calculators which it sells to a limited number of exclusive dealers. Accuro's normal production rate is 260 units per week at a total cost of $3,200. At full capacity it can produce 340 units per week at a total cost of $3,800.

   a. What is the average cost per calculator under normal operating conditions?
   b. How much is the average variable cost per calculator.
   c. What is the total fixed cost?
   d. How much is the average fixed cost per calculator under normal operating conditions?
   e. A foreign distributor offers to buy 50 calculators per week from Accuro over a one-month period, to be marketed under a different brand name. The distributor offers a price of $10 per calculator. Should Accuro accept the offer? What is the least price Accuro should accept for this kind of arrangement?

13. An accountant in your company plotted a scatter diagram of production and cost data for the firm, as shown by the dots in the following exhibit. He then sketched in the total cost curve, TC, and presented it to you for an evaluation.

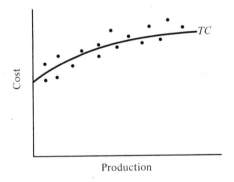

On the basis of what you read in this chapter, what is he assuming by employing this TC curve? (HINT: What type of equation does the curve represent? What can you say about the equations for ATC, AVC and MC, and the elasticity of total cost?

14. Fill in the following table representing the cost schedule for a manufacturer of children's shoes. Then, on a single chart, sketch the graphs of ATC, AVC, AFC, MC. (SUGGESTION: It will suffice to fill in the table below for even values of X only, i.e., for X = 2, 4, 6, . . . , 20. Various odd values of X may then be used to facilitate graphing if desired.)

Cost Schedule of a Shoe Manufacturer

Quantity of Production Q	Total Fixed Cost TFC	Total Variable Cost TVC	Total Cost TC	Average Fixed Cost AFC	Average Variable Cost AVC	Average Total Cost ATC	Marginal Cost MC
1	$50		$ 55.00				
2			58.00				
3			60.50				
4			63.00				
5			65.00				
6			68.00				
7			72.75				
8			78.00				
9			86.00				
10			95.00				
11			104.50				
12			115.20				
13			130.00				
14			149.10				
15			174.75				
16			212.00				
17			259.25				
18			319.50				
19			399.00				
20			500.00				

15.

CASE PROBLEM: MARVEL DAIRY
PRODUCTS CORPORATION
CONSTRUCTING NEW PLANTS

The Marvel Dairy Products Corporation is a leading producer of milk, ice cream, cheese, and various other dairy products. Recently, after many years of research, the company succeeded in developing a very low calorie type of ice cream. Extensive taste tests have indicated that this new ice cream is every bit as delicious as any of the leading brands. Accordingly, the management of the company has decided to produce and market the new ice cream on a "test" basis within one region of the country, and to construct the necessary production facilities for this purpose.

The Marvel Company conducted a market survey of the three largest population areas of the region. The results of the survey indicated that the company could expect to sell 10,000, 5,000, and 2,500 gallons in each area, respectively, per week. An engineering consultant for the company has suggested either of two alternatives with respect to the construction of ice cream plants: one alternative is to construct a single plant equidistant from the three population areas, with a production capacity of 20,000 gallons per week at a fixed cost of $5,000 per week and a variable cost of 70 cents per gallon; the other alternative is to construct three plants (one in each market area) with capacities of 12,000, 6,000, and 3,000 gallons, respectively, and with weekly fixed costs of $4,000, $3,000, and $2,000 respectively, and a variable cost in all three plants of only 60 cents per gallon due to the reduction of shipping costs.

Questions:

a. Assuming that the market survey is correct, which alternative should management select? At a price of $1.99 per gallon, how much profit (or loss) per gallon and in total would the company have?

b. If demand were to increase to production capacity, which alternative would be better?

c. Suppose that management selects the second alternative rather than the first, and that demand is at the level of production capacity in all three markets. If the company wanted to make a profit of $1 per gallon in each of the three markets, what price per gallon would it have to charge in each of these markets? Can management be sure of realizing its expected profit? Explain why.

16.   **CASE PROBLEM: CITY OF NORTHFIELD**
                    REPLACEMENT OF GAS MAINS

The city of Northfield buys gas from Public Gas Company for distribution and resale. The monthly charge which the city pays is based on the following wholesale rate.

DEMAND CHARGE: $3.50 per month times the maximum number of cubic feet of gas used during any 24-hour period during the previous 12 months

                         PLUS

COMMODITY CHARGE: $0.20 per cubic foot of gas used during the previous 12 months.

During the preceding 12 months the city used 300,000 cubic feet of gas and its peak consumption on the maximum day of the year was 2,000 cubic feet. The city's annual bill may thus be computed as follows:

Demand charge: $3.50 × 12 × 2,000.	$ 84,000
Commodity charge: $0.20 × 300,000	60,000
Total annual bill	$144,000

The average cost of gas to the city is therefore $144,000 ÷ 300,000 = $0.48 per cubic foot.

There are a number of old gas mains in the distribution system, as a result of which there is a moderate amount of gas leakage. City engineers have established the fact that the amount of leakage is due entirely to pressure rather than gas consumption. Therefore, by maintaining a constant pressure the gas loss per day is kept constant and well within safe limits. Nevertheless, the city controller, in a report to the City Council concluded:

. . . According to bids received by engineering firms, the cost of replacing the leaking gas mains amounts to an average annual expense of $0.35 per cubic foot of gas lost. On the other hand, since the average annual cost of gas to the city is $0.48 per cubic foot, replacement of the leaking gas mains would result in an average annual saving to the city of $0.13 per cubic foot. I therefore recommend that the City Council authorize the replacement of the leaking gas mains.

Question:

Assuming the controller's facts are correct, would you advise the City Council to accept his recommendation? Explain.

REFERENCES

BAIN, JOE S.   *Barriers to New Competition.* Cambridge, Mass: Harvard University Press, 1956.

BASSETT, LOWELL   "Returns to Scale and Cost Curves." *The Southern Economic Journal,* vol. 36, no. 2 (October 1969), pp. 189–90.

BAUMOL, WILLIAM J.   *Economic Theory and Operations Analysis,* chap. 11, "Production and Cost," pp. 250–69. Rev. ed, Englewood Cliffs, N.J.: Prentice-Hall, Inc., 1965.

———, and SEVIN, C.   "Marketing Costs and Mathematical Programming." *Harvard Business Review,* vol. 35, no. 5 (September–October 1957), pp. 52–60. Discusses the approach to distribution cost analysis as outlined in this chapter.

CLARK, J. M.   *Studies in the Economics of Overhead Costs,* chaps. 3 and 9. Chicago: University of Chicago Press, 1923. Contains a more extensive treatment of cost concepts than the one presented in this chapter.

DORFMAN, ROBERT; SAMUELSON, PAUL A.; and SOLOW, ROBERT M.   *Linear Programming and Economic Analysis.* New York: McGraw-Hill Book Co., 1958.

FABRYCKY, W. J., and TORGERSEN, PAUL E.   *Operations Economy,* chap. 4, "Models of the Production Process." Englewood Cliffs, N.J.: Prentice-Hall, Inc., 1966.

FERGUSON, C. E., and GOULD J. P.   *Microeconomic Theory,* chap. 7. 4th ed. Homewood, Ill.: Richard D. Irwin, Inc., 1975.

———, and SAVING, T. R.   "Long-Run Scale Adjustments of a Perfectly Competitive Firm and Industry." *American Economic Review,* vol. 59, no. 5 (December 1969), pp. 774–83.

GRANT, EUGENE L., and IRESON W. G.   *Principles of Engineering Economy,* chap. 14, 4th ed. New York: Ronald Press, 1960. Contains a discussion of incremental cost analysis with several applications to public utilities.

JOHNSTON, J.   *Statistical Cost Analysis,* chap. 5, pp. 136–68. New York: McGraw-Hill Book Co., 1960. These pages summarize, in a few paragraphs each, the main features and conclusions of more than two dozen well-known statistical cost studies. Chapter 6, pp. 169–94, presents criticisms and evaluations of statistical cost analyses.

KOOT, RONALD S. and WALKER, DAVID A.   "Short-Run Cost Functions of a Multiproduct Firm." *The Journal of Industrial Economics,* vol. 18, no. 2 (April 1970), pp. 118–28.

McElroy, F. W.   "Return to Scale of Cost Curves: Comment." *The South-ern Economic Journal*, vol. 37, no. 2 (October 1970), pp. 227–28.

Riggs, James L.   *Economic Decision Models: For Engineers and Managers*, pp. 82–115. New York: McGraw-Hill Book Co., 1968.

Shephard, A. Ross   "A Note on the Firm's Long-Run Average Cost Curve." *Quarterly Review of Economics and Business*, vol. 11 (Spring 1971), pp. 77–79.

chapter 9

Profit: Theories and Measurement

Profit is the ultimate test of a firm's well-being and a comprehensive indicator of management's ability to fulfill its coordinative function of decision making and planning. Since the search for profit is, after all, the reason for a business firm's existence, this chapter presents an analysis and treatment of the forces which determine profit or the lack thereof.

A detailed examination is undertaken of various profit aspects with a major view to relating the theoretical with the "practical." This involves a discussion of various profit theories that have been put forth over the years, an analysis of profit measurement, and a presentation of some techniques for profit planning and control.

PROFIT THEORIES

The history of the development of economic thought reveals an abundance of profit theories which in varying degree are based upon some one or a combination of the aspects of profit—whence it derives, the economic function it performs, to what productive factor or factors it is distributed, and so forth. We will, therefore, present a brief summary of profit theories, not individually or comparatively but in terms of the three major categories in which all profit theories may be more or less classified.

1. Compensatory or functional theories.
2. Friction and monopoly theories.
3. Technology and innovation theories.

This classification is not all-inclusive, nor does it imply that particular theories may not contain elements of others. It merely points out the different lines that have been followed historically in the course of thinking on the subject and represents a logical arrangement of ideas for approaching the problems of managerial decision making.

Compensatory or Functional Theories

This group of theories holds that economic profits (surplus) are the necessary payments to the entrepreneur in return for the services performed in coordinating and controlling the other productive factors. It is the entrepreneur who organizes the factors of production into a logical sequence, combines them efficiently, establishes policies and sees that they are carried out, and in other ways acts in both a coordinative and supervisory capacity. Profits, therefore, are the entrepreneur's compensation for fulfilling these functions successfully. In like manner, losses are the penalty for unsuccessful entrepreneurship.

This group of theories, propounded in the early 19th century, were adequate to explain the individual-proprietorship type of business enterprise which was predominant at that time. However, when attempts were made to apply the theory to the modern large corporation with its separation of ownership and control, the results appeared confusing and contradictory. In this form of business organization, the coordinative function is usually delegated by the owners (stockholders) to salaried executives. If the latter's remuneration is taken to be "profits," despite its contractual form, the theory still leaves unexplained the residual income of the enterprise that goes to stockholders who exercise no active control. The only alternative, if these theories were to be consistent with their original definition, was to allocate a share of the entrepreneurial function to stockholders. But attempts to do this are not in accord with reality where the corporation is an organization of active leadership by managers and passive ownership by stockholders. Hence, around the turn of the century, with the growing importance of the large corporation as a dominant type of business organization in the American economy, this set of profit theories lost its meaning and a new group of "friction theories" emerged in its place.

Friction and Monopoly Theories

By the year 1900, the theory of a stationary economy was well on its way toward becoming a complete and unified system of thought. Against this setting the noted American economist J. B. Clark constructed an economic model that was intended to be a reconciliation between static laws of theory and the dynamic world of fact.

According to stationary theory (or, roughly, the theory of perfect

competition as it is commonly called today), the economy is characterized by a smooth and frictionless flow of resources, with the system
automatically clicking into equilibrium through the free play of market
forces. Changes may occur that will occasion a departure from equilibrium, but so long as resources are mobile and opportunities are equally
accessible to all economic organisms (i.e., knowledge is perfect), the
adjustment to change and a new equilibrium will be accomplished
quickly and smoothly. In this type of economic equilibrium all factors
of production would receive their opportunity costs; the revenues of
each enterprise would exactly equal its costs (including the imputed
wages and interest of the owner), and hence no economic surplus or
profit residual could result.

In the real world, however, such surpluses do occur, and in accordance with the theory they can only be attributed to the frictions (or
obstacles to resource mobility) and changes that actually characterize
a dynamic economy. In the long run, according to the theory, the forces
of competition would eliminate any surpluses, but the surpluses continue
to recur because new changes and new frictions continually arise. Profits,
therefore, in contrast to the earlier compensatory theories outlined above,
are not attributable to any particular function; they are the result of
institutional rigidities in the social fabric that prevent the free play
of competitive forces and are to the temporary advantage of the surplus
recipient.

Such imperfections in resource fluidity made it possible for economic
and social critics to generalize about "unearned" incomes: rising rents
attributed to enhanced values of limited land resources, and the natural
pressure of growing population and increasing urbanization (Henry
George); "abnormal" profits ascribed to the existence of monopolistic
and even exploitative elements of a favored capitalist minority (a modern-
ized restatement of Karl Marx); and, in fact, all surpluses preempted
by owners of any resources (including labor, capital, and managerial
skills) because of the institutional frictions of an otherwise fluid system
(Thorstein Veblen and John Hobson).

There are many illustrations from real life to substantiate the friction
theory as a cause of economic surplus. The construction of military
posts during a war brings profit bonanzas to neighboring cities; cold
war crises have often rescued domestic industries from threatening over-
supplies of their products; the existence of patents and franchises enables
many firms to reap profits by legally excluding competitors from the
field; a favorable location for a business may result in the value of
the site exceeding the rental payment for it; or, in general, the control
of any resource whose supply is scarce relative to its demand provides
a basis for pure or windfall profits. In such instances a surplus would
not arise if resources were sufficiently mobile to enter the market, or
if the economy were frictionless (perfect) in its competitive structure.

At best, if any surpluses did arise, they would be short-lived and would vanish entirely when the adjustments had time to exert their full effect in the market. But social processes—customs, laws, traditions, and so forth—make these rapid adjustments impossible.

Technology and Innovation Theories

An innovation theory of profits can be developed which when cast into an uncertainty framework probably goes further than any other theory toward explaining in a realistic way the historical development of business enterprise.[1] An *innovation* is defined as the creation of a new production function. A "production function" is the physical relation between the output and various kinds of inputs (capital, land, labor, etc.) in a production process.

From a broad business standpoint, an innovation may embrace such a wide variety of activities as the discovery of new markets, differentiation of products (thereby yielding wider consumer acceptance), the development of a new product, or in short, a new way of doing old things or a different combination of existing methods to accomplish new things. There is an important distinction to be made between invention and innovation: invention is the creation of something new; innovation is the adaptation of an invention to business use. Many inventions never become innovations.

The original purpose of the innovation theory as propounded by Schumpeter was to show how business cycles result from these "disturbances" and from successive adaptations to them by the business system. He never stated (as is sometimes implied) that innovation alone was the cause of change or disturbance in the economic system. His procedure was to assume a stationary system in equilibrium—in which all economic life is repetitive and goes on smoothly, without disturbance. Into this system a shock—an innovation—is introduced by an enterprising and forward-looking entrepreneur who foresees the possibility of extra profit. The quietude and intricate balance of the system is thus shattered. The successful innovation causes a herd of business executives (followers rather than leaders) to plunge into the new field by adopting the innovation, and these mass rushes create and stir up secondary waves of business activity. When the disturbance has finally ironed itself out, the system is settled in equilibrium once again, only to be disturbed later on by another innovation. Economic development thus takes place as a series of fits and starts (cycles) rather than progressing in a smooth and continuous manner.

The manager who is considering the introduction of an innovation

---

[1] The innovation theory as originally expounded by the late Professor Joseph Schumpeter was an attempt to explain business cycles, not so much the causes and distribution of profits.

must subjectively forecast the effect of that innovation on expected profits. The expected profit is the sum of expected receipts less the sum of expected expenses at all moments of time within the economic or planning horizon. This horizon is the length of time over which managers plan economic activity. If future sales and costs (and hence profits) were known with certainty, the span of the planning horizon would be infinite. But in a world of uncertainty where forecasts must be subjective, the time length of the planning horizon will differ among managers and will depend on the extent to which they formulate effective expectations and plans in a temporal vein. "Effective" expectations, therefore, are expectations that are held by managers with a degree of "subjective certainty" sufficient to cause action or the establishment of a plan (as would occur, for example, if discounted returns exceeded costs).[2]

Status of Innovation Theory

As it stands, the innovation theory is a "great-man" theory of history and thus provides a useful hook on which to hang the development of business in capitalist countries. The innovating decision maker is here cast in the role of determining the intensity and pace of economic growth.

When conceived in its broadest business sense as a new way of doing things, the innovation theory can go a long way in helping to explain such great historical episodes as the rise of mercantilism and the industrial revolution itself, as well as the underlying structural changes that took place in American business during the latter half of the 19th century and which have been in continued evidence since then. In terms of present-day experience, the broader aspects of the innovation theory can be seen in business, in industry, in government, in science, in agriculture, in education, in almost every aspect of life in our society. Since the advent of the electronic computer, which itself is certainly one of the most important innovations of recent decades, the shock waves of computer-generated or computer-supported innovation have been coming faster and faster. Since World War II we have seen the development

---

[2] Thus, in an uncertainty framework, an innovation may be defined as "such changes in production functions, that is, in the schedules indicating the relation between the input of factors of production and the output of products, which make it possible for the firm to increase the discounted value of the maximum effective profit obtainable under given market conditions." By market conditions is meant prices, or demand and supply schedules. Discounted expected prices and schedules as well as current ones are included. An increase in discounted maximum effective profit means an increase in the sum of surpluses of effective receipts over effective expenses. (See O. Lange, "A Note on Innovations," *The Review of Economic Statistics*, vol. 25, 1943, pp. 19–25.)

of vast new markets, revolutionary products, amazing therapeuticals, new forms of consumer credit, new metals, new sources of energy, and new fuels.

Innovation theory places stress on the dynamic, uncertain, ever-changing nature of capitalism. It points out quite vividly that the only limits to human progress are the inherent limits upon humans themselves. And even now, this may not be a seriously restraining factor with the advent of the computer-controlled automatic firm of the electronic age.

Innovation Theory and Managerial Economics

From the standpoint of managerial economics, the value of a theory is not so much determined by how well it explains the past or even the present but how well it can predict the future. For this purpose, innovation theory is of little use. For since the scientific principles, technical know-how, materials, and skills—all the ingredients necessary to bring to the business world the reality of a new product, service, or method of production or of distribution—are, at any time, known and available long before the innovation bursts forth on the business world, why does the explosion take place when it does, and neither sooner nor later? On the surface, the answer is that an innovation takes place when the possibility for profit is recognized by individuals willing and able to exploit the potentials they believe to be inherent in the opportunity they see and, moreover, when these individuals are willing to assume the risks required in the new business venture. Basically, however, the answer lies in the structural environment of complex underlying pressures, institutional and otherwise, which bring the innovator onto the scene. For innovation theory to be complete, it must be reshaped in terms which facilitate the prediction of the innovation and its ramifications. In this form innovation theory would serve to reduce the uncertainty that is inherent in forward planning. And in its broader application such a theory would actually explain the entire course of economic development. This is really what Karl Marx attempted, and failed to accomplish, a century ago in building his theory of economic history. It appears, at least intuitively, that innovation theory may provide the point of departure for a similar venture, in which case we would not merely have an innovation theory but a *theory of innovations*.

PROFIT MEASUREMENT

The Allocation Problem

When it comes to measuring profit, the major difficulty is introduced by the requirement to allocate to a given accounting period the "correct" revenues and costs deemed to be attributable to that period as distinct from previous and subsequent periods. *The true profitability of any investment or business operation cannot be determined until the ownership of the investment or business has been fully terminated,* so that the need to measure profits over a particular segment of the total life span of the investment imposes a degree of arbitrariness which cannot be avoided. Although arbitrary allocation to a given accounting period is necessary with respect to both revenues and costs, it is the latter which has received the greatest amount of attention, particularly with respect to depreciation accounting and inventory valuation. Aside from the accounting aspects of cost (and profit) measurement, there are certain important economic considerations which we would like to deal with first.

Economic versus Accounting Measures of Profit

In economic literature dealing with the determination of profit, much attention is paid to the possible discrepancies that might arise out of the failure to account for all costs. The point made is that certain portions of accounting profit may actually include elements of cost; therefore, it is important to recognize these economic costs, as well as the more obvious cash outlays, and such items as development costs and capital expenditures which are amortized over the future. There are, in fact, at least three possible sources of discrepancy:

1. The entrepreneur's wages (which the entrepreneur could earn by working for someone else).
2. Rental income on land employed in the business (which the owner could receive by leasing the property to another firm).
3. A minimum or "normal" profit (which would be just enough to compensate the owner for his (or her) capital investment and which he presumably could earn by putting his money to work in somebody else's business at equivalent risk).

The above items are all deemed to be costs for the simple reason that an entrepreneur who failed to secure a net revenue at least equal to their total would, in the long run, withdraw from the business, hire out to another firm, lease or sell his (or her) property, invest his funds in some alternative undertaking, and improve his economic position. Thus arises the technical, *economic* meaning of *cost—that minimum compensation necessary to keep a given resource or factor of production in its stated employment in the long run.* Frictions and various other market imperfections will cause resources to remain in their existing employment at less than economic cost, and there are many situations in which resource owners receive compensation in excess of economic costs, but in the long run there is sufficient mobility of resources which tends to eliminate these discrepancies (under dynamic, real-world conditions, changes always occur to redistribute the discrepancies and introduce new ones).

Cost, in the *economic* sense, is thus viewed as a *payment necessary to keep resources out of (the next most attractive) alternative employment,* since a payment which is below economic cost will result in an eventual shift of the resource to the alternative opportunity—hence the term "opportunity cost."

Our specific concern with the problem of profit measurement raises the question of how to deal with these potential discrepancies between accounting and economic profit, for it follows from the above that economic profit or "true surplus" is equal to accounting profit less certain unaccounted-for costs. Actually, the discrepancies are not too serious as applied to the corporation, and are most likely to exist in the small proprietorship. Thus, in the corporation, management is hired and receives, presumably, an opportunity cost wage. These wages are treated as expenses, along with the wage payments to all employees, and are deducted in determining final profit. Properties are ordinarily rented, and these rents are deductible in determining the final profit. To the extent that real estate is owned rather than rented, it is frequently segregated into a special real estate or building corporation subsidiary from which the property is "rented." Where the latter device is not used, the real estate is treated as part of the total investment which the firm seeks to employ profitably (the rental value being readily determinable). We are, therefore, left with this one possible source of discrepancy between accounting and economic profit—the earnings on the invested capital.

A corporation derives its long-term capital from any one or a combination of three external sources: the sale of bonds, preferred stock, and common stock. The bondholder's contribution is obtained, however, at an opportunity cost interest rate, and this cost is recognized in determining profit. As for the preferred stockholder, while legally an owner so that profit is computed before the distribution of the preferred dividend, his (or her) position is really that of a "limited partner." Thus, from the point of view of the common stockholder, the preferred dividend constitutes an opportunity cost payment for the use of the preferred stockholder's capital. This is, of course, objectively determinable, and in fact is always deducted in determining "net profits available for the common stock." We are then left with only one significant element of discrepancy between accounting and economic profit: the cost for the use of the common stockholder's contribution (including reinvested earnings) to the corporation. This "normal profit" on the stockholders' capital is the amount by which accounting profit exceeds economic profit in the corporation. This element is, furthermore, measurable—it is the amount that would be earned elsewhere on investments of equivalent risk, and unless the existing investment process is capable of producing this opportunity rate of return, the capital will be gradually withdrawn from its employment in search for "greener pastures."

Problems in Measuring Accounting Profit

In addition to errors arising from a failure to give consideration to certain economic costs, there are the even more serious errors which arise from the accounting techniques themselves. The difficulties are not due to the failure of the accounting profession to produce the right techniques. As stated earlier, they arise simply out of the fact that the true profitability of an investment cannot be precisely determined until the process has been terminated, and that for any period other than the full life of the investment profits can only be estimated. This in turn means that revenues and costs must, to some extent, be arbitrarily allocated to the period in question.

However, various factors impel the periodic determination and reporting of profits. Stockholders wish to know how their investment is faring; the government wants its taxes; and management needs a guide for future decision making and a measure of the success (or lack of it) of past decisions made. Thus, despite the dilemma that exists, the bull must be grasped by the horns. In doing so, we will attack the problem from the economist's point of view.

The accountant, at least for legal reasons if for no other, is primarily concerned with historical fact, so that to the accountant profit is an *ex post* concept based on past transactions. The economist views profit as a surplus in excess of all opportunity costs so that past outlays are only of partial significance, for the cost allocations arising from these past transactions must be modified by current facts. To state this in more concrete terms, the economist would say that the profit earned in period "A" is equal to the growth in value of the enterprise from the beginning of the period to the end of the period (after adjusting for any distributions by, or contributions to, the firm during the period). This increase in value is a reflection not only of what we ordinarily understand to be the results of operations during the period but of changes in asset values (plant, equipment, inventories) as well. Thus, *profit, in an economic sense, would be the difference between the cash value of the enterprise at the beginning and end of the period.*

We have thus laid a base from which we can proceed to evaluate certain accounting conventions used in arriving at accounting profit. The two major areas in which discrepancies are most likely to be produced, and which will receive detailed consideration here, are depreciation accounting and the significance of price-level changes on asset valuation.

Depreciation

The accounting measurement of profit depends in a very direct way upon the firm's practice with respect to depreciation. In carrying on business activity, the firm's buildings, machines, and other equipment wear out with time and use so that eventually a company's entire investment in such assets becomes worthless. In order, therefore, that the corporation's income be properly stated and that the cost, less salvage value, be recovered by the time the assets are abandoned, the accountant makes as a charge against annual income the amount of the decrease in value during that period. This charge is called depreciation[3] and is prorated over the life of the asset. The exact amount charged is by and large a function of company policy, with many companies taking advantage of tax laws to replace their "straight-line" methods with accelerated depreciation approaches.

Stated thus, there would appear to be little more to be said about the subject, except perhaps to recognize that the importance of this operating cost to the enterprise will vary widely from one company to another, depending on the composition of the firm's assets. Characterized by extremely large depreciation charges are companies that are engaged in steelmaking, railroad and airline transportation, chemical processing, and the production of primary aluminum; while insurance companies, banks, investment funds, and advertising and merchandising establishments bear relatively small depreciation costs. The subject, however, does not end with this simple observation, for it is complicated by controversy over the true function of depreciation, the proper method for measuring it both for purposes of reporting net income to stockholders and taxable income to the government, and (a recent development) its proper use as a tool for stimulating capital formation and directing investments along lines deemed to be in the national interest.

A prime example of this latter consideration is the percentage depletion allowance permitted by the federal government for income tax purposes. It is available only to those with economic interest in oil and gas wells, mines, and quarries. It allows recovery of the cost of the well or mine, or of a percentage of production, whichever is higher. Since the owners may thus recover many times the actual cost of a good producer, capital formation from what would otherwise be paid in taxes is encouraged for the exploration and discovery of new sources of gas, oil, and minerals.

With respect to reporting income, the accounting profession, amid much controversy, has been unable to arrive at any satisfactory improvement on the current method, which is to deduct a prorated recovery

---

[3] The charge for depreciation also includes the charge for ordinary obsolescence. There is no set rule for determining the rate of obsolescence.

of historical cost from current operating revenue. To the economist who is concerned with the replacement of assets that are necessary for the survival and growth of the firm, the resulting income statements exaggerate the true financial position of the firm. In this era of substantial inflation, the mere recovery of capital spent years ago is not sufficient to replace the asset today, even with an identical make and model. The replacement problem is further complicated by the fact that the 20th century has also been an era of rapid technological change; it may well be that an identical replacement simply is not available. The improved replacement may provide greatly increased earnings in the future and thus be well worth its greater cost. Nevertheless, provision for its purchase requires that a certain portion of the reported income be made unavailable either for expansion of the firm or for distribution to its owners.

Measuring Depreciation.   While the straight-line method has been by far the most widely used in industry, the depreciation pattern has undergone substantial change over the years because of the federal government's desire to stimulate and direct investment in new plant and equipment. This was first done by permitting, for tax purposes, a five-year write-off or amortization of all or part of the cost of "defense-certified" facilities. First instituted in World War II and adopted again after the outbreak of the Korean War, this device was designed to increase the cash flow of corporations engaged in defense work by permitting them to write off in 5 years a facility which might have an economic life of as much as 20 or 30 years. The greatly inflated depreciation charge had the effect of reducing taxable net income and, thereby, the impact of income taxes, serving to stimulate activity in the building of facilities regarded as essential for national defense.

Congress subsequently extended the principle of fast write-offs—but at a slower rate—to nondefense facilities as well, that is, to *any* new machinery and buildings. Thus, two accelerated methods of depreciation were made available as alternatives to the straight-line method. These are the "declining balance" method and the "sum-of-the-years' digits" method, respectively. The differences among the three methods, none of which require special authorizations like the fast write-off initiated during the war, are described below.

Before looking at these, however, it should be noted that in 1962, Congress enacted the investment tax credit to spur capital investment in machinery and equipment, including research and development facilities. Unlike depreciation, which merely reduces taxable income, the investment tax credit as originally formulated allows the firm to reduce directly its tax liability by an amount up to 7 percent of the cost of a qualified investment. (The remaining cost of the investment must be recovered through depreciation.)

The tax credit worked all too well and in 1966 was suspended on the grounds that it was a stimulus to inflation. Since then, the tax credit has been instituted when Congress and the Administration felt that the economy needed stimulation, and rescinded when the economy appeared to be overheating. Thus the credit became available to business in 1967, unavailable in 1969, and available again in 1971.

Methods of Depreciation

1. *Straight-Line Method.* Under the straight-line method the cost of a new machine or building is spread equally over its expected life. For instance, with a machine costing $1,000 and having a life expectancy of ten years, a company would depreciate the asset at a 10 percent rate on original cost, or $100 a year.

2. *Declining Balance Method.* Under the declining balance method, the company can deduct up to double the straight-line rate, but on the "undepreciated" balance each year rather than on the original cost. Thus, for the $1,000 machine, the second year's deduction would be 20 percent of the remaining $800, or $160; the third year's deduction would be 20 percent of the remaining $640, or $128; and so on. This method never permits a 100 percent depreciation of the asset no matter how long the process is carried on. Therefore, the balance which remains at the end of the asset's economic life is treated, for accounting purposes, as salvage value.

3. *Sum-of-the-Years' Digits Method.* Under the sum-of-the-years' digits method, which is actually a variation of the declining balance method, a diminishing depreciation ratio is employed which is derived and used in the following manner: (*a*) The years of expected useful life of the asset are summed, and the resulting figure is the denominator of the ratio. Thus, for the machine example with a life expectancy of 10 years, the total of the digits 1, 2, 3, . . . , 10 is 55, and this 55 becomes the required denominator. (*b*) The numerator of the ratio represents, each year, the number of years of life which the asset has remaining, and thus declines by one each year. In the machine example, the numerator would be 10 in the first year, 9 in the second year, and so on down to 1 in the tenth year. (*c*) The depreciation ratio is thus composed of a varying numerator and an unvarying denominator, and this ratio is applied each year to the asset's original cost. In the machine illustration with the original cost at $1,000, the first year's depreciation deduction would be $10/55$ of $1,000, or $181.82; the second year's deduction would be $9/55$ of $1,000 or $163.64; and so on down to the tenth year, for which the depreciation deduction would be $1/55$ of $1,000 or $18.18. By using this method, the depreciation charged declines consistently, and the sum of the depreciation allowances always amounts to exactly the cost of the machine so that the asset is fully depreciated at the end of its economic life.

Exhibit 1 reveals some of the important differences among the three depreciation methods.

Depreciation and Tax Policy. Manifestly, the accelerated methods provide larger depreciation charges in the early years of the asset's life,

EXHIBIT 1
Three Methods of Depreciation* (estimated life of asset: ten years) (original cost of asset: $1,000)

Year	Straight-Line (10%) Annual Charge	Cumu-lated	Declining Balance (20%) Annual Charge	Cumu-lated	Sum-of-the-Years' Digits Annual Charge	Cumu-lated
1.....	$100	$ 100	$200	$200	$182	$ 182
2.....	100	200	160	360	164	346
3.....	100	300	128	488	145	491
4.....	100	400	102	590	127	618
5.....	100	500	82	672	109	727
6.....	100	600	66	738	91	818
7.....	100	700	52	790	73	891
8.....	100	800	42	832	55	946
9.....	100	900	34	866	36	982
10.....	100	1,000	27	893	18	1,000

* Figures are rounded to nearest dollar.

and correspondingly smaller taxable income and taxes than is the case with straight-line depreciation. If the asset in question is kept in the business for all or most of its useful life, the depreciation charges would fall off rapidly in the later years to levels substantially below those that would prevail under straight-line depreciation. Assuming no change in tax rates or in income before depreciation, taxable income and income taxes would be substantially larger, thereby offsetting the lower taxes of earlier years. All other things being equal, however, the corporation would still have the advantage, under the accelerated methods, of having had the productive use of cash that would otherwise have been paid out in taxes had the straight line method applied. This cash, in effect available to the company as an interest-free loan from the federal government, could, depending on the useful life of the asset, be employed in the business for a number of years for any of the numerous corporate purposes upon which management might decide, thereby reducing the need for outside financing.

Whether a company's choice of one of the accelerated methods will, in the future, prove to have been wise depends a great deal on at least two factors each of which is subject to change. Since the accelerated methods result only in a postponement of taxes rather than a permanent avoidance of them, the wisdom or folly of adopting a given course of action depends on (1) the income tax rates prevailing at the time the deferred tax has to be paid, and (2) the level of corporate taxable income at that time. Corporate management must, therefore, evaluate the future in terms of these uncertainties when adopting a given depreciation policy. With respect to the course likely to be followed by income tax rates, no single corporate management is in a particularly superior position for predicting their level at any time in the future. However, the international situation and our domestic economic policies both tend to inject an inflationary bias into our economy which, if too rapid an erosion of the purchasing power of the dollar is to be prevented, calls for a continued high level of taxes. On the other hand, the dangers of an onerous tax are well recognized so that at any given time when tax rates are already high, as they are today, the probability of their going much higher is rather small—except for temporary measures, in the form of something like an excess-profits tax, in unusually critical periods. Conversely, when and if tax rates are low, the possibility of their going substantially higher becomes quite real.

With respect to a given company's future income, no one is in a better position to evaluate this than the company's own management, for business income is, at least to some extent, subject to management's control. If income is expected to increase, then other things being equal, future tax payments will be greater than present ones, and this consideration alone would favor the adoption of straight-line depreciation. But other considerations complicate the picture so that the choice becomes necessarily individualistic, varying from one company situation to another. Among the more important complicating factors are (1) current versus anticipated future working capital requirements, (2) extent and timing of planned capital expansion programs, and (3) the fact that a present dollar is worth more than a future dollar, that is, the company's cost of capital.

In light of the foregoing, it would seem that accelerated depreciation offers a clear advantage to young, growing companies with limited access to capital markets and relatively great needs for immediate funds to finance expansion. Even well-established companies with excellent credit will find this an attractive alternative to straight-line depreciation if these companies are engaged in a program of rapid and continuing capital expansion and/or are subject to very rapid plant obsolescence. The latter is particularly true of the chemical industry, for example, where new products rapidly replace existing ones.

Furthermore, as long as a rapid rate of growth is anticipated, accelerated depreciation on new facilities will serve to make up for the rapid decline in the depreciation charges on facilities installed a few years earlier. But managements of such rapidly growing enterprises will have to realize that as soon as the rate of expansion starts to flatten out, a sudden "burst" of taxable earnings will occur; and if tax rates are still high at the time this happens, the tax bill will be inordinately large. On the other hand, this in itself need be no cause for alarm if it is also realized that the adoption of accelerated depreciation by such expansion-minded managements will have made possible a rate of growth which could not otherwise have been achieved—at least not as rapidly, and certainly not as cheaply.

Price-Level Changes and Asset Valuation

In preparing balance sheets and income statements, accountants operate on the "going-concern" convention that the business will continue indefinitely. Hence, on the assumption that the company will not sell its fixed assets, it is customary to value these in terms of original cost rather than current market value. Therefore, depreciation charges represent what may be regarded as a proration of historical dollar cost.

Conservative accounting practices prevent market fluctuations from entering into the fixed asset accounts. With respect to inventories, however, conservatism has led to the development of the "lower-of-cost-or-market" rule which, interestingly enough, does recognize down-side price fluctuations of sufficient amplitude. This special treatment accorded to inventories is perhaps justified because during the production process a certain amount is continually being used up and replaced. If prices were constant and the size of stock always the same, accounting for inventory use would present no particular problem. But when prices fluctuate, inventory replacement at varying cost levels raises the problem of measuring the costs to be applied to the utilized inventory. Accountants have devised various methods of measurement, two of which, called first-in, first-out (Fifo) and last-in, first-out (Lifo), are most common.

Valuation by Fifo. Under the Fifo method of valuation, the production sequence is viewed as a continuous historical process. The units that are the first to go into the plant as raw materials are also the first to come out of the plant as part of the finished product. Hence, when prices are rising, the goods used up are costed out at the earlier, lower price levels so that the operating statement reflects an inventory profit, and the remaining unused inventory is carried at the more recently prevailing prices. Conversely, when prices are declining, the higher cost inventory acquisitions are charged against current operations resulting in a narrowing of profit margins, or even a reporting of operating losses, and the remaining inventory is valued at the lower prices at which the material was recently acquired.

This was the state of affairs, with respect to inventory accounting, until the advent of World War II. Because it seemed to comply with the actual way in which a business managed its physical inventory, getting rid of its old stocks first and keeping on hand the fresh, most recently acquired materials, the Fifo method was logically correct and almost universally followed. The criticisms directed at Fifo inventory accounting—that it permitted inventory profits and losses (as the result, respectively, of rising and falling prices) to distort the "true" picture of a company's operations—were not taken seriously enough to have any great impact on business accounting practices. Not, that is, until World War II made it quite obvious that the prewar cost structure was rapidly becoming an antiquated relic, and that the price level was reaching a plateau from which there was not likely to be a return.

The sharp rise in the general price level that began in 1940 and has continued to the present time has led to seriously distorted results in corporate financial statements, and raised a considerable amount of discussion among business executives, accountants, and economists as to the proper treatment of assets. For instance, in the late 1940s Joseph E. Pogue, vice president of Chase National Bank (now Chase Manhattan Bank), said, "It thus becomes apparent that the changing value of the dollar distorts the income account so that the reported net income ceases to be synonymous with profit." And Eugene Holman, president of Standard Oil of New Jersey, commented, "Our depreciation allowances are based on original cost. Therefore our accounting profit does not give now, as it did before the war, a measure of the funds available for increased capacity and for dividends." These comments are as appropriate today as when they were first made.

Valuation by Lifo. The remarks quoted above reflected the concern of most business executives with the effect of price rises on inventory accounting and on depreciation allowances. The response with respect to the latter culminated in revision of the revenue laws as discussed earlier, though pressure continues to be exerted for other changes to be considered shortly. With respect to inventory accounting the result was a rather widespread adoption of Lifo, with the underlying reasoning running somewhat as follows.

Under the Lifo method, the last units acquired in inventory are the first to enter production. This means that the prices paid for the last units become the costs of the raw materials in current production. From this it follows that if the firm maintains a fairly stable inventory, the cost of raw materials is always close to market value, and only when the inventory is reduced do the earlier purchases of stock enter into the computation. Consequently, in a period of rising prices, the Lifo method yields a higher cost of goods sold since the most recent acquisitions are the first to be costed out in production. The result of these higher costs is to reduce the profit increase in a period of rising prices. Conversely, when prices are falling, the last units acquired are the first to enter production, so costs are thus lower and the profit fall is reduced. As compared to Fifo, therefore, which tends to magnify the profit increase in periods of rising prices and the profit decrease in periods of falling prices, Lifo, it was argued, would act as a restraining influence and stabilizer by holding back both a profit increase in prosperity and a profit decrease in recession.

Both in business and in academic circles, an almost naïve enthusiasm was engendered among those who felt that the cure had at last been discovered which would solve what had been an ever-present problem in inventory valuation. For, although Lifo valuation was an artificial approach contrary to the business practices of maintaining inventories as fresh and new as possible, the accounting function did not necessarily have to be tied to actual business practice. Besides, there was the obvious advantage of ironing out fluctuations in the profit and loss statement to the extent that they stemmed from inventory price movements.

Where naïvete did exist, it was among those who failed to realize that only in periods of more or less normal price and inventory changes did Lifo really work as was expected of it, and that under the wrong conditions distortions in the profit and loss statement were much more serious than were likely to be caused by the condemned Fifo method. These conditions are:

1. A sharp drop in price, bringing the level below the cost basis of the original inventory established when Lifo was first instituted.
2. A decline in the physical stock to the point where earlier and very-low-cost inventories are brought into the cost of goods sold.

In the first case, the sharply lower price forces a revaluation of the original inventory stock (through the application of the "lower-of-cost-or-market" rule) with concomitant inventory losses to be recognized. In the second case, very strange results become possible. For example, suppose that a company has been on Lifo for a ten-year period during which prices were moving up steadily and operations were proceeding at a pace which permitted stocks to be maintained at desired physical levels. Labor difficulties set in, and a strike is called which forces the company to operate out of inventory for a prolonged period. Soon the inventory which has been carried at prices which prevailed ten years earlier is brought into sales, and huge inventory profits are realized. It is even conceivable, in fact, that these very large profits result in reported earnings far in excess of those realized for the equivalent period before the strike began. For these reasons there has developed evidence in some quarters of a disenchantment with Lifo valuation and a desire to return to what is felt to be the more logical and realistic Fifo approach.

Inflationary Effects upon Depreciation. With respect to the recognition of fixed asset depreciation, price-level changes also work great havoc. While accelerated depreciation provides a large cash shelter during the early life of an asset, the sharp drop in depreciation charges in later years results, as we have seen, in sharply higher taxes (other things being equal), thereby offsetting in large measure the lower tax payments in earlier years.

Business executives are still concerned with the fact that as capital expenditures taper off, depreciation charges will likewise decline and events will catch up with them in the form of higher taxes. This in itself is no justification for directing criticism at the tax law. The law does, at least, make it possible to postpone the payment of taxes, and in this respect it fulfills a pressing need for all businesses engaged in heavy capital expansion programs, and is particularly beneficial to smaller companies which are going through a period of rapid growth. But there is still legitimate cause for complaint on the part of business executives who see the forces of inflation consistently eroding the purchasing power of their replacement funds and who recognize that consistent growth of dollars is necessary just to stand still in terms of physical facilities. If we accept the premise that this will continue to be a long-term problem because we have a long-term inflationary bias built into our economy, then no depreciation method will make available sufficient replacement allowances so long as it is tied to historical cost.

Appreciation of Land. Another problem in asset valuation is the appreciation of land values. As a case in point, we take Castle and Cooke, Inc., parent of Dole Company, the packers of Dole pineapple. In the 19th century Castle and Cooke acquired extensive pineapple-growing land in Hawaii. In accordance with generally accepted accounting principles, this land is carried on the company balance sheet at its original cost of approximately $30 million, although its current market value is many times that amount.

The significance of this understatement of land value depends upon one's point of view. If profit is measured by the increase in value of the firm from one accounting period to the next, then we must conclude that the profitability of this concern has been grossly understated. On the other hand, if we assume that the firm will continue to use this land for growing pineapple, the appreciation of the land is irrelevant because it cannot be realized in terms of cash flow. However, much of this land represents potentially valuable building sites, and Castle and Cooke has already responded to growing population pressures by converting some of the land into housing development. Therefore, the increased market value of the land can hardly be ignored when evaluating the profit potential of the company. The implication is that valuation of land assets must go beyond either cost or market value alone. Consideration of ways in which the assets will be used is necessary to establish the economic value of land assets.

Conclusion. As is well known, we are committed to a policy of full employment to be achieved within a framework of free and collective bargaining. These two objectives can be achieved, but probably at a sacrifice of stable money. A shift to a stable money policy, on the other hand, is likely to require a sacrifice of one or both of the other objectives. Why? Since our national policy has emphasized full employment without undue restrictions being imposed on collective bargaining, we must learn to live with inflation and to deal with it as effectively as possible.

How, then, can our tax policy take cognizance of "built-in" inflation features and their effect on replacement funds for plant and equipment? Facilities put in place 20 or 25 years ago, replacement of which might now be contemplated, have furnished far from adequate depreciation allowances because of the sharp rise in construction costs that has taken place during the period (many costs have more than tripled). To the extent that allowances are inadequate, the deficiency must be made up from retained earnings or from new financing. In any case it is clear that reported earnings are substantially overstated and that replacement costs are greater than the depreciation allowances which appear on the income statement. Such costs can, in the long run, be recovered only by shifting them to consumers in the form of higher prices. At the same time the continuing overstatement of earnings provides labor leaders with motives and arguments for wage increases in excess of what productivity improvements alone might justify. While such demands can hardly be attributed directly to our tax policy, it seems reasonable to believe that the latter is at least a contributing cause.

Assuming a 50 percent tax on corporate income, every dollar of retained (after-tax) earnings used to supplement a deficient depreciation reserve represents about $2 of pretax income. Clearly, the long-run effect of forcing such deficiencies to be made up out of retained earnings must necessarily mean a higher price level than would prevail if depreciation allowances were realistically computed. A more reasonable approach would therefore require that depreciation be tied to replacement rather than historical cost—a method not yet permitted by the tax laws—for only in this way could the effects of inflation on depreciation allowances be properly offset.

Replacement cost accounting, while not allowed for most assets, is actually being performed when the Lifo method of inventory valuation is employed, and can be reasonably extended to long-term assets as well. However, because of the undesirable aspects of Lifo, a more generalized replacement cost approach would be preferred, to be uniformly applied to both inventories and fixed assets. The essential idea is to arrive at a reported profit figure that reflects the revenues and costs of the present period, not the revenues of the present year and the costs of previous years. For practical purposes under the present circumstances, perhaps the best method of attack is to adjust the data by the application of index numbers. This is readily enough done by making the adjustments with the aid of appropriate indexes, depending on the nature of the asset or account being adjusted.[4] An illustration of the procedure is shown in Exhibit 2.

EXHIBIT 2
Illustrations of Depreciation Adjustment for Fixed Assets

(1)	(2)	(3)	(4) Annual Depreciation Rate (straight-line)	(5) Unadjusted Depreciation (2) × (4)	(6)	(7) Price Index Conversion Factor to Year 11 Dollars	(8) Adjusted Cost of Asset (2) × (7)	(9) Adjusted Depreciation (4) × (8)
Year Purchased	Cost of Asset	Estimated Life			Price Index			
Year 1	$ 50,000	50 yr.	2%	$1,000	80	$\frac{240}{80} = 3.0$	$150,000	$ 3,000
Year 4	80,000	20 yr.	5%	4,000	100	$\frac{240}{100} = 2.4$	192,000	9,600
Current: Year 11	100,000	25 yr.	4%	4,000	240	$\frac{240}{240} = 1.0$	100,000	4,000
	$230,000			$9,000			$442,000	$16,600

Interpretation: The unadjusted depreciation in column (5) totaled $9,000. After adjusting for price changes, the new total of $16,600 in column (9) is found to be $7,600 greater. This $7,600 is a "gain" that accrues to stockholders because they held fixed assets during a period of inflation. The company's operating income, of course, is decreased by this amount.

PROFIT OBJECTIVES OF THE FIRM

Before we study profit planning and control in the next chapter, it seems appropriate to develop an analytical framework for discussion of the firm's profit objectives.

Difficulty of Recognizing Aberrations

It is extremely difficult to assert unequivocally that business firms do not strive to maximize profits. For one thing, it is necessary to segregate short-run from long-run policies, and it is clear that many policies which may reduce short-run profits are designed to establish a better long-run situation. In this regard we may point to such programs as aggressive research for new products, costly development of new markets, and fringe benefits to employees aimed at developing long-run loyalties.

Another complicating factor which makes an unequivocal answer impossible is that each company approaches the profit problem differently

---

[4] For example, plant assets might be adjusted by a construction index; agricultural implement sales by an agricultural equipment price index; and so forth. There is a wide area for research in finding the most suitable index for each purpose.

and what to one enterprise may seem a wise policy is deemed unnecessary and, perhaps, even folly to another. This is true particularly in the field of employee relations: pensions, health and accident insurance, and even coffee breaks. One firm considers such benefits as important in raising labor productivity; another considers them at best a necessary evil.

Nevertheless, it does seem clear that the maximizing principle cannot be accepted without qualification. Studies conducted in recent years have pointed to the conclusion that profit maximization is frequently not the ultimate goal of management. To be sure, in industries characterized by pure competition, the horizontal demand curve confronting the seller leaves no room for price discretion, and maximum profit becomes synonymous with normal profit in the long run. But in most of industry where oligopoly market structures prevail in one form or another, the drive to maximize profits is often modified and compromised with other objectives that may reduce earning power.

What are these other objectives? They may be referred to as limitational factors which, in general, are believed to reduce profits below the level that would have prevailed had maximizing motives been the sole driving force. Yet, in almost every case, it is possible to argue that these factors are only superficially limitational, and that the goal of attaining maximum long-run profit levels requires that they be blended into the operating picture as part of the total pattern of internal and external forces which management must reckon with in its drive for maximum profits. This must be kept in mind in evaluating the discussion which follows.

Profit-Limiting Factors

A number of causes have been suggested as factors responsible for limiting management's drive for profit maximization. These may be classified into two distinct but related groups:

1. Those that are largely internal to the firm's operations are often indirect in their effect on curbing profit, and may go unrecognized by management as profit-limiting factors.
2. Those that are usually external in nature are known and recognized by management, and may be serious enough to warrant the establishment of plans that will specifically provide for nonmaximum profit.

Although this classification may allow for some overlapping, it appears to be fairly reasonable for outlining some of the more common limitational factors.

In the first group are the actions of management that serve in an indirect manner to dampen profits.

1. *Desire for Company Prestige.* Some managers place (excessive) emphasis on establishing the firm as a leader in its industry, even at the expense of lower profits, on the supposition that the company's sales growth is its best measure of success. This occurs, for example, when management devotes a disproportionate amount of effort to broadening the product line by introducing new products, without sufficient attention paid to costs, in order to build a reputation of being largest in the field.

2. *Resistance to Change.* Managers often have a fear or reluctance to make a decision when the expected outcome is other than a near certainty. Rather than chance the possibility of penalty (such as loss of status or even job) in the event of an unfavorable outcome, they prefer to operate on an assumption of "nothing ventured, nothing lost." Preserving the status quo for the security it offers is to them more important than the "risk" of sacrifice that is attendant with progress.

3. *Excessive Desire for Liquidity.* Where increased profits depend on entering new areas of production, this often requires an increased investment in fixed assets and hence a reduction in liquidity. Some industrial companies have balance sheets that look more like bank statements and, of course, reflect extreme pessimism over the business outlook. Such companies have consistently lost ground to their more aggressive competitors. For many managers, "sound" financial conditions are more important than maximum profits.

In the second group are those reasons why a firm consciously and purposely avoids maximizing (short-run) profits, although the execution of these policies may be argued to be best for profits in the long run.

1. *Discouragement of Competitive Entry.* If profits should be large due to higher prices rather than lower costs and superior efficiency, or if the company has a weak monopoly position in the industry, management may prefer lower profits in order to discourage potential competitors from entering the industry. In this case a long-run price policy that is in line with the rest of the industry will be more advantageous to the firm than one which exploits current market conditions for immediate profit.

2. *Discouragement of Government Interference.* Profits have been one of a number of criteria sometimes employed as evidence of monopolistic market control. This can seem somewhat of a paradox when contrasted with the previous consideration. On the one hand, management may maintain lower profits in order to exclude competitors and thereby strengthen its monopoly control. Yet the antitrusters sometimes consider high profits, not low profits, as one of several indexes of monopoly power.

3. *Restraint of Union Demands.* Reducing the possibility of having to pay higher wages is another factor prompting management to restrain

profits. This is particularly applicable in industries with strong labor unions. As long as the economy is prosperous and profits are rising, unions can more easily demand a higher wage rate without inflicting damage to the firm. But in a recession when prices are falling faster than wages, the profit margin is squeezed at both ends. Those companies that curbed wage increases in the beginning would then have a better opportunity to cope with changing market conditions.

4. *Maintenance of Consumer Goodwill.* Management may choose to limit profits in order to preserve good customer relations. Consumers frequently have their own ideas as to what constitutes a "fair" price, whether such ideas are based on "what used to be in the old days" or whether they are the results of "comparison shopping."

5. *Discharge of Social Responsibility.* The large gifts to charity that are regularly made by corporations can hardly be explained by the profit motive. "Social responsibility" has become a major topic for discussion in annual reports and at stockholders' meetings, and it is likely to continue as a permanent long-run goal of many corporations.

Profit Standards

It does seem clear that the profit-maximization principle is a questionable premise. When management itself admits to nonprofit motives in its decision making, and when these motives rule to an extent which causes others to issue warnings about the harm likely to follow from "going off the profit standard," it would seem foolish for anyone to deny that such departures do take place.

There are, of course, times when the drive for profits must give way, at least somewhat, to other factors—national defense in time of war, and responsibility to the community. But these considerations should result in no more than temporary or fairly minor departures from what can be the only meaningful measure of corporate success and managerial effectiveness. Since the decision-making role of management must be cast in a profit-seeking framework, it is desirable to employ some kind of profit yardstick as a measure of what constitutes acceptable performance for a given enterprise from management's own point of view as well as the stockholder's. While "maximum profit" is suitable, to the extent that it is realistic, as an economic principle, it is unwieldy as a standard because, as pointed out earlier, it is possible to support every decision and action as one aimed at maximizing long-run profits even though it may obviously result in reducing current or short-run profits. Besides, how can we hope to recognize "maximum" profits even if we were to see them?

The problem is at best a highly complex one, and it is possible here only to point out some of the reefs and shoals in the search for the desired profit standard. Unfortunately, it is not a case of looking for a beacon in the dark because no one measure will suit all purposes best. Two sets of profit standards can be developed, however, that will be of frequent use to managers in guiding their performance: one of these is a group of overall measures for the firm as a whole; the other consists of internal standards to be employed by the heads of divisional units in the decentralized firm.

Overall Standards. The choice of an appropriate profit standard for the company as a whole depends on the use to be made of it by management—whether for excluding potential competitors, acquiring capital to finance expansion, maintaining control against creditors, restraining union demands, or other considerations. The following overall standards may be proposed as relevant criteria.

1. *Comparative Earnings Standard.* The rate of return in comparison with other companies is a commonly used standard by business firms. The measure may take several forms such as the ratio of net income to net worth, the ratio of company profits to industry profits, or the ratio of current profits to profits in some average or normal period in the past (i.e., an index number).

Measures of these types have been proposed in antitrust investigations in an attempt to establish that excessively high profits when compared with other firms are a possible indication of monopoly power. Labor unions have employed similar measures as an indication of management's ability to pay higher wages. In any event, the use of these measures requires recognition that, especially for industry leaders, the laws of growth will make themselves felt eventually; and even the very large company must inevitably accept a declining rate of secular development. Even the industry, as it matures, will be subject to these forces from which there is no escape.

2. *Capital-Attracting Standard.* To finance continued growth may eventually require recourse to the capital markets, and the ability to acquire needed funds can be used as a reflection of the company's status in the investment community, where a continued evaluation of alternative investment outlets is always being made. Since capital is obtainable by any established business at *some* price, the mere ability to acquire capital is not in itself a measure of success. If a company is able to acquire capital, it may be necessary to evaluate such financing in terms of dilution of stockholders' equity. For example, the principle underlying this standard might be that the corporation's net profits should, on the average, support a level of market prices for its equity securities such that the issuance of new shares does not reduce the proportionate share of present stockholders in the company's assets when valued at current prices. In any event, successful financing should result in little or no

dilution of the stockholders' equity in terms of the measure employed. Typically, such measures as book value per share, earnings per share, and market value per share are favored. These measures, however, tend to be rather unwieldly because no consistent relationship exists among them, and because much will depend on the type of financing undertaken, especially as between equity and debt.

Where debt is employed, the problem is relatively simple since we may then merely compare the cost of such financing with what seems to be the prevailing rates paid by other established firms in the industry or even in other industries. Where common stock is employed as the financing medium, the acquisition of new funds tends to be tied to some discount (large or small) from current market value. If, then, the stock is selling at several times book value (e.g., International Business Machines), it follows that common stock financing will increase the shareholders' book equity. Conversely, where the market price is as much as one half the book value (e.g., many textile companies), common stock financing will dilute book value per share. This problem is not solved by simply reevaluating book values in terms of current replacement costs (a process which would be desirable for other reasons) unless we were arbitrarily, and improperly, to raise or lower book values so as to make them coincide with the market prices of the stocks.

Of the measures that might be employed, perhaps the most suitable would be earnings yield. This would involve using an average of, say, the last five years' earnings as a percent of the price per share received from the sale of new stock. Since the market tends to evaluate the future potential as well as the past performance of the company, this ratio would reflect the investment community's evaluation of the company's position, and the cost it must incur in acquiring equity funds as compared with other capital seekers in the market.

3. *Stockholder Purchasing Power Standard.* Since a business corporation is organized for making profits which will be the source of an income stream for the stockholders, a suitable measure, and one rather easy to employ, is the *relative* position of the stockholders' purchasing power in the industrial economy. Thus, a company's success may be measured in terms of the growth of dividends per share. If such growth has been sufficient not only to offset purchasing power erosion resulting from inflation but to maintain the *relative* income position of the stockholder as well, for example, dividend growth at least equal to the growth in industrial wages, then the company has performed quite satisfactorily for the stockholder.

This measure is suitable only for long-run applicability as a profit standard. Applied in the short run it can too readily break down because (1) many companies maintain the same dividend for a period of time until they feel they can reasonably expect to maintain a higher dividend; (2) companies undergoing rapid growth do not pay out much of their earnings until expansion projects have begun to taper off; and (3) profits are typically unstable, and companies that are particularly subject to earnings instability are likely to permit dividends to fluctuate rather than follow a very difficult stable dividend policy.

4. *Market Appraisal Standard.* Another standard that may be used is to allow a rate of profit for the firm that will preserve the historical relationship between the market price of its equity shares and a broad average of common stock prices. The standard may be a time series expressing the ratio of the price of the stock to the value of the stock index. The latter may be the Dow-Jones Industrial Average or any one of several indexes that are available, or analysts can devise their own index which for particular purposes might be deemed superior. The approach may also be applied to earnings or to dividends, as well as to market prices; and it might even be the wish of the analyst to compose an overall index which utilized all three elements in some weighted or unweighted combination. This standard could also be of use in guiding management's plans for long-term growth by providing a favorable setting for capital attraction.

Since market prices, in the long run, tend to reflect the pattern of earnings and dividend growth, the advantage of economy of labor tends to favor series based on price movements rather than a combination of price, earnings, and dividends. On the other hand, since a small, less-known company is not likely to find its operation properly reflected in the market price of its stock (or the stock might be closely held so that a realistic market appraisal does not exist), an earnings index would be preferable.

SUMMARY AND CONCLUSIONS

In this chapter we have noted that the search for profit is the reason for a firm's existence and have discussed the three major categories of profit theories, that is, compensatory or functional theories, friction and monopoly theories, and the more recent technology and innovation theories.

We have also noted that economists and accountants have conflicting views on how profits should be measured, and that accounting methods permit wide variations in the measurement of profit. The main sources of variation are in the valuation of inventories and in the measurement of depreciation. Appreciation of land also creates a problem.

Finally we have noted that although we assume throughout this book that profit maximization is the basic economic policy of the firm, there is considerable doubt that this premise reflects the real world. Many factors, both internal and external, conspire to limit the firm's profit, to say nothing of the difficulty of determining when maximum profits have been reached.

PROBLEMS

1. Profits are a flow over a period of time. If this is so, can you write an equation for profit using all of the following five variables?
   a. Value of ownership of firm at beginning of period.
   b. Value of assets distributed to owners during period.
   c. Value of ownership of firm at end of period.
   d. Profit during period.
   e. Value of assets contributed by owners during period.

2. Using the five variables listed in Problem 1, write an equation which represents as closely as possible the accounting measure of the change in surplus between two successive points in time.

3. Distinguish between *accounting profit* and *economic profit*.

4. Contrast the three major groups of profit theories as to—
   a. Their explanation of the source or derivation of profits.
   b. The distribution of income shares to a factor or factors of production.
   c. The shortcomings of the theory in explaining income distribution.
   d. Relationship to the condition of uncertainty.

5. Evaluate the following statements:
   a. "A firm in general adopts profit maximization as its goal in the short run but not in the long run."
   b. "In a real-world situation, a firm could maximize its profit."
   c. "The profit maximization model is not closely related to the theory of the firm."

6. There may be limited incentives for most business firms to maximize their profits. Why?

7. If accounting methods do not provide a true measure of profit, why are they used?

8. Describe carefully three currently acceptable methods of depreciation accounting and explain the profit-reporting consequences of each.

9. What kind of enterprise would most greatly benefit by adopting an accelerated depreciation accounting method? Can you indicate any enterprises that would not benefit from such a method? Explain.

10. "The use of both accelerated depreciation and shorter service lives are merely substitute methods of adjusting depreciation for changes in the price level." True or false? Explain.

11. List five factors that limit profit and show that one might argue, in each case, that they are only apparently limitational.

12. Discuss three overall profit standards. Can you suggest two or three others not mentioned in the chapter? Which standard seems best to you?

13. Suppose you bought a house 20 years ago for $15,000 and sold it this year for $25,000. During this period the accumulated depreciation on the house was $12,000, leaving a book value of $3,000.
    a. Did you make an accounting profit? If so, how much?
    b. Is your accounting profit your "real" profit? Explain.

14. The Midwest Electric Power Company purchased plant and equipment in the following years:

Year	Asset	Estimated Life (years)	Price Index
1952	$ 20,000	25	50
1955	40,000	20	100
1961	100,000	40	150
1972	125,000	25	200
1973	60,000	10	300

a. Assuming that these assets were purchased on January 1 of the year in which they were acquired, compute the total depreciation charge for 1967 based on original cost. Assume straight-line depreciation.

b. Compute the total depreciation charge for 1967 in terms of 1967 dollars.

c. The company's revenues for 1967 were $100,000. Fuel expenses were $18,000; labor expense, $9,000; taxes, $25,000. Prepare two profit and loss statements, one without the adjusted depreciation and one with depreciation adjusted according to the price index.

d. On the basis of your calculations, what is the effect of the adjustment in depreciation on the company's operating income? Are stockholders better or worse off? Discuss.

15. Mr. Smith bought an automobile for $4,700 six years ago. He received 10 percent of its original cost when he traded it in on a new car. He had driven the old car 76,000 miles. His investments earned 5 percent interest. What was the cost per mile for capital recovery *plus* return during his period of ownership?

REFERENCES

ANTHONY, ROBERT N. "The Trouble with Profit Maximization." *Harvard Business Review*, vol. 38, no. 6 (November–December 1969), pp. 126–34.

———— *Management Accounting Principles*. Rev. ed. Homewood, Ill.: Richard D. Irwin, Inc., 1970.

CURRAN, WARD S. "Depreciation in Economic Theory and Capital Budgeting." *The Quarterly Review of Economics and Business*, vol. 8 no. 1 (Spring 1968), pp. 61–68.

KNIGHT, FRANK H. *Risk, Uncertainty, and Profit*. Boston: Houghton Mifflin Co., 1921.

PAPANDREOU, A. G. "Some Basic Problems in the Theory of the Firm." *Survey of Contemporary Economics*, vol. II, pp. 183–219. Homewood, Ill.: Richard D. Irwin, Inc., 1952.

SIMON, H. A. *Models of Man—Social and Rational*. New York: John Wiley & Sons, Inc., 1957.

SOLOMONS, DAVID "Economic and Accounting Concepts of Incomes." *The Accounting Review*, vol. 36, no. 3 (July 1961), pp. 374–83.

chapter IO

Profit Management: Planning and Control

Profit management is a function of the financial executive of a firm and refers to the executive's operating decisions in the areas of product line, volume of production, and pricing. Whatever the firm's profit goals may be, profit planning must take into account the expected demand for the firm's products, its capacity to meet the demand, and all of its costs. A good profit management plan will establish objectives, prescribe the ways and means of achieving the objectives, and establish a timetable for actions necessary to carry out the plan. Profit management is not only a vital function for directing short-run operations but is also essential for optimizing investment and financing decisions in the long run.

There are at least five approaches to profit planning and control that are in common use by accountants, business economists, and managers:

1. The profit budget.
2. Break-even analysis.
3. Decentralized control.
4. Time-series projections.
5. Regression analysis.

Each of these may be used separately or in combination with others depending on the information available and the purpose of the analysis.

THE PROFIT BUDGET

A budget is a plan, and a profit budget is a projected or *pro forma* income statement. It is based upon the most recent income statement of the firm, with appropriate adjustments for forecast changes in costs, prices, and anticipated demand over the period covered by the profit budget. From these figures, of course, either a profit or a loss can be forecast.

The profit budget is used for coordination and control, as well as for planning, and good accounting practice requires that it be flexible, with periodic review and revision. The planning aspect of profit budgeting enables managers at all levels to anticipate their needs for manpower, materials, equipment, and financial resources, and act accordingly.

The coordination aspect of profit budgeting is a side effect of the preparation and periodic revision of the budget. The executive who is responsible for drawing up the budget cannot perform the necessary duties without extensive consultation with, and input from, the various department heads. The very process of drawing up a budget forces a coordination of the firm's activities that otherwise might not take place.

The control aspect of the profit budget, unlike coordination, is not automatic. However, when the budget is used properly, it enables management to maintain a systematic check on the results of current operations with relation to previous forecasts. When a wide variation is observed, the causes can be analyzed to discover ways to improve profitability.

BREAK-EVEN ANALYSIS

A technique of profit control that came into use many years ago and has since gained increasing popularity among accountants, business executives, and some economists is break-even analysis. The economic basis of break-even analysis stems from the cost-output and revenue-output functions of the firm, as illustrated in Exhibit 1. These curves should be familiar to you from your study of elementary microeconomics. The diagram in Exhibit 1 shows the total revenue curve *TR*, the total cost curve *TC*, and the corresponding net profit curve *NP*, as these relationships are commonly expressed. It represents the short-run cost and revenue data for a single firm under static conditions, that is, a fixed plant, no change in technology, or in general, "a given state of the art." The total revenue curve, determined by price per unit times the number of units sold, is concave to the origin, indicating that the firm can sell additional units only by charging a lower price per unit on all units sold.[1] Total revenue starts at zero output indicating that when there

---

[1] If the firm participated in a perfectly competitive market and could sell additional units at the same price, the *TR* curve would be a straight line. For firms with some

EXHIBIT 1
Generalized Total Cost, Total Revenue, and
Net Profit Curves

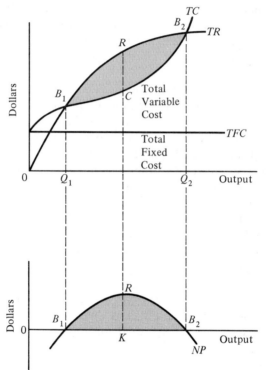

is no output, there is no revenue. Inventories are assumed not to exist so that the firm sells all it produces.

The total cost curve represents the sum of both total fixed costs and total variable costs $(TC + TVC)$. As outlined in a previous chapter, total fixed costs are those costs which do not vary with (are not a function of) output. They include "franchise" payments such as real estate taxes, contractual payments such as rent and interest on capital for the use of specific resources over a fixed time period, and all other constant payments for a flow of services provided by fixed resources during the production period and irrespective of the level of output.

Total variable costs are those costs that vary with (are a function of) output. They include all payments made for the flow of services provided by resources in the production period which vary according to the level of production. Examples of variable costs are direct labor and raw material expenses. In Exhibit 1 the variable cost area lies be-

---

measure of price control, the *TR* curve will usually first increase, but may eventually decrease. The *TC* curve need not cut *TR* when *TR* is increasing, as traditional charts usually imply.

tween the *TC* and *TFC* curves. In short, at any given level of production, total cost equals total fixed cost plus total variable cost. The total cost curve or cost function thus represents the dependent relationship between cost and output.

The difference between total revenue and total costs is, of course, net profit, *NP*, as shown by the shaded area in Exhibit 1 (upper portion), and may be plotted as a separate function (lower portion). The curve can, of course, be negative, reflecting a situation where total costs exceed corresponding revenues. Total net profit is maximized where $TR - TC = $ maximum, as at output *K*.

The chart reveals two break-even points; that is, two levels of output at which the firm's revenues just cover its costs so that net profit is zero. These output levels occur at Q_1 and Q_2. At both of these levels, however, the firm is assumed to be receiving "normal" profits, since costs are assumed to be determined by the returns to productive inputs in alternative employments, that is, opportunity costs. Hence, the profit function is actually plotting only "excess profits." Also, of the two break-even points, only the first of these is usually considered, because it is at this point that the firm first covers its costs and beyond which it can hope to make a profit.

Contribution Margin

REV. PER UNIT.

$P - AVC = C.M$

OUT OF POCKET EXP.

Business executives do not usually think of profit in the economic sense as total revenue less total cost. Instead, for short-run decisions where a portion of the firm's capital is already a sunk investment and hence immobile, they use a more appropriate profit concept known as *contribution* margin or contribution profit—the difference between unit receipts and unit variable costs. Thus, if a product sells at $1 per unit and the variable expenses are 30 cents, each unit sold covers its variable expenses, and the remaining 70 cents is contribution margin, since it contributes to the recovery of fixed expenses and the earning of profit. In economic terms, assuming linear cost and sales relationships with total fixed costs, *TFC*, imposed as a net addition to total variable costs, *TVC*, the total contribution margin, *TCM*, as distinguished from total net profit, *TNP*, is shown in Exhibit 2. Total contribution margin is thus equal to total net profit plus total fixed costs ($TCM = TNP + TFC$), or total revenue less total variable costs ($TCM = TR - TVC$). Also, total revenue is seen to be the sum of total contribution margin and total variable cost ($TR = TCM + TVC$).

As Exhibit 2 stands, it conveys all of the information commonly used by break-even analysts in profit planning and control. The original data for the construction of the chart are frequently obtained directly from the published profit and loss statement of the firm. Sometimes a single statement is used and the lines are extrapolated backwards on the as-

EXHIBIT 2
Contribution Margin

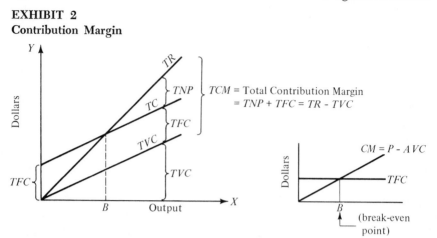

sumption that linear relationships prevail and that the observations selected are typical. Sometimes several statements are employed representing different output levels; the points are plotted as a scatter diagram and the revenue and cost curves may then be sketched in as freehand regression lines.

On the horizontal axis, any measure of output, such as physical units, percent of capacity, or dollar sales, may be employed. When the company's income statement is the source of the data, sales are usually the measure of output since the other indicators are not ordinarily given. In any event, when used for profit planning, the chart shows (1) the output required to net a given revenue, (2) the revenue to be expected from a given output, (3) the sales volume required to break even (output level B in Exhibit 2), and (4) variations of these concepts in terms of net profit and contribution margin (right panel). For levels of output beyond those shown by the diagram, the revenue and cost curves are generally projected on the assumption that the underlying relationships remain unchanged up until the level of full capacity, however defined.

Algebraic Techniques

The assumption of linear revenue and linear cost functions permits the development of simple algebraic procedures for handling problems that would otherwise be solved more inefficiently by graphic techniques. Thus, let us define the following symbols:

Q = quantity of output in units

$TR = PQ$, the total revenue received from the sale of Q units of product

$P = \bar{R}$, the price per unit of output, or average revenue, assumed a constant

TFC = total fixed cost

AVC = average variable cost, that is, variable cost per unit of product

TC = total cost, equal to $TFC + Q \cdot AVC$, the sum of the total fixed and total variable cost

$NP = TR - TC$, the net profit from sale of Q units of product

B = break-even point

The basic formula for calculation of the break-even point is to divide the fixed costs by the contribution margin which may be expressed either as a dollar value or as a percentage, depending upon how the break-even point is to be stated. The break-even point may be expressed as a quantity of units that must be produced and sold, or as a percentage of plant capacity that must be produced and sold, or as a dollar volume of sales that must be realized. Each of these calculations requires a different expression of the contribution margin.

Thus, if the break-even point is desired in terms of unit quantity, the contribution margin is a dollar value per unit, calculated as the difference between price and average variable costs:

$$B(\text{quantity}) = \frac{TFC}{P - AVC} \tag{1}$$

If the break-even point is desired in terms of a percentage of plant capacity, the contribution margin is an aggregate dollar value, calculated as the difference between total revenue and total variable cost at maximum capacity:

$$B(\text{percent of plant capacity}) = \frac{TFC}{(P - AVC)} \times \frac{100}{Q_{\text{max}}} \tag{2}$$

where Q_{max} is the plant capacity in units of production.

If the break-even point is desired in terms of sales dollars, the contribution margin is a percentage, calculated as the fraction of price or revenue that contributes to payments of fixed costs and profit:

$$B(\text{sales}) = \frac{TFC}{1 - \dfrac{AVC}{P}} \tag{3}$$

or

$$B(\text{sales}) = \frac{TFC}{1 - \dfrac{TVC}{TR}} \tag{4}$$

In equation (3) the contribution margin is calculated on a per unit basis from the ratio of average variable cost per unit price (AVC/P). In equation (4) the contribution margin is calculated on a total-sales basis from the ratio of total variable cost to total revenue (TVC/TR). The resulting ratio is the same in either case, and in both cases the calculated ratio is subtracted from 1 to yield the percentage of revenue which contributes to payment of fixed costs.

Example of Break-Even Calculation. An airline can carry a maximum of 10,000 passengers per month on one of its routes at a fare of $50. Variable costs are $10 per passenger, and fixed costs are $300,000 per month. What load factor (i.e., average percentage of seating capacity filled) must be achieved to break even?

First we note that $P - AVC = \$50 - \$10 = \$40$. Then, by equation (2), we calculate:

$$B(\text{load factor}) = \frac{\$300,000}{\$40} \times \frac{100}{10,000} = 75 \text{ percent}$$

If we want the number of passengers necessary to break even, we calculate by equation (1):

$$B(\text{passengers}) = \frac{\$300,000}{\$40} = 7,500 \text{ passengers}$$

If we want the ticket sales necessary to break even, we calculate by equation (3):

$$B(\text{sales}) = \frac{\$300,000}{1 - \dfrac{\$10}{\$50}} = \frac{\$300,000}{.8} = \$375,000$$

Break-Even Point Alternatives

As was previously shown in Exhibit 1, profit is represented on a break-even chart by the area between total revenue and total cost beyond the first break-even point. Obviously, this area can be enlarged by increasing the volume of sales; however, the increase in units sold is eventually limited by plant capacity. The profit area can also be enlarged by shifting the break-even point to a lower level of production and sales. This can be achieved by reducing fixed or variable costs, or by increasing the unit price.

To illustrate these concepts, suppose that we have the situation depicted in Exhibit 3(A) involving linear cost relationships, based on the following data:

$$\text{Plant capacity} = 100 \text{ units}$$
$$AVC = \$7 \text{ per unit} \qquad TFC = \$400$$
$$P = \$12 \text{ per unit} \qquad B = 80 \text{ units}$$
$$TR \text{ (at capacity)} = \$1,200$$
$$TC \text{ (at capacity)} = \$1,100$$

EXHIBIT 3
Break-Even Point Alternatives

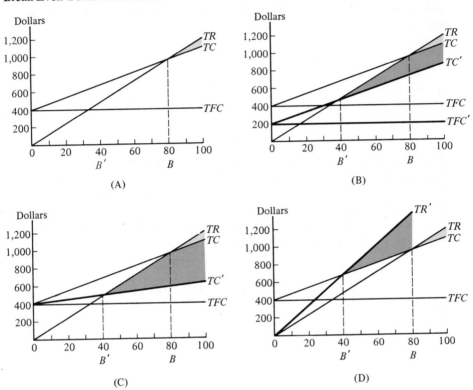

(A)   (B)
(C)   (D)

The shaded area in Exhibit 3(A) represents profit at levels of production beyond the break-even point.

Suppose now that we want to reduce the break-even point to 40 units (*B′*). From equation (1) we note that the break-even point could be reduced in direct proportion to a decrease in total fixed cost.[2] Therefore, we can reduce the break-even point to 40 units if we can cut fixed costs (*TFC′*) to $200, because

$$B' = \frac{TFC'}{(P - AVC)} = \frac{\$200}{\$12 - \$7} = 40 \text{ units}$$

This situation is illustrated in Figure 3(B), where the darker, shaded area represents the gain in profit.

---

[2] If there seems to be a contradiction of terms when we speak of reducing fixed costs, remember that, by our previous definition, fixed costs are those that do not vary with the volume of production. If the company's "overhead" has grown too fat, it may be possible to reduce fixed costs in the next short-run period.

As an alternative to reducing fixed cost, reduction of the break-even point to 40 units (B') might be achieved by a reduction in average variable costs (AVC'). This alternative reduction in variable cost may be computed from equation (1) as

$$B' = \frac{TFC}{P - AVC'}$$

or

$$AVC' = P - \frac{TFC}{B'} = \$12 - \frac{\$400}{40} = \$12 - \$10 = \$2 \text{ per unit}$$

This situation is illustrated in Exhibit 3(C), where the darker, shaded area points out the increase in profit. However, it should be noted that a 50 percent reduction in the break-even point requires more than a 70 percent reduction in total variable cost.

The increase in price necessary to achieve a break-even sales volume of 40 units (B') may be computed from equation (1) as

$$B' = \frac{TFC}{P - AVC}$$

or

$$P = \frac{TFC}{B'} + AVC = \frac{\$400}{40} + \$7 = \$17$$

This situation is illustrated in Figure 3(D). With an increase in price, a decrease in sales might be expected, but Figure 3(D) shows that even with sales reduced to 80 percent of capacity, a sizable increase in profits could result.

Margin of Profit

In the preceding illustrations, only one of the variables (price, total variable cost, or total fixed cost) was changed at a time, but in reality they may all be changed simultaneously. One way of measuring the overall effect of multiple changes is to look at the ratio of gross annual profits to total fixed costs. This ratio may be thought of as a margin of profit, or margin of safety. Since the break-even point is the unit quantity at which total fixed costs are fully recovered and gross profits are obtained by sale of a quantity in excess of the break-even point, the margin of profit may also be computed as $(Q - B)/B$.

To illustrate this concept, let us suppose a firm producing solid-waste disposal units which are sold to stores, factories, and other commercial users for $35,000 each. The plant is currently operating at 60 percent of its capacity of 80 units per year, at a total fixed cost of $600,000 and an average variable cost of $20,000 per unit. The firm is contemplating a change in design which will increase the average variable costs by $1,000 per unit. Also an advertising campaign will be launched, at a cost of $120,000, to announce that the new improved model will sell for $2,000 less than the old one. The marketing manager estimates that these measures will increase sales to 90 percent of plant capacity. Assuming that the marketing manager is right, what will be the effects on the break-even sales volume and on annual profits?

To answer these questions, we note first of all that under current conditions the break-even point is

$$B = \frac{TFC}{P - AVC} = \frac{\$600,000}{\$35,000 - \$20,000} = 40 \text{ units}$$

The annual net profit is

$$NP = Q(P - AVC) - TFC$$
$$= .60(80)(\$35,000 - \$20,000) - \$600,000 = \$120,000$$

The margin of profit is calculated as

$$\frac{NP}{TFC} = \frac{\$120,000}{\$600,000} = .20$$

The same result can be obtained by calculation of

$$\frac{Q - B}{B} = \frac{48 - 40}{40} = .20$$

If all of the contemplated changes are carried out, there will be a new break-even point (B') and a different level of net profit.

$$B' = \frac{\$600,000 + \$120,000}{\$33,000 - \$21,000} = \frac{\$720,000}{\$12,000} = 60 \text{ units}$$

At 90 percent capacity, $.90(80) = 72$ units will be manufactured and sold. The net profit will be

$$NP = 72(\$33,000 - \$21,000) - \$600,000 - \$120,000 = \$144,000$$

which is an increase of $24,000. The margin of profit, however, has not changed, since it is

$$\frac{Q - B}{B} = \frac{72 - 60}{60} = .20$$

To get the same net profit without the additional advertising, the break-even point would be

$$\frac{\$600,000}{\$12,000} = 50 \text{ units}$$

and the quantity sold would be

$$Q = \frac{NP + TFC}{P - AVC} = \frac{\$144,000 + \$600,000}{\$12,000} = 62 \text{ units}$$

The margin of profit would increase to

$$\frac{62 - 50}{50} = .24$$

To get the same gross profit with the advertising but without the price cut, the break-even point would be

$$\frac{\$720,000}{\$14,000} = 52 \text{ units}$$

and the quantity sold would be

$$\frac{\$144,000 + \$720,000}{\$14,000} = 62 \text{ units}$$

The margin of profit would decrease to

$$\frac{62 - 52}{52} = .19$$

Production above Normal Volume

Practical situations arise where a firm must sometimes produce more than its normal output for some period of time. This may occur, for example, when the company has an opportunity to fill a special order, to replace an unexpected drop in inventory, or to increase its inventory above the normal level in anticipation of a decline in production due perhaps to an expected strike or a shortage of materials. Whatever the reason, break-even analysis can be applied as a guide for decision making. For example, suppose we have a situation in which total fixed cost = $20, average variable costs = $5 per unit, price = $10 per unit, and the normal production volume = 8 units per time period. The net profit for this operation is

$$NP = Q(P - AVC) - TFC = 8(\$10 - \$5) - \$20 = \$40 - \$20 = \$20$$

Now let us say that we receive an order for two additional units per time period. If we accept the order, the additional units will have to be produced on overtime and the average variable cost of the additional units will rise to $7 per unit. Should we accept the order?

Letting Q' and AVC' stand for the quantity and average variable cost of the additional units, we can easily calculate the net profit from 10 units as

$$NP' = Q(P - AVC) + Q'(P - AVC') - TFC$$
$$= 8(\$10 - \$5) + 2(\$10 - \$7) - \$20 = \$26$$

which is certainly more than the $20 earned at standard production rates.

The foregoing concepts and analyses are illustrated graphically in Exhibit 4. The diagram provides a clear demonstration of the application

EXHIBIT 4
Incremental Revenues, Costs, and Profits Resulting from a Decision to Expand Production

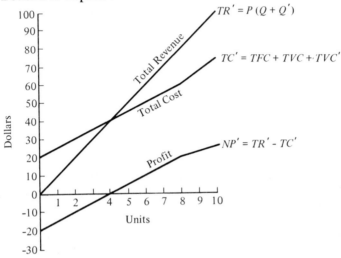

of *incremental profit analysis* as a guide for management decision making. Thus, any act which adds more to revenues than it does to costs should be undertaken, since the result will be a net addition to profits. In this case, a decision by management to produce two additional units beyond its normal eight units resulted in an incremental revenue of $10 \times 2 = \$20$, an incremental cost of $7 \times 2 = \$14$, and hence an incremental profit of $20 - \$14 = \$6$. The company has thus earned an additional $6 of profit over and above the $20 it ordinarily earns on its normal production of eight units.

Price Reductions to Expand Sales

A firm may realize a constant price per unit over a limited range of output; beyond this limit, the price may have to be reduced if sales are to be further expanded. Returning to the above example, suppose the firm is able to sell six out of the eight units it normally produces at its regular price of $10 per unit, and decides to put the remaining two units "on sale" at the reduced price of $7 per unit. Letting Q' represent the two units at the sale price $P' = \$7$, the profit on all eight units becomes

$$NP = Q(P - AVC) + Q'(P' - AVC') - TFC$$
$$= 6(\$10-\$5) + 2(\$7 - \$5) - \$20 = \$14$$

The, incremental revenue on the two "sale" units is $\$7 \times 2 = \$14$, the incremental cost is $\$5 \times 2 = \$10$, and hence the incremental net profit from the sale of these two units at the reduced price is $\$14 - \$10 = \$4$. Since these two units would not otherwise have been sold at the usual price of $10, the seller has made a profit on the first six units of $6(\$10 - \$5) - \$20 = \$10$, and a profit on the last two units of $2(\$7 - \$5) = \$4$. *Note that fixed cost was not considered in calculating the profit on the two last units.* That is, fixed cost did not enter into the decision of whether to sell the last two units at the sale price of $7 each. (Why not?)

Planning for Profit

In order to calculate the production and sales necessary to meet a planned profit goal, the planned profit may be treated as an additional increment of fixed cost.

Since the total dollar volume of sales, S, is equal to the sum of total contribution profit TCP and total variable cost TVC, we have

$$S = TCP + TVC$$

Dividing through by S, we can obtain an equation for average contribution profit, ACP, in the following way:

$$1 = \frac{TCP}{S} + \frac{TVC}{S}$$
$$= ACP + \frac{TVC}{S}$$

Therefore,

$$ACP = 1 - \frac{TVC}{S}$$

Thus, average contribution profit is defined as the ratio of total contribution profit to sales. If total variable cost is expressed as a percentage of sales, it can be seen from the equation above that the contribution profit percentage and the variable cost percentage are complementary, that is, they total to 1.

The break-even sales volume, *BES*, can now be expressed in terms of total fixed cost, *TFC*, and either *ACP* or *TVC/S*. Thus:

$$BES = \frac{TFC}{ACP} = \frac{TFC}{1 - \dfrac{TVC}{S}}$$

This formula can be extended further by setting a planned profit goal and then calculating the minimum sales level required to attain that goal. This is done by treating the planned profit as an additional fixed cost, as follows:

$$BES_{\text{PLANNED}} = \frac{TFC + \text{Planned profit}}{ACP}$$

The above relationships are illustrated by the following example.

A company estimates its fixed costs for the coming year at $800,000 and its profit target at $200,000. Each unit of product is sold at $10, and variable cost per unit is $8. What sales level must the company achieve in order to realize its profit goal?

Since variable cost per unit is 80 percent of the price, the contribution margin is 20 percent. Using the above formula,

$$BES_{\text{PLANNED}} = \frac{\$800,000 + \$200,000}{.20} = \$5,000,000$$

Thus, the company's minimum sales level needed to obtain its planned profit target of $200,000 is $5,000,000. Of this, 80 percent or $4,000,000 will cover variable costs, and the remaining 20 percent or $1,000,000 will go toward the fixed cost of $800,000 and a profit of $200,000.

In this example, no provision was made for the payment of income taxes. If profit after taxes of $200,000 is desired with income taxes at the rate of 50 percent, the profit figure in the above equation would have to be twice as great, namely $400,000. Likewise, if the tax rate were, say, 40 percent, the profit after taxes would be equal to 60 percent of the profit before taxes. In general, if r denotes the tax rate expressed in decimal form, then profit after taxes, *PAT*, is related to profit before taxes, *PBT*, in the following way:

$$PAT = (1 - r)PBT$$

and hence

$$PBT = \frac{PAT}{1 - r}$$

Thus, in the example above, a planned profit of $200,000 after taxes is, at a 40 percent tax rate, equivalent to a before-tax profit of

$$PBT = \frac{\$200,000}{.60} = \$333,333$$

That is, a 40 percent tax on $333,333 is $133,333, leaving $200,000 profit after taxes.

This calculation can be incorporated directly into the *BES* planning formula if desired:

$$BES_{\text{PLANNED}} = \frac{\$800,000 + \dfrac{\$200,000}{.60}}{.20} = \$5,666,667$$

Similarly, if management is contemplating an action which will involve additional fixed commitments (e.g., the floating of a new bond issue which will require the firm to make periodic interest payments in the future), these increments in fixed cost can be added to the numerator of the above formula, and the additional sales revenue needed to cover these extra costs can thus be calculated.

Evaluation

Break-even analysis is a general method of profit planning and control, based on the assumption that there is a unique functional relationship between the profits of a firm and its level of output. Output, as stated earlier, may be measured in terms of physical units, dollar value of sales, percent of plant capacity, or any other relevant index. Profit, on the other hand, is a more explicit notion in break-even analysis and usually represents the difference between receipts and expenses for the period under study. As an analytical device, break-even methods have as their chief advantages simplicity, ease of comprehension by management, and relative inexpensiveness compared to other more sophisticated techniques. Most, and sometimes all, of the data required are taken directly from the published income statements of the firm, and hence break-even analyses can be conducted on a monthly, quarterly, and annual basis.

The static profit-output relation, which underlies the notion of break-even analysis, contains certain implications which are the basis for most of the criticisms leveled against the method. It states that profit, the dependent variable, depends on output, the independent variable; and hence given the level of output, the corresponding level of profit can be determined if the mathematical or graphic relationship is known. Realistically, however, profit is dependent on a great many factors other than output, which the break-even analysis fails to recognize because of the oversimplified construction of its two essential components: the cost function and the revenue function, the difference between which establishes the profit function. With dynamic forces continually at work to shift and modify the underlying elements determining costs and revenues, any attempt to represent these relations in the form of static functions is immediately suspect.

On the cost side, the chief difficulty is this: by assuming a constancy in the state of the arts, that is, technology, plant scale and depth, efficiency, and so forth, traditional break-even methods cannot solve the problems of profit forecasting with much precision. A substantial improvement would be accomplished if there were a careful selection of the enterprise and sample period, and if careful statistical adjustments could be made in order to account for changes in factor prices, product mix, cost-output relations, and similar variations that are influential in their effect on profit. However, the increased expense and know-how necessary to accomplish this in a break-even analysis overcome the practical advantages of the method, namely its inexpensiveness and ease of comprehension by management.

On the revenue side, the use of a static revenue function assumes a constancy of sales mixture, selling prices, and proportion of total output allocated to each distribution channel (i.e., channel ratio), at the very least. But even granted that management can control reasonably well the second and third of these factors, changes in sales mixture are due largely to the whims of consumers. Such changes (as well as changes in the channel ratio), where the contribution profit between products or product classes differs and the changes are not closely correlated with output, may seriously distort the static sales or revenue line and hence the profit forecast.

In short, the break-even analysis applied to profit planning assumes a continuation of the same relative sales and expense patterns, and hence takes no account of uncertainty influences as manifested by probable changes in revenues and costs as business conditions change.

Thus, the assumption in break-even analysis that profit is a *simple relation* with output alone is an oversimplification of the facts. Profit depends on output, to be sure, but it also is affected by production processes, selling effort, the composition of demand, and a multiplicity of other factors both internal and external to the firm. A more general statement closer to the facts would thus be to express profit as a *multiple relation*. To the extent that firms experience rapid changes in their main cost components, in their sales mixture, and their advertising and promotional policies, and in their technology and product design, the use of oversimplified "traditional" break-even techniques is of doubtful validity.

DECENTRALIZED CONTROL

Determining and employing profit measures for purposes of internal control is a more difficult and controversial matter than establishing profit measures for the company as a whole. Economic literature has traditionally concerned itself with the theory of the firm as a profit-making whole; and relatively little energy has been directed, until rather recently, at profit-making subcenters within the firm.

The need for appropriate profit measures (for evaluating performance of subordinate executives and guiding decisions of the subcenter managements) exists in any real sense only in a firm which is decentralized and where management responsibility has been delegated to the heads of the divisional units. In a monolithic organization where all important decisions are made by the firm's top management, the divisional managers are preempted from exercising any discretion over most factors which will shape the profits of their units, so that the problem of evaluating their performance becomes merely a problem of determining how quickly and how effectively they are carrying out the orders which flow down from their superiors at the home office.

The truly decentralized firm is organized as a combination of semiautonomous units and, largely as a result of the fabulous success achieved by General Motors with this type of organization, has won increasing favor among many of our larger manufacturing companies. It has been adopted, among others, by such well-known industrial giants as General Electric, Ford, Chrysler, and Westinghouse Electric. Divisional managers are given authority to plan their selling campaigns, establish selling prices, determine their material and personnel requirements, select their sources of supply either from within or outside of the company as they see fit, and determine their marketing and distribution channels. Responsibility, in other words, tends to be complete with respect to all short-run decision making. Matters of long-run policy, particularly with respect to capital expenditures, remain the responsibility of the top executive group.

From the above it follows that a profit measure which will function properly should be so designed as to exclude all factors over which the divisional managers have no control. This means that it must be independent not only of the decisions handed down from the top but, as well, from the superior or inferior performance of other divisions with which the one in question "does business."

We can begin to appreciate now why the problem of internal profit measurement is such a difficult one. Many facilities and services may be used jointly by two or more divisions of the company; for example, general administrative services, research, maintenance personnel, and equipment. Furthermore, one division is likely to use more of these common facilities and services than another; and the amount of such use is not necessarily related to the volume of a division's business, thereby complicating the problem of allocating such costs among the operating units. It is also very likely that one division will have a "business relationship" with another involving a transfer of semiprocessed goods, by-products, and/or services. Where established market prices exist for such product and service transfers the problem is relatively simple; but where no market prices exist, a system of (arbitrary) transfer prices must be established. Since the purchasing division has no control over the efficiency with which such products and services have been produced (and for which no established market prices exist to permit objective testing of their supply prices), it should not be placed in a position of having its own performance hindered or bettered by the supplying division's performance.

The foregoing discussion leads to the conclusion that divisional net profit is a highly unsatisfactory measure to be employed for internal day-to-day decision making and executive evaluation. To this figure should be added back two major cost groups:

1. Nondivisional expenses which have been charged to the division as part of its burden for supporting the company overhead.
2. Nonvariable or overhead costs of the division itself, incurred either by decisions made by a predecessor divisional manager or by the top executive group with which rests responsibility for long-term capital commitments made by the division.

We then come up with a figure which may be called *controllable divisional profit* and which is essentially the earnings available after deducting from divisional revenues all variable divisional costs such as materials and administrative and selling expenses, as well as any overhead costs directly subject to the control of division managers.

TIME-SERIES PROJECTIONS

Income statement projections are also commonly used in profit planning. Thus, sales and cost figures are taken directly from past income statements, and growth trends are passed through the data by conventional statistical procedures; the profit forecast is then the residual of these sales and cost projections. Or, instead of forecasting sales and costs first and then taking the difference as the profit forecast, an alternative is to project the past-profit figures directly. Either of the two methods involve the identical statistical procedures, and may also be applied to every item on the profit and loss statement, thereby arriving at a projected-income statement for any period in the future. Cyclical and seasonal variations can, of course, also be measured; and the appropriate projected income statements can be built up to show these factors as well. In short, the measurement techniques employ the methods traditionally described in all elementary statistics textbooks.

How valid is the use of time-series analysis as a general approach to forecasting profits? Some brief comments may be given at this point.

First, the forward extrapolation of secular trend is essentially a projection of past or historical relationships, and hence assumes that future profits will be affected by the same relative relationships between sales and costs as existed previously. Consequently, traditional time-series analysis takes no account of changing technology, efficiency, plant scale and depth, and so forth, as factors affecting costs, nor of changes in product mix, prices, distribution channel ratios, and so forth, as factors affecting sales. It is essentially a static method and in this respect has shortcomings similar to those of break-even charts.

Second, there are the statistical problems themselves, such as (a) the assumed relationships between the elements of the time series, particularly as to whether they are additive (i.e., $O = T + S + C + I$), multiplicative (i.e., $O = TSCI$), or whether they stand in some other relationship to each other; (b) whether the traditional residual method should be used in isolating the cycle or whether another procedure would be more appropriate; and (c) whether the trend should be represented by a straight line or a curvilinear relationship, and the correct choice of curve if the latter is chosen. These are some of the considerations that must be taken up in any time-series analysis.

REGRESSION ANALYSIS

A fifth method commonly employed in profit planning is regression analysis. How does this procedure relate to profit prediction?

Essentially, the goal is to discover a functional relationship between the company's profits and one or more indicators of national economic change such as the Federal Reserve Board's Index of Industrial Production, disposable income, bank debits, and so forth. Frequently, "time" is used as one of the independent variables. The underlying assumption in the use of this method for profit prediction is that the well-being of the firm as measured by its profits is directly determined by business conditions in the economy; the company, in other words, is a product of its environment. Profits are thus treated as a dependent variable and the relevant measures of national economic change as independent variables.

In practice, this approach to profit forecasting is greatly enhanced when some logical lead-lag relationship can be found between the company's profits and one or more of the external variables. For example, the American Radiator & Standard Sanitary Corporation (now known as American Standard, Inc.) utilized the fact that there was approximately a four-month lag between its own sales and the regularly published Dodge index of residential contracts awarded,[3] thereby facilitating its profit forecast on plumbing and heating supplies.

Where logical lead-lag relationships cannot be found, however, the independent variables must themselves be forecast before a prediction of profits can be made. In that event, the accuracy of the profit forecast will depend directly upon (1) the accuracy of the forecast made for the independent variables, and (2) the extent to which these external

---

[3] Contained in *Dodge Construction Statistics Services* (New York: F. W. Dodge Corporation).

variables are truly related to the company's profits. The first condition can be partially hedged against by selecting indicators that are frequently forecast by various governmental and private agencies—variables such as GNP, disposable personal income, the FRB index of industrial production, and so forth—so that the various predictions can be cross-checked, weighted, and evaluated. The second condition requires more of a subjective judgment supported by economic reasoning as to which variables will most closely affect the company's present and future earnings. Discovering the relevant data and choosing the appropriate period for the analysis (such as the most recent business cycle with the data expressed quarterly) are probably the most difficult aspects of this type of regression analysis.

NATURE AND DYNAMICS OF PROFITS

Profits Planned and Unplanned

From a managerial standpoint, a central notion in the concept of uncertainty is that anticipations of the future are framed in terms of a range of possible outcomes distributed in some way around a single most-expected outcome. As applied to incomes this means that there will result a deviation of actual returns from planned returns. This follows from the fact that not all future revenues and costs can be known, so that not all resources in the production process can be engaged on a contractual basis. Since the payments to some resource owners are contractual, it follows that other resource owners will receive residual returns. By the very nature of the typical production process, these residual returns will include unanticipated positive or negative components.

Profits, it should be made clear, are a mixture of both anticipated and unanticipated residuals. The latter component is a true surplus (positive or negative) and as such is a part of economic profit in the fullest sense. The former component, however, is not necessarily a surplus; and whether it is or not depends on the particular case in question. In the typical well-managed enterprise, the planning process is directed toward planning for profits and tight financial control and proper capital budgeting require that profits be planned. To the extent that the planned or anticipated profits are just large enough to warrant bringing together the necessary resources for carrying the plan through to fruition (the project would be scrapped if the estimated returns were expected to be less than this minimum)—to that extent they would more properly constitute a functional or compensatory return (long-run cost) and as such would not qualify as "true" surplus.

However, projects are frequently undertaken with the expectation of securing something more than the planned required profits. This extra may, in contrast, be thought of as a planned surplus profit—a return in excess of that necessary to bring the project into being and is, therefore, a "true" profit. In addition, there exist unplanned positive or negative residuals which will increase or decrease the planned surplus. In short, *profits may be either anticipated or unanticipated, required or surplus, but in any case they are always uncertain, and will always be so as long as the future cannot be forecast with known error.*

Profit over Time

By its very nature, planning involves the future, and the future introduces the element of uncertainty. In static analysis, profit maximization extends only to the time interval in which business transactions are completed. Thus, if management starts production in "year 1" with the aim of selling in "year 2," its forecasts extend only as far as "year 2." That is, management formulates plans in the current time periods t_1 in anticipation (forecasts) of events that will take place in future time periods t_2, t_3, and so forth. If the events which are expected to occur within this time period are forecast with certainty, plans can be formulated in a static vein and no further decisions beyond the initial one of establishing operations are necessary. Profit maximization then reduces itself to the problem of making the initial decisions required for arriving at maximum profits over the given (planned) time period.

But even in such a situation, a forecast of a $100 profit in some future time period is not the equivalent of a $100 profit in the current one. This is due to the fact that the interest obtainable on a perfectly certain investment, such as government bonds, is greater than zero so that there exists a time preference which favors the present as against the future. Thus, if a government bond maturing in one year is available at a yield of 4 percent, a profit of $100 to be made available one year from today from a production process involving no uncertainty would have a present value of $100/1.04 (= $100/104 percent) or approximately $96.15. [Conversely, at 4 percent the value next year of $96.15 today is 104 percent of that amount, or $96.15(1.04) = $100.] Similarly, if a two-year government bond were available at a 4 percent yield, then $100 obtainable two years from today from a production process with no uncertainty would have a present value of $100/(1.04)^2$, or approximately $92.46. If this same process were to produce a stream of $100 to be available at the end of one year and another $100 to be available at the end of the second year, the present value of these two payments would be the sum of their separate present values, or $188.61.

In the real (dynamic) world, however, uncertainty is an ever-present element in the economic environment. Related to the above discussion this means that future receipts must be discounted (capitalized) at a rate in excess of that available on an investment of perfect certainty, with the result that the present value of such future receipts are accordingly lowered. We may express this concept in general terms, namely:

$$I = \frac{R}{(1 + r)^n} \qquad (1)$$

where I represents an investment which will produce a revenue, R, available at the end of n periods in the future, and discounted at a rate represented by r per period (expressed in decimal form). Where a stream of income is expected over a period of years, the equation can be expanded as below, where R_1, R_2, R_3, and R_4 represent flows of cash earnings in the first, second, third, and nth years:

$$I = \frac{R_1}{1 + r} + \frac{R_2}{(1 + r)^2} + \frac{R_3}{(1 + r)^3} + \cdots + \frac{R_n}{(1 + r)^n} \qquad (2)$$

Just what the profit-maximizing firm seeks to maximize was discussed in a previous chapter, so at this point we will simply say that it is desirable to maximize the stream of future income. In static analysis, where the current period's profits are simply extended repetitively into the future, the problem of maximizing an earnings stream reduces simply to the problem of maximizing R. But in a dynamic situation, where fluctuating values for R are projected, the problem of maximizing is greatly complicated. However, as a practical approach to the problem, it is often useful to estimate a uniform (average) annual profit and to project this into the future until a change in conditions (such as installation of a new plant) calls for a new projection. Where the flow of expected uniform annual profit. U, is for an indefinite period of time, the following equation defines the value, I, of this income sequence into perpetuity:

$$I = \frac{U}{r} \qquad (3)$$

where r is the appropriate capitalization rate.

This approach is employed universally in the valuation of stocks by investors who multiply estimated earnings by a factor known as the price-earnings multiple to arrive at an estimated value for the stock in question. The price-earnings multiplier is simply the reciprocal of r, the capitalization rate. It is a technique also commonly employed in the real estate industry, whereby the estimated annual rentals are multiplied by some figure (the reciprocal of the capitalization rate) to arrive at an estimate of the real estate value.

SUMMARY AND CONCLUSIONS

In this chapter we have discussed five approaches that are commonly used for profit planning and control. The profit budget sets the pace for the firm and is used for both planning and control. The techniques of break-even analysis as a profit-planning tool were discussed in considerable detail, and we have concluded that they are of doubtful validity in firms which experience rapid changes in costs, sales, promotional policies, or technology.

The problems of measuring the profit performance of decentralized autonomous divisions have been discussed, and we have noted that the division should be judged only on its controllable divisional profit. Finally, we have explained the ways in which the statistical methods known as time-series analysis and regression analysis can be used for profit planning.

PROBLEMS

1. If a firm were to operate at the "break-even" point, as defined in this chapter, would it remain long in business? Why or why not?

2. What is meant by contribution margin? Can it be positive while total profit is negative? Can it be negative when total profit is positive?

3. Critically evaluate the following methods of profit planning and control in terms of managerial decision making:
   a. The profit budget.
   b. Break-even analysis.
   Suggest possible modification or improvement of these methods.

4. List and discuss five important factors that must be considered in profit planning in the following industries:
   a. Toy manufacturing.
   b. Airline industry.
   c. Color television manufacturing.
   d. Auto repair business.
   e. CPA firm.
   f. Construction materials.
   g. Petroleum industry.
   h. Computer manufacturing.

5. For the XYZ company, the cost (overhead and wholesale price) for handling of dishwashers is $C = 150 + 72q$. The q dishwashers are sold at $\$p$ per unit per month where $p = 180 - 30q$ (the demand function). What retail price per unit is required for profits to be maximized?

6. This & That Boutique offers all its merchandise for sale at $20 per unit. The total cost of producing q units is given by $C = 40 + 4q + .02q^2$.
   a. How many units must be produced to maximize profit?
   b. Show that marginal revenue equals marginal cost at the profit-maximizing value of q.

7. Kona Coast Inn manages 7 two-bedroom apartment units which rent for $55 a night and 20 one-bedroom cabin units which rent for $40 a night. The Inn also manages 30 single-room units and 15 double-room units, which rent for $20 and $30 a night, respectively. The maintenance cost including cleaning and preparation for new occupants is $12 each

for the apartment and cabin units, and $6 each for all other types of accommodations. Annual lease for the property is $150,000, and other fixed costs for managing the property are $125,000 on a 300-day annual basis. The average stay at the facility is 2½ days, and the occupancy closely follows the proportion of available facilities.

    a. What percentage of facilities must be rented each night to break even?

    b. How many of each type of accommodation must be rented each day to make an annual profit of $50,000?

8. An electric pencil sharpener currently sells for $15. The fixed costs are 30 percent of selling price, and 20,000 units have been sold annually for the last 5 years. Annual net profit is $55,000. Due to severe competition, the company's promotion manager proposes some modification of the products design to attract more customers. The modification will increase average variable costs by 22 percent and total fixed costs by 10 percent, but sales may be expected to increase to 24,000 units per year. What should the selling price be in order to earn the same net profit?

9. Suave Hats, Inc., manufactures men's hats and sells them at $15 each. Its total fixed cost is $5,000 per week, and its average variable cost is $10 per unit.

    a. What is the company's break-even sales volume?

    b. What would the company's profit be at its normal production capacity of 2,000 hats per week?

    c. The company has been operating at its normal production capacity. The union threatens to strike, so the management of Suave decides to produce an additional 500 hats for inventory at an estimated average variable cost of $13 per hat. What will be the incremental profit (or loss) on the sale of the 500 additional hats?

    d. After some negotiation, the company and the union agree on a new labor contract. Meanwhile, the company has been able to dispose of only 300 of the 500 additional hats at its regular price of $15. However, a department store has offered to take the remaining 200 hats under a private label at $11 each. If the management of Suave accepts the offer, what will the incremental effect be of these 500 units?

10. Last year, Superior Paint Company sold 250,000 gallons of paint for which the variable cost of manufacture was $4.20 per gallon. Each gallon contributes 30 percent of its revenue to fixed costs and profits. This year the company is contemplating a price reduction of 5 percent.

    a. How many more gallons will the company have to sell at the 5 percent price reduction in order to earn the same profit this year as last?

    b. Suppose that average contribution profit had been 20 percent and the selling price $7. What would your answer be then?

11. National Outerwear manufactures and sells men's raincoats at a price of $40 each, for which the average contribution profit is $15 per coat. Last year total fixed costs were $5.4 million; this year, through a major cost reduction effort, they are expected to be $3.9 million.

a. How many raincoats did National Outerwear need to sell last year in order to break even?

b. How many must it sell this year in order to break even?

c. How many raincoats must the company sell this year in order to earn a profit before taxes equal to 20 percent of sales?

12.   **CASE PROBLEM: URBAN D. RICKERT, INC., PUBLISHER**
         PROFIT PLANNING FOR A NEW TEXTBOOK

The Urban D. Rickert Company is a major publisher of college text-books in the fields of business and economics. Recently, Dr. Notlim H. Recneps, a professor at a large midwestern university, submitted a manuscript to the company for publication.

In order to decide whether or not to publish the book, the management of the Rickert company drew up estimates of the number of copies that it might expect to sell at various prices. These estimates were based on what were believed to be the approximate sales volumes of three competing books on the same subject published by three other major companies, namely Prentick-Hill, McGrew-Hall, and Macmulen.

According to the Rickert company's estimates, it would expect to sell 20,000 copies at a price of $12 per copy. However, since the book was unusually comprehensive and covered a rather wide array of topics in business and economics, the publisher felt that many professors would advise students to purchase the book for their personal reference use, even if the book were not used as a required text for a particular course. Accordingly, the Rickert company estimated that at $11 per copy it would expect to sell 40,000 copies; at $10 per copy, its sales volume would increase by 50 percent; and for each further reduction of $0.50 in price the sales volume would increase by 20,000 copies until a total of 160,000 books was sold.

Fixed costs are $200,000 but rise to $240,000 when 100,000 copies or more are produced and sold. At an output volume of 140,000 books, fixed costs increase to a level of 260,000.

Variable costs amount to $4 per copy for the first 100,000 copies, $5 per copy on *all* copies if more than 100,000 books are produced and sold, and $6 per copy at an output of 140,000 books.

Questions:

a. Construct a break-even chart depicting this situation. Your chart need show nothing more than total revenue total cost, and the break-even points if any.

b. Suppose the Urban D. Rickert company decides to price the book at $9.50, and that it sells no more than 80,000 copies. Construct another break-even chart showing total revenue, total cost, and the break-even points if any.

c. Can you estimate the break-even sales volumes from your two charts?

d. At what output volume is profit maximized?

REFERENCES

HAWKINS, C. M. "On the Sales Revenue Maximization Hypothesis." *The Journal of Industrial Economics,* vol. 18, no. 2 (April 1970), pp. 129–40.

McRAE, T. W. *Analytical Management.* New York: Wiley-Interscience, 1970.

MANTELL, LEROY H., and SING, FRANCIS P. *Economics for Business Decisions.* New York: McGraw-Hill Book Co., 1972.

MAO, JAMES C. T. *Quantitative Analysis of Financial Decisions.* Toronto: The Macmillan Co., 1969.

RIGGS, JAMES L. *Economic Decision Models for Engineers and Managers.* New York: McGraw-Hill Book Co., 1968. The discussion of break-even analysis, on which portions of this chapter are based, is particularly recommended.

chapter 11

Advertising

How can we evaluate the effectiveness of our advertising? What criteria should we employ to determine the size of the advertising budget? Given the size of the total advertising budget, how should it be allocated among different products and media?

These are the kinds of *decision* questions that are often asked by managers who are engaged in the budgeting of advertising expenditures. In addition, there are *social* questions which crop up from time to time, such as whether the net effect of advertising is "good" or "bad" for society as a whole and whether the functions of advertising in today's economy should be subject to a serious revaluation.

Needless to say, intelligent executives are interested in both classes of questions. Hence a discussion of the problems will comprise the subject matter of this chapter. But first a word about the relationship between advertising and demand may be appropriate.

It is often said that the purpose of advertising, from the seller's standpoint, is to make the demand curve more inelastic, thus allowing a higher price to be charged for each unit sold. If this statement is true, it would mean, as shown in Exhibit 1, that the seller would prefer to be confronted with the demand curve D_1 rather than D_2. Yet if his most profitable output is beyond ON_1, say at ON_2, then D_2 is clearly preferable to D_1 because it allows for sales at a higher price even though D_2 is more elastic than D_1. On the other hand, if his most profitable output were ON_3, then he would prefer D_1 to D_2. Therefore, the argument

EXHIBIT 1
Advertising and Demand

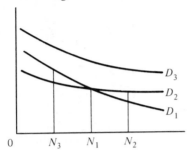

that advertising is desirable for the seller because it results in a more inelastic demand curve may be only partially true and in many instances may be completely false.

The statement can be correctly reformulated by noting that what the seller really wants is not necessarily a more inelastic demand curve but rather a new and higher curve *level*. This is illustratd by D_3. With this demand curve the seller can charge a higher price per unit relative to either D_1 or D_2, irrespective of the most profitable output volume indicated on the chart.

THEORETICAL ADVERTISING—SALES MODEL

Our purpose is to construct a model showing the relationship between sales and advertising. This means that we want a theoretical model in which total advertising expenditure is viewed as the independent variable and sales as dependent. Of course, there may be other factors besides advertising that will influence sales, but they will not be taken into account at the present time. The model we construct will serve as a guide for deciding on the total size of the advertising budget. Once this decision is made, the next step is to develop a procedure for allocating the given budget among competing uses.

Exhibit 2 contains some "typical" advertising-sales relationships. Each curve shows that sales are some positive amount even when advertising expenditures are zero. This is to be expected since there are factors other than advertising that influences sales.

In Chart A, *equal* increases in advertising result in *equal* amounts of change in sales. Hence the functional relationship is linear. In Chart B, *equal* increases in advertising produce *increasing* amounts of change in sales. The relationship in this case is exponential. In Chart C, *equal* increases in advertising produce *diminishing* increases in sales. This relationship is that of a power function.

EXHIBIT 2
Advertising-Sales Relations

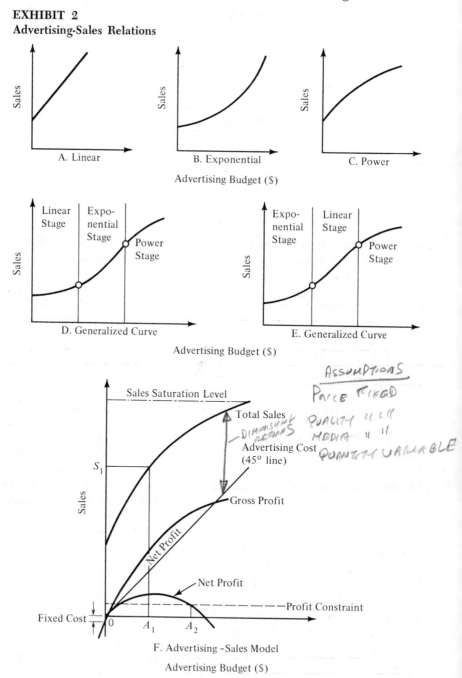

A. Linear

B. Exponential

C. Power

Advertising Budget ($)

D. Generalized Curve

E. Generalized Curve

Advertising Budget ($)

Sales Saturation Level

Total Sales

Advertising Cost (45° line)

S_1

Gross Profit

Net Profit

Net Profit

Profit Constraint

Fixed Cost

A_1 A_2

F. Advertising –Sales Model

Advertising Budget ($)

You don't have to be an economist to guess that no one of these functions is likely to be typical for all levels of advertising expenditures. That is, any real advertising-sales curve based on actual data covering a wide enough domain of expenditures on advertising is likely to exhibit some features of all three curves. For example, Chart D illustrates a case in which the sales curve goes through three stages: a slow linear growth stage at low advertising levels, a rapid exponential growth stage when advertising passes beyond a certain threshold or critical level, and a slowing down or power stage at high levels of advertising expenditure. A different type of advertising-sales curve with the first two stages reversed is presented for comparison in Chart E. Of course, several other generalized curves, each representing a plausible hypothesis, could be shown.

Despite the probability that the curves shown in Charts D and E are perhaps more representative of reality, they are not the types of curves that are likely to be fitted in an actual statistical investigation. There are several reasons for this, all of which may be roughly summed up by the statement that their shapes tend to make them too complicated relative to the data that are usually available and the reliability of the statistical analysis. Hence a simpler curve such as one of the first three is usually selected. Of these, the power function in Chart D may be chosen for further discussion because it has at least one important economic property that the linear and exponential functions do not possess: it is the only one of the three curves that allows for diminishing (marginal) returns to advertising. (The linear curve in Chart A, on the other hand, allows only for constant returns whereas the exponential curve in Chart B allows only for increasing returns.)

Consider the diagram in Chart F. The rising 45° line represents advertising costs. That is, at any point along this line the amount spent on advertising is exactly equal to the amount received as sales revenue. The curved line labeled gross profit represents the difference between sales and all costs except advertising. Net profit is thus the area between gross profit and advertising costs, and the net profit curve when plotted separately takes the inverted "bathtub" shape as shown in the diagram.

The analysis assumes that price, quality, media, and other factors that may affect sales are held constant so that different sales levels can be attributed to variations in advertising expenditures, that is, the size of the advertising budget. With larger doses of advertising expenditures, the sales curve rises by decreasing amounts indicating that diminishing returns to advertising are at work. That is, each increment in advertising, say in $1,000 expenditure blocks, produces a less than proportional increase in sales so that the ratio of the change in sales (ΔS) to the change in advertising expenditure (ΔA) decreases. Since the type of sales curve chosen is one which is asymptotic to the saturation level, the ratio $\Delta S/\Delta A$ will approach zero as a limit as advertising increases. Note, however, that if maximum short-run net profit is the objective,

the optimum advertising budget is OA_1. This expenditure level will produce OS_1 in sales, which is considerably below the saturation level.
We may conclude from this that the amount of advertising expenditure
which will produce maximum profit may be quite different from the
amount of advertising expenditure that will yield anything approaching
maximum sales.

A somewhat greater degree of realism can be built into the diagram
by introducing the notion of a profit constraint, that is, a minimum
long-run profit or target rate of return which management is striving
to attain. This is shown by the horizontal dashed line near the bottom
of the chart. Assuming that management wants the largest volume of
sales consistent with this constraint, it will select an advertising budget
equal to OA_2. This decision rule can thereby result in a substantially
higher advertising budget as compared to OA_1. Distinctions between
short-run and long-run considerations are thus seen to be quite important
in decisions involving advertising budgeting and profit policy.

Advertising Elasticity of Sales

In measuring short-run advertising effectiveness, a useful concept to
employ is the *advertising elasticity of sales* (or *demand*). Like other
elasticity notions, it may be defined as the percentage change in quantity
sold (or market share) resulting from a 1 percent change in advertising
outlay. If we represent sales in units by S and advertising expenditure
by A, the point formula is:

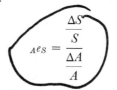

$$_A e_S = \frac{\dfrac{\Delta S}{S}}{\dfrac{\Delta A}{A}}$$

This formula gives the elasticity at any point along the sales curve.
In many cases it may be desirable to estimate the elasticity over a
segment of the curve. If the segment is linear or nearly linear, the following arc elasticity formula for advertising elasticity of sales can be
used:

$$_A E_S = \frac{\dfrac{S_2 - S_1}{S_2 + S_1}}{\dfrac{A_2 - A_1}{A_2 + A_1}}$$

where (A_1, S_1) and (A_2, S_2) are the coordinates of the two endpoints
of the linear segment. As with all arc elasticity formulas, this one measures the average elasticity for the segment as a whole.

The advertising elasticity coefficient may be affected by a number of factors such as (1) the stage of the product's market development; (2) the extent to which competitors react to the company's advertising, either by further advertising or by increased merchandising efforts; (3) the quality and quantity of the company's past and present advertising relative to that of competitors', since variations in *qualitive* factors (e.g., choice of media) obscure the effects of *quantitative* variations in advertising outlay; (4) the importance of nonadvertising demand determinants such as growth trends, prices, incomes, and so forth, and the extent to which these can be averaged out in conducting the analysis; (5) the time interval that elapses between the advertising outlay and the sales response, which is difficult to predict because it depends on the type of product, advertisement, and so forth; and (6) the influence of the "investment effect" of the company's past advertising and the extent to which this may be influential in affecting current and future sales as manifested by delayed and cumulative buying. In measuring advertising effectiveness, these are the sorts of considerations that must be taken into account. Since the goal of the analysis is to discover what sales are as a result of advertising, compared to what they would have been without advertising, measurement methods must be devised that will allow and compensate for the above complexities. Several of these methods may be described as follows.

Basically, the figures necessary for studying advertising effectiveness can be obtained either from historical data within the firm or from controlled experiments. (A third approach is to base the analysis on the historical data of several firms. But this requires that products, prices, and other market characteristics be as similar as possible so that differences in sales can be attributed to advertising outlay. Such uniformity is sufficiently rare, however, to make this approach quite impractical in most cases.) Historical data are often inadequate because they cover a period of time during which many unknown factors may have been significant in affecting sales, in addition to advertising as such. However, for companies whose market share is otherwise quite stable, variations in advertising outlay over time may reveal significant sales differences so that a meaningful advertising-sales relation can be established and an elasticity coefficient computed. In actual measurement, statistical regression analysis must often be used in order to isolate advertising from other factors that may be responsible for sales. But regression analysis also requires that the significant causal factors affecting sales be measurable. Since this is not always the case, the use of regression techniques is not always possible. Controlled experiments, on the other hand, offer the opportunity for creating data, but they are usually more costly, particularly when the results must be subjected to further statistical analyses.

ADVERTISING BUDGETING

What are the economic implications of planning and allocating advertising budgets both under short-run and long-run conditions? This question often arises in discussions relating to the economics of advertising.

It should be noted that a distinction exists in economic theory between production costs and sales costs. Production costs are those resulting from the production of the product itself; sales costs arise from those activities designed to influence the demand curve, as when firms incur expenses of salespeople, public relations, gifts to purchasing agents, and the use of various advertising media such as radio, television, newspapers, and so forth. In theory the distinction between the two classes of cost is usually clear-cut; in practice, a sharp line between the two cannot always be drawn because some costs, for example, packaging, may fall partly in each category. Nevertheless, the distinction is conceptually useful, at least as a beginning to the discussion of short- and long-run budgeting, even though some expenditures will occasionally defy precise classification.

Short-Run Budgeting

Three approaches to the short-run budgeting of sales costs may be outlined: (1) the incremental method, (2) percent-of-sales method, (3) objective-and-task method. The first draws entirely on principles of economic theory and is useful as a guide to thinking about the subject as well as pointing out clearly where empirical research is really needed. The remaining two are the methods in more common use by advertisers today.

Incremental Method. An important assumption underlying the incremental method is that the firm will seek to adjust its selling expenditures to the level which will allow maximum profit. Various methods for attacking the problem have been developed by a number of economists.

In all instances three variables are involved: price, selling costs, and sales. Sometimes either price or selling cost is varied with the other held constant to determine the effect on sales; sometimes both price and selling cost are varied and the effect on sales is noted. In all cases the ultimate objective is to arrive at a combination of price and selling costs that will result in a sales figure which yields maximum net profit to the firm.

It is not within the scope of this discussion to go into the details of the theoretical structure concerning the nature of these adjustments. However, some essential theoretical concepts can be presented based on the elementary principles of production economics.

Basically, the procedure used is to regard selling cost as a kind of productive resource, variations in which will cause changes in sales if price is held constant. There are thus two classes of optimization problems:

1. To determine the optimum relation of total selling cost expenditure to sales.
2. Given the total selling cost expenditure or budget, to determine the optimum allocation of that expenditure among competing advertising media.

The first problem is akin to that of a simple input-output or factor-product type of production function, except that now the input factor would be varying doses of selling costs for a homogeneous medium (instead of labor, capital, or some other factor of production) and the production would be sales (instead of units of output). The result should take the form of a selling-cost–sales function somewhat similar to the typical production function of economics textbooks, although it may of course be linear over a range of inputs.

Similarly, if both price and selling costs are varied, the principles parallel the factor-factor type of production function analysis where the object is to determine either:

1. The optimum combination of price and selling cost to produce a given profit level from sales; or
2. The maximum profit level from sales that can result from a given combination of price and selling cost.

The second problem, that of allocating a given budget among competing media, is also an extension of principles derived from production economics. Using the incremental notation Δ, let $\Delta S_1, \Delta S_2, \Delta S_3, \ldots, \Delta S_n$ represent the increase in sales at a given price from advertising media 1, 2, 3, ..., n, and let $\Delta A_1, \Delta A_2, \Delta A_3, \ldots, \Delta A_n$ denote the additional expenditure sum on various forms of advertising, say in $1,000 blocks. For (equilibrium) optimum allocation of expenditures, it is necessary that the corresponding incremental ratios be equal. That is, if medium 1 represents radio time, medium 2 is spot television commercials, and so forth, then optimum allocation requires that

$$\frac{\Delta S_1}{\Delta A_1} = \frac{\Delta S_2}{\Delta A_2} = \frac{\Delta S_3}{\Delta A_3} \cdots \frac{\Delta S_n}{\Delta A_n}$$

For if the ratios are not equated, as when

$$\frac{\Delta S_1}{\Delta A_1} > \frac{\Delta S_2}{A_2}$$

medium 1 in this case would be preferred to medium 2. Hence it would pay to reduce (or withdraw) expenditures on medium 2, thereby raising the value of that ratio, and increase expenditures on medium 1, thereby reducing the value of that ratio. When the ratios are equal, profit is at a maximum.

Theory thus leads to the conclusion that basically similar principles are involved in regarding sales costs in the same manner as the hiring of productive factors. Further, it infers that there is a law of diminishing returns to advertising in that constant increments of advertising expenditure shift the demand curve to the right in ever-decreasing amounts (assuming price is unvaried).

These conclusions, plus the advantages cited above—that the incremental method provides a guide for thought clearing and empirical measurement—are offset by some limitations:

1. The theory makes <u>no allowances for the investment or cumulative effects of advertising,</u> nor does it recognize the effect of lagged responses.
2. <u>It takes no account of the effect of competitors' reactions to advertising.</u>
3. <u>It assumes that the effect of advertising on sales volume can be measured so that the results can serve as a basis for budgeting.</u>

Concerning this last limitation, it may be noted that some empirical studies have yielded good results, particularly with respect to the allocation problem. Using the incremental concept outlined above, controlled experiments were set up for various test markets. In one such study, five different media treatments were taken and the treatments were rotated between the relevant cities during the week. Covariance analyses were then conducted, and tests of significance were made. The results of the study revealed significant differences in advertising media sufficient to warrant a reshuffling of the company's selling costs for its next fiscal period, with substantially larger sales and profits as a result. But in this case the firm was particularly suited to this type of analysis because its product was a service—a unique type of insurance plan—on which it had a near-monopoly status in its own regional area.

Normally, however, the incremental method may not as easily be adapted to other business firms because of the limitations cited above, although the use of mail order and of keyed response techniques offers another area in which the approach could be successfully developed. In view of these limited applications, most companies normally employ either of the other two more "practical" or expedient approaches to short-run budgeting discussed next.

Percent-of-Sales Method. The percent-of-sales method is self-explanatory. <u>It consists of taking a fixed percentage of the previous period's sales or of an average of several period's sales and using this as a budget for the company's next fiscal period.</u> An alternative approach is to select a percentage based on a forecast of sales. In either case, the short-coming of the method is essentially that it places the cart before the horse by not recognizing that advertising expenditures are made for the purpose of influencing sales. Using a percentage figure based on past experience gives no indication of how much should be budgeted to *increase future* sales, that is, shift the demand curve to the right, which is the way in which advertising should be viewed. Used in its present manner, the percent-of-sales approach to advertising budgeting is more an effect of sales than a cause. Its widespread use, however, is probably due to the fact that it offers a simple and mechanical method of budgeting and control, and that it permits the advertising expense to pay its own way because the expenditure fluctuates according to sales.

Objective-and-Task Method. In this method, the sales objective is established first, usually on the basis of the difference between the sales level that would be expected with and without advertising. This difference becomes the objective, and the "task" is to determine the advertising budget needed to reach the objective. In this simple form, the method suffers from the weakness that it takes no account of whether the predetermined increase in sales—the objective—is worth the increased cost needed to attain it, that is, whether or not the ultimate result will be an increase in net profit. If the appropriate measures could be obtained for comparison and evaluation, the objective-and-task method would come closer to the incremental approach described above. Unfortunately, such measures are usually difficult to establish, and the result is that the approach is used by most companies in its simpler form. In fact, studies indicate that the great majority of American advertisers probably use this method in one form or another.

Long-Run Budgeting: Cyclical Considerations

The above discussion of short-run budgeting took no account of business cycles and the bearing they may have on a firm's advertising expenditures over the years. It is a truism, of course, that a company's long-run advertising outlay will either be constant or it will fluctuate. If it fluctuates, the rate of change may in some manner be related to the firm's sales or profits. Therefore, can a set of principles be established that would serve as a guide to management in formulating a cyclical advertising policy?

Unfortunately, no systematic program can be presented that would be applicable to all firms, partly because of the differences among companies as to size, products, and marketing methods, and partly because economists have still much to learn about the nature and causes of business cycles. Regarding the latter, many single-cause theories have been proposed, but economists generally agree that cycles are the result of a multiplicity of causes rather than any single factor. This places a chief obstacle in the way of developing a unified budgeting policy.

NOTE: One suggestion that has been made is that a fund be accumulated in prosperity periods from which constant advertising expenditures could be maintained over the cycle. This assumes a "psychological theory" of business cycles, that is, that optimistic and pessimistic errors, once under way, are self-generated in an endless chain, as expounded in the twenties by such economists as A. C. Pigou, *Industrial Fluctuations,* and F. Lavington, *The Trade Cycle.*

In view of this, we can only point out a few of the important concepts gained from business cycle theory and experience that may be useful as a tool to management when considering long-term advertising policy. The chief task is to see if certain guides are available that can be used to improve the efficiency of the advertising expenditure over the business cycle. Some key guides may be listed as follows:

The income elasticity of demand, which measures the percentage change in quantity demanded resulting from a given percentage change in income, when applied to particular products or classes of products, might serve as a useful indicator. Products with a high elasticity, such as durables and luxuries, would require advertising to overcome consumer resistance when incomes are low. Other elasticity measures such as price, substitute, and promotional elasticities, and their interrelations, can provide further quantitative evidence on which to base a cyclical advertising strategy.

A rational program for timing product improvement and new-product development, combined with the appropriate type of advertising depending on the phase of the cycle, offers a further area for improved sales-cost budgeting. Occasional "cyclical" considerations on the part of some major durable goods manufacturers to turn out smaller and more economical models of their products in anticipation of consumers becoming more cost conscious, may be a case in point.

A planned program of "investment advertising" over the full course of the business cycle can yield two broad advantages. (1) In depression periods it can help maintain consumers' brand preferences at a time when price competition is relatively more severe. This assumes that it would cost more for the firm to regain lost buyers through advertising than it would to maintain at least a minimum level of advertising in depression periods. (2) In prosperity periods, the firm that has strongly entrenched itself by continuous advertising can exploit the fact that buyers are less price conscious, while simultaneously incurring some savings in sale costs by not having to match the heavier advertising expenditures of competitors at a time when charges (e.g., newpaper space rates) are more expensive.

In summary, the proposals amount to the suggestions that—

1. Firms direct their long-run advertising strategy to exploiting the various elasticity characteristics of particular products and product classes.
2. Firms time their rate of product development and improvement to accord with the need for effective advertising in depression periods.
3. Firms stabilize their selling expenditures somewhat by cutting off the peaks and troughs so as to maintain continuous advertising over the business cycle.

A NOTE ON DISTRIBUTION COSTS

The study of distribution costs from the firm's-eye viewpoint has become an increasing concern of business economists and marketing analysts. Perhaps a chief reason has been the development of operations research procedures, particularly mathematical programming techniques, that are especially well suited to the solution of problems involving distribution costs. In this section a few brief comments will be made concerning the techniques that management can profitably use in the area of distribution cost analysis.

The Problem

The main objective of distribution cost analysis is to reduce distribution costs that are otherwise out of line because of a misallocation or maldistribution of marketing effort.[1] Ultimately, the hope is that enough information can be obtained, particularly with respect to cost data, on the basis of which the firm's marketing expenditures and resources can be reallocated so as to yield maximum profits.

Why does the problem exist? Primarily because in most businesses, whether manufacturing, retailing, or wholesaling, there is a distorted pattern of relationship between the costs and profits attached to each segment of the business; to items in the product line; to customers, orders, and territories; and to selling, advertising, and other marketing efforts. The result is that for many if not most firms, a great majority of the customers may be responsible for a very small percentage of sales volume, or a large percent of products manufactured may account for hardly more than a few percentage points of total sales.

Evidently, management fails to recognize that each dollar's worth of marketing effort, in terms of salesmen's time, advertising, warehouse space, and so forth, should be directed to where it yields the largest

---

[1] Cf. W. Baumol and C. Sevin, "Marketing Costs and Mathematical Programming," *Harvard Business Review*, vol. 35, no. 5 (September–October 1957), pp. 52–60.

increment in net profit. This failure causes a disproportionate spreading of marketing effort, which in turn results in the company's profits as a whole being substantially less than they might otherwise be if marketing resources were reallocated in a more efficient manner.

The Solution

In theory, the approach to the solution of the problem could be framed in terms of an incremental ratio notion as will be seen below. In practice, however, it is difficult to determine which parts of the firm's marketing process contribute to its costs, sales, and profits. Unfortunately, prevalent accounting techniques do not provide satisfactory answers, and although most business executives think they do, the fact is that they are laboring under a serious misapprehension.

The typical accounting procedures for recording the results of marketing activities are not sufficiently detailed because they show only the averages; further, their information is distorted by arbitrary cost calculations and their figures are only part of what is actually required. The correct approach to the solution of the problem, therefore, lies first in providing a finer breakdown and a reclassification of the company's average cost and profit data.

The firm's overall distribution costs must be allocated to the *specific segments* of the business *for which they are incurred.* Thus, the sale of 100 dozen watches to medium-sized retail jewelers in a particular city may require x dollars worth of salesman time, y dollars in transportation and warehousing costs, z dollars in advertising expenditure, and so on. By segmenting the cost and profit data, the net profits or losses for each segment can be calculated separately. The object, therefore, is to divide the business of the company into segments classified, for instance, by categories of customers and products, and then to determine the marketing costs, production costs, and net profits or losses for each segment separately. There are thus two basic principles and techniques that may be summarized:

1. The distribution expenses of the firm should be reclassified from a *natural* expense basis into *functional* cost groups, bringing together all of the indirect costs associated with each marketing activity or function performed by the company.
2. The functional cost groups should be allocated to products, customers, and other segments of sales according to measurable factors, or product and customer characteristics which bear a cause-effect relationship to the total amounts of these functional costs.

In order to perform the required calculations for each segment and each functional cost group, it is necessary to distinguish between three classes of *marketing* costs for which data are needed.

Common Fixed Distribution Costs. These are costs that are incurred in common for different sales segments, and their magnitudes do not vary with the volume of sales in any one segment. An example is the advertising expense of a company's name, which probably influences sales in all segments in varying degrees. These costs are excluded from the distributional cost and profit analysis.

Variable Distribution Costs. These are distribution costs that vary with sales and hence can be allocated. An example is the increased freight bill resulting from additional sales, which is clearly variable and can be readily assigned. Some variable and fixed marketing costs are more difficult to distinguish, however. Warehousing cost, for example, is a fixed cost when not used to capacity, but becomes variable when storage space fills up and management considers the construction of more space to eliminate a bottleneck. Despite the difficulties of segregating costs, it is necessary since the variable costs must be included in the analysis.

Separable Fixed Distribution Costs. These are fixed marketing costs that can and should be allocated to sales. For example, the value of a sales manager's time devoted to a particular sales segment is variable, although the salary received in return is not. Hence, the time should be allocated even though the salary is a fixed cost. It follows that the incremental cost of separable fixed expenses, such as the cost of the manager's time required to make *additional* sales in each segment of the business costed, should be computed if possible and these figures should be kept distinct from variable costs.

When these figures are obtained, marketing efforts can be redistributed to yield greater profits. Expressed in words: the condition for maximum profit is that marketing efforts be reallocated to those segments of sales where an additional unit of marketing effort will yield the largest contribution to net profits and overhead, after deduction of variable costs. Expressed in symbols: letting Δ represent incremental contribution profit defined as the difference between incremental sales, ΔS, and incremental variable costs, ΔVC, and letting ΔR denote the additional resource or effort devoted to a sales sector, effort should be increased in a sector until

$$\frac{\Delta S - \Delta VC}{\Delta R} = \frac{\Delta P}{\Delta R} = \text{Maximum}$$

Using the subscripts 1, 2, 3, . . . , n to code each market sector, such as New York, Chicago, San Francisco, and so forth, optimum allocation of marketing efforts among sectors requires that

$$\frac{\Delta P_1}{\Delta R_1} = \frac{\Delta P_2}{\Delta R_2} = \frac{\Delta P_3}{\Delta R_3} \cdot \cdot \cdot \frac{\Delta P_n}{\Delta R_n}$$

For if the ratios are not equal, as for example if

$$\frac{\Delta P_1}{\Delta R_1} > \frac{\Delta P_2}{\Delta R_2}$$

it implies, as in all types of resource allocation problems, that net profits can be increased by reducing or withdrawing effort in market sector 2, thereby raising that ratio, and increasing it in market sector 1, thereby reducing that ratio.

The analysis thus brings to the forefront the notion that there is a law of diminishing returns with respect to the allocation of marketing effort—an assumption that is not unreasonable by any standards and certainly in accord with the experience of business firms. Framed in this manner, the analysis is capable of a practical solution by employing methods of mathematical programming. But this is part of the science of operations research, a full discussion of which is beyond our present scope.

SOCIOECONOMIC ASPECTS OF ADVERTISING

Advertising has been the subject of much economic and social controversy. Proponents of advertising have argued, for example, that it educates buyers, broadens the market for goods, increases the scale of operations of firms, and encourages mass production and lower prices. Critics, on the other hand, have said that it wastes resources, misinforms consumers, distorts their "natural" preference patterns, and contributes to the monopolization of markets. These statements, both pro and con, are typical of the contentions that various scholars have advanced in their assessment of advertising's role in the total economy. An examination of some of the socioeconomic issues implied by these arguments should therefore be fruitful.

Information versus Persuasion

Social scientists who have studied the role of advertising have usually taken the position that advertising is both informative and persuasive. Hence to the extent that it is informative it may be condoned; to the extent that it is persuasive it should be condemned. The following quotation by an economist specializing in the structure of American industry is fairly typical:

> Advertising has its good and bad points. On the good side, it informs us of the goods available and tells us about market conditions so that we know where to go for the lowest price or the model best suited to our needs. To this extent, advertising makes markets more perfect than they otherwise would be. On the other hand, much advertising

aims not to inform us but to misinform us. It seeks to change our preference patterns and create wants which our private introspection would deny. It aims at making us believe statements which may be scientifically unverifiable or false. At the point where advertising departs from its function of informing and seeks to persuade or deceive us, it tends to become a waste of resources.[2]

The doctrine thus appears to boil down to the following syllogism:

Consumer sovereignty is a necessary condition for optimal resource allocation in our economy.

Advertising, to the extent that it persuades rather than informs, distorts consumer sovereignty.

Therefore, persuasive advertising causes a misallocation and waste of resources.

This criticism, as indicated above, has been widely adopted by many social reformers and by a substantial proportion if not a majority of economists. As a practical matter, however, it is an inadequate argument for the following reasons:

1. The doctrine evaluates advertising by comparing it with the results that would be expected in the economic theory of perfect competition—a theoretical model which, as the eminent British economist Nicholas Kaldor has pointed out, is "built on notions of questionable validity and employs a technique that is apt to conceal the true complexity of the problems presented by competition in imperfect markets."[3] The evaluation, in other words, ought to be made in relation to existing real-world alternatives, not in relation to some ideal but practically nonexistent system.

2. The distinction between advertising that informs and advertising that persuades seems to smack of academic speciousness, for in reality it is usually impossible to distinguish between the two. Nor is it at all clear that persuasive advertising which results in the creation of new wants is necessarily bad per se, since new wants are undoubtedly a powerful stimulant for raising the standard of living.

3. Economists have long agreed that advertising may add utility to products, and to the extent that it does so this added usefulness is indistinguishable from the utility inherent in the commodity itself. Admittedly, however, advertising may sometimes have the reverse effect: it may be deceptive or even false, thereby resulting in disutility. Of course, laws exist to prevent these possibilities, but they are necessarily broad and sometimes difficult to enforce, so that these adverse effects of advertising can at best be only greatly reduced rather than eliminated.

---

[2] Richard Caves, *American Industry: Structure, Conduct, Performance* (Englewood Cliffs, N.J.: Prentice-Hall, Inc., 1964), p. 102.

[3] Nicholas Kaldor, *Essays on Value and Distribution* (Glencoe, Ill.: Free Press, 1960), pp. 4–5.

Thus, no one will deny that advertising provides some useful information to consumers. But is this the relevant social issue? Clearly not. *The real problem is whether this method of transmitting product information is better or worse than any realistic alternative method that might be devised.* This question, like others posed below, is left for the reader to decide, for social scientists have for the most part failed to orient their theoretical and empirical research in this direction.

Efficiency versus Waste

A second class of arguments pertains to the question of whether advertising leads to higher or lower product costs.

Proponents of advertising have contended that it familiarizes the consumer with new products and thereby broadens the market. This stimulus encourages further investment and innovation by business executives, resulting in a larger scale of operations and therefore lower cost mass production. At the same time, expansion in advertising tends to make expenditures on other forms of selling (e.g., salesmen) less necessary, and to the extent that advertising replaces some more costly selling activity it may lower selling costs by reducing the amount of retail sales effort per unit of retail sales.

Critics of advertising have argued that it encourages artificial product differentiation among goods that are physically similar, and that in imperfectly competitive markets most of the advertising done by competing firms tends to have a canceling effect. This duplication of effort results in a waste of resources and higher product costs. Competition tends to be in terms of advertising rather than price, and any real economies of scale, even if they exist, are lost through inefficiencies.

What can be said about these arguments?

1. According to neoclassical economic theory, firms will tend to approach their optimum size in the *long run* on the basis of price and cost relationships exclusively. Therefore, there is no need for advertising nor is there even any room for it in the economist's theoretical model. But in the real world the long run may take years or perhaps decades; therefore advertising, if it does provide for a larger scale of operations, tends to hasten the process and is thus desirable.

2. In neoclassical theory, it is shown via certain technical procedures involving tangencies of demand curves with average cost curves that product differentiation is undesirable and that the degree of social welfare varies inversely with the extent of product differentiation. However, this theory fails to acknowledge the fact that the establishment of identifiable brand names through advertising has been a major force responsible for the stabilization and enhancement of product quality. Even in the Soviet Union, for example, where product differenti-

ation and advertising were long deplored, a substantial effort has been expended since the late 50s to employ these same methods as means for improving the quality, performance, and appeal of both consumer and industrial goods.

Thus, when real-world alternatives are considered, the problem is not whether advertising makes for more product differentiation and for greater economies of scale, for it undoubtedly contributes significantly to both. *The real issue is whether a reduction in product differentiation is desirable in light of the probability that there would be a consequent reduction in product quality, and whether the same economies of scale could be attained by some means other than advertising, perhaps by price reductions as some economists have frequently suggested.* The fact is that there is no empirical evidence to suggest either an affirmative or negative answer to either of these questions.

Competition versus Concentration

Those who have defended the role of advertising in our economy have argued that it tends to encourage competition in various ways. Thus it has been said that advertising, by making product information available to a larger number and wider distribution of consumers, reduces the opportunities for firms to earn local monopoly profits. Also, it enables firms, both young and old, to introduce new products and gain market acceptance for them much more rapidly than would be possible without advertising. And finally, with the trend in American industry toward organization based on diversified product lines, it has been contended that advertising may enhance the effective entry of these new lines and thereby encourage more efficient organization structures within firms as well as more effective competition between them.

Critics of advertising have argued that it facilitates the growth of oligopolistic industries and therefore enhances market concentration. This occurs, they say, because of the existence of economies of scale. Thus, the costs of advertising exposures per unit of product sold are lower for firms with large sales volumes than those with small sales volumes, and successive exposures are usually necessary for advertising to be effective. In addition, many advertising media grant substantial quantity discounts (sometimes as much as 30 percent) to large advertisers, with the discount rate applying to the advertiser's total advertising rather than to a particular product. For these reasons, it has been argued that advertising works a hardship against small firms which are seeking to gain market acceptance for their products, while it tends to favor established multiproduct firms whose gross revenues from sales are substantial enough to support continuous heavy advertising.

Most economists would undoubtedly agree that a distinction should be made between concentration in total productive capacity and concentration in the sale of a particular type of product. Advertising probably contributes to the former, but it is not at all evident that it does the same for the latter. Nor is it clear that further concentration would be avoided if all advertising were eliminated. In short, the fundamental question is not whether advertising enhances concentration and restriction of entry into markets, for it is likely that it does—especially for certain classes of products with the requisite production and promotion characteristics. *The real issue is how the resulting oligopolistic industry structures dominated by a few large firms would compare with the "competitive" structures of many small firms.*[4] The economic theory of perfect competition assumes that consumer wants are independent of producer influence. In the real world of imperfect competition and imperfect knowledge, this assumption is obviously incorrect. There is no theoretical or empirical evidence to support the view that a large number of small competing firms with limited distribution can provide new and better quality products at lower prices than can a few large firms with national distribution and substantial economies of scale.

Conclusion

Many social scientists have a tendency to evaluate the performance of a system in relation to Utopia, not to the real world. In this connection, economists all too often employ the neoclassical model of perfect competition as their basis for judgment, and any aspects of the problem that do not readily fit the model are often discarded. Thus with respect to advertising, the criticisms of it that have been made by economists— namely that it results in excessive prices, costs, inefficiencies, concentration, and profits—are based largely on the premise that in a world of perfect competition where consumers are assumed to know their alternatives, the only beneficial advertising is that which furthers consumer knowledge. But as David Blank, economist for the Columbia Broadcasting System has pointed out, this model has no need for advertising other than perhaps classified advertising and the Sears, Roebuck catalog.

Advertising is obviously a phenomenon of significant social and economic importance, and should be evaluated in terms of operational alternatives. Yet there is no apparent tendency on the part of social scientists and economists to couch their theoretical or empirical studies in this framework. Thus we simply do not know the net effect of advertising on product prices and quality, nor do we have empirical evidence to judge the possible extent of relationships between advertising and concentration.

We suspect that advertising as it currently exists may not inspire

---

[4] James D. Shaffer, "Advertising in Social Perspective," *Journal of Farm Economics*, vol. 46, no. 2 (May 1964), p. 394.

in people the most desirable wants and values, yet we are unprepared to state precisely what we mean by most desirable. As Shaffer has pointed out, if achieving a so-called "good life" is our objective, then advertising seeks to define this good life in terms of service or contribution to society. *As far as advertising is concerned, the good life is to have goods, not to be good*—as evidenced by the liberal use which is made of prestigious members of society to identify specific products with this good life.

The role of advertising in our economy is clearly in need of revaluation by social scientists. It is to be hoped that when and if this revaluation is undertaken, it will be done in meaningful and realistic terms, reflecting both its beneficial and deleterious effects in a manner suitable as a guide for executives and policy makers. This is the only basis on which proper market rules can be formulated for the well-being of society.

PROBLEMS

1. The Widget Company has recently developed and marketed a new product. Management eventually plans to budget $10,000 a month to advertise the product throughout the country, but it first wishes to have your advice on how it might judge the effectiveness of its advertising. What do you suggest?

2. Comment on the following dialog between the economist and the sales manager of the Zilch Soap Company.

    ECONOMIST: Two years ago we cut our advertising and our sales increased. Last year we increased our advertising and our sales fell.

    SALES MANAGER: How can that be? Anyone knows that the more you spend on advertising, the more you sell; and the more you sell, the more profits you make.

    ECONOMIST: Ugh!

3. During periods of economic recession, many business firms tend to reduce advertising expenditures as a means of cutting expenses. Can you give at least three reasons for this?

4. Schultz's Frankfurter Company recently conducted a carefully controlled market experiment and obtained the following data (in thousands of dollars):

Weekly advertising, x	0	1	2	3	4	5	6	7	8
Weekly sales, y	1	2	4	8	16	32	64	128	256

   a. Assuming that this relationship between advertising and sales is exact, write the equation which expresses the relationship.
   b. Write the equation in a form which is linear in x.
   c. Plot the data on an ordinary (arithmetically scaled) chart. Then plot the data on a chart for which the horizontal axis is arithmetically

scaled and the vertical axis is logarithmically scaled. You may transfer the following logarithmic scale in Exhibit 3 (or a scale taken from a slide rule) to the vertical axis of ordinary graph paper for this purpose.

EXHIBIT 3
Logarithmic Scale

```
 ┌──┬──┬──┬─┬┬┬┬┬──────┬────┬──┬──┬┬┬┬┬───────┬─────┬───┬──┬─┬┬┬┐
 1     2  3  4 5       10    20  30 40 50      100   200 300 500  1,000
```

5. A marketing executive in your company feels that since his advertising budget is very limited, he would prefer to spread it thin by maintaining some advertising in all markets rather than withdrawing funds from some territories to concentrate on others. Evaluate this reasoning.

6. A British engineer by the name of F. W. Lanchester once wrote a classic article entitled "Mathematics in Warfare." (See J. R. Newman, *The World of Mathematics*, vol. 4 [New York: Simon and Schuster, 1956], pp. 2138–57.) In an analysis of combat between opposing forces, Lanchester shows that the forces are equal when

$$aN_1{}^2 = bN_2{}^2$$

where

N_1 = number of units of A's force
N_2 = number of units of B's force
a = striking power per unit of A
b = striking power per unit of B

Lanchester's formula states that the strength of a force is directly proportional to its striking power per unit and to the square of the number of units. Does this formula have any applicability to advertising? If yes, what specific advertising variables might be suggested as an analog?

7. Several mathematical theories of epidemics have been developed to describe and predict the spread of contagious diseases through a host population. In most of these theories the spread of the disease is a function of such factors as the number of contacts with infected individuals, the length of contact time, the probability of contagion through contact, immunity characteristics, and so forth. Do such theories have any applicability to advertising? If yes, what specific advertising variables might be suggested as an analog?

8.   **CASE PROBLEM: SOAP AND DETERGENT INDUSTRY**
            COMPETITION AND ADVERTISING

The following item is adapted from an article in *Business Week,* November 5, 1966:

A full-scale investigation of advertising spending in the packaged soap and detergent industry—and whether it leads to higher prices—has been launched by the Justice Dept.

The probe, involving Procter & Gamble, Colgate-Palmolive, and Lever Bros., is the first move in what could become a major challenge by anti-trusters to the power of big advertisers. What's more, it could be a prelude to similar investigations in other consumer-goods industries, from cereals to cigarettes, if it follows the policy line laid down by Antitrust Div. Chief Donald F. Turner. Turner said he believes heavy advertising outlays lead both to dominance of an industry by a few companies and to high prices.

Outcome. Some economists have reasoned that the high cost of heavy advertising is passed on to the consumer, thus artificially raising prices in the supermarket. But Justice seems primarily concerned with suspected violations of the Sherman Act's ban on monopolization.

Turner's theory is that heavy advertising spending heightens the barriers a new company must overcome to enter an industry. The result is that a new company without the resources to advertise heavily and overcome established consumer preferences is locked out of the business, no matter how good its product may be.

What will grow out of the probe, now in its infancy, isn't clear. It may turn up nothing; it may lead to an antitrust suit; or it may turn up situations that Justice looks on as serious but which are outside the scope of antitrust laws.

Alternatives. If antitrusters think they can prove that packaged-soap manufacturers have violated the Sherman Act, they probably will ask a court to limit ad spending. This would be the first time such a request has been made, and would mark the case as a test vehicle for a major new antitrust approach.

Turner favors absolute or percentage limitations on promotional expenditures in cases where these restrictions may "dissipate the consequences of illegal acts." He believes they are appropriate even though the spending itself is entirely legal.

However, if government lawyers conclude that advertising in the soap industry poses a problem beyond the reach of antitrust laws, they undoubtedly will seek alternative solutions. Turner has urged that the government provide financial support to consumer research organizations, whose reports on product testing, if widely distributed, could dilute advertising's effects on the public.

The thrust of the investigation ultimately may reach far beyond the soap box. Besides soaps and detergents, Turner has singled out the drug industry as one earning "very high rates of return" and spending heavily on various forms of promotion.

Higher Take. A statistical study by Harvard economist William S. Comanor adds to the list cereals, cigarettes, soft drinks, perfumes, and hand tools—all industries that have high advertising-to-sales ratios and profit rates of 10% or more. Autos, on the other hand, had high profit rates but had a low ad-to-sales ratio.

Comanor, who was chief economist at the Antitrust Div., found that high ad spending in consumer-goods industries leads to an increase of roughly 50% in profit rates. He proposed that the effects of high promotional spending be taken into account in antitrust enforcement.

Turner agrees that the anticompetitive consequences are important, not only because new companies are shut out but also because the mere threat of a new company coming in may prevent established companies from running up higher price tags. When an industry is dominated by a few giants, he feels, the threat of newcomers may be the most significant factor promoting competition.

Where heavy advertising outlays aggravate this situation, he feels, becomes clear in this example: In packaged soap, where promotion is high, the four top companies in 1958 controlled 74% of the market; in the case of bulk soaps sold mainly to industrial customers, on the other hand, advertising is less important and the big four accounted for only 30% of the total output.

Question:

Assume that you are employed as a consulting economist for the industry. What arguments would you offer against the charges made by the Department of Justice? (NOTE: You may find it helpful to refer to Backman's or Groner's books cited in the reference section below.)

REFERENCES

BACKMAN, JULES   *Advertising and Competition.* New York: New York University Press, 1967.

COMANOR, WILLIAM S., and WILSON, THOMAS A.   "Advertising and the Advantages of Size." *The American Economic Review,* vol. 59, no. 2 (May 1969), pp. 87–98.

GREER, DOUGLAS F.   "Advertising and Market Concentration." *The Southern Economic Journal,* vol. 38, no. 1 (July 1971), pp. 19–32.

GRONER, ALEX   *Advertising: The Case for Competition.* New York: Association of National Advertisers, 1967. This booklet, available free from the publisher, summarizes Backman's book cited above.

HOROWITZ, IRA   "A Note on Advertising and Uncertainty." *The Journal of Industrial Economics,* vol. 18, no. 2 (April 1970), pp. 151–60.

KALDOR, NICHOLAS   "The Economic Aspects of Advertising." *Essays on Value and Distribution,* chap. 6. Glencoe, Ill: The Free Press, 1960. An excellent economic analysis of advertising.

MARCUS, MATITYAHU   "Advertising and Changes in Concentration." *The Southern Economic Journal,* vol. 36, no. 2 (October 1969), pp. 117–21.

MELROSE, KENDRICK B.   "An Empirical Study on Optimizing Advertising Policy." *The Journal of Business,* vol. 42, no. 3 (July 1969), pp. 282–92.

SHAFFER, JAMES D.   "Advertising in Social Perspective." *Journal of Farm Economics,* vol. 46, no. 2 (May 1964), pp. 387–97.

SPENCER, MILTON H.   "Socioeconomic Aspects of Advertising." *Business Horizons* (Indiana University), vol. 10, no. 4 (Winter 1967), pp. 75–78.

TELSER, L. G.   "Some Aspects of the Economics of Advertising." *The Journal of Business* (The Graduate School of Business of the University of Chicago), vol. 41, no. 2 (April 1968), pp. 166–73.

chapter 12

Pricing

If a study of pricing is to be of much practical value, it should concentrate on the development of concepts that serve as a guide for executive decision making and control. Accordingly, our primary attention will be devoted to analyzing and interpreting the pricing practices and policies of (1) manufacturing firms in oligopolistic markets, that is, markets characterized by fewness of sellers and similarity of products, for this is the most common type of competitive situation in American industry, and (2) monopolistically competitive firms in American distribution and retailing. The topics to be considered will be those that seem to be of greatest relevance to the practical pricing decisions of top management in the light of current thinking.

PRICING CONCEPTS, THEORIES, AND MARKETING POLICIES

Various price concepts such as "odd prices," "customary prices," "price lining," and so forth, are discussed in elementary marketing texts, but purely from a descriptive standpoint without any indication of the relation of these notions to economic theory. It is appropriate, therefore, to develop a discussion of various marketing price policies, paying particular attention to the fact that these policies are merely special cases of the general theory of monopolistic competition. The chief advantages of presenting these concepts in an analytical framework are that the theory provides (1) a sounder basis for discussion and evaluation, and (2) an indication of what it is that really needs to be measured.

The procedure followed will be to present, first, a few statements about the general theory of pricing that are now common to elementary economics textbooks but which stem originally from the writings of Chamberlin and Robinson in the early thirties; and, second, an illustration of various common pricing concepts from the viewpoint that they represent nothing more than an implicit assumption regarding the nature of the particular demand curve.

General Theory of Pricing

The general theory of pricing, that is, the theory of pricing under monopolistic competition, is basic to most of the concepts, practices, and policies discussed in the literature of pricing. The fundamental scheme, therefore, may be sketched briefly as follows:

Theoretical Formulation. Exhibit 1, Chart A, represents the demand and cost structure of a firm under monopolistic competition. Because

EXHIBIT 1
General Theory of Pricing

A. Traditional Theoretical Formulation

B. Break-Even Formulation

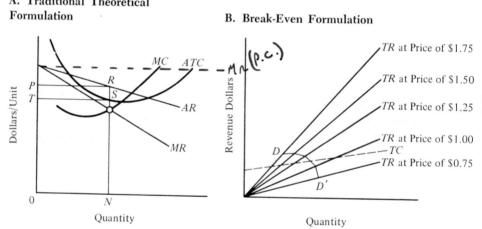

of product differentiation, the seller will have some degree of monopoly power. This is indicated by the negatively sloping demand or average revenue curve, AR, showing that at higher prices, the firm loses some sales but not all sales (as compared to a seller in pure competition for whom the demand curve is horizontal).

From this the marginal revenue curve, MR, representing the change in total revenue resulting from a unit change in output, is derived. Similarly, total cost per unit of output, or average total cost, ATC, and the marginal cost curve, MC, are shown. The condition for establishing the price and output that will yield maximum short-run profit is then determined: the firm should produce to where the marginal cost equals marginal revenue, which is where the rate of change in total costs equals the rate of change in total receipts. In terms of the diagram, the most profitable output is ON units, to be sold at a price of $OP(=NR)$ dollars per unit, which, as determined by the demand curve, is the highest price per unit that can be charged to clear the volume ON. The total receipts would then be the price times quantity or the area of the rectangle OPRN; the total cost is the average cost times the number of units or the area OTSN. Net profit is thus the area of the rectangle PRST, or the difference between the larger (total revenue) and smaller (total cost) rectangle. This net profit rectangle is maximized only when the production is carried to the $MC = MR$ level. At any other output, the area of the rectangle would be smaller under the given demand and cost conditions.

Break-Even Formulation. Business executives, accountants, and engineers, who are more familiar with break-even charts, will prefer a translation of these theoretical principles into the break-even formulation of Exhibit 1, Chart B. Some modifications of the chart are necessary, however, because the conventional break-even chart shows only the various sales possibilities at a *single price* and the volume required to break even at that price.

In Chart B, several total revenue curves (TR) are drawn, each assuming a different price per unit. Each TR curve thus reveals the total receipts that would be realized over a range of sales at a given price. The lower the price, the flatter the TR curve, indicating a wider sales range; similarly, higher prices indicate steeper TR curves and narrower sales ranges, evidencing some degree of monopoly power on the part of the firm due to product differentiation or other factors.

On each TR curve a point is estimated showing the sales volume actually realized at that price as a result, say, of a controlled price experiment in several markets. The locus of these points is then the curve DD', which may be thought of as a kind of "demand curve" except that it shows total revenue rather than average revenue as does the usual demand curve such as AR in Chart A. The condition for profit maximization would then be to maximize the vertical distance between DD' and the total cost curve TC.

Although appearing distinctly dissimilar, there is an intimate relationship between Charts A and B. The alternate prices hypothesized in Chart B correspond to alternate levels of the variable plotted along the vertical axis of Chart A. Consider, for example, the price level, P, of Chart A indicating a price of say, $1.25, and therefore corresponding to the middle revenue line in Chart B. Then the point marked off on this revenue line is simply determined by requiring its horizontal distance to correspond with ON—the number of units actually expected to be sold in the market at that price. Notice that this implies that only points on *DD'* are viable as far as business decision making is concerned—all others on the revenue lines of Chart B are fictitious in the sense that given demand, only one point on each of them—the one corresponding to the actual amount sold in the market—is appropriate.

This formulation thus yields an actual advantage over the traditional marginal-cost–marginal-revenue formulation of Chart A because it shows not only the correct price and volume but also total cost, total revenue, and net profit. In the following discussion of price policies, however, the conventional *AR* curve is used because it conveys the various concepts more clearly and precisely. (Of course, the theoretical formulation of Chart A could also have been presented in terms of the total revenue and total cost curves of economic theory, but the method shown is more common, and often more practical.)

Odd-Number and Critical-Number Pricing

It is a practice among some companies, particularly noticeable in retailing, to set prices in such a way that they end either in an odd number of just under a round number.

In the case of odd-number pricing, for example, the assumption is made that it is possible to sell a greater number of items priced at 21 cents rather than 20 cents, or at 99 cents rather than $1. The idea applies to higher priced merchandise as well, such as a suit of clothes at $81 instead of $80, or an automobile at $2,999 or $3,001 rather than $3,000. These notions, expressed in virtually all marketing textbooks, can be illustrated more meaningfully by the use of the average revenue or demand curve of economic theory.

Exhibit 2, Chart A, shows the type of demand curve *assumed* by a seller who sets prices by the odd-number "rule," that is, that sales are larger when the price ends in an odd number than when it ends in the adjacent lower even number. Thus the quantity demanded is greater at $1.99 than at $1.98, and greater at $1.97 than at $1.96. Although this type of demand curve must be believed to exist by sellers who price by this odd-number method, there is no conclusive evidence that an odd-price policy actually results in larger sales as is assumed by those who employ it.

The second concept, that of critical-number pricing, is illustrated in Exhibit 2, Chart B. The assumption here is that sales will be larger when the price is set just under a critical point, such as $20 or $25 in the diagram. At prices slightly below these critical numbers, demand is elastic in that a small decrease in price from the critical point brings a more than proportional increase in sales, regardless of whether the

EXHIBIT 2
Odd-Number and Critical-Number Pricing

A. Odd-Number Pricing

B. Critical-Number Pricing

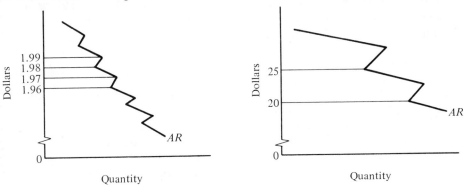

Psychological Prices

price is an odd or even number. As with odd-number pricing, this assumption about the shape of the demand curve by those who practice critical-number pricing has never been subjected to any extensive tests.

Psychological Prices

Somewhat similar to the demand pattern in Exhibit 2 is that found in Exhibit 3A. The phenomenon represents the type of demand curve

EXHIBIT 3
Demand Curves for Psychological Prices and Customary Prices

A. Psychological Prices

B. Customary Price

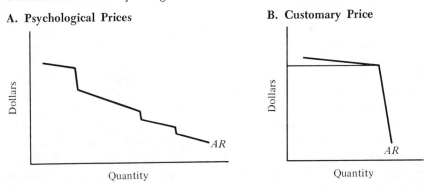

that would exist for what some writers have called "psychological prices." It has been found in some pricing experiments that a change in price has little effect over certain ranges of demand, thus yielding a step-type of average revenue (AR) curve. This differs from the concept of odd-number pricing in that the curve need not have any positively inclined segments, and the critical points are not necessarily located at each round number but only at prices that are psychologically significant to buyers. Some pricing experiments conducted many years ago at the R. H. Macy department store in New York have revealed the occasional existence of such stepshaped demand curves. Thus, the demand curve had substantially different elasticities at different points.

Customary Prices

Examples of products with customary prices are candy bars, chewing gum, soft drinks, and similar types of "convenience" goods, the prices of which are largely a matter of tradition. For this reason the prices of such items have tended to persist for long periods because management assumes a type of kinked demand curve as in Exhibit 3B. At prices above the customary price shown by the horizontal line, sales fall off rapidly thus evidencing high elasticity; at prices less than the customary price sales increase less than proportionately thereby indicating relative inelasticity. The demand curve thus contains a kink at the customary price.

Examples of this situation are not difficult to find. Most candy manufacturers, for instance, have tended to reduce the size of candy bars in the face of inflation and higher costs over the years, rather than alter their long established prices. In the public transportation industries, some firms have preferred to postpone the costs of replacement and maintenance of equipment, thereby permitting a deterioration in quality of service, rather than petition the transit commission for a rate increase.

Pricing at the Market

The kinked demand curve of Exhibit 3B also represents a type of policy sometimes referred to as "pricing at the market." It arises in instances where (1) management is ignorant of the true shape of the demand curve confronting it and hence adopts a "safe" policy of matching its price with competitors, or (2) where oligopoly markets prevail and a policy of matching competitors' prices minimizes the chance of a price war. In either case, consumers must regard product differentiation between competitors as basically insignificant if the kink is to exist. In that case, a small increase in price above the kink by any firm will bring it a large loss in sales, while a decrease in price will be followed by competitors and the resulting increase in sales will be relatively small for each. The frequent price wars between gasoline stations in many states are a typical example.[1]

---

[1] Gasoline price wars came to an abrupt halt with the Arab oil embargo and the consequent gasoline shortage in the winter of 1973–74. When alternate sources of energy make gasoline plentiful once more, we may see the price wars again, albeit at higher price levels.

Prestige Pricing

Where buyers judge the quality of a product by its price, the resulting demand curve will be positively inclined over a range of quantity, and may eventually bend back again as in Exhibit 4. The curve shows that

EXHIBIT 4
Prestige Pricing

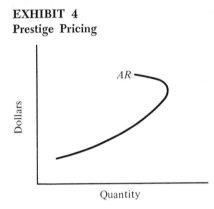

a larger quantity is actually demanded at higher prices, until finally the price is sufficiently high that smaller quantities are demanded. From a theoretical standpoint, a positively inclined demand curve represents an extreme case of irrational consumer behavior.

> NOTE: Are positively inclined demand curves contradictions or exceptions to economic theory? Not if they exist because consumers regard price as one of the product's qualities. In that case the demand curve does not measure the same product but rather "different" products along the same curve, and hence the demand curve is not the demand curve of economic theory. (Can you see why? Explain.) Of course, from the seller's standpoint of pricing policy, what really counts is his ability to judge what *he* believes is the true shape of the *AR* or demand curve for his product.

Despite the upsetting influences which positively inclined demand curves may have in economic theory, the probability is strong that such situations exist, at least for limited ranges and conditions, in the real world. Concrete examples occur for such products as fine furs, diamonds, and expensive trips, and even in the more everyday buying habits of consumers, at least in the "conspicuous consumption" sense inferred by Thorstein Veblen in his socioeconomic writings several decades ago.

Price Lining

The policy of price lining, frequently found in retailing and usually practiced by department stores, refers to the marketing of a class of merchandise in a limited number of price lines according to differences in workmanship, materials, design, or other characteristics. The types of products to which the practice is often applied include coats, suits, dresses, furniture, hosiery, novelty jewelry, and a wide range of other items. Price lining is thus a manner of exploiting quality differentials. Once the lines are decided upon, they are usually held constant for long periods of time, with changes in market conditions accommodated by changes in quality rather than in prices. Frequently, only three basic price lines are deemed necessary for each type of merchandise, on the assumption that the customer needs some basis of comparison before he can make a decision to buy at a particular price. The three price lines represent a "good," "better," and "best" plan, the lowest prices being for a stripped item and the medium and higher prices representing improved quality, styling, and other selling appeals. Sometimes each price line is actually a range of prices, called "price zones," according to differences in customer preferences.

Two chief advantages claimed for price lining are that—

1. It simplifies the price structure, thereby enabling manufacturing and selling effort to be concentrated on the most profitable price lines;
2. It avoids the need for making frequent pricing decisions after the establishment of the initial price and with the exception of special sales.

With respect to the first argument, in periods of rising manufacturing and selling costs, quality may have to be reduced to preserve customary price lines, or else frills may be added to the product to raise it into the next higher price line. If the retailer has heavily promoted a particular price, the retailer may have to accept a lower margin and/or reduce quality in order to maintain an advertised price. In periods of declining business activity, wholesale and retail prices tend to be "sticky" because better materials and workmanship are added to preserve the higher price lines of prosperous times. Price flexibility is thus lessened, creating an obstacle to the dynamic sort of pricing that would be more advantageous both to the company and to the economy as a whole over the long run. (Why?)

Concerning the second argument, a price lining policy does not avoid management's problem of making price decisions. In fact, it presents the seller with precisely the same choice of alternatives as does a variable price policy, namely, whether to price by (a) equating marginal cost with marginal revenue or (b) using a customary percent of markup. The decision, however, concerns the prices paid for merchandise rather than the selling prices. The widespread use of price lining by retailers has resulted in manufacturers and wholesalers giving increasing attention to tailoring their own prices in order to fit retail prices. Retailers, however, do have some choice with respect to the quality of goods they purchase; and, presumably, the more they pay or the lower their percent of markup, the larger their sales volume must be to yield a given profit.

In Exhibit 5, if P is the established retail price, it is also the average

EXHIBIT 5
Price Lining

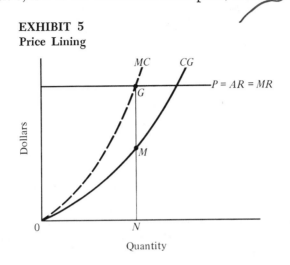

revenue and marginal revenue curve since the line is horizontal. The line CG represents the cost of goods in various quantities that can be bought by the retailer. Evidently, the retailer should equate MC with MR (the price), paying NM for the merchandise and selling the quantity ON, thereby obtaining the maximum gross margin, GM, times ON. Alternatively, the retailer may buy at a price that provides a customary or arbitrary percent of markup, but then it would be a matter of pure chance as to whether the maximum gross margin would be obtained.

Actually, other than cost of goods, there are relatively few variable costs associated with sales at retail. The retailer's goal, therefore, should be generally one of maximizing *gross margin dollars*. To the extent that other variable expenses are important, however, they may be added to cost of goods, and the CG curve in Exhibit 5 would then become a variable cost curve instead.

The foregoing analysis hinges on the assumptions of (1) a rising cost-of-goods curve, and (2) an absence of a demand curve because the firm is assumed to be able to sell all it wants at the given price. Often, however, the retailer encounters just the opposite situation—quantity discounts (discussed more fully in the next section) offered by the manufacturer result in cost breaks yielding a downward-trending step function for marginal costs. In that case it is more realistic to assume that the retailer can charge a variety of prices for these goods, thus suggesting the possibility of a demand schedule.

To expand the analysis to include these assumptions, let us hypothe-

EXHIBIT 6
Price Lining with Quantity Discounts

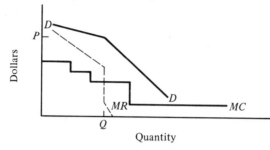

size the situation illustrated in Exhibit 6, in which the firm confronts the demand curve *DD*, kinked at the established retail price, *P* (that is, the same price as Exhibit 5). Marginal costs are represented by the step function, *MC*, indicative of the quantity discount assumption; the marginal revenue curve, *MR*, as derived from the average revenue, or *DD* curve, is also shown.

To determine an optimal quantity of goods to purchase, the retailer sets marginal cost equal to marginal revenue. While many values of *Q* are possible, the fact that the kink in the demand curve determines a discontinuous marginal revenue curve means that there is a wide range of dollar values (*MR* values) for which the optimal purchase of goods for the retailer is *Q* units. Hence, often, there is a pure economic incentive for the purchaser to maintain actively the fixed ("suggested") retail price set by the distributor or supplier.

Two further points might be made with regard to the analysis. The first is that there is no guarantee that the optimal quantity to purchase will always be at *Q*, that is, this is not a foregone conclusion. The correct purchase quantity will of course be entirely dependent upon where marginal cost intersects marginal revenue; specific cost and demand structures will of course determine different *MC* and *MR* curve patterns. The second point is that legal restrictions may bind the seller from deviating from an established retail price, thereby barring the previous analysis. More of this is discussed below.

Resale Price Maintenance

Resale price maintenance is a form of vertical price control. It occurs when a price agreement is made between two sellers at different levels in the distribution channel, such as a manufacturer and wholesaler, manufacturer and retailer, or wholesaler and retailer, whereby the minimum or actual wholesale or retail price of a product bearing the producer's trademark, brand, or name are fixed by contract. The states in the United States that have on various occasions upheld such contracts have done so under what are commonly known as "fair-trade" laws or "unfair practices" acts.

From our present standpoint, resale price maintenance is interesting because the assumption is frequently made that retailers, for example, have no pricing decisions to make when a manufacturer maintains resale prices under fair-trade contracts. Actually, retailers in this instance will always have at least one decision to make and possibly a second as well. They must choose between a pricing policy that equates marginal costs and marginal revenue as against one that employs a customary percent of markup. A selection of the latter may well result in their refusal to push or even to handle many low-markup items that actually would be very profitable to them. In those states where the fair-trade laws permit only minimum rather than specified prices, retailers must choose between selling at the minimum or some higher price. Selecting the latter would involve still further decisions as to what price policy to adopt.

What is the nature of the pricing decision for a *manufacturer* using resale price maintenance? Exhibit 7 provides an illustration. At any given

EXHIBIT 7
Resale Price Maintenance

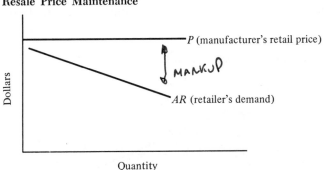

retail price, *P*, the manufacturer who sets the price will be confronted with a particular demand curve by retailers, *AR*, the shape of which will depend on their attitudes concerning the amount of markup they can obtain on the manufacturer's selling price. If the markup is low, some retailers will refuse to take the item and others will refrain from pushing it. If the markup is relatively high, dealers will tend to push the item and hence sell more than consumers would otherwise have taken at the given retail price. The appropriate price policy of the manufacturer, therefore, is to establish an optimum price by first computing marginal revenue from average revenue, and then equating marginal revenue with marginal cost. Since there will be a different *AR* curve associated with each retail price, the calculations must be made for each retail price, and the combination of retail and wholesale prices that will yield the maximum profits is then selected.

Quantity Discounts

In marketing literature and in statements made by business executives, quantity discounts are usually justified in terms of (1) the lower *unit* costs of handling larger orders because certain costs remain fairly constant or else increase less than proportionately to the increased volume (e.g., bookkeeping costs), and (2) the desire to utilize excess capacity thereby further reducing unit costs.

What type of price policy should a seller adopt if quantity discounts are to be offered to buyers? As before, the rules can be derived from the construction of simple model situations. Two types of quantity discount problems can be examined: the first, where the seller offers the product to the *same buyer* at quantity discounts; the second, where the seller offers the product to different buyers at quantity discounts. We shall discuss the first of these in this section but defer an examination of the second until a later section of this chapter, where it may be examined within the broader framework of price discrimination.

Exhibit 8 illustrates the process of quantity discounting to one buyer.

EXHIBIT 8
Quantity Discounts: One Buyer

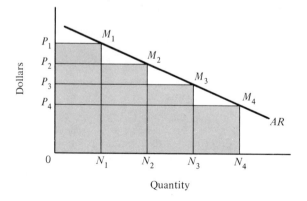

Assuming *AR* to be the buyer's demand curve, the seller may simply charge a price of OP_4 per unit and thereby sell ON_4 units. Since there is no discount involved, the seller's total revenue is then the area of the rectangle $OP_4M_4N_4$. However, the seller can enlarge total receipts considerably if quantity discounts are offered. Thus, the seller may first charge a price of OP_1 and thereby sell only ON_1 units, giving a total revenue of $OP_1M_1N_1$. Then the price may be lowered to OP_2 per unit and an additional N_1N_2 units sold, then the price may be lowered to OP_3 and an additional N_2N_3 units sold, and finally the price may be lowered to OP_4 where a further N_3N_4 units are sold. Although the seller still ends up selling the same number of units, namely ON_4, the total receipts are now the entire shaded area instead of the area $OP_4M_4N_4$ when a price of OP_4 per unit was charged without quantity discounts. Evidently, the smaller the seller can shade discounts, the narrower the steps under the demand curve become and hence the larger the total revenue becomes. Theoretically, the limit would be a total revenue equal to the entire area under the curve, but this would require discounting in infinitesimal amounts. In practice, of course, the discounts are in blocks of units.

Examples of this type of pricing, called "differential pricing," are not uncommon. They illustrate not only one of several types of quantity discounting but may also account for why electric utility companies charge decreasing rates in blocks of kilowatt-hours, based on different price scales for industrial and residential users, why photocopy services price on a decreasing scale which is dependent upon the volume of copying, or why dry goods in grocery stores such as sugar or flour tend to be cheaper, per volume or weight unit, in larger sizes. In all instances, the seller is assuming a downward-sloping demand curve and is attempting to "tap" the consumer surplus portion of it by chiseling away with successive price reductions for larger purchases.

The question of legality with regard to quantity discounts appears to involve a moot point of law. The Federal Trade Commission (FTC) has at times found quantity discounts permissible if justified by differences in costs, for example, Kraft-Phenix Cheese case [25 FTC 537, (1937)] and American Optical Company case [28 FTC 169, (1939)]. But in the circumstances of the famous Morton Salt case, the FTC found that the company's carload as well as cumulative discounts were not justified by differences in cost and hence were injurious to competition. The firm was ordered to desist from selling to retailers at prices lower than those charged wholesalers whose customers compete with them, and the order was later sustained by a Supreme Court decision [334 U.S. 47, (1948)].

Two other types of quantity discounts are also particularly worth noting: cumulative discounts and functional discounts.

Cumulative Discounts. Cumulative discounts are based upon total quantity bought over a period of time (such as a year). They are granted by sellers primarily as a concession to large buyers, or for the purpose of encouraging greater buyer loyalty, or because they may reduce costs by facilitating forward planning in production, stabilize seasonal output variations, and reduce investment in inventories. In any event, a cumula-

tive discount is worthwhile to the seller if a saving is realized from
sales made to a particular buyer over a period of time, where such
savings were not reflected in the price paid by the buyer but which
are reserved and refunded to the buyer at the end of a period of time.

As for their legality, however, the Federal Trade Commission observed in the H. C. Brill case [26 FTC 666, (1938)] that any system
of discounts based on the amount of annual sales is a price discrimination
in violation of the Clayton Antitrust Act [Section 2(a), as amended]
if it tends substantially to lessen competition, unless justified by due
allowance for differences in cost not previously allowed. In other words,
cumulative discounts by themselves *may* not be illegal if a cost saving
can be shown in the firm's accounting records, and if the discounts
are proportional to the saving.

Functional Discounts.   Based upon the trade classification of the
buyer (e.g., wholesaler, jobber, retailer, etc.), functional discounts are
also commonly referred to as "distributor discounts." Since these discounts are granted to distributors according to the latter's position in
the product's channel of distribution, the various differentials have the
purpose of inducing distributors to perform their particular marketing
functions.

From a legal standpoint, it has been held that when buyers are in
competition with one another, as when dealers are at the same level
in the distributive structure, discriminatory practices between them
("horizontal" discounts) are in violation of the law. But differences in
discounts at different levels in the structure ("vertical" discounts) have
been held to be legal and, accordingly, the FTC has never issued an
order against such discounts [in re: Standard Brands, 30 FTC 1117,
(1940); Caradine Hat Co., 39 FTC 86, (1944)]. From the seller's standpoint, therefore, the following problems must be considered in setting
an appropriate structure of differentials.

1.   Buyers must be classified, not on an arbitrary basis, which would
be illegal, but according to their strict nature of operations or functions
undertaken. Buyers at the same level, such as mail-order houses, chain
stores, and independent retailers, must be placed in the same class and
then the discounts granted must not exceed cost savings [in re: Pittsburgh Plate Glass Co., 25 FTC 1228 (1937); American Oil Co., 29
FTC 857, (1939); Sherwin-Williams, 36 FTC 25, (1943)].

2.   Properly classified, a retailer might thus be given a larger discount
than a wholesaler. But where the buyer performs more than one function,
as selling both at retail and wholesale, the FTC has ruled that the
larger discount can be applied only to the portion of the order for
which that function alone is performed. In practice, however, the rule
is difficult to enforce because the seller must take the buyer's word
as to how different portions of the order will be handled, and the buyer

may tend to overstate the quantity on which the higher discount applies [in re: *Southgate Brokerage Co.* v. *FTC*, 150 F. 2d 607, (1945); *Standard Oil Co. of Indiana* v. *FTC*, 173 F. 2d 210, (1949)]. But the rule is also open to criticism when applied to the dual-function dealer, since he is denied a rightful discount for performing the wholesale function on that part of the order which he retails himself.

3. Discounts must provide adequate margins to cover operating costs and normal profits of dealers. Excessive margins will encourage entry of new distributors while deficient ones will result in lost orders. Since this entails the practical difficulties of knowing dealers' costs, two useful guides to the seller for judging those costs are:

a. The cost of selling through alternative channels (including the alternative of bypassing dealers and performing the function himself), which sets an upper limit to the size of the discount in each case;
b. The extent to which price cutting prevails at successive stages in the channel, with large cuts indicating that margins are too high, or perhaps that the least efficient dealers should be dumped and that a discount structure for the most efficient ones should be devised.

4. Industry tradition and competitive practices with respect to discounts are further factors to be considered. The seller who offers an unusually high margin may or may not succeed in increasing turnover rate, depending upon whether the dealer can push the product and upon the seller's market share. Where product differentiation is negligible, consumers are relatively indifferent except to price, and salesmanship may have little effect despite the dealer's greater incentive to sell. Yet, if the dealer passes the greater margin along to the consumer by cutting price, the result may be a price war unless the seller's market share is small enough so that larger competitors do not deem it necessary to meet the lower price. Sugar refineries, gasoline stations, and several other oligopolistic industries provide many actual examples of this situation.

The above comments as to quantity differentials serve once again to emphasize the dangers inherent in using ordinary cost accounting data as a basis for management decisions. The ambiguous nature of such data must be recognized by any management interested in establishing a differential price structure, since the burden of proof of cost differences is on the seller and not on the government. The pattern that seems to be emerging from various cases reveals a tendency of the courts to place increasing reliance on the FTC's interpretation of the situation. Management, therefore, must consider the legal as well as the economic aspects of differential pricing if such pricing is to become a basis for future policy.

Geographic Pricing

Finally, a comment on the spatial aspects of pricing is in order. This involves the problem of establishing an optimum geographic pricing policy which in turn revolves largely around the nature of transportation costs and certain legal considerations. Omitting the more detailed aspects of these factors, some essential points may be noted at this time.

The appropriate price policy is *not* simply one that charges all buyers the same base price with the result that buyers closer to the plant pay less and buyers farther away pay more, according to differences in transportation costs. Instead, each buyer's average revenue curve should be conceived as a *net* demand curve after deduction of transportation costs. The elasticity of each buyer's curve then becomes the important factor, in that the correct net price to each buyer is the one that equates the marginal cost of the seller's entire output with marginal revenue.

Under the Robinson-Patman Act, a seller is not allowed complete freedom of differential price discretion. Thus, it is illegal for price differentials to be disproportionately larger than cost differentials. However, some discretion does exist. For example, the seller may, at least within limits, legally employ a differential pricing policy:

1. By giving discounts that are less than the amount of his (or her) cost saving when buyers are not in competition with one another.
2. Where he is himself "meeting" competition but not "beating" it.
3. By selling slightly different products under different brand names.

Thus, it appears that economic theory does offer a guide for management decisions involving geographic pricing policies.

Conclusion

This discussion has had two main purposes:

1. To provide a theoretical background against which to formulate intelligent pricing policies.
2. To show that most pricing behavior, which is treated in a purely descriptive way in virtually all marketing literature, can actually be integrated with the general theory of monopolistic competition.

This second consideration has two particular advantages. First, it enables marketing managers and business economists to learn more about the pricing policies actually used by business firms and hence provides a sounder means for proposing improvements in these policies. Second, it provides a guide for empirical measurement by focusing sharply on what it is that actually needs to be measured. The result is thus a stronger foundation on which to construct a plan for future action by management.

PRICING OBJECTIVES

Some time ago, the Brookings Institute, a prominent research organization in Washington, D.C., sponsored a well-known study of the pricing objectives of 20 major American corporations.[2]

The typical and collateral pricing goals of these 20 companies cited tended to fall into four categories, namely: (1) pricing to achieve a target return on investments, (2) pricing to stabilize prices and outputs, (3) pricing to realize a target market share, and (4) pricing to meet or match competition.

Although today, in light of inflationary experience and higher capitalization costs, the rates of returns on investment uncovered by the study would probably be considered outdated, the pricing goals by which they were obtained are still viable decision criteria worthy of consideration. We therefore examine each of the above pricing objectives, using the Brookings study as a framework for our discussion.

Pricing to Achieve a Target Return on Investment

A *target-return price* is a price which is designed to yield a predetermined average return on capital employed for specific products, product groups, and divisions. Most firms tend to use stockholders' equity (net worth) plus long-term debt in measuring return on capital. In allocating fixed costs among products or divisions, firms usually employ a standard cost system based on an assumed rate of production—typically 70 to 80 percent of capacity—and an assumed product mix as "normal."

Some of the essential features of target-return pricing which were brought out in the Brookings study may be conveniently listed as follows.

1. Company accountants and industrial engineers establish estimates of standard costs based on standard volume—the latter usually measured by the long-run rate of plant utilization. The margins added to these standard costs are designed to yield the target rate of return on investment over the long run. The margins are thus based on the averaging of fluctuations in cost and demand over the business cycle; hence, short-run changes in volume or product-mix do not unduly affect price.

2. Companies are aware of the fact that a rigid adherence to target-return pricing may not always be possible, depending on the degree of market protection afforded the particular product. This is especially true of new products, where an orderly "stepping down" of prices may be necessary over the long run as competing products become available.

3. Since target returns are established on the basis of "normal" or average periods, year-to-year profits may at times be higher or lower than the predetermined targets. This is a further bit of evidence which

[2] See Robert V. Lanzillotti, "Pricing Objectives in Large Companies," *American Economic Review,* vol. 48, no. 5 (December 1958), pp. 921–40.

tends to support the belief that firms probably do not as a general rule set prices so as to "maximize" profits, at least in the short run. However, there may of course be specific and quite realistic situations where exceptions to the rule are possible. (Can you think of any examples?)

4. New products have been particularly singled out for target-return pricing by most companies. At firms such as Du Pont, Union Carbide, Alcoa, International Harvester, and General Foods, either of two types of pricing strategies are often employed: (*a*) a relatively high price policy may be adopted with planned step-down rates for "skimming" the market by exploiting the inelasticity of demand in different markets (as long as current or potential competition permits); (*b*) a relatively low or "penetration" price policy may be adopted to develop mass markets quickly, in anticipation of a rapid expansion of the market and higher returns later. It should be emphasized, however, that the target approach to pricing is not limited to new products; it has also been applied extensively to high-volume, low-unit-profit items including steel, aluminum, and chemicals.

A concomitant issue with regard to the target-return criterion is the selection of the profit target itself. Executives who have been asked this question have responded by saying that their company's margins are based on one or more of the following considerations: (1) what is believed to be a "fair" or "reasonable" return, (2) industry custom, (3) a desire to equal or better the company's recent average return, (4) what the company felt it could get, and (5) use of a specific profit target as a means of stabilizing industry prices. Independent of the specific criteria of choice, however, is the fact that the target rate in most cases is regarded by the various firms as a long-run objective. It tends to average about 15 percent after taxes, with a range of from 10 to 20 percent.

In general, it may be noted that there appears to be an increasing tendency for more and more companies to adopt target-return pricing objectives. There are various reasons for this, including the growing awareness on the part of executives that the subtle concept of "rate of return" can be a valuable analytical tool, as evidenced by the long history of success which Du Pont and General Motors are known to have experienced in using this concept for many kinds of decision-making problems.

Pricing to Stabilize Prices and Outputs

Several companies emphasized the drive for *stabilized prices* as an important objective. Their justification for specifying this goal was presumably based on a philosophy which holds that if a firm's general level of prices is sufficient to yield adequate returns during periods of recession, the level should not be raised as high as the traffic will bear in periods of prosperity. This also implies, of course, that in pricing individual products, an effort will be made—conditioned in each case by the pricing executive's conscience—not to exploit the situation by raising prices beyond reasonable limits of "cost-plus."

There is thus a close relationship between target return on investment as a pricing *objective* and cost-plus as a pricing *method*. In most companies cost-plus pricing, in one form or another, is the chief means of obtaining the objective. The "cost" may be based on an estimate of standard cost and standard volume for a specific group of products; the amount of the "plus" may vary with the pricing executive's goal—whether it be a target return on investment, price stabilization, or some other objective.

Pricing to Realize a Target Market Share

Pricing to achieve a minimum or maximum *market share* was an objective cited very frequently by the various companies. However, the use of a target market share concept as a guide for pricing decisions was not typically employed by firms which at one time or another enjoyed a patent or innovative monopoly in a certain product.

For example, Du Pont made no mention of striving for a particular share of the cellophane or nylon market, nor did Union Carbide for its automobile antifreeze product, Prestone. General Electric, on the other hand, stated that its products rarely have more than 25 percent of any given market, and that it is the company's policy not to exceed 50 percent because it would then become too vulnerable to competition. And Johns-Manville, as another example, stated as company policy that for those building materials in its product line for which it was *not* the price leader, it strives for a maximum of 20 percent of competitive markets. Moreover, it tries to achieve this goal by stressing service and superior quality of its products—rather than price reductions—and indeed even maintains its prices somewhat above those of its competitors.

It appears, therefore, that there is no substantial uniformity of policy among many business firms in their use of market share as a guide for pricing decisions. However, there is undoubtedly some incompatability between a target-return approach and a market-share policy: a company desiring to increase its share of the market will probably find that it must place decreasing emphasis on a strict adherence to a predetermined target.

Pricing to Meet or Match Competition

Pricing to "meet" or to "match" competition was sometimes cited as the objective of a pricing policy. To some extent, this type of policy, if it can be called such, may be due largely to executive "fears"—fear of losing competitive status in the marketplace, and fear of violating the antitrust laws concerning price discrimination.

Regarding the former, it is clear that at least in the case of standardized products such as flour and frozen fish sold by General Foods, or wholesale meat by Swift, a pricing policy to "meet" competition is meaningless since it is the going market price rather than "competition" which each firm must meet. With respect to the latter, the Robinson-Patman Act (1936) permits a seller who is charged with price discrimination to offer the defense that the lower price "was made in good faith to meet an equally low price of a competitor," and not to undercut it. Paradoxically, therefore, the law in some cases may actually be forcing companies to prevent competition instead of creating it.

Conclusions

1. Managements have fairly well-defined pricing objectives that are based upon *planned* profits and long-range profit horizons. Specific pricing policies may differ among firms, reflecting different orders of priorities among competing objectives rather than any simple concept of profit maximization.

2. There is a realization among managements that the typical situation of multiproduct and multimarket operations requires a simultaneous decision with respect to price, cost, and product characteristics. Pricing and marketing strategies pertaining to individual products and markets thus tend to be viewed not in isolation but in the global context of the entire firm as a decision-making enterprise.

3. In large multiproduct and multimarket firms, there are particularly complex problems of joint production and joint distribution costs, as well as considerable lack of knowledge with respect to basic cost-output and cost-sales relationships. Pricing, therefore, is frequently done for broad product groups within the framework of the company's overall profit position and objective. Hence it is possible that the costing of products ends up as a result rather than a cause of price policy. (Can you see why?)

4. In oligopolistic industries such as steel, economic theory leads to the conclusion that price leadership by the dominant firm in the industry will tend to prevail. In the light of the Brookings study, however, the conclusions are not that simple. The extent to which a follower will adhere to a price established by a leader will depend on whether the leader's price results in a target return that is acceptable to the follower. This, in turn, will be conditioned by various factors such as the degree of product differentiation among the competitors, the profit-importance of the product in the follower's product line, and the follower's marketing strategies as related to overall company objectives.

5. Finally, from a social standpoint, target-return pricing makes for more rigid or stable prices over long periods of time. This price inflexibility tends to magnify cyclical fluctuations in income and employment, thereby impeding the operation of corrective public policy measures which are undertaken to combat such fluctuations.

PRICING METHODS AND APPROACHES

Industry pursues its pricing objectives through a variety of methods and approaches, and it is to these that we next turn our attention. In particular, we shall examine seven policies: (1) cost-plus pricing, (2) variable markup pricing, (3) intuitive pricing, (4) experimental pricing, (5) stabilization pricing, (6) control pricing, and (7) incremental cost pricing. Of course some of these approaches are more widely employed in practice than others, and specific circumstances most obviously weigh heavily on the choice of pricing model ultimately made. Further, the methods and approaches discussed below need not always be mutually exclusive. It is likely that some of them may sometimes complement and supplement one another, and hence should be considered with this possibility in mind.

Cost-Plus Pricing

The most widely used method of pricing employed by business firms is known as cost-plus pricing. It is a procedure whereby the price is determined by adding a fixed markup of some kind to the cost of the good (as distinguished from a variable markup, which is discussed later under "flexible markup pricing").

Thus the typical cost-plus calculation for pricing a job usually proceeds in steps somewhat as follows:

1. Estimate the job's direct cost—mainly material and labor.
2. Add a charge for indirect costs or overhead—usually by allocating them at some rate per unit of direct labor, machine-hours, and so forth.
3. Add a margin for profit—usually calculated as some percentage of the total arrived at in the two previous steps.

In short, if pricing is done by the cost-plus method, a price of $10 on a good costing $8 would represent a 25 percent markup on cost, or a 20 percent margin on the price (which is the customary form of quotation). Evidently, two decision problems confront the manager who uses cost-plus formula pricing: (1) arriving at an estimate of cost, and (2) selecting an appropriate margin or markup. How are these done by most firms?

In practice, most manufacturers using cost-plus pricing usually employ some notion of standard cost as their basic cost figure. They arrive at the figure by estimating unit costs of labor and materials and by computing unit overhead costs for operations at some arbitrary percentage of capacity. In other words, they typically calculate their costs for a "standard output," commonly between two-thirds and four-fifths of capacity, irrespective of the actual volume of operations. Other cost measures sometimes used, however, are actual cost, or the cost for the most recent accounting period, and expected cost, which is a forecast of actual cost for the future pricing period based on a forecast of operating rates for that period. Still another method, but one that is relatively rare in industry except where special products are concerned, is to construct a cost figure based on engineering estimates of efficiency and various physical relationships. In any case, regardless of the method employed to estimate costs, the overall nature of the cost-plus pricing formula is essentially the same.

How is the size of the markup determined? Numerous surveys of pricing practices have been made by economists, and the evidence continues to indicate no definite answer to this question, other than the feeling on the part of business executives that their margins represent what they believe to be a "fair" or "reasonable" profit. The evidence also indicates that there are wide variations in the percentage of markup both within industries and between industries, due to differences in pricing objectives, competition, cost structures, accounting methods, inventory turnover, and industry custom.

This last factor, custom, appears to be of considerable importance. Margins used in the past are considered "fair" simply because of their long use over the years. Scarcely a business executive surveyed believes that the margin used is the most profitable one; all seem to stress the ethics rather than the economics of price setting; and most if not all are aware that a more profitable pricing policy may be possible.

Advantages of Cost-Plus Pricing. Some of the chief reasons cited by business executives for using cost-plus pricing are:

1. It offers a relatively simple and expedient method of setting price by the mechanical application of a formula.
2. It provides a method for obtaining adequate ("fair") profits when demand is unknown.
3. It is a method of establishing a stable price uninfluenced by fluctuations in demand, which is particularly important to firms that commit themselves on price through their catalogs, advertising, and so forth.
4. It is desirable for public relations purposes even at the expense of short-run profits, presumably because consumers will accept price increases when costs rise.

Some Disadvantages. Despite its prevalence, cost-plus formula pricing has at least three important disadvantages to firms employing it as a pricing method.

1. It fails to take account of demand as measured in terms of buyers' desire and purchasing power. Moreover, where price planning for the future is involved, what is needed is a forecast of both future costs and future demand if the best pricing decision is to be made, and not an estimate of past or even of present costs.

2. It attempts to make an accurate estimate of what usually amounts to the wrong cost concept rather than even an approximate estimate of the right cost concept. It does this by failing to recognize the roles of such important cost concepts as avoidable cost and opportunity cost as guides for pricing decisions.

   Avoidable costs are the firm's expenses of doing a job as compared with its expenses if it does nothing. The difference represents the sacrifices or potential savings that the firm can avoid by not doing the job or anything else.

   Opportunity costs are the foregone net revenues which the firm sacrifices by putting its resources into a particular job rather than applying these same resources to their next best use. Thus if the firm's resources (including plant, materials, managerial talent, etc.) could have been employed to yield a 15 percent return in some other alternative, then that is the cost of applying these same resources to a particular job.

   For pricing decisions, the total sacrifice involved in doing a job may include both avoidable cost and opportunity cost. Yet, those who employ cost-plus pricing procedures neglect these considerations entirely by basing their decisions on historical cost data which are largely irrelevant for pricing purposes. Further, there is even some doubt as to how accurate the measures of full (past or present) costs usually used in the formula really are, especially in multiple-product firms where common costs exist and are hardly more than arbitrarily apportioned to products in typical cost accounting systems.

3. It fails to reflect competition in terms of rivals' reactions and the possible entry of new firms. For example, in an industry that prices by the cost-plus method, if company margins are above the level necessary to cover operating costs and yield "normal profits" per unit at capacity, new firms will tend to enter the industry as long as no considerable excess capacity is already present. The results will be a smaller market share for each firm, and therefore higher unit overhead costs and lower profits per firm.

Flexible or Variable Markup Pricing

A pricing practice that is closely related to cost-plus pricing, but is by no means as widespread in industry, has been termed flexible or variable markup pricing. Essentially, it is a pricing method that takes some cognizance of changing economic conditions by providing for a variable markup over the course of a business cycle. In periods of prosperity when incomes are high and buyers are less price conscious, sellers add larger margins to their base cost; in recession or in relatively low income periods, buyers are more sensitive to competitive price differences, so sellers add smaller margins to their base cost.

Flexible markup pricing, despite its advantage over cost-plus pricing in that at least it takes some recognition of demand, is not a common pricing practice used by business firms for the following reasons:

1. It requires frequent estimates of demand which may involve more time, effort, and money than most industrialists care to expend. Besides, there is a common and sometimes well-founded belief among many managements that the longer run sale of their products is more affected by changes in determinants other than price, primarily incomes, advertising, and "demographic" factors such as number of families where consumer durables are concerned, and buyers' profit anticipations where the purchase of durable producer's goods are involved. In addition, buyers of consumer durable goods often react to major price cuts not by immediate purchase increases, but by postponing their purchases in anticipation of still further price reductions. All of these factors tend to indicate that many sellers frequently regard the cyclical demand for their products as relatively price inelastic, which probably accounts to a large extent for the more widespread use of cost-plus rather than flexible markup pricing.

2. Sellers will tend to prefer cost-plus pricing to flexible markup pricing during recession periods, in the belief that they deserve a larger margin when business declines. When sales decrease, cost per unit (exclusive of merchandise) increases, and the seller sees the margin, which allows for overhead costs, eroding. For even if the margin percentage remains the same, the absolute amount declines because of the drop in base costs; hence sellers feel that their charges to buyers are lower.

3. The goal of a "fair" price is lost if margins are allowed to vary, and instead there is a flavor of "charging what the traffic will bear." The objective of "reasonable" profits is not uncommon and seems to be an important motive guiding many management decisions.

Intuitive Pricing

Intuitive pricing, or pricing by the "feel of the market," is a fairly common method practiced by many executives. The degree of its application can vary from prices based on pure hunches or guesses to prices based on an examination of past data and future trends in costs and demand.

A common procedure in many firms is to arrive at a preliminary price estimate based on a cost-plus formula and then adjust the price upward or downward in accordance with executive opinion as to expected demand, competition, and other market forces. In a certain sense, therefore, it combines cost-plus pricing with flexible markup pricing. The emphasis, however, is on the subjective "weighting" of factors believed to be influential in affecting price, and thus is a type of "psychological" rather than mechanical pricing method.

Evidently, intuitive pricing requires a high degree of self-confidence, since the firm's well-being will depend to a large extent on how accurately management can "feel" future business conditions. Despite its vagueness, a possible justification of the method is that the extreme subjectivity involved in this type of pricing often requires that the pricing decision be the result of group action, which thereby removes the responsibility of a wrong decision from the shoulders of any one executive.

Experimental Pricing

A technique for arriving at an optimum price that has gained increasing acceptance by companies in recent years is a kind of trial-and-error, or experimental, pricing. The procedure is to select a sample of test markets, establish a statistical experimental design, and manipulate the "treatments" or prices among markets, thereby arriving at a price that maximizes profit. However, because of the difficulty of deriving empirically the price that actually maximizes profit, the more common practice is usually to choose the price that maximizes sales. Experimental pricing thus offers at least a partial solution to the problem of establishing an optimum price by taking some recognition of the influence of demand.

Experimental pricing methods have found particular application in the pricing of new products at the retail level. Conducted properly, these experiments can yield rich marketing information for later use as well as a sounder base on which to construct a more profitable pricing structure. As in researching demand, however, the approach through controlled experimentation can be hazardous, whether for new products or for established ones, when:

1. Oligopoly conditions prevail in the test markets so that there is a danger of rivals' reactions to downward price movements by the experimenting firm; or
2. Buyers cannot be sealed off into separate markets so as to prevent their infiltration from higher to lower priced markets.

Stable and Imitative Pricing: Oligopoly Problems

A company that adheres strictly to any one or combination of the above pricing methods would, in view of the dynamic economic environ-

ment, be in almost a continuous process of rebuilding its price structure.
The fact is, however, that many firms do not recalculate their price
structures frequently, but instead establish prices either by building on
stable prices of the recent past or by imitating the prices charged by
competitors. The reasons behind each of these pricing methods may
be examined briefly.

Stable Pricing. Price stability for a period of months and sometimes
for years is the rule for most companies rather than the exception. Official
quotations in catalogs and other media, wage contracts, and product
differentiation are only a few of the important factors making for price
stability of manufactured goods. But in oligopolistic industries characterized by few sellers and very similar products, which is the typical
situation in American manufacturing, there are further price-stabilizing
influences as well.

1.   Sellers in industries with few firms will normally tend to maintain
the prevailing price, since, in theory, competitors will not usually follow
price increases but will match price reductions, at least in particular
market areas. This is the familiar situation of the kinked demand curve.

2.   Even aside from the oligopolistic aspects of the problem, there
are less complex reasons why price stability is an important element
of a firm's price policy. Changes in price can be costly to the company
as well as disturbing to salespersons and purchasers. In the past, many
firms that reduced their prices in recession periods found it extremely
difficult to raise them later, even in the face of rising costs and general
inflation.

Imitative Pricing. Imitative pricing occurs when a firm chooses to
set its price equal to, or at some proportion of, the price of another
firm in the industry. The advantages to the imitator of pricing products
this way are that:

1.   The firm it imitates may be more experienced and better able to
      establish the appropriate price.
2.   It saves the expense of deriving demand and cost estimates.
3.   It leaves management more time to concentrate on nonprice competi-
      tive forms, such as advertising, merchandising, product development,
      personal selling, and services.

The importance of these conditions that make for imitative pricing
should not be underestimated. The tendency to rely on an experienced
competitor in setting prices, the tendency to avoid price cutting because
of its retaliatory effects, and the likelihood that nonprice competitive
practices would, in the long run, increase industry demand more than
would lower prices, have created a unique type of competition in oligopolistic industries. One aspect of this competitive pattern is a type
of imitative pricing known as "price leadership."

Price Leadership. When firms tend to establish their prices in a manner dependent upon the price charged by one of the firms in the industry, price leadership exists. The firm that takes the initiative in announcing its changes in price is called the price leader; all other firms in the industry that either match the leader's price or some differential of it are termed price followers. The price leader will sometimes be a leader in all markets, although it frequently happens that a firm will sometimes follow in some markets and lead in others. Custom, industry demand and cost structures, and changing economic pressures vary between firms, and such changes are frequently sufficient to destabilize existing patterns for unpredictable periods of time.

Price leadership can easily exist without explicit agreements and, indeed, this form may well be the rule rather than the exception. That is, price leadership frequently arises as a natural growth within an industry; and the price leader is usually the firm with a successful profit history, sound management, substantial market share, and long experience in marketing matters. The remaining firms in the industry accept the leader, not necessarily because of an explicit agreement but because of the leader's ability to coordinate the industry's growth with that of its members. In effect, the leader's overall judgment of market conditions replaces the separate judgments of the followers. Evidence of a leader-follower relationship has existed in such industries as agricultural implements, cement, cigarettes, copper, gasoline, lead, newsprint, nonferrous alloys, steel, sulphur, and tin cans, to mention only a few.

Not in all cases, it may be noted, do small firms only follow the leader down, in accordance with economic theory and the dictates of competition; in reality, they frequently follow a price increase as well—a fact not often emphasized in theoretical discussions but one that is readily observable in practice. The reasons may be (1) a fear or desire on the part of the price follower to avoid provoking a price war with the leader, (2) a belief by the follower that profits are larger in the long run under the refuge of the leader's price umbrella for the industry as a whole, (3) the follower finds it easier or more convenient to follow the leader, or (4) suppliers to the industry have raised their prices and a "justified" (cost-induced) price increase is merely initiated by the price leader.

In any case, as long as the leader's price is high enough to allow at least normal profits for the less-efficient followers, the industry may operate fairly smoothly with little or no price warfare. The challenge to the leader may thus involve not only an ability to forecast changing demand and cost conditions but also sometimes to evolve an industry-wide pattern of price differentials that would be acceptable to members and that would allow for differences in brand name, service, and quality, particularly in differentiated oligopolistic industries. Failure to comply with these conditions and to revise the differential structure with changes in underlying market conditions and business cycles may easily result in a loss of leadership, despite the firm's historical dominance in the industry.

Incremental-Cost Pricing

"The economist who understands marginal analysis has a full-time job in undoing the work of the accountant!"

This quotation is indicative of a viewpoint that has long been held by many business economists. Stated simply, it refers to the fact that accounting practices and most business executive's thinking are permeated with cost allocation directed at average rather than incremental cost. Thus, in any business, there is likely to be a substantial difference between the costs of each company activity as it is carried on the accounting books and the "extra" costs—the so-called incremental costs—which determine whether or not the activity should be undertaken. For many kinds of pricing decisions, it is the incremental costs that are the only "true" and relevant costs to be considered.

The typical manager comment—that nobody ever made a profit without meeting all costs—is a misleading statement which causes many firms to lose potential profits. True, the company as a whole must cover its average unit costs in order to make a profit, *but covering average unit costs should not determine whether a particular activity should be undertaken.* Managers who fail to recognize this actually forgo various opportunities for extra gains.

How does the notion of incremental cost apply specifically to pricing? We can answer the question by first defining incremental cost and then pointing out some of its important implications.

> DEFINITION: *Incremental cost* is the increase in total costs resulting from an expansion in a firm's volume of business or level of activity.

Technically, therefore, incremental cost is not the same as "marginal cost," for in economic theory the latter term represents the change in total cost resulting from a unit change in output. But in many practical discussions and in much of the business literature, the two expressions are frequently used synonymously. This should be no cause of confusion, however, since the distinction, if any, is normally clear from the context.

Incremental cost provides business executives with an essential guide for production and pricing decisions. For if a business executive is considering, say, a reduction in price in order to increase sales, the executive must know whether the resulting gain in revenue from the additional volume, that is, the incremental revenue, will more than cover the increase in costs. If the incremental revenue exceeds the incremental cost, profits will be expanded accordingly.

NOTE: Even for the economy as a whole, it can be argued that incremental cost, rather than average or "fully distributed" cost, is the relevant cost guide to employ in allocating resources among various lines of production. The reason is that incremental cost measures the additional resources that will be used up when more of anything is produced, and this is what represents the real cost to society. For each alternative there is associated a given incremental cost and a corresponding incremental revenue. By comparing these sets of data, it can be decided whether additional outputs of any commodity are worth producing, and which of the alternative ways of satisfying wants is most efficient.

Thus, while incremental costs should not *determine* a product's price, they should set a "floor"—and demand conditions a "ceiling"—within which the range of many profitable pricing decisions should be made. "Fully distributed" cost, on the other hand, is an economically invalid criterion for specific pricing decisions, since it is based on arbitrary apportionments of unallocable costs among various products, departments, and divisions. It is manifestly absurd and illogical to hold a certain product or group of products economically responsible for any given share of unallocable costs. Whether the particular price of a product is above or below its fully distributed cost is of no economic significance as far as its minimum price is concerned in a particular pricing decision.

Consider the following vivid illustration of these principles, adapted from an article that appeared in *Business Week* on April 20, 1963:

CONTINENTAL AIR LINES, INC.

During a given year, Continental sometimes fills only half the available seats on its jet flights, a record some 15 percentage points worse than the national average.

By eliminating just a few runs—less than 5 percent—Continental could raise its average load considerably. Some of its flights frequently carry as few as 30 passengers. But the improved load factor would mean reduced profits.

For Continental bolsters its corporate profits by deliberately running extra flights that aren't expected to do more than return their out-of-pocket costs—plus a little profit. Such marginal flights are an integral part of the overall operating philosophy that has brought small Continental through its bumpy growth years.

Chief Contribution

This philosophy leans heavily on "marginal" or incremental analysis. And the line leans heavily on Chris F. Whelan, vice-president in charge of economic planning, to translate marginalism into hard, dollars-and-cents decisions.

Getting management to accept and apply the marginal concept probably is the chief contribution any economist can make to his company. Put most simply, *marginalists maintain that a company should undertake any activity that adds more to revenues than it does to costs—and not limit itself to those activities whose returns equal average or "fully allocated" costs.*

The approach, of course, can be applied to virtually any business, not just to air transportation. It can be used in consumer finance, for instance, where the question may be whether to make more loans—including more bad loans—if this will increase net profit. Similarly, in advertising, the decision may rest on how much extra business a dollar's worth of additional advertising will bring in, rather than pegging the advertising budget to a percentage of sales—and, in insurance, where setting high interest rates to discourage policy loans may actually damage profits by causing policyholders to borrow elsewhere.

Approach

Whelan finds all such cases wholly analogous to his run of problems, where he seeks to keep his company's eye trained on the big objective: *net profit.*

Whelan's approach is this: He considers that the bulk of his scheduled flights have to return at least their fully allocated costs. Overhead, depreciation, insurance are very real expenses and must be covered. The out-of-pocket approach comes into play, says Whelan, only after the line's basic schedule has been set.

"Then you go a step farther," he says, and see if adding more flights will contribute to the corporate net. Similarly, if he's thinking of dropping a flight with a disappointing record, he puts it under the marginal microscope: "If your revenues are going to be more than your out-of-pocket costs, you should keep the flight on."

By "out-of-pocket costs" Whelan means just that: the actual dollars that Continental has to pay out to run a flight. He gets the figure not by applying hypothetical equations but by circulating a proposed schedule to every operating department concerned and finding out just what extra expenses it will entail. If a ground crew already on duty can service the plane, the flight isn't charged a penny of their salary expense. There may even be some costs eliminated in running the flight; they won't need men to roll the plane to a hangar, for instance, if it flies on to another stop.

Most of these extra flights, of course, are run at offbeat hours, mainly late at night. At times, though, Continental discovers that the hours aren't so unpopular after all. A pair of night coach flights on the Houston-San Antonio-El Paso-Phoenix-Los Angeles leg, added on a marginal basis, have turned out to be so successful that they are now more than covering fully allocated costs.

Alternative

Whelan uses an alternative cost analysis closely allied with the marginal concept in drawing up schedules. For instance, on his 11:11 P.M. flight from Colorado Springs to Denver and a 5:20 A.M. flight the other way, Continental uses Viscounts that, though they carry some cargo, often go without a single passenger. But the net cost of these flights is less than would be the rent for overnight hangar space for the Viscount at Colorado Springs.

And there's more than one absolute-loss flight scheduled solely to bring passengers to a connecting Continental long-haul flight: even when the loss on the feeder service is considered a cost on the long-haul service, the line makes a net profit on the trip.

Continental's data handling system produces weekly reports on each flight, with revenues measured against both out-of-pocket and fully allocated costs. Whelan uses these to give each flight a careful analysis at least once a quarter. But those added on a marginal basis get the fine-tooth-comb treatment monthly.

The business on these flights tends to be useful as a leading indicator, Whelan finds, since the off-peak traffic is more than normally sensitive to economic trends and will fall off sooner than that on the popular-hour flights. When he sees the night coach flights turning in consistently poor showings, it's a clue to lower his projections for the rest of the schedule.

Unorthodox

There are times, though, when the decisions dictated by the most expert marginal analysis seem silly at best, and downright costly at worst. For example, Continental will have two planes converging at the same time on Municipal Airport in Kansas City, when the new schedules take effect.

This is expensive because, normally, Continental doesn't have the facilities in K.C. to service two planes at once; the line will have to lease an extra fuel truck and hire three new hands—at a total monthly cost of $1,800.

But when Whelan started pushing around proposed departure times in other cities to avoid the double landing, it began to look as though passengers switching to competitive flights leaving at choicer hours, would lose Continental $10,000 worth of business each month. The two flights will be on the ground in K.C. at the same time.

Conclusion

The gist of the thinking which illustrates the technique of applying incremental cost analysis at Continental is summarized [below]:

Incremental Analysis in a Nutshell

PROBLEM: Shall Continental run an extra daily flight from City X to City Y?

THE FACTS: Fully allocated costs of this flight $4,500
Out-of-pocket costs of this flight $2,000
Flight should gross $3,100

DECISION: Run the flight. It will add $1,100 to net profit—because it will add $3,100 to revenues and only $2,000 to costs. Overhead and other costs, totaling $2,500 [$4,500 minus $2,000], would be incurred whether the flight is run or not. Therefore, fully allocated or "average" costs of $4,500 are not relevant to this business decision. It's the out-of-pocket or "marginal" costs that count.

One of the main lessons to be learned from Continental's experience is that even a rough application of marginal principles may come closer to the right answer for business decision makers than an analysis based on precise average or unit cost data. In short, *it is better to have an approximate estimate of the right concept than an accurate estimate of the wrong one.*

Conclusion

Business executives employ a variety of pricing methods of which cost-plus formula pricing, because of its simplicity and mechanical nature, is most common. Though these methods frequently provide adequate profits, they do not maximize profits because they ignore demand in general and its elasticity in particular.

Perhaps the most important factor coloring managerial price decisions are business executive's notions of "fair" or "reasonable" profits as a goal of the firm. It is quite possible, however, indeed even likely, that the concept of a just price is a rationalization by executives to compensate for their economic ignorance rather than a means of securing only a moderate profit as the company's objective. If a management could, on the basis of well-founded demand and cost calculations, estimate the most profitable price consistent with other company objectives, it seems plausible that competitive forces would prompt it to charge that price at least in the long run. To the firm that knows its costs and demand, therefore, the notion of a fair profit can readily be reconciled with that of maximum profit; to the firm that is ignorant of its demand, costs, and market structure, however, any profit—even if not a maximum—would obviously be "fair." Evidently, there is a need for serious reconsideration on the part of many managements as to the profitability of their present and often outdated pricing practices and policies.

PRODUCT-LINE PRICING

Most of economic theory with respect to pricing is based on the assumption that the firm produces only one product. If "product" is defined broadly—for example, to mean automobiles, shoes, or locomotives—this assumption is not unrealistic and, in fact, goes a long way in describing a very important part of business behavior. But for many management problems such a broad definition is unsatisfactory because it fails to explain why a firm produces diverse commodities and what the relationship is among their prices.

In modern industry the typical firm produces multiple products, and therefore a definition of "product" is needed that is more suitable for attacking the kind of pricing problems encountered by such firms. The most meaningful definition is simply that *a product is any homogeneous commodity*. But what is the criterion of homogeneity? In everyday terms, the test is that buyers must not distinguish between any portions of the stock, or, in other words, that they be indifferent as to separate portions. Thus the key economic feature with respect to the pricing of a company's product line is the nature of the interrelated demands for parts of the firm's output, which when measured in quantitative terms takes its most common form as the *cross elasticity of demand*. This coefficient represents the percentage change in the demand for product Y resulting from a 1 percent change in the price of product X, the price of Y remaining constant. On this narrow definition of product, it is evident that virtually all firms are multiple-product firms and that the emphasis from a pricing standpoint is to define a company's product line in terms of demand interrelationships.

A firm produces multiple products either because (1) the demands for the various products are related or (2) production costs are lower when products are jointly produced. Keeping this in mind, some implications for product-line pricing may be noted under the separate conditions where goods are substitutes for each other and where they are complements. The overall problem in product-line pricing is to manipulate the combination of prices until the optimum or most profitable price structure is achieved.

Pricing Substitute Goods

From the standpoint of product-line pricing, the production of substitute goods by a firm should be viewed as an effort to segregate (or segment) individuals or market sectors with different demand elasticities, in order to profit from the different taste idiosyncrasies. Striking examples of firms producing competing, that is, substitute products, are numerous: meat-packers, automobile manufacturers, tire companies, clothing producers, cigarette firms, soap companies, and pharmaceutical houses are only a few. Evidently, these firms compete with themselves to some extent in the sense that they produce products to fill similar needs. At any given time, the more they sell of one product, the less they may sell of others. How then should these products be priced? In practice, two common methods of product-line pricing for substitute goods can be distinguished.

The procedure followed by most producers is to set prices on their entire line of products by the same method. Essentially, a markup method of pricing is used on the entire line of products, with the same margin employed for all similar products in the line. The specific technique is to price the products in proportion to costs, with the choice of costs being either full costs or "transformation" costs, the latter representing the labor and overhead expenditures required to transform (convert) raw materials into finished products.

A second approach commonly employed in product-line pricing is to price the product by varying the size of the margin with the level of costs. Thus, the more costly the product, the higher the margin, and hence the higher the price.

Both of these methods, despite their widespread use in industry, suffer from the shortcomings that they take no account of differences in demand, differences in competitive conditions, and differences in the degree of market maturity of each product in the line. Further, the accounting methods employed to divide joint costs among products of the same firm are not at all justified economically, being wholly arbitrary and thus resulting in prices that reflect at least partly the arbitrary allocation of common costs.

What, then, should be the appropriate method for setting price? Ideally, the optimum price in a market sector is the one that yields the largest "contribution margin," tempered by expected secular shifts in demand, and by competitive forces as measured, for instance, by market share, the possibility of entry by new competitors, and other criteria of competitive intensity that may be selected as guides to action. Approached in this way, the product-line price structure would aim at the correct objective: that of *exploiting the differences in demand elasticities between market sectors.* More is said of this in the following section on price discrimination.

Pricing Complementary Goods

The second type of demand interrelation is complementarity. The degree of complementarity among users can take one near-extreme form of fixed proportions (e.g., watch cases and watch mechanisms, automobiles and engine blocks, houses and furnaces); it may take different degrees of variable proportions (e.g., turpentine and paint, cameras and film, stereo phonographs and records); or it may take the most remote form where the various products in the line are not jointly related in use but merely augment the firm's general reputation (e.g., dentifrices and soap by a firm such as Procter and Gamble, where the ultimate product being sold is "personal hygiene"). In the last case, all multiple products of a firm can be viewed as complementary if they enhance one another's acceptability, but in any event the fundamental pricing principles are not materially altered.

The ultimate objective, as with substitute goods, is to arrive at a price structure that produces the largest "contribution margin" according to the separate demand elasticities of market segments. An essential difference, however, is this: where complementary goods are concerned, a decrease in the price of one leads to an increased demand for the others, so that the cross elasticity is substantially negative. The direct price elasticity of demand would then be less than unity or inelastic. (Why?) The practical consequence of this is that sellers will frequently find it more profitable to price an item low or even at a loss, in the hope of selling the complementary item at an above-average margin. Three illustrations of this and of similar pricing strategies for complementary goods, which are frequently encountered in descriptive form in marketing literature, may be noted.

   1. Loss Leaders. Loss leaders illustrate one type of product-line pricing of complementary goods. Most commonly encountered in retailing, this practice refers to the sale of a commodity at less than invoice cost or at a price sharply below customary price, and publicizing of the fact through advertising. The intention is (1) to draw in customers who will buy other products and/or (2) to arouse consumer interest that will eventually shift the demand curve to the right.

   In the first case, the complementarity is between different products at the same time, and the direct losses on the loss leader are unimportant if they are more than offset by the indirect gains in the complementary items. In the second case, the complementarity reveals a time dimension between present and future demand, with the hope that present losses will encourage future sales and profits, for example, magazine trial subscriptions, student rates on theater tickets, and so forth.

   For a loss leader to be effective, the negative cross-elasticity coefficient between the loss item and the other products must be large (ideally, infinite); the direct or price elasticity should be low (ideally, zero); and the supply elasticity should be high so that the direct losses do not merely outweigh the indirect complementary gains. Frequently, the purchasers of loss leaders will be rationed (e.g., one to a customer) at the submerged price. Implicitly, this serves to reduce the demand elasticity and limits the direct losses suffered by the seller while still evoking sales on the complementary commodities. Further, the good should be well known, widely and frequently purchased, unsuitable for storage by consumers, and standardized so that its customary price is widely known and its "bargain" price quickly recognized.

   Thus, the phrase *loss leader* is actually a misnomer, for an intelligent management can in reality increase its profits by careful selection and pricing of loss leaders. Given the prices of other products, a change in the price of the loss leader produces larger sales of all products so that the increment in revenues exceeds the increment in costs. Hence the fact that the leader's marginal cost is greater than its marginal revenue is irrelevant; the true marginal revenue of the leader is the change in the firm's *total* revenue with other outputs (or prices) remaining the same. Therefore, a good loss leader is always a "profit leader."

   2. Tie-In Sales. Tie-in sales or contracts afford a second concrete illustration of complementarity commonly discussed in marketing literature. The practice consists of requiring buyers to combine other purchases with the featured goods so that in effect the seller is offering the purchaser a joint product. Normally, the featured or "lever" commodity, if the tie-in is to be effective, must be difficult to substitute, not easily dispensed with, and relatively more inelastic in demand than the subsidiary item. An ideal opportunity for tie-in sales exists when the seller possesses an exclusive and essential patent, as in the classic example of the American Shoe Machinery Company, which compelled shoemakers to purchase other materials and intermediate products as a condition of purchasing shoe machinery.

A variation of tie-in sales is "full-line forcing," where the dealer must accept the parent firm's entire product line as a condition of purchasing one item in the line. From the seller's standpoint, this may effectively seal off or at least curb sharply the distributive facilities of competing producers because of the limited financial and physical facilities of dealers. It also has a socioeconomic welfare effect, however, in that it reduces competition in distribution and narrows the alternatives open to consumers, thereby involving certain antitrust issues as to its legality. In any event, the pricing aspect involves a recognition of the relatively inelastic demand for the main product and hence a higher price, coupled with a lower price for the subsidiary items because of their greater demand elasticity. Packaged sales, with the offer to "buy one and get one free," may be considered a type of tie-in practice, and are often encountered as a method of introducing a new product.

3. Two-Part Tariff. Still another illustration of complementarity in pricing and somewhat similar to tie-in sales is the "two-part" tariff. Here the buyer pays two prices for a joint product consisting of a fixed and a variable component. For the fixed portion, the buyer pays a set price independent of utilization; and for the variable flow of services, the buyer makes separate payments. Examples include the basic installation charge for electric wiring or gas transmission lines and the variable payments dependent upon use; the minimum charge for public utility services and the variable payments for units purchased; the entry fee to an amusement park (or the cover charge in a night club) and the variable payments for each individual entertainment; and so on.

Economically, the two-part tariff can be used as a device to cover initial costs with further income to be derived from the variable service (e.g., college registration fees and separate course rates per credit hour) or as a source of profit from both components of the product. In the latter case the product should be viewed as consisting of complementary items in variable proportions, with a relatively inelastic demand for the fixed component and a more elastic demand for the variable flow.

Conclusions

The problems of product-line pricing are essentially twofold: (1) to decide on what it is that management wants and can expect from a structure of product prices, and (2) to manipulate the price structure until the desired combination of prices for producing the desired end is achieved.

If the objective is maximum profits, it must be recognized that each price structure will produce a different sales mixture and therefore a different combination of total revenue and total cost. Hence the optimum price structure is the one that produces the greatest expected difference between total revenue and total cost, or in other words the largest expected net profit. To achieve this goal requires a knowledge of product interrelationships, particularly from the demand standpoint, since it is the demand elasticities, rather than cost considerations alone, that are usually more relevant for pricing purposes.

The importance of cost, however, should not be underestimated. For instance, certain kinds of cost estimates are crucial when decisions must be made as to: (1) whether to drop the product or retain it, in which case the cost saving (i.e., avoidable cost) is relevant; (2) whether to market one of two or more new products, in which case a comparison of each product's incremental cost and price is needed and, when combined with sales forecasts, indicates the contribution profit for each product; and (3) whether to accept a sales commitment (e.g., government contract) for a fixed future period or quantity of supply, in which case the relevant criterion is again incremental cost, the size of which will depend to a large extent on future variations in capacity due to seasonal and cyclical factors. Hence, various kinds of cost and demand estimates may be needed.

Product-line pricing is thus seen to be closely related to general problems of product-line policy. One of the chief differences, however, is this: from the production viewpoint, the problem of product-line policy is one of manipulating the component items of the product line in order to maximize profit; from the pricing viewpoint, the problem of product-line pricing is to manipulate the price structure of the component items in order to maximize profit. Both independent variables—the product line and its price structure—are necessarily interrelated in their effects on the dependent variable, net profit. The role of management in this respect, therefore, is to keep a continuous weather-eye open for possible additions and deletions to the commodity belt if it is to maintain an optimum product line.

Finally, stress was placed on the segmentation of markets and the pricing of substitute and complementary goods. Where products are neither substitutes nor complements, or only faintly substitutable or complementary, as reflected by cross-elasticities of demand close to zero, they should be treated as independent goods for pricing purposes, but the importance of identifying the needed types of demand and cost estimates are still applicable.

PRICE DISCRIMINATION

Differential pricing, or price discrimination, has been a subject of heated controversy for years, involving both economic implications and regulatory problems. The economic aspects will be the main area of our concern in this section; the regulatory considerations are treated for the most part in the literature of antitrust.

What is meant by the term "differential pricing?" Specifically, it may be defined as the practice by a seller of charging different prices to the same or to different buyers for the same good, without corresponding differences in cost.

> NOTE: From a theoretical standpoint, a better statement would be one which defines differential pricing or price discrimination as the sale of technically similar products at prices that are not proportional to *marginal* costs. However, the law that deals with price discrimination does not distinguish as to the type of cost, thus leaving wide room for interpretation as will be discussed below.

For analytical purposes, it is convenient to distinguish between three classes of differential pricing.

First Degree. Differential pricing of the first degree means that the seller charges the same buyer a different price for each unit bought, thereby extracting the maximum total receipts. This is a familiar price discrimination situation studied in elementary economics. By shading the price down to the buyer for each unit purchased, the seller obtains a larger total revenue than if he were to charge the same price per unit for all units bought.

Second Degree. Differential pricing of the second degree involves the same underlying principle as first-degree pricing, except that the seller charges different prices for blocks of units instead of for individual units. The result is the "stair-step" pricing effect discussed previously under quantity discounts and illustrated graphically in Exhibit 8. The yield is still a larger total revenue to the seller than if the same price was charged, but not as large as would be realized if the price could be shaded for each unit so that the total receipts approached in magnitude the entire area under the demand curve as in first-degree pricing.

Third Degree. Differential pricing of the third degree occurs when the seller segregates buyers according to income, geographic location, individual tastes, kinds of uses for the product, or other criteria, and charges different prices to each group or market despite equivalent costs in serving them. Thus, as long as the demand elasticities among different buyers are unequal, it will be profitable to the seller to group the buyers into separate classes according to elasticity, and charge each class a separate price. This is what has been referred to more generally in earlier discussions as market segmentation, that is, the carving up of a total market into homogeneous subgroups according to some economic criterion.

Exhibit 9 illustrates one type of discriminatory pricing. In the diagram, the market for the firm's product has been segmented into two

EXHIBIT 9
Price Discrimination of the Third Degree

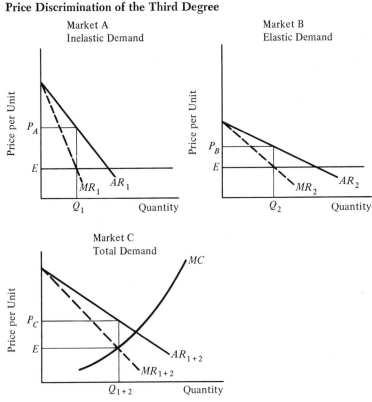

distinct groups, A and B, each with its own characteristic demand curve and attendant elasticity. Total demand for the firm's product is equal to the horizontal sum of the two independent demand curves AR_1 and AR_2, and is represented as market C or demand curve AR_{1+2}.

Decision making for the firm begins with this latter total demand curve, from which a marginal revenue curve, MR_{1+2}, is deduced. Of course the firm need not price-discriminate. If it chooses not to, then its most profitable policy would be to set marginal revenue equal to marginal cost (at level E on the figures above), and hence determine a single price P_C as shown in the graph for market C. It would charge this same price in both market A and market B.

The firm can do better, however, if it price-discriminates. As before, marginal revenue is set equal to marginal cost, E, for the market as a whole; but this time the firm explicitly identifies separate markets and discriminatorily charges the price that maximizes profit in each. In particular, this means that the firm will equate the marginal revenue of A, MR_1, to marginal cost, E, and therefore will charge price P_A in market A. Similarly, in market B, the firm will equate marginal revenue with marginal cost, E, and charge indicated price P_B. Of course, the analysis can be extended to as many marketing segments as can be distinguished and separated by the firm. In general, the correct pricing policy (in the sense of profit maximization) will be the one that results in a higher price scale to buyers with the less elastic demand (market A), and a lower price scale to buyers with the more elastic demand (market B). If the demand elasticities for both markets are the same, the optimal pricing policy would be to charge the same price in both markets.

The Conditions for Differential Pricing

Three practical conditions are necessary if a seller is to practice price discrimination effectively: (1) multiple demand elasticities, (2) market segmentation, and (3) market sealing.

Multiple Demand Elasticites. There must be differences in demand elasticity among buyers due to differences in income, location, available alternatives, tastes, or other factors. If the underlying conditions that normally determine demand elasticity are the same for all purchasers, the separate demand elasticities for each buyer or group of buyers will be approximately equal and a single rather than multiple price structure may be warranted.

Market Segmentation. The seller must be able to partition (segment) the total market by segregating buyers into groups or submarkets according to elasticity. Profits can then be enhanced by charging a different price in each submarket.

Market Sealing. The seller must be able to prevent—or natural circumstances must exist which will prevent—any substantial resale of goods from the lower to the higher priced submarket. Any leakage in the form of resale by buyers between submarkets will, beyond minimum critical levels, tend to neutralize the effect of differential prices and narrow the effective price structure to where it approaches that of a single price to all buyers.

In view of these conditions, what practical techniques can sellers use to establish a structure of price differentials? In the following paragraphs the techniques employed will be differential structures based on (1) geographic location, (2) time, and (3) product use. This classification, it will be seen, cuts across the three degrees (forms) of price discrimination but places major emphasis on the most interesting and important one—price discrimination of the third degree.

Geographic Differentials

Unlike quantity differentials, which attempt to exploit differences in quantity purchased, geographic price differentials can be used by sellers to exploit the differences in buyer locations. Before considering this type of pricing policy, some preliminary definitions are in order.

Sellers may quote prices either at the point of origin of their goods or at the point of destination. Point-of-origin prices are more commonly known as "f.o.b. shipping point" prices, the idea being that the seller agrees to deliver the goods without charge, that is, to place them "free on board" the conveyance provided by the buyer or the nearest common carrier (such as the nearest dock, railway station, or airport). Point-of-destination prices, called "delivered prices," include the cost of shipping the goods to the buyer's location or to the common carrier (e.g., dock, station, or airport) nearest him.

It is commonly believed, by many business executives and even by some antitrust lawyers and economists, that delivered prices are discriminatory and f.o.b. prices are not. The facts are that this is usually true, but not always, and that both kinds of price quotations may sometimes be discriminatory and sometimes not, depending on particular circumstances. *The ultimate economic test,* it will be seen later, *is not the form in which the price is quoted but a comparison of the seller's realized receipts from different sales.* In practice, a seller will frequently adopt one of several alternative geographic pricing policies, depending on the nature of the seller's product and the transportation costs, and the industry's competitive structure. The resulting price structure will vary in each case, as indicated by the following common geographic pricing alternatives available to most companies.

Uniform F.O.B. Mill Pricing. Under this type of pricing, the seller charges all buyers in the same trade classification the same mill price for goods of the same quality purchased in similar quantities. Two variations may be employed:

1. The buyer pays the mill price and then selects the means of transportation and pays the freight costs.
2. The seller quotes a delivered price which is composed of the uniform mill price plus the actual freight to the buyer.

Neither of these methods involves any price discrimination. In both instances the seller's price structure is the same, and the return received on every sale, or mill net, is the same, regardless of the buyer's location. The cost to buyers will differ only according to their distance from the mill. From the seller's standpoint, the only difference in policy between the two alternatives is that if the second is chosen so that a delivered price is being quoted, the seller retains title while the goods are in transit and hence must be the one to file claims with the carrier in the event of loss or damage to the goods.

What economic conditions must prevail if a firm is to practice uniform f.o.b. mill pricing successfully? Some of the more essential characteristics may be noted as follows:

1. The ratio of the value of the good to its transportation cost must be high. That is, transport costs must be a relatively small proportion of buyer's cost, or else the sale of the good will be confined to the seller's local market.
2. Products must be differentiated, that is, have a low cross-elasticity of demand, so that sellers are not under pressure to meet competing prices of nearby rivals.
3. Fixed costs must be a relatively small percentage of total costs, and marginal costs must be close to average costs at average output levels, so that there is a minimum of pressure on sellers to extend themselves into distant markets in order to break even or earn a profit.
4. Plants must be geographically distributed in close conformity with their markets so as to minimize the number of distress (excess production) and shortage (excess demand) areas.

The above conditions are clearly the opposite of what prevails in typical oligopolistic industries, and hence raise serious doubts as to whether a general system of uniform f.o.b. mill pricing could ever be established (as many economists and legislators have proposed) without wreaking havoc with the competitive structure of most American industries. Normally, oligopolistic sellers must be allowed to absorb freight charges if they are to meet the prices of rivals in distant markets. In oligopolistic industries, a forced adherence to f.o.b. pricing without freight absorption would inevitably have the effect of reducing the number of firms in each market area and increasing the average size of the firm instead. The result would be a long-run movement toward more, rather than less, monopoly in American industry, as pointed out further below. At one time or another, f.o.b. pricing has been employed in the sale of such goods as automobiles, agricultural machinery, apparel, household furniture, standard drugs, staple foodstuffs, and textiles.

"Postage-Stamp" or Uniform Delivered Pricing. This type of geographic pricing is defined simply as the charging of the same delivered price at all destinations in the economy irrespective of buyer location. The actual method of quoting price may take either of two forms:

1. The seller may quote the same price at every destination, in which case the price already covers the average expenditure for freight.

2. The seller may quote a uniform f.o.b. price to all buyers but make allowances by permitting customers to deduct their full freight charge from their bill.

In either of these cases economic discrimination is involved, for although prices at different destinations are the same, buyers located nearer to the seller pay more for freight than those located farther away. The Supreme Court, however, has held this type of pricing to be legal, even though it involves discrimination in the economic sense.

"Postage-stamp" or uniform delivered pricing is most commonly employed for goods that have a high value-transport ratio, and where the product is branded and has national distribution. The seller can thus maintain a uniform resale price at all locations and can quote the price in advertising. Examples of goods that have been priced in this way include appliances, hardware, auto accessories, typewriters, cosmetics, soft drinks, and candy bars. Occasionally, capital goods, for example, light construction equipment and machinery replacement parts, have also been priced in this manner.

Zone Pricing. Under this type of pricing, the seller divides the economy into zones or regions and charges the same delivered price within each zone but charges different prices between zones sufficient to cover average freight costs as a whole. As before, the seller can either pay the freight or permit the buyer to pay it and then deduct it from the invoice. In either case, the seller's average mill net is the same in every zone. However, the seller will be discriminating within each zone and along each boundary because (1) less freight will be allowed than is paid at a farther boundary of a zone and more than is paid at a nearer one, while (2) less freight will be allowed to buyers on the nearer side of a boundary than to buyers just across the line.

What are the legal implications of zone pricing? Evidently, if the seller's price zones are the same as the freight-rate zones, then this type of pricing is the same as f.o.b. pricing and no legal difficulties are involved. However, if the price zones do not conform with the freight-rate zones, the seller's mill net is higher for nearby customers in the zone than for those farther away, thus involving economic discrimination similar to that found in postage-stamp pricing. This is the more common case in industry and, in the light of court decisions on basing-point pricing, may be open to serious questions as to legality.

Generally speaking zone pricing is preferred where the freight cost on branded goods is too high to permit their sale throughout the country at a uniform delivered price. The larger the freight charge, the greater the number of zones and the smaller their size. Conversely, for products that have a relatively low transportation cost, zones are normally few but large. Prices quoted in newspaper or magazine advertisements with such qualifying statements (usually in small print) as "slightly higher west of the Rockies" or "west of the Mississippi" are typical examples. Zone pricing has been widely used for a tremendous variety of products including major appliances such as washing machines, refrigerators, and ranges, and also transformers, elevators, paint, power cables, soap, and book matches, to mention only a few.

Freight-Equalization Pricing. Under freight-equalization pricing, the seller charges the buyer a freight cost which he would pay in getting delivery from a nearer supplier. The seller may accomplish this either by quoting a delivered price that covers freight from his competitor's mill but paying the higher freight from his own mill, or he may quote an f.o.b. price or a delivered price covering his own freight and allow the customer to deduct from his bill the excess freight over and above that which would be charged by a competitor closest to the buyer.

In either case the seller quotes identical delivered prices of competitors by absorbing freight. The seller's return, or mill net, thus varies, depending on the amount of freight absorbed on each sale; hence, the seller is discriminating in price.

The seller may follow this type of policy occasionally in order to utilize excess capacity. If done generally and *systematically*, however, it is likely to be illegal. Typically, freight-equalization pricing has been found in industries characterized by standardized products, many sellers, high fixed costs, heavy investment in fixed assets, and a low value transport ratio. Examples include bituminous coal, lumber, and gasoline, among others.

Time Differentials

As a second classification of differential pricing, we can consider the phenomenon of temporal discrimination. Market segmentation, instead of being achieved by exploiting differences in quantity purchases or buyer locations, as in the two previous classifications, is now accomplished through the medium of *time*. As in other kinds of price differentials, the object from the seller's standpoint is to capitalize on the fact that buyers' demand elasticities vary, but in this case as a function of time. Thus two classes of price differentials may be distinguished, extending from the narrowest to the broadest "slice of time."

Clock-Time Differentials. When demand elasticities of buyers vary within a 24-hour period, the seller has the opportunity of exploiting these differences through price differentials. The most common examples of this are the differences between day and night rates on long-distance telephone calls, and the differences between matinee and evening admission charges in movies and theaters.

When price differentials are based on clock time, the object of the seller is to charge a higher price for the product in the more inelastic period and a lower price during the more elastic interval. Telephone rates and theater prices are thus an interesting contrast. With the former, the more inelastic demand period is during the day and with the latter it is during the evening; conversely, demand for long-distance phone calls is more elastic in the evening, while the demand for movies and theater is more elastic in the daytime. Prices are thus structured accordingly so as to utilize the advantages of these differences in buyers' time preferences.

Calendar-Time Differentials. Price differentials may be based not only on elasticity differences within a day but on differences between days, weeks, months, or seasons as well. Examples of calendar-time price differentials are found in the sale of services by recreational facilities such as golf courses, tennis courts, and swimming pools; the sale of food by some restaurants; and seasonal variations in the sale of clothing, resort accommodations, and vacation trips. Calendar-time differentials thus refer to any variable price structure based on time that extends beyond the 24-hour period of clock time.

Seasonal variations, since they occur within a year and are due strictly to weather and custom, are more broadly a function of time in that variations in weather and in custom (e.g., Christmas and Easter buying) are recurrent and fairly periodic. Hence, seasonal variations may justifiably be placed in the category of calendar-time differentials from the standpoint of the seller who is considering this type of pricing structure. Perhaps cyclical variations could also be included if they were fairly regular and periodic in the calendar sense, which they are not for the economy as a whole but may be for certain (relatively few) business firms.

In any case, as with clock-time differentials, the object of the seller is to derive a price structure that exploits the time preferences of buyers. For many products the economic characteristics stated above with respect to time preferences, cost considerations, and the nonstorability of product use are relevant in setting calendar-time differentials as well. But other than these factors, special conditions may prevail in particular circumstances that would make any general statement inapplicable.

Legality. The setting of such prices is discriminatory when they are unrelated to cost differences or to differences in satisfaction provided by the product. Conversely, maintaining the same price despite variations in cost would also be a form of temporal price discrimination, but the law is not concerned with this. Since demonstrated differences in cost as shown by the seller are the chief test as to the legality of a discriminatory pricing policy, there is the problem of calculating costs to show fluctuations over time.

Thus, the accounting problem of measurement is again posed. For instance, should fixed costs be allocated among sales made at different hours, days, weeks, and months, or should they be distributed equally for each dollar of sales irrespective of the time factor? The first alternative would raise sharply conflicting theoretical problems and hence measurement difficulties, while the second may miss the real target by a wide mark.

As of this time, the antitrust agencies have paid relatively little attention to temporal price discrimination and, in the light of their limited budgets, it seems likely that this trend will continue.

Product-Use Differentials. A third basis for price discrimination is to segregate buyers according to their use of the product. The classical application of product-use differentials dates back to the 19th century in the long- and short-haul pricing practices of railroads. These amounted simply to charging farmers what the traffic would bear by sometimes pricing a short haul higher than a long haul over the same line under substantially similar circumstances, according to competition at various points.

In the service industries, electric and gas companies establish separate rate structures for residential and commercial users; telephone companies distinguish between residential and business phones; movie theaters, barber shops, and public carriers set separate charges for adults and children despite equal time and space costs of serving both groups; and railroads sell freight transportation service at different prices to different groups according to the goods shipped. In manufacturing, the glass container industry sold identical containers as domestic fruit jars and as packer's ware, the former at substantially higher prices because of a much lower demand elasticity; Du Pont and Rohm and Haas sold methyl methacrylate for commercial purposes at 85 cents per pound but for denture purposes it was sold to the dental profession at $45 per pound; the Aluminum Company of America used to sell aluminum ingots at a higher price per pound that it sold aluminum in cable form (on the condition, in the latter case, that the buyer would not melt it); and similarly, plate glass manufacturers sold their product at a substantially higher price per square foot for large pieces than for small pieces even though all plate glass is produced in large sheets, the reason being that competition in the small-piece market was much more severe due to the competition of ordinary window glass. Finally, in agriculture, it is well known that the price paid farmers for milk usually depends on the use to be made of the milk, whether for bottling or for manufacture into butter, cheese, or ice cream.

Legality. In principle, as always, a chief antitrust test of legality in price discrimination is whether differences in prices are warranted by differences in costs. In practice, it is impossible to state categorically whether product-use differentials (or other forms of price discrimination) are legal or not. The procedure of the courts is to consider each case separately. Nor are there necessarily any clear-cut trends toward illegality emerging. The difficulties of measuring cost, the widespread application of product-use discrimination in industry, and the obscure nature of the law on the subject of discrimination in general—all these are factors to consider if management is to establish an appropriate policy of differential pricing.

Summary

Although there are many ways in which a firm may practice differential pricing, four common ones include quantity differentials, geographic differentials, time differentials, and product-use differentials. In many industries it is possible to employ these approaches in combination as well as separately.

Market segmentation and market sealing are necessary if differential pricing is to be effective. Several techniques for accomplishing segmentation and sealing are available, including variations in product design, quality, branding, choice of channel, time of sale, conditions of sale, patents, packaging, and advertising. Each of these offers opportunities for dividing the market and increasing revenues, and hence represents a vast area for management research and experimentation.

The legal aspects of differential pricing are not at all clear in many respects, and are treated more fully in discussions of antitrust economics. Perhaps the only general statement that can be made is that all systems of pricing other than f.o.b. mill pricing *may* be subject to legal attack by governmental agencies such as the Federal Trade Commission and the Department of Justice, particularly when there are implications of collusion, conspiracy, and attempts to monopolize. Since this is not the case in many instances, various forms of differential pricing are widespread and probably will continue to exist for a long time to come.

PROBLEMS

1. Discuss the implications of the following sets of quotations taken from some well-known sources. Reconcile where necessary.

   a. *All the money we are ever going to get we are going to get from [the customer]. And so we know that ultimately he sets our price. . . . So we start by estimating the possible quantities of our products customers will take at any one price or in any price class. Then, looking two or three years ahead, we design to that tentative price.*

      Ernest Breech, formerly Chairman, Ford Motor Co.

   b. *We start with clearly defined cost targets and we make cost estimates at each step. We revise our design or engineering specifications as necessary to make sure that a particular model can be mass produced at costs suitable for the price class for which it is intended.*

      L. L. Colbert, formerly President, Chrysler Corp.

c. *We might as reasonably dispute whether it is the upper or the under blade of a pair of scissors that cuts a piece of paper as whether value is governed by utility or cost of production.*

>Alfred Marshall, *Principles of Economics,* 8th ed. London: Macmillan and Company, Ltd., 1920), p. 348.

d. *Management is justified in studying direct costs [such as the cost of materials, labor, directly chargeable factory services, etc.] not so much to guide pricing decisions as to help in deciding whether to continue making and marketing products whose prices pay little or nothing above direct costs.*

>R. S. Alexander, memorandum to Merck & Company, in "Hearings on Administered Prices," United States Senate, Part 15, p. 8688.

e. *After all, my fees are no different, in principle, from the government's philosophy of a progressive income tax. The higher income groups have to pay more to compensate for the lower fees—and sometimes no fees—that I charge poorer people for the same services.*

>Statement by a prominent surgeon.

f. *The other common basis for defending [price] discrimination is equity, that it is proper, for example, for physicians to tax rich patients and subsidize poor patients. This argument raises major questions such as whether both classes of patients will not gain if the redistribution is made directly of income, and whether rich healthy people are not an even more appropriate group to finance poor sickly people. These questions, like so many others, we leave to the reader to answer.*

>George Stigler, *The Theory of Price,* rev. ed. (New York: The Macmillan Company, 1952), pp. 219–20.

2. Identify the pricing principle(s) involved in each of the following, non-constant, pricing practices:

   a. The price of liquid detergent, per ounce, is found to decrease with larger-sized containers.

   b. A movie theater charges one price for adults, a second for children, and a third for students.

   c. A bakery charges only half as much for day-old bread as it does for fresh bread.

   d. There is a several-hundred-dollar difference between comparably equipped Chevrolets, Pontiacs, and Cadillacs.

   e. A photo processing concern charges 35 cents each for between 1 and 5 prints from a negative, 30 cents for between 6 and 10 prints from the same negative; and 25 cents each for more than 10 prints from the negative.

   f. On a certain round-trip flight, an airline charges $30 less of passengers flying weekdays than those taking the same flight on weekends.

   g. Subscriptions to many periodicals are cheaper if more than a year's subscription is purchased. Also, often, the publisher offers a substantial discount to students and educational institutions.

    h. Many utilities charge different prices to private versus industrial users.

3. An economist for the Kahala Corporation estimates a demand equation for the company's product as $P = 600 - 30Q$, where Q is quantity, expressed in number of carloads. The economist has also found the total cost function for the company's product, again in carloads, represented by the equation $TC = 300Q - 15Q^2 + Q^3$. (Fixed costs are negligible.)

    a. Develop a traditional cost analysis for the company, and graph your results as in Exhibit 1A of the chapter.

    b. Determine graphically an optimal production schedule (output quantity) and price.

    c. Perform the same analysis for a break-even formulation such as found in Exhibit 1B.

    d. What is the optimal quantity to produce in part *c*?

    e. Using either analysis, what is the profit per unit? total profit?

4. Are prices determined by costs of production or are costs of production determined by prices? Discuss.

5. If most firms tend to set prices on the basis of costs, for example, "cost-plus," why should companies ever show losses on their profit-and-loss statements?

6. An economist at the Roberts Company estimated a demand equation for the company's product as $Q = 6{,}000 - 4{,}000P$, where Q denotes the weekly number of units purchased and P represents the price per unit. The company's total cost when it sells nothing is $1,500, and increases by 15 cents for each unit produced.

    a. Construct a demand schedule for prices from $0 to $1.50, in multiples of 25 cents.

    b. Write the equation for total cost, TC, and for average total cost, ATC.

    c. Construct an average total cost schedule for production quantities from 1,000 to 6,000 units, in multiples of 1,000 units.

    d. Write the general equation for net profit, NP, in terms of P, Q, and TC alone (i.e., your equation should contain the letters N, P, Q, and TC).

    e. Making appropriate substitutions in your answer to (*d*) above, derive an equation for NP in terms of P. What will NP be at a price of $1 per unit?

    f. Graph the net profit equation derived in (*e*) above. What is the optimum production, price, and net profit? (If you are familiar with elementary calculus, you should be able to answer this question without sketching a graph).

    g. What assumption about competitors' market behavior has been made in this problem? Explain.

7. "Nothing is free." If this is so, explain why—

    a. An automobile tire center offers a two-for-one tire sale in which a customer gets one tire "free" when the other tire is bought at full price.

    b. A drugstore offers a "1-cent sale," in which, for example, a second bottle of aspirin is obtained for a penny (virtually free!) when the first is purchased at regular price.

c. Many companies provide "free" tours of their plants.

d. Airlines provide "free" meals on board longer flights.

8. New products are probably the most difficult for which to establish pricing policies, and the decision to "skim" versus "penetrate" the market is ordinarily based on a variety of factors peculiar to industry and market conditions. Identify probable explanatory factors for each of the following:

   a. The price of the first ball-point pen in the early 1940s was approximately $12.

   b. New detergent soaps are customarily introduced at a "sale" price.

   c. The prices of hand ("pocket") calculators have decreased substantially since their introduction around 1970.

   d. Cigarette companies often give away free samples of a new brand of cigarettes.

9. A firm's total cost curve is estimated to be:

$$TC = 250Q - 20Q^2 + 2Q^3$$

   (Fixed costs are negligible.)

   a. Graph the firm's average total cost curve (ATC) and the firm's marginal cost curve (MC).

   b. Suppose the firm produces in a perfectly competitive market. What would be the expected long-run equilibrium price for the market?

   c. If the competitive price per unit is $314, should the firm operate or shut down? What is the expected profit or loss if the firm operates?

   d. Answer part (c) for a market price of $175.

   e. What is the firm's "shutdown" price?

   f. What would be the firm's optimal pricing decision if it were an oligopoly with individual demand curve given by the equation $P = 700 - 25Q$?

10. Saturn Publishing Company publishes two monthly magazines called *Action* and *Brisk*. The company charges the same price for both magazines, but the sales of *Brisk* are about twice those of *Action*. Both magazines are among the leaders in their field, with combined sales of 5 to 6 million copies a month. In this sales range, therefore, the marginal cost of producing the two magazines is practically constant. Further, it has been established on the basis of previous pricing experiments in various markets that the elasticity of demand is equal for the two magazines at the present price.

   Recently, the president of the company posed the question of whether it is consistent with profit maximization for the two magazines to carry the same price. The sales manager replied that in order for Saturn to maximize its profits, it ought to charge a higher price for *Brisk* than for *Action*, since demand is greater for the former.

   The president has called you in as a consulting economist to settle the question. Both the president and sales manager studied a considerable amount of economics while in college and are fairly familiar with such concepts as average revenue, marginal revenue, marginal cost, and so forth. Can you provide them with an analytical (i.e., graphic) solution to the problem?

11. In the book publishing business, it is inherent in the royalty arrangement that the publisher's pricing policy results in an economic conflict between the author and the publisher. Thus, in the great majority of cases, the author's royalty is a percentage of the total revenue which the publisher receives on the sale of the book. The publisher, however, determines the price of the book (and also incurs all costs of manufacturing, promotion, and distribution). It follows that *the price which maximizes profit for the publisher is higher, and the output lower, than the price and output which maximize royalty payments for the author!* Why? Demonstrate this proposition graphically, using marginal analysis.

12. Scrumptious Pizza Company operates a national chain of pizza parlors on a franchise basis. The company maintains a closely controlled, uniform set of production standards and selling prices as a condition for granting franchises. One of the unique features of Scrumptious pizzas is that they are made with a special blend of imported exotic cheeses.

Recent cost increases of cheeses, dough, and other ingredients has made it necessary for the company to consider a revision of its pricing and product policies for all its franchisees. Three alternatives have been proposed:

a. Increase price by some specified percentage but maintain quantity and quality.
b. Reduce quantity by some specified percentage but maintain price and quality.
c. Reduce quality but maintain price and quantity.

The company hired the services of a marketing consulting firm to estimate the effects on profits of each of these choices. In its report, the consulting firm submitted the following *payoff matrix*—a table showing the probable level of profit that will result from each alternative and its associated sales level.

Alternatives, Profits, and Probabilities	Average Daily National Pizza Sales			
	6,000	7,000	8,000	9,000
Alternative A:				
Profit.	$2,000	$2,800	$4,000	$4,200
Probability	.15	.25	.30	.30
Alternative B:				
Profit.	$1,500	$3,000	$5,000	$5,100
Probability	.25	.25	.40	.10
Alternative C:				
Profit.	$1,200	$2,500	$4,500	$4,800
Probability	.05	.05	.40	.50

a. Which alternative should the company choose, assuming it wants to maximize its profit?
b. Which alternative should the company choose in order to maximize its sales?

c. Is it possible to have a situation in which one alternative would maximize profit and another would maximize sales, or must the same alternative do both? Explain.

13.   **CASE PROBLEM: AUTOMOBILE INDUSTRY**
                DEMAND ELASTICITY AND PRICE REDUCTION

Union leaders, government economists, and various other people have contended from time to time that since the overall demand for automobiles is relatively elastic, an across-the-board price cut of, say 10 percent would increase the sale of automobiles and, therefore, the profits of the companies. These arguments are particularly prominent during periods of recession, since an increase in the sale of a product like automobiles would have substantial beneficial effects on other industries, for example, steel, rubber, and so forth, and would thereby help boost the level of employment, national income, and economic activity in general.

On the face of it, this argument may seem plausible. Upon further analysis, however, it becomes apparent that there are actually two sets of elasticities to be considered:

1. *Demand elasticity,* since there is a question of the effect which the price reduction will have on demand and thus on revenues.
2. *Cost elasticity,* since there is a question of the effect which the increased sales volume will have on production and thus on costs.

Obviously, both questions would have to be considered by automobile manufacturers if they were contemplating a general price reduction. However, those who have suggested such price reductions have usually considered only the former and have completely neglected the latter.

Economists who have conducted demand analysis for new automobiles have estimated price elasticities of demand ranging from .5 to 1.5. Obviously, the higher the coefficient of elasticity, the greater the percentage increase in quantity demanded which will result from a given percentage decrease in price. Thus, if we assume an elasticity as high as 1.5, this means that a 1 percent decrease in price would produce a 1.5 percent increase in quantity demanded, and hence a larger total revenue for the seller than he would obtain with a lower elasticity coefficient. Therefore, let us agree on this liberal elasticity measure of 1.5 and proceed to explore the question of whether it pays, even with such a high elasticity, for an automobile manufacturer to reduce the list price of a line of cars by, say, $200.

We must assume, of course, that a price reduction by one producer will be met by his competitors so that we are not considering a relative price advantage but rather the effect of a general price change by all sellers. In addition, the following conditions may also be specified:

Average price of the line of cars. . . . . $3,500 per car
Expected sales volume @ $3,500 per car . . . .   1,000,000 cars
Average total cost of the line of cars . . . . $3,200 per car
Total variable cost $2,500,000,000

Questions:

a. What is the change in total revenue, if any, resulting from a price reduction of $200?

b. What will profit be before the price reduction?

c. Find total fixed cost, average fixed cost, and average variable cost before the price reduction.

d. What will profit be after the price reduction?

e. The price reduction of $200 has reduced revenues per car by $200. How much did it change the cost per car? What will average total cost be at the new sales volume?

f. What do you conclude from your calculations?

g. What is the proportion of total variable cost to total cost? Total fixed cost to total cost? Are these proportions realistic?

h. "In general, the higher the level of total fixed cost relative to total cost (or the lower the level of total variable cost relative to total cost), the lower the price elasticity of demand must be in order to justify a price reduction, and vice versa." True or false? Why?

i. The following formula may be used to determine the price elasticity of demand that is needed for a given price reduction, leaving profits unimpaired, when the respective ratios of fixed and variable cost to total cost within the expected volume range are known.

Q = percentage increase of output quantity required
P = price decrease in dollars
$\bar{N}$ = net profit per unit at the old price
$\bar{C}$ = cost per unit (i.e., average total cost) at the old price
V/C = ratio of total variable cost to total cost

$$Q = \frac{P}{\bar{N} - P + \left(1 - \dfrac{V}{C}\right)\bar{C}}$$

The elasticity coefficient is then

$$\text{Elasticity} = \frac{Q(\bar{N} + \bar{C})}{P}$$

How much would the elasticity have to be in order to justify a price reduction? How does your answer compare with measures of demand elasticity for automobiles that have been estimated by various scholars? Interpret your result.

j. What conclusion do you draw as to the advisability of a price reduction in order to increase the sale of automobiles?

REFERENCES

Asch, Peter   "'Antitrust and Efficiency: Product Extension Mergers': A Comment." *The Southern Economic Journal,* vol. 37, no. 1 (July 1970), pp. 100–101.

CARROLL, D. T. "Conglomerates Revisited." *Business Horizons,* vol. 13, no. 4 (August 1970), pp. 42–44.

COWLING, KEITH, and RAYNER, A. J. "Price, Quality, and Market Share." *Journal of Political Economy,* vol. 78, no. 6 (November–December 1970), pp. 1292–1309.

DARDEN, B. R. "An Operational Approach to Product Pricing." *Journal of Marketing,* vol. 32, no. 2 (April 1968), pp. 29–33.

HAVEMAN, ROBERT, and BARTOLO, G. D. "The Revenue Maximization Oligopoly Model: Comment." *The American Economic Review,* vol. 58, no. 5 (December 1968), pp. 1355–58.

LANZILLOTTI, ROBERT V. "Pricing Objectives in Large Companies." *American Economic Review,* vol. 48, no. 5 (December 1958), pp. 921–40.

MAYER, M. L.; MASON, J. B.; and ORBECK, E. A. "The Bordon Case—A Legal Basis for Private Brand Price Discrimination." *MSU Business Topics,* vol. 18, no. 1 (Winter 1970), pp. 56–63.

OKUGUCHI, KOJI "On the Stability of Price Adjusting Oligopoly Equilibrium under Product Differentiation." *The Southern Economic Journal,* vol. 35, no. 3 (January 1969), pp. 244–46.

PYATT, F. G. "Profit Maximisation and the Threat of New Entry." *The Economic Journal,* vol. 81, no. 322 (June 1971), pp. 242–55.

SCHNABEL, MORTON "An Oligopoly Model of the Cigarette Industry." *The Southern Economic Journal,* vol. 38, no. 3 (January 1972), pp. 325–35.

SCHNEIDAU, R. E., and KNUTSON, RONALD D. "Price Discrimination in the Food Industry: A Competitive Stimulant or Tranquilizer?" *American Journal of Agricultural Economics,* vol. 51, no. 5 (December 1969), pp. 1143–48.

SILBERSTON, AUBREY "Surveys of Applied Economics: Price Behavior of Firms." *The Economic Journal* vol. 80, no. 319 (September 1970), pp. 511–82.

SIZER, JOHN "The Accountant's Contribution to the Pricing Decision." *The Journal of Management Studies,* vol. 3, no. 2 (May 1966), pp. 129–49.

WILLIAMSON, OLIVER E. "Allocative Efficiency and the Limits of Antitrust." *The American Economic Review,* vol. 59, no. 2 (May 1969), pp. 105–18.

YANDLE, BRUCE, JR. "Monopoly-Induced Third-Degree Price Discrimination." *The Quarterly Review of Economics and Business,* vol. 11, no. 1 (Spring 1971), pp. 71–75.

chapter 13

Government and Business

The American economy is primarily a free market economy, and as such most decisions that are made by managers are essentially competitively oriented. It is appropriate, therefore, to discuss the nature of competition and its framework of legal controls. For management decision making does not take place in an economic vacuum, but rather in a sociopolitical environment that must be recognized as a limiting factor in the process of adjusting to uncertainty. Decisions and plans, in other words, may sometimes have to be modified from what they otherwise would have been if economic principles were the sole guide for action.

It is beyond our scope to delve into the wide variety of areas that would normally be included in a full-scale study of antitrust. Instead we shall examine a few of the more important topics that are of particular interest to business executives from the standpoint of market economics and marketing policy. These include the nature of the antitrust laws, which are the basis for the discussion, and the relation of these laws to competitive practices in the area of monopolistic behavior, patent and trademark policy, exclusion and discrimination, delivered pricing, distribution, and the measurement of economic concentration. Thus, the protection and regulation of agriculture, labor, investors, utilities, and so forth, which are discussed in most books dealing with government and business, will not be treated here.

THE ANTITRUST LAWS

The antitrust laws are a number of acts passed by Congress since 1890 by which the U.S. government is committed to prevent monopoly and to maintain competition in American industry. Although there are also state antitrust laws in almost every state in the country, these are largely ineffectual and spasmodically enforced, since they are powerless to control agreements or combinations in major industries whose activities extend into interstate commerce. This, coupled with inadequate funds, has left the task of maintaining competition via antitrust law enforcement almost entirely to the federal government. Thus it is the federal antitrust laws that will be of concern to us here. These laws include the Sherman Antitrust Act, the Clayton Antitrust Act, the Federal Trade Commission Act, the Robinson-Patman Act, the Wheeler-Lea Act, and the Celler Antimerger Act. There are also others, but they are of relatively lesser significance.

The substantive provisions of the antitrust laws may be outlined as follows.

The Sherman Act (1890)

This was the first attempt by the federal government to regulate the growth of monopoly in the United States. The provisions of the law were concise (probably too concise). It declared as illegal:

1. Every contract, combination, or conspiracy in restraint of trade which occurs in interstate or foreign commerce.
2. Any monopolization or attempt to monopolize, or conspiracy with others in an attempt to monopolize, any portion of trade in interstate or foreign commerce.

Violations of the act were made punishable by fines and/or imprisonment and persons injured by violators could sue for triple damages.

The act was surrounded by a cloud of uncertainty by failing to state precisely which kinds of actions were prohibited. Also, no special agency existed to enforce the law until 1903, when the Antitrust Division of the U.S. Department of Justice was established under an Assistant Attorney General. In order to put some teeth into the Sherman Act, therefore, Congress passed the Clayton Act and the Federal Trade Commission Act.

The Clayton and Federal Trade Commission Acts (1914)

The Clayton Act. Aimed at practices of unfair competition, the Clayton Act was concerned with four specific areas: price discrimination, exclusive and tying contracts, intercorporate stockholdings, and inter-locking directorates. About each of these it had this to say:

1. For sellers to discriminate in prices between purchasers of commodi-ties is *illegal*. However, such discrimination is permissible where there are differences in the grade, quality, or quantity of the com-modity sold; where the lower prices make due allowances for cost differences in selling or transportation; and where the lower prices are offered in good faith to meet competition. Illegality exists where the effect is substantially to lessen competition or tend to create a monopoly.
2. For sellers to lease, sell, or contract for the sale of commodities on condition that the lessee or purchaser not use or deal in the commodity of a competitor is *illegal* if such exclusive or tying con-tracts substantially lessen competition or tend to create a monopoly.
3. For corporations engaged in commerce to acquire the shares of a competing corporation, or the stocks of two or more corporations competing with each other, is *illegal* if such intercorporate stockhold-ings substantially lessen competition or tend to create a monopoly.
4. For corporations engaged in commerce to have the same individual on two or more boards of directors is an interlocking directorate, and such directorships are *illegal* if the corporations are competitive and if any one has capital, surplus, and undivided profits in excess of $1 million.

Thus, price discrimination, exclusive and tying contracts, and intercor-porate stockholdings were not declared by the Clayton Act to be abso-lutely illegal but rather, in the words of the law, only when their effects *"may be substantially to lessen competition or tend to create a monopoly."* On interlocking directorates, however, the law made no such qualifica-tion; the fact of the interlock itself is illegal, and the government need not find that the arrangement results in a reduction in competition.

The Federal Trade Commission Act. The Federal Trade Commission Act served primarily as a general supplement to the Clayton Act by stating broadly and simply that "unfair methods of competition in com-merce are hereby declared unlawful." But what significant contribution to monopoly control was made by these laws?

Essentially, both the Clayton Act and the Federal Trade Commission Act were directed toward the prevention of abuses, whereas the Sher-man Act emphasized the punishment of abusers. To be sure, the practices that were prohibited in the two later laws could well have been attacked under the Sherman Act as conspiracies in restraint of trade or as attempts to monopolize, but now the nature of the problem was brought more sharply into focus. Moreover, under the Federal Trade Commission Act, the Federal Trade Commission (FTC) was established as a governmental antitrust agency with federal funds appropriated to it for the purpose of attacking unfair competitive practices. No longer was it necessary to await private suits brought by private parties upon their own initiative and at their own expense in order to curb unfair practices in commerce.

In addition to the heart of the Federal Trade Commission Act, which makes unfair methods of competition illegal as quoted above, the FTC is also authorized under the act to safeguard the public by preventing the dissemination of false and misleading advertisements with respect to foods, drugs, cosmetics, and therapeutic devices used in the diagnosis, prevention, or treatment of disease. In this respect it supplements in many ways the activities of the Food and Drug Administration which, under the Food, Drug, and Cosmetic Act (1938), outlaws adulteration and misbranding of foods, drugs, devices, and cosmetics moving in interstate commerce.

The Robinson-Patman Act (1936)

Frequently referred to as the "Chain Store Act," the Robinson-Patman Act was passed for the purpose of providing economic protection to independent retailers and wholesalers such as grocers and druggists, from "unfair discriminations" by large sellers attained "because of their tremendous purchasing power." The law was an outgrowth of the increasing competition faced by independents that came with the development of chain stores and mass distributors after World War I. Those who favored the bill contended that the lower prices charged by these large organizations were attributable only in part to their lower costs, and more so if not entirely to the sheer weight of their bargaining power which enabled them to obtain unfair and unjustified concessions from their suppliers. The act was thus a response to the cries of independents who demanded that the freedom of suppliers to discriminate be more strictly limited.

The act, which amended Section 2 of the Clayton Act relating to price discrimination, contained the following essential provisions:

1. The payment of brokerage fees where no independent broker is employed is *illegal*. This was intended to eliminate the practice of some chains of demanding the regular brokerage fee as a discount when they purchased direct from manufacturers. The argument posed was that such chains obtained the discount by their sheer bargaining power and thereby gained an unfair advantage over smaller independents that had to use and pay for brokerage services.

2. The making of concessions by sellers, such as manufacturers, to buyers, such as wholesalers and retailers, is *illegal* unless such concessions are made to all buyers on proportionally equal terms. This provision was aimed at preventing advertising and promotional allowances from being granted to large-scale buyers without allowances being made to competing buyers on proportionally equal terms.

3. Other forms of discrimination, such as quantity discounts, are *illegal* where they substantially lessen competition or tend to create a monopoly, either among sellers or among buyers. However, price discrimination is not illegal if the differences in prices make "due allowances" for differences in cost or if offered "in good faith to meet an equally low price of a competitor." But even where discounts can be justified by lower costs, the FTC is empowered to fix quantity limits beyond which discounts may not be granted, if it believes that such discounts would be "unjustly discriminatory or promotive of monopoly in any line of commerce."

4. It is *illegal* to give or to receive a larger discount than that made available to competitors purchasing the same goods in equal quantities. Also, it is *illegal* to charge lower prices in one locality than in another for the same goods, or to sell at "unreasonably low prices," where either of these practices is aimed at "destroying competition or eliminating a competitor."

The Wheeler-Lea Act (1938)

An amendment to part of the Federal Trade Commission Act, the Wheeler-Lea Act was passed for the purpose of providing consumers, rather than just business competitors, with protection against unfair practices. The act makes *illegal* "unfair or deceptive acts or practices" in interstate commerce. Thus, a consumer who may be injured by an unfair trade practice is, before the law, of equal concern with the merchant who may be injured by an unfair competitive practice. The act also defines "false advertising" as "an advertisement other than labeling which is misleading in a material respect," and makes the definition applicable to advertisements of foods, drugs, curative devices, and cosmetics.

The Celler Antimerger Act (1950)

The Celler Antimerger Act is an extension of Section 7 of the Clayton Act relating to intercorporate stockholdings. The latter law, as stated earlier, made it illegal for corporations to acquire the stock of competing corporations. But that law, the FTC argued, left a loophole through which monopolistic mergers could be effected by a corporation acquiring the *assets* of a competing corporation, or by first acquiring the stock and, by voting or granting of proxies, acquiring the assets. Moreover, the Supreme Court in several cases held that such mergers were not illegal under the Clayton Act if a corporation used its stock purchases to acquire the assets before the FTC's complaint was issued or before the Commission had issued its final order banning the stock acquisition.

The Antimerger Act plugged the loophole in the Clayton Act by making it illegal for a corporation to acquire the stock *or assets* of a competing corporation where the effect may be "substantially to lessen competition, or to tend to create a monopoly." The act thus bans all types of mergers—*horizontal* (similar plants under one ownership, such as steel mills), *vertical* (dissimilar plants in various stages of production, integrated under one ownership), and *conglomerate* or *circular* (dissimilar plants and unrelated product lines)—provided the Commission can show that the effects *may* substantially lessen competition or tend towards monopoly.

It should be noted, however, that the intent of Congress in passing the act was that there be a maintenance of competition. Accordingly, the act was intended to apply to mergers with large firms or large with small firms, but not to mergers among small firms which may be undertaken to strengthen their competitive position.

Enforcement of the Laws

A few comments should be made as to the enforcement of the antitrust laws. In general, the application of the antitrust laws is effected on a case-by-case basis. That is, an order or decision resulting from an action is not applicable to all of industry but only to the defendants in the particular case. Cases tried under the Sherman Act may originate in the complaints of injured business executives, suggestions made by other government agencies, or in the research of the Antitrust Division of the Department of Justice, since it is this organization which may bring into the federal courts criminal or civil suits against violators of the act. About 90 percent of the cases, it has been estimated, arise from complaints issued by injured parties; and at the present time most of the ensuing investigations are conducted by the FBI. The Federal Trade Commission Act, on the other hand, is enforced by the FTC and, when their orders become final, through suits brought by the Department of Justice. Finally, with respect to the Clayton Act, both the FTC and the Justice Department have concurrent jurisdiction in its enforcement, and in practice it is usually a matter of which agency gets there first.

Sherman and Clayton Acts. Section 14 of the Clayton Act fixes the responsibility for the behavior of a corporation on its officers and directors and makes them subject to the penalties of fine or imprisonment for violating the laws. Under the Sherman Act, the fine is limited to $50,000, but fines have actually been pyramided into several hundred thousand dollars in a single case by exacting the $50,000 on each count of an indictment (e.g., monopolizing, attempting to monopolize, conspiring, and restraining trade) and by imposing the fine on each of the defendants in a suit (e.g., a trade association, each member of the association, and each of the directors and officers of the member firms). Other penalties are also possible as provided in other acts.

Business executives who want to avoid risking violation of the law may consult with the Justice Department by presenting their proposed plans for combination or other particular practices. If the plans appear to be legal, the Department may commit itself not to institute future criminal proceedings, but it will reserve the right to institute civil action if competition is later restrained. The purpose of a civil suit is not to punish but to restore competition by providing remedies. Typically three classes of remedies are employed:

1. *Dissolution, divestiture,* and *divorcement* provisions may be used. Examples include an order to dissolve a trade association or combination, to sell intercorporate stockholdings, or to dispose of ownership in other assets. The purpose of these actions is to break up a monopolistic organization into smaller but numerous competitors.
2. An *injunction* may be issued. This is a court order requiring that the defendant refrain from certain business practices, or perhaps take a particular action that will increase rather than reduce competition.
3. A *consent decree* may be employed. This is usually worked out between the defendant and the Justice Department without a court trial. The defendant in this instance does not declare himself guilty, but agrees nevertheless to abide by the rules of business behavior set down in the decree. This device is now one of the chief instruments employed in the enforcement of the Sherman and Clayton Acts.

Finally, the laws are also enforced through private suits. Under the Sherman Act, injured parties (individuals, corporations, or states) may sue for treble damages including court costs; and under the Clayton Act, a private plaintiff may also sue for an injunction—a restraining order—whenever threatened by loss or damage resulting from some firm's violation of the antitrust laws.

Federal Trade Commission Act. Under this law, the FTC is authorized to prevent unfair business practices as well as to exercise, concurrently with the Justice Department, enforcement of relevant provisions of the Clayton Act as amended by the Robinson-Patman Act. Accordingly, the FTC has taken action against agreements that have tended to curtail output, fix prices, and divide markets among firms, thereby striving to maintain competition as well as to prevent unfair methods.

In enforcing the laws relating to monopoly, unfair trade, and deception (including such laws as the Export Trade Act, the Wool Products Labeling Act, the Fur Products Labeling Act, and the Flammable Fabrics Act), the FTC utilizes three procedures:

1. The *cooperative* method, which involves conferences on an individual and industrywide basis in order to secure voluntary compliance

by business executives with respect to the rules of fair competition.
2. The *consent* method, whereby the Commission may issue a stipulation to the violator stating that he discontinue his illegal practices.
3. The *compulsory* method, which involves legal action based upon the issuance of formal complaints.

In general, the Commission obtains its evidence for making complaints from its own investigations, from injured competitors, from consumers, and from other governmental agencies. About 10 percent of the cases actually selected arise from the Commission's own investigations; the remaining 90 percent are derived from the other sources, particularly from the complaints of injured parties.

Summary

The chief prohibitions contained in the antitrust laws, together with the relevant sections and acts, may now be summarized.

1. It is flatly *illegal*, without any qualification, to:
    a. Enter a contract, combination, or conspiracy in restraint of trade (Sherman Act, Section 1).
    b. Monopolize, attempt to monopolize, or combine or conspire to monopolize trade (Sherman Act, Section 3).

2. When and if the effect may be substantially to lessen competition or tend to create a monopoly, it is *illegal* to:
    a. Acquire the stock of competing corporations (Clayton Act, Section 7).
    b. Acquire the assets of competing corporations (Clayton Act, Section 7, as amended by the Antimerger Act in 1950).
    c. Enter exclusive and tying contracts (Clayton Act, Section 3).
    d. Discriminate unjustifiably among purchasers (Clayton Act, Section 2, as amended by Robinson-Patman Act, Section 1).

3. In general, it is also *illegal* to:
    a. Engage in particular forms of price discrimination (Robinson-Patman Act, Sections 1 and 3).
    b. Serve as a director of competing corporations of a certain minimum size (Clayton Act, Section 8).
    c. Use unfair methods of competition (Federal Trade Commission Act, Section 5).
    d. Use unfair or deceptive acts or practices (Federal Trade Commission Act, Section 5, as amended by Wheeler-Lea Act, Section 3).

Thus the laws taken as a whole are designed not only to prevent the growth of monopoly but to maintain competition as well.

Conclusion

As we have seen, the antitrust laws have various things to say about monopoly, competition, and related concepts. Specifically, the Sherman Act forbade restraints of trade, monopoly, and attempts to monopolize; the Clayton Act forbade certain practices where the effects may be to lessen substantially the degree of competition or tend to create a monopoly; and the Federal Trade Commission Act forbade unfair methods of competition. But although Congress succeeded in passing these laws, it failed to define, and left up to the courts to interpret in their own way, the meaning of such terms as "monopoly," "restraint of trade," "substantial lessening of competition," "unfair competition," and so on. For business executives, therefore, these are areas of uncertainty that need to be understood if decisions are to be made and plans formulated that will guide the firm's future course of action.

But how are these areas to be understood, and in what connection? The most suitable method is to approach the problem from the standpoint of particular issues they raise. Since judicial interpretation has been crucial in determining the applications and effects of the antitrust laws, we shall attempt to sketch briefly the nature of each issue, some leading court decisions, and the major trends.

RESTRICTIVE AGREEMENTS

The state of the law as to restrictive agreements of virtually any type among competitors is reasonably clear, and the courts have almost always, with few minor exceptions, upheld the government in such cases. In general, a restrictive agreement is regarded by the government as one that results in a restraint of trade among separate companies. It is usually understood to involve a direct or indirect, overt or implied, form of price fixing, output control, market sharing, or exclusion of competitors by boycotts or other coercive practices. It makes no difference whether the agreement was accomplished through a formal organization such as a trade association, informally, or even by habitual identity of behavior frequently referred to as "conscious parallel action" (e.g., identical price behavior among competitors). It is the effect, more than the means, that is judged.

Thus, in the second American Tobacco case in 1946, it was charged that the "big three" cigarette producers exhibited striking uniformity in their buying prices on tobacco and in their selling prices on cigarettes, as well as in other practices. Despite the fact that not a shred of evidence was produced to indicate that a common plan had even so much as been proposed, the Court declared that conspiracy "may be found in a course of dealings or other circumstances as well as in an exchange of words"; hence the companies were held in violation of the law [328 U.S. 781, 810].

In other words, no secret meetings in a smoke-filled room and no signatures in blood are needed to prove the conspiracy provisions of the Sherman Act. Any type of agreement, explicit or implicit, any practice, direct or indirect, or even any action with the knowledge that others will act likewise to their mutual self-interest, is likely to be interpreted as illegal if it results in exclusion of competitors from the market, restriction of output or of purchases, division of markets, price fixing, elimination of the opportunity or incentive to compete, or coercion.

To some extent, the doctrine of conscious parallel action by which firms can be convicted on rather flimsy circumstantial evidence has, fortunately, been partially repudiated by judges in more recent cases. However, it still remains as a relevant antitrust barometer and is likely to be used, though perhaps more sparingly, in the foreseeable future.

The Electrical Equipment Case. In February 1961 the first phase of one of the most important antitrust cases in the history of the United States was concluded. Several dozen companies in the electrical equipment industry, including General Electric and Westinghouse, and a number of corporate officials were convicted of unlawful price fixing and dividing the market. As brought out during trial, the various conspiracies were remarkably well organized, involving regular meetings of executives in resorts and hotel rooms, coded communications, and complicated formulas for rigging bids on government contracts.

Nearly two million dollars in fines were levied, and seven executives were sentenced to jail terms of 30 days each. The fines were huge, but it was the jail sentences that were most noteworthy. Sending men to jail for antitrust violations was not unheard of, but it had been rather unusual, especially when the defendants were considered to be "pillars of the community."

From 1890 to 1959 a total of about 200 people had received prison sentences for violating the Sherman Act. Most of these were union members and petty racketeers, and a few were wartime spies. Only seven were business executives, all of whom received suspended prison sentences. Thus, until 1959, no important business executive ever spent a day in jail for violating the Sherman Act.

In 1959, however, a Federal District Court in Columbus, Ohio, decided that four officials of garden tool companies who pleaded *nolo contendere* (no contest or no defense) to price-fixing charges should not, as was typically the case, get off merely with fines and lectures. Accordingly, even though the government had not sought jail terms, the judge nevertheless gave 90-day sentences to each of the four.

At this time, the government was also conducting its investigation of the electrical industry, and these jail sentences undoubtedly encouraged formerly reluctant witnesses to "volunteer" information to the grand jury in hopes of obtaining immunity from criminal prosecution.

COMBINATION AND MONOPOLY

Concerning monopoly, the state of the law is less certain and the position of the courts less consistent than in cases involving restrictive agreements. There are three aspects of the problem to be considered: monopoly per se, vertical integration, and mergers.

Monopoly per Se

Here there has been a fundamental change in the attitude of the courts since 1945. Prior to that time, it was the position of the Court that the mere size of a corporation, no matter how impressive, is no offense, and that it requires the actual exertion of monopoly power, as shown by unfair practices, in order to be held in violation of the law. This has been called the "good-trust-versus-bad-trust" criterion.

But the decisions handed down in various antitrust cases since 1945 have reversed this outlook almost completely. In the case against the Aluminum Company of America in 1945, in which Judge Learned Hand turned the trend in judicial thinking on monopoly [148 F 2d 416], it was the Court's opinion that:

1. To gain monopolistic power even by growing with the market, i.e., by reinvesting earnings rather than by combining with others, is nevertheless illegal.
2. The mere size of a firm *is* an offense, for the power to abuse and the abuse of power are inextricably interwined [pp. 427–28].
3. The Company's market share was 90 percent and that "is enough to constitute a monopoly; it is doubtful whether 60 or 64 percent would be enough; and certainly 33 percent is not" [p. 424].
4. The good behavior of the Company which, prior to 1945, would have been an acceptable defense to the Court, is no longer valid, for "Congress did not condone 'good' trusts and condemn 'bad' ones; it forbade all" [p. 427].

With this decision, Judge Hand put an end to the "good-trust-versus-bad-trust" criterion that had been used by the courts for almost a quarter of a century, beginning with the U.S. Steel case in 1920 and supplemented by the International Harvester case in 1927. And despite the doubtfulness of the measure of monopoly power and hence whether the charge of monopoly was really proven in this case, subsequent court decisions have never repudiated the doctrines enunciated by Judge Hand, although they have tempered them somewhat. Thus, at the present time, the judgment of monopoly is based on such factors as the number and strength of the firms in the market, their effective size from the standpoint of technological development and competition with substitutes and with foreign trade, national security interests in maintaining strong productive facilities and maximum scientific research, and the public's interest in lower costs and uninterrupted production (as later stated in 1950 by Judge Knox in his decree for a remedy in the aluminum case).

The trend, on the basis of subsequent cases, indicates that monopoly may be held illegal without requiring proof of intent and even if the power were lawfully acquired; and the power may be condemned even if never abused, especially if it tends to limit or bar market access to other firms. (See the Brown Shoe Case below.)

Vertical Integration

Here the Court stated, in the Paramount Pictures case in 1948, that such integration might be illegal if it were undertaken "to gain control over an appreciable segment of the market and to restrain or suppress competition," or if there was evidence of a power and intent to exclude competitors [334 U.S. 131, 174]. But integration per se, it said, was not illegal.

The Paramount case, which was one of the most important disintegration cases in years, involved five major motion-picture producers operating first-run theaters in large cities and a chain of smaller theaters throughout the country. The government charged them with impeding and restraining competition through such practices as blocked bookings, discrimination in favor of their own theaters, charging minimum admission prices, and protracting the intervals between successive showings of films, thereby affecting adversely and unfairly the independent producers and distributors.

When the case finally reached the Supreme Court in 1948, the decision of the Court was that production and exhibition be separated from each other. In 1952, after reorganization, the five companies became ten, consisting of five producers and five operating chains of theaters. Thus, as stated previously with respect to monopoly, the Court had felt that there was sufficient power and its abuse to bar effective competition, and hence the firms were held in violation of the law.

Mergers

The final effects of the Antimerger Act of 1950, which forbade the acquisition of assets as well as shares where the effect may be "substantially to lessen competition or tend to create a monopoly," remains to be seen. According to the trends, the antitrust agencies will use their own judgment as to what constitutes a substantial lessening of competition or a tendency to create a monopoly in each particular situation, rather than wage an all-out war against mergers in general.

Vertical and Horizontal Mergers. Thus, in a 1953 case involving Pillsbury Mills, the company had acquired two other milling firms thereby raising its market share for flour-base mixes from 16 percent to 45 percent. In a preliminary hearing on the matter, the FTC concluded that there was *prima facie* evidence that competition might be substantially impaired. Similarly, requests by Bethlehem Steel to merge with Youngstown Sheet and Tube, which would increase its capacity to one fifth of the industry's, have been disapproved by the Department of Justice. On the other hand, in three instances involving a merger of automobile manufacturers—Kaiser and Willys, Nash and Hudson, and Packard and Studebaker—the enforcement agencies entered no complaint, probably believing that these mergers would increase competition with General Motors, Ford, and Chrysler. On balance, it seems that the antitrust agencies are concerned with distinguishing between mergers that will tend to lessen competition as against those aimed at product diversification, vertical integration, and the strengthening of weaker competitors.

Further support for this conclusion can be found in a 1962 benchmark decision involving the Brown Shoe Company. The basis of the suit was the legality of a shoe manufacturer (Brown Shoe Company) merging with a shoe retailer (Kinney Shoes). The Court decided against the merger on the grounds that it might lessen competition both in the production and retail sales of men's, women's, and children's shoes. The following concise account of this important case is adapted with changes from an article in *Business Week*, June 30, 1962:

THE BROWN SHOE CASE

The government won a major antitrust victory that may turn out to be a precedent for a number of future cases. In the most important antitrust case in years, the Supreme Court ordered Brown Shoe Co., Inc., to give up G. R. Kinney Corp., and did so in language that encouraged government attorneys to take a new look at growing concentration in industries where there are many competitors.

The decision, written by Chief Justice Warren but agreed to by the other six justices participating, said that Brown's acquisition of Kinney in 1955 violated Sec. 7 of the Clayton antitrust law. The decision takes an especially hard view of growth through acquisition on the part of retail chains, and broadly interprets geographic markets that fall under antitrust jurisdiction.

Both the Antitrust Div. and FTC have filed a number of actions hinging on judicial definition of a "line of commerce" and of a geographic area in which competition must be considered. Many of these cases have been languishing until the Supreme Court handed down a decision in the Brown Shoe case.

First Test

The Brown Shoe case gave the court its first chance to make a detailed examination of the 1950 amendments of the antimerger law to forbid corporate acquisitions of stock or assets in "any line of commerce in any section of the country" where the effect "may be substantially to lessen competition or to tend to create a monopoly."

At the time of its merger with Kinney in 1955, Brown was the nation's fourth-largest shoe manufacturer, producing 4% of the total. Brown also controlled a number of retail outlets. Kinney operated the largest retail chain, with over 400 stores in 270 cities. Its outlets accounted for about 1.2% of national retail shoe sales. In addition, Kinney was the nation's 12th largest shoe manufacturer.

The Justice Dept. asked the courts to restrain the merger, charging that it might lessen competition both in the production and retail sale of men's, women's, and children's shoes. A federal district court in St. Louis ordered Brown to divest itself of Kinney. It is this decision that the Supreme Court upheld.

Trends

In deciding the case against Brown, Warren stressed that while the shoe industry is presently made up of many competing companies, the number of manufacturers and retailers in recent years has been declining, and the "vertical" integration of manufacturers with retailers increasing. Brown Shoe, Warren said, was a "moving factor in these industry trends."

One of Congress' purposes in passing the 1950 merger amendments, Warren said, was to provide machinery to prevent fragmented industries from becoming concentrated ones.

Competition

In evaluating whether products compete, the Chief Justice said that there are broad markets—in this case shoes—and "submarkets"—men's, women's, and children's shoes. Potential competitive damage to any one of these submarkets can be illegal, Warren said.

On the competitive effects of a merger, Warren said that a company's share of market, while important in considering competition, is of absolute importance only when the market share approaches monopoly proportions. So the court must look behind the market share in deciding whether a merger is legal, and must study the "very nature and purpose of the arrangement."

In this regard, Warren placed special emphasis on testimony by Brown's Pres. Clark R. Gamble that "Brown would use its ownership of Kinney to force Brown shoes into Kinney stores."

Further, Warren said, the courts should examine the character of the industry to get an idea of the "probable future effect of the merger." He referred to the trend in the shoe industry for manufacturers to acquire retail outlets. Brown had argued that there were still many competitors in the industry, but Warren said: "Remaining vigor cannot immunize a merger if the trend in that industry is toward oligopoly."

Two Factors

The vertical aspect of the marriage of Brown's manufacturing facilities with Kinney's retail outlets would likely "foreclose competition from a substantial share of the markets for men's, women's, and children's shoes, without producing any countervailing competitive, economic, or social advantages."

In considering the horizontal aspects of the merger—the marriage of Brown's retailing outlets with those of Kinney—Warren agreed with the government that a relevant retail market could be the entire nation, or a single metropolitan area. "The fact that two merging firms have competed directly on the horizontal level in but a fraction of the geographic markets in which either has operated does not, in itself, place their merger outside the scope of Section 7," he said.

Warren made clear that he views the amalgamation of chain operations as having more serious competitive effects than the merger of independent retailers. Some chain operations benefit consumers, he acknowledged, and the simple fact that independent competitors may be damaged does not make the expansion of a chain unlawful. But, the Chief Justice said, the courts must recognize "Congress' desire to promote competition through the protection of viable, small, locally owned businesses."

The conclusion to be drawn from this case can be stated briefly. Basically, it now appears that the changes in the law on corporate acquisitions made in the Celler Antimerger Act of 1950 have been given specific meaning. Under the new policy, both *vertical* mergers (those involving dissimilar plants in various stages of production, integrated under one ownership) and *horizontal* mergers (those involving similar plants under one ownership) are likely to be held illegal unless the companies can clearly demonstrate that the mergers are likely to increase competition and thus promote the public interest.

Conglomerate mergers or those where the merging firms are neither competitors nor have a supplier-customer relationship, have proved to be the most popular form of combination since the great "second" merger wave that started in the mid 1950s. (The "first" wave, involving vertical and horizontal mergers, started after World War II.) Some well-known examples include: American Tobacco's acquisition of Sunshine Biscuits, Inc.; Radio Corporation of America's purchase of Random House, Inc., publishing company; and Procter and Gamble's acquisition of Clorox Company.

The P&G–Clorox case involved a conglomerate merger which took place in 1957 between a major producer of a diversified line of soaps and a leading manufacturer of household bleach. When the Supreme Court, exactly ten years later, ordered the dissolution of this marriage, Justice William O. Douglas who wrote the decision for the Court pointed out that a conglomerate merger is likely to be illegal if it combines two key features:

1. The acquired firm is a major factor in an oligopolistic industry. (In this instance, Clorox's sales were 48 percent of the national total, and the top four bleach producers had 80 percent of the market.)
2. The acquiring company is in a closely related line. (Thus, P&G is in the detergent-soap-cleanser business, whereas Clorox sells bleach. Both companies sell low-cost, high-turnover household goods to the same customers by the same marketing methods in grocery stores, and both companies' products are largely "presold" through large-scale advertising and promotions.)

Justice Douglas also pointed out that P&G, by acquiring Clorox, injured competition in three ways: (1) P&G became a wealthy giant in a relatively small industry, and hence smaller firms in the industry, for example, Purex Corp., Ltd., would become more cautious in competing due to their fear of retaliation by P&G; (2) P&G could effectively block the entry of new firms into the household bleach industry by its ability to divert large portions of its advertising budget to meet the threat of a newcomer; (3) P&G, because of its sheer size, had already exerted a restraining influence before 1957 on the prices charged for bleach, when it stood at the edge of the industry— implicitly threatening to break in. Indeed, P&G was one of the few companies which, according to Douglas, could have entered the bleach industry on its own with "the temerity to challenge a firm as solidly entrenched as Clorox."

Conclusion

Although guidelines are proposed from time to time which could be of some help to business executives who are contemplating merger, it seems certain that no definitive set of rules will ever be devised which will be universally applicable for all situations. The most that can be predicted is that according to the trend of antitrust attitudes:

1. Internal growth is preferable to growth by merger.
2. Any merger, no matter how small, in a concentrated or oligopolistic industry like automobiles, chemicals, or steel, will be subjected to an evaluation.
3. Any industry which has ever been charged with price fixing will automatically draw attention on a matter of mergers.
4. Mergers on the part of top companies within industries, as well as between industries, will be scrutinized.
5. The larger a company, the more carefully it will be watched, especially if it seeks merger in an industry characterized by small companies.

In short, the antitrusters and the Supreme Court are likely to look with disfavor at a merger when the industry is concentrated, entry into the market is difficult, the firm being eliminated is a particularly vigorous competitor, there is a merger trend in the industry, or one or both of the companies are large in relation to competitors.

PATENTS

The Constitution of the United States (Art. 1, Sec. 8, Par. 8) empowers Congress "To promote the progress of Science and useful Arts, by securing for limited Times to Authors and Inventors the exclusive Right to their respective Writings and Discoveries . . ." Though this power was not denied to the states, it came in time to be exercised solely by the federal government, and upon this authority the American patent and copyright system is based. In the present discussion our attention will be devoted exclusively to patents and their particular legal-economic aspects that are of concern to management.

A patent is an exclusive right conferred by a government on an inventor, for a limited time period. It authorizes the inventor to make, use, transfer, or withhold his (or her) invention, which he might do even without a patent, but it also gives him the right to exclude others or to admit them on his own terms, which he can only do with a patent.

Patents are thus a method of promoting invention by granting temporary monopolies to inventors. But the patent system, it is held, has also been employed as a means of controlling output, dividing markets, and fixing prices of entire industries. Since these are perversions of the patent law which have a direct effect on competition, they have been subject to criticism by the antitrusters, and the courts have increasingly come to limit the scope and abuses of patent monopoly. Among the chief issues have been the standard of patentability, the right of nonuse by the patentee, the use of tying contracts, the employment of restrictive licenses, and the practices of cross-licensing and patent pooling. The recent trends based on court decisions in each of these areas may be outlined as follows.

Standard of Patentability

The chief standard employed by the courts is the so-called "flash of genius" test. Thus, in the Cuno Engineering Corporation case in 1941, involving the patentability of a wireless lighter, Justice Douglas, speaking for the Court, said that usefulness and novelty alone do "not necessarily make the device patentable. . . . The device must not only be 'new and useful,' it must also be an 'invention' or 'discovery.' . . . The new device, however useful it may be, must reveal the *flash of creative genius,* not merely the skill of the calling. If it fails, it has not established its right to a private grant on the public domain" (314 U.S. 84, 91; italics supplied).

The "flash of genius" test has been criticized as resting on the subjective judgment of the Court, and as not taking sufficient recognition of inventions that are the product of teams rather than individuals, especially in large corporations. In response to these arguments, Congress passed the Patent Act of 1952 which provides that a formula, method, or device, in order to be patentable, must be "new" in that it must be unknown to the public prior to the patent application, or it must be "useful" in that it evidences a substantial degree of technical advance in the object invented or in the process of producing something. But the courts have not found in the act an adequate definition of "invention" and continue to rely on case law and their own judgment in determining what constitutes an invention. It appears, therefore, that the "flash of genius" test, tempered perhaps by the political and economic attitudes of the courts with respect to the public interest, will be the chief criterion of patentability at least in the foreseeable future.

Right of Nonuse

The right of a patentee to withhold an invention from use has been upheld by the courts. In numerous cases tried since the turn of the century, the courts have viewed a patent as a form of private property and hence have upheld the patentee's right to refuse putting it to use. In response, it has been argued by some that a patent is a privilege and not a right, that the practice of nonuse may result in retarding technological progress and economic development, and hence that the courts should exercise more judgment and discretion in such cases. And even the courts in recent decades have spoken of patents as privileges contingent upon the enhancement of public welfare. But the right of nonuse appears nevertheless to be supported by the law, for as stated by the Supreme Court in the Hartford Empire case in 1945: "A patent owner is not . . . under any obligation to see that the public acquires the free right to use the invention. He has no obligation either to use it or to grant its use to others" (323 U.S. 386).

Tying Contracts

These are viewed by the antitrusters as attempts to extend the scope of monopoly beyond the limits of a patent grant, and the courts have upheld this view by striking down consistently and repeatedly all such agreements. Two common forms of tying contracts that have been held illegal may be noted:

1. *Attempts by the patentee to prevent a competitor from selling an unpatented product in a patented combination.* In a case tried in

1944 involving Minneapolis-Honeywell against the Mercoid Corporation, the latter had sold an unpatented switch for use in connection with a patented combination of thermostats for controlling furnace heat. The Court found no patent infringement. It held that Honeywell's attempt to extend the scope of its patent was illegal; and in the words of Justice Douglas speaking for the Court, "An unpatented part of a combination patent is no more entitled to monopolistic protection than any other unpatented device" (330 U.S. 680).

2. *Attempts by the patent holder to require in the license contract that the licensee purchase other products from the patentee.* Before the passage of the Clayton Act such tying contracts were upheld by the courts, some well-known examples being the A. B. Dick case in 1912 and the United Shoe Machinery case in 1913. But since the passing of the Clayton Act, which outlaws such contracts in Section 3, a number of tying contracts involving firms such as Radio Corporation of America, International Business Machines, and International Harvester, have been struck down by the courts where such agreements were found substantially to lessen competition within the meaning of the act. It appears, therefore, that the trend of the courts is to disallow tying clauses of any kind, regardless of circumstances, where the effect is to extend the scope of a patent monopoly. An extreme example existed with respect to Eastman Kodak prior to 1954. The company sold amateur color film at a price which included the charge for finishing, thereby tying the sale of the film itself to the business of providing finishing services. In 1954 the company signed a decree, agreeing to sell the film alone and thus admit competitors to the finishing business.

Restrictive Licensing

This refers to the practice of licensing patents among competitors with certain restrictions imposed. Typically, the restrictions may include the patentee's fixing the geographic area of the licensee, the level of output of the licensee, or the price that can be charged in selling the patented goods. Usually such licensing is motivated by considerations of reciprocal favor (e.g., the exchange of patents among competitors) or perhaps performed for the purpose of minimizing the incentive of the licensee to develop an alternative process. In any case, since it is the legality of particular practices that concerns us here, the following trends may be noted.

1. The right of a patentee to fix the licensee's prices on patented products has been and still is upheld by the courts. The leading case in this respect, decided as long ago as 1926, concerned the question of whether General Electric could, under its basic patents on the electric lamp, fix the prices charged by Westinghouse, the licensee. The Supreme Court answered in the affirmative. It should be observed, however, that

this case involved a *single* patentee, a *single* licensee, and a *single* product.

2. The right of the patentee to fix the prices charged for unpatented products made by patented processes (e.g., a patented machine) has been doubtful since the 1940s.

3. In contrast with the General Electric case cited above, the use of restrictive licensing is illegal when employed for the purpose of eliminating competition among many licensees. In the Gypsum case decided in 1948, involving a price-fixing arrangement among the licensed producers of gypsum wallboard, the Supreme Court upheld the government's charge. In the words of Justice Reed: "Lawful acts may become unlawful when taken in concert," and therefore "the General Electric case affords no cloak," no precedent, "in this case" [*U.S.* v. *U.S. Gypsum Co.*, 333 U.S. 364,400]. Thus there is now a sharp restriction as to the extent to which a patent may be licensed by a patent owner. On the basis of this and the Line Material case of 1948, when each of several licensees accepts restrictive terms on condition or with the knowledge that others will do likewise, they are committing a conspiracy in restraint of trade in the opinion of the Court and hence are guilty of violating the law.

Cross Licensing and Patent Pooling

These are not held to be illegal as such, but they generally are declared illegal when, in the eyes of the courts, they are used as a means of eliminating competition among patent owners and licensees. But what constitutes elimination of competition? In the Hartford Empire case, decided in 1945, it was held that Hartford employed the patents in its pool to dominate completely the glass container industry, curtail output, divide markets, and fix prices through restrictive licenses, and therefore this was unlawful conspiracy. In the National Lead case in 1947, a cross-licensing agreement that divided markets and fixed the prices of titanium pigment was also declared illegal. And in the Line Material case of 1948, mentioned previously, the Court was most emphatic in its denouncement of a cross-licensing arrangement that fixed the price of fuse cutouts used in electric circuits.

In general, it appears that although patent pooling per se is not illegal (the automobile industry being frequently cited as an outstanding example of successful and desirable patent pooling), the courts will declare it illegal when it seems to be abused. And the courts will tend to declare that abuse exists either when the pool is restricted to certain competitors or available only at excessive royalty payments, or when the pool is used as a device to cross-license competitors for the purpose of fixing prices and allocating markets.

Concentration of Patent Ownership

Patent concentration in the hands of a single firm has also come under consideration in recent years. Prior to another United Shoe Machinery case in 1953, the ownership of many patents by a single company was held to be legal. But the United case appears to represent what may be a definite turning point in the trend of the Court. Thus, the Court found that the company (1) had almost 4,000 patents, about 95 percent of which came from its own research and the remainder purchased from others; (2) put about a third of these patents to use; (3) had not abused its patents by suppressing them or by using them as a threat over competitors; (4) had not been offered or asked to grant licenses, but had not refused to do so; (5) had not resorted to litigation as a means of harassing competitors but instead acted in good faith in bringing infringement suits; (6) had leased rather than sold its machines, and in a manner so as to discriminate against customers who might install competing machines; (7) required lessees to use the machines at full capacity in the manufacture of shoes; and (8) required that lessees purchase United's supplies and services along with the leasing of machines. None of these policies, the Court held, was illegal per se, but their combined effect, in view of United's dominant position in the industry, was sufficient to constitute monopolization and hence the firm was held in violation of Section 2 of the Sherman Act.

It might be added that the Court decision in 1953 did not end United's troubles. By 1965 the company managed to reduce its market share from 85 percent to 60 percent, but that was not enough in the eyes of the Justice Department. The case was finally settled by a consent decree in 1969 in which the company agreed to new divestitures which would eventually limit it to one third of the total market.

Far and away the most important implication of the United Shoe settlement was the reinforcement of the legal precedent in which even "accidental monopolies" are considered illegal. Hence, whereas concentration of patent ownership in and of itself may not violate the law, the company enjoying such concentration may be prosecuted under the antitrust laws if patent ownership results in "undue" industry dominance. Thus Eastman Kodak agreed to provide other color-film finishers with up-to-date manuals on its processing technology and to provide technical representatives to assist competitors in using the methods described. In a number of other cases involving Standard Oil of New Jersey, the Aluminum Company of America, Merck & Co., A. B. Dick, Libbey-Owens-Ford, Owens-Corning Fiberglas, American Can, and General Electric, as well as about 25 other firms, somewhat similar provisions have been arrived at since the forties. Hundreds of patents involving a wide variety of manufacturing areas have thus been freed, and it is to be expected that the courts will continue to move in this direction in future years.

More recently, lower courts have found against IBM, the giant in the computer industry, primarily on such grounds. Although, at the time of this writing, the final outcome of this suit is unclear, this much is certain: strong remedies have been used by the courts against patent holders who have been declared in violation of the antitrust laws. These remedies, which are now quite typical, include compulsory licensing, sometimes on a royalty-free basis for a company's existing patents, and on a reasonable royalty basis for future patents; and the provision of necessary know-how in the form of detailed written manuals and even technical consultants, available at nominal charges, to licensees and competitors.

TRADEMARKS

The purpose of a trademark, as originally conceived, was to identify the origin or ownership of a product. In an economic sense, however, managements have come to look upon trademarks as a strategic device for establishing product differentiation and, through advertising, strong consumer preference. In this way firms have sometimes been able to establish a degree of market entrenchment that has remained substantially unrivaled for as long as several decades. Moreover, by establishing product differentiation through trademarks, firms have exploited this advantage in various ways with the aim of enhancing long-run profits. Five examples may be noted:

1. *Price discrimination* has been implemented. Rohm & Haas sold methyl methacrylate as Lucite and Crystalite to manufacturers at 85 cents per pound, and as Veronite and Crystalex to dentists at $45 per pound. The decision, rendered in 1948, was against the company for using trademarks in this discriminatory manner.

2. *Output control* has been accomplished. U.S. Pipe and Foundry licensed companies to produce under its patents at graduated royalty rates on condition that they stamp their products with the trade name "de Lavaud." The decision, rendered in 1948, was against the company for using a trademark in controlling output.

3. *Exclusive markets* have been attained. General Electric was able to persuade procurement agencies to establish specifications requiring the use of Mazda bulbs. It licensed Westinghouse to use the name but denied its other licensees the same right. The decision against General Electric was rendered in 1949, on the grounds that the company had used the trademark as a device for excluding competitors from markets.

4. *Market sharing* has been maintained. The procedure is somewhat as follows. A trademark is advertised throughout the world, and each

cartel member is granted the exclusive right to use it in his own territory. If a member oversteps his market boundary, he is driven back by an infringement suit. Trade names that provide examples of such regional monopolies include Mazda, Mimeograph, Merck, and Timken, and the trademarks of General Storage Battery, New Jersey Zinc, American Bosch, and S.K.F. Industries.

In a number of cases tried during the late 1940s, the courts found such arrangements to be in violation of the Sherman Act. In the Timken Roller Bearings case of 1949, it rejected the licensing of trademarks as a defense; in the Merck & Co. case of 1945, it canceled trademarks and enjoined their renewal; and in the Electric Storage Battery case in 1947 it forbade cartel members the right to grant their foreign partners exclusive trademark rights abroad, to sell in American markets, and to interfere with American imports.

In short, where trademarks have been employed to implement market sharing arrangements by cartels, the courts have usually upheld the government with stringent remedies, and probably will continue to do so. Where trademarks have supported purely domestic monopolies, however, the government has trodden more lightly. Thus in the American Tobacco case of 1946, the leading manufacturers of cigarettes were found guilty of violating the Sherman Act. Nevertheless, the government did not request dissolution, probably because it would have resulted in the destruction of property values, that is, brand names (Camel, Chesterfield, Lucky Strike) worth millions of dollars. It appears, therefore, that the exclusive right to a name that has been widely advertised may continue to be held as an important consideration in the applications of the antitrust laws.

5. *Resale price maintenance* has been implemented, even where patents and copyrights have failed. Although contracts which maintain the resale price of trademarked goods were held to be unlawful as early as 1911 in the Dr. Miles case, they were subsequently legalized and have had an interesting history.

TYING CONTRACTS AND EXCLUSIVE DEALING

Tying contracts and exclusive dealings have sometimes been used to obtain and extend a position of monopoly. In the opinion of the antitrusters, such agreements affect the ability of producers to compete with one another in obtaining access to markets, and the ability of distributors to compete with one another in the purchase and resale of goods. And in most cases, the courts have upheld the government in its view by striking down such arrangements, its decision usually hinging on whether it believed the effect was "to substantially lessen competition or tend to create a monopoly."

But when is competition substantially lessened? Congress never ex-

plained this when it passed the Clayton Act, and it has been left to
the courts to decide in each case. Opinions have varied and, in general,
it cannot be predicted that exclusive arrangements will be outlawed
per se, despite the pressure exerted by the FTC. At best, all that can
be said is that the Commission tends to confine its orders to cases in
which it believes it can actually show substantial injury or the probability
of such injury to competition. Perhaps this is due to the courts which,
at times, have dismissed a suit or two because of insufficient evidence,
declaring that the use of coercive methods to secure exclusive dealerships
is unlawful, but exclusive dealerships as such are not illegal. This, in
essence, is where the issue now stands.

PRICE DISCRIMINATION—GENERAL LEGALITY

With respect to price discrimination, the antitrust laws have been
applied primarily to two classes of practices: the first is discount structures; the second is delivered pricing systems. Both of these are considered in the following sections after a discussion of the general legality
of price discrimination.

The Robinson-Patman Act, which amended Section 2 of the Clayton
Act dealing with price discrimination, made the following practices
illegal:

1. Charging different prices to different buyers on sales that are otherwise identical.
2. Selling at different prices in different parts of the country "for the
   purpose of destroying competition or eliminating a competitor."
3. Selling "at unreasonably low prices" where the purpose is to destroy
   competition or a competitor.
4. Discriminating in price.
5. Paying brokerage commissions to buyers or to intermediaries under
   their control.
6. Granting allowances, services, or facilities by sellers to buyers,
   whether for services rendered by the buyer or not, that are "not
   accorded to all purchasers on proportionally equal terms."

The first of these offenses is too narrowly defined to be of much
practical importance; the second is definite; and the third is too vague
and difficult to enforce, that is, when are prices "unreasonably low"?
These first three provisions constitute the criminal portion of the act
and have been relatively insignificant. It is in civil aspects or in the
last three provisions that the act has been of major importance, and
these will concern us here.

Under the Robinson-Patman Act, price discrimination is illegal not
only where the effect is "substantially to lessen competition or tend
to create a monopoly," as in the Clayton Act, but also where it may

be "to injure, destroy, or prevent competition with any person who either grants or knowingly receives the benefit of such discrimination, or with the customers of either of them." The act thus makes *injury to competitors* the test of illegality. It also, however, allows the seller charged with discrimination to offer two defenses: (1) that the differentials in price "make only due allowance for the differences in cost of manufacture, sale or delivery . . ."; and (2) that the lower price "was made in good faith to meet," not competition, as in the Clayton Act, but "an equally low price of a competitor," and not to undercut it. That is, discriminatory price cutting to "meet" competition is legal; discriminatory price cutting to "beat" competition is illegal. Finally, the act also permits the FTC to set limits on quantity discounts, even though justified by cost differences, "where it finds that available purchasers in greater quantities are so few as to render differentials on account thereof unjustly discriminatory or promotive of monopoly," and makes it illegal for buyers "knowingly to induce or receive" a prohibited discrimination in price.

With this as a background, we now turn our attention to the legal status of discounts and delivered pricing as the two most important specific areas of price discrimination, and the major court trends in each.

Price Discrimination—Discounts

The courts have, under the Robinson-Patman Act as under the Clayton Act, upheld the government in cases involving local price discrimination. Discounts, however, have been treated less sympathetically, depending primarily on the form of the discount. In the following paragraphs the current legal status of various kinds of discounts are surveyed, along with enforcement problems, in the light of relatively recent court trends.

Brokerage and Allowances. The illegality of brokerage payments has been consistently upheld in a number of different circumstances. In fact, about half the orders issued by the Commission under the Robinson-Patman Act have been to prohibit such payments. Two typical classes of circumstances may be noted:

1. Where brokerage has been given as an advantage to a single buyer, it has been held illegal. Thus, in the A&P case of 1940, the company was charged with receiving commissions which were granted to it in the form of quantity discounts and price reductions. In the Webb-Crawford case in 1940, involving the owners of a wholesale grocery firm who were also partners in a brokerage organization, the court held that the collection of commissions through a dummy firm was illegal.

2. Where brokerage has been passed on to the benefit of smaller firms, it has also been held illegal. Examples include the Oliver Bros.

case of 1939, a firm which sold marketing information to its clients and passed its commissions on to them in the form of lower prices; and the Modern Marketing Service case of 1945, a purchasing firm for wholesale and retail grocers which passed on to them the commissions it received from suppliers. In these and similar cases, some involving cooperatives, payments that were deemed helpful to small independents, and not to mass distributors, were nevertheless prohibited.

Allowances and services have been given much less attention, possibly because of the ambiguity of the law. The Robinson-Patman Act states that allowances and services must be made available to all buyers "on proportionally equal terms," but it does not state a criterion for proportionality nor has the Commission defined one. In any event, only a few cases have ever reached the courts, but on the basis of these and on several complaints issued by the Commission, the interpretation of "allowances" seems to be this:

1. They must not be secretly rendered but must be publicly announced.
2. Their terms must not be such as to confine them to a few large buyers but must be available to all.
3. They must be made only for services actually rendered.
4. They must not be excessively greater than their cost to distributors or their value to manufacturers.

In general, therefore, it appears that the courts, as in the past, will continue to follow the FTC in the latter's strict interpretation of the sections of the act dealing with brokerage and allowances.

Quantity Discounts. These have never been held, either by the Commission or by any court, to be illegal per se. In fact, in the Bruce's Juices case in 1947, Justice Jackson, speaking for the majority of the court, said: "The economic effects on competition of such discounts are for the Federal Trade Commission to judge. . . . It would be a far-reaching decision to outlaw all quantity discounts. Courts should not rush in where Congress fears to tread." And the Commission, possessing the power to judge the effects of discounts on competition, has frequently exercised that power. It has prohibited discounts where it could not find sufficient savings in delivery, selling, or production costs to justify a price difference, and it has forbidden cumulative discounts, that is, discounts on purchases over periods of time, claiming that such purchases do not evidence a reduction in seller's costs. Further, the Commission has sometimes ruled that discounts at a given time and place may be justified by differences in cost, as with the Kraft-Phenix Cheese Corporation in 1937 and the American Optical Company in 1939, and sometimes not, as in the landmark Morton Salt Company case in 1948.

Morton's prices, it was charged, were unjustly discriminatory and injurious to competition because its discount structure, though in principle available to all the company's purchasers, was in practice available only to the largest few. That is, the company's prices ranged from $1.60 to $1.35 per case for quantities ranging from less-than-carload lots to 50,000 cases, purchased within a year. The evidence showed that only a few large grocery chains could buy enough within a year to take advantage of the $1.35 price, while independent retailers had to buy from wholesalers who paid around $1.50. Both the Commission and the Court held this as substantially injurious to competition, and the company has since withdrawn all discounts on quantity buying.

The practical outcome of the Morton Salt decision should be noted, in view of its unfortunate economic consequences as well as the problems it has left unresolved. Manifestly, it is within the discretion of the Commission to decide whether a price difference, no matter how small, is discriminatory or not. The burden of proof—and a heavy burden it frequently is—then passes to the seller, who must justify the difference either by "due allowance" for differences in cost, or by "good faith" to meet, but not undercut, a competitor. By thus failing to distinguish between a price difference and a price discrimination, the Commission can conceivably declare any quantity discount, no matter how small, a violation of the law.

Of what significance is this? The answer is that the power held by the Commission may result in the elimination of quantity discounts by many sellers, even though such discounts, after long and expensive litigation in the courts, might have been upheld as nondiscriminatory. The outcome is twofold: quantity buyers who otherwise might have passed their savings on to consumers are unable to do so, at least in the short run; and the public, through higher prices, preserves small business on the questionable assumption that such preservation is *in and of itself* desirable.

Functional Discounts. In general, the attitude of the Commission with respect to trade (or functional) discounts is that they are legal, and that discrimination between buyers is not unlawful, provided that the buyers are not in competition with one another. Is it possible, therefore, for sellers to evade the law relating to quantity discounts by establishing special customer classes for the purpose of granting discounts that cannot be justified by cost differences, or, in other words, by cloaking unjustifiable quantity discounts as functional discounts? The answer is no, not readily, because the Commission, on the basis of several cases, views the conditions of classification as follows:

1. Buyers must be classified according to their strict nature or level of operations. Different types of customers who nevertheless are at the same level, for example, chain stores, independent retailers, and mail-order houses, must be placed in the same class, and the discounts granted must not exceed the cost savings.

2. For split-function customers, such as a dealer who is both a wholesaler and a retailer and thus performs two functions, the discount allowed for any function must be applied only to the portion of the order for which that function alone is performed. This rule, however, has two shortcomings:

a. It is difficult to enforce because the seller can only take the buyer's word as to which quantities will be employed in each function, and the buyer may naturally tend to overstate the quantity on which the larger discount will apply.

b. It denies the split-function dealer the discount rightfully deserved for performing the wholesale function on that part of the goods retailed by the dealer.

The rule thus attempts to maintain a rigid stratification of functions in distribution by trying to prevent dealers who perform both wholesale and retail functions from reducing the retail price of their goods. And the Commission, it appears, is on fairly solid ground, despite the dubious assumption on which it operates that everything that "injures" (hurts) competitors "injures" (hinders) competition.

Assessment of the Robinson-Patman Act

At least two classes of problems, involving measurement and policy, appear to cloud the Robinson-Patman Act. As regards the measurement problem, the underlying principle of the act is that differences in price should be proportionate to differences in cost. However, anyone familiar with cost accounting knows that the assignment of costs resulting from manufacturing is open to interpretation. The allocation of overhead provides a typical example. Further, the writers of the act did not specify which costs are to be considered: total costs, average variable costs, marginal costs, and so forth.

The Federal Trade Commission has provided no guides of accepted cost accounting principles and, until recently, has frequently rejected cost estimates offered in defense of price differences. In general, its policy has been to (1) permit discounts justified by savings in selling and delivery costs; (2) reject discounts based on savings in manufacturing costs; (3) establish average total cost of an order (total expenditures ÷ total output) rather than incremental or added cost as its standard or, in other words, require a uniform allocation of overhead to all units sold, thereby denying the role of incremental cost as a management guide in production and pricing; and (4) put the burden of proof on the seller as to whether there is really a cost difference.

As regards policy, the law is inherently contradictory in that it *sometimes outlaws discrimination, sometimes permits it, and sometimes even requires it.* Thus, sellers may legally discriminate among consumers, and among noncompeting business buyers in the channel of distribution (e.g., manufacturers, wholesalers, and retailers). They may also charge identical prices where costs differ, which is also discriminatory, or give discounts that do not reflect cost differences. And they may discriminate *against* the firm that buys in quantity.

A better rationale for the Robinson-Patman Act may be found when the legislation is put in historical perspective. The authors of the Clayton Act were concerned with the effects of discrimination on competing sellers; the authors of the Robinson-Patman Act were concerned with the effects of discrimination on competing buyers. The latter law was designed to reduce the buying advantages of chains and mass distributors; it aimed not at eliminating discrimination in general but at preventing discrimination in favor of larger buyers and permitting or even requiring it in favor of smaller ones. And it has been applied in a manner that has served not only to handicap the chains but also to check the advantages obtained by agencies that buy collectively for independent firms. In short, compared with the Clayton Act, it was concerned more with the maintenance of small competitors and less with the maintenance of competition. But on balance, whether the effect has been actually to strengthen or weaken competition, it is not possible to say. Some experts believe that if anything, it even helped the A&P, for example, by forcing it into the supermarket business.

Conclusion. Two defenses are available to the seller who is charged with illegal discrimination: one of these is to show that the differences in the seller's price made due allowance for differences in cost; the other is that the lower price was made in good faith to meet, but not undercut, the price of a competitor. From what has been said in the previous paragraphs, it is clear that the Federal Trade Commission has seriously impaired both of these defenses. Evidently, the FTC's policy is to lend encouragement to "soft" competition and to frown on "hard" competition as required by the Sherman Act. Under a policy of hard competition, price discrimination would still be controlled, but there would be some important differences. Since the application of the law hinges on two considerations, namely (1) the test of illegality, and (2) the respondent's defense, the following amendments to the Robinson-Patman Act would seem advisable as an initial step in the right direction.

1. The test of illegality should be changed from injury to a competitor to injury to competition in general, with emphasis on the probability rather than the mere possibility of injury being shown. As implied previously, not everything that hurts competitors hinders competition. A price discrimination may frequently hurt a competitor, as does any price cut, but whether it hinders competition in general is much less certain. There is as much if not a greater likelihood that it promotes competition rather than hinders it.

2. The two defenses, that is, the "cost defense" and the "good faith defense," should be reconsidered along the following lines:

a. Accounting rules should recognize savings in manufacturing as well as in selling and delivery costs, and utilize incremental rather than average costs as a criterion.
b. Brokerage allowances and services should be revised so as to permit price concessions provided they are related to the cost and the value of the services involved.
c. The commission's power to limit quantity discounts, even when justified by lower costs, should be repealed.
d. The opportunities for business to lower prices discriminately so as to meet competition should be expanded.

With appropriate amendments along the lines indicated, the Robinson-Patman Act would improve the rivalry among business firms, and the maintenance of competition would thus become more nearly self-enforcing. As it stands now, the act is concerned more with the survival of small competitors than with maintaining competition. Thus intended, it does not prevent discrimination in general but merely prevents discrimination in favor of larger buyers and permits or even requires it in favor of smaller ones.

Price Discrimination—Delivered Pricing

The preceding discussion of discrimination was rooted primarily in the economic functions performed by purchasers. In the present section we turn our attention to another form of discrimination—geographic price discrimination—which arises because of the particular locational differences that exist between buyers and sellers. Such differences may result in *delivered pricing systems,* which means essentially that the price to the buyer includes not only the cost of the goods themselves but a delivery charge as well. The result of this is that the seller's mill net will vary depending on the amount of freight charges absorbed, and by thus accepting varying net returns on sales to different customers, the seller is discriminating between customers.

Geographic price discrimination becomes potentially dangerous where (1) transportation cost is a large proportion of the final price, or in other words, where the value-transport ratio is low; or (2) sellers are pricing on the basis of mutual understanding, either tacitly or explicitly, so that the effect is to restrain competition. Geographic discriminatory pricing may exist under the opposite of these conditions, that is, a high-value–transport ratio and independence of sellers' actions; it may also occur with either one of the conditions. But it is mainly when both exist, and especially the second, that the antitrusters have been particularly concerned.

The economic aspects of delivered pricing systems, such as basing points, zones, and freight equalization, involve familiar pricing concepts. Since most of the litigation has centered on basing point systems and their ramifications, the discussion below will be oriented around these practices. The procedure followed will be to outline first the implications of the basing point controversy, and then the legality of basing point systems.

The Basing Point Controversy

The basing point system is a method of quoting delivered prices that has been used mainly in sales by manufacturers to other producers. A basing point price consists of a factory price plus a transportation charge. The transportation charge, however, does not always correspond to the actual cost; instead the charge is usually from some designated production center known as a "basing point." Under such a system the seller may calculate delivered price by using either single or multiple basing points.

The outstanding and classic example of the *single* basing point system is "Pittsburgh Plus," employed by the steel industry and ordered discontinued by the FTC as long ago as 1924 in a landmark case against the United States Steel Corporation. Under this system, every seller, regardless of location, would quote a buyer, also regardless of location, the Pittsburgh mill price of steel plus the rail freight from Pittsburgh to the destination, irrespective of the actual origin of the shipment or its actual freight cost. Hence the term "Pittsburgh Plus." All firms in the industry tended to follow the same practice, the price leader being the U.S. Steel Corporation; and hence buyers were usually quoted the same prices by competing sellers on most steel products.

The basing point system has been debated off and on in economic literature and court cases since the time of World War I. Out of the complicated mass of facts and interpretation, two distinct schools of thought have emerged. One of these is the opponent group, composed of the Federal Trade Commission and perhaps the majority of academic economists, who hold that basing point systems are monopolistic and the result of collusion, and should be generally outlawed; the other is the proponent group, consisting of executives of basing point industries and some business and academic economists, who argue that such systems are competitive, that they emerge naturally in certain (oligopolistic) industries, and that to outlaw them would result in less desirable pricing systems.

Legality of Basing Points

The first set of cases to reach the Supreme Court in the postwar period involved the Corn Products Refining Company and the A. E.

Staley Manufacturing Company, both decided on the same day in 1945, and commonly referred to as the "glucose cases."

Both companies were engaged in the sale of glucose to candy manufacturers. The Court held that the companies' adherence to a single basing point system was in violation of the law; that this pricing method, which resulted in freight absorption on some sales and phantom freight on others, was discriminatory between customers and injurious to competition; and that the Staley company's defense that its prices were made "in good faith to meet the equally low prices of a competitor," was not acceptable since such prices had been quoted systematically. In subsequent decisions, handed down by a Court of Appeals in 1945 and 1946, the FTC was upheld in orders issued, involving not only single basing point systems but also plenary systems (i.e., where each producing point is a basing point) and zone systems. Thus, in each of these cases, involving the sale of malt, milk and ice cream cans, and crepe paper, the Court held that the characteristics of delivered pricing systems are such as to infer that there is agreement to avoid competition.

The second set of cases came in 1948. These involved the Cement Institute case, decided by the Supreme Court, and the rigid steel conduit case, decided by a Court of Appeals. In the cement case, the Court upheld the Commission, declaring that the collective adherence by competitors to a multiple basing point system was "an unfair method of competition prohibited by the Federal Trade Commission Act"; that such a practice was injurious to competition; and that the good faith defense is unacceptable when the evidence reveals that price matching is consistent rather than sporadic for the purpose of meeting individually competitive situations. And in the rigid steel conduit case, involving the sale of pipe shielding for electric wiring, the Court of Appeals upheld the Commission, finding strong evidence of agreement and declaring that the basing point system as such might be regarded as an unfair method of competition.

These decisions led eventually to a settlement in steel. The industry accepted an FTC order in 1951, agreeing not to participate in any pricing practices of a formula nature "which produces identical price quotations or prices or delivered costs," although delivered pricing or freight absorption is specifically permitted by the order "when innocently and independently pursued . . . with the result of promoting competition."

Conclusion

The outcome of all this may be summarized as follows:

1. The Commission's policy now is to accept the good faith defense as absolute, and its attention is focused on cases where *probable,*

rather than mere possible, injury to competition is evidenced by illegal practices.

2. The courts will rely more on the Commission's own factual interpretation of the situation.

3. The Commission, in repeated assertions, has stated that it has never acted to prohibit delivered pricing or freight absorption when such practices were independently pursued with the result of promoting competition, nor does it intend to do so.

In other words, a policy of f.o.b. pricing with sporadic freight absorption has come to replace basing point systems in cement and several other industries. Although discrimination is still practiced, it is not systematic; the all-rail freight charge and common rate books have been abandoned, as have phantom freight and nonbasing points.

DISTRIBUTION

It is evident by now that in the area of distribution, the administration of the antitrust laws has not been with the aim of enforcing competition or preventing monopoly. The objective has been to protect the independent against the competition of the chains. The form which the attack has taken has centered around the advantages of size: the legal issue has been whether these advantages are great enough to restrict competitive opportunities sufficiently to constitute restraint of trade; the public policy issue has been whether the small competitor should be protected at the risk of impairing vigorous competition, or whether competition should be preserved at the risk of impairing the small competitor. The famous A&P case is an illustration in point.

The A&P Case

In a major civil suit brought against A&P in 1949, the government charged three classes of violations: (1) illegal sales practices, (2) illegal buying practices, and (3) vertical integration.

Illegal Sales Practices. It was charged that the company engaged in local price cutting and selling below cost with the intent of eliminating competitors, while setting higher prices in less competitive areas to offset losses. In effect, the company was criticized for placing relatively greater emphasis on demand elasticity (in full accordance with profit maximizing theory) than on costs in its pricing policy. No evidence was shown that the company increased its market share by using such a system, but the government still claimed that the company should more appropriately have followed a cost-plus pricing procedure.

Illegal Buying Practices. It was charged that A&P used coercive tactics to secure preferential treatment from suppliers. But what were these tactics? The company announced that it would buy only direct from suppliers and not through brokers, and that it would manufacture for itself if suppliers did not accept its terms. Accordingly, A&P was able to secure a broker's commission for performing a broker's services; it received promotional allowances for advertising the products it handled; and it received discounts for the services it rendered producers. In other words, here was a company that because of its oligopolistic position was able to extract from other oligopolists certain concessions which it passed on to consumers in the form of lower prices. Certainly, consumers were not unhappy. But could it be argued that A&P exercised a monopsonistic (buyer's monopoly) position, leaving suppliers with no other alternative but to deal? Hardly. The evidence showed that the company purchased only about 10 percent of the foodstuffs sold in national markets, and about 20 percent of those sold in regional markets. Suppliers, therefore, if they were displeased with A&P's offers, could certainly have dealt with others. It seems that the government's charge of coercion should more correctly have been called successful bargaining.

Vertical Integration.   The final charge leveled by the government was twofold in nature.

1.   It held that A&P offset the low profits or even losses of its discriminatory retail operations with the profits of its manufacturing subsidiary. This it accomplished by having its factories charge higher prices to competitors than it charged its own stores.

The meaningfulness of this charge may be questioned on at least three counts. First, many integrated firms subsidize the losses of one subsidiary with the profits of another (and hence violate the antitrust laws?). Second, A&P was evidently justified in doing so, for it realized definite savings by being able to consolidate shipments and by not having to incur the costs of soliciting business and transferring ownership. And third, the charge was absurd from a technical standpoint because, accounting-wise, the company could just as well have recorded lower transfer prices in its factory accounts thereby showing smaller profits or even losses in that subsidiary, and consequently higher profits in its retailing operations.

2.   The government also claimed that the company's main central purchasing agency, Atlantic Commission Company (ACCO), which served as a produce broker for A&P as well as other distributors, had abused its dual function purpose. ACCO, it was charged, had sought to obtain produce at lower prices for A&P than it did for other distributors, and had attempted to establish exclusive dealings with suppliers and jobbers for the purpose of cutting rivals off from their sources of supply.

Whether it could be clearly inferred that ACCO abused its dual function in favor of A&P is doubtful, for the evidence revealed that ACCO never attained a position even approaching that of monopoly. Suppliers and jobbers who were "victimized," therefore, could readily have taken their business elsewhere without being any the worse off.

The case was settled by a consent decree in 1954, the company being enjoined on several points: (1) In selling, A&P was forbidden to set low markups in particular stores with the intent of eliminating competitors by operating at a loss; but such intent would have to be proven, and could not be inferred from mere operation at a loss. (2) In buying, A&P was forbidden to exert pressure on suppliers that would prevent them from selling to competitors through brokers, offering discounts, or raising prices. (3) Concerning its vertically integrated structure, the company dissolved ACCO and was forbidden to buy food for, or sell food to, competitors, except the food processed in its own plants.

Conclusion. The A&P case was not aimed at preventing monopoly or at enforcing competition; it was an attack by the government against the advantages of size. Certain relevant conditions that have come about with the growth of competing chains—a more competitive grocery industry, improved distribution methods at lower costs, better products at lower prices—in short, all the desirable consequences of competition, were hardly considered. The antitrusters, bent on preserving small business per se at the possible risk of impairing efficiency, were successful with the help of the court in imposing limitations on A&P that do not apply to its competitors such as Kroger, Food Fair, and others. This was accomplished despite the fact that the chains were carrying only a minor share of the business and that entry of new competitors with new methods is still occurring at a rapid rate. And it appears, in view of these happenings, that this pattern will continue in the future.

BIG BUSINESS AND GOVERNMENT: RECENT DEVELOPMENTS AND ISSUES

The growth and importance of big business in the United States has resulted in charges, frequently made and widely believed, that: (1) the concentration of economic power is centered in the hands of a few corporate giants; (2) this concentration has grown over the years; and (3) there has been a "decline of competition." In addition, the controversy over the role of big business in the American economy has become more intensified since the late 1960s owing in part to recent inflationary experiences, monetary devaluations, trade imbalances, and energy crises. This section of the chapter traces recent developments, and attempts to assess the implications to business resulting from governmental policy.

Merger Mania

The mid- and late 1960s heralded an era of business mergers and acquisitions of unprecedented proportions in the United States. Placed in historical perspective, the phenomenon was truly spectacular, with the number of consummated agreements made in the peak year of 1969 (almost 2,500) more than doubling the previous record of 1929, and more than quadrupling the earliest record of 1902. Although a large number of mergers and acquisitions during the 1960s was probably motivated on sound principles of diversification, in which companies sought to acquire unrelated enterprises in attempts to stabilize earnings and diversify risks, a number of others appeared to be predicated upon less reasonable objectives. Foremost on this list would have to be the questionable, but legal, method of fattening corporate profits through "pooling of interests" accounting procedures available at that time. Under these provisions, free-wheeling conglomerate chiefs were able to pyramid their corporate structures to new financial heights, and their income statements to ever loftier levels, largely though what now appears to have been more the adroit use of accounting wizardry than the generation of any genuine economic value.

Be that as it may, diversification and corporate expansion were not the only reasons for mergers; a number of acquisitions were clear examples of vertical or horizontal integration, and hence, at least potential violations of the Sherman and Clayton Acts. Yet, despite the fact that the combined assets of such "jumbo" mergers as McDonnell Company with Douglas Aircraft Company and Atlantic Refining Company with Richfield Oil Company were enormous ($1.2 and $1.4 billion, respectively), the Justice Department only very selectively pressed antitrust charges. At that time, and in marked contrast to the courts, which appeared quite willing to strike down such integration under a loose interpretation of the antitrust laws, the Department tended to overlook size and the potential implications of such power and concentrate on the competitive aspects of the resulting merger. Under this approach, an acquisition was not challenged just because the resulting company was big, but only if it could be shown that the integration tended to restrict or reduce competition. Hence, under this "new" view, and in marked contrast to earlier cases such as A&P and United Shoe in which size itself lent weight in the divestiture proceedings, corporate executives had, with a few exceptions, a free ticket to merge and acquire at will.

The above facts do not tell the whole story, however, for they fail to examine the period following the peak of the merger wave, 1969. With the passage of time, the evolution of new economic realities, the establishment of a new presidential administration, and a change in the attitude of the Justice Department, the "concentration pendulum" has appeared to swing back once again. A pure economic explanation would attribute this turn-around to the 1970 recession and the resultant "shake-out" in the stock market (firms could no longer afford to float stock issues for acquiring company securities), as well as the burdensome debt to which some companies resorted in their expensive efforts to bid for smaller acquisitions. Undoubtedly, however, crackdowns by the FTC and the Justice Department had some influence. The former, for example, began to require advanced notice from all companies with assets of over $250 million intending to acquire companies with sales over $10 million, and the Attorney General announced as early as mid-1969 that the government would seriously entertain a move to bar any merger involving the nation's biggest corporations. Also, a number of trial suits were instigated against selected conglomerates on the grounds of anticompetitive industrial concentration.

Perhaps of greatest interest, however, was the ironic discovery that the conglomerates themselves sometimes didn't know how to run the companies they had so hastily acquired, and thereby disproved their own theory that pure management capability could replace expertise in the subsidiary. General weakness in the economy and specific weaknesses within merged firms thereby conspired to force many conglomerates to conduct "remnant sales" in order to raise needed cash and liquidate themselves of unprofitable acquisitions.

What of the future? In early 1973, signs of a brightening economy and partial recovery from the 1970 recession appeared to spark a second interest in merger negotiations, but economic expectations were not fulfilled and acquisition activity slackened. Hence, the future road of corporate integration is, at the present time, still uncertain. Yet, this much does seem clear: mergers and acquisitions have tended to be greatest when the economy has been in a state of expansion, when the Justice Department has not pressed antitrust too harshly, and, perhaps most importantly, when public sentiment, as expressed in the courts, has not been too ready to condemn big business simply for its size. Dramatic merger activity has only occurred three times since the turn of the century, with intervals of nearly 30 and 40 years between each one. Hence, the small likelihood of favorable concurrent circumstances as well as historical perspective suggest that the possibility of another bout of "merger mania" is not too great in the near future.

Measurement of Economic Concentration

The degree of corporate pooling that has transpired during the last few years reopens the old saw, "Is big business really big, or does it just look that way?" However, answering this question obviously hinges on what we mean by "business," and what we mean by "big." In short, the problem boils down to a choice of base (all businesses, manufacturing only, all nonfinancial corporations, etc.), a choice of measurement unit (plant or firm, company or manufacturing subsidiary, etc.,), and, finally, the choice of concentration index (assets, employment, income, sales, etc.). Though a good case could probably be made for any combination of these three measures, depending upon the purpose of the study, most conventional estimators of economic concentration have tended to look at the assets of the 200 largest manufacturing and mining (or nonagricultural) firms in the country. (*Fortune* magazine periodically compiles a list of the 500 top companies, ranked by assets and by sales.)

On the basis of this or similar evaluators, studies prior to 1950 had generally concurred in the conclusion that some economic concentration existed, but was not growing, or at least not growing as rapidly, as alarmists were claiming. In an article entitled "The Measurement of Industrial Concentration" in the *Review of Economics and Statistics* (1951), for example, Professor M. A. Adelman found that in 1947 the nation's 200 largest corporations held 40 percent of all corporate assets and between 20 to 25 percent of all income-yielding wealth. Even as late as 1963, the National Industrial Conference Board, in its *Business Management Record* (July 1963), reported the results of a concentration study for the period 1954–58 in which it was found that some concentration ratios for individual industries, product groups, and product classes advanced while others fell; but on balance, the composite ratios for manufacturing were stable or declining.

More recent studies have yielded conflicting results on the nature and extent of economic concentration in the United States. What appears to emerge from the different analyses is that assessments are highly dependent upon industrial classifications and, perhaps more importantly, on the methodological measure of concentration. Although assets or four-firm concentration ratios have been popular, value added, employment, value of shipments, and number of firms have also been used to test the hypothesis that industrial concentration has been growing since the early 1950s. As a result, the conclusions are contradictory, depending upon which measure and which precise time frame has been used in the study.

With the flurry of merger activity during the last decade, the level of economic concentration must be reassessed. Exhibit 1 indicates the trend of such mergers. As revealed in the charts, the trend has declined substantially since 1968.

Conclusion

In summary, a clear trend in economic concentration has not yet been established. At present it appears that only in the manufacturing sector of our economy is the problem of excessive concentration substan-

EXHIBIT 1
Acquisitions of Manufacturing and Mining Firms with Assets of $10 Million or More

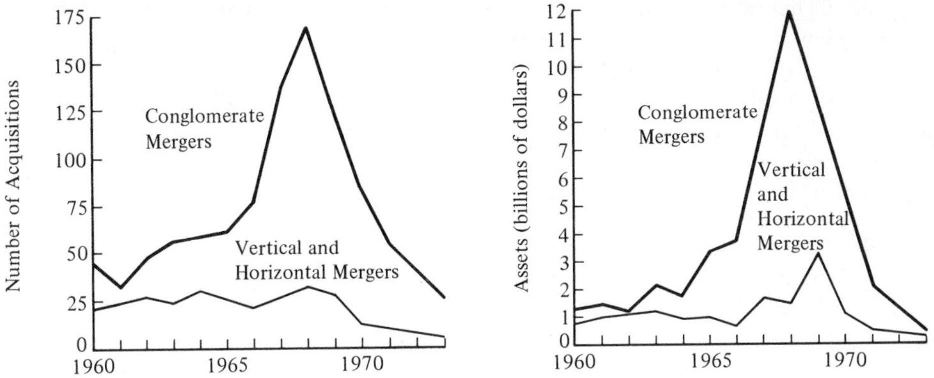

Source: Federal Trade Commission.

tial, and even here the scope is narrowed down to a select group of industries where concentration is high. Some of these include, in the industrial field, petroleum, rubber, glass, primary metals, newsprint, and heavy equipment; in consumer durables, autos, radios, sewing and washing machines, refrigerators, and vacuum cleaners; and in lighter consumer products, cigarettes, soap, matches, and light bulbs. The tendency of economic reformers to identify the major producers in these fields as monopolies, merely because of their size, only serves to distort the real nature of the problem. Production in these industries is characterized by a small number of large firms so that the antitrust problem is one of oligopoly not monopoly. And economic theory does not say that oligopoly is not fiercely competitive; it only states that there may be a stronger tendency to avoid price (as compared to nonprice) competition.

PROBLEMS

1. Although the Procter and Gamble decision represents a landmark case in the field of antitrust, the Court has left many questions unanswered. How far-reaching could the standards applied to this type of merger ultimately be? Would this merger, which created a technical conglomerate, have been declared illegal if the industries involved were not so closely related? What might have happened if P&G had acquired a smaller company—or, perhaps more significantly, if Clorox had been acquired by a less powerful firm than P&G?

2. What constitutes a merger? Are mergers the same as "acquisitions?"

3. "When corporations fix prices, it is called collusion; when the government fixes prices, it is called regulation." Discuss.

4. In 1973 the federal government froze the retail price of beef and ranchers withheld their stocks in anticipation of higher prices later on when the freeze ended. For the most part, their patience was rewarded. Under

present-day antitrust law, could the ranchers be prosecuted for restraint of trade?

5. "The rationale underlying restrictive agreements among competitors is based on the potential danger arising from the existence of the power of sellers to manipulate prices. Where this power does not exist, the laws pertaining to restrictive agreements are practically meaningless. Thus, there is no point in holding unlawful an agreement among competitors to fix prices, allocate customers, or control production, when the competitors involved are so small that they lack significant power to affect market prices." Evaluate.

6. Suppose that tomorrow morning, all grocers in Chicago, without previous public notice, raised their prices for milk by 3 cents per quart. Does this action prove the existence of an agreement, or constitute an offense on the part of the grocers? What would your answer be if the automobile manufacturers without notice announced a 5 percent price increase next year on all new model cars? Explain.

7. In an industry characterized by price leadership without prior arrangement, is there likely to be a charge of combination or conspiracy leveled against that industry if (a) prevailing prices are announced by the industry's trade association rather than by a leading firm; (b) all firms in the industry report their prices to their industry trade association; (c) all firms in the industry quote prices on a basing point system, that is, the delivered price is the leader's price plus rail freight from the leader's plant; and (d) all firms follow the leader not only in price but in product and sales policies as well? (These four questions should be answered as a group rather than individually.)

8. In the Columbia Steel case (1948), the Supreme Court said: "We do not undertake to prescribe any set of percentage figures by which to measure the reasonableness of a corporation's enlargement of its activities by the purchase of the assets of a competitor. The relative effect of percentage command of a market varies with the setting in which that factor is placed." Does this conflict with Judge Hand's statement in the ALCOA case? Explain.

9. "Many trustbusters and economists forget that *concentration is a function of consumer sovereignty,* and that the same consumers who make big businesses big can make them small or even wipe them out by simply refraining from the purchase of their products. This is a not-so-obvious principle of our free enterprise system which needs to be better understood." Do you agree? Explain.

10. "To say that the degree of competition depends on the number of sellers in the marketplace is like saying that football is more competitive than tennis." Do you agree? Explain: (HINT: Can you describe different forms of competition, in addition to price competition, that exist in American industry?)

11. Suppose that General Motors, the largest firm in the automobile industry, were to reduce prices on its automobiles to levels which yield only a "fair" profit for itself but not for its competitors. As a result, consumer purchases shift to General Motors because of its lower prices, and the other automobile manufacturers subsequently find themselves driven out

of business as a result of bankruptcy. In the light of the ALCOA case, would General Motors be guilty of monopolizing the market and hence violating the Sherman Act?

12. It is generally stated that growth, stability, and flexibility are three primary objectives of mergers. (*a*) With respect to growth, it has been said that "a firm, like a tree, must either grow or die." Evaluate this statement. (*b*) Why may instability be a motive for merger? Instability of what? (*c*) What is meant by flexibility as a motive for merger? (HINT: Compare flexibility versus vulnerability.)

13. Explain the differences between vertical mergers, horizontal mergers, conglomerate mergers, and concentric mergers. (HINT: Concentric mergers have "multiplicative" effects on the sales or profits of the merged firms, as distinguished from the other types of mergers which may have only "additive" effects. What do you suppose this means? Keep this in mind as you develop your answer.)

14. Section 7 of the Clayton Act of 1914 and its amendment, the Celler Antimerger Act of 1950, states:

"No corporation engaged in commerce shall acquire, directly or indirectly, the whole or any part of the stock or other share capital and no corporation subject to the jurisdiction of the Federal Trade Commission shall acquire the whole or any part of the assets of another corporation engaged also in commerce, where in any line of commerce in any section of the country, the effect of such acquisition may be substantially to lessen competition, or to tend to create a monopoly."

Assume that you are a business economist for a large corporation and you are asked to prepare a report on why this legislation should be repealed. What main points would you bring out in your argument?

15. (Library research) Examine the Electrical Equipment Case in detail. (A good source is *Time* Magazine, Februrary 17, 1961.) What were the principle antitrust provisions that were broken? Were the damages thought to result from the antitrust violations considerable, or was the simple act of collusion the major concern? Was corporate morality ever an issue? Did governmental prosecutions have any effect on future corporate policies?

16. (Library research) In the last few years, the firm of ITT (International Telephone and Telegraph) has come under the scrutinous eye of government investigators for various questionable practices. What, specifically, has the government been concerned about?

17. (Library research) The federal government's suit against IBM is expected to continue for some time. Yet this more recent suit is not the first time antitrust investigators have found fault with the company. Discuss the company's "Consent Decree." What is the present status of the government's case?

18. ## CASE PROBLEM: PRICE DISCRIMINATION

A new management has recently assumed control of the fifth largest company in one of the nation's major industries. The industry is strongly oligopolistic and has had a long history of price leadership.

The new management is headed by an aggressive president who has announced his interest in expanding the company's market share through planned price reductions. The president, however, is aware of the likelihood that any general price reductions would be promptly matched by competitors, and hence little if anything would be gained. Moreover, the four larger firms in the industry control about 90 percent of the output, and are therefore in a relatively stronger position to withstand the damaging effects of a price war.

The president has decided, therefore, to adhere to the outward historical pattern of price leadership as far as the industry is concerned, but to engage in secret price concessions with potential customers whenever necessary to attract their business. For example, he will continue to publish his previous prices and he will follow the price leader as long as total demand is high and there is no major price resistance by buyers. However, if it ever becomes apparent that an important sale may be lost because of the price, a lower price will be negotiated in order to retain the customer.

Questions:

The president of the company has hired you as an antitrust economist to advise him on the following questions:

a. How will the president's strategy stand up in view of the Robinson-Patman Act?

b. The president proposes to cut prices in New England where the demand for the product is more elastic, and to maintain prices elsewhere. What do you advise with respect to the Robinson-Patman Act?

c. The president has several personal friends in Congress. What would you advise him to do about the Robinson-Patman Act? Be specific.

19.   **CASE PROBLEM: SHOULD MEDICAL
                              DOCTORS BE LICENSED?**

Should doctors be licensed in order to practice? How about dentists, lawyers, and other professionals?

These questions usually take the great majority of people by surprise. After all, they ask, "Who in his right mind would want to allow unlicensed individuals to call themselves doctors and to practice medicine? That would be quackery, pure and simple!"

The fact is, however, that a number of distinguished scholars advocate precisely that; but they call it "free enterprise," not quackery. The question is really part of a larger issue dealing with the general purpose of licensing and the way it has been used as a device for restricting competition by keeping newcomers out of a field.

A summary of the subject as a whole makes for an interesting research project, or for a class report by an ambitious student. The following sources, and the references cited therein, may be used as a starter:

FARMER, RICHARD N., and KASSARJIAN, HAROLD H. "The Right to Compete." *California Management Review,* vol. 6, no. 1 (Fall 1963), pp. 61–68.

FRIEDMAN, MILTON *Capitalism and Freedom,* Chap. 9. Chicago: University of Chicago Press, 1962. Professor Friedman, one of America's foremost economists, opposes the licensing of doctors.

KESSEL, REUBEN A. "Price Discrimination in Medicine." *Journal of Law and Economics,* vol. 1 (October 1958), pp. 20–53.

MOORE, THOMAS G. "The Purpose of Licensing." *Journal of Law and Economics,* vol. 4 (October 1961), pp. 93–117.

REFERENCES

"Antitrust: New Life in an Old Issue." *Time,* June 28, 1971, pp. 70–72.

BAIN, JOE S. "Changes in Concentration in Manufacturing Industries in the United States, 1954–66: Trends and Relationships to the Levels of 1954 Concentration." *Review of Economics and Statistics,* vol. 52, no. 4 (November 1970), pp. 411–16.

——— "Economies of Scale, Concentration and the Condition of Entry in Twenty Manufacturing Industries." *American Economic Review,* vol. 44, no. 1 (March 1954), pp. 15–39.

BEMAN, LEWIS "What We Learned from the Great Merger Frenzy" *Fortune,* April 1963, p. 70 ff.

BOCK, BETTY "Antitrust Issues in Conglomerate Acquisitions." *Studies in Business Economics,* no. 110. New York: National Industrial Conference Board, 1969.

FRIEDMAN, MILTON *Capitalism and Freedom,* chap. 8; "Monopoly and the Social Responsibility of Business and Labor," pp. 119–36. Chicago: University of Chicago Press, 1962. A penetrating discussion by a distinguished economist.

HAILSTONES, THOMAS J.; MARTIN, BERNARD L.; and MASTRIANNA, FRANK V. *Contemporary Economic Issues and Problems.* Cincinnati: South-Western Publishing Co., 1970. A lively, contemporary discussion of the 1970s most controversial issues. The federal role in pollution abatement, urban renewal, and income, as well as business is discussed at length.

KEYES, LUCILE SHEPPARD "Price Discrimination in Law and Economics," *Southern Economic Journal,* vol. 27, no. 4 (April 1961), pp. 320–28.

LAWYER, JOHN Q. "How to Conspire to Fix Prices." *Harvard Business Review,* vol. 41, no. 2 (March–April 1963), pp. 95–103. A facetious but clever discussion by a prominent antitrust attorney who prefers to remain anonymous.

LOCKLIN, D. PHILIP *Economics of Transportation,* 7th ed. Homewood, Ill.: Richard D. Irwin, 1972. A comprehensive guide to transportation economics.

MARKHAM, JESSE "Antitrust Trends and New Constraints." *Harvard Business Review,* vol. 41, no. 3 (May–June 1963), pp. 84–92. A survey of some of the issues and interpretations of antitrust policy.

MUND, VERNON A., and WOLF, RONALD H.   *Industrial Organization and Public Policy*. New York: Appleton-Century-Crofts, 1971. This is a standard text in the field. The authors advocate strong antitrust laws and increased government intervention to curb monopolistic practices.

OSBORN, RICHARDS C.   "Concentration and the Profitability of Small Manufacturing Corporations." *Quarterly Review of Economics and Business*, vol. 10, no. 2 (Summer 1970), pp. 15–26.

PETERSON, WILLIAM H.   "The Case against Antimerger Policy." *Business Horizons*, vol. 4, no. 4 (Winter 1961), pp. 111–20. A critical evaluation of antitrust policy.

"Taking the Crusade Out of Antitrust." *Business Week*, May 20, 1967, p. 59 ff.

"The War on Mergers Escalates." *Business Week*, April 19, 1969, pp. 36–37.

VAN CISE, JERROLD G.   "How to Live with Antitrust." *Harvard Business Review*, vol. 40, no. 6 (November–December 1962), pp. 119–26.

WESTON, J. FRED, and ORNSTEIN, STANLEY I., EDS.   *The Impact of Large Firms on the United States Economy*. Lexington, Mass.: Lexington Books, 1973. This is a volume of articles dealing with motives of concentration, industry structure and profits, decision processes in large business firms, price decisions, and the performance of large firms, including conglomerates, in terms of market structure, growth, and profitability. Both theoretical and empirical studies are found among the 16 chapters provided.

WILCOX, CLAIR, and SHEPHERD, WILLIAM G.   *Public Policies toward Business*, 5th ed. Homewood, Ill.: Richard D. Irwin, Inc., 1975. This is perhaps the most comprehensive book in the field. More than just a text, it represents a superb contribution to the subject, reflecting the late Professor Wilcox's mature thought. On various controversial issues, it often takes somewhat of a more "conservative" view, and thus contrasts interestingly and provocatively with a text like Mund and Wolf cited above.

chapter 14

Capital Budgeting

Capital budgeting involves the planning of expenditures for assets, the returns from which will be realized in future time periods. Thus, typical classes of decision problems in capital budgeting include:

1. *Expansion decisions,* such as the building or acquiring of additional plant facilities.
2. *Replacement decisions,* such as the replacement of existing equipment.
3. *Buy or lease decisions* involving the problem of whether to purchase a particular asset or to lease it from another source.
4. *"Seed" investment decisions,* such as research and development, advertising, market research, training, and professional consulting services.
5. *Operating investment decisions,* such as increasing inventories or accounts receivable, or development of a new product line.

Each of these types of problems requires, for correct solution, a comparison of rates of return and costs of capital on alternative investments. Hence an explanation of the theory and measurement of these concepts is necessary.

RATE OF RETURN

Among laymen, the common conception is that the *rate of return on an investment is simply the ratio of annual receipts to original cost.*

This meaning, it should be noted, is only approximately correct; it is precisely true for a special type of investment, namely, a permanent, nondepreciating, nonappreciating asset, producing a periodically uniform income stream. To the extent that the liquidating or resale value of the asset is, at the time the investment is terminated, greater or less than the original outlay, the true rate of return will be greater or less than the rate as defined above.

In reality, it is rarely possible to predict the precise liquidating or resale value of an investment; hence, in the typical case, the *true* rate of return on an investment to a given owner cannot be known until the ownership has terminated and the actual liquidation value is known. This liquidation value and the income stream produced by the investment are combined to obtain a measure of the true rate of return. However, for many practical situations we want to be able to estimate the rate of return before, rather than after, the investment is made, in order to have some preliminary idea of the investment's profitability. The method of accomplishing this is described below.

Time Value of Money

A fundamental concept which must be understood when talking about rate of return is the notion of the *time value of money*. By this is meant that dollars at different points in time cannot be made directly comparable unless they are first expressed in terms of a common denominator. The common denominator which is used is the interest rate.

Thus, if money can be invested at 6 percent interest, then a dollar today is not the same as a dollar next year, because a dollar today can be invested so that it is worth $1.06 next year. Similarly, $1.06 next year is not equivalent to $1.06 in the following year, because $1.06 next year can be invested at 6 percent so as to be worth $1.06 plus 6 percent of that amount, or a total of $1.124 in the following year.

It is clear that this process, which is known as *compounding,* can be extended as far into the future as we like. Further, by this process, we can equate a given sum of money at the present time with another sum of money at any future time. Thus, in line with the above example, the sum of $1 today is, at 6 percent interest, equivalent to $1.06 next year, or to $1.124 in the following year, or to still greater amounts in later years.

The reverse of compounding is *discounting.* Whereas, in compounding we move from the present into the future, in discounting we move from the future back to the present. Thus, at 6 percent interest, how much is $1.124 two years from now worth today? We know from the previous example that $1 now is worth $1.124 two years from today at 6 percent. Therefore, we may say that $1.124 two years hence discounted at 6 percent has a *present value* of $1.

By showing how dollars at different points in time can be made equivalent through the common denominator of an interest rate, we may define and illustrate the meaning of "rate of return."

> DEFINITION: The *rate of return* on an investment is the interest rate which equates the present value of the cash returns on the investment with the present value of the cash expenditures relating to the investment. That is, the rate of return on investment is the interest rate at which an investment is repaid by its discounted receipts.

As already stated, many people think of the rate of return on an investment as the annual net receipts or cash flow from the investment divided by the total amount of the investment. Thus, if an investment of $1,000 in a parcel of land were to yield forever a rent of $200 per year, then the rate of return would be $200 ÷ $1,000 = 20%. In this case the entire $200 is return on capital, since no part of this amount is used to pay back the original investment of $1,000. To obtain the present value of this investment, we must "capitalize" it. This is done by dividing the income ($200) by that rate of interest (20 percent) which will make the present value of the investment equal to the present cost of the investment. Thus, $200 ÷ .20 = $1,000. Hence, according to the above definition of rate of return on investment, the reason why 20 percent is the rate of return on this investment is because it is the only interest rate which equates the present value of the income stream to the present value of the cost of the investment. That is, it is the only interest rate which, when applied to the cash flow or net receipts, will precisely recover the investment.

If the $1,000 had been invested in an asset with a finite life, then part of the cash flow of $200 would represent return on capital, and part would represent the amount needed to recover the initial investment. In such cases where the annual receipts include both interest and principal, the rate of return is more difficult to compute. For this purpose, interest tables have been devised to facilitate the computations.

Case I. Present Value of a Uniform Series: PVUS

There are many types of problems that arise in calculating rate of return. They involve the nature of the variations in cash flow, the length of life of the investment, and, of course, the amount of the investment. Most of the problems, however, can usually be grouped into three classes of situations. The first involves the present value of a uniform series, abbreviated PVUS. This case relates to an investment which will yield a constant income stream over its life.

> EXAMPLE: A new machine costs $10,000, requires no increased investment in working capital, and is expected to yield a $3,000 (before tax) profit per year for 10 years, at which time its scrap or resale value will be negligible.

Assume straight-line depreciation and a 50 percent tax rate. (*a*) What is the rate of return on this investment? (*b*) If management requires at least a 10 percent return on any new investment, would this investment qualify? (*c*) At a 10 percent rate of return, what is the present value per dollar of investment? Of what use is this type of measure?

SOLUTION: (*a*) One way of conveniently solving for rate of return is to begin by setting up a table such as Exhibit 1.

EXHIBIT 1
Calculation of Cash Flow
Cost of Asset: $10,000
Life of Asset: 10 years

(1)	(2) Operating Profit and Capital	(3) Depreci- ation— Straight-	(4) Taxable Income	(5) Taxes @ 50% 50% of	(6) Income After Taxes	(7) Cash Flow (2) – (5) or
Year	Recovery	line	(2) – (3)	(4)	(4) – (5)	(6) + (3)
1....	$3,000	$1,000	$2,000	$1,000	$1,000	$2,000
2....	3,000	1,000	2,000	1,000	1,000	2,000
3....	3,000	1,000	2,000	1,000	1,000	2,000
4....	3,000	1,000	2,000	1,000	1,000	2,000
5....	3,000	1,000	2,000	1,000	1,000	2,000
6....	3,000	1,000	2,000	1,000	1,000	2,000
7....	3,000	1,000	2,000	1,000	1,000	2,000
8....	3,000	1,000	2,000	1,000	1,000	2,000
9....	3,000	1,000	2,000	1,000	1,000	2,000
10....	3,000	1,000	2,000	1,000	1,000	2,000
CR*...	0	—	—	—	—	0

* CR denotes capital recovery. It includes the forecasted resale or scrap value of the asset, plus the return of additional working capital which may have been needed due to the investment.

Note that depreciation is calculated only for the purpose of arriving at income after taxes. As far as cash flow (column 7) is concerned, it may be estimated by subtracting taxes from operating profit, or by adding in the amount of depreciation when income after taxes (column 6) has been determined. Thus, depreciation is conceived as a *source of cash* in the sense that profits are reduced because expenses are increased each year by the amount of depreciation, leaving that much less profit for distribution to stockholders and that much more for the replacement of fixed assets.

Thus, by investing $10,000 now, management expects a cash flow of $2,000 a year for ten years. What interest rate will equate these sums? To answer this question, we shall have to utilize an interest table or chart as in Appendix A which gives the present value of an annuity of $1 at specified interest rates for a given number of years. That is, the figures in the body of the table tell us the amount that must be invested now, at the rate of compound interest shown across the top, to produce an income of $1 a year for the years shown on the left side of the table. The chart, of course, shows similar information.

First, we set up our equation, using r to denote the interest rate and n the number of years.

$$\$10,000 = \$2,000 \begin{bmatrix} \text{PVUS} \\ r = ? \\ n = 10 \end{bmatrix}$$

$$\text{Therefore,} \begin{bmatrix} \text{PVUS} \\ r = ? \\ n = 10 \end{bmatrix} = \frac{\$10,000}{\$\ 2,000} = 5$$

Thus, an investment of $10,000 which yields $2,000 per year is proportional to an investment of $5 which yields $1 per year. Looking at Appendix A, we note that at $n = 10$, the closest number to the present value or discount factor 5 is represented by an interest rate of 15 percent. Hence, 15 percent is very nearly the rate of return on this investment. (A closer estimate can be obtained by linear interpolation, resulting in 15.1 percent, but the slight gain in accuracy thus obtained is probably not worth the extra effort.)

(b) If management requires at least a 10 percent return on capital, then this investment would surely qualify since its rate of return is about 5 percent greater than the minimum acceptable rate.

NOTE: The concept of a minimum acceptable rate of return on an investment has been given the technical name of *cost of capital*. In this case, therefore, the cost of capital is said to be 10 percent. A fuller discussion of cost of capital is presented below.

(c) At a rate of return (or cost of capital) of 10 percent, the present value factor in Appendix A for $n = 10$ is 6.145. Hence 6.145 × $2,000 = $12,290, which is the present value of the discounted cash inflow. The net present value of the investment, then, is $12,290 − $10,000 = $2,290; and the present value per dollar of investment, called the profitability index or benefit/ cost ratio, is $12,290 ÷ $10,000 = 122.9 percent. The profitability index provides a convenient method for screening proposals, and for ranking investments that require identical cash outlays. For investments of differing magnitude, however, ranking by a profitability index should be used with caution, as illustrated in Exhibit 2.

Clearly, these projects are ranked correctly if the only criterion is the

EXHIBIT 2
Profitability Index versus Net Present Value

	Funds Required	Profitability Index or Benefit/Cost Ratio	Net Present Value
A. Buy new machine	$ 100,000	127% or 1.27	$ 27,000
B. Expand advertising.	100,000	122% or 1.22	22,000
C. Expand plant	1,500,000	119% or 1.19	285,000
D. Renovate existing plant	800,000	115% or 1.15	120,000
E. Replace truck fleet	900,000	102% or 1.02	18,000

amount returned per dollar invested. However, if the firm is able to raise the capital to execute project C, or even project D, the overall benefit to the firm will be much greater even though the profitability index is less. Project C, for example, will yield more than ten times as much as project A, even though its profitability is 8 percent less.

Case II. Present Value of a Nonuniform Series, or Present Value of Single Payments: PVSP

When the income stream or cash flow varies substantially from year to year, it is necessary to obtain a separate discount factor for each year's cash flow. This requires the use of the table or chart in Appendix B. Here the figures in the body of the table reveal the amount that must be invested now, at compound interest, to yield a single payment of $1 in a specified future year. The table thus gives the present value of $1, and hence can be used to find the present value of any single payment. The corresponding chart, of course, conveys similar information. There are also "canned" computer programs available to calculate the discounted value of any payment.

EXAMPLE: The cash flow (i.e., after taxes and before depreciation) on an investment of $1,000 with an expected life of five years is, for each year, estimated to be: $400, 350, 300, 250, and 200. Capital recovery at the end of the five years is expected to be zero. (*a*) What is the rate of return on this investment? (*b*) If the firm's cost of capital is 12 percent, what percent would it lose (or gain) by undertaking this investment? What about a cost of capital of 25 percent? Discuss.

SOLUTION: (*a*) In this case the cash flow is already given, in contrast to the previous example where it first had to be calculated before the rate of return could be determined.

A convenient procedure for handling this type of problem (i.e., where the cash flows are nonuniform) is shown in Exhibit 3. First, from the note at the top of the table we see that we wish to find the interest rate at which the ratio of the present value of the investment to the present cost of the investment is equal to 1. In order to do this, we adopt a trial-and-error procedure as shown in the table. Thus the actual cash flow is also the flow at 0 percent interest, or equivalently, at 0 percent interest the actual cash flow has the same present value no matter when it is received. In this case, the present value at 0 percent is $1,500, and the ratio, therefore, is 1.5. For convenience, we plot this point on the chart of Exhibit 3 and label the point with the number 1 to represent trial number 1.

Note that this point lies to the right of the heavy vertical line at which $B/A = 1$. This means that we have discounted the cash flow at too low a rate of interest, and that a higher discount rate is necessary.

As a second trial, we try 10 percent, and we enter the appropriate discount factors from Appendix B which gives the present value of $1. These discount factors are then multiplied by the corresponding cash flow figures and the resulting products are totaled. The B/A ratio is now 1.17, and this point

EXHIBIT 3
Calculation of Rate of Return (nonuniform payments)

A. Present Cost of Investment: *$1,000*

Year	Cash Flow	*Trial No. 1* 0% Interest Discount Factor†	*Trial No. 1* Present Value	*Trial No. 2* 10% Interest Discount Factor†	*Trial No. 2* Present Value	*Trial No. 3* 20% Interest Discount Factor†	*Trial No. 3* Present Value	*Trial No. 4* _% Interest Discount Factor†	*Trial No. 4* Present Value
1	$ 400	.91	$ 364	.83	$332				
2	350			.83	291	.69	242		
3	300			.75	225	.58	174		
4	250			.68	170	.48	120		
5	200			.62	124	.40	80		
CR*.	0	.0		.0	0	.0	0		
B. Total	$1,500				$1,174		$948		
Ratio B/A	1.50				1.17		.948		

* CR denotes capital recovery. It includes the forecasted resale or scrap value of the asset, plus the return of additional working capital which may have been needed due to the investment.

† Discount factors may be rounded to nearest hundredth.

Note: The true rate of return is the interest rate at which the present cost of the investment (A) equals the present value of returns on the investment (B), or the interest rate at which $B/A = 1$.

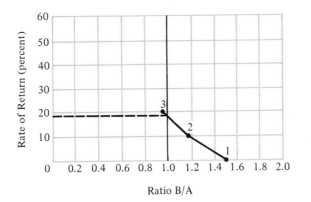

is plotted as the point 2 on the chart. Since point 2 is still to the right of the heavy vertical line, a third trial is necessary.

On trial 3, we try a 20 percent discount rate. The present value now results in a B/A ratio of 948, which we plot as point 3 on the chart. Connecting the points, we thereby perform a graphic linear interpolation between points 2 and 3, resulting in a rate of return of about 18 percent as shown by the dashed line. Of course, the closer the two points are on each side of the heavy vertical line, the closer will be the estimate of the true rate of return as determined by the line which connects the two points. This is because we are performing a *linear* interpolation of a *curvilinear* function, since the data in Appendix B is derived from the power function:

$$PSVP = (1 + r)^{-n}$$

where r is the rate of interest per period and n is the number of periods. Note that a straight line between points 1 and 3 does *not* pass through point 2; rather, the straight-line segments 1–2 and 2–3 suggest the underlying curve.

In most instances, a close estimate can be obtained by the third trial. Sometimes, however, a fourth trial may be necessary, and hence space has been left in the table for this purpose.

Of course, the interpolation can be done directly, without the use of a graph. Thus, at the interest rates of 10 percent and 20 percent, we have:

Interest Rate	Present Value

$$.10 \left\{ x \left\{ \begin{matrix} .10 \\ ? \\ .20 \end{matrix} \right. \quad \left. \begin{matrix} 1174 \\ 1000 \\ 948 \end{matrix} \right\} 174 \right\} 226$$

Setting up the proportion:

$$\frac{x}{.10} = \frac{174}{226}$$

Cross multiplying:

$$226x = 17.4$$

and hence

$$x = .077$$

Therefore,

$$\text{Rate of return} \approx .10 + .077 = 17.7\%$$

We can get a closer approximation of the rate of return if we choose interest rates which are closer together, such as 15 percent and 20 percent. At an interest rate of 15 percent, the discounted cash flow amounts to $1,055. (The student should verify this figure, using the discount factors in Appendix B, rounded to two decimal places.) Then following the same procedure for interpolation, we have:

Interest Rate	Present Value

$$.05 \left\{ x \left\{ \begin{matrix} .15 \\ .? \\ .20 \end{matrix} \right. \quad \left. \begin{matrix} 1055 \\ 1000 \\ 948 \end{matrix} \right\} 55 \right\} 107$$

Setting up the proportion:

$$\frac{x}{.05} = \frac{55}{107}$$

Cross-multiplying:

$$107x = 2.75$$

and hence

$$x = .026$$

Therefore,

$$\text{Rate of return} \approx .15 + .026 = 17.6\%$$

The student should verify that if 16 percent and 18 percent are chosen and the discount factors are rounded to two decimal places, interpolation again gives an estimated rate of return of 17.6 percent.

(*b*) If the firm's cost of capital is 12 percent, it would earn nearly 6 percent over that amount by undertaking this investment. At a cost of capital of 25 percent, it would lose more than 7 percent by undertaking this investment. Note that the B/A ratio computed in the table becomes the profitability index by converting the ratio into percent (i.e., by moving the decimal point two places to the right).

Case III. Present Value of a Uniform Series and Present Value of a Single Payment: PVUS & PVSP

This case combines some of the features of the two previous cases, and hence may be treated briefly.

EXAMPLE: The cost of a new machine is $44,000, and requires an additional $6,000 in working capital due to the added inventory and accounts receivable which will result from the estimated increase in sales. The economic life of the machine is expected to be seven years, at which time the scrap or resale value is predicted to be about $9,000.

Assuming straight-line depreciation, and a forecasted cash flow of $12,000 a year, calculate the rate of return on this investment, using both graphic and formula methods.

SOLUTION: Note that the predicted cash flow is given, and hence need not be derived as was done in the first problem. We may, however, begin by listing the essential factors to be considered.

(1)	Cost of asset	$44,000
(2)	Working capital needed.	6,000
(3)	Total investment	$50,000
(4)	Scrap or resale value	9,000
(5)	Economic life: 7 years	
(6)	Allowed depreciation (1) – (4)	35,000
(7)	Depreciation per year (6) ÷ (5)	5,000
(8)	Capital recovery (2) + (4)	15,000

Graphic Method. The solution is shown in Exhibit 4. Note that on the first trial, the B/A ratio of 1.98 is relatively high or far to the right of the heavy vertical line. Hence, as a second trial, let us try 15 percent. At this discount rate, which gives a discount factor of 4.2 for the uniform portion of the cash flow, and .38 for the single payment portion, the B/A ratio comes to 1.12. This is much closer to the true rate, as can be seen by the chart. Hence, only one more trial should be necessary for a graphic interpolation. Thus, on the third trial of 20 percent, we can then estimate graphically a true rate of return of about 19 percent, as shown by the dashed line on the chart.

Formula Method. When the formula approach is used, we calculate the present value at two different rates of interest, just as in the graphic method

EXHIBIT 4

Calculation of Rate of Return (uniform and nonuniform payments)

A. Present Cost of Investment: *$50,000*

Year	Trial No. 1 0% Interest Cash Flow	Trial No. 2 15% Interest Discount Factor†	 Present Value	Trial No. 3 20% Interest Discount Factor†	 Present Value	Trial No. 4 __% Interest Discount Factor†	 Present Value
1	$12,000 ⎫						
2	12,000						
3	12,000						
4	12,000 ⎬	4.2	$50,400	3.6	$43,200		
5	12,000						
6	12,000						
7	12,000 ⎭						
CR*.....	15,000	.38	5,700	.28	4,200		
B. Total	$99,000		$56,100		$47,400		
Ratio B/A	1.98		1.12		.95		

* CR denotes capital recovery. It includes the forecasted resale or scrap value of the asset, plus the return of additional working capital which may have been needed due to the investment.

† Discount factors may be rounded to nearest hundredth.

Note: The true rate of return is the interest rate at which the present cost of the investment (A) equals the present value of returns on the investment (B), or the interest rate at which $B/A = 1$.

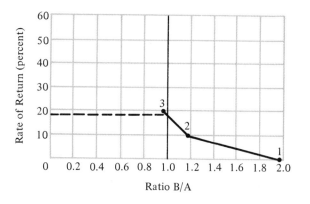

above, and then interpolate algebraically. Thus suppose we decide to start at a trial interest rate of 15 percent.

$$\$12,000 \begin{bmatrix} \text{PVUS} \\ r = 15\% \\ n = 7 \end{bmatrix} + \$15,000 \begin{bmatrix} \text{PVSP} \\ r = 15\% \\ n = 7 \end{bmatrix} = ?$$

$$\$12,000(4.2) + \$15,000(.38) = \$56,100$$

This means that in order to receive the given cash flow, the required investment at 15 percent interest would have to be $56,100 instead of $50,000.

This interest rate, therefore, is too low. Hence we try a higher interest rate, say 20 percent.

$$\$12,000 \begin{bmatrix} \text{PVUS} \\ r = 20\% \\ n = 7 \end{bmatrix} + \$15,000 \begin{bmatrix} \text{PVSP} \\ r = 20\% \\ n = 7 \end{bmatrix} = ?$$

$$\$12,000(3.6) + \$15,000(.28) = \$47,400$$

This means that in order to receive the given cash flow, the required investment at 20 percent interest would have to be $47,400 instead of $50,000. This interest rate, therefore, is too high.

To find the correct interest rate, which is somewhere between 15 percent and 20 percent, we interpolate as follows.

	Interest Rate	Present Value		
.05 $\left\{ x \left\{ \right. \right.$	.15	$56,100 $\left. \right\}$ $6,100	$\left. \right\}$ $8,700
	?	$50,000		
	.20	$47,400		

Setting up the proportion:

$$\frac{x}{.05} = \frac{\$6,100}{\$8,700}$$

Cross multiplying:

$$\$8,700x = \$305$$

and hence

$$x = .035$$

Therefore,

$$\text{Rate of return} \approx .15 + .035 = 18.5\%$$

Note, therefore, that the so-called formula method involves the same calculations as the graphic method, until the interpolation stage is reached. At that point, the graphic technique provides results that are quite adequate for decision purposes, while the algebraic interpolation provides only a slightly more accurate estimate. Either method may be used for most practical problems. The only advantage of the graphic technique is that it provides a good visual indication of the closeness of each approximation to the desired $B/A = 1$ ratio.

SOME ANALYTICAL ASPECTS OF
RATE OF RETURN

The approach employed in previous sections to calculate the yield on an investment in assets is called the *discounted cash flow* method. Despite various short-cut devices that have been developed to give rough approximations to the rate of return, the discounted cash flow method is the only one which produces the correct measure. In order to see why this is so, it is first necessary to review and clarify some technical points which were stated at the beginning of this chapter.

The Common Concept of Rate of Return

Let us recall that most people think of the rate of return on investment as simply the ratio of annual receipts to original cost. Actually, however, this definition is only correct for a special kind of investment, namely a permanent, nondepreciating, nonappreciating asset, producing a periodically uniform income stream. To the extent that the liquidating value or resale value of the asset is, at the time of liquidation or sale, greater or less than the original outlay, the true rate of return will be greater or less than the rate as defined above. Since at the time the investment is made one rarely is able to predict its precise liquidating or resale value, it follows that in the typical case the *true rate of return on an investment to a particular owner cannot be known until the ownership has terminated.* Hence, prior to actual termination of ownership, it is necessary to accept the best estimated rate of return as a reasonable measure of the investment's profitability.

The Technically Correct Concept

What, then, is the technically correct meaning of rate of return? As we have seen, a precise definition is:

> DEFINITION: The *rate of return* on an investment is that interest rate which equates the present value of cash receipts expected to flow from the investment over its lifetime with the present value of all expenditures relating to the investment.

To minimize unnecessarily complicating aspects without doing violence either to the concept or the conclusions, it is usual to assume that the investment involves only an initial outlay of funds. Where additional outlays are expected to be required in the future, however, these are simply discounted down to the present and added to the original outlay to determine the total present value of outlays. Thus, the total cost of the investment may be expressed as:

$$I = C + \frac{O_1}{1 + r} + \frac{O_2}{(1 + r)^2} + \cdots + \frac{O_n}{(1 + r)^n} \tag{1}$$

where C is the initial cost outlay, $O_1, O_2, \ldots, O_n$ are a series of future outlays, I is the sum of all outlays properly discounted to represent the present value of the investment, and r is the interest or discount rate.

The project will also produce a flow of cash earnings over its life which must be similarly discounted down to the present. Thus:

$$I = \frac{R_1}{(1 + r)} + \frac{R_2}{(1 + r)^2} + \cdots + \frac{R_n}{(1 + r)^n} + \frac{S}{(1 + r)^n} \tag{2}$$

where $R_1, R_2, \ldots, R_n$ are a series of cash revenues received at the end of each of the respective periods over the life of the investment, S is the liquidating or salvage value at the end of n periods, and I is the present value of this stream of future receipts.

Equation (1) expresses the present value of the investment in terms of the outlays connected with it; equation (2) expresses the investment's value in terms of the cash revenues that will flow from it. If we select that rate of discount, r, in such a way that I will be the same in both equations, as we have tacitly done above, then r is defined as the *true rate of return on the investment.*

Simplified Version of Rate of Return

For many practical purposes, equations (1) and (2) are too cumbersome to work with, so we can usually make certain simplifying assumptions which, as stated above, do no violence either to the rate of return concept or to the conclusions reached. The typical assumptions are:

1. The original cost is the total cost (no future outlays will be required), so that equation (1) reduces to $I = C$.
2. The cash earnings flow is uniform, so that we simply represent each year's cash flow by a uniform receipt, U.
3. The salvage value is small relative to the original outlay and the present worth of the salvage value, being still less, may be ignored, so that the term $S/(1+r)^n$ in equation (2) drops out.

From the last two of the above assumptions, equation (2) simplifies to:

$$I = \frac{U}{1+r} + \frac{U}{(1+r)^2} + \cdots + \frac{U}{(1+r)^n} \tag{3}$$

and is easily recognized as a geometric progression in which each term differs from the preceding one by a factor of $1/(1+r)$. This enables us to apply the formula for the sum of a geometric progression to equation (3), giving us:

$$I = \frac{\frac{U}{1+r}\left[1 - \left(\frac{1}{1+r}\right)^n\right]}{1 - \frac{1}{1+r}} \tag{4}$$

which simplifies down to:

$$I = \frac{U}{r} - \frac{U}{r}\left(\frac{1}{1+r}\right)^n \tag{5}$$

Equation (5) is to be interpreted as saying that for an investment, I, from which it is estimated that there will be a uniform annual cash flow of U, the true rate of return is that value of r which will equate the total cash inflow with the investment outlay.

For any specific problem to which the foregoing simplifying assumptions do not apply, equation (5) should not be used—obviously. In such cases it will be necessary to find that value of r which equates equation (1) with equation (2). [NOTE: setting the right-hand side of equation (1) equal to the right-hand side of equation (2) constitutes a mathematical expression of the precise meaning of rate of return.] But for analytical purposes, equation (5) is far the more desirable form, and will be applicable to a wide range of practical problems as well.

Rate of Return, Economic Theory, and Decision Making

The rate of return on investment, technically defined by the set of equations (1) and (2), is a well-conceived theoretical concept that goes by various "aliases" in the economic literature. Among the more important of these are *marginal efficiency of capital*, a phrase made famous by John Maynard Keynes, and the closely related concept of *internal rate of return*, used by Kenneth E. Boulding and others. But while it is a concept well founded in theory, it presents many practical problems to anyone desiring to apply it to actual cases, for it involves a great amount of trial and error work if one were to insist on solving for the precise rate of return from any of the applicable equations discussed above. Such precision is actually unnecessary and would, in fact, be misleading, for we must realize that the solution for r depends on the value assigned to (estimated for) U. Hence, the rate of return can itself only be an estimate, so that insistence on a precise solution for r would be unrealistic. It is worth repeating at this point that the *rate of return on an investment can never be stated with precision until the ownership of the investment has been terminated.*

What guides are needed for making correct capital budgeting decisions? Actually, two measures are required: one is the internal rate of return, r; the other is the firm's cost of capital on the project. Given these two choice indicators, economic theory states that profit maximization requires adherence to the following fundamental principle of marginal analysis:

> FUNDAMENTAL PRINCIPLE: All projects whose estimated rate of return exceed the cost of capital are undertaken to the point of the marginal product where the rate of return just equals the cost of capital.

As an alternative and more practical approach to choosing projects, r may be set equal to the firm's cost of capital, and the sum of the cash flows from alternative projects can be discounted by the value of r. Projects may then be ranked according to their present value per dollar of investment. As a further step, greater realism can be incorporated in the ranking process by "weighting" each project with an appropriate risk factor which reflects the probability of realizing the estimated return.

RANKING OF CAPITAL INVESTMENTS

Capital budgeting theory holds that the firm should raise the necessary capital for all nonconflicting proposals that promise to increase the value of the stockholders' shares. In the real world, however, there are many reasons why the firm cannot or should not raise enough capital for all of the investment opportunities that it faces. Hence the decision maker may be confronted not only with conflicting or mutually exclusive proposals (e.g., buy new machines or renovate machine shop) but also with the necessity for capital rationing. In either case, the decision maker's problem is to rank investment proposals in such a way that the available capital may be fully invested in the most profitable combination.

The critical factor in ranking investments is the measurement of the expected return. In the preceding sections of this chapter, we defined two methods of measuring the return, one being the net-present-value method and the other being the rate-of-return method (which some financial writers call the internal-rate-of-return or discounted-rate-of-return method). The relationship between the two methods is illustrated in Exhibit 5.

EXHIBIT 5
Relationship between Net Present Value and Rate of Return

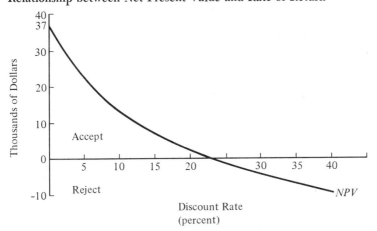

Exhibit 5 depicts evaluation of an investment proposal that will cost $23,000 and that will provide net cash inflows of $6,000 per year for ten years. The *NPV* line traces the net present value of the investment at various discount rates. If we ignore the time value of money, the project will return $60,000 — $23,000 = $37,000. Ignoring the time value of money is equivalent to a discount rate of zero, so we can establish the y-intercept at $37,000. The net-present-value (NPV) line curves downward and to the right, indicating that NPV decreases as the discount rate increases, and the rate of return is measured at the x-intercept where the NPV is zero. In Exhibit 5 the rate of return is 22.7 percent. The zone of acceptance is the area under the NPV line and above the x-axis, where the cost of capital (discount rate) is less than or equal to the rate of return and the corresponding NPV is equal to or greater than zero. The zone of rejection is the area under the NPV line and below the x-axis where the cost of capital (discount rate) is greater than the rate of return and the corresponding NPV is therefore negative.

Despite the harmony between net present value and rate of return illustrated in Exhibit 5, there can be a conflict between conclusions reached via the net-present-value method and those reached via the rate-of-return method, because of implicit assumptions with respect to reinvestment of cash flows. The net-present-value method assumes that cash inflows are reinvested at a rate equal to the cost of capital (or whatever discount rate is chosen as the cutoff criterion), and all projects are evaluated against the same assumed rate of reinvestment. In contrast, the rate-of-return method assumes that cash inflows are reinvested at the rate of return for the project, which means that different projects have different assumed rates of reinvestment. This can lead to conflicting conclusions with respect to ranking of investments, as illustrated in Exhibit 6.

Here in Exhibit 6 we have two different proposals to be ranked in

EXHIBIT 6
Cash Flows for Two Mutually Exclusive Proposals

	Cash Flow	
Year	Project A	Project B
0	$(22,856)	$(22,856)
1	8,500	0
2	8,500	5,000
3	8,500	10,000
4	8,500	15,000
5	8,500	19,516
Total cash inflow	$ 42,500	$ 49,516
Less initial investment	22,856	22,856
Net cash inflow	$ 19,644	$ 26,660
Net present value*	$ 5,636	$ 5,783
Rate of return	25.0%	22.0%

* At discount rate of 15 percent.

order of desirability. Both proposals have the same initial cost, but the magnitude and timing of the cash flows are quite different.

If we evaluate by the net-present-value method, all cash flows in both projects are discounted by the same 15 percent cost of capital, and the implicit assumption is that all cash flows can be reinvested to yield 15 percent. This seems to be an even-handed basis for judgment; and project B clearly is superior, since it has a larger net present value.

If we evaluate by the rate-of-return method, we see that project A has a rate of return of 25 percent, compared to only 22 percent for project B. But this is because we have made the implicit assumption that the cash flows from project A will be reinvested at 25 percent, while the cash flows from project B can be reinvested at only 22 percent. There seems to be no logical reason why the $8,500 received from project A in year 2 would bring 25 percent in another investment while the $5,000 received from project B in the same year would yield only 22 percent. We must conclude, then, that ranking by rate of return is erroneous in this case.

Which method should be used? The answer depends upon what is the appropriate rate of reinvestment for the cash flows. The net-present-value method is theoretically superior because all projects under consideration are rated against the same assumed rate of reinvestment, which should be the cost of capital. However, the cost of capital may be difficult to calculate, and in any case it is predicated upon a specific degree of business and financial risk which may or may not be present in the contemplated investment. In cases where the assumed cost of capital is merely a rough estimate, as when it must be adjusted for extraordinary risk or when it is known that reinvestment can be made at rates higher than the cost of capital, the rate-of-return method may permit a more realistic comparison of projects, particularly those that are nearly equal in magnitude. When there is a wide disparity in the amount of capital required, comparison of rates of return can be misleading. (After all, one percent of something is greater than 100 percent of nothing.) The net-present-value method provides a direct measurement of the amount by which the stockholders' shares may be increased by the proposed investment. This, in essence, is what capital budgeting is all about.

SHORT-CUT METHODS AND BUSINESS PRACTICES

Although either the internal rate-of-return formulation or the cost-of-capital method can be employed to solve the problem of selecting economically worthwhile investments, neither of these approaches have the widest use in business. This is due chiefly to the difficulty on the part of most business executives of comprehending the basic theoretical and computational features that are involved. Consequently, a number of short-cut devices and "rule-of-thumb" techniques have been developed to facilitate capital budgeting decision making. None of these, it should be emphasized, yield the correct answer that is obtained by the discounted cash flow procedure; at best they provide only rough approximations. Nevertheless, one of the more interesting procedures and techniques is described briefly below.

Payout, Payoff, or Payback Period

Business executives have frequently employed a short-cut method of allocating capital funds by estimating the length of time required for the cash earnings on a given investment to return the original cost to the owner. This measure is referred to in various parts of the literature as either the payout, payoff, or payback period. It is used both as a before- and after-tax measure (the latter being the more important), and its expression in terms of cash earnings is a recognition of the fact that depreciation and depletion charges should be included in the earnings figures, that is, earnings are measured before depreciation and depletion.

By way of simplifying the employment of this tool, it is typical to estimate a uniform flow of annual earnings over the life of the project. Hence, if the original investment is represented by I and the uniform (average) annual cash flow is represented by E, the payout period, P, is expressed as:

$$P = I/E$$

Under the conditions stated above it is clear that given the life of the project, profitability will vary inversely with the payout period, and that, given the payout period, profitability will vary directly with the life of the project. It is, therefore, easy enough to understand the insistence of management on short-payout investments. However, the tool is often too blunt to be used in selecting among alternative projects which differ as to cost, payout, and productive life. In such cases, a more precise instrument is needed. It is worth pointing out, at the risk of being obvious, that a short payout is not necessarily coincident with high profitability. Thus, if the productive life of the project is even shorter than the payout period, the return on the investment will be negative; and if the project life and payout period are equal, the invesment return is zero. In either case, an economic loss is incurred. (Why? Can you explain?)

Effect of Corporate Income Tax on Payout. The relationship between the pre-tax and after-tax[1] payout depends both on the tax rate

---

[1] Discussion of an after-tax payout seems meaningful only for projects which are actually profitable, that is, the productive life is greater than the pre-tax payout period.

and the productive life of the project. Representing depreciation by D and assuming a 50 percent tax rate, the after-tax payout becomes:

$$P' = \frac{2I}{E + D}$$

As a limiting value, for projects of perpetual life (or, for practical purposes, extremely long-lived projects such as hydroelectric plants and dams), the depreciation charge approaches zero and the after-tax payout approaches twice the value of the pre-tax payout. Hence, with a 50 percent tax rate, the after-tax payout will, for all depreciable investments, lie somewhere between the pre-tax payout at the lower limit and twice that value at the upper limit.

Approximating the Rate of Return. Although the payout concept as such does not yield an estimate of rate of return, it is nevertheless one of the most widely used notions which businessmen employ in making investment decisions. Surprisingly, however, it can also be adapted as a device for approximating the rate of return. This may be done in the following manner.

Let us first rewrite equation (5) by solving for r. We then get:

$$r = \frac{U}{I} - \frac{U}{I}\left(\frac{1}{1 + r}\right)^n \tag{6}$$

Since U is the uniform annual cash flow, and I is the investment outlay, it is clear that U/I is the *reciprocal of the payout period.* The formula states, then, that the rate of return is the difference between the reciprocal of the payout period and some quantity equal to the product of the payout reciprocal and

$$\left(\frac{1}{1 + r}\right)^n$$

or

$$\frac{1}{(1 + r)^n}$$

It is immediately obvious, especially from the latter ratio, that for large values of n (long-lived projects) the ratio will be small and, therefore, *the rate of return will be approximated by the value of the payout reciprocal.*

For a project whose life is permanent (or practically so, as a hydroelectric dam and other very-long-lived investments) n is, of course, infinitely large and the value of $U/I(1/1 + r)^n$ becomes zero, so that the return on such investments is exactly equal to the reciprocal of the payout period.

It thus seems clear that a rule-of-thumb method employed by business executives for a great many years is actually a reasonably good approximation of the theoretically correct measure. Further, this method has a rather wide applicability to business investment problems, for the rate at which the factor $1/(1+r)^n$ approaches zero, as n becomes large, increases rapidly as r itself increases. Since few business executives would be willing to consider a project offering anything less than 20 percent (before taxes), the payout period (and its reciprocal) becomes, for practical purposes, a very handy tool.

Employment of the tool requires recognition of the fact that the *payout reciprocal is always a maximum estimate of the true rate of return*, for, as pointed out above, the solution for r from equation (6) is obtained by subtracting some quantity from the payout reciprocal. Hence, in using the payout reciprocal as an estimate of the rate of return we are ignoring the quantity which must be subtracted. This quantity may properly be ignored, in theory, only when n is infinitely large; but, in practice, the payout reciprocal would appear to be a very satisfactory estimate of r in all cases where the project life is substantially greater, that is, *more than twice*, the payout period. In most business situations, the projects that are typically given major consideration are those for which the payout period is very short relative to the project life. Therefore, the payout reciprocal can often serve as a useful practical tool for estimating quickly a project's approximate rate of return.

COST OF CAPITAL

As we have seen, a firm's cost of capital is an essential choice criterion for investment decision making. Accordingly, the theory and measurement of cost of capital are of fundamental importance in business finance.

> DEFINITION: The *cost of capital* is the minimum rate of return which a firm requires as a condition for undertaking an investment.

How do we measure a firm's cost of capital? The most widely recommended method is to calculate the weighted average of the current cost of funds to the firm from all sources. This amounts to calculating the cost of debt and the cost of equity, as explained below.

First, let us note a fallacy in reasoning which often arises when calculating cost of capital. Suppose that the cost of debt funds is 6 percent before taxes (or 3 percent after taxes) and the cost of equity money is 15 percent. Then if an investment project under consideration is to be financed by debt, there are some who think that the cost of capital for the project is the cost of debt, because the new project is giving rise to additional debt financing. This thinking is *fallacious* for the following reasons.

In order for a firm to be able to borrow money, that is, engage in debt financing, it must have an adequate equity base. This is necessary because when a firm incurs debt, it also incurs the legal obligation to make periodic interest payments before its earnings can be distributed to owners or stockholders. Hence the existence of an equity base provides a safety cushion for creditors.

Obviously, the greater the proportion of total assets that are financed by debt as compared to equity, the greater the potential economic loss to the owners in case of a decline in earnings. On the other hand, if the firm can earn more on its total assets than the interest rate it pays on its debt, the owners will benefit by receiving higher earnings. This is known in business finance as "trading on the equity," or by the preferred term *leverage*.

Calculating Cost of Capital

This leads to the notion that an "optimum" or "best" financial structure exists for each firm, or at least a range exists within which the proportions of debt and equity, or the debt/equity ratio, is approximately ideal. Accordingly, when a firm incurs additional debt financing, it is thereby using up some of its existing equity base. If it continues, the financial structure (i.e., the entire right-hand side of the balance sheet as may be summarized by the ratio of debt-to-equity) will become unbalanced in favor of debt.

Logically, therefore, it is often recommended that the calculation of cost of capital be based on a weighted average of *all forms of financing* which the firm currently employs, including all forms of debt as well as equity. Further, the estimates should be based on current market costs of debt and equity rather than on historical costs or book values, because decisions for investment are to be made in the present on the basis of current rather than past information. Exhibit 7 illustrates the weighting procedure involved for calculating cost of capital in this way.

EXHIBIT 7
Calculating Cost of Capital

(1)	(2)	(3)	(4)	(5)	(6)
				Current Market Cost	
	Current	Propor-		After	Weighted
Method of	Market	tion of	Before	Taxes	Cost
Financing	Value	Total	Taxes	(50%)	(3) × (5)
Long-term debt	$ 35,000	35%	8%	4%	1.4%
Preferred stock	10,000	10	8	8	0.8
Common stock	30,000	30	20	20	6.0
Retained earnings	25,000	25	18	18	4.5
Totals	$100,000	100%			12.7%

Note from this example that the cost of debt is an expense or deductible item for income tax purposes, whereas the cost of equity is not.[2]
The cost of capital, in this case 12.7 percent, is the minimum that must
be earned on the total assets of any project. Of course, management
may also wish to add a "safety" margin to this estimate, but the current
cost of capital at least indicates the minimum prospective profitability
necessary to undertake a particular investment.

In order to use the weighted average cost of capital to evaluate investment decisions, certain explicit assumptions must be made. It is assumed
that the business-risk complexion of the firm as a whole will not change
as a result of the contemplated projects, that the dividend payout policy
of the firm will not change, and, most critical of all as we shall see
later, that the financing mix will not change from the one used to calculate the firm's cost of capital.

Each method of financing brings some net amount of funds into the
firm (after paying costs such as underwriting) and requires some future
cash outflows, such as interest payments, repayment of principal, or
payment of dividends. The discount rate that equates the present value
of the net income with the present value of the expected outflows is
the explicit cost of the particular source of financing involved. The general equation, then, for the explicit cost of any method of financing
is:

$$I_0 = \frac{C_1}{(1 + k)} + \frac{C_2}{(1 + k)^2} + \cdots + \frac{C_n}{(1 + k)^n} \qquad (7)$$

where I_0 is the net income, or yield, of the method of financing, C_t
is the cash outflow in the period t, $t = 1, 2, \ldots, n$, and k is the discount
rate that expresses the before-tax cost of the method of financing.

Cost of Debt

The cost of debt is determined not only by the rate of interest specified in the debt instruments but also by the method of repayment, the
yield of the debt issue (i.e., the net cash inflow after paying all expenses
of the debt issue), and the assumptions that are made about the tax
rates expected over the life of the debt.

The first step in calculating the cost of debt is to determine the
periodic cash outflows which are the C_t in equation (7). The interpolation technique used in Case II and Case III in the preceding section
can then be used to find the before-tax cost of debt, which is k in
equation (7).

---

[2] Of course, if the firm does not earn a profit, there are no income taxes and
the cost of debt is the full interest rate. Likewise, if the firm earns $25,000 or less,
the tax rate is less and the cost of debt is more.

For example, let us suppose that a firm which normally pays a 48 percent income tax issues one hundred 8 percent bonds, each with a face value of $1,000, all maturing in five years. The payout will be a uniform series of $8,000 per year for five years, plus a single payment of $100,000 to retire the bonds at the end of five years. From present value tables for a discount factor of 8 percent, we calculate the present value of the cash outflow as ($8,000 × 3.99271) + ($100,000 × .68058) = $100,000, which, of course, is the total face value of all the bonds. Thus we see that if the yield is equal to the face value, the cost is equal to the stated interest rate. The after-tax cost in this case would be .08 × (1.0 − .48) = 4.16 percent.

If the yield is less than the face value of the securities, the before-tax cost will be greater than the stated interest rate. For example, if the yield were $95,000, we would interpolate to find the cost of debt as follows:

$$\textit{Discount Rate} \qquad\qquad \textit{Present Value}$$

$$x \left\{ \begin{matrix} .08 \\ ? \\ .10 \end{matrix} \right\} .02 \qquad\qquad \$5,000 \left\{ \begin{matrix} \$100,000 \\ \$\ 95,000 \\ \$\ 92,428 \end{matrix} \right\} \$7,572$$

At a discount rate of 8 percent the present value of the cash outflow would be $100,000, as previously calculated. At a discount rate of 10 percent, the present value of the cash outflow would be 3.791 × $8,000 + .621 × $100,000 = $92,428. The yield we seek lies between these two figures; therefore the discount rate lies between .08 and .10 (See the tables in Appendix A and B.)

Setting up the proportion:

$$\frac{x}{.02} = \frac{\$5,000}{\$7,572}$$

Cross-multiplying:

$$\$7,572x = \$100$$

and hence

$$x = .0132$$

Therefore, the before-tax cost of debt = .08 + .0132 = 9.32 percent, and the after-tax cost is 9.32 × .52 = 4.85 percent.

If the yield is greater than the face value, the before-tax cost of debt will be less than the stated interest rate. For example, if the yield were $105,000, the before-tax cost of debt would be 6.81 percent, and the after-tax cost would be 3.54 percent.

In the case of mortgages and serial bonds, periodic payments are made on the principal as well as on the interest. For example, suppose that one hundred 8 percent serial bonds yield $95,000 and are scheduled to be retired at the rate of 20 bonds per year. The cash outflow would be:

Cash Outflow	Year				
	1	*2*	*3*	*4*	*5*
Principal	$20,000	$20,000	$20,000	$20,000	$20,000
Interest	8,000	6,400	4,800	3,200	1,600
Total outflow	$28,000	$26,400	$24,800	$23,200	$21,600

The present value of the cash outflow at 8 percent discount is: $28,000 × .92593) + ($26,400 × .85734) + ($24,800 × .79383) + $23,200 × .73503) + ($21,600 × .68058) = $100,000. At a discount rate of 11 percent, the present value is $92,887. Then by interpolation, the before-tax cost of debt is 10.11 percent, and the after-tax cost is 5.26 percent.

Cost of Preferred Stock

Although some of the current literature on the theory of finance classifies some preferred stock as debt and some as equity, preferred stock actually stands somewhere in between, with features of both debt and equity. Like bonds or mortgage loans, preferred stock specifies a rate of return to the investor that is fixed as a percentage of the face (par) value of the instrument. Unlike debt, however, the payment of these dividends is not a legal requirement. If the company falls upon hard times, the directors can pass the preferred dividend without danger of being forced into bankruptcy.

The tax collector regards payment of dividends on preferred stock as a distribution of earnings rather than a tax-deductible expense. Thus it is that although preferred stock provides financial leverage, the cost is much higher than for debt as long as the firm is profitable. On the other hand, the financial risk of debt is largely avoided when preferred stock is used instead.

In determining the cost of preferred stock financing, we assume that the directors intend to pay the preferred dividends on time, and we therefore treat preferred stock as a perpetual debt. The cost, then, is simply the annual dividend divided by the yield. For example, if a firm obtains a yield of $98 per share on an issue of par $100, 7 percent preferred stock, the cost is $7/$98 = 7.14 percent. If the preferred stock has a call option and the company intends to call it in after some specific time, equation (7) may be used to calculate the cost.

Nature of Equity Capital

Equity capital consists of the aggregation of funds obtained from the sale of common stock plus the retained earnings of the firm. The market price of a common stock is based upon the investors' expectations and attitude toward risk. Each investor has in mind some minimum rate of return (from dividends and capital gains) that constitutes his[3] own threshold of investment; and he will invest when the expected rate of return is at or above his threshold, and disinvest when it falls below. Thus the cost of equity capital may be defined as the minimum rate of return that will leave the market price of the common stock unchanged.

The rate of return upon which the investor establishes his threshold reflects both his perception of the risk involved and his attitude toward risk. His perception is based upon information emanating from the firm's investment and financing policies and upon his knowledge about the nature of the business. His attitude toward risk, however, is the result of his own utility function, which is based upon the familiar economic concept of the marginal utility of income. The individual's utility (i.e., degree of satisfaction) comes, of course, not from the income itself, but from what it can buy.

Risk and the Marginal Utility of Income

Conceptually, there are three different ways in which utility might relate to income, as depicted on Exhibit 8.

Looking at curve A on Exhibit 8 we see that an increase in income from I_1 to I_2 produces an increase in utility from U_1 to U_2. An increase of the same size in income, from I_2 to I_3, produces a still larger increase in utility from U_2 to U_3. Thus curve A describes a situation where marginal utility increases as income rises. This reflects the case of the compulsive gambler, who places a higher utility on the dollar won than he does on the dollar lost. The rising curve thus depicts the abnormal behavior of a risk seeker.

Curve B of Exhibit 8 is a straight line, indicating that the marginal utility of a dollar lost is exactly the same as of a dollar gained. This curve also reflects pathological behavior. The individual with such a utility curve would be a miser who values money for its own sake rather than for what it would buy. The slope of the line indicates the individual's attitude toward risk. The line B has a slope of 1, and is therefore neutral toward risk. If the slope is greater than 1, as in line B', it would indicate that the individual is inclined to seek risk for the sake of acquir-

---

[3] Masculine pronouns are being used for "investor" for succinctness and are intended to refer to both females and males.

EXHIBIT 8
Utility versus Income

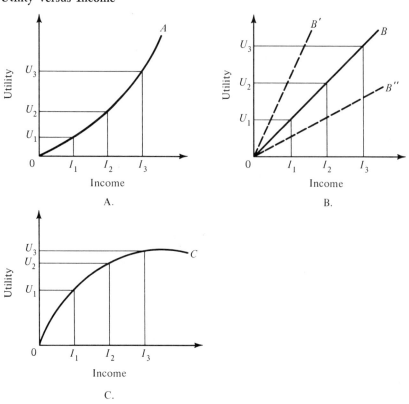

A.

B.

C.

ing money. If the slope is less than 1, as in line B'', it would indicate that the individual is still a miser, but a more cautious one.

Curve C in Exhibit 8 depicts the utility function of a typical investor. His total utility increases as his income increases, but at a decreasing rate: that is, his marginal utility decreases. Eventually in accordance with the law of diminishing returns, the curve will level off and may even turn downward. Can you think of a situation where the curve might turn downward?[4]

Exhibit 8C depicts three equal changes in income, from 0 to I_1, from I_1 to I_2, and from I_2 to I_3, and the corresponding changes in utility.

---

[4] In terms of money, it is unlikely that the curve would ever turn downward. In terms of what money can buy, however, it may be that additional possessions become more hindrance than help. For example, if a person already has one car, an additional car of identical make and model would serve no useful purpose, but would impose the burden of maintenance, insurance, and the other costs of ownership. Acquisition of the additional car would be a disutility, causing the curve to turn downward.

Within this region the slope of the curve, which indicates the marginal utility of income, is decreasing. This means that the utility of a dollar gained is less than the utility of a dollar lost. This will cause the investor to be averse to risk to a greater or lesser degree, depending upon his position on the curve. If he is in the region $0 - I_1$, the utility to be gained is much greater than if he is in the region $I_1 - I_2$. Therefore, he will be less willing to take a chance if he is in the region $I_1 - I_2$, and still less willing if he is in the region $I_2 - I_3$.

The investor's aversion to risk is manifested in many ways. Grade AAA bonds sell for more than grade B bonds; investors diversify either by individual portfolios or by investing in mutual funds; people deposit their funds in insured savings accounts at 4 or 5 percent even at a time when high-grade corporate bonds are yielding 7 percent or more; and people buy all kinds of insurance.

Why, then, if they are averse to risk, do investors put their money into common stocks? The answer is that an investor will not do so unless he expects to receive a risk premium.

To illustrate the concept of risk premium, suppose an investor has a utility function as in Exhibit 9, and he is asked to bet $1000 on the

EXHIBIT 9
Utility of Bet with No Risk Premium

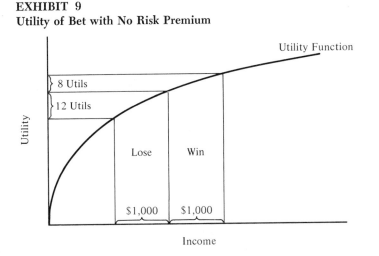

flip of a coin at even odds; thus, if he wins he gets $1,000, if he loses he pays $1,000. Should he take the bet? To get the answer, let us look at Exhibit 9.

Exhibit 9 illustrates an investment without risk premium. If the investor wins $1,000, he gains 8 utils of utility; but if he loses, he loses 12 utils. In other words, the utility of winning is .008 per dollar, while the disutility of losing is .012. Since the probability of winning or losing is the same (.5), the expected value in utils or average return is

.008(.5) — .012(.5) = —.002. Since the expected value is negative, it is clear that the investor should not take this bet.

Now let us suppose that the same investor is offered a premium if he will take the bet. If he loses, he loses $1000; but if he wins, he wins $1800. Should he take the bet? Let us look at Exhibit 10.

EXHIBIT 10
Utility of a Bet with Risk Premium

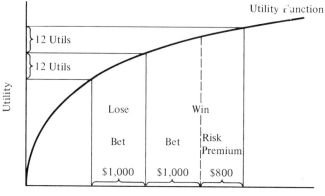

Income

The answer depends upon the investor's utility function. As the curve is drawn in Exhibit 10, a loss of $1,000 will bring a disutility of 12 utils, while a win of $1,800 will provide a utility of 12 utils. The expected value of the bet then is .012(.5) — .012(.5) = 0, meaning that the investor may be indifferent to the bet. If the risk premium is increased, he will accept the bet; but if the risk premium is decreased, he will not accept.

Now let us suppose that the same investor is offered another bet for $500, again on the flip of a coin. Will he also require an $800 premium on the $500 bet? This time we look at Exhibit 11.

Exhibit 11 shows that the loss of $500 for this investor involves the loss of 5 utils. In order to win 5 utils the investor requires a risk premium of $100. But this is only one eighth of the risk premium required for the $1,000 bet. That is to say that when the bet is increased two times, the risk premium demanded is increased eight times. How can this be?

The answer, of course, lies in the shape of the investor's utility function or curve. The risk is measured by the dispersion of possible outcomes. Since the dispersion of ±$1000 is twice as great as the dispersion of ±$500, it would seem that the risk should be twice as great. But we have seen in Exhibits 10 and 11 that when a risk premium is added to the winning side of the bet, the dispersion of the possible outcomes is changed, hence the risk is also changed.

EXHIBIT 11
Risk Premiums for a Smaller Bet

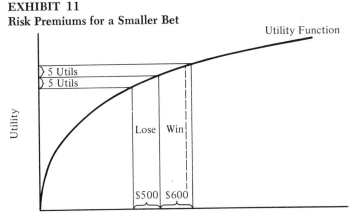

The investor's attitude toward risk depends first of all upon the shape of his utility curve, and secondly upon his current position on the curve, which is determined by his current income. If his current income is low, his marginal utility of income (measured by the slope of the curve) is high, and he will accept risk for a much lower premium than when his income is at a higher level.

To a firm, the risk premium may be viewed as having two components, a business risk and a financial risk. Business risk is always present to some degree, since no business is guaranteed success. The degree of risk depends upon the nature of the business and the demonstrated skill of its management. Certain types of businesses are inherently more risky than others. Within any type of business, an investor would usually perceive more risk in a newly established firm than in one with a longer record of earnings. On the other hand, a long-established firm whose products or business methods have become outdated may present a high degree of risk.

Financial risk is incurred whenever the firm includes long-term debt in its capital structure. Earnings must go first to payment of interest on the debt. If the firm is unable to make these payments, it may be forced into bankruptcy. To a lesser degree, financial risk is also incurred by the sale of preferred stock, since preferred stock dividends must be paid before the equity investor can receive any return on his investment.

Cost of Equity Capital

The investor makes his decision to invest, hold, or disinvest, based on the market price of the common stock. In return for the price of a share of common stock, the investor expects to receive a future stream of income composed of periodic dividends and, finally, the market price of the stock when he chooses to sell it. Since these increments of income are to be received in the future, they must be discounted to reflect the time value of money. The market price of common stock, then, is simply the present value of the expected value of a future stream of income.[5]

To show why this is so, suppose that an investor buys a share of common stock at a price of $100, expecting to receive a dividend of $5 at the end of one year, and then be able to sell the stock for $110. His return will be the gain over his original investment, $15, divided by the investment, which gives a return of 15 percent. If we substitute the data into equation (2) and solve for r, we get the same answer.

Now let us suppose that the investor decides to keep the stock for two years before he sells, basing his decision on information or belief that the second-year dividend will be $6.26, and that the price of the stock at the end of two years will be $120. When we substitute into equation (2) and solve for r, we again get r = 15 percent. This illustrates that the price of the stock is the present value of a discounted stream of dividends plus a discounted terminal value. But the terminal value is just the price that another investor is willing to pay, which is a discounted stream of dividends plus a discounted terminal value, and so on. Thus we see that the price of a stock is based on a stream of earnings in perpetuity.

If the company's dividends are expected to grow at some constant rate, then the dividend in any period is equal to the most recent dividend multiplied by the compound growth factor. By manipulation of equation (2) it can be shown that the cost of equity capital is the ratio of the next expected dividend to the current price, plus the rate of growth; however, this assumes that dividends will grow at a constant rate forever. There may be firms where this is a reasonable expectation, but in most cases the rate of growth can be expected to taper off from time to time. If both the timing and the magnitude of changes in the growth pattern can be estimated, then equation (2) can be used to derive the cost of equity capital.

But what about companies that pay no dividends? Not only do their stocks often sell well, but sometimes for very high prices. How does this happen? The answer, of course, is that investors expect a high

---

[5] Of course, the market price of a given stock fluctuates from day to day. These fluctuations are caused by trading activity in which buyers buy and sellers sell for reasons which have nothing to do with investors' valuations of the firm, such as taking capital gains or losses that will affect buyers' and sellers' personal tax positions. Over a period of time, however, the *trend* of the stock's price will reflect the expectations of all those who *hold* the stock as well as of those who have bought or sold the stock.

terminal value, high enough that they are willing to forego dividends. In the meantime the company is reinvesting its earnings, and, hopefully, this will mean greater earnings in the future. How can the cost of capital be estimated for a company that pays no dividends? One way to estimate the return that investors expect is by examining the growth in the market price of the stock. For example, if the stock price has grown over several years at a compound rate of 10 percent and this growth is expected to continue, one might accept 10 percent as the cost of equity capital.

Earnings-Price Ratio. The earnings-price ratio is just one of many pieces of information that investment analysts may use to evaluate a stock. In two special situations, the earnings-price ratio may reflect the firm's cost of equity capital. The first case is that of the firm whose earnings per share are expected to remain constant and which pays out all earnings as dividends. The other case is that of a firm which does not have investment opportunities yielding more than the cost of equity capital, but can invest a constant proportion of its earnings in projects that provide a perpetual return just equal to the cost of equity capital. In situations where the investors expect growth in the corporation's earnings, the earnings-price ratio is a very uncertain measure of the firm's cost of equity capital, since earnings-price ratios of less than the yield on government bonds are quite common.

Cost of New Stock Issues. When a new issue of stock is sold, the net yield to the firm will be somewhat less than the market price of the stock because of flotation costs. Consequently, the cost of equity capital on new financing will be somewhat higher than the market would indicate. Flotation costs include the difference between the sale price and the proceeds received by the company (called the underwriting spread), registration expenses, and other out-of-pocket costs such as printing and postage.

Cost of Retained Earnings

Although today it is recognized that the use of retained earnings is not cost-free as some writers have contended in the past, there still is much controversy over the measurement of the cost. Some authorities feel that the cost of equity capital should be adjusted downward to reflect the tax effect, but a strong case can be made for simply using the cost of equity capital as the cost of retained earnings.

There is general agreement that the cost of retained earnings is an opportunity cost equal to the value of the dividend foregone by the stockholders. This cost may be defined as the rate of return that permits the shareholder to be indifferent between (*a*) a cash dividend payment and (*b*) the investment project financed by retained earnings.

In a world free of taxes, we might reason that if the firm paid out all of its earnings as dividends, then the only way the firm could attract these earnings back into its capital structure would be to sell stock. The price of the stock would be determined by the cost of equity capital as previously defined, hence the cost of retained earnings is just the cost of equity capital. However, there are those who point out that even in a world without taxes, there still are brokerage fees. Therefore the stockholder could not be indifferent unless the cost of equity capital were somewhat higher than the cost of retained earnings. More precisely, the cost of retained earnings would be the cost of equity capital multiplied by 1 minus the brokerage rate. For example, if the brokerage rate is 1 percent, the cost of retained earnings would be 99 percent of the cost of equity capital.

In the real world, however, there are taxes as well as brokerage fees and they are levied at different rates. The personal income tax rate on ordinary income is twice as much as the rate on capital gains; dividends, with the exception of a small exemption, are taxed as ordinary income. It can be shown that the cost of retained earnings is the cost of equity capital multiplied by the ratio $(1 - t_p)/(1 - t_g)$, where t_p is the personal income tax rate on ordinary income and t_g is the personal income tax rate on capital gains. For example, if the investor were paying 32 percent personal income tax and 1 percent brokerage fees, the cost of retained earnings would be $(1 - .32)/(1 - .16) \times (1 - .01) = 80$ percent of the cost of equity capital.

This is a very neat solution except for the problem of determining the composite personal tax rate for all stockholders. Rough estimates suggest that for the average investor the personal tax rates are 40 percent on personal income and 20 percent on capital gains, but there can be very large institutional stockholders who are tax-exempt. In very small firms or closely held corporations it might be possible to ascertain the tax rate by questioning all stockholders. In large publicly held firms this would be an impossible task.

Another approach to evaluation of the cost of retained earnings is the external-yield criterion. In this approach, the cost of retained earnings is defined as the opportunity foregone to invest in other firms of similar risk. This criterion is not affected by, and need not be concerned with, personal tax rates, as it simply measures what the firm could get by direct investment. The external-yield criterion is economically justifiable and can be applied consistently. As a general rule, however, since we assume equilibrium in the marketplace between risk and return, we would expect the external yield to be the cost of equity capital.

Cost of Depreciation Funds

Depreciation represents the recovery over a period of time of cash previously invested in depreciable assets, and these funds are not free.

Like retained earnings, they have an opportunity cost, and the opportunity cost of depreciation funds is the overall cost of capital. To illustrate why this is so, suppose that a firm begins with $100,000 from common stock, borrows an additional $100,000, and invests the entire $200,000 in depreciable assets. The firm's beginning balance sheet is as shown in Exhibit 12.

EXHIBIT 12

Assets

Depreciable assets.	$200,000
Total Assets.	$200,000

Liabilities and Equities

Debt	$100,000
Common stock	100,000
Total Liabilities and Equities	$200,000

Now suppose that the firm depreciates its assets on a straight-line basis over a life of ten years. Suppose also that during the first year of operation, the firm's net income is zero. The balance sheet at the end of the first year would be as shown in Exhibit 13.

EXHIBIT 13

Assets

Cash		$ 20,000
Depreciable assets.	$200,000	
Less allowance for depreciation	20,000	180,000
Total Assets.		$200,000

Liabilities and Equities

Debt	$100,000
Common stock	100,000
Total Liabilities and Equities	$200,000

Now suppose that there are no investment opportunities available and that the firm's policy is to distribute excess cash by reducing debt and equity in the same proportion in which they were used to acquire the assets. Since the original proportion of debt and equity was 50/50, they would pay off $10,000 of the debt and buy back $10,000 worth of common stock at the current market price. But the cost of repaying the debt and buying back the stock is just the weighted average cost of capital. We conclude, then that the opportunity cost of depreciation funds is simply the firm's overall cost of capital. Therefore, depreciation funds need not be considered in computation of the firm's cost of capital.

Summary

The problem of capital budgeting is to provide management with guides for investing in fixed assets. Essentially, the procedure may be summarized as follows.

1. Estimate the cash flow from the investment. This includes earnings after taxes, plus depreciation, plus capital recovery (which is made up of working capital recovered, plus net receipts from sale of the asset).
2. Calculate the rate of return. This is the interest rate which equates the present value of the investment with its present cost.
3. Calculate the cost of capital. This is the weighted cost of the financial structure that is appropriate for the particular project. A project with greater risk and uncertainty would entail more equity financing (at a higher cost); a project whose returns are fairly safe or relatively certain can be financed more by debt (at a lower cost).
4. Rank the investment opportunities when alternate opportunities exist and a decision must be made to select from among these alternatives. Considerations in ranking investments are the rate of return, the present value of the discounted cash flows, the present value per dollar invested (also called the profitability index, or benefit-cost ratio), and the degree of risk.

The rate of return on an investment is defined as the interest rate which equates the present value of the investment with the present cost of the investment. The only scientific way of measuring this rate is by the discounted cash flow (DCF) method.

The DCF approach employs either of two techniques:

1. Measure the rate of return by finding for each project the discounting rate which makes the present value of the stream of net receipts just equal to the present value of the outlay stream, or
2. Discount cash flows of all projects at a uniform rate, usually the company's cost of capital, and rank the various investment alternatives by their present value per dollar of investment.

Both techniques require that future economic cost, revenue, and taxes be forecasted, and that these data be arranged in a year-by-year timetable of net cash flows extending into the future for the life of the project. The timetable thus reveals for each year the net after-tax effect on the company's cash receipts and payments. No distinction is made between capitalized outlays and current operating transactions except to the extent that these affect corporate income taxes. Finally, the net cash flows are discounted, yielding a measure of rate of return or of present value which then becomes the choice indicator or criterion for comparing—and accepting or rejecting—particular investment proposals.

Although the DCF method is the only scientific way of measuring rate of return, short-cut or rule-of-thumb devices may be useful either because they give rough approximations or because they actually employ the cash discount method with some built-in assumptions. One widely used short-cut approach is the payback method which measures the number of years required to recover the original investment by earnings or savings before depreciation but after taxes. Thus if an investment of $1,500 is expected to earn or save $500 a year before depreciation but after taxes, the payback period is three years. Various surveys have found that well over half of all industrial firms employ the payback method for investment decisions, usually requiring short paybacks of a few years in order to permit a quick recovery of investment. A chief criticism of the payback method is that it fails to account for the interest factor. However, it can be demonstrated that the *reciprocal of the payback period approaches the correct rate of return as the project life increases beyond twice the payback period.*

Risk in capital budgeting arises from the fact that all calculations are based upon estimates of future events. Variability of cash flows, both income and outgo, is to be expected, and the actual results may be quite different from the planning estimate. Analysis of the risk is possible by means of a number of approaches, one of which involves statistical estimation using probability distributions.

PROBLEMS

1. How do you distinguish between operating expenditures and capital expenditures, and how are these distinctions reflected on the company's financial statements?

2. Which of the following, if any, should be added to, or deducted from, the cost of a new machine in deciding whether to purchase it? (Disregard all tax considerations.)

   a. A $2,000 fee paid to a consultant for advice on whether the machine should be acquired or not.

   b. The cash salvage value of the old machine is $1,000.

   c. The original cost of the old machine was $5,000, and its book value is now $3,000.

   d. Removal of the old machine costs $400.

   e. Installation costs on the new machine are $300.

   f. The cost of training operators for the new machine will be $600.

   g. An additional investment of $6,000 in accounts receivable and inventory will be needed.

3. Under what conditions might a firm be better off to select a project with a rapid payback than one with the highest rate of return?

4. What critical areas or problems should be analyzed when calculating the rate of return for a prospective capital investment?

5. What factors other than rate-of-return analysis should be considered in determining capital equipment expenditures?

6. Calculate each of the following:
   a. The present value of $7,000 to be received at the end of five years, discounted at 12 percent.
   b. The present value of receiving $3,000 a year for six years, discounted at 10 percent.
   c. The present value of $4,000 a year for five years, and an additional $1,000 at the end of five years, both discounted at 6 percent.

7. Concrete Products Company, a large manufacturer of concrete building materials, needed $240,000 worth of aggregates (at then current prices) over a period of two years. They learned that the Acme Sand and Gravel Company owned deposits which were more than enough for their needs. However, Acme was a small company without enough equipment to produce at the required rate and without enough capital to expand. In order to secure the necessary supply of raw materials, Concrete Products agreed to supply Acme with the necessary capital by paying for one year's supply in advance, discounted at 12 percent. Acme in return agreed to provide a constant daily flow of sand and gravel into the Concrete Products plant, with monthly billings against the prepaid amount. The contract was signed and Concrete Products paid Acme $107,160.

   At the end of the first year Concrete Products, wanting to insure itself against a price increase, again proposed to make advance payment of $107,160 for the second year's supply, but Acme's new controller objected. "The 12 percent discount rate is reasonable," he told Acme's president, "but you were cheated on the payment for the first year and you shouldn't let yourself be cheated again. The correct amount is $112,550."

   Explain the controller's objection.

8. The XYZ Company is considering two mutually exclusive projects, each requiring an initial investment of $15,000, and each lasting for five years. The estimated cash inflows are as follows:

| Project | Period | | | | |
	1	2	3	4	5
A	5,000	5,000	5,000	5,000	5,000
B	–	5,000	12,000	8,000	5,000

   The firm's cost of capital is 20 percent. Find: (a) the net present value, (b) the rate of return, and (c) the profitability index for each proposal.

9. The Jason Company is considering replacing one of its old machines with a new and more efficient one. The old machine is still in good working condition and will last, physically, for at least 20 more years.

   The new machine, delivered and installed, costs $10,000, and is expected to save $1,900 annually in direct costs as compared to the old machine. The new machine has a ten-year economic life, with zero salvage value.

The Jason Company can borrow money at 10 percent, but it does not expect to negotiate a loan for this particular purpose. The management of the company requires a return of at least 20 percent before taxes on this type of investment. Disregard all taxes for the time being.

a. Assuming that the old machine has a zero book value and a zero salvage value, should the company buy the new machine?

b. Suppose the present machine, now four years old, originally cost $8,000 and has been depreciating at a straight-line rate of 10 percent. Its present *book value*, therefore, is equal to original cost less accumulated depreciation, or $8,000 − $3,200 = $4,800. Its salvage value, however, is zero. Should the Jason Company buy the new machine?

c. Suppose, in Part (*b*), that the salvage value is currently $3,000, but will decline to zero if held for another ten years. Should the company purchase the new machine?

d. What if the annual savings were cut in half and the economic life were doubled? In other words, if the annual savings were $950 for 20 years, should the company purchase the new machine? (Assume everything else is the same as in Part (*a*) above.)

e. Assume now that the Jason Company must pay a 50 percent tax, that it uses straight-line depreciation, and that the company's cost of capital is 10 percent after taxes. If the facts are the same as for Part (*a*), should the company buy the new machine?

10. The London Shipping Company is considering investing $28,000 in new conveying equipment. It is estimated that the new equipment will result in direct labor savings of $11,000 annually over the ten-year life of the equipment, and that an additional $10,000 in working capital will be required which will be entirely recovered at the end of the ten-year period. If the company requires a 20 percent minimum return on investment, should it go ahead with this project? (Disregard tax and depreciation considerations, and assume a zero salvage value.)

11. The Steadfast Corporation maintains a capital structure of 40 percent debt and 60 percent equity, and pays a 50 percent tax rate. At the present time, the costs of raising various amounts of debt and equity financing are given below:

Total Amount	Cost of Debt Portion	Cost of Equity Portion
$100,000	10.00%	15.00%
200,000	10.50	16.00
300,000	11.00	17.00
400,000	12.00	18.00
500,000	14.00	20.00
600,000	16.00	22.00

a. What is the overall cost of capital if $300,000 is raised?

b. If a project promises an after-tax return of 12 percent, under what conditions would it be adopted?

REFERENCES

BAUMOL, WILLIAM J., and MALKIEL, BURTON G.   "The Firm's Optimal Debt-Equity Combination and the Cost of Capital." *The Quarterly Journal of Economics,* vol. 81, no. 4 (November 1967), pp. 547–78.

BAUMOL, WILLIAM J., and QUANDT, RICHARD E.   "Investment and Discount Rates under Capital Rationing—A Programming Approach." *The Economic Journal,* vol. 75, no. 299 (June 1965), pp. 317–29.

BERNHARD, RICHARD H.   "Mathematical Programming Models for Capital Budgeting—A Survey, Generalization, and Critique." *Journal of Financial and Quantitative Analysis,* vol. 4, no. 2 (June 1969), pp. 111–58.

BIERMAN, HAROLD, JR., and SMIDT, SEYMOUR   *The Capital Budgeting Decision,* 2d ed. New York: The Macmillan Co., 1966.

HERTZ, DAVID B.   "Investment Policies That Pay Off." *Harvard Business Review,* vol. 46, no. 1 (January–February 1968), pp. 96–108.

———   "Risk Analysis in Capital Investment." *Harvard Business Review,* vol. 42, no. 1 (January–February 1964), pp. 95–106.

MAO, JAMES C. T.   "Survey of Capital Budgeting: Theory and Practice." *Journal of Finance,* vol. 25, no. 2 (May 1970), pp. 349–60.

———   "The Internal Rate of Return as a Ranking Criterion." *Engineering Economist,* vol. 11, no. 4 (Winter 1966), pp. 1–3.

QUIRIN, G. DAVID   *The Capital Expenditure Decision.* Homewood, Ill: Richard D. Irwin, Inc., 1967.

SOLOMON, EZRA   "Alternative Rate of Return Concepts and Their Implications for Utility Regulation." *The Bell Journal of Economics and Management Science,* vol. 1, no. 1 (Spring 1970), pp. 65–81.

THIERAUF, ROBERT J., and GROSSE, RICHARD A.   *Decision-Making Through Operations Research.* New York: John Wiley & Sons, Inc., 1970.

VAN HORNE, JAMES C.   *Financial Management and Policy.* 2d ed. Englewood Cliffs, N.J.: Prentice-Hall, Inc., 1971.

chapter 15

Capital Management and
Financial Policy

A good deal of material has been written on the development of concepts and techniques related to the computational or "quantitative" aspects of capital budgeting. Much less, however, has been said about the "qualitative" considerations—namely, the overall philosophies and attitudes that should shape a sound financial policy relating to capital management. Yet, this aspect of capital budgeting is undoubtedly the most interesting—and perhaps the most valuable—to top management.

Apparently, any discussion of capital management must relate in various ways to the extremely important and controversial notion of "cost of capital," since this is a concept which, either explicitly or implicitly, permeates the literature in the field. Accordingly, we shall proceed by formulating and integrating a number of ideas—some old and some new—on the basis of which an overall financial policy relating to capital management is then constructed.

ESTABLISHING THE ACCEPTANCE CRITERION

The measurement of a project's rate of return, or establishing its superiority or inferiority relative to other projects by whatever measure one might choose, is only one important step toward the construction of the final capital budget. Thus, having determined that the rate of return on a project is, say, 15 percent, do we accept it or not? It would be manifestly imprudent to rely on some intuitive figure which "sounds" good or "seems" attractive, and so it becomes necessary to consider the establishment of some standard that will divide projects into two broad groups: those that are acceptable and those that are not.

Equilibrium of Supply and Demand

It was the great British economist Alfred Marshall who once depicted the forces of supply and demand as the two blades of the scissors, both of which were necessary for performing the function of determining equilibrium price. The analogy might be adapted to the problem under discussion. Thus, if the various proposed projects were arrayed in descending order according to their estimated rates of return, together with the dollar amounts of capital required by the respective projects, we would then have constructed what constitutes the firm's *demand* schedule for capital. The problem would then be to determine a capital *supply* schedule; and, theoretically, the intersection point would indicate the desired volume of investment to be undertaken. All projects promising a return in excess of the intersection rate would be accepted; those with estimated rates less than the critical rate would be rejected.

As nice and as neat as this approach seems to be, it is not readily useful for the problem at hand. The reason is that it is extremely difficult to establish a uniquely determinable capital supply schedule that will intersect the demand schedule at always the same point, which could then be accepted as the "cutoff rate." In other words, the supply of funds available to the firm (currently and potentially) is conditioned by a vast complex of factors: dividend policy, the firm's asset and liability structure, capital projects instituted in the past, current profitability, and many other factors which, in greater or lesser degree, are subsumed under the foregoing list. It is, therefore, an arbitrary oversimplification of the case to assume a given availability of capital (internal or otherwise) and to apply this (usually as a vertical supply curve) to the demand curve, with a resulting "equilibrium" cutoff rate. Since the firm's supply of liquid capital can be altered at will by changes in plans respecting debt retirement, dividend policy, working capital position, sales expansion, asset conversions, and so on, it is clearly necessary to exercise a great deal of precaution in designating the firm's capital supply.

The Potential Internal Supply of Capital. To any firm, the full potential internal supply of liquid capital consists of cash plus the funds that can be acquired by the sale of all other assets, less those conversions which result in the creation of accounts receivable. From this total must be deducted currently maturing cash obligations as representing a preemptive claim on the cash fund. As a practical matter, the internal cash supply to be made available for the acquisition of new assets is substantially less than that defined above, for it is necessary to reduce this sum by that portion which will be "reinvested" in existing assets— that is, that sum represented by the existing assets which will *not* be sold.

The foregoing comments might well seem to the pragmatic decision maker to take on the appearance of a flight of fancy, for one is naturally inclined toward the attitude that a firm's operating assets are hardly ever seriously considered as a source of cash (except through their gradual conversion in the normal business process). While this is generally true, it is so for reasons which do not necessarily negate the above considerations.

Theoretically, the decision to "reinvest" in any of the firm's existing assets should be taken only if the present value of their anticipated revenues exceeds the cash value of their current sale. Otherwise it would pay to exchange existing assets into others which, for the same investment, will produce a higher capitalized revenue stream. The fact that firms ordinarily do "reinvest" in existing assets might be interpreted as implicit recognition of this fact, though it is unlikely that specific thought along the lines suggested here are ever pursued, except in unusual circumstances.

Thus, in late 1947 and in 1958, the Penn Texas Corporation engaged in a liquidation of several divisions of the company in order to meet debts incurred in its unsuccessful attempt in 1957 to wrest control of Fairbanks Morse & Co. This is clearly a case of "unusual circumstances."

In practice, however, an explicit calculation is usually not necessary because the assets in question are frequently too specialized (or involve dismantling costs or other substantial cash leakages) to provide, when sold, sufficient cash which, through investment in other assets, will enhance the firm's present value. Such considerations are nevertheless quite realistic and may play a vital role in decision making. For example, the airline companies have for years relied on asset conversions as a major source of investible funds, and the capital gains from such sales have, in many instances, contributed the lion's share of net income. (This is, however, an extreme example of equipment replacement economy.)

Before leaving this particular topic, let us be sure we have conveyed the opinion that while it is probably a theoretically sound approach, the supply-and-demand technique is not a good workable method for solving the problem of determining an acceptance criterion. The method, it seems, is so capricious for this purpose that no two independent investigators are likely to arrive at the same solution for any given situation. In fact, it appears likely that no method can be expected to give precise and predictable results, but at least one of the techniques discussed below offers a promise of greater uniformity and accuracy.

Allotted Funds

Many firms meet the problem under discussion by allocating, either arbitrarily or by some simple "formula," a specified sum to be expended for capital purposes during a given fiscal period. Hence, the "allotted funds" method may embrace as wide a variety of techniques as there are firms that employ it.

To the extent that the allocations are arbitrarily determined, it is clear that a correct decision will be made only by coincidence, for no arbitrary allotment can possibly result in the establishment of an optimum cutoff point. And where allocations have been tied to some "formula," here too the optimum cutoff can be attained only by coincidence.

The major weakness of this approach is that the amount of funds allocated to the capital budget is predetermined—or tied to some consideration which has no direct connection with the contributions that the proposed projects are expected to make to the enterprise. Thus, many firms adopt some arbitrary dividend payout ratio (percentage of earnings paid out in dividends) and tie their capital expenditure programs strictly to the earnings that are retained, plus depreciation flows. It is typical to "earmark" depreciation funds for reinvestment, whatever the allocation method employed; and because of the inflation most firms have reconciled themselves to requiring something in addition to depreciation funds to replace wornout or obsolete facilities.

Debt Aversion.   Many firms place an upper limit on capital expenditures in terms of most or even all of the cash earnings, the restriction being, in effect, that the firm avoid recourse to outside financing, especially with respect to the acquisition of debt funds. This aversion to debt has been true of many companies and is, at least to some extent, an outgrowth of the separation of ownership and control in the modern corporation. That such aversion does widely exist has been reported with remarkable consistency in many investigations of the subject.

The practical reasons for debt aversion seem to be based largely on the view that the greater profits engendered by trading on equity during favorable periods do not properly compensate management's risk exposure during times of economic reversal. In the latter case, management faces the possibility of stockholder revolt, or raids by outsiders—in either event, a threat to well-paying jobs. Since the executive's salary represents to him, in the typical case, a much more important source of income than his stock ownership—(many executives, in fact, own little or none of their company's stock, though the widespread use of stock options as a form of managerial compensation has done much to alter this situation)—it is quite understandable that "conservative" financial policies are so widely adopted. Nevertheless, many industrial companies have engaged in debt financing to an increasing degree. This development is due to a combination of two things: long-run growth and prosperity and a high level of taxes that has placed a premium on debt financing.

Inverted Reasoning of Allotted Funds Method.   It seems clear enough that what is wrong with the allotted funds method of capital budgeting and any of its variations is that they all smack of "putting the cart before the horse." A rational approach requires that the volume of capital expenditures be determined by profit-making considerations, and not by any arbitrary methods which are at best only remotely related to considerations of profit. However, it must not be inferred that matters such as dividend policy, liquidity, capital structure, and the like should be ignored in executing the capital budget. It will be seen later that such considerations have an appropriate place in the total picture.

Cost of Capital

It would seem a perfectly logical principle, from the concepts of marginal cost and marginal revenue, that a firm would improve its earning power if the expected rate of return on a given project proposal exceeded the cost of acquiring the funds necessary for bringing the project into being. However, where there is widespread agreement about the theoretical meaning of the rate of return on a project, the same cannot be said of the concept of cost as it relates to this particular problem. An immediate realization of the complexities involved is induced by questions such as the following:

1. What is the cost, if anything, of retained earnings?
2. How is the cost of new equity funds measured?
3. How is the cost of funds determined when both debt and equity sources are tapped in financing capital expansion?
4. In what way does dividend policy enter into the picture in its effect on capital costs, and if a firm pays no dividends does this mean that its equity funds are "free"?

These and many other difficult questions must be settled in arriving at a satisfactory solution to the problem at hand.

Confusion Regarding the Cost of Capital. The questions raised above relate to a concept that is discussed in the literature as *cost of capital,* and it is fairly well accepted that the *cost of capital to a firm provides the optimum cutoff rate or acceptance criterion for project proposals.* The obstacle still to be surmounted, and a major one it is, is how to measure a firm's capital cost. The nature of the difficulty is indicated by the above questions: to take into account the different kinds of equity and debt capital the firm might rely upon, including such diverse sources as retained earnings, common equity, preferred equity, and all kinds of debt; and to "unify" or "subsume" them into some sort of overall measurable concept which can be used as the firm's cost of capital or cutoff rate.

Cost of Capital as an Opportunity Cost. It is generally accepted that a firm's cost of capital is an *opportunity cost* concept. Some go still further by making a distinction between what they call a "borrowing rate" and a "lending rate." The borrowing rate is conceived to be a rate at which firms or entrepreneurs can borrow; and for any given firm (credit rating) at any given time the rate will vary directly with the credit risk to which the lender is subjected. On the other hand, entrepreneurs have available to them the opportunity of investing any free funds they might have either in their own firms or in some alternative outlet. The outside rate of interest available to them is the "lending rate" which, to them, is constant because of the substantially perfect competition that exists in the market for funds, and because their activity in the outside market is likely to have no more than an imperceptible effect.

This distinction between a borrowing rate and a lending rate points up one of the major sources of the confusion that has developed about the cost of capital concept. For purposes of fund raising, by whatever means, the borrowing rate is the appropriate measure of what the firm may be expected to pay for new capital; for purposes of discounting future cash flows to the present, the lending rate is the appropriate one because it reflects investment alternatives available to, and outside of, the firm.

Structure of Rates. The confusion is further compounded by the fact that the borrowing and lending rates are themselves complexes, just as is "the interest rate"—a phrase so commonly employed in the economic literature. Actually, there exists not a single interest rate but a pattern or structure of interest rates. In the capital markets, a separate interest rate exists for every class of claims to be found there, varying as to maturity, issuer, protective covenants, nature and priority of rights, and so forth. These, together, comprise the complex structure of interest rates, and it is this complexity which is too often glibly glossed over in the frequent references to "the interest rate." Further, there also exists a huge and diverse volume of equities, on which no interest is paid, but which, by virtue of the dividends currently being paid on them or of the expectational receipts of dividends in the future, are tied to, or find their place in, the complex interest rate structure.

Much the same may be said of the "borrowing rate" and "the lending rate," each of which have been suggested as the measure of the firm's cost of capital. As a "borrowing" agent, or fund raiser, the firm might have open to it a wide range of possibilities: various types of debt differing as to security, maturity, priority, and so forth, and equity, or common stock and various types of preferreds. But what, then, is "the borrowing rate?" As a "lending" agent, or supplier of funds to others, an even wider range of possibilities exists, from riskless investments such as government bonds (of varying maturities and yields) to highly speculative equities. What, in this case, is "the lending rate?" In arriving at the answers to these two questions we will have achieved a solution to one of the most vexing problems in the theory and budgeting of capital expenditures.

The Earnings Yield

The two questions raised above are actually tied up rather closely with one another, but we will approach the "lending" aspect first. In doing so it seems that it would be more meaningful to think of the function as that of investing rather than lending, since the investing function more clearly includes the acquisition of equities and titles, as well as claims.

Internal and External Opportunities. The rates of return on the investment opportunities confronting the entrepreneur outside the firm constitute, together with the returns on the investment opportunities within the firm, a vast array of alternatives available for selection. Because the many alternatives involve varying degrees of risk and non-monetary advantages and disadvantages as well, it is not simply a matter of selecting those opportunities offering the greatest rate of return. It is, rather, necessary to recognize that the entire structure of rates represents a range of opportunities within which the firm itself may be fitted, and that the returns available on opportunities existing within the firm are strictly comparable only to those opportunities outside the firm which involve equivalent degrees of risk. Given sufficient freedom of flow of capital from industry to industry, opportunities of equivalent risk can be expected to provide comparable rates of return. Thus, the opportunity cost rate (outside investing rate) to be used is that which is available on investments equivalent in risk to that within the firm itself.

Expected Earnings Yield. What is the correct measure of this opportunity cost rate? The most logical answer appears to be what might be called the "expected earnings yield" on the common stock. The reasoning goes as follows:

1. If the rate of return on a project exceeds the cost of the new funds needed to finance it, the future earnings available to the stockholders will be increased by accepting the project. And in terms of the profit-making goals of business firms, improvement in earnings available to the stockholders is a necessary condition for investment action.

2. Investors make their decision to invest, hold, or disinvest based upon their perception of the relationship between the market price of a share of common stock and its expected earnings. The market price of common stock, then, is the present value of the expected stream of income perceived by investors.

3. The cost of the new funds is the rate of return required by investors. It is properly measured as the discount rate that equates the present value of all expected earnings without the project with the current net price per share. The latter is a measure of the dollars the firm can receive from the sale of stock (net of underwriting and flotation expenses); the former represents the expected productivity of existing

capital in the firm. Thus, unless newly employed funds can produce incremental earnings at the same rate as or better than the existing funds, the earnings available per share will decline.

The above reasoning assumes that the new funds will be acquired by sale of common stock so that earnings dilution will result if the new funds are employed to finance projects which promise a rate of return less than that represented by the expected earnings yield on the existing stock.

The argument as it stands, however, is incomplete for it must be made to encompass funds derived from other sources: retained earnings, sale of debt securities, and sale of preferred stock. And the solution will be meaningful only if we are able somehow to relate these diverse sources to one another. The basic element to which all these diverse sources and the costs of funds derived from them must be related is the opportunity cost rate defined earlier and described above as the "expected earnings yield." In expounding upon the relationships existing among the costs of the diverse capital sources that a firm might tap, we hope to make clear why we were justified in saying earlier that the "borrowing rate" and "lending rate" concepts are inextricably intertwined.

Retained Earnings

If it were not for various leakages (the most important of which is the income tax) and other overriding considerations, all earnings could be distributed as dividends and, to the extent that expansion were deemed desirable by the directors, could be recouped by selling new stock in sufficient quantity to bring in the desired equity funds. This idealistic proposal has been made from time to time by various economists as a desirable means of turning over to the stockholders complete control of the corporate capital.

For various practical reasons, however, this would not be a very satisfactory procedure. Nevertheless, for the purposes of treating the problem under discussion, a 100 percent distribution policy associated with the sale of whatever amount of stock is necessary for acquiring an adequate volume of funds to finance internal expansion does serve as a useful point of departure.

Thus, considering only the leakages resulting from the income tax, and ignoring exclusions and the other smaller leakages due to brokerage fees and underwriting expenses, a dollar of retained earnings is equivalent to two dollars of dividends paid to a stockholder in the 50 percent tax bracket, since such a stockholder would be able to put back into the corporation (or into any other investment) only one dollar after paying taxes. What this means, then, is that if the opportunity cost rate as measured by the expected earnings yield is, say, 12 percent (so that projects promising less than this should be rejected if they are to be financed by sale of new stock), it would be to the economic advantage of the stockholders to accept projects promising substantially less than 12 percent if financing is to be done from retained earnings. How much less than 12 percent, that is, how much below the earnings yield it would be desirable to go, would depend on the tax brackets of the corporation's stockholders.

In the closely-held corporation, where the insiders own as well as control the enterprise, the tax situation of the managerial team can be readily enough applied as a guide to policy. But in the publicly held corporation where the tax brackets are likely to range from zero for the tax-exempt institutional stockholder to extremely high percentages for the very wealthy individual, the problem is not so easily solved. Perhaps a workable solution would be to assume a median tax bracket, or something above that based on the logic that the lower income groups in the economy do not own stock (at least not to a degree sufficient to warrant undue concern on the part of the management). If the 30 percent tax bracket were assumed to be the appropriate guide to employ, it would mean that a project need promise only 70 percent as much a return when financed by retained earnings. Hence, a cutoff rate of 12 percent applied to projects to be financed by sale of new stock would be equivalent to a rate of 8.4 percent where retained earnings are to be used.

Another approach to evaluation of the cost of retained earnings is the *external-yield criterion*, which determines the cost of retained earnings by what they would yield if invested in other firms of similar risk. This criterion need not be concerned with personal income taxes since it simply measures what the firm could get by direct investment. The external-yield criterion is economically justifiable and can be applied consistently.

Sale of Senior Securities

The use of bonds and preferred stock as media for acquiring long-term capital is referred to as *trading on equity*—a concept which is generally explained in elementary textbooks in finance. The underlying principle involved is that the profits available to the stockholders will be increased if the rate paid on the senior capital proves to be less than the rate earned on that capital when employed in the firm. This advantage is, unhappily, offset by the risk exposure resulting from trading on equity, for the profits available to the owners will be less, and the losses greater, if the rate earned on the senior capital should prove to be less than its cost.

How can we reconcile this with the opportunity cost rate defined earlier in terms of earnings yield? From what we know about the costs of debt funds, it would appear that the cutoff rate expressed in terms of the earnings yield is much higher than debt capital costs, so that the principle of applying such a rate for cutoff purposes runs quite contrary to the suggestions flowing from the trading-on-equity principle. Thus, a firm whose opportunity cost rate is, say, 15 percent would apparently be missing many profitable opportunities by rejecting projects promising less than that if it can finance them by borrowing at, say, 5 percent. This simple logic seems reasonable enough, and is the sort usually employed in the typical textbook treatment of trading on equity.

Equally simple and reasonable logic, however, indicates that the above conclusion is erroneous. Can a firm that has shown vigorous growth—such as Xerox or International Business Machines—continue its exceptional rate of growth by accepting projects with low earning power simply because the funds of financing such projects are available to it at or slightly above the prime rate? Obviously not! And if it did follow such a course, the very high price-earnings ratio (low earnings yield) of its stock would fall (rise) precipitously, reflecting a sharp increase in the cost of any new equity funds it might later seek. In a less spectacular fashion the same would happen to any stock, though the reasons may not be quite so apparent. There are actually many subtleties involved which are typically ignored (often unconsciously) in the elementary textbook treatment of trading on equity, for the ramifications that result from combined debt and equity financing are very complex.

It is generally quite well understood that when a firm engages in debt financing it exposes itself to risks which, once the debt begins to approach a rather sizable amount relative to the total capital structure, increase in rapid geometric fashion compared to the increase in the debt itself. This reflects itself, of course, in the leveraged effect on corporate earnings; but it reflects itself also in the earnings yield (price-earnings ratio) of the stock in adverse fashion. The increase in the cost of new equity funds to the firm is directly traceable to the debt financing and therefore must be properly considered as part of the real cost of borrowing.

It has been suggested, in fact, because of this interplay of forces between debt and equity financing, that the true measure of all financing costs be taken to be the cost of equity funds. The reasoning involved is that managements recognize the hidden costs of borrowing—in the form of the risks of default mentioned above, as well as the loss of managerial flexibility and freedom of action in the form of dividend restrictions, working capital requirements, and other constraints imposed by the bond indenture.

Thus, *given the firm's capital structure, management will undertake new financing in that medium—debt or equity—which is least costly, so that there will exist, or tend to exist, an equality between the marginal* (*real*) *cost of borrowing and the marginal cost of equity.* Because of this equality, the best way to measure cost is to look at the earnings yield on the stock, for this is objectively measurable, whereas most of the "real" borrowing costs are subjective and not readily measurable due to default risks and constraints.

The Optimum Capital Structure Approach

The above argument has a great deal to commend it. Most important is that it recognizes the significance of the interaction of debt and equity. But because many of the real costs of borrowing are subjective, it means that what might be a moderate cost to one management is excessively burdensome to another. The result is that it becomes impossible, in the first place, to state objectively the combination of debt and equity that must be sought in striving for the point at which the marginal real cost of debt financing equals the marginal cost of equity financing; and, in the second place, it would seem to follow from the argument presented above that management always strives to achieve this balance anyway, and in its own way, so that whatever the capital structure might be, it is always at, or tending toward, an optimum combination.

The Significance of the Firm's Capital Structure. The last conclusion has an almost teleologic quality and, for that reason at least, is suspect. It is, of course, a principle or precept that could well become a part of the normative structure of neoclassical economics; but, as it stands, the equation of marginal borrowing and equity costs in the individual firm is presumed *somehow* to occur, and this is neither probable nor useful as a guide to the management that would like to have some concrete suggestions on how to achieve this goal. A solution does exist, however, and that is to accept again the impersonal dictates of the market.

As indicated earlier, the market reflects the cost of borrowing in the valuation which it places on the common stock of the company. But borrowing need not necessarily involve positive real costs over and above the nominal out-of-pocket interest charges. If the borrowed funds are expected to produce earnings at a rate that is at least equal to the earnings yield, and if the total debt is a very small portion of the capital structure, the market might welcome the decision to borrow by reducing the rate at which the firm's earnings are capitalized. Thus the real cost of borrowing might actually be less than the interest charge. This implies that there is, in the opinion of the market, an *optimum capital structure* which reflects the firm's desire to take advantage of the benefits provided by leveraging, while at the same time keeping the risk of default under control.

Variability of Optimum Structure. The optimum ratio of debt to equity in the capital structure will vary considerably from one industry to another and, to a significant extent, among companies within a given industry. This variability enormously complicates the problem of establishing criteria to serve as guides on constructing optimum financial structures. As a result it is necessary to settle for general principles rather than rules of precision, but even general principles will help greatly to fill the void that exists.

We might well approach the problem by asking what it is that the earnings yield is supposed to reflect. As a relationship between average future annual earnings and recent average price, the earnings yield actually reflects a host of factors, some of them imponderable. However, it may be reasonably assumed that in the long run all significant factors, whether tangible or not, will reflect themselves in the record of earnings and dividends. Hence, it may be argued that it is unnecessary to attempt to evaluate such difficult elements as managerial ability, personnel relations, competitive position, new product development, operating efficiency, and so on. These are all important considerations, and they help to explain why the earnings pattern is what it is. But they are important also for the effect they are expected to have on future *earnings* and *dividends*. Hence, these basic series provide us with the materials we need.

The next step is to fashion these materials into the forms in which they are used by investors. Since it is the market's attitudes and psychology that determine the cost to the firm seeking new capital, it is upon these attitudes that a meaningful and measurable cost of capital concept must be built.

Defining Anew the Cost of Capital. From what has been said above, our earlier definition of the cost of capital simply in terms of earnings yield is not suitable. Rather, a more fruitful approach would be to define the cost of capital as the *cost of equity funds* (still measured by earnings yield) *when the firm has what the market considers to be a well-balanced capital structure.* For with such a structure it may be assumed that the marginal real cost of borrowing equals the marginal cost of equity funds. If a firm is considered to be excessively leveraged, the marginal real cost of borrowing (because of the risks involved) will exceed the marginal cost of equity financing; where a firm is too conservatively capitalized, additional borrowing should involve lower costs than would be required on equity funds.

It may further be pointed out that each new financing, whether by debt or by equity means, can be expected to affect the marginal cost of financing by the alternative method. For example, a firm that is already believed to be too highly leveraged would cause the marginal cost of equity funds to increase if it were to engage in additional borrowing; on the other hand, if the same firm were instead to employ equity financing, this would reduce the marginal real cost of borrowing.

Some Unsolved Problems

The problems that remain to be solved, with respect to the actual determination of a firm's cost of capital, taking into consideration the impact of the firm's capital structure on its capital costs, are (1) the establishment of standards of optimum capital structures, and (2) a means of relating the variations of those structures which depart from the optimum to the cost of that particular firm's capital.

If it were necessary, for practical applications, to set down a precise system of standards and procedures, we would have before us an impossible task. As it is, the problem is a difficult one, but it can be coped with. Our concern is only that we arrive at a useful and usable measure of the cost of capital; and this requires, from what we have said thus far, that we recognize, and try to adapt to, the tastes and attitudes of the market. While a precise measure of these tastes and attitudes would be desirable, it is by no means necessary for adopting a meaningful course of action.

Investment Ratings. Actually, standards exist which have been employed for many years by the investment community and which can be adapted to the problem being presently considered. We refer to those standards that have been employed to distinguish among different qualities of stocks and bonds.

It is the practice in security analysis to rate both stocks and bonds for their investment quality. These ratings are particularly important with respect to bonds, for the investment status given to debt securities by the leading rating services (Moody's, Standard and Poor's, and Fitch) will determine whether or not they will find their way into the portfolios of institutional investors. This means, as well, that the yield basis on which the bonds will be taken up will be accordingly affected—in fact, the ratings on these securities will even affect the terms under which subsequent sallies into the capital markets could be made. This applies to a firm's equity financing too, though perhaps in somewhat lesser degree.

These investment ratings thus have a clear connection with a firm's cost of capital in that they both reflect and influence the firm's credit standing in the capital markets. However, the security ratings are based on statistics and qualities which have, in many cases, no direct connection with the composition of the firm's capital structure. For the purpose of coping with this particular problem, it is necessary to narrow down to those factors which relate to what the market would consider to be an optimum capital structure, and the way in which these considerations affect the security ratings and the earnings yield on the common stock. In doing so it is necessary to classify companies into various groupings.

Thus, an electric power company would obviously have a different optimum structure than a steel warehousing firm; the former would be expected to be much more highly leveraged. In fact, an electric power company that had only 30 percent of its capital structure represented by debt and preferred stock would be exceedingly conservative, and would be considered so to the detriment of the common stockholders. Such a company would obviously have been financing much of its growth via sale of common stock, the result of which would have meant repeated dilution of common stock earnings. This would further mean that the company's growth trend was being unnecessarily dampened; and it would result in the capitalization of the company's earnings, by the market, at a higher rate than necessary, that is, a higher cost of capital for the firm.

We have here not only an example of how the composition of a firm's capital can affect its earnings record and, through it, its cost of capital, but an illustration as well of what was meant earlier when it was stated that all factors—tangible or intangible, quantitative or qualitative—will in time reflect themselves in the earnings and dividend records of the company.

The typical classification for security investment purposes is the quadripartite grouping of public utility, railroad, financial, and industrial. This classification is unsatisfactory for our purposes, however, because of the heterogeneity of the individual groups—especially the industrial category. For example, the dairy, food chain, and tobacco companies have better records of earning and dividend stability than most railroads and even some public utilities. Thus, the quadripartite arrangement serves only as a useful point of departure.

The Omnipresence of Uncertainty

One might well argue that uncertainty is the only factor that explains the discrepancies in the earnings yields existing in the market at any given time. It is very common, however, for investment analysts to discuss growth as a factor distinct from investment risk, and to explain extremely low earnings yields (as measured in terms of current price and latest 12 months' earnings) in terms of the growth potential anticipated by the market.

A classic example is afforded by IBM stock. It has often sold at an earnings-price ratio of less than 3 percent, which is below the yield on Treasury bonds. It would obviously be false to conclude that IBM was considered to be "safer" than government bonds. The answer lies rather in the fact that the investor in either case is actually buying a stream of future income; and that for the government bonds, the future stream was to flow at a constant rate, while it was expected that the stream produced by the IBM investment would flow at a rapidly expanding rate. For this reason, the earnings yield as a measure of cost of capital must be defined, and has so been defined here, in terms of *future* rather than current annual earnings.

While the growth factor seems to explain certain discrepancies in current earnings yields, uncertainty here too plays an important part. For there is uncertainty concerning (1) whether a given investment will produce a *growing* stream of earnings; (2) the *rate* of growth that will be achieved; and (3) the general level of earnings and dividend yields prevailing in the market in the future, which will, of course, affect the liquidating value of the investment at that time. If the market is performing its valuation function properly, all of these factors are reflected in the current earnings yields of common stocks.

The Need for Continued Research

The foregoing considerations point out the route along which a fruitful investigative research of the problem might proceed; but at this point, we are not as yet able to make too definitive a statement. There is reason to believe, for example, that a public utility might safely carry a capital structure represented by less than 30 percent in common stock, and that 50 percent would probably be too conservative. On the other hand, a cyclical business would possibly demand, in the interest of safety, little or no debt and, perhaps, up to a maximum of 25 percent of preferred stock if leveraging is to be employed at all.

Exactly what the optimum capital structure should be for any given type of business, that is, what the capital market seems to view as an optimum structure, remains to be determined, and would make a very interesting and useful study. (A number of studies have been made, but the results have been inconclusive and controversial.) It would provide the basis for making fairly accurate estimates of a company's cost of capital. While rather crude approximations are currently possible for any given industry—investment attitudes are always making themselves felt—such estimates would be greatly improved by a careful research survey. And once it is possible to accept confidently a given capital structure as the optimum for a certain type of company, that company can (1) gradually adjust its structure toward that optimum, thereby improving (reducing) its cost of capital; and (2) estimate fairly accurately what its cost of capital is and use it as its cutoff rate for its current capital planning. Until this "scientific" approach becomes possible, business managements will simply have to content themselves with less reliable estimates.

DETERMINANTS OF CAPITAL COSTS

The discussion of the pattern of interest rates earlier in this chapter applies in full to the determinants of the pattern of capital costs. It is clear that the two concepts are closely related, if not more or less synonymous, when we recognize that the forces which determine bond yields (as costs of debt capital) also determine the place of these yields within the interest rate structure.

However, capital costs are determined by a host of forces that exert their influence on the capital markets; and since these forces do not all work in the same direction, it is not always an easy matter to explain the net effects, let alone to predict the direction of new and longer term changes.

The Federal Authorities

The single most important determinant of the interest rate structure (and therefore of the cost of debt capital) is the federal government, making itself felt through the operations of the Treasury Department and the policies of the Federal Reserve authorities. While matters pertaining to money and credit are officially the province of the "Fed," the Treasury's operations are much too important for its effects on the capital markets to be ignored.

The Treasury enters the money market each Monday with an offer of 91-day bills which during a given year may run in the neighborhood of several billion dollars. Generally, this offering is simply a refunding of a similar volume of maturing bills, but even when this is the case the Treasury must still set a rate that will (1) be taken by the market without shaking it unduly; and (2) be in general line with the objectives of the Federal Reserve authorities. In addition to these weekly bill offerings, the Treasury enters the market less regularly with longer maturities for sale. These must not only be fitted into the existing structure and be reasonably consistent with monetary objectives but must also suit the Treasury's own purposes, namely: (1) to provide the desired volume of funds, and (2) to lengthen or shorten the average debt as desired by the Treasury's policy-making officials.

The Fed, in which is vested the responsibility for pursuing monetary and credit policies designed to promote economic growth and stability, actually "sets" the pattern of rates which prevail in the market. Through the exercise of controls over the rediscount rate, member bank reserve requirements, and selective credit controls (such as margin requirements for stock purchases), the Fed produces a marked effect on the general level of the rate structure. On the other hand, its open-market operations, a tool that was originally supposed to enable the Reserve authorities to "make the rediscount rate effective," are capable of shaping the rate structure itself. This is possible by concentrating market operations on the shorter or longer end of the maturity scale, as the case might be.

While other forces, discussed below, have important effects on the general structure of rates, the government bond market is almost entirely subject to the operations of what amounts to the monolithic force of the federal authorities. One might argue that the manner and direction in which this force is applied is not entirely self-willed but must suit the more basic dictates of economic conditions and objectives. Thus, Treasury operations depend on fiscal requirements and congressional appropriations; the Fed's controls are relaxed or more stringently imposed depending on whether conditions call for credit relaxation or restriction. Be this as it may, the federal force does not automatically arise out of market conditions themselves but is imposed upon the market as a result of *positively determined policy.*

Public Psychology

For lack of space we will here interpret "public psychology" very broadly and treat it rather briefly. It includes such elements as "consumer optimism," "investor confidence," and "business outlook." These frequently point in the same direction at the same time, and their effects are most importantly felt on the yields which prevail on security issues other than Treasury debt obligations. Thus, while it is true that the federal authorities have an enormous effect on all yields by setting the pattern through their government bond operations, the question of how, and to what degree, other yields will respond depends on "public psychology."

Except for the so-called "money-rate bonds" (issues which are of such high quality that the possibility of default is virtually nonexistent, so that their prices fluctuate strictly in line with government bonds), corporate bonds and common and preferred stocks will move in varying sympathy with the yields available on government bonds. Thus, whether the spread between bond and stock yields will be narrow or wide, or whether it will favor one type of investment as against another, depends more on the factors subsumed under "public psychology" than it does directly on the Fed's credit policies.

For example, one would expect that dividend yields on good quality stocks would "normally" exceed the yields available on high-grade corporate bonds. This has happened more often than not (in varying degree), but it was not true from 1921 to 1929, and in 1933 and 1934.

Thus, one is likely to find bond yields to exceed or be only slightly less than stock yields during booming prosperity or deep depression. In the latter situation stock yields decline sharply as dividends are cut or omitted, while the fixed interest charges on high-grade bonds usually continue to be paid. During sanguine periods of prosperity, buoyant optimism may lead investors to project unlimited economic growth, motivating them to buy equities at prices that provide absurdly low income and earnings yields.

Individual Factors

Thus far we have considered the market forces which affect the general level and patterns of rates. Within this pattern must be fitted each individual security (investment), and the forces that have been discussed above apply also to the individual issue. But, in addition to those general forces, the individual investment is subject to specific forces.

The decision to raise the tariff on lead imports, or to reduce further the allowable days of crude oil production in Texas, can be expected to affect specific industries or companies more than others, although it is conceivable that their effects might be traceable to many other segments of the economy. Similarly, if the outlook for automobile or housing demand is unpromising, the yields on the securities of the companies involved will reflect this fact. In short, many of the factors discussed above as part of "public psychology" can be found to apply, at times, with particularly telling force to specific companies rather than to industry in general. All of these factors, both those of general and specific import, can, in fact, be classed under the heading of that all-embracing term "uncertainty." We are then able to say, simply, that yields on treasury securities are lowest because there is no question of default involved; that money-rate bonds offer somewhat higher yields; and so on down the scale to low-grade equities on which dividend and earnings yields are large. For any given equity, of course, current dividends and earnings might be zero. But the possibility exists, reasonable or not, that future earnings will permit payments of such order as to make the current price attractive, that is, at least in line with prices of other securities.

Corporate Income Taxes

Finally, the single most important determinant of the pre-tax cost of equity capital has been the corporate income tax. To verify this fact one need only note the close correlation that exists between the corporate tax rate and the pre-tax cost of equity capital.

Compare, for example, the year 1920 with the more recent period. In 1920, when the corporate tax rate was only 10 percent, the pre-tax cost of equity capital was barely larger than the post-tax cost; in recent decades, with a corporate tax rate averaging slightly less than 50 percent, the pre-tax cost has been almost twice the post-tax cost. With a rising long-run trend in corporate income taxes, it is no wonder that reference is frequently made to the fact that our tax policies have placed debt financing in a favorable position.

Of course, where post-tax costs are relatively low, as has been the case from time to time, even the present corporate tax does not produce pre-tax costs of great enormity: doubling a small number results at most in something which is itself not much more than small or moderate. However, compared with the costs of debt capital, post-tax equity costs have usually not been particularly small, and a doubling of the more typical post-tax equity costs leads to pre-tax costs of rather shocking size. The implications for managerial decision making are obviously of vital significance to all business firms.

POLICY IMPLICATIONS FOR MANAGEMENT

We now turn to the matter of defining or proposing an overall policy approach to the capital management function—an approach that seems logically to be called for in light of what has thus far been said.

Broadly speaking, the implications for managerial decision making can be summed up in a single sentence:

> *Management should pursue policies which are designed to reduce, or maintain at as low a level as possible, the company's cost of capital.*

We will complete this chapter with a discussion of these policies.

Stockholder Relationships

The implications in this area are very broad but can be discussed under two headings: (1) taking the stockholders into management's confidence, and (2) managing the corporation for the stockholders' benefit.

1. Taking the Stockholders into Management's Confidence. There is an old saying that "nothing succeeds like success," and, certainly in the field of business management this old saw is as true as it might be anywhere else. A company that shows a consistently superior performance can, with respect to stockholder-management relations, pursue virtually any policy it wishes without doing any particular harm to the company's position in the capital market. An exceptionally good return earned on the stockholder's investment, achieved year after year, will induce most, if not all, stockholders to place complete faith in their company's management without any concern as to whether management tells them of the company's plans and objectives, or even whether the published financial statements are at all adequate for intelligent and critical analysis by the outsider. But such cases are exceptionally rare. Most companies cannot qualify in this regard, and so should be concerned with the state of existing relations, and should strive to improve it if there is a possibility of doing so.

A stockholder body which is kept well informed of the company's activities and objectives, which is treated explicitly by the management as the respected owners to whom the management is fully accountable for its acts, and which is given the clear impression that it is for the group's benefit that the corporation is being managed, is an extremely valuable asset. These stockholders are potentially the prime and most fruitful source of future capital, particularly equity capital (the expensive kind), and the favorable regard in which they hold their company and their stock can mean substantial dollar savings when outside capital is sought. It could even mean the difference between whether the funds will or will not be available in sufficient quantity and at a cost that makes the proposed capital projects worth undertaking.

2. *Managing the Corporation for the Stockholders' Benefit.* There is no doubt that the publicly held corporation has obligations to groups other than its owners. The community, the creditors, the management, the employees—all are vitally interested in the corporation's welfare and well-being. But only if corporate action is governed by considerations of stockholder interest will the correct economic decisions be made. Thus, in considering a specific project proposal, we have seen that only if the project is evaluated in terms of whether it will increase the earnings available to the shareholders will the management make the correct economic choice.

In a broad sense, all managerial decisions can be related to this general heading of "stockholders' benefit." However, we may single out certain areas of managerial action that deserve special emphasis and discuss them as follows.

Dividend Policy

The most explicit and meaningful expression of the stockholders' relationship with their company is the dividend they receive on their stock. If only for this reason, then, the matter of dividend policy deserves the most thoughtful attention of top management.

In electing the corporation's directors, the stockholders delegate to them full authority over dividend policy; and it becomes a matter for the directors' discretion to determine what portion, if any, of the earnings shall be distributed to the owners. Recourse to the courts is always open to the shareholders, but this is a practical course of action only when there has been what amounts to an almost flagrant abuse of fiduciary responsibility. Even where earnings are very much larger than the current dividend, the penalty tax on improper surplus accumulation (imposed by Section 102 of the Internal Revenue Code) cannot be made to take effect as long as the earnings are put into physical plant, equipment, inventories, and so forth, or used to repay debt. Of course, as has already been pointed out, the consistently successful company with an outstanding earnings performance record will not make its stockholders unhappy even with a very low dividend payout policy, but we are not concerned here with the exceptional case.

Because of the great importance which the typical stockholder attaches to dividends, it is mandatory that a corporate management striving to improve its capital costs give consideration to the establishment of a dividend policy which will contribute to that end. The policy established should be consistent with the company's potentials and prospects. While dynamic growth is still going on, even a very low payout is justifiable, but an indiscriminate investment of earnings into bank balances and government bonds is both unfair to the stockholders and harmful to the long-run position of the corporation. Briefly, for that is all that space permits, management should announce a policy which it intends to pursue and will stick to unless required by circumstances to deviate from it. This policy should include a decision to maintain a regular quarterly dividend which the company feels it can reasonably do, and an aim at improving the dividend whenever circumstances permit. Many companies already pursue such a policy; too many others do not.

Just as it may be said that nothing succeeds like success, so we must also point out that in the business world there is no permanent substitute for success. A company can hardly make up for consistent losses by tackling the problem of dividend policy. Mediocre earnings will not suddenly blossom into large returns because regular dividends are paid out. But just as operating economies can be effected in production, materials handling, distribution, and marketing, so capital cost economies can be produced by giving adequate attention to such matters as dividend policy, and others discussed below.

Retained Earnings Policy

The decision to pay out 30 percent of earnings is, at the same time, a decision to retain 70 percent. Yet this area is important enough to justify a discussion of both aspects, while at the same time keeping in mind the fact that one cannot be decided without in effect deciding the other.

The emphasis on dividend policy is intended to point up the need for management to recognize its responsibility to the corporate owners, and the desirability of developing a loyal stockholder body and a regard for the corporation which will redound to the long-run benefit of all concerned. The emphasis on retained earnings is intended to point up the importance of this major source of equity capital and its advantages over alternative sources. Because of the "double tax" on distributed corporate income (once before and once after distribution), retained earnings have a lower net cost than do dividends returned to the company by way of new stock financing. But whereas the latter is a voluntary subscription, the retention of earnings amounts, in effect, to an involuntary subscription on the part of the stockholders. For this reason, retention policies should be carefully weighed against the desirability and benefits (to the corporation's long-run position) of greater dividend distributions. In many cases investment of retained earnings may serve the stockholder better than payout of dividends. Aside from the aspect of double taxation, investment of retained earnings in such things as plant expansion or research and development of new products may result in vastly increased earnings in the future. The increase in earnings will, in turn, yield either greater dividends or greater capital gains.

As a result of the rising demand for capital, the huge amount of internal financing that has taken place in recent decades has been accomplished at almost a consistent increase in the cost of equity financing. But the personal income tax, as explained earlier, places retained earnings at a great advantage over externally derived equity funds; and this is one of the basic principles on which retained earnings policy (dividend policy) should be built.

No matter what the cost of equity funds may be, it is mandatory that the project to be financed shall be profitable. Where retained earnings are employed, project profitability can be substantially less, and it would still be in the stockholders' interest that these projects be carried through. However, this should not be an excuse for drastic reductions in dividends and continued low payouts in all cases, unless economically justified. And even where such action seems desirable, management should advise the stockholders of the reasons for the dividend retrenchment and should give all necessary assurances that dividend improvement will be forthcoming as soon as possible.

The Corporate Income Tax

In attempting to meet head-on the problem posed by the corporate income tax, those firms contemplating the employment of new equity capital would undoubtedly find it desirable to be able to predict the future course of such taxes. Depending on one's analysis of the major forces involved, this particular prediction can be either very simple or very difficult. The former belief would be held by those who felt that corporate income taxes will remain high indefinitely, if not necessarily at their present relatively high level; the latter opinion would be held by those convinced that conditions are always altering sufficiently to permit wide swings in tax rates from time to time.

The forces involved are economic and political, domestic and international, changing and ever present. Pressing for continued high corporate taxes are:

1. The international situation which calls for a high level of defense spending.

2. A full-employment policy which, together with the organized labor movement's pressing for regular wage increases for its members, must necessarily produce price inflation.
3. The productivity of this revenue source and the difficulty of replacing it with another that would be politically less unpopular.
4. The increasing size of the "hard core" portion of federal expenditures—interest payments, farm subsidies, social welfare, highways, and numerous other demands that tend to become part of a permanent program rather than a "one-shot" proposition.
5. Pressures for new spending areas, such as pollution control.

Arrayed against these forces is the basic and powerful desire on the part of everyone—corporations, stockholders, nonstockholders, low- and high-income groups—to minimize the tax bite. But whenever economic conditions seem to warrant a reduction in taxes, even stockholders would prefer a cut in personal taxes to a reduction in corporate assessments; and in terms of popularity, an increase in personal exemptions would have much greater political appeal than a cut in corporate income taxes. Even if a 38 or 40 percent corporate tax rate were a near-term possibility, these rates would still be high and would have great impact on the pre-tax cost of equity capital.

If the above conclusion is acceptable, it would follow that managements which have been traditionally conservative in their financing plans would do well to consider a shift in their approach and permit greater use of debt financing. A sharp shift in that direction is not necessarily called for, but where earnings typically indicate a substantial coverage of fixed charges (actual or potential), debt financing would be a reasonable course to pursue, though the traditionally conservative management might prefer to do so cautiously.

The Investment Timing Problem

An inseparable part of any investment decision is the timing of the expenditures involved. Historically, the wide swings that have occurred in the costs of capital are apparent enough, and the importance of timing can be more clearly brought home by a simple illustration.

Forecasting. Some years ago, Public Service Electric & Gas Company (New Jersey) offered $60 million of 30-year, first-mortage bonds, rated Aa (i.e., second only to the highest rating of Aaa) at a yield of 4.81 percent. The bonds sold, but rather sluggishly. Six months later, Union Electric Company (Missouri) sold a 30-year first-mortgage issue, also rated Aa, to yield 4.22 percent, and it was quickly taken by the market. This difference of 59 basis points (slightly over one half of 1 percent) meant that had the Public Service company been able to market its bonds six months later, it would have saved $354,000 per year in interest charges—hardly a saving to be ignored.

Situations like this occur frequently. But in a broader sense, the timing problem is only one part of the bigger problem of forecasting. As related to capital expenditure planning specifically, it has already been shown that the investment decision is based on cash flow estimates (forecasts) expected over the life of the project. There arise, then, two considerations with respect to investment timing:

1. Planning the expenditure so that the new capital will be sought at opportune (low-cost) moments.
2. Selecting investments so that the cash flows are available for reinvestment at the most attractive rates.

Both of these aspects impose a demand on the decision maker to predict the future course and pattern of rates, and it would certainly be desirable to develop the skill and foresight that this would require. Suffice it to say, in this connection, that this is a goal worth striving for, but how difficult it is to attain has already been indicated in the above illustration.

Let us turn now to the second aspect of the timing problem before reaching any specific conclusions to serve as guides for managerial decision making.

The Reinvestment Problem. The task of selecting among investments with full consideration to the timing and availability of the generated cash flows is usually referred to as "the reinvestment problem." The point is made that it is not enough to determine that project A provides a 15 percent rate of return as against 12 percent for project B and that therefore A is to be preferred to B. For, the argument goes, it might be that the cash flow patterns are such that the heavier flows from project A are anticipated at a time in the future when reinvestment opportunities are less attractive than those expected to exist at the time when the cash flows from project B are made available.

To take a simplified example, assume that both A and B have an economic life of two years, that A will produce one tenth of the expected cash at the end of the first year and nine tenths at the end of the second year, while B is expected to generate nine tenths of the total cash stream at the end of the first year and one tenth at the end of the second. Assuming that the size of the respective cash incomes were such that A indicated a higher rate of return, we would presumably select it rather than project B.

But suppose the forecast indicates that reinvestment opportunities will be very attractive one year from today and rather unattractive two years from today. This means, then, that a very large amount of cash will be available for attractive reinvestment if we select project B, whereas most of the cash flow forthcoming from project A will be available for reinvestment at substantially lower rates of return. Hence, the combined results of initial investment plus reinvestment of cash proceeds points to project B as the more profitable alternative.

The argument as it stands is completely valid and cannot as such be refuted. But consider what this line of reasoning leads to. The corporation has a life in perpetuity so that the investment function it performs is a permanent and continuing one. Therefore, where is the justification in considering only a first stage of reinvestment of cash proceeds? Theoretically, all current investment decisions must be based not on a selection of profit alternatives as measured by rates of return on the respective investments, or even on these rates adjusted for the reinvestment returns on the cash proceeds as they become available in the future, but on a *total investment and reinvestment plan that stretches indefinitely into perpetuity.* Each investment produces cash flows which are, typically, reinvested and which in turn will produce other cash flows to be reinvested, and so on. This is what we mean by the permanent and continuing investment function of the corporation. Ideally, then, the optimum investment decision is the one which selects from among an infinite number of infinitely long-term investment plans, that one which will produce the best investment results (verifiable only many years later with hindsight knowledge).

There may exist, then, a discrepancy between the investments to be selected on the basis of the anticipated *rates of return* on the individual alternative projects and the selection of alternative investment plans on the basis of the anticipated best *investment results* from a long-run continuing investment and reinvestment process. While the latter basis is the proper one upon which to build the investment function, the seeming discrepancy between the two alternative approaches may frequently be more imagined than real. This point is further amplified below.

Reinvestment and the Rate of Return

Implicit in the rate-of-return analysis is the assumption that all cash flows can be reinvested in other projects of *equivalent risk yielding the same rate of return.* This is a necessary premise in the analysis. Otherwise it is possible to make any investment superior to all other by assuming a reinvestment rate which will make it so. We will illustrate this implicit and basic principle in two important applications:

1. The borrower of $1,000 for ten years at 10 percent compound interest might arrange to repay the loan in one of many ways. Two equivalent alternatives would be:
   a. Have the interest added to the principal at the end of each year and make a single lump-sum payment at the end of ten years, amounting to $2,593.73.

  b. Pay $100 annual interest charges, and repay the principal sum of $1,000 at the end of ten years.

  Both of these alternatives involve *compound* interest (though most people are likely to think that latter case involves only simple interest), and what makes them exactly equivalent is the *implicit assumption* that the annual interest payments, as they are received by the lender in the second case, can be *reinvested at exactly the same degree of risk at* 10 percent.

2. A bridge is to be constructed across a river and the choice (to simplify the illustration) is between steel and wood. A steel bridge would last, say, 40 years; a wooden bridge would have to be replaced in, let us say, 8 years. The advantage of the steel bridge is its lower annual maintenance costs. Its major disadvantage is the much larger investment required. Assuming that there is no preference for either type of bridge in terms of the quality of service, the investment decision will hinge on a comparison of annual costs (comprising maintenance costs and the investment's capital recovery cost), and the alternative involving the least annual cost would be the proper economic choice. The fact that the steel bridge would be much more durable does not alter the decision, for implicit in the analysis is the assumption that the wooden bridge can be replaced after each eight-year period at *exactly the same* cost, maintenance disbursements, durability, and salvage value (if any), and that the same will be true for the steel bridge when the time comes to replace it. Thus, the annual costs computed for the original bridge are implicitly assumed to repeat indefinitely into the future.

This is, in short, an "other things being equal" approach. Where it is not possible to plan otherwise, or to predict whether the "other" things will change in one direction rather than another, it is the only meaningful approach to employ. In terms of the above example, the choice between the less durable wooden bridge and the longer lived steel bridge is determined by what we consider today to be the correct economic decision. Our hope is that it will prove to be the right decision in the long run, and whether it does will depend on economic and technological conditions eight years from now. Any factors that would make the replacement economics more favorable eight years from today (lower prices and wage costs, more efficient construction methods, more durable materials which cost as much as or less than the wood does today) would be added reasons for selecting the wooden bridge today. Inflationary factors will make the choice of the steel bridge more attractive.

Thus, "the reinvestment problem" as stated earlier is not a newly discovered one, and is only one aspect of all investment decisions which must be made today in a continuing and perpetuating society or firm. The sophisticated decision maker takes all factors into consideration, whenever possible, and acts accordingly. The more dynamic the industry and the more uncertain the external forces which act upon the firm, the greater the number and importance of the factors likely to cause discrepancies between anticipated and actual results. In such cases, investment decisions are likely to be biased in favor of very short payouts. In more stable and predictable industries (such as public utilities), long payout investments are much more common.

Notwithstanding the theoretical weight of the foregoing discussion, there is something to be said for limiting investment decisions to a strict rate-of-return analysis without encumbering (and endangering) the analytical process with what are frequently rather tenuous and intractable factors—namely, those involving particular time patterns of cash proceeds and their relative profitabilities. This is not a denial of the desirability of estimating these factors whenever possible; it is rather an expression of caution against attempting to put too much weight on these estimates in the typical investment decision.

Certain investment processes, for example, mutual investment trusts, are more suited for this type of decision making; it is not so for the typical manufacturing enterprise. In the latter case, there is, in the first place, substantially less fluidity in the asset structure, which in turn places greater emphasis on the need for making the correct decision *today* rather than being able to correct today's wrong decision tomorrow (the "sunk" nature of capital investments); and in the second place, the investment results of a business enterprise over time are much more importantly dependent on the correct estimate of the cash flows expected from a given project than upon the reinvestment of these cash flows at opportune moments "brilliantly" anticipated (more likely by pure chance, if at all).

To state the last thought somewhat differently: those who point to the "reinvestment problem" as a discrepancy-producing source in the rate-of-return analysis are either reflecting an excessively pessimistic view of the availability of attractive investment opportunities, or are with gross optimism suggesting that the difficult problem of estimating profitability can be further compounded by adjusting the rates of return by the profitability of reinvesting cash proceeds of varying pattern over a variety of time spans, without at the same time making the problem an impossible one.

For the pessimistic view it need only be said that there is never, at any time, a shortage of profitable investment opportunities—there is more likely to be a shortage of risk takers capable of seeing the opportunities that are available; and while a given investment opportunity might more profitably (opportunely) be undertaken at one time than at another, there are always other opportunities whose right moment is *now*.

For the optimistic view it bears repeating, in somewhat different terms, the point made earlier, viz, why stop at the "first stage" of reinvestment? If it will improve investment results to modify the dictates of the rate-of-return analysis by what the reinvestment estimates indicate, why not carry the logic still further with a third, fourth, and fifth modification of what the reinvestment of the reinvested proceeds (etc.) would indicate?

Obviously, it is all a matter of degree of difficulty. But our point is that stopping at the "first stage"—with the rate-of-return analysis—is as far as we should *ordinarily* go. In an investment process where it is possible to go beyond this, it should be done. Otherwise, the intrepid forecaster who is willing to venture into the dark unknown should be wise enough to place a heavy premium on the rate-of-return results, and give only slight weight to the suggestions of the reinvestment estimates. In a sense, this tends to be done in the business decisions biased in favor of short payouts.

Public Relations with the Financial Community

We have already discussed under a separate heading the matter of stockholder relationships, wherein was emphasized management's responsibility to the owners. In this section we concern ourselves with the corporation's financial public relations with the general financial community in which investment opinion is formed and develops and which, in turn, can have tremendous importance to the future of a business enterprise.

Departing from Tradition. Product advertising—employing aggressive, persistent, and repetitive techniques—is a widely accepted part of promoting business and expanding profits. Yet, many of the companies that are well known for "hard selling" of their product lines have been manifestly unaware (at least they have not done anything to show their awareness) of another type of selling—*cultivating the investor!*

The background and traditions of business practices and attitudes probably explain this difference. To make profits it is necessary to sell the company's products and services and, up to a point, the more that can be sold at a given price per unit the greater will be the profit. Since products and services do not sell themselves, successful selling techniques become an important part of this logic. On the other hand, competition has traditionally induced business executives to feel that the less known by those outside the management the better, with the result that a "none-of-your-business" attitude toward the outside investors tended to prevail at one time. In the recent past, however, it has been giving way to a more enlightened attitude of telling investors all that possibly can be told. This trend has, of course, been accelerated by Securities and Exchange Commission regulations requiring full disclosure before securities can be offered to the public.

Advantages of a Broad Ownership Base. The spread of public ownership of most large corporations has brought an awareness to many managements that a change in attitude was necessary. Among the first companies to recognize this change and take advantage of it were those engaged in selling products directly to consumers (foods, oils, autos, appliances, beverages, etc.). Realizing the potential market represented by the stockholders, many of these companies have made it a point to advertise their products in the annual reports and other materials which are sent out to the owners, and to maintain, by means of stock dividends and splits, as broad an ownership base as possible by keeping the price of the stock within a reasonable buying range. High-priced stocks are unpopular with investors; stock splits bring the price down to a range that will have broader appeal. Such considerations are important: purchasers of automobiles, for example, might, other things being more or less equal, give preference to the product of the company in which they are stockholders. There are other advantages to a broadened ownership base: (1) it facilitates retention of control by making it more difficult for ownership to become concentrated in unfriendly hands; (2) it means a larger source of equity and debt capital, or at least a larger ready market to which an appeal for such capital can be made; (3) it provides added incentive to independent financial services to give some attention to the affairs of the company; and (4) it adds stability to the market price of the corporation's common stock.

Required—A New Selling Technique. The financial public relations program that seems desirable involves the adoption of a long-run policy to which the firm must commit itself unwaveringly, and which cannot be switched on and off as readily as one switches advertising media and techniques. The approach required is radically different from that of product advertising:

1. The items for sale are the company's financial record and its future prospects.
2. The "market" to which the appeal must be directed is made up of investors, the most important one of whom is the institutional investor. The latter is an "enlightened professional," so to speak, with large resources for investigating and analyzing situations, and many connections for checking information.
3. The underlying philosophy must be a willingness to deal as honestly and openly as possible with the present and potential investors in the company's future.

Rules of Conduct. It is impossible, of course, to consider here in detail the many ramifications of this subject. The arguments are not all on one side, but there seems to be taking place an awakening, so to speak, on the part of American managements to the importance of cultivating the investor. This is at least evidence of the fact that an increasing number of managements have come to the conclusion that the effort might prove rewarding. It is no simple matter to lay out a program that will be suitable for all companies alike, but some generalities are possible. The basic approach is what might be described as "sincere aggressiveness" on the part of the management to secure for the company the advantages of a favorably inclined capital market.

Hold regional stockholder meetings (depending on the size of the company and the concentration of stockholders in various parts of the country). This gives many of the stockholders an opportunity to see their management, hear their plans (in a general way, of course), and ask questions. Contrast such an approach with the current policy of so many large corporations which select a rather inaccessible, out-of-the-way meeting place for the annual stockholder meeting—obviously an attempt to minimize stockholder attendance.

Aggressively seek, and graciously accept, invitations to speak at the various investment analysts' societies throughout the country. The members of such societies are typically the representatives of the largest institutional investors in the country—major banks, insurance companies, and mutual funds—as well as representatives of brokerage firms and investment counselors whose reactions ultimately are made known to most investors active in the market. At these meetings, executives are invited to discuss their company's operations, plans, problems, and prospects. These forums present an ideal opportunity for a profitable selling job of the executive talent, and the company's future. Social contact of this sort between the company executives and the investment analysts adds an element of realism to the performance of the latter's duties and makes the company more than just a "name." From the company's point of view, a presentation effectively carried out can enhance its standing in the investment community, though any permanent enhancement would have to be supported by operating results over the future.

Build investor confidence by requiring all management personnel to own and retain a reasonable minimum amount of stock in the company, such stock to have been acquired by direct purchase in the market over a period of five years (so as not to force acquisition at times when stock prices are generally believed to be too high). This ownership should be related to the individual's position and salary, *and should come outside of any stock option plan that the company might have.* The latter is a justifiable means, when reasonably employed, of compensating management for a job well done, but is not an expression of management's confidence in the business. A properly expressed vote of confidence by management will go a long way to calling forth a vote of confidence by the stockholders in the company and its management (in the form of higher price-earnings ratios on the stock, and a ready willingness to subscribe to new security issues at prices attractive to the company).

In meeting with a group of investors, whether actual or potential, management should discuss their questions frankly and approach them with a ready willingness to state some of the problems confronting the company—how long it seems likely it will take for the solution of problems to be forthcoming, the amount of sales and earnings currently being budgeted for, a clear-cut statement of the company's present and probable dividend policy, and the direction in which the company expects to move in the future. The investors are actually entitled to such treatment, and will react favorably toward a management which accords it to them. This will show itself in enhanced stockholder loyalty and a generally better price-earnings ratio—important considerations, of course, when new capital is sought.

The Need to Sell Success. The point was made earlier that nothing succeeds like success. This is generally true, but we must modify this adage by the comment that sometimes success has to be sold. The psychology of the investor—even the well-staffed institutional investor—can cause him (or her) to act in peculiar fashion. How else to explain the fact that company A has a much better record of dividend and earnings growth than company B in the same or allied industry, yet consistently sells at a significantly lower price-earnings ratio? To a great extent this can be due to a lack of close familiarity with the undervalued company on the part of the investment community. No investor, institutional or otherwise, is able to follow very closely the affairs of all companies listed on the securities exchanges, let alone those of the many unlisted companies. The result is that a given company might be undervalued indefinitely, in spite of a consistently good operating record, and the only remedy for such a situation is to "sell" the company to the investment community by means of a wisely conceived financial public relations program comprising most of the suggestions put forth herein.

CONCLUSION

The quantitative aspects of capital budgeting are of great importance, but the final decisions must be based on qualitative aspects as well. Aside from the many obstacles to making an accurate determination of the cost of capital, capital budgeting decisions must be made within a framework of corporate financial policy. Financial policy will, of course, reflect management decisions at the highest level with respect to such considerations as debt limitation, tax rates, interest rates, and the necessity for payment of dividends to the stockholders (which is the obverse of retention of earnings).

In establishing financial policy, the directors must consider public psychology and the prospective money market, as well as the corporate relationship with the stockholders. Above all, the directors must discover and examine the investment opportunities available to the firm, and determine whether policy changes are necessary to take advantage of the opportunities.

PROBLEMS

1. If capital were treated as a commodity to be obtained by the corporation from financial institutions, private investors, and its own internal sources, it should be theoretically possible to establish supply and demand schedules for capital. The point of intersection, or equilibrium point, of these schedules could then be used as the "cutoff rate" for evaluating investment proposals. Why is this approach not practical in the real world?

2. What is a firm's potential internal supply of capital?

3. The L Company follows a policy of paying 35 percent of cash earnings in dividends and reinvesting 65 percent in replacement of existing facilities and for expansion. Assuming that this is their guiding principle in determining capital expenditure planning, what name is given to this method of resource allocation? What do you think of this method? Can you see why, if used in a more sophisticated manner along with other guides, it might be a very suitable (practical) approach to the problem of capital budgeting?

4. Why would management be reluctant to engage in debt financing of capital investments? What developments have tended to lessen management's aversion to debt?

5. When is it appropriate to use the "borrowing rate" and when to use the "lending rate"? What sort of costs are these? Are they ever the same?

6. Are there really such things as "the borrowing rate," "the lending rate," and "the interest rate"? If so, how are they determined? If not, why do we use such terms?

7. Is financing by retained earnings less costly than financing by the sale of new stock? What difficulty is encountered in determining the cost of retained earnings?

8. When may a firm be considered to have an optimal capital structure?

9. Distinguish between "earning yield," as that phrase is typically employed, and rate of return on investment.

10. "A truly democratic policy which all businesses should pursue is 100 percent distribution of cash earnings, the corporate capital being replenished by offer of stock subscriptions. Only in this way would the stockholders truly control the corporation's capital, and the free market forces will truly allocate resources among competing firms in the most optimum manner." Discuss.

11. What is meant by trading on equity? Why is this principle, as it is

usually stated, an inadequate guide for appropriate managerial action for maximizing profits?

12. Explain what is meant by "the marginal real cost of borrowing." How is this concept useful in defining optimum capital structure? What is important about capital structure as it relates to a firm's cost of capital?

13. Why would an investor purchase stock with an earnings-price ratio less than the yield on treasury bonds?

14. What are the principal determinants of the cost of capital?

15. How do the U.S. treasury and the Federal Reserve affect the cost of capital?

16. What is the most significant factor in determining the relative costs of debt and equity capital?

17. You have been appointed to the post of director of public relations for your firm, a publicly held corporation. The president has asked you to study and present in writing what you feel would be an integrated public relations program aimed at improving the firm's cost of capital and accessibility to the capital markets. What are your recommendations?

18. What is meant by the "reinvestment problem"? Discuss in full, indicating the nature of the "problem," the proposed "solution," and the shortcomings of the "solution."

REFERENCES

BARGES, ALEXANDER   *The Effect of Capital Structure on the Cost of Capital.* Englewood Cliffs, N.J.: Prentice-Hall, Inc., 1963.

BAUMOL, WILLIAM J., and MALKIEL, BURTON G.   "The Firm's Optimal Debt-Equity Combination and the Cost of Capital." *Quarterly Journal of Economics,* vol. 81, no. 4 (November 1967), pp. 547–78.

BAXTER, NEVINS D.   "Leverage, Risk of Ruin, and the Cost of Capital." *Journal of Finance,* vol. 22, no. 3 (September 1967), pp. 395–404.

LEWELLEN, WILBUR G.   *The Cost of Capital.* Belmont, Calif.: Wadsworth Publishing Co., Inc., 1969.

PORTERFIELD, JAMES T. S.   *Investment Decisions and Capital Costs.* Englewood Cliffs, N.J.: Prentice-Hall, Inc., 1965.

QUIRIN, G. DAVID   *The Capital Expenditure Decision.* Homewood, Ill.: Richard D. Irwin, Inc., 1967.

ROBICHEK, ALEXANDER A., and MYERS, STEWART C.   *Optimal Financing Decisions.* Englewood Cliffs, N.J.: Prentice-Hall, Inc., 1965.

SOLOMON, EZRA   "Measuring a Company's Cost of Capital." *Journal of Business,* vol. 28, no. 4 (October 1955), pp. 240–52.

VAN HORNE, JAMES C., ED.   *Foundations of Financial Management.* Homewood, Ill.: Richard D. Irwin, Inc., 1966.

―― *The Function and Analysis of Capital Market Rates.* Englewood Cliffs, N.J.: Prentice-Hall, Inc., 1970.

―― *Financial Management and Policy.* 2d ed. Englewood Cliffs, N.J.: Prentice-Hall, Inc., 1971.

chapter 16

Linear Programming and Operations Management

Linear programming is somewhat of a misnomer since there is a tendency to confuse the terms "linear programming" and "computer programming." Linear programming is of course related to computer programming to the extent that linear programming problems may be solved with the aid of a computer. But here the analogy ends. In actuality, linear programming is a mathematical modeling technique in which the "best" of a set of decision variables is chosen when the relationships between variables is linear. Technically, as will be seen below, linear programming may be formally defined as a method of optimizing (i.e., maximizing or minimizing) a linear function of several variables subject to a set of linear constraints.

ELEMENTARY GEOMETRY OF LINEAR PROGRAMMING

Since linear programming deals with problems of optimization, it evidently has a wide variety of applications in economics and business. The field of production economics may be taken as a concrete illustration.

Production Processes

The notion of a production *process* forms a convenient starting point for a discussion of linear programming. The concept of a process is illustrated in Exhibit 1 as several lines radiating from the origin. This chart is based on the data in Exhibit 2.

Process line I, for example, indicates how total output changes as inputs X and Y are increased proportionately. Thus, distance

EXHIBIT 1
Lines Representing Five Different Processes

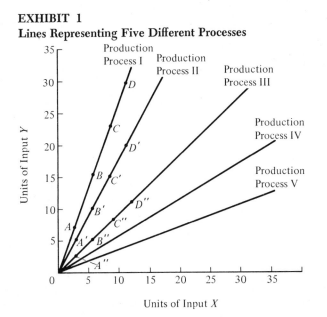

$OA = AB = BC$. Further, at point A total product is equal to 10Z, at point B it is equal to 20Z, and at point C it is equal to 30Z, as can be verified from Exhibit 2. Also, at point B, inputs of X and Y are exactly twice as large as at point A; and at point C they are three times as large as at point A. Thus, along line I, output increases in proportion to increases in input.

Likewise, along process line II, output increases proportionately, and the same is true along the other process lines, III, IV, and V. However, the output points designated as A, A', and A'' are not equidistant from the origin on all these lines. Output points such as A, B, C, and A', B', C' are evenly spaced along any given line, but $OA > OA'$, $AB > A'B'$, and so forth.

Thus, along each process line, total output changes proportionately to fixed proportionate changes in inputs, and the only differences among the process lines are the combinations of input proportions as shown in Exhibit 2.

Further, since changes in output are proportional to changes in all inputs along a process line, the production function is *linearly homogeneous*. Evidently, the number of such lines which can be drawn in

EXHIBIT 2
Quantities of Product Z Obtainable from
Given Inputs, X and Y

Production Process	Quantity of Output, Z, and Output Points		Quantity of Input, X	Quantity of Input, Y
I	10	A	2.5	7.5
	20	B	5.0	15.0
	30	C	7.5	22.5
	40	D	10.0	30.0
II	10	A'	2.5	5.0
	20	B'	5.0	10.0
	30	C'	7.5	15.0
	40	D'	10.0	20.0
III	10	A''	3.0	3.0
	20	B''	6.0	6.0
	30	C''	9.0	9.0
	40	D''	12.0	12.0
IV	10		5.0	2.5
	20		10.0	5.0
	30		15.0	7.5
	40		20.0	10.0
V	10		7.5	2.5
	20		15.0	5.0
	30		22.5	7.5
	40		30.0	10.0

a given case depends on the divisibility of X and Y. If the inputs are perfectly divisible, an infinite number of processes is possible.

Derivation of the Isoquants

If we join the corresponding points (such as A, A', and A'') with straight lines, we produce contour lines, or *isoproduct* curves such as AA'A'', BB'B'', and CC'C'' in Exhibit 3. The isoproduct curve AA'A'' is labeled as $I_q 10$. This curve may be described as the locus of points along which substitution between any two processes occurs at a constant rate, yielding the same amount of output for alternate levels of inputs. However, the rate of substitution among all five processes is not the same. Thus, in linear programming, the isoquants are treated as straight-line segments having corners at points such as A, A', A'', and so forth, instead of being treated as continuous curves.

Determination of Quantities of Inputs Employed

It is possible to combine *isocost* curves with *isoquants* in order to obtain an optimum or equilibrium position for the firm. Thus, in Exhibit

EXHIBIT 3
Linear Isoquants

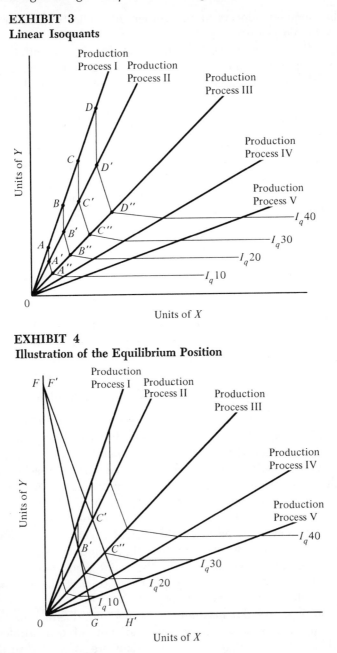

EXHIBIT 4
Illustration of the Equilibrium Position

4, the line FG represents the isocost line when the price of input X, say, is \$8 per unit, the price of input Y is \$1 per unit, and the firm budgets a total outlay of \$50 for inputs. As shown in Exhibit 2, the firm at B' uses 10 units of Y and 5 units of X to produce 20 units of Z (the product). The point of tangency between the isocost curve, FG, and the isoquant appears at the corner, B', indicating that process II is the optimum process.

Let $F'H'$ represent a line indicating that the company attains a higher level of output (30 units of Z, as represented at C'') with a smaller total outlay ($45) at different relative prices of X and Y. The line $F'H'$ is tangent to I_q30 *over the range* $C'C''$, which indicates that at the new given relative prices of X and Y, both process II and process III are optimal and any combination of the two processes is also optimal. Along $F'H'$, the price of X is $4 per unit, and the price of Y is $1 per unit. Thus, the optimum production program depends on the relative prices of the factors or inputs. In the diagram, the firm need never use more than a single process in order to produce the given output. At C', for example, the firm uses 15 units of Y and 7.5 units of X as seen in Exhibit 2. At the given relative prices we have:

$$(\$4)(7.5) + (\$1)(15) = \$45$$

At C'' the company uses nine units of Y and nine units of X. Hence,

$$(\$4)(9) + (\$1)(9) = \$45$$

Thus, the slope of the isoquant between C' and C'' is $(15 - 9)$ divided by $(9 - 7.5) = 6/1.5 = 4$, and this is equal to the ratio of the prices of X and Y indicated by the slope of the isocost line $F'H'$.

The Complete Description Method: Maximization Problem

A graphic method of solving a linear programming problem is practical when it involves two or three variables. But whenever it is complex—involving more than three variables—it cannot be shown geometrically because there is no way of illustrating four or more dimensions in space. In such cases we must resort to algebraic procedures. First, however, a linear programming problem involving two products is presented, in order to convey some elementary geometric relationships.

Let us assume that the assembly lines of a certain automobile plant are identical in all respects, and that these lines are used to produce both sedans and convertibles with the same labor force. In a given amount of time, at most four sedans or two convertibles can be assembled completely on one assembly line.

Exhibit 5 shows the maximum combinations diagrammatically. We measure units of sedans on one axis and units of convertibles on the other. It can be seen that when four sedans are assembled in the given amount of time, no convertibles are produced; and when two convertibles are assembled in the given amount of time, no sedans come off the line. Likewise, three sedans and one half a convertible can be assembled in the same amount of time, as defined by point P_1. Also, two sedans and one convertible can be produced, as defined by point P_2.

EXHIBIT 5
The Automobile Plant's First
Functional Constraint

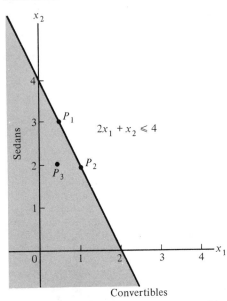

The region of combinations of convertible
versus sedan assemblies in a given time period.
(Note that the shaded area extends beyond the
axes, indicating the possibilities of negative
values of x_1 and x_2.)

Clearly, any point along the line defines the maximum combination of
sedans and convertibles that can be produced in the given time period.

However, the maximum combinations are not always available, due
to the fact that the assembly lines cannot always be expected to function
smoothly. For example, parts shortages, changes in personnel, machine
or assembly-line breakdowns may slow down the line. As a result, the
diagram depicting the maximum combinations has to be modified.

The shaded area under (and to the left) of the line represents the
region of combinations available to the auto manufacturer. Situations
may arise in which it is possible to produce, say, two sedans and only
one half a convertible in a given time period, as shown by point P_3.
Similarly, any other point in the shaded region represents a different
output combination of convertibles and sedans which is less than any
maximum combination shown by the line.

The First Functional Constraint

The line in Exhibit 5 can be algebraically represented by the linear
equation:

$$2x_1 + x_2 = 4$$

where x_1 is expressed in terms of convertibles, and x_2 in terms of sedans. Thus, when two convertibles, x_1, are assembled in a given time period, no sedans, x_2, are produced; hence:

$$2(2) + (0) = 4$$

Likewise, when four sedans are produced, no convertibles come off the line in a given time period, that is,

$$2(0) + (4) = 4$$

Similarly, $x_1 = 1$, and $x_2 = 2$, describe another possible combination in a given time period, namely:

$$2(1) + (2) = 4$$

as defined by point P_2 in Exhibit 5.

The shaded area under and to the left of the line shown in the figure can be algebraically represented by the inequality:

$$2x_1 + x_2 \leqq 4$$

This relationship is composed of the linear equation and the linear inequality described above. Thus, it is satisfied by all points located on the line and in the area below the line, as shown in Exhibit 5. (Note that the shaded area extends beyond the axes, indicating the possibilities of negative values of x_1 and x_2. The implications of this will be discussed shortly.) The above inequality is called a *functional constraint*.

Derivation of the Second Functional Constraint

Let us assume further that depending on the particular model of sedan being produced as compared to the particular model of convertible, a maximum of 50 percent more storage space and raw material, including steel, iron, glass, rubber, fabric, and so forth, is used up in the assembly of a sedan. Thus, either three convertibles or two sedans can be produced with the same material at a given time. The relationships are exhibited in Exhibit 6, which shows the region of combinations satisfying the second functional constraint. Again, all points on the line and in the region satisfy the second inequality, which can be algebraically represented as:

$$2x_1 + 3x_2 \leqq 6$$

where x_1 is to be expressed in terms of convertibles, and x_2 in terms of sedans.

EXHIBIT 6
The Automobile Plant's Second
Functional Constraint

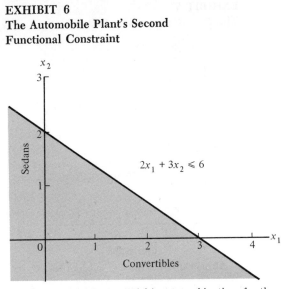

The region of raw material input combinations for the convertible and the sedan.

Derivation of the Nonnegativity Restrictions

Conceptually, the firm could be thought of as producing a negative number of cars if it were to purchase autos from other firms. Since we desire to rule out this possibility, all production may be thought of as positive, thereby permitting us to operate entirely in the first quadrant, that is, the region where x_1 and x_2 are each equal to or greater than zero. We are introducing what are appropriately called *nonnegativity restrictions*.

Exhibit 7 shows the nonnegativity restrictions for convertibles, written as $x_1 \geq 0$, and the nonnegativity restrictions for sedans, written as $x_2 \geq 0$.

When the two functional constraints and the two nonnegativity restrictions appear simultaneously on one graph, the resulting region is displayed as shown in Exhibit 8. The boundaries of the region are defined by:

$$2x_1 + x_2 = 4$$
$$2x_1 + 3x_2 = 6$$
$$x_1 = 0$$
$$x_2 = 0$$

Likewise, the interior of the region is defined by the following inequalities:

$$2x_1 + x_2 < 4$$
$$2x_1 + 3x_2 < 6$$
$$x_1 > 0$$
$$x_2 > 0$$

EXHIBIT 7
The Two Nonnegativity Restrictions

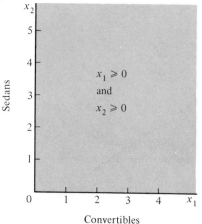

Convertibles

All points inside the first quadrant as
well as on the two lines $x_1 = 0$ and $x_2 = 0$
satisfy the two nonnegativity restrictions
simultaneously.

EXHIBIT 8
The "Feasible" Region

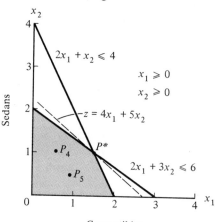

Convertibles

All points inside the first quadrant and
bounded by the two nonnegativity restrictions
and the two functional constraints are feasible
solutions of the linear programming problem.

The shaded area and its boundaries in Exhibit 8 represent the region
of feasible solutions to the linear programming problem, that is, the
set of all combinations of (x_1, x_2)—convertibles and sedans—which
satisfy the constraints of the linear programming problem as outlined
above. For example, any point such as P_4 or P_5 satisfies the two func-

tional constraints and the two nonnegativity restrictions. However, a feasible solution of a linear programming problem is not necessarily the optimal solution. To obtain the optimal solution, the *objective function* of the linear programming problem must first be determined, and then considered simultaneously with the functional constraints and the nonnegativity restrictions.

Derivation of the Objective Function

Let us further assume that each sedan yields $500 and each convertible $400 above its individual cost. The profit relationship defines a plane in a three coordinate system which is restricted to the first quadrant by the two nonnegativity restrictions and is constrained in height (profit) by the two functional constraints. Exhibit 9 shows all of these relationships diagrammatically. Profits are measured on the vertical axis, while convertibles and sedans are measured on the two horizontal axes, x_1 and x_2 respectively.

EXHIBIT 9
Geometrical Representation of the Linear Programming Problem

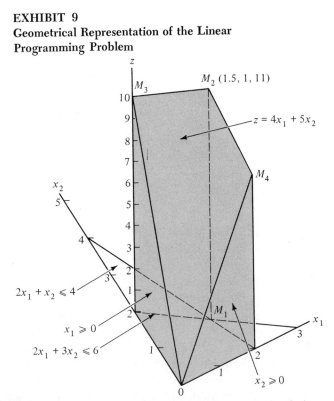

Each point inside the volume represents a feasible solution. The optimal solution is the uppermost point of the bounded volume, defined by point M_2.

The profit relationships are defined by the objective function which can be algebraically determined as the plane:

$$z = 4x_1 + 5x_2$$

where z is to be expressed as profit in hundreds of dollars, x_1 in terms of units of convertibles, and x_2 in terms of units of sedans.

Any point in or on the volume bounded by the two functional constraints, the two nonnegativity restrictions, and the objective function, is a feasible solution of the linear programming problem.

One of the feasible solutions is also the optimal solution. The optimal solution is the point in or on the volume which yields the maximum profit, that is, the largest possible value of z subject to the two nonnegativity restrictions and the two functional constraints. Thus, the optimal solution must lie graphically on the uppermost point of the bounded volume.

The uppermost point of the bounded volume is the point defined by M_2, as shown in Exhibit 9. At point M_2, $z = 11$, $x_1 = 1.5$, and $x_2 = 1$. Thus, the optimal solution for the automobile company's production process occurs when $z = \$1,100$, $x_1 = 1.5$ convertibles, and $x_2 = 1$ sedan for each given amount of assembly-line time.

An alternate way of determining the optimal value for z would be to note that since z is a positive function of x_1 and x_2, z gets larger as each of these variables does. Arbitrarily setting z to some positive number, say 20, the objective function can then be collapsed into the two-dimensional space of Exhibit 8, and the equation becomes:

$$x_2 = \frac{z}{5} - \frac{4}{5}x_2 = 4 - \frac{4}{5}x_2$$

for $z = 20$. With the equation written in this form, note that the slope of the objective function remains the same as z varies, only the "intercept" of the equation changes. Hence, alternate values of z will determine an entire family of lines parallel to one another on the graph, with larger values of z, and therefore greater profit, represented by lines further from the origin. The optimal solution to the two-dimensional linear programming problem at hand is therefore the value of z corresponding to the line furthest from the origin that still satisfies the constraints—or the line just tangent to the feasible region at the single point, $P^* = (1.5, 1)$, as indicated in Exhibit 8. Here, z cannot be increased any more without violating the linear restrictions on the variables, and of course it would be silly to make z any smaller by looking at lines to the left of the one illustrated. Hence, an optimal solution is determined with optimal values of x_1, x_2, and z as identified above.

One might also note that the optimal solution to the graphical linear programming problem need not always occur at the intersection of the functional constraints—that is, at a point such as P^* in Exhibit 8. This will depend on the relative slopes of the objective function, as reformulated above, and the constraints. For example, if instead of $-\frac{4}{5}$, the objective function had a slope more negative than -2 or less negative than $-\frac{2}{3}$, a "corner" solution would result, in which the optimal production strategy would be to make either all convertibles or all sedans.

ELEMENTARY ALGEBRA OF LINEAR PROGRAMMING

When a linear programming problem involves more than two of the x variables (x_1 and x_2), the problem can no longer be solved graphically. However, problems involving even more than three different variables can be solved by algebraic means, since algebra is not restricted by three-dimensional space.

An Algebraic Example

Consider a manufacturer of commercial electronic equipment who markets three transistorized portable radios, x_1, x_2, and x_3, at $11, $17, and $20, respectively. The radios are alike in most respects, differing only in the number of various electronic components which are required for their assembly. The purchasing department of the electronics firm provides the information shown in Exhibit 10.

EXHIBIT 10
Components Required to Build Each of the Three Different Radios

Component	Product x_1	Product x_2	Product x_3
Component Type 1 (a_{1j})	6 per unit	4 per unit	3 per unit
Component Type 2 (a_{2j})	12 per unit	10 per unit	14 per unit
Component Type 3 (a_{3j})	5 per unit	10 per unit	12 per unit
Component Type 4 (a_{4j})	2 per unit	6 per unit	8 per unit

Assume further that the electronics firm is producing for inventory, so that it has a free choice as to whether to assemble x_1, x_2, or x_3, or any combination thereof. Due to the fact that all three radios are functionally similar, they require the same labor costs and overhead expense. In deciding what to manufacture in a given day, the production manager of the firm needs only to consider his (or her) inventory of

EXHIBIT 11
Quantities of the Four Components on
Hand on a Particular Day with Their
Associated Unit Costs

Component	Number in Stock (q_i)	Cost per Unit
Component Type 1 (a_{1j})	210	30¢
Component Type 2 (a_{2j})	960	10¢
Component Type 3 (a_{3j})	600	90¢
Component Type 4 (a_{4j})	400	50¢

components. On a particular day the production manager obtains the inventory of components shown in Exhibit 11, from the production control supervisor.

Utilizing the information in Exhibits 11 and 12, the production manager sets out to determine the production schedule for the day which will

EXHIBIT 12
Gross Profit per Radio

Component	Unit Cost	Per Unit of x_1 No.	Per Unit of x_1 Cost	Per Unit of x_2 No.	Per Unit of x_2 Cost	Per Unit of x_3 No.	Per Unit of x_3 Cost
1	30¢	6	$ 1.80	4	$ 1.20	3	$ 0.90
2	10¢	12	1.20	10	1.00	14	1.40
3	90¢	5	4.50	10	9.00	12	10.80
4	50¢	2	1.00	6	3.00	8	4.00
Total cost			$ 8.50		$14.20		$17.10
Selling price			11.00		17.00		20.00
Gross profit			2.50		2.80		2.90

earn the maximum gross profit for the company. Gross profit in this problem means the difference between the selling price of each radio and the total of its component costs. (The costs of labor and overhead have been omitted since it was determined that these were identical for all three products.)

The first step in solving the problem is to determine the gross profit to be earned by each unit of x_1, x_2, and x_3, based entirely on the costs of components. See Exhibit 12.

Next, the availabilities of the components must be considered, since they will constrain choices regarding the number and types of radios to be assembled. The production manager algebraically determines the inventory constraints as follows:

$$6x_1 + 4x_2 + 3x_3 \leq 210 \quad \text{[Component } a_{1j}\text{]}$$
$$12x_1 + 10x_2 + 14x_3 \leq 960 \quad \text{[Component } a_{2j}\text{]}$$
$$5x_1 + 10x_2 + 12x_3 \leq 600 \quad \text{[Component } a_{3j}\text{]}$$
$$2x_1 + 6x_2 + 8x_3 \leq 400 \quad \text{[Component } a_{4j}\text{]}$$

Plotting the four inventory constraints simultaneously on one graph, four overlapping planes as shown in Exhibit 13 are obtained. Only values of x_1, x_2, and x_3 inside the shaded volume satisfy the four inventory constraints simultaneously.

EXHIBIT 13
Geometrical Representation of the Four Inventory Constraints

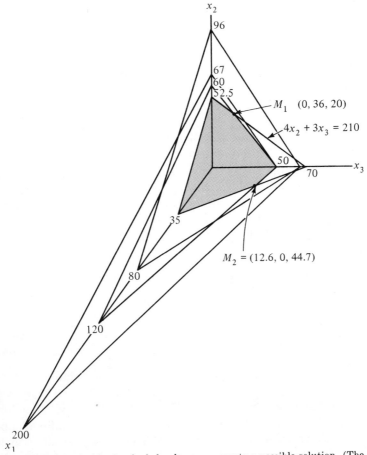

Each point inside the shaded volume represents a possible solution. (The feasible solutions are drawn from this volume after values of x_1, x_2, and x_3 are inserted into the objective function.)

Why are the four planes in Exhibit 13 drawn only in the first octave of a three-coordinate system? The answer is based on the existence of the nonnegativity requirements. Thus, since the manufacturer does not intend to purchase radios from competing firms, the following non-negativity restrictions apply:

$$x_1 \geq 0, \; x_2 \geq 0, \; x_3 \geq 0$$

The objective function derived from the profit figures in Exhibit 12 is thus:

$$\text{Maximum profit} = z = 2.5x_1 + 2.8x_2 + 2.9x_3$$

where z is to be expressed in dollars of profit.

Solving the Problem: The Simplex Method

In order to solve the linear programming problem algebraically, we first transform all of the inventory constraints into equalities. The transformation is achieved by introducing additional nonnegative variables whose sole purpose is to take up the difference or *slack* between the inequality and the equation.

As an example, we can transform the inequality $6x_1 + 4x_2 + 3x_3 \leq 210$ into the equation $6x_1 + 4x_2 + 3x_3 + x_4 = 210$ where x_4 is the *slack variable* and must be nonnegative, that is, $x_4 \geq 0$. When x_4 equals 0, the sum of $6x_1 + 4x_2 + 3x_3$ will equal exactly to 210; when x_4 is any value larger than zero, the sum of $6x_1 + 4x_2 + 3x_3$ will be less than 210 by an amount equal to x_4. Note that when x_4 equals 210, x_1, x_2, and x_3 all equal zero; also, x_4 can never become larger than 210 because of the nonnegativity restrictions for x_1, x_2, and x_3.

Introducing the slack variables into the four inventory constraints we obtain:

$$6x_1 + 4x_2 + 3x_3 + x_4 \qquad\qquad\qquad = 210 \qquad (1)$$

$$12x_1 + 10x_2 + 14x_3 \qquad + x_5 \qquad\quad = 960 \qquad (2)$$

$$5x_1 + 10x_2 + 12x_3 \qquad\quad + x_6 \quad = 600 \qquad (3)$$

$$2x_1 + 6x_2 + 8x_3 \qquad\qquad\qquad + x_7 = 400 \qquad (4)$$

We now have an "undetermined" system of four equations in seven unknowns, that is, x_1, x_2, x_3, x_4, x_5, x_6, and x_7. That is, there are not enough equations to determine each variable uniquely. Therefore, in such a system there are either no solutions or an infinite number of solutions. However, a solution can be obtained algebraically which will optimize the linear programming problem, by means of the *simplex method*.

The simplex method requires that we start with a "basic feasible" solution. A feasible solution is one in which the variables satisfy the nonnegativity conditions and the constraints; a basic feasible solution requires that, in addition, we have only as many positive variables in the solution as there are independent equations in the system. Hence, for the problem at hand, the basic feasible solution implies that exactly four variables be positive and the rest zero.

For production problems in which constraints are of the "less than" variety, a basic feasible solution is easily determined by letting the slack variables be positive, and the others zero. This means that $x_1 = 0$, $x_2 = 0$, and $x_3 = 0$ for the present system of equations; and because of the "canonical" (identity-matrix-like) form of the slack system, we can immediately also tell the values of the slack variables: $x_4 = 210$, $x_5 = 960$, $x_6 = 600$, and $x_7 = 400$.

As noted previously, any basic feasible solution is not necessarily an optimal solution to the linear programming problem because the ultimate determinant of optimality is measured by the value of the objective function. For the present basic feasible solution, this value is zero because the slack variables do not enter the objective function. In effect, the present solution corresponds to the situation in which we are actually storing our components and, of course, making no profit.

In order to improve this situation, we next wish to exchange a slack variable for a "real" (manufacturing) variable. If we set x_2, x_3, and x_4 equal to 0 in equation (1), we see that $x_1 = 35$. Likewise, if we set x_1, x_3, and x_4 equal to 0 in equation (1), we get $x_2 = 52.5$. In the same manner, if we set x_1, x_2, and x_6 equal to 0 in equation (3), we get $x_3 = 50$. Also, if we set x_1, x_2, and x_7 equal to 0 in equation (4), we get $x_3 = 50$. Through inspection, it is easy to verify that when $x_1 = 35$, while x_2 and x_3 are equal to 0, equations (1) through (4) are simultaneously satisfied, and no value of x_1 larger than 35 will satisfy the four equations simultaneously. Likewise, when x_1 and x_3 are equal to 0, no value larger than 52.5 will satisfy the variable x_2 in each of the four equations. When x_1 and x_2 are both equal to 0, the greatest value of x_3 is 50 in each of the four equations.

Since the maximum profit for the firm occurs when

$$z = 2.5x_1 + 2.8x_2 + 2.9x_3$$

is maximized, we see that $z = \$87.50$ when $x_1 = 35$, $x_2 = 0$, and $x_3 = 0$. Likewise, $z = \$147$ when $x_1 = 0$, $x_2 = 52.5$, and $x_3 = 0$. Also, $z = \$145$ when $x_1 = 0$, $x_2 = 0$, and $x_3 = 50$.

The points (x_1, x_2, x_3) corresponding to $(35, 0, 0)$, $(0, 52.5, 0)$ and $(0, 0, 50)$ determine three of the "extreme points" of the feasible region for the problem at hand. Exhibit 13 graphically depicts the complete feasible region as the shaded portion of the figure.

By theorem, to determine the optimal solution to the linear programming problem, it is only necessary to evaluate the objective function at each of these extreme points: if an optimal solution to a linear programming problem exists, then at least one extreme point will be optimal. Referring again to the figure, we see that only five points need be examined for the problem at hand: the three points enumerated above, plus point $M_1 = (0, 36, 20)$ and $M_2 = (12.6, 0, 44.7)$. The value of the objective function at each of these two points is \$158.80 for M_1 and \$161.32 for M_2. Hence, the optimal solution to this linear programming program is to produce 12.6 units of product 1, no units of product 2, and 44.7 units of product 3, yielding a net profit of \$161.32. Due to the manufacturing constraints, an excess of 182.1 components of type 2 and 16.8 components of type 4 will be incurred. The complete solution is, therefore: $x_1 = 12.6$, $x_2 = 0$, $x_3 = 44.7$, $x_4 = 0$, $x_5 = 182.1$, $x_6 = 0$, and $x_7 = 16.8$.[1]

To convince yourself of the optimality of the proposed solution, consider feasible points lying near point M_2. For example, if we set $x_1 = 12$, then we can increase x_3 to 45 with $x_2 = 0$. But the value of the objective function is reduced to 160.50. Similarly, if we set $x_1 = 13$, x_3 will equal 44 with $x_2 = 0$, and the value of the objective function is 160.10. Finally setting $x_1 = 10.7$, $x_2 = 1$, and $x_3 = 44.7$, we still have a suboptimal solution since $z = 159.23$. In all three cases, a lower profit level is observed. Only at the extreme point M_2 does our objective function achieve its highest value, and hence determines the product mix of maximal profit.

General Description of the Simplex Method

As noted, the above method of solution is called the simplex method. Basically, this method is concerned with determining when the maximum total profits from given inputs is being obtained by computing the *changes in total profit* (Δz) which would occur by moving in any direction from a given corner point, such as M_1 in Exhibit 13 or M_1, M_2, M_3, and M_4 in Exhibit 9. If the change in total profit is positive ($\Delta z > 0$), thus signifying that total profit can be increased by moving in a given direction (increasing the output of one of the products at the expense of another or changing the proportions in which the outputs are produced), the computation process is repeated, using new corner positions as a basis for further computations. Finally, when a corner position is reached (such as M_1 for the electronics firm) so that a movement away from it in any direction results in a decrease or negative change in total profit ($\Delta z < 0$), the problem has been solved in that

---

[1] More precisely, these numbers are 12.6316, 0, 44.7368, 0, 182.105, 0, and 16.8421, respectively.

an optimal solution has been found. For, in this case, the total profit obtainable from the given inputs must be at a maximum.

A Basic Theorem of Linear Programming

The solution illustrated above, and in the previous section, illustrates a basic theorem of linear programming:

> THEOREM: *In the optimal solution, there will usually be exactly as many outputs produced as there are inputs used to capacity.*

In the present case, two products, x_1 and x_3, are produced and two of the four inputs, a_{1j} and a_{3j}, are used to capacity, so that there are virtually no unutilized or leftover amounts (in the integer or noncontinuous case as above) of these inputs at the optimal point M_2 in Exhibit 13.

THE DUAL PROBLEM

In general, every linear programming problem has a *dual.* The dual of the maximization problem just discussed is a counterpart of the linear programming problem and addresses the question: What is the value to the electronics firm of additional units of inputs?

"Shadow" or "Accounting" Prices

Consider input a_{2j} which is not being fully employed in the electronics firm's input allocation problem discussed above. Other things remaining the same, what are additional units of input a_{2j} worth to the electronics firm?

Since additional inputs of a_{2j} do not increase total output in terms of their effect on total profit, additional units of a_{2j} have a zero value to this company. On the other hand, additional units of a_{3j} and a_{1j} (which are fully employed) do have a positive value to the firm: for if the company obtained additional units of these inputs, it could combine them with inputs a_{2j} and a_{4j} (which are not scarce insofar as the activities of this company are concerned) to increase total product and hence total profit.

The dual of the problem of resource allocation or of maximization of the total profit obtainable from the production of x_1 and x_3 in our case is thus the problem of determining the values to the firm (or the imputed values) of the inputs employed at the margin. Such imputed values are sometimes referred to as "shadow prices" or as "accounting prices" of the inputs.

The Electronic Firm's Equations Rearranged

The above problem can be easily solved by rearranging the data and the equations which have already been used in the algebraic example above. In order to develop the new equations, consider the fact that the value to the company of all the inputs used to produce one unit of x_1 must be greater than or equal to the amount of profit obtained by the firm from the sale of one unit of x_1.

The same can be said of x_2 and x_3. In the form of a series of equations:

$$6s_1 + 12s_2 + 5s_3 + 2s_4 \geq P_{x_1} = \$2.50$$
$$4s_1 + 10s_2 + 10s_3 + 6s_4 \geq P_{x_2} = \$2.80$$
$$3s_1 + 14s_2 + 12s_3 + 8s_4 \geq P_{x_3} = \$2.90$$

where each P represents gross profit per radio.

In these equations, s_1, s_2, s_3, and s_4 represent the "shadow prices" or imputed values of the respective inputs (a_{1j}, a_{2j}, a_{3j}, and a_{4j}) employed. The shadow prices in this case are really "shadow profits" due to the fact that we are interested in maximizing the profit of the electronics firm.

It follows from the above discussion that the imputed unit values of the inputs multiplied by their corresponding quantities available, when summed, equals the total value of the resources employed, and must be just equal to the maximum total profit obtained from the sale of the products at the current prices (and therefore profits).

Accordingly, the objective equation in the case of the dual problem can be written as:

$$V(\min) = 210s_1 + 960s_2 + 600s_3 + 400s_4$$

which is equal to total profit also.

This formulation of the objective function thus states that the respective imputed unit values or "shadow profits," s, of the resources, multiplied by the amounts of each of them which are available, must be equal to the total profit obtained from the sale of the three products produced by means of the four inputs.

The Optimum Solution to the Dual Problem

Normally, the dual problem like the primal problem is solved with the assistance of a computer. In this case, however, we can use what we already know about the shadow prices of the electronics firm's inputs to solve the dual problem graphically. We have observed that at optimality, "slack" appears in the second and fourth input constraints of the primal problem. We may therefore conclude that additional units of inputs a_{2j} and a_{4j} are useless to the firm. This implies that the shadow prices s_2 and s_4 of these inputs are zero. Recognizing this fact, the reduced set of equations for the dual problem is therefore:

$$6s_1 + 5s_3 \geq 2.50$$
$$4s_1 + 10s_3 \geq 2.80$$
$$3s_1 + 12s_3 \geq 2.90$$

$$(\text{min.})210s_1 + 600s_3$$

which is a system of inequalities in only two unknowns. Plotting these constraints as in Exhibit 14, the optimal values of the dual variables

EXHIBIT 14
A Geometric Interpretation of the Dual

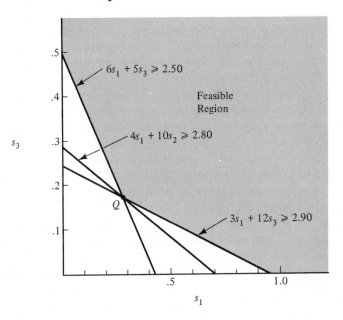

are determined to be $s_1 = .272$, $s_2 = 0$, $s_3 = .174$, and $s_4 = 0$, or point Q in Exhibit 14.[2]

To test these results, we must have the value of the dual objective

---

[2] More precisely, $s_1 = .27193$ and $s_3 = .173684$. This point is found as the intersection of the first and third equations of the system. The second constraint is found to lie outside the feasible region defined by these equations.

function equaling the value of the primal objective function at optimality. Substituting:

$$210(.272) + 600(.174) = \$161.32$$

as desired.

THE GENERALIZED LINEAR PROGRAMMING
PROBLEM AND METHODS

Based on the geometrical and algebraic solutions of the two linear programming problems above, certain fundamental relationships which represent the generalized properties of all linear programming problems may be observed.

The Objective Function

All linear programming problems are concerned with either minimizing or maximizing something. In general, the quantity to be minimized or maximized is called the *objective function*. There is some temptation to classify linear programming problems into two types according to whether the objective function is to be minimized or maximized. This is pointless, however, because there is no real difference between the two problems. Every time a quantity is minimized, some other quantity—for example, its negative—is maximized, and vice versa. Thus, one cannot distinguish between minimizing and maximizing problems and we can discuss the linear programming problem in terms of whichever type or extreme degree seems most convenient at the time.

It is assumed that the typical manager normally desires either to maximize the profits or minimize the costs of his operations. Examples of such objectives are optimizing production processes, selecting optimum product mixes, determining the least-cost combination of meeting specifications, and finding the least costly transportation routes. There is, however, no reason why the objective should be so restricted. If one wishes to make certain other specifications so as to modify an objective, these can be easily included. Thus, one may be interested in keeping the good will of the customer, and thus deviate somewhat from the optimum product mix. Or, one may be willing to maintain a fully employed labor force in order to placate the union, even if it involves a financial sacrifice.

It should be strongly emphasized that if sensible results are to be obtained from linear programming, the objective must be clearly specified before computations take place. Thus, solving an automobile company's production question, the problem may be one of determining which assembly lines should produce a quantity of a particular automobile consistent with a given level of demand. The objective should be stated accordingly. The objective of a linear programming study may be expressed in physical, monetary, or other terms, depending upon the problem being analyzed.

The Functional Constraints

Another property of the linear programming problem is that it contains functional constraints expressed as linear inequalities which state the special conditions of the problem. Thus, it can unequivocally be stated that a linear programming problem does not exist unless resources are restricted or limited. The majority of planning problems contain constraints which set limits on the kinds of plans which can be considered. For a producing company, constraints are defined by the fixed quantities of certain resources. Thus, a manufacturing firm will have a fixed number of machines and floor space. The firm in general will also be limited in the amount of money it has or shall have in the future. Scarce labor resources may also limit the operations of a company. The manager himself may place restrictions on the minimum or maximum size of certain enterprises. In a transportation problem the constraints are the supplies of commodities at production centers and the quantities demanded at consuming centers.

The Nonnegativity Requirements

A third property of the linear programming problem is that the solution to the problem cannot be negative. The equations that define this restriction are called nonnegativity restrictions, and are mathematically expressed as $x_1 \geq 0$, $x_2 \geq 0$, . . . , $x_n \geq 0$.

An Algebraic Representation of the Linear Programming Problem

The three generalized properties of the linear programming problem described above can be algebraically represented as follows:

Values should be assigned to the j individual unknowns, x_1, x_2, x_3, . . . x_j, in such a way as to maximize or minimize the objective function defined by:

$$z = p_1x_1 + p_2x_2 + \cdots + p_jx_j$$

subject to the i conditions defined by the functional constraints:

$$a_{11}x_1 + a_{12}x_2 + \cdots + a_{1j}x_j \leq q_1$$
$$a_{21}x_1 + a_{22}x_2 + \cdots + a_{2j}x_j \leq q_2$$
$$a_{31}x_1 + a_{32}x_2 + \cdots + a_{3j}x_j \leq q_3$$

$$a_{i1} + a_{i2}x_2 + \cdots + a_{ij}x_j \leq q_i$$

and the nonnegativity restrictions:

$$x_1, x_2, x_3, \ldots, x_j \geqq 0$$

The x_j unknowns are usually called the choice variables in linear programming problems. Quite frequently, but not always, each choice variable indicates the extent to which something is to be done. For this reason it is convenient (and usually sufficiently accurate) to think of each choice variable as indicating the level of some operation, called an "activity" or a "process." A process is some physical operation such as selecting something, discarding something, or perhaps manufacturing something in a particular manner. It is often convenient to think of fictitious processes which do not correspond to any physical operation, as, for example, the non-use of resources represented by "slack" variables.

The essential characteristic about a process from the point of view of linear programming is not its physical nature (the process may be entirely fictitious and have no nature), but the way it enters into the objective function and the constraints plus restrictions. This characteristic is contained entirely in the coefficients by which the choice variable corresponding to the process is multiplied in the objective function and in the constraints. These coefficients, p_j, a_{ij}, and q_i are parameters; they represent quantities that are to be specified in advance. The coefficient p_j by which the choice variable is multiplied in the objective function is known as the *payoff coefficient* or the *value* of the process. The list of coefficients by which the choice variable is multiplied in the functional constraints is known as either the *input-output coefficient* or the *process vector*, and is designated as a_{ij}. Some of these coefficients may, of course, be zero. Likewise, each of the individual q_i in the functional contraints is called a *right-hand-side constant*.

Just as each choice variable specifies the level of operation or process to be used, so a list of choice variables that occur in a problem specify the levels of operation or processes considered to be used. Such a list is therefore called a *program*. If the list satisfies all the functional constraints, it is called a *solution*, a *feasible solution*, a *feasible program*, or a *feasible strategy*. If the solution maximizes (or minimizes, as the case may be), the objective function, it is known as an *optimal solution*, an *optimal program*, or an *optimal strategy*.

The "Unsolvable" Linear Programming Problem

It should be pointed out that not all linear programming problems are solvable. However, the linear programming problems which are not solvable are really not linear programming problems or even problems in the pure sense of the word. They are, unequivocally, dilemmas. An example of a dilemma or "unsolvable linear programming problem" follows:

Suppose we set $i = 2$ and $j = 2$ in the generalized linear programming equation and inequalities described above. Since $i = 2$, we have two generalized functional constraints; and since $j = 2$, we have two input-output coefficients in each generalized inequality, that is:

$$a_{11}x_1 + a_{12}x_2 \leqq q_1$$
$$a_{21}x_1 + a_{22}x_2 \leqq q_2$$

Now, if we set the input-output coefficients as follows:

$$a_{11} = -2 \quad a_{12} = 2 \quad a_{21} = 3 \quad \text{and} \quad a_{22} = -3$$

plus the right-hand-side constants as:

$$q_1 = -4 \quad \text{and} \quad q_2 = 3$$

we see that upon substituting the above numbers for the input-output coefficients and the right-hand-side constants into the two functional constraints, we obtain:

$$-2x_1 + 2x_2 \leqq -4$$
$$3x_1 - 3x_2 \leqq 3$$

Likewise, the objective function can be written as follows when $j = 2$:

$$z = p_1x_1 + p_2x_2$$

If we set $p_1 = 5$ and $p_2 = 7$, and substitute these values into the generalized objective function above, we obtain:

$$z = 5x_1 + 7x_2$$

The nonnegativity restrictions for $j = 2$ are simply:

$$x_1 \geqq 0$$
$$x_2 \geqq 0$$

After a simple algebraic manipulation the functional constraints may be rewritten as follows:

$$x_1 \geqq x_2 + 2$$

and

$$x_1 \leqq x_2 + 1$$

or

$$x_2 + 1 \geqq x_1 \geqq x_2 + 2$$

which is impossible mathematically, or in other words, a dilemma.

OPERATIONS RESEARCH IN PRODUCTION
MANAGEMENT

The foregoing analysis has focused upon the product mix problem of the firm and has stressed the usefulness of the linear programming model in solving this type of production problem. From the standpoint of the operations manager, however, it perhaps goes without saying that production problems encompass a great deal more than estimating a hypothetical production function, or simply solving the product mix problem with a linear programming model. The practitioner must face the challenges involved in day-to-day decisions regarding product design and manufacturability, purchasing, packaging, scheduling, warehousing, and even shipping. When one adds to these "expected" problems the unanticipated ones involving industrial relations, work disputes, strikes, shipping tie-ups, price controls, supplier failures, machine malfunctions, and just plain human error, few of us, it would appear, would really envy the production manager.

In the last two or three decades various approaches to the solution of at least some of the more common problems in production management, particularly approaches employing mathematical modeling, have been developed and successfully applied by management scientists or operations researchers. It is an issue of some controversy as to what, exactly, operations research or management science is, but fortunately that need not concern us here. However our ability to solve business, economic, and more recently, urban and other social problems through operations research (OR) and contributions in such diverse areas as inventory control, scheduling, transportation planning, and, of course, product-line choice should not go unmentioned in a chapter such as this.

It is impossible to adequately cover, even without detail, the many models and approaches developed in the recent past, as this would require the presentation of material comparable to a second textbook. It must therefore suffice to confine our comments to introductory remarks, from which at least some indication of operations research contributions may be gained. The reader interested in a more thorough understanding of the many diverse applications in this area, as well as the reader merely wishing to become more familiar with this approach, is directed to the references at the end of this chapter.

Inventory Models. Basically, the inventory models developed by operations researchers are prescriptive models which attempt to answer the question: "Given a cost structure for the inventory system, when and how much of each commodity should be ordered or produced by the firm?" Three of the more fundamental models are "lot size systems" in which the size of the replenishment "lot" becomes the chief concern; "order level systems" in which the replenishment period is fixed but shortages are allowed; and "order-level–lot-size systems" in which both shortages and a variable replenishment period are permitted. All three systems have a common goal: to strike a balance among ordering, holding, and shortage costs so as to minimize the total cost of the system per unit time. More sophisticated models which formally recognize lead times required when ordering, discontinuities in demand patterns, scheduling constraints, space limitations, transportation restrictions, and union policies have also been developed.

Scheduling. If demand is known and the firm's inventory system has been determined, then the production or ordering schedule is also determined since the firm must produce just enough to satisfy its stocking policy. On the other hand, scheduling and dispatching must also be viewed as separate issues in their own right, since the specification of completion times of finished goods still does not determine the order of work processes prior to completion or the optimal allocation of fixed resources for the multiproduct problem. Predictably, linear programming has been of primary importance in solving, for example, such problems as the "assignment model," in which the allocation of jobs to machines, or men to jobs, is under consideration. Network models have also been employed in scheduling work, especially where the coordination of several tasks at once is required. The PERT example discussed in Chapter 3 provides an example. Queueing models, which attack the "bottleneck" problem in waiting lines, such as in customer service applications, or in assembly line work, have also been successfully utilized in solving a special class of scheduling problems.

Transportation Planning. Perhaps the best known of all linear programming models is the classic "transportation model," in which the distribution of goods from several supply centers, such as production plants or storage warehouses, to several demand centers, such as retail outlets, is at issue. Basically, the transportation problem attempts to find the least-cost way of satisfying demand for a given product, subject to supply constraints associated with the production and storage capacities of the various supply centers. Given linear transportation costs, the problem is perfectly suited to a linear programming formulation, although nonlinear models and network models have also been applied successfully in this area.

Optimum Product Lines. This application has already been discussed at length in the earlier portion of this chapter. However, it should also be emphasized that the judicious use of the linear programming model may also indicate (1) what reapportionment of product line is necessitated by market developments which affect production, transportation, or selling costs; (2) what product line changes would be required in the face of new "technical coefficients" resulting from new production processes; (3) what policy implications could be recommended in the face of raw materials shortages, further resource constraints, or environmental impact restrictions; and (4) by how much production costs must fall, or profit margins rise, in order to make the production of any particular product profitable in relation to "competing" goods.

Conclusion: The Efficacy of Linear Programming

Linear programming is an efficient way of determining optimum plans only if there are numerous enterprises or processes and numerous constraints in attaining a specific objective such as maximizing manufacturing profits or minimizing production costs. Thus, if there are 1,000 possible enterprises or processes but only one limiting resource or constraint, the optimum plan will contain only one process. In this particular case the optimum solution can be determined more easily by simple arithmetic than by linear programming. If there are two processes or products and several constraining resources, the optimum plan can be obtained from simple graphic procedures as outlined in the "complete description method." When j equals 3 or more, it behooves the specialist to utilize formal programming procedures, such as the "simplex method" described above, in order to arrive at the optimum solution.

PROBLEMS

1. Sketch the region (set of points) which corresponds graphically to each of the following constraints. (Do not assume nonnegativity unless this is implied by the constraints.)

    a. $x_1 \leqq 4$

    b. $x_2 \geqq 4$

    c. $\begin{cases} x_1 \leqq 6 \\ x_1 \geqq 0 \end{cases}$

2. Sketch the region (set of points) which corresponds graphically to the following nonnegativity restrictions and functional constraints. (See Exhibit 8.)

$$x_1 \geqq 0$$
$$x_2 \geqq 0$$
$$x_1 + 2x_2 \leqq 4$$
$$4x_1 + x_2 \leqq 8$$

3. In Problem 2 above, if the objective function is:

$$z = 3x_1 + 6x_2$$

what would be the optimum solution? (Show the result graphically, similar to that of Exhibit 8.)

4. Two men, Bill and John, work in a small garden implement factory. They may be employed for any number of hours as they are both part-time employees. Bill receives $2 per hour while John's wage is $3 per hour. Bill can produce 10 shovels and 3 rakes per hour. John can produce 5 shovels and 7 rakes per hour. A rush order from a local hardware store calls for 50 rakes and 50 shovels. Because of the expense of running the machines, no more than 11 man-hours can be spent on the manufacture of these rakes and shovels. How many hours should Bill work, and how many hours should John work to keep the payroll at a minimum?

5. The Grand Motor Company manufactures two basic auto models, the luxurious Grand Paree and the inexpensive Garson. These are sold to their auto dealers at a profit of $400 per Grand Paree and $200 per Garson. A Grand Paree requires, on the average, 150 man-hours for assembly, 50 man-hours for painting and finishing, and 10 man-hours for checking out and testing. The Garson averages 60 man-hours for assembly, 40 man-hours for painting and finishing, and 20 man-hours for checking and testing. During each production run, there are 30,000 man-hours available in the assembly shops, 13,000 man-hours in the painting and finishing shops, and 5,000 man-hours in the checking and testing division.

   How many Grand Parees and how many Garsons should the Grand Motor Company plan to produce, in order to realize the greatest possible profit from each production run?

6. In Problem 5 above, suppose the demand for luxury cars were to increase to the point where the company could realize three times as much profit on a Grand Paree as on a Garson. Show that it would then no longer pay to produce the smaller car at all. In that case, how many Grand Parees should the company produce?

7. An appliance dealer has stores in Detroit, Cleveland, Chicago, Cincinnati, and Pittsburgh. He has eight extra color television sets in Detroit and six extra in Cleveland. He would like to move five of them to Chicago, five to Cincinnati, and four to Pittsburgh. The transportation costs per color television set between the cities are given in the table:

	Chicago	*Cincinnati*	*Pittsburgh*
Detroit	$16	$10	$15
Cleveland.	10	12	10

How should the color television sets be distributed to keep transportation costs at a minimum?

8. A plant has three different types of polishers, P_1, P_2, and P_3, and two finishers, F_1 and F_2, available for the completion of five products. Given the data below, formulate a model to find the most profitable allocation of machines among the five products. Ignore any other costs or consideration.

Hours of Polishing or Finishing Time Required of Different Machines to Complete One Unit of Products 1, 2, 3, 4, 5

	Product 1	Product 2	Product 3	Product 4	Product 5	Hours Available
Polisher 1 . . .	.7	–	–	.5	.3	35
Polisher 2 . . .	.5	.2	.8	.2	–	28
Polisher 3 . . .	.3	.2	–	.1	.8	40
Finisher 1 . . .	–	.6	1.2	.3	.1	35
Finisher 2 . . .	–	.3	–	.4	.2	26
Gross profit per unit of output	$2.00	$1.75	$1.05	$3.50	$2.50	

9. Using the linear programming package available at your school's computer center, solve Problem 8 and interpret your results.

10. (A media selection model) The J. G. Brody Company is trying to decide which advertising media it should use to promote a new product. Prior market experience indicates that three distinguishable types of clients would be interested in the product, and the company has set "exposure goals" of at least 300, 400, and 250 clients for each of the respective client types. Also, through careful investigation, the company's staff has found that the number of exposures to potential customers which can be expected from the different media are all linearly related to the number of ads which are placed in any single investment source. The relevant data is provided in the table below. Formulate as a linear program in such a way as to find the least-cost advertising campaign satisfying the exposure goals of the Brody company.

Expected Exposures per "Standard" Ad Placed in Selected Media by the J. G. Brody Company

Clients	Media Source						Advertise-ment Goal
	1	2	3	4	5	6	
Type 1 . . .	6	1	2	3	6	3	300
Type 2 . . .	3	1	0	2	5	2	400
Type 3 . . .	2	4	5	4	8	1	250
Costs per ad	$25	$40	$60	$70	$80	$10	

11. (Manpower recruitment problem) The Pay-Later Insurance Company is involved in the development, underwriting, and retail sales of life insurance policies in a national market. The chief executives of the company have anticipated a sharp upswing in the insurance market in the coming years, and have decided to embark upon a substantial

manpower development program in anticipation. There are four different training programs, designated A, B, C, and D, which take, respectively, 1, 2, 3, and 4 years to complete. A maximum of 60, 45, 90, and 80 representatives can be trained in programs A, B, C, and D, respectively, at any one time. The costs of providing this training are dependent upon the duration and type of program, and total (multiyear) costs to the company for providing this job education are provided in the table below. The company can recruit in each of the five years prior to the termination of the manpower "drive," and would like to field 200 company representatives (independent of program and from all three programs) by the end of the third year, 300 new representatives (including the previous 200) by the end of the fourth year, and 525 new representatives (including the previous 300) by the end of the fifth year. One final restriction is that due to a lack of office space, the total number of trainees in all four programs at any one time is limited to 185 people. Formulate as a linear programming problem. (HINT: Let X_{ij} be the number of company representative trainees recruited in year i for program j, $i = 1, 2, 3, 4, 5$; $j = $ A, B, C, D).

Total (Multiyear) Training Costs for Pay-Later Insurance Company in Thousands of Constant (Year 0) Dollars

Year of Entry	Program A	Program B	Program C	Program D
Year 1	$3.0	$5.0	$6.0	$7.5
Year 2	2.7	4.5	5.4	6.9
Year 3	2.5	4.1	4.9	*
Year 4	2.1	3.6	*	*
Year 5	1.9	*	*	*

* Program costs not considered because programs in these years extend beyond planning horizon.

12. (Mining problem with demand constraints) The JKL Mining Company mines at four locations. Each location has a different grade of ore, and each grade can be mined to extract four different minerals, which, for simplicity, will simply be numbered 1, 2, 3, and 4. The extraction processes are such that approximately the same percentage of minerals will be obtained from each ton of raw material. As noted in the table below, the "loss" or unusable material is a consistent 10 percent from each of the sources, but the yields (composition) of the ores will vary from location to location. Hence, so will output levels of product per unit input.

At three of the four mining stations, the plant capacity is limited to 100,000 units per year. The fourth mining station is also limited to a total of 100,000 units per year, but two methods of extraction are possible, and each method will determine a slightly different yield. The relevant data concerning all extraction processes are provided below.

At present, production costs are such that the gross profit, per ton of ore, for each of the locations has been computed to be $100, $200,

$70, for the first three locations, and $150 and $250 for the two processes of the fourth location. On the company's books are orders for 150, 70, 20, and 110 units (thousand tons) of minerals 1, 2, 3, and 4, respectively. The company's policy is to try to meet this demand. However, under no circumstances can the company mine more than the amount demanded of any mineral because it has no place to "warehouse" the processed material. Hence, JKL is willing to supply less than what is demanded on a "holdover" or back order basis, carrying the order on its books until the next year.

Formulate as a linear programming problem.

Demand, Capacity, Profit, and Mineral Content for JKL Mining Company

Mineral Type	Ore Locations					Amount of Final Product on Order
	1	2	3	4		
1	.6	.5	.3	.4	.4	150
2	.2	.2	.3	.3	.1	70
3	0	0	0	0	.2	20
4	.1	.2	.3	.2	.2	110
Loss.	.1	.1	.1	.1	.1	
Plant capacity* . . .	100	100	100	100		
Profit per ton of ore.	$100	$200	$ 70	$150	$250	

* In thousands of tons.

REFERENCES

BAUMOL, WILLIAM J.   *Economic Theory and Operations Analysis.* 3d ed. Englewood Cliffs, N.J.: Prentice-Hall, Inc., 1972.

DANTZIG, GEORGE B.   *Linear Programming and Extensions.* Princeton, N.J.: Princeton University Press, 1963.

DORFMAN, ROBERT; SAMUELSON, PAUL A.; and SOLOW, ROBERT M. *Linear Programming and Economic Analysis.* New York: McGraw-Hill Book Co., 1958.

HILLIER, FREDERICK S., and LIEBERMAN, GERALD J.   *Introduction to Operations Research.* San Francisco: Holden-Day, Inc., 1974.

LEE, SANG M.   *Goal Programming for Decision Analysis.* Philadelphia, Auerback Publishers Inc., 1972.

PLANE, DONALD R., and KOCHENBERGER, GARY A.   *Operations Research for Managerial Decisions.* Homewood, Ill.: Richard D. Irwin, Inc., 1972.

TAHA, HAMDY A.   *Operations Research: An Introduction.* New York: Macmillan Co., 1971.

WAGNER, HARVEY M.   *Principles of Operations Research.* Englewood Cliffs, N.J.: Prentice Hall, Inc., 1969.

Appendix: Discount Tables and Charts; Common Logarithms

A. PRESENT VALUE OF A UNIFORM SERIES: PVUS

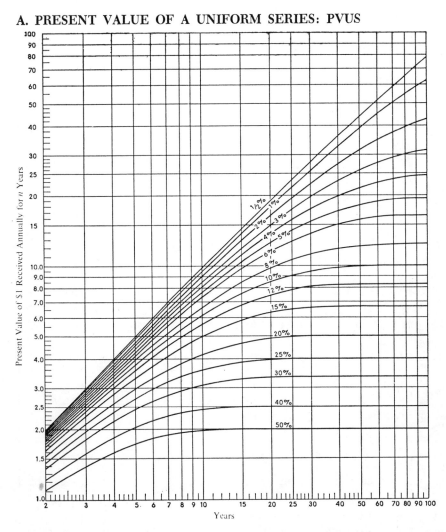

Source: This and the following chart are adapted from Norman Barish, *Economic Analysis For Engineering and Management Decision Making* (New York: McGraw-Hill, 1962).

A. PRESENT VALUE OF A UNIFORM SERIES: PVUS

Present Value of $1 Received Annually for N Years

Years (N)	1%	2%	4%	6%	8%	10%	12%	14%	15%	16%	18%	20%	22%	24%	25%	26%	28%	30%	35%	40%	45%	50%
1	0.990	0.980	0.962	0.943	0.926	0.909	0.893	0.877	0.870	0.862	0.847	0.833	0.820	0.806	0.800	0.794	0.781	0.769	0.741	0.714	0.690	0.667
2	1.970	1.942	1.886	1.833	1.783	1.736	1.690	1.647	1.626	1.605	1.566	1.528	1.492	1.457	1.440	1.424	1.392	1.361	1.289	1.224	1.165	1.111
3	2.941	2.884	2.775	2.673	2.577	2.487	2.402	2.322	2.283	2.246	2.174	2.106	2.042	1.981	1.952	1.923	1.868	1.816	1.696	1.589	1.493	1.407
4	3.902	3.808	3.630	3.465	3.312	3.170	3.037	2.914	2.855	2.798	2.690	2.589	2.494	2.404	2.362	2.320	2.241	2.166	1.997	1.849	1.720	1.605
5	4.853	4.713	4.452	4.212	3.993	3.791	3.605	3.433	3.352	3.274	3.127	2.991	2.864	2.745	2.689	2.635	2.532	2.436	2.220	2.035	1.876	1.737
6	5.795	5.601	5.242	4.917	4.623	4.355	4.111	3.889	3.784	3.685	3.498	3.326	3.167	3.020	2.951	2.885	2.759	2.643	2.385	2.168	1.983	1.824
7	6.728	6.472	6.002	5.582	5.206	4.868	4.564	4.288	4.160	4.039	3.812	3.605	3.416	3.242	3.161	3.083	2.937	2.802	2.508	2.263	2.057	1.883
8	7.652	7.325	6.733	6.210	5.747	5.335	4.968	4.639	4.487	4.344	4.078	3.837	3.619	3.421	3.329	3.241	3.076	2.925	2.598	2.331	2.108	1.922
9	8.566	8.162	7.435	6.802	6.247	5.759	5.328	4.946	4.772	4.607	4.303	4.031	3.786	3.566	3.463	3.366	3.184	3.019	2.665	2.379	2.144	1.948
10	9.471	8.983	8.111	7.360	6.710	6.145	5.650	5.216	5.019	4.833	4.494	4.192	3.923	3.682	3.571	3.465	3.269	3.092	2.715	2.414	2.168	1.965
11	10.368	9.787	8.760	7.887	7.139	6.495	5.988	5.453	5.234	5.029	4.656	4.327	4.035	3.776	3.656	3.544	3.335	3.147	2.752	2.438	2.185	1.977
12	11.255	10.575	9.385	8.384	7.536	6.814	6.194	5.660	5.421	5.197	4.793	4.439	4.127	3.851	3.725	3.606	3.387	3.190	2.779	2.456	2.196	1.985
13	12.134	11.343	9.986	8.853	7.904	7.103	6.424	5.842	5.583	5.342	4.910	4.533	4.203	3.912	3.780	3.656	3.427	3.223	2.799	2.468	2.204	1.990
14	13.004	12.106	10.563	9.295	8.244	7.367	6.628	6.002	5.724	5.468	5.008	4.611	4.265	3.962	3.824	3.695	3.459	3.249	2.814	2.477	2.210	1.993
15	13.865	12.849	11.118	9.712	8.559	7.606	6.811	6.142	5.847	5.575	5.092	4.675	4.315	4.001	3.859	3.726	3.483	3.268	2.825	2.484	2.214	1.995
16	14.718	13.578	11.652	10.106	8.851	7.824	6.974	6.265	5.954	5.669	5.162	4.730	4.357	4.033	3.887	3.751	3.503	3.283	2.834	2.489	2.216	1.997
17	15.562	14.292	12.166	10.477	9.122	8.022	7.120	6.373	6.047	5.749	5.222	4.775	4.391	4.059	3.910	3.771	3.518	3.295	2.840	2.492	2.218	1.998
18	16.398	14.992	12.659	10.828	9.372	8.201	7.250	6.467	6.128	5.818	5.273	4.812	4.419	4.080	3.928	3.786	3.529	3.304	2.844	2.494	2.219	1.999
19	17.226	15.678	13.134	11.158	9.604	8.365	7.366	6.550	6.198	5.877	5.316	4.844	4.442	4.097	3.942	3.799	3.539	3.311	2.848	2.496	2.220	1.999
20	18.046	16.351	13.590	11.470	9.818	8.514	7.469	6.623	6.259	5.929	5.353	4.870	4.460	4.110	3.954	3.808	3.546	3.316	2.850	2.497	2.221	1.999
21	18.857	17.011	14.029	11.764	10.017	8.649	7.562	6.687	6.312	5.973	5.384	4.891	4.476	4.121	3.963	3.816	3.551	3.320	2.852	2.498	2.221	2.000
22	19.660	17.658	14.451	12.042	10.201	8.772	7.645	6.743	6.359	6.011	5.410	4.909	4.488	4.130	3.970	3.822	3.556	3.323	2.853	2.498	2.222	2.000
23	20.456	18.292	14.857	12.303	10.371	8.883	7.718	6.792	6.399	6.044	5.432	4.925	4.499	4.137	3.976	3.827	3.559	3.325	2.854	2.499	2.222	2.000
24	21.243	18.914	15.247	12.550	10.529	8.985	7.784	6.835	6.434	6.073	5.451	4.937	4.507	4.143	3.981	3.831	3.562	3.327	2.855	2.499	2.222	2.000
25	22.023	19.523	15.622	12.783	10.675	9.077	7.843	6.873	6.464	6.097	5.467	4.948	4.514	4.147	3.985	3.834	3.564	3.329	2.856	2.499	2.222	2.000
26	22.795	20.121	15.983	13.003	10.810	9.161	7.896	6.906	6.491	6.118	5.480	4.956	4.520	4.151	3.988	3.837	3.566	3.330	2.856	2.500	2.222	2.000
27	23.560	20.707	16.330	13.211	10.935	9.237	7.943	6.935	6.514	6.136	5.492	4.964	4.524	4.154	3.990	3.839	3.567	3.331	2.856	2.500	2.222	2.000
28	24.316	21.281	16.663	13.406	11.051	9.307	7.984	6.961	6.534	6.152	5.502	4.970	4.528	4.157	3.992	3.840	3.568	3.331	2.857	2.500	2.222	2.000
29	25.066	21.844	16.984	13.591	11.158	9.370	8.022	6.983	6.551	6.166	5.510	4.975	4.531	4.159	3.994	3.841	3.569	3.332	2.857	2.500	2.222	2.000
30	25.808	22.396	17.292	13.765	11.258	9.427	8.055	7.003	6.566	6.177	5.517	4.979	4.534	4.160	3.995	3.842	3.569	3.332	2.857	2.500	2.222	2.000
40	32.835	27.355	19.793	15.046	11.925	9.779	8.244	7.105	6.642	6.234	5.548	4.997	4.544	4.166	3.999	3.846	3.571	3.333	2.857	2.500	2.222	2.000
50	39.196	31.424	21.482	15.762	12.234	9.915	8.304	7.133	6.661	6.246	5.554	4.999	4.545	4.167	4.000	3.846	3.571	3.333	2.857	2.500	2.322	2.000

B. PRESENT VALUE OF A SINGLE PAYMENT: PVSP

B. PRESENT VALUE OF A SINGLE PAYMENT: PVSP

Present Value of $1

Years Hence	1%	2%	4%	6%	8%	10%	12%	14%	15%	16%	18%	20%	22%	24%	25%	26%	28%	30%	35%	40%	45%	.50%
1	0.990	0.980	0.962	0.943	0.926	0.909	0.893	0.877	0.870	0.862	0.847	0.833	0.820	0.806	0.800	0.794	0.781	0.769	0.741	0.714	0.690	0.667
2	0.980	0.961	0.925	0.890	0.857	0.826	0.797	0.769	0.756	0.743	0.718	0.694	0.672	0.650	0.640	0.630	0.610	0.592	0.549	0.510	0.476	0.444
3	0.971	0.942	0.889	0.840	0.794	0.751	0.712	0.675	0.658	0.641	0.609	0.579	0.551	0.524	0.512	0.500	0.477	0.455	0.406	0.364	0.328	0.296
4	0.961	0.924	0.855	0.792	0.735	0.683	0.636	0.592	0.572	0.552	0.516	0.482	0.451	0.423	0.410	0.397	0.373	0.350	0.301	0.260	0.226	0.198
5	0.951	0.906	0.822	0.747	0.681	0.621	0.567	0.519	0.497	0.476	0.437	0.402	0.370	0.341	0.328	0.315	0.291	0.269	0.223	0.186	0.156	0.132
6	0.942	0.888	0.790	0.705	0.630	0.564	0.507	0.456	0.432	0.410	0.370	0.335	0.303	0.275	0.262	0.250	0.227	0.207	0.165	0.133	0.108	0.088
7	0.933	0.871	0.760	0.665	0.583	0.513	0.452	0.400	0.376	0.354	0.314	0.279	0.249	0.222	0.210	0.198	0.178	0.159	0.122	0.095	0.074	0.059
8	0.923	0.853	0.731	0.627	0.540	0.467	0.404	0.351	0.327	0.305	0.266	0.233	0.204	0.179	0.168	0.157	0.139	0.123	0.091	0.068	0.051	0.039
9	0.914	0.837	0.703	0.592	0.500	0.424	0.361	0.308	0.284	0.263	0.225	0.194	0.167	0.144	0.134	0.125	0.108	0.094	0.067	0.048	0.035	0.026
10	0.905	0.820	0.676	0.558	0.463	0.386	0.322	0.270	0.247	0.227	0.191	0.162	0.137	0.116	0.107	0.099	0.085	0.073	0.050	0.035	0.024	0.017
11	0.896	0.804	0.650	0.527	0.429	0.350	0.287	0.237	0.215	0.195	0.162	0.135	0.112	0.094	0.086	0.079	0.066	0.056	0.037	0.025	0.017	0.012
12	0.887	0.788	0.625	0.497	0.397	0.319	0.257	0.208	0.187	0.168	0.137	0.112	0.092	0.076	0.069	0.062	0.052	0.043	0.027	0.018	0.012	0.008
13	0.879	0.773	0.601	0.469	0.368	0.290	0.229	0.182	0.163	0.145	0.116	0.093	0.075	0.061	0.055	0.050	0.040	0.033	0.020	0.013	0.008	0.005
14	0.870	0.758	0.577	0.442	0.340	0.263	0.205	0.160	0.141	0.125	0.099	0.078	0.062	0.049	0.044	0.039	0.032	0.025	0.015	0.009	0.006	0.003
15	0.861	0.743	0.555	0.417	0.315	0.239	0.183	0.140	0.123	0.108	0.084	0.065	0.051	0.040	0.035	0.031	0.025	0.020	0.011	0.006	0.004	0.002
16	0.853	0.728	0.534	0.394	0.292	0.218	0.163	0.123	0.107	0.093	0.071	0.054	0.042	0.032	0.028	0.025	0.019	0.015	0.008	0.005	0.003	0.002
17	0.844	0.714	0.513	0.371	0.270	0.198	0.146	0.108	0.093	0.080	0.060	0.045	0.034	0.026	0.023	0.020	0.015	0.012	0.006	0.003	0.002	0.001
18	0.836	0.700	0.494	0.350	0.250	0.180	0.130	0.095	0.081	0.069	0.051	0.038	0.028	0.021	0.018	0.016	0.012	0.009	0.005	0.002	0.001	0.001
19	0.828	0.686	0.475	0.331	0.232	0.164	0.116	0.083	0.070	0.060	0.043	0.031	0.023	0.017	0.014	0.012	0.009	0.007	0.003	0.002	0.001	
20	0.820	0.673	0.456	0.312	0.215	0.149	0.104	0.073	0.061	0.051	0.037	0.026	0.019	0.014	0.012	0.010	0.007	0.005	0.002	0.001	0.001	
21	0.811	0.660	0.439	0.294	0.199	0.135	0.093	0.064	0.053	0.044	0.031	0.022	0.015	0.011	0.009	0.008	0.006	0.004	0.002	0.001		
22	0.803	0.647	0.422	0.278	0.184	0.123	0.083	0.056	0.046	0.038	0.026	0.018	0.013	0.009	0.007	0.006	0.004	0.003	0.001	0.001		
23	0.795	0.634	0.406	0.262	0.170	0.112	0.074	0.049	0.040	0.033	0.022	0.015	0.010	0.007	0.006	0.005	0.003	0.002	0.001			
24	0.788	0.622	0.390	0.247	0.158	0.102	0.066	0.043	0.035	0.028	0.019	0.013	0.008	0.006	0.005	0.004	0.003	0.002	0.001			
25	0.780	0.610	0.375	0.233	0.146	0.092	0.059	0.038	0.030	0.024	0.016	0.010	0.007	0.005	0.004	0.003	0.002	0.001	0.001			
26	0.772	0.598	0.361	0.220	0.135	0.084	0.053	0.033	0.026	0.021	0.014	0.009	0.006	0.004	0.003	0.002	0.002	0.001				
27	0.764	0.586	0.347	0.207	0.125	0.076	0.047	0.029	0.023	0.018	0.011	0.007	0.005	0.003	0.002	0.002	0.001	0.001				
28	0.757	0.574	0.333	0.196	0.116	0.069	0.042	0.026	0.020	0.016	0.010	0.006	0.004	0.002	0.002	0.002	0.001	0.001				
29	0.749	0.563	0.321	0.185	0.107	0.063	0.037	0.022	0.017	0.014	0.008	0.005	0.003	0.002	0.002	0.001	0.001	0.001				
30	0.742	0.552	0.308	0.174	0.099	0.057	0.033	0.020	0.015	0.012	0.007	0.004	0.003	0.002	0.001	0.001	0.001					
40	0.672	0.453	0.208	0.097	0.046	0.022	0.011	0.005	0.004	0.003	0.001	0.001										
50	0.608	0.372	0.141	0.054	0.021	0.009	0.003	0.001	0.001	0.001												

C. TABLE OF MANTISSAS FOR COMMON LOGARITHMS

N	0	1	2	3	4	5	6	7	8	9
10	0000	0043	0086	0128	0170	0212	0253	0294	0334	0374
11	0414	0453	0492	0531	0569	0607	0645	0682	0719	0755
12	0792	0828	0864	0899	0934	0969	1004	1038	1072	1106
13	1139	1173	1206	1239	1271	1303	1335	1367	1399	1430
14	1461	1492	1523	1553	1584	1614	1644	1673	1703	1732
15	1761	1790	1818	1847	1875	1903	1931	1959	1987	2014
16	2041	2068	2095	2122	2148	2175	2201	2227	2253	2279
17	2304	2330	2355	2380	2405	2430	2455	2480	2504	2529
18	2553	2577	2601	2625	2648	2672	2695	2718	2742	2765
19	2788	2810	2833	2856	2878	2900	2923	2945	2967	2989
20	3010	3032	3054	3075	3096	3118	3139	3160	3181	3201
21	3222	3243	3263	3284	3304	3324	3345	3365	3385	3404
22	3424	3444	3464	3483	3502	3522	3541	3560	3579	3598
23	3617	3636	3655	3674	3692	3711	3729	3747	3766	3784
24	3802	3820	3838	3856	3874	3892	3909	3927	3945	3962
25	3979	3997	4014	4031	4048	4065	4082	4099	4116	4133
26	4150	4166	4183	4200	4216	4232	4249	4265	4281	4298
27	4314	4330	4346	4362	4378	4393	4409	4425	4440	4456
28	4472	4487	4502	4518	4533	4548	4564	4579	4594	4609
29	4624	4639	4654	4669	4683	4698	4713	4728	4742	4757
30	4771	4786	4800	4814	4829	4843	4857	4871	4886	4900
31	4914	4928	4942	4955	4969	4983	4997	5011	5024	5038
32	5051	5065	5079	5092	5105	5119	5132	5145	5159	5172
33	5185	5198	5211	5224	5237	5250	5263	5276	5289	5302
34	5315	5328	5340	5353	5366	5378	5391	5403	5416	5428
35	5441	5453	5465	5478	5490	5502	5514	5527	5539	5551
36	5563	5575	5587	5599	5611	5623	5635	5647	5658	5670
37	5682	5694	5705	5717	5729	5740	5752	5763	5775	5786
38	5798	5809	5821	5832	5843	5855	5866	5877	5888	5899
39	5911	5922	5933	5944	5955	5966	5977	5988	5999	6010
40	6021	6031	6042	6053	6064	6075	6085	6096	6107	6117
41	6128	6138	6149	6160	6170	6180	6191	6201	6212	6222
42	6232	6243	6253	6263	6274	6284	6294	6304	6314	6325
43	6335	6345	6355	6365	6375	6385	6395	6405	6415	6425
44	6435	6444	6454	6464	6474	6484	6493	6503	6513	6522
45	6532	6542	6551	6561	6571	6580	6590	6599	6609	6618
46	6628	6637	6646	6656	6665	6675	6684	6693	6702	6712
47	6721	6730	6739	6749	6758	6767	6776	6785	6794	6803
48	6812	6821	6830	6839	6848	6857	6866	6875	6884	6893
49	6902	6911	6920	6928	6937	6946	6955	6964	6972	6981
50	6990	6998	7007	7016	7024	7033	7042	7050	7059	7067
51	7076	7084	7093	7101	7110	7118	7126	7135	7143	7152
52	7160	7168	7177	7185	7193	7202	7210	7218	7226	7235
53	7243	7251	7259	7267	7275	7284	7292	7300	7308	7316
54	7324	7332	7340	7348	7356	7364	7372	7380	7388	7396

C. TABLE OF MANTISSAS FOR COMMON LOGARITHMS

N	0	1	2	3	4	5	6	7	8	9
55	7404	7412	7419	7427	7435	7443	7451	7459	7466	7474
56	7482	7490	7497	7505	7513	7520	7528	7536	7543	7551
57	7559	7566	7574	7582	7589	7597	7604	7612	7619	7627
58	7634	7642	7649	7657	7664	7672	7679	7686	7694	7701
59	7709	7716	7723	7731	7738	7745	7752	7760	7767	7774
60	7782	7789	7796	7803	7810	7818	7825	7832	7839	7846
61	7853	7860	7868	7875	7882	7889	7896	7903	7910	7917
62	7924	7931	7938	7945	7952	7959	7966	7973	7980	7987
63	7993	8000	8007	8014	8021	8028	8035	8041	8048	8055
64	8062	8069	8075	8082	8089	8096	8102	8109	8116	8122
65	8129	8136	8142	8149	8156	8162	8169	8176	8182	8189
66	8195	8202	8209	8215	8222	8228	8235	8241	8248	8254
67	8261	8267	8274	8280	8287	8293	8299	8306	8312	8319
68	8325	8331	8338	8344	8351	8357	8363	8370	8376	8382
69	8388	8395	8401	8407	8414	8420	8426	8432	8439	8445
70	8451	8457	8463	8470	8476	8482	8488	8494	8500	8506
71	8513	8519	8525	8531	8537	8543	8549	8555	8561	8567
72	8573	8579	8585	8591	8597	8603	8609	8615	8621	8627
73	8633	8639	8645	8651	8657	8663	8669	8675	8681	8686
74	8692	8698	8704	8710	8716	8722	8727	8733	8739	8745
75	8751	8756	8762	8768	8774	8779	8785	8791	8797	8802
76	8808	8814	8820	8825	8831	8837	8842	8848	8854	8859
77	8865	8871	8876	8882	8887	8893	8899	8904	8910	8915
78	8921	8927	8932	8938	8943	8949	8954	8960	8965	8971
79	8976	8982	8987	8993	8998	9004	9009	9015	9020	9025
80	9031	9036	9042	9047	9053	9058	9063	9069	9074	9079
81	9085	9090	9096	9101	9106	9112	9117	9122	9128	9133
82	9138	9143	9149	9154	9159	9165	9170	9175	9180	9186
83	9191	9196	9201	9206	9212	9217	9222	9227	9232	9238
84	9243	9248	9253	9258	9263	9269	9274	9279	9284	9289
85	9294	9299	9304	9309	9315	9320	9325	9330	9335	9340
86	9345	9350	9355	9360	9365	9370	9375	9380	9385	9390
87	9395	9400	9405	9410	9415	9420	9425	9430	9435	9440
88	9445	9450	9455	9460	9465	9469	9474	9479	9484	9489
89	9494	9499	9504	9509	9513	9518	9523	9528	9533	9538
90	9542	9547	9552	9557	9562	9566	9571	9576	9581	9586
91	9590	9595	9600	9605	9609	9614	9619	9624	9628	9633
92	9638	9643	9647	9652	9657	9661	9666	9671	9675	9680
93	9685	9689	9694	9699	9703	9708	9713	9717	9722	9727
94	9731	9736	9741	9745	9750	9754	9759	9763	9768	9773
95	9777	9782	9786	9791	9795	9800	9805	9809	9814	9818
96	9823	9827	9832	9836	9841	9845	9850	9854	9859	9863
97	9868	9872	9877	9881	9886	9890	9894	9899	9903	9908
98	9912	9917	9921	9926	9930	9934	9939	9943	9948	9952
99	9956	9961	9965	9969	9974	9978	9983	9987	9991	9996

D. TABLE OF AREAS OF NORMAL DISTRIBUTION THAT IS TO THE LEFT OR RIGHT OF Z (ONE-TAILED TEST)

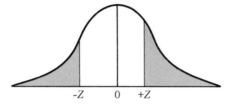

Plus or minus Z is the number of standard deviations to the right or left, respectively, of the mean; that is, $Z = (X - \bar{X})/\sigma$. An entry in this table represents either one of the shaded areas, and is equal to the probability of that area.

Second Decimal Place of Z

↓Z→	.00	.01	.02	.03	.04	.05	.06	.07	.08	.09
0.0	.5000	.4960	.4920	.4880	.4840	.4801	.4761	.4721	.4681	.4641
0.1	.4602	.4562	.4522	.4483	.4443	.4404	.4364	.4325	.4286	.4247
0.2	.4207	.4168	.4129	.4090	.4052	.4013	.3974	.3936	.3897	.3859
0.3	.3821	.3783	.3745	.3707	.3669	.3632	.3594	.3557	.3520	.3483
0.4	.3446	.3409	.3372	.3336	.3300	.3264	.3228	.3192	.3156	.3121
0.5	.3085	.3050	.3015	.2981	.2946	.2912	.2877	.2843	.2810	.2776
0.6	.2743	.2709	.2676	.2643	.2611	.2578	.2546	.2514	.2483	.2451
0.7	.2420	.2389	.2358	.2327	.2297	.2266	.2236	.2206	.2177	.2148
0.8	.2119	.2090	.2061	.2033	.2005	.1977	.1949	.1922	.1894	.1867
0.9	.1841	.1814	.1788	.1762	.1736	.1711	.1685	.1660	.1635	.1611
1.0	.1587	.1562	.1539	.1515	.1492	.1469	.1446	.1423	.1401	.1379
1.1	.1357	.1335	.1314	.1292	.1271	.1251	.1230	.1210	.1190	.1170
1.2	.1151	.1131	.1112	.1093	.1075	.1056	.1038	.1020	.1003	.0985
1.3	.0968	.0951	.0934	.0918	.0901	.0885	.0869	.0853	.0838	.0823
1.4	.0808	.0793	.0778	.0764	.0749	.0735	.0721	.0708	.0694	.0681
1.5	.0668	.0655	.0643	.0630	.0618	.0606	.0594	.0582	.0571	.0559
1.6	.0548	.0537	.0526	.0516	.0505	.0495	.0485	.0475	.0465	.0455
1.7	.0446	.0436	.0427	.0418	.0409	.0401	.0392	.0384	.0375	.0367
1.8	.0359	.0351	.0344	.0336	.0329	.0322	.0314	.0307	.0301	.0294
1.9	.0287	.0281	.0274	.0268	.0262	.0256	.0250	.0244	.0239	.0233
2.0	.0228	.0222	.0217	.0212	.0207	.0202	.0197	.0192	.0188	.0183
2.1	.0179	.0174	.0170	.0166	.0162	.0158	.0154	.0150	.0146	.0143
2.2	.0139	.0136	.0132	.0129	.0125	.0122	.0119	.0116	.0113	.0110
2.3	.0107	.0104	.0102	.0099	.0096	.0094	.0091	.0089	.0087	.0084
2.4	.0082	.0080	.0078	.0075	.0073	.0071	.0069	.0068	.0066	.0064
2.5	.0062	.0060	.0059	.0057	.0055	.0054	.0052	.0051	.0049	.0048
2.6	.0047	.0045	.0044	.0043	.0041	.0040	.0039	.0038	.0037	.0036
2.7	.0035	.0034	.0033	.0032	.0031	.0030	.0029	.0028	.0027	.0026
2.8	.0026	.0025	.0024	.0023	.0023	.0022	.0021	.0021	.0020	.0019
2.9	.0019	.0018	.0018	.0017	.0016	.0016	.0015	.0015	.0014	.0014
3.0	.00135	.0013	.0013	.0012	.0012	.0011	.0011	.0011	.0010	.0010
4.0	.0000317									

Illustration: For Z = 1.96, shaded area is .0250 out of a total area of 1.0.

Index

*This book has been set in 10 and 9 point
Caledonia, leaded 2 points. Chapter numbers
are in 30 and 60 point Kennerly and chapter
titles are in 18 point Kennerly. The size of the
type page is 27 × 46½ picas.*